THE WAYS OF THINKING OF EASTERN PEOPLES

by

HAJIME NAKAMURA

JAPANESE NATIONAL COMMISSION
FOR UNESCO

1960

Classics of Modern Japanese Thought and Culture

The Ways of Thinking of Eastern Peoples
Hajime Nakamura

A Study of Good
Kitaro Nishida

Climate and Culture: A Philosophical Study
Tetsuro Watsuji

Time and Eternity
Seiichi Hatano

Studies in Shinto Thought
Tsunetsugu Muraoka

The Japanese Character: A Cultural Profile
Nyozekan Hasegawa

An Inquiry into the Japanese Mind as Mirrored in Literature
Sokichi Tsuda

About our Ancestors: —The Japanese Family System
Kunio Yanagita

Japanese Spirituality
Daisetz Suzuki

A Historical Study of the Religious Development of Shinto
Genichi Kato

THE WAYS OF THINKING OF EASTERN PEOPLES

by

HAJIME NAKAMURA

Professor, Tokyo University

Compiled by

JAPANESE NATIONAL COMMISSION FOR UNESCO

1960

Greenwood Press
New York • Westport, Connecticut • London

Library of Congress Cataloging-in-Publication Data

Nakamura, Hajime, 1912-
The ways of thinking of Eastern peoples.

Translation of: Tōyōjin no shii hōhō.
Reprint. Originally published: Toyko : Monbushō, 1960.
1. Asia—Intellectual life. 2. Philosophy, Oriental. 3. Asia—Civilization. I Title.
DS12.N3513 1988 001.1′095 88-21947
ISBN 0-313-26556-9

British Library Cataloguing in Publication Data is available.

Library of Congress Catalog Card Number: 88-21947
ISBN: 0-313-26556-9

First published in 1960

Reprinted in 1988 by Greenwood Press, Inc. in cooperation with Yushodo Co., Ltd., Tokyo with the permission of the Ministry of Education, Japan

Printed in the United States of America

The paper used in this book complies with the Permanent Paper Standard issued by the National Information Standards Organization (Z39.48-1984).

10 9 8 7 6 5 4 3 2 1

Unesco, at its 9th session of General Conference, held at New Delhi, India, in November, 1956, decided to launch the Major Project on the Mutual Appreciation of Eastern and Western Cultural Values. In response to this decision, this Commission initiated in 1958 the project of introducing Japanese philosophical works to foreign countries within the framework of the Project.

For the implementation of this project, this Commission has set up a committee of leading Japanese scholars of philosophy and language experts to work out the detailed plan.

The programme is divided into two parts. One is to publish complete translations of individual books, such as "The Ways of Thinking of Eastern Peoples" by Hajime Nakamura, published in 1948, and "A Study of Good" by Kitaro Nishida, published in 1932. The former was rendered into English in 1958, the latter in 1959. The other is to bring out annual publication in English of a collection of philosophical papers produced by contemporary authors, or excerpts or adaptations thereof.

The Commission hopes that the project will contribute to the cultural exchanges and the better understanding between the Orient and Occident.

March, 1960

Japanese National Commission
for Unesco

Foreword on behalf of the Japanese National Commission for Unesco

When the external shells of the manifold and diversified languages of the human race are eliminated, the internal, essential and universally human thought common to all mankind appears and man is able to understand his fellowman. The same may be applied to the ethics, arts and cultures of the numerous and diversified peoples of the human race. On the surface they appear very different, mysterious and hard to comprehend. This is due to the historical and environmental background of peoples. But when we remove those external layers and penetrate into the inner recesses of the substance of these peoples and their cultures we find the universally common human element which makes us understand each others' aspirations and spiritual values.

The philosophers of the end of the last century and those of the beginning of this century concerned themselves with solving the spiritual and mental problems of man in the light of his historical and environmental background. The two great World Wars have intensified interest in this field and this interest is strong even today.

Our Japanese philosophy of life has been under the influence of Buddhism introduced from India and that of Confucianism introduced from China. This condition lasted for over 1,400 years. However, when, about four centuries ago, European civilization and culture began to make its influence felt through such missionaries as Zavier and others, the Japanese people found themselves in a state of confusion. The civilization introduced from Europe seemed so entirely strange, peculiar and difficult to grasp that they made no effort to attempt to study the differences and come to a mutual understanding. Instead, unfortunately, the Japanese people then, lacking discretion, fell into a state of nervous tension and considered the new wave from overseas a danger to the survival of their culture. The feudal lords especially agitated the people to avoid any contact with anything European fearing the destruction of Japanese traditions and way of life. As a result of such agitation the doors were completely shut to the West. This policy was enforced even at the price of much bloodshed. Thus for two and a half centuries Japan was completely isolated. During these two and a half centuries, however, the West made immeasurable strides and fast progress in many fields of knowledge. Japan as a result of her isolation remained much behind in its civilization. How wise it would have been for Japan to have overlooked the existing differences and compromised instead. How much richer our civilization would have been today and how much more advanced!

A century ago, when finally Japan opened its doors to America and Europe, it found itself faced with the serious problem of how to catch up with the remarkable progress made in the West during Japan's isolation. A feverish haste to make up what she had neglected to accomplish during the long period of isolation directed all Japan's efforts toward the accomplishment of this goal, allowing no time for the continued research of the traditions of Buddhism and Confucianism.

In our feverish haste to catch up with the West in such a short span of time as a century, we were naturally bound to make mistakes and as a result, our civilization is full of weak points. During that century it seems people were in such a hurry to imitate European civilization that they looked upon Buddhism and Confucianism as barriers to their complete absorption of European civilization. This they did without any attempt at understanding the foundations upon which European civilization was built, namely, Greek, Roman and Christian. Likewise they did not thoroughly analyze the peculiarities inherent in their own civilization and way of life. In the process of our intensive effort to make up for our two and a half centuries of "backwardness", we almost completely neglected or refused to understand that despite the strikingly different peculiarities in culture and civilization of both the East and West, they, nevertheless, are alike essentially in essence and universality of purpose.

Now is the time to begin to correct the mistakes of the past. The peoples of both the East and the West must begin to understand themselves and each other. By a full understanding of our own individual peculiarities, we may break down the barriers which prevent us from understanding each other. No efforts other than our own can remove restricted areas or "no man's lands" which separate us.

If all the peoples of the world would only try to understand each other by forgetting for a moment apparent peculiarities which history, tradition, habits and environment have shaped and would think solely of common problems facing them as human beings since the dawn of civilization, the universal character of all peoples would appear and all causes of prejudice and misunderstanding would disappear and all mankind would unite in their efforts to enrich their lives with spiritual values and happiness.

The purpose and goal of Unesco expressed in the motto "Mutual Appreciation of Eastern and Western Cultural Values" is what we the Japanese people and our scholars in all branches of knowledge are trying to accomplish. It is our hope that we may be able to contribute toward the shedding of light upon the path which mankind is to pursue by following the ideals expressed in the motto of Unesco.

September, 1959 Tetsuro Watsuji

Foreword on the Works of the Author

It seems to me singularly appropriate that an English version of Professor Nakamura's work should appear under Unesco auspices. In 1958 Unesco embarked on a major project designed to promote the "mutual appreciation of Eastern and Western cultural values." One who has read Mr. Nakamura's book and studied the Unesco project in outline will note a striking convergence of interest. Two problems in particular are of primary concern to Mr. Nakamura and central to the Unesco program.

One of these problems is the identification in some meaningful way of the "East" and the "West." How may one define such entities and how may they be systematically compared one with another? False antitheses and monolithic comparisons cast in tarnished cliches have long beclouded the minds of Europeans and Asians alike as they contemplated each other's cultures across time and space. Mr. Nakamura sweeps these aside and sets out to analyze, with rigor and objectivity, the characteristic thought patterns of four Asian peoples as these are revealed in their language, their logic and their cultural products. In this analysis he speaks neither of an "Oriental mind" nor of an undifferentiated "West." He speaks of the Indians, the Chinese, the Japanese and the Tibetans, and when he makes comparative references to Western thought and culture he is careful to specify which "West" at which point in history he is referring to. These differentiations seem like the most obvious good sense. But it is a commentary on the need for the new Unesco program that Mr. Nakamura is one of the very few who have begun to make them and thus, I believe, to raise the whole level of discussion from the muddy and impressionistic level on which it has long reposed.

The second major problem dealt with in this study is equally relevant to the Unesco program. Mr. Nakamura poses it in this way: No people in the world today is isolated from those world-wide movements of thought and belief which are tending to transform the lives of all peoples. But each people accepts or rejects, adapts and modifies the universal ideologies which reach them. What governs this process, and what is it which produces within each culture an amalgam which is at once part of a world-wide movement and distinctively its own? Mr. Nakamura considers the spread of the universal religion of Buddhism, and in Chinese, Japanese, and Tibetan responses to Buddhism—as well as in the history of Buddhism in India—Mr. Nakamura finds clues to certain fundamental and persisting characteristics of their differing modes of thought. These characteristics in turn help to explain their fundamental historical and cultural differences one from another and their variant responses to Western culture in our time.

The magnitude of this study, encompassing as it does four civilizations, four literary traditions, two and half millenia of history and some of the most intractable problems known to scholarship inevitably directs attention to its author. What sort of a man is he and under what circumstances did he conceive and carry through this impressive work? Mr. Nakamura completed his study in 1947, when he was in his middle thirties. Its earlier stages were a part of a broader project headed by Professor Kichinosuke Ito, but the design and the final product are distinctively Mr. Nakamura's own. He graduated from Tokyo Imperial University in 1936 and was awarded the degree of Doctor of Letters (*Bungaku Hakase*) in 1943. He is currently Professor of Indian and Buddhist Philosophy at the University of Tokyo and in 1957 was awarded the Imperial Prize by the Academy of Japan for his four volume history of early Vedānta philosophy. His books and numerous articles have stamped him as an intellectual innovator and a major force in the modernization of Indian studies in Japan. His training in Indian and Buddhist studies was both wide and deep; it involved intensive work in Indian philology and in the Buddhist traditions of China, Tibet and Japan. He thus acquired the broad knowledge of language and culture requisite for such a study as this. Yet philology seldom inspires or sustains work of such sweep and boldness, and for the sources of Mr. Nakamura's ideas and methods we must look elsewhere.

The catastrophe which befell Japan in 1945 inspired Japanese intellectuals to undertake new analyses of their culture and nation; a number of these took the form of fresh comparative studies which, it was hoped, would place the Japanese ethos in one or another comparative spectrum. Mr. Nakamura, as his preface indicates, was drawn to this new effort at self-knowledge through intercultural comparisons. His training in Indian and Buddhist studies drew him to examine four societies (including his own) which had been affected in different ways by their experience with

Buddhism. Other intellectual influences dictated the way in which he went about that task.

Mr. Nakamura had long been interested in Western philosophy. Through Professor Nagano's *Logic* he was introduced to the thought of such Anglo-American philosophers as Dewey, Creighton and Jevons. At this stage he also read widely in the writings of Deussen, Keyserling and Schopenhauer. Through Professor Shinkichi Sudo's *Logic* he was led to study the German logicians, notably Wundt and Sigwart. Thereafter he became deeply interested in Windelband's "problem approach" to the history of philosophy.

Like many scholars throughout the world, Mr. Nakamura was influenced by the general breakdown of absolutist philosophies. He was impelled to ask the question, not, are these views in accord with some absolute system, but rather how is it that some men in some societies come to hold such views? How will men's behavior be affected by those views and under what altered circumstances will they change them? In formulating questions of this kind, Mr. Nakamura was influenced by Marx, Max Weber, and by Professor Watsuji whose book, *Climate* explored the broad problem of the relation between environment and thought. His studies in philosophy thus led ultimately, not to the study of philosophic systems but to the study of "modes of thought"—those distinctive and slowly evolving ways by which people sort and classify experience, argue with one another, and make their decisions. It is this approach which is exemplified in the present volume.

These problems and a comparative interest in four civilizations deeply influenced by Buddhism thus determined the design of the study. As the reader will note, each of the four principal sections of the study is built on a common plan. First there is a discussion of language and logic, of the characteristic ways in which certain types of judgments and inferences are made in the four cultures. In each section the author then proceeds to the manifestations of these patterns in different types of literature and cultural activities; it is in these portions of the work that the interaction of Buddhist and pre-Buddhist patterns is studied in detail.

Mr. Nakamura is acutely conscious of the fact that explicit logic and abstract formulations of all kinds are the particular property of the small educated elites in the societies he is considering. But, if I interpret him correctly, he regards the philosophizing of the elite as a kind of translation into more general and abstract terms of the problems encountered in the common life of the society. And, in turn, folk sayings, proverbs, everyday thought reflect a translation downward or a seeping downward of what the philosophers have voiced. To find evidence of how this occurred and of how Buddhist ideas and values entered into this process in the four societies, Mr. Nakamura has cast a wide net. He has combed folk literature, prayers and the scriptures of popular cults, collections of proverbs, descriptions of everyday life and, wherever possible, he has used the accounts of foreign observers whose fresh eyes often register characteristics that escape the native critic of his own society. Thus, in the end we are shown not only how each elite grappled with the problems of Buddhist thought and belief but also how this process affected habits of thought and modes of behavior in the society as a whole.

It will be noted that Mr. Nakamura's interest in the effects of Buddhism on the modes of thought of these peoples has led him to a more dynamic approach than that found in many other studies. For example the great Marcel Granet isolated many of the same characteristics of pre-Buddhist thought in China that Mr. Nakamura discusses. Yet Granet was convinced that Chinese thinking had taken its permanent forms by the Han Dynasty (206 B.C.–A.D. 222) and consequently restricted himself largely to pre-Han sources. Mr. Nakamura, on the other hand, has pursued the changes in Chinese thinking brought about by Buddhism and by Chinese reactions to Indian ideas and beliefs. In the Chinese case, as in the other societies considered, Buddhism brought changes in ways of thinking. At the same time, the history of those changes places in sharp relief those characteristic native attitudes and habits of thought that proved most enduring and impervious to change.

The reader may occasionally be puzzled by the lack of reference to certain important Western writers whose work bears directly on the problems with which Mr. Nakamura is concerned. It is well therefore to recall that the flow of Western ideas into Japan has been, in the best of times, uneven and haphazard. In the war years during which Mr. Nakamura emerged as a mature scholar the flow diminished and for a few years virtually ceased. It became clear, during a year at Stanford University when Mr. Nakamura discussed his findings with interested members of the faculty, that he would now be disposed to make certain changes in his approach and methods in the light of his recent studies in symbolic logic and the philosophy of language.

This fact only serves to underline what the reader will discover in the pages of this book: that Mr. Nakamura is a tireless explorer on the frontiers of knowledge, a scholar whose virtuosity in research is matched by his relentless drive towards new understandings.

Arthur F. Wright

Yale University

September 7, 1959.

Author's Preface to the Japanese Edition

The Japanese nation is now confronted with the stark realities resulting from the World War II. In the crisis that now faces us, we should reflect upon our civilization and philosophy; this will, I feel, give us the answers to some of our problems. We have so far made few conscious efforts to investigate our characteristic ways of thinking which, often unknown to us, condition our attitudes and our actions. Many Japanese intellectuals place great emphasis on the necessity of modernizing Japan or of accomplishing in our thought and behaviour a synthesis of East and West. To realize any such objective, however, we must first investigate the ways of thinking or the thought processes of the Japanese people.

Professor Kichinosuke Ito who was commissioned by a Ministry of Education Committee to promote the comparative study of the ways of thinking of different peoples, asked me to collaborate in his study from 1945 to 1946. I accepted his proposal, proceeded with the necessary research and submitted reports to the committee. The problems which Professor Ito had asked me to deal with were in particular "the ways of thinking of the Indians as revealed in language and logic" and "the ways of thinking of the Chinese and the Japanese as they appear in the modes of introducing Buddhist thought."

In proceeding with these studies, I first wanted to determine the procedure I should adopt and the form in which I should embody the results. If I was not clear on methodology, I realised that I would not achieve the scientific preciseness which I desired. So, in order to accomplish the study systematically, I adopted the following methods. When possible, I aimed to isolate the characteristic features of the ways of thinking of each people in the form of expression of judgments and of inferences; such features are, I believe, most clearly revealed in these forms of expression. I refrained from discussing them *in toto*; but using the characteristic features thus isolated occasionally, I intended to proceed with investigations of concrete cultural phenomena which also reflect the ways of thinking and the thought process of each people. To clarify the particular ways in which Buddhism and Indian logic were introduced from India into China, Japan and Tibet, that is, how a universal religion and logic has modified itself according to the native characteristics of each people, was the special focus of my research. I therefore applied *the same methods* in investigating the ways of thinking of each people. (Concerning the Japanese ways of thinking, I realized I should deal also with the problem of the introduction and modification of Confucianism. However as this problem lies beyond my ability, I touched it only occasionally.) The contrasts with Occidental ways of thinking were not made a separate topic but were made an integral part of the study. As a result, I took special care to indicate the contrasts presented by the ways of thinking of the ancient occidental peoples in that part of my study in which Indian ways of thinking are explained. Although the ancient Indians and the ancient Occidentals were ethnographically and linguistically related, there are many differences in their individual ways of thinking. I feel that a clarification of these differences is a scientific problem of great importance. I do not refer here to a study of differences as revealed in their cultural philosophies, but to a specific and positive study on the characteristic features of their ways of thinking through cultural phenomena.

This book is a result of my studies conducted independently as well as for the Committee on this subject.

Many of the problems raised in the present work would require a large monograph for adequate treatment. Therefore I have not here attempted detailed descriptions but have sought to isolate and define various features of the ways of thinking and their logical interconnections.

I am acutely conscious of the defects of this work, particularly when it is concerned with areas outside my special competence. But the general subject seemed to me worthy of study. It is my hope that further scholarship will correct, expand and refine many of the problems here stated. I am greatly indebted to the teachers and friends who aided me in my studies and encouraged me to complete and publish this study.

April 18, 1947 [rewritten, June 16, 1959]

Hajime Nakamura

Preface to the English Translation

On the occasion of publishing an English translation of this work, the author would like to give a few words of thanks to those who worked for bringing the English translation to this form of perfection.

When Dr. Charles B. Fahs, Director of the Rockefeller Foundation came to Tokyo in 1950, he urged to translate tentatively some chapters of this work into English on the advice of Urof. Shunsuke Tsurumi. A grant was conferred by the Rockefeller Foundation on the Institute for the Science of Thought, Tokyo, whose virtual organizer Mr. Tsurumi was. A board for the translation was established; the chapters of "Introduction" and "the Japanese Ways of Thinking" were translated by Professors S. Tsurumi, Saburo Ichii, Masaaki Kawaguchi, Arata Ishimoto, and Miss Kazuko Tsurumi. Professor Shokin Furuta was an adviser to them, and Mr. Kyojun Inoue and Miss Mieko Shimizu were assistants.

When the author went to Stanford University as visiting professor of philosophy in September, 1951, a seminar was established by the faculty for discussing the contents of the translated portions, the members being Professors John David Goheen (Philosophy), Arthur F. Wright (History), Nobutaka Ike (Political science), Bernard Joseph Siegel (Anthropology), Bert Alfred Gerow (Anthropology), David Shepherd Nivison (Chinese Philosophy), Donald Herbert Davidson (Philosophy), Thomas Carlyle Smith (History), and Raymond K. Waters (Japanese). The session was held every other week, and reports were distributed each time. Part of the translation was looked over.

Since the author left America in July, 1952, Professors Nivison and Waters were continuing the work of editing the English manuscript, which has finally been brought to this state of perfection. The portions of "Introduction" and "the Japanese Ways of Thinking" of this book owe their finishing touch to them.

Some portions of the chapter on "the Chinese Ways of Thinking" were translated by the author during his stay in London, 1952, and was later edited by Professor Wright and distributed by the Committee for Chinese Thought at Aspen, Colorado. This manuscript has been incorporated in this book.

It was a great honor for the author that this work was taken up by the Japanese National Commission for Unesco, Government of Japan, as the first attempt of translating philosophical works by Japanese scholars. The Editorial Board, set up in the Commission for this task, helped the Secretariat in the arrangement of translation, the members being Professors Tetsushi Furukawa, Shokin Furuta, Shinsho Hanayama, Takeo Iwasaki, Takezo Kaneko, Joken Kato, Juichi Katsura, Hideo Kishimoto, Yoshinari Muraji, Seizo Ohe, Yasumasa Oshima, Torataro Shimomura, Seiichi Uno, Mr. Mitsuaki Maeda, Deputy Secretary-General of the Commission, and myself, with such prominent scholars as Teiyu Amano, Kichinosuke Ito, Hakuju Ui, Tetsuto Uno and Tetsuro Watsuji as advisors. The author was requested to collaborate for the project by Mr. Yoshio Muto, Secretary-General of the Commission on August 21, 1958. The translation was finished in June 1959.

The chapter of "the Indian Ways of Thinking" have been translated by Messrs. Shintei Kawasaki, Shoyu Hanayama, Junkichi Imanishi, Ryushin Uryuzu, Shinko Sayeki, Ishii Yamada, Jikido Takasaki and the remainder of the chapter of "the Chinese Ways of Thinking" by Messrs. Eisho Sonoke, Shoyu Hanayama, Kyoyu Tamura, Hiroo Kashiwagi, that of "the Tibetan Ways of Thinking" by Mr. Jikido Takasaki, and that of "Conclusion" by Mr. Shojun Bando. Mr. Mitsuyoshi Saigusa, and later Mr. J. N. Takasaki, took all the responsibility in launching the whole project, always keeping in touch with the Commission. Miss Hideko Kobayashi worked in the secretariat. Various passages were translated by the author himself.

To look over the drafts of the translation also was a painstaking job. Messrs. Akira Hata, Stanley Weinstein, Kenneth Kameo Inada, Tetsuo Unno, and Minoru Kiyota, who were all educated in America and were studying at the Department of Indian and Buddhist Philosophy, University of Tokyo, as graduate students, kindly engaged themselves in the work of checking. V. C. Trivedi, First Secretary, Embassy of India, Tokyo was good enough to look over some part of the English manuscript personally and gave me good suggestions for revising it. The results were finally looked over by Rabbi Milton J. Rosen who has been studying at our Department so that the newly translated portions will be brought to unity in style.

The author feels himself greatly honored by the goodwill of Dr. Tetsuro Watsuji and Professor Arthur F. Wright who have introduced this work into the international scope by their prefaces to the English version.

Part of this work had already been published in Western languages as follows:

(1) The Ways of Thinking of the Chinese as Revealed in Chinese Buddhist Thought. Edited by Prof. Arthur F. Wright and distributed by the Committee for Chinese Thought, Aspen, Colorado, U.S.A., 1952.

(2) Influence of Confucian Ethics on the Chinese Translations of Buddhist Sutras. (The *Dr. Liebenthal Commemoration Volume: Sino-Indian Studies* 10. Santiniketan, India. 1957, pp. 156–70.)

(3) Une Caractéristique de la Pensée Japonaise. La Dévotion Absolu à une Personnalité Determinée. (*Monumenta Nipponica,* published by Sophia University, Tokyo, 1952. vol. VIII, Nos. 1/2, pp. 99–129.)

(4) Japanese Ambiguity Revealed in the Process of Introducing Buddhism and Indian Logic. (*The Science of Thought,* No. 1, 1954, pp. 25–44. Published by the Institute for the Science of Thought, Tokyo. Agency: The Kyobunkan Publishing Company, Ginza, Tokyo.)

(5) The Japanese Emphasis upon Social Activities. (In *the Science of Thought,* No. 2, 1956, pp. 20–39. Tokyo, the Institute for the Science of Thought.)

(6) The Humanitarian Tendency of the Japanese. (*Berkeley Bussei,* No. 1, 1955, pp. 4–6. Published by the Young Buddhist Association, 2121 Channing Way, Berkeley, California, U.S.A.)

(7) Some Features of the Japanese Way of Thinking. (*Monumenta Nipponica,* vol. XIV, Nos. 3–4, 1958–59, pp. 31–72. Published by Sophia University, Tokyo.)

(8) A Tendency toward the Intuitive and the Emotional ———A Study on a Way of Thinking of the Japanese. Translated by Rabbi Milton J. Rosen. To be published in a collection of essays, ed. by Prof. Seizi Uyeda and published by the Waseda University Press, Tokyo, 1959.

From among the above-mentioned eight translations, No. (1) alone has been incorporated in this book *in toto,* and the remaining seven were not incorporated, the reason being that they were translated by other translators than those who engaged in the work of translating the whole work, and that the author wanted to keep unity in style; otherwise the whole translation might look like a magazine. Considering the possibility that they may also help researchers in some respects, the author listed them all here. Some portions of the work have been translated into French by Mr. Masao Kamata who has been studying at Strassburg. The late Professor Kenzo Ikegami took good offices for his getting in touch with the author. The French manuscript has not yet been published.

The author should not fail to express his indebtedness to all gentlemen who have been connected with the Commission, especially to Mr. Tamon Maeda, ex-Chairman, Dr. Tatsuo Morito, present Chairman, of the Commission, Mr. Yoshio Muto, Mr. Mitsuaki Maeda, Mr. Kazumasa Ohnishi, Mr. Toshio Hara and Mr. Nagahiro Yamashida. In the last, but not least, the author is very thankful to Mr. Yasushi Kohno, Mr. Akira Yoshikawa, Mr. Tetsuhiko Yasui, Miss Haruko Tsuchiya, Mrs. Sakae Naoi and Mr. Nobuo Miyamoto of the External Relations Section of the Commission who greatly helped the author in clerical affairs, and collaborated with him day and night at the final stage of publication.

Herewith the author expresses his sincere gratitude to all these gentlemen for their kind help and advice.

March, 1960

Hajime Nakamura

CONTENTS

Page

Foreword by Tetsuro Watsuji i

Foreword by Arthur F. Wright v

Preface to the Japanese Edition xi

Preface to the English Translation xiii

PART I. INTRODUCTION 1

1. The ways of thinking of East Asian peoples 1
2. Ways of thinking and other terms 3
3. Ways of thinking and language 4
4. Ways of thinking and logic 6
5. Ways of thinking and cultural phenomena 9
6. Ways of thinking as revealed in the pattern of adoption of a foreign culture 10
7. The order in which the ways of thinking of the various Eastern peoples will be considered 11

PART II. THE WAYS OF THINKING OF THE INDIAN PEOPLE 13

—Special Features of the Ways of Thinking Characterized in Cultural Phenomena—

Chapter 1. Introduction 13

Chapter 2. Laying stress on the universals 16

(1) Preponderance of abstract notion 16

(2) The bestowal of substantiality to the abstract conception 20

Chapter 3. The negative character 23

(1) Fondness for the negative expression 23

(2) Negatively grasping the absolute 25

(3) Attraction to the Unknown 30

Chapter 4. Disregard for the individual and the particular .. 32

(1) Desregard for the individual and the particular appearing in language 32

(2) Disregard for the individual and the particular in the speculation in general 37
Chapter 5. The concept of the unity of all things 39
Chapter 6. The static quality 45
(1) Comprehension of this quality through static aspects of language 45
(2) The static quality in thought process 49
(3) Lack of common sense concepts of time 53
(4) Contemplative attitudes 55
(5) Passive and forbearing attitudes toward behavior 58
Chapter 7. Subjective comprehension of personality 61
(1) Subjective comprehension of personality as revealed in language 61
(2) Subjective comprehension of personality as revealed in philosophy 63
Chapter 8. Supremacy of the universal self over the individual self 68
(1) The unobstructed extension of the self as revealed in language 68
(2) The continuity of one's self and other selves 71
(3) Consciousness of the existence of the self 76
(4) Ethics of the non-duality of one's self and other selves. 81
Chapter 9. Subservience to universals 84
(1) Subservience to universals as revealed in language ... 84
(2) The extension of the subject of action 85
(3) Reverence for universal standards in behavior 89
(4) Perceiving the truth: Faith and rationalism 95
(5) Transcendence of limited ethical systems 98
Part 1. Transcendence of national and racial consciousness 98
(6) Transcendence of limited ethical systems 104
Part 2. The problem of caste 104
(7) Consciousness of living beings: Indian concept of man. 106
(8) The conservative character of Indian thinking 110
(9) The development of nomothetical learning 113
Chapter 10. Alienation from the objective natural world 114
(1) Loss of the notion of order in the objective natural world 114

(2) Imagination which ignores natural law 122
(3) The tendency to resort to extremes 129
(4) Fondness for myths and poetry 130
(5) Lack of historical consciousness 133
(6) The concept of truth 135
(7) Non-development of natural sciences 136
Chapter 11. The introspective character of Indian thought: The development of the sciences of inner reflexion 141
Chapter 12. The metaphysical character of Indian thought .. 146
(1) The religious character of Indian thought 146
(2) The tendency to transcend this world 151
(3) The tendency of thought to transcend the gods 157
Chapter 13. The spirit of tolerance and conciliation 159

PART III. THE WAYS OF THINKING OF THE CHINESE 166

—Characteristics of the Ways of Thinking as Revealed in Various Cultural Phenomena, Particularly in the Process of Accepting Buddhism—

Chapter 1. Introduction 166
Chapter 2. Emphasis on the perception of the concrete 167
(1) Graphic character of the writing 167
(2) The concrete expression of concepts 168
(3) Explanation by means of perceived symbols 171
(4) Diagrammatic explanation 172
Chapter 3. Non-development of abstract thought 176
(1) Lack of consciousness of universals 176
(2) Non-logical character of verbal expression and thought. 177
(3) Lack of comprehension through conscious use of general laws 180
(4) Acceptance of Indian logic in a distorted form 181
(5) The non-logical character of Zen Buddhism 184
Chapter 4. Emphasis on the particular 187
(1) Emphasis on particular instances 187
(2) Explanation on the basis of particular instances 189
(3) Development of descriptive science in regard to the particular 191

Chapter 5. Conservatism expressed in exaltation of antiquity .. 196
(1) Importance attached to past events 196
(2) Continuity of the identical way of thinking 198
(3) Influence on the reception of Buddhism 201
(4) Non-development of free thought 205
(5) Traditional character of scholarship 206
Chapter 6. Fondness for complex multiplicity expressed in concrete form 208
(1) The concrete character of the artistic imagination 208
(2) Fondness for ornate diction 210
(3) Exegetical and literary predilections of Chinese 213
Chapter 7. Formal conformity 218
(1) Fondness for formal conformity 218
(2) External conformity 223
Chapter 8. The tendency towards practicality 226
(1) The anthropocentric attitude 226
(2) Worldly tendency of religions 229
(3) Non-development of metaphysics 239
Chapter 9. Individualism 243
(1) The tendency towards egoism 243
(2) The spiritual leadership of Buddhism and its transformation 244
(3) Non-formation of religious sects 250
(4) Universality of Tao 252
Chapter 10. Esteem for hierarchy 256
(1) The moral personality 256
(2) Elegant attitude on sexual matters 258
(3) Formalism in behavior 262
(4) Esteem for superiority in status 263
(5) The high value placed on patriarchal kinship 267
(6) Religion's struggle against the state and its defeat ... 270
(7) Racial pride and reverence for lineage 274
Chapter 11. Esteem for nature 276
(1) Conformity to nature 276
(2) Relationship of mutuality between heaven and man ... 282
Chapter 12. Reconciling and harmonizing tendencies 284
(1) The absolute character of existence 284

(2) Acknowledgment of all heretical doctrines 286
(3) Syncretism within Buddhism 290
(4) Chinese characteristics of reconciling and harmonizing. 292

PART IV. THE WAYS OF THINKING OF THE JAPANESE 298

—Characteristics of Japanese Ways of Thinking, as Revealed in Various Cultural Phenomena, Particularly in the Process of Accepting Buddhism—

Chapter 1. Introduction 298
Chapter 2. The tendency to emphasize particular social nexus. 304
(1) Overstressing of human relations 304
(2) Superseding of human relationships takes precedence over the individual 306
(3) Unconditional belief in a limited human nexus 311
(4) Observance of the family morals 315
(5) Emphasis on rank and social position 326
(6) Problems of ultra-nationalism 337
(7) Absolute devotion to a specific individual 355
(8) Emperor worship 377
(9) Sectarian and factional closedness 396
(10) Defense of a human nexus by force 407
(11) Emphasis upon human activities 414
(12) Acuteness of moral self-reflection 438
(13) The lack of awareness of religious values 450
Chapter 3. Irrationalistic tendencies 462
(1) The tendency to be illogical (to neglect logical rules) .. 462
(2) Lack of the ability to think with logical coherence 471
(3) Immaturity of logic in Japan 476
(4) Some hopes for development of logical thinking in Japan 484
(5) Intuitive and emotional tendencies 486
(6) Lack of ability of forming complicated ideas 492
(7) Fondness for simple symbolic expressions 500
(8) The lack of knowledge concerning the objective order .. 511
Chapter 4. Problem of shamanism 515
Chapter 5. The acceptance of actuality 527

(1) Apprehension of the absolute in the phenomenal world. 527
(2) This-worldliness 540
(3) The acceptance of man's natural dispositions 553
(4) Emphasis on the love of human beings 563
(5) The spirit of tolerance 567
(6) Cultural multiplicity (consisting of several strata still preserved) and weakness of the spirit of criticism 587

PART V. THE WAYS OF THINKING OF THE TIBETAN PEOPLE 595

—Characteristics of Tibetan Ways of Thinking as Revealed in Cultural Phenomena, Especially in the Process of Accepting Buddhism—

Chapter 1. Introduction 596
Chapter 2. Weakness of consciousness of association among individuals 596
Chapter 3. Absolute submission to a religiously charismatic individual 601
Chapter 4. Absolute adherence to the Lamaist social order 608
Chapter 5. Shamanistic tendencies 611
Chapter 6. Logical tendencies 616

PART VI. CONCLUSIONS 623

Chapter 1. General consideration of the ways of thinking of East Asian peoples 623
(1) Various cultural phenomena and the ways of thinking of East Asian peoples 623
Chapter 2. The universal character and the particular character of East Asian thought 636
(1) The concept of the "East" and previous comments on it . 636
(2) East Asian thought and its universality 639
(3) Comparative study of ways of thinking and philosophy. 645
Chapter 3. The cognitive basis and the existential basis for the difference of ways of thinking 649

PART I. INTRODUCTION

1. The ways of thinking of East Asian peoples

Our sense of belonging to one world has never been keener than at the present moment. Each and every individual is now caught up in the ceaseless flow of world events. At the present time it is no more possible for an individual to exist apart from the world than heretofore it has been possible for him to exist apart from his pople or nation. And yet, the present emphasis on this evident fact itself shows that while each individual is influenced by world currents and keenly aware of them, nonetheless he is still strongly affected by the ways of life and ways of thinking of his own nationality.

It is commonly said that following the Meiji Restoration, Japan in a short space of time rapidly and skillfully adopted and assimilated Western civilization; yet as has often been pointed out in these post-war days, this acceptance was extremely selective and superficial. Today there is a demand for a reappraisal of Western civilization with a view to a fuller acceptance of it. But may we say that it is actually being accepted in its entirety? And how much the less may this be said of those great peoples of Asia, the Indians and the Chinese; for despite their close relations with Westerners for several hundred years, industrialism and capitalism have failed to take root among them. In many respects these peoples still preserve their traditional ways, and it is the less surprising therefore that verbal expressions, beliefs, ritual practices, etc. show no signs of being easily transformed. Western thought, from its first arrival in these lands, was theoretically rather well understood among the educated classes as a part of their general cultivation. And yet it certainly did not govern completely the practical and concrete behavior of any of these peoples. How are we to explain this? We cannot dismiss these phenomena simply by calling them "backward" or "Asiatic", but must rather seek the answer in the characteristics of the traditional ways of thinking of each individual people.

There has long been a tendency in Japan to think in terms of a dichotomy between East and West. The device has been to take two mutually opposed value concepts, labelling one "Occidental" and the other "Oriental". Thus the Oriental way of thinking is represented as "spiritual", "introverted", "synthetic" and "subjective", while the Occidental is represented as "materialistic", "extroverted", "analytic" and "objective". This sort of explanation by paired opposites is often met with in the West as well. However, the meanings of the concepts "Orient" and "Occident" are extremely complex. If we inquire into what these words refer to, we are struck with the fact that the sense of each is composite, embracing a range of various narrower concepts. For example, the Greek and Hebrew civilizations which are the components of Western civilization differ markedly one from the other. Moreover the civilization formed by the fusion of these two strains is divisible into the ancient, medieval and modern periods, each of which has its peculiar characteristics; and further, modern Western civilization takes on different characteristics from nation to nation. Consequently, without a thorough grasp of these differences it is impossible to generalize about the ways of thinking of Westerners.

So likewise, in the case of Eastern peoples,[1] we must first explain the characteristics of the ways of thinking of each of the various peoples involved. If we are to reach any conclusions about Eastern peoples as a group, it must be as the final step in a process of comparative study of the data. Generalized conclusions drawn before such individual preparatory studies have been made will perforce be hasty and dogmatic. Thus, in order to deal with the ways of thinking of Eastern peoples, it is first necessary to examine the ways of thinking of each of the peoples individually. However, such a study of all the peoples of the East is, from a practical point of view, impossible at this time. I intend to concentrate on India, China, Tibet and Japan. My reason is that among these four peoples alone did there exist—however imperfectly—a study of logic, which came first from India to the other three areas, and then developed independently in each. I believe that the various other peoples of the East have nearly the same ways of thinking as one or another of these four. Specifically, one may say that Ceylon, Burma, Siam, and southern French Indo-China (Cambodia and Laos) are akin to India. Central Asia and Mongolia are at present akin to Tibet. Manchuria, Korea and northern French Indo-China (Vietnam) are akin to China. Thus, an examination of the ways of thinking of these four is, in effect, a study of the most influential peoples of the East. It is only after such a study, if at all, that a generalized view of the ways of thinking of the Eastern peoples can emerge.

1) In this book the term "Eastern" refers to India, China, Tibet and Japan, and their cultural satellites.

2. Ways of thinking and other terms

In order to furnish an explanation for the problems raised above, first we will define several related concepts, fixing at the outset their usage as they appear in this work.

(1) "Rules of logic" (sometimes called "Laws of Thought") are those explicitly expressed formal rules put forward by logicians. When interpreted, such rules usually claim to give universally valid results, that is, to lead from true assumptions to true conclusions. Traditional logic claimed special priority for the "laws" of identity, contradiction and the excluded middle; alternative systems suggest other rules. The rules of a logic do not purport to describe how people think. Hence the present work, not being a work in logic, does not deal with them from a logical and formal point of view. But of course, it is a historical fact that certain people have at certain times accepted, organised and promulgated logical systems and rules, and from this fact, among others, conclusions can be drawn about how people think. In this sense alone, the present book is concerned with rules of logic and logical systems.

(2) "Ways of thinking" (Denkweise) refer to any individual's thinking in which the characteristic feature of the thinking habits of the group to which he belongs is revealed. "Ways of thinking" as here used will designate especially ways of thinking about concrete, empirical questions, which may, on some occasions, involve also value judgments and questions of value. The thinker need not consciously be aware of any way of thinking himself when he is engaged in operations of thinking. However, his ways of thinking are, in fact, conditioned by the group when he engages in these operations. We have adopted the phrase "ways of thinking" in the title of this work as the main subject of our study.

On some logical or other problems all members of a people or a group may think in the same way. But concerning other concrete problems of daily experience, all members of one and the same people do not necessarily think in the same way, and so we can only point out a general tendency of thinking of the people concerned. Thus, as each member may think in a slightly different way, our work can only mention the predominant tendency of each people.

(3) Based on several "ways of thinking" which have been mentioned above, any thinker might have formed a coherent, self-conscious system of thought. We call this system and its tradition a "system of thought". For example, any well-organized, coherent system of theology or philosophy is a "system of thought". We refer to it, only when it is necessary.

3. Ways of thinking and language

In studying the ways of thinking of a people, we will find one of the first clues in their language. Language is basic to the life of a people; so basic that when a special language system comes into being, we may say that a people has come into being. The existence of a common language can serve as a criterion for the existence of a people. Even though linguistic activity is common to all mankind, a universal language has never existed, and consequently there has never been a single speech community. Several international languages have been devised, and some have, moreover, actually begun to be used as international languages. These, however, are languages used only by people who, faced with the actual situation of many different languages existing in conflict, wish to overcome this confusion. Practically speaking, these languages also are in a sense only *special* languages themselves.

Forms of expression by means of language become, in the inner consciousness of people, norms for psychologically ordering in a fixed pattern and carrying to conclusion the operations of thought. Therefore the special forms for developing the effectiveness of a given language, especially the grammar of that language and more especially its syntax, express the concrete ways of thinking of the people using the language, and what is more, may be said to regulate such ways of thinking.

In the past a good deal of discussion has taken place in Western scholarly circles concerning the relation between linguistic forms and ways of thinking. Many scholars believe that between the two there exists a relationship of parallel development and mutual correspondence. However, there are other scholars who either deny such parallel development and mutual correspondence entirely or assert that the relationship is not a significant one.

Recently, especially in America, the relation between language and action based upon verbal communication has been discussed as one of the most important philosophical problems.

Recognizing that many theories exist as to the relationship between linguistic forms and ways of thinking, in this book I have nevertheless followed what seems to be the general assumption that, to a certain extent, between the two there is a relationship of correspondence or parallel development—that language is a representation in sound of the concept which is produced as a result of the operation of thinking within our consciousness.

If there is such a relationship between the operations of language and thinking, it is worth while and indeed necessary to use forms of linguistic expression as a key in studying forms and ways of thinking.

Studies have already been partially undertaken which attempt to clarify the differences between the ways of thinking of various peoples, using as a key the differences in the forms of grammatical construction in the languages used by these peoples. For example, Wilhelm von Humboldt thought it possible to study the differences between the structural constitutions of different languages by making a study of such questions as how a given form of grammatical structure is handled in each language, what sort of grammatical position it has, and what sort of relationship it has to other grammatical forms. As one instance of this he made an investigation of duals.[1] Thus with this method as a key he proposes to attack the problem of the forms of thinking of a people. Again, the sinologist Granet said, "Just as linguistic research permits the analysis of the *mechanism* of thoughts transmitted in language, in the same way the analysis of the guiding principles of thought can verify the analysis of its means of expression".[2] Taking this position he endeavored to explain the ways of thinking of the Chinese as a whole, by using the analytical study of the Chinese language as a key.

In this work it is my aim to carry out an investigation in broad scope with regard to the most important people of the East, following a similar scheme of analysis for each people. The procedure I followed with each people is to use their forms of expressing judgments and inferences as initial clues to their ways of thinking, and then to attempt to elucidate these ways of thinking by analysing the various cultural phenomena conditioned by them. But for comparative purposes I have placed particular emphasis upon Buddhism—a cultural phenomenon common to all.

1) This famous article is incorporated in Wilhelm von Humboldt: *Gesammelte Werke,* VI, S. 562 f.

2) M. Granet: Quelques particularités de la langue et de la pensée chinoisse, *Revue Philosophique,* 1920, pp. 101–102.

4. Ways of thinking and logic

Although the forms of linguistic expression involve many different things, since we are concerned with the ways of thinking, it will be proper for us to give primary emphasis to the forms of expression of judgment and inference; because these are the basic forms for expressing the operations of thinking. I will defer for the present such questions as what varieties of these forms of judgment and inference there are, and how these varieties ought to be classified, for these are, properly speaking, problems of logic. Accordingly, although it would be desirable to examine the special characteristics of the ways of thinking of each people, taking up all the forms of expression of judgment and inference one by one, yet insofar as the problem of their classification is concerned, the actual fact is that the content of logic in this respect is not yet definitely fixed, and so in the present general discussion I will omit this problem, and even among these judgments and inferences I would like to select for consideration merely those which are fundamental or especially characteristic.

First, as to judgments, I shall consider the most fundamental and simple forms, namely judgments of identity, judgments of classification, judgments of inference, and judgments of existence.[1] In Western logic the problem of *impersonal judgments* has been widely discussed but propositions (such as "it rains", for example), which in the West are considered impersonal judgments, cannot be so considered in Japanese and Chinese, differing as they do from Western languages in their linguistic forms. Furthermore, in the ancient Indian language, which is on a par with Western languages in its linguistic forms, very often the same idea is not an impersonal judgment but is expressed as an operational judgment ("it rains" equals "devo varṣati"). Consequently, since the question whether or not it is well to recognize the "impersonal judgment" must first be argued out logically, in this work comparisons of the linguistic forms of various languages in the matter of the impersonal judgement will not be carried out as an independent topic, but will merely be discussed by way of reference at necessary points. Moreover in recent years there have been many logicians who have emphasized the "judgment of relation" (*Relationsurteil*).[2] However, inasmuch as the views of scholars vary conspicuously as to the meaning of the concepts of "relational judgments", in the present work it will suffice to mention them when necessary without bringing them together and examining them under an independent heading.

Moreover, among the various forms of inference, I should like to give my attention especially to the forms of expression of simple inference. In Western formal logic this problem is examined under the "syllogism". but in everyday life very often the method is used of demonstrating the conclusion by advancing only one premise, in the manner "x, therefore y". We must in addition consider the joining together of several inferences. However, the compound syllogism—i.e. a form which joins together complete syllogisms—is in actual fact seldom used; in almost all situations a form is used which links together abbreviated syllogisms. This is called in formal logic the *sorites* or *Kettenschluss.* We must of course also be concerned with the question how these chains of inference are differently applied by various peoples.[3]

Since these forms of expression we have discussed, it seems to me, exhibit especially well the typical features of the ways of thinking of a people, when we have made an investigation of these, we will, I believe, be able to come to a provisional conclusion as to what these features are.

Such, then, is the use of linguistic expressions as basic material for clearly understanding the features of the ways of thinking of a given people; but even better material is offered by logic, whether it be originated or adopted by the people. Since the original name for logic, ἡλογικὴ τέχνή means skill in regard to *logos* (word), the features of the ways of thinking which are unconsciously embodied in language, may possibly become conscious in logic and may moreover be displayed in a systematized, organized state. In this I single out the most important key for the study of the features of the ways of thinking of a people. Accordingly, by studying the logic of the East, while at the same time comparing it with the logic of the West, we should be able to apprehend the features of the ways of thinking of the various Eastern peoples. Logic in the East originally appeared in India, but when it was introduced into Tibet, China and Japan, it was practiced in different ways in each place, and in each country it was considerably changed in appearance. Although logic should be the most universal form of learning, as a matter of historical fact it has by no means been transmitted to these other peoples in its original state. Naturally, the characteristic features of ways of thinking, differing with each people, are conspicuously reflected in such mutual differences in native or imported patterns of logic.

But it ought to be noted here that those who have mastered logic and actually apply it are the *intellectual class* within a given people. Some of the intellectual class within a given people think in conformity to logic, and logic becomes a standard for them in the orderly statement of the content of their thoughts.[4] In spite of the fact that the masses use language constantly every day, the use of logical forms of expression by them is almost non-existent. Consequently it is difficult to say that logic regulates in their entirety the ways of thinking of a given people to the same extent as do linguistic forms. It is impossible to hold absolutely that conclusions obtained from the examination of the systems of logic of the past are directly appropriate to the entire people who study this logic. In order to take logic as a key for the examination of the ways of thinking of a given people, it is necessary to take into consideration just such facts as these.

The comparison of the systems of logic of East and West is in itself a great problem and an independent topic of study. Since it is impossible to discuss this problem fully in this work, I shall discuss it *only insofar as it is related to the ways of thinking of the people at large.*

---

1) Although every judgment can be expressed in the simple form "A is B", we must divide it into several kinds. The meaning of this simple judgment may be different on different occasions. Concerning this problem Joseph says, "Thus we may take the proposition, and point out that in every affirmative categorical proposition there is a subject about which something is said and a predicate, or something which is said about it. This is true equally of the propositions 'A horse is an animal', 'First-class railway tickets are white', and '*Londre* is London'. We may, if we like, because in all propositions there is formally the same distinction of subject and predicate, take symbols which will stand for subject and predicate, whatever they are, and say that all affirmative categorical propositions are of the form 'S is P'. But when we ask for the meaning of this form, and in what sense S is P, it is clear that the meaning varies in different propositions. *Londre* is just the same as London; but a horse is not just the same as an animal; it may be said that 'animal' is an attribute of horse, and 'white' of first-class railway tickets, but animal is an attribute belonging to horses in quite a different way from that in which white belongs to first-class railway tickets; these might well be of any other color, and still entitle the holder to travel first-class by the

railway; a horse could not cease to be an animal and still continue to be a horse. The meaning of the formula 'S is P' cannot possibly be fully known merely by understanding that S and P are some subject and predicate; it is necessary to understand what kind of subject and predicate they are, what the relation is between them, and in what sense one is the other; and if this sense is different in different cases, just as animal is something different in a dog and a starfish, then the thorough study of the form of thought involves the consideration of material differences in the thoughts also". H.V.B. Joseph: *An Introduction to Logic*, 2nd ed., Oxford 1916, pp. 6–7.

My method is slightly different from that of Joseph. My classification will be discussed on another occasion.

2) Pfänder classifies this kind of judgment according to the following four classes:

1) Vergleichungssachverhälte
2) Zugehörigkeitssachverhälte
3) Abhängigkeitssachverhälte
4) intentionale Sachverhälte.

(*Logik*, S. 184 ff.: K. Ikegami: *Ronrigaku*, p. 243) Sigwart means by the word "Relationsurteil" the full wing propositions, e.g., A is similar to B: A is different from B; A is bigger than B; A is left to B; A is faster than B, etc.

3) The differences displayed by Chinese, Indians and Greeks in their employment of the chain of reasoning was pointed out briefly by P. Masson-Oursel: Esquisse d'une theorie comparée du sorite (*Revue de Metaphysique et de Morale*, 1912, pp. 810–824.)

4) "Logic makes us realize better what the general forms of speech that we habitually use really means, and familiarises us with the task of examining our reasonings and looking to see whether they are conclusive." (Joseph: *op. cit.* p. 11)

5. Ways of thinking and cultural phenomena

Here, as above, we shall not concern ourselves with logical systems as such, nor shall we deal with questions of *comparative philosophy*.[1] The reason for this is that, in studying the ways of thinking of a given people, one should consider the ways of thinking adopted by all the members of that group. In so doing, it is preferable to exclude from consideration the characteristic ways of thinking of the individual philosophers. Of course every philosopher, however great, is conditioned by a certain region and a certain time. He cannot, moreover, avoid a certain social conditioning as a member of a particular people. Thus, the ways of thinking of philosophers cannot be freed completely from national or historical tradition. On the other hand, however, a great philosopher not infrequently follows a way of thinking which differs from that of the nation which gave him birth. Indeed, a philosopher is often considered great for this very reason. Therefore, the ways or patterns of thinking of individual philosophers will generally be disregarded in this work, and will be referred to only when necessary. However, we will deal with the matter when the ways or patterns of thinking of the majority of the philosophers of a given people exhibit certain common tendencies.

On the other hand I shall take up, in my study of the ways of thinking of a people, the characteristic popular sayings, proverb and folklore of that people. Nor will it be out of place to include within the limits of this study all such generally current expressions even when found in the writings of formal philosophers. One must, however, exercise considerable caution in determining which of the numerous expressions found among the people are universal and truly of the people. In addition, such things as myths, religious scriptures, and works of literature in general must, of course, be considered as important sources for our study. Since such documents are found in great number among all peoples, one must choose as source material those among them which are particularly esteemed by *the people in question.* Those works which are not esteemed by the people, even though they may be interesting from the point of view of the modern reader, will be of little significance as sources for determining the ways of thinking common to the entire people. But on the other hand, works which furnish a critique of the ways of thinking of a given people written by *foreigners*, in spite of the fact that the people in question may know nothing of such works, are very important sources in that they clarify the differences between the ways of thinking of the two nations involved.

1) The term "comparative philosophy" was used by Masson-Oursel: *La philosophie comparée*, 1925. We can regard the following works as of the same line, G. Misch: *Der Weg in die Philosophie*: Y. Ruben: Indische und griechische Metaphysik (*Zeitschrift für Indologie und Iranistik.* VIII, 1931, S. 147 f.)

6. Ways of thinking as revealed in the pattern of adoption of a foreign culture

The *modern* investigator draws his conclusions about the ways of thinking of peoples by means of comparative study, with linguistic forms, logic, and general cultural phenomena furnishing the bases for such study. There are, however, instances of a given people, in the course of its *past* history, elucidating concretely its own ways of thinking which differ from those of another people. This insight is furnished by the way in which one people adopts the ways or patterns of thinking of another. One people does not adopt the ways or patterns of thinking of another in their original forms, but rather criticizes them, selects from them, and modifies them in the course of adoption. In this process the characteristics of the ways of thinking of this people are clearly indicated. The problem of the interplay of cultures has been investigated a great deal, but such studies have been made mainly from the historical and philological point of view. The subject has not been sufficiently explored from the standpoint of the ways of thinking. It is this problem to which I address myself in this book.

Speaking from the standpoint of the ways of thinking, the reception of a universal religion, among the various phenomena of cultural interplay, would seem to furnish a most valuable clue to the understanding of the characteristic ways of thinking of a people. In what form does this people adopt the universal religion, and in what way is the religion modified? Now the universal religion in the East is, of course, Buddhism. (In the case of Japan, Confucianism should also be considered.) It will be important to study the ways in which the characteristic ways of thinking of the various peoples directed the adoption of Buddhism. There have been many studies of the spread (adoption, from the point of view of the people) of Buddhism. These too have been principally historical and philological, and it appears that there has been no consideration of the problem from the standpoint of ways of thinking. This is the problem I should like to consider.

7. The order in which the ways of thinking of the various Eastern peoples will be considered

In accordance with the methodology outlined above, I intend to proceed with this study in the following way. First, in my study of each of the Eastern peoples, I shall bring out the characteristics of their ways of thinking as discernible in the forms of expression of the simplest judgments and inferences. These characteristics are among the most fundamental to the ways of thinking of a people. Next I shall examine the ways in which such characteristic ways of thinking operate in connection with actual cultural phenomena (especially the mode of acceptance of Buddhism). These phenomena most certainly have a logical relationship with the characteristics discernible in the mode of expression of simple judgments and inferences. My study will concern itself with this relationship.

In studying the characteristics of the ways of thinking of Eastern peoples, the question arises as to the proper order in which to deal with the several peoples. In my opinion, to study India, China, and Japan in that order is most in accordance with historical actuality. Since the Indians are, in the main, of the same racial, linguistic and cultural family as Occidentals, I shall first contrast these two groups and point out their differences from the standpoint of their ways of thinking. Then I shall discuss the Chinese, who are a completely different people in origin. Lastly I shall come to Japan, which was influenced culturally by India and China (note that in contrast to this, pre-modern India had practically no cultural influence from Japan and China). One would have to discuss India and China even if one began with Japan. Therefore, out of practical considerations I have decided upon the first-named order. Further, Tibet, although not an important region from the political or economic point of view, cannot be overlooked in *a consideration of ways of thinking,* in that it was there that Indian logic found widest acceptance. Consequently we shall give collateral consideration to the ways of thinking of the Tibetans.

I should further like to point out here that "the Chinese" as used in this book refers to the Han race, and not to the citizens of the Republic of China. From the standpoint of nationality Tibetans are Chinese. "Chinese national" is a *political* concept, whereas "the Chinese", "the Tibetans", are cultural concepts. In a consideration of the ways of thinking, the Chinese and the Tibetans must of course be distinguished. (In the Occident this is regarded as a truism.)

[In each of the following parts II–V the forms of expression of judgment and inference of the people concerned are discussed in the Japanese original as the first section of each part. However, due to shortage of space, these sections have not been translated in this English version.]

PART II. THE WAYS OF THINKING OF THE INDIAN PEOPLE

Special Features of the Ways of Thinking Characterized in Cultural Phenomena

Chapter 1. Introduction

By what method can we grasp the special features of the ways of thinking of the Indians? Going back to the various cultural phenomena in Indian history, to examine their cultural phenomena widely and impartially will not be an easy task. If a student, who was careless of methodology, judged on the bases of his optional and partial data that the Indian racial characteristics were such and such, he may reach the right conclusion but he may also draw wrong conclusions. For instance a study of the ancient Indian society resulted in completely opposite conclusions; those who based themselves on Brahmanic literatures and those who used Buddhist literatures derived conflicting conclusions. In our present study of the ways of thinking there would be such a danger, because it would be impossible to exhaust all existing sources and data.

Therefore, in order to formulate *objective* conclusions, we must consider the methodology to be employed.

At first we must lay stress on the expression of language; in this chapter we will examine some of the major problems related to expression. It is important—it is the first step as I have said before—to compare the Indian language with the Greek and Latin languages in respect to their grammers and syntaxes. If we had some concrete examples of Greek or Latin translation, of the Indian languages or vice versa, they would be very convenient for our study, but unfortunately we have nothing like them. Although the *Bhagavadgītā*, a famous religious book of India, and "the *Dhammapada*", a sacred book of Buddhists, were translated by modern European scholars, the Greek and Latin translation of the former and the Latin translation of the latter offer us important data for reference.[1] The archeological relics and epigraphs, in which Indian languages are written together with European classical languages, are limited only to certain coins so they are of little use in our present study.

Secondly as a source of data, we must lay stress on the way the Indians have taken in foreign cultures; but we regret that the evidences of this have not remained in clear form. This is due to the fact that they did not accept Chinese culture, and because the degree of recipiency in which they accepted Greek culture has yet to be clarified sufficiently. But it is a fact that to a certain degree they accepted Greek and Latin cultures, so we admit it as a part of our investigation.

Thirdly we must lay stress on the criticism of Indian thought by foreigners as important datum for our study. In ancient time some Greeks, Romans and Chinese criticized Indian thought from their respective standpoint. And there were some Japanese who criticized Indian thought, basing their criticism on the Chinese translation of sacred Buddhist books. And again it is a well known fact that in modern times many European scholars examined and criticized Indian thought.

Lastly we must select data from the sentences written by the Indians themselves. This appears simple, but in reality this is very difficult. What datum to choose from infinite available sources? By what can we know the characteristic of racial ways of thinking? First of all we consider those literatures which have been considered authoritative by the majority of people. For example about "the *Praśnottararatnamālika*" (Treasure garland of question and answer),[2] Brahmanic tradition says it was written by the Vedāntist Saṅkara, Jain tradition says it was written by the Jain King Amoghavarṣa or the Jain Vimala, and Buddhist tradition says it the was written by a Buddhist; we can really find its Tibetan translation in the Tibetan Tripiṭaka. From this we can say that this book is an important datum, though it is relatively unknown, in our examination of the Indian ways of thinking or racial inclination in general. Again the *Kural*, which has been called the Veda in Tamil language, has been admitted as the sacred book by each of Jain, Buddhist, Viṣṇu and Śiva schools; thus, it falls into the same category as that of the *Praśnottararatnamālikā*.

On the contrary, even though a book is famous to foreigners, if its thought content had not been known as widely to the Indians, we should be very careful when we use it as a datum for our investigation. As there are only a limited number of books which were admitted by the followers of all religions as their authority, we must carefully compare every datum with one another on each point. Especially, when the same sentence is found in various books belonging to different sects,[3] this reveals its general acceptance and may be referred to in determining the characteristics of the ways of thinking of a race.

We shall be able to reach the right conclusion by which the characteristics of the ways of thinking of a race will be shown, when we shall have compared this or that datum with each other and examined all data completely.

In the following, I will combine the conclusion gained through examining these data with the conclusion gained through examining the form of judgment and inference; and then around these results, I will consider synthetically the characteristics of the ways of thinking of the Indians.

---

1) Greek trns. of the *Bhagavadgītā* (Bhag.) in Sanskrit:
Gita, e Thespecion Melos. metaphrastheisa ek tou Brakhmanikou para Dēmētriou Galanou, en Athēnais, 1848.
Latin trans. of it:
Bhagavad-Gita, textum recensuit adnotationes criticus et interpretationem Latinam adiecit, Aug. Guil. von Schlegel. Editio altera auctior et emendatior cura Christiani Lasseni. Bonnae, 1846.
Latin trans. of the *Dhammapada* (Dhp.) in Pāli:
Dhammapadam, ex tribus codicibus hauniensibus Palice edidit, Latine vertit, excerptis ex commentario Palico notisque illustravit, V. Fausböll, Hauniae, 1855.
In the following I will often use these two books, which seem to be representative of Indian spiritual culture, as a key in the comparative study of the ways of thinking.

2) I quoted from the text ed. by Yenshō Kanakura in his *Indo Seishin Bunka no Kenkyū* (印度精神文化の研究 *Study of Indian Spiritual Culture*), pp. 297 ff.
This seems to be written in its original form by a Buddhist before the 10th century. Its content was so excellent that other religions plundered its whole sentences and each maintained mutually that it had been written by someone belonging to their own religion. The book, which was inherited by Brahmanic schools, contains later addition, so the small books of Buddhists and Jains are worth studying.

3) The same sentences can be seen in early Buddhist canons, early Jain canons, Mahābhārata and Brahmanic sacred books. These can be seen pan-Indian thought. But sometimes they might have been influenced by the common restriction of the age when they were written, so that we might be careful to compare them with various thoughts in later ages.

Chapter 2. Laying stress on the universal

(1) Preponderance of abstract notion

Indian people are inclined to consider the universal seriously in their thinking process. This can be easily seen in the fact of their verbal usage in which they have willingly used abstract nouns. In Sanskrit, abstract noun is formed adding -tā (f.) or -tva (n.) suffix to the root. These suffixes correspond to -*τη* (Greek), -tas (Latin), -tät (German), -té (French), -ty (English) and etymologically they have close connection. In these European languages, however, abstract nouns are scarcely used except in scientific essays or formal sentences, while in Sanskrit they are often used even in the usual speeches. For examples, 'He becomes old.',[1] 'Er wird alt.' is expressed in Sanskrit 'He goes to oldness.' (*vṛddhatām* (-tvam, -bhāvam) *gacchati* (āgacchati, upaiti etc.)); 'The fruit becomes soft.', 'Die Frucht wird weich.' is expressed in Sanskrit 'The fruit goes to softness.' (*phalaṃ mṛdutām* (-tvam, -bhāvam, mārdavaṃ) *yāti*); 'He goes as a messenger.', 'Er geht als Bote.' is expressed 'He goes with the quality of mesenger.' (*gacchati dautyena*); 'A man was seen to be a tree.' is expressed 'A man was represented by the quality of tree.' (*pumān kaścid.* v. *vṛkṣatvenopavarṇitaḥ*).[2] The European languages express the individual by its attribute or quality realized concretely by the individual itself, while the Sanskrit expresses the individual only as one of instances belonging to the abstract universal.

In Sanskrit, furthermore, any noun or adjective can become an abstract nouns by addition of -tā or -tva suffix, i.e., the abstract noun can be made without limit in Sanskrit. On the contrary, in the Greek or Latin language the abstract noun is made by addition or -*τη* or -tas, and does not allow such freedom. Here we can also find one of Indian characteristics to think anything abstractly and universally.

The expression using cognate object more often appears in early Indian languages than in European languages. In English there are some expressions using cognate object as 'to fight a battle', 'to die the death', 'to live a good life' etc., but such usage is limited. On the contrary in classical Indian languages such expression have been widely and freely allowed through all ages.[3] Therefore it is often impossible to translate from Indian directly into the European languages; e.g., *kāmakāmaḥ* = amori dediti

(*Dhp.* 83) (those who persuit their desire), abhijñānābhijñātaiḥ (be possessed of occult power),[4] varṣam varṣate, tapas tapate etc..

That Indians were skillful in abstract speculation can be seen in their skillful expression of the ideas of numbers. A great number or infinitesimal number often appears in religious books and literary works. This reveals their rich imagination and analysis. The Arabic numerals of today had been invented by the Indians, and the Arabians only transmitted it into European countries. The manner of writing by numbering order and the idea of zero were both invented by the Indians. In Sanskrit zero is represented by '*śūnya*' which is translated as '*kōng*' (空) in the Chinese translation of Buddhist canons.

The characteristics of ways of thinking, by which the Indians think the individual or the particular as only one example belonging to the universal, appears clearly even in their theoretical philosophy.

There is no idea of the individual in the Vaiśeṣika Philosophy which organized the systematical natural philosophy objectively. So the Vaiśeṣika philosophers used the technical term of 'the particular in the ultimate' (antyaviśeṣa, biān yi, 邊異) to represent the notion of the individual. Of course in other philosophy there was the conception of the individual and its unique meaning was investigated in India. But in Indian philosophy the position of the individual was not compatible with the particular and the universal, differing from European philosophy in which the individual, the particular, and the universal were equally admitted to have their respective meaning and position.

This way of thinking appears not only in their philosophy but also in their usual speeches; e.g., in Sanskrit *the plural form* of the abstract noun often appears, i.e., *lakṣmyaḥ* means 'happiness of a person', *kīrtayaḥ* means 'honour of a person' and *bhayeṣu* (lit. in horrors) means 'when he was filled with horror' (= *bhayakāleṣu*). There are a few usages like this in European languages, but they are generally used with special meaning, while in Sanskrit many plural forms of abstract nouns are used in the meaning not dissimiliar to its singular form. Moreover in modern European languages like German and French, the exactly opposite phenomenon can be seen, i.e., the plural form of a proper noun means those who belong to him, whose families including all servants and maids, those who can be ascribed to that person's type; e.g., 'die Goethe' means 'the family of Goethe', 'men who are self-conceited themselves as Goethe' or 'people who have a brilliant talent', 'les Périclès' means 'people who are self-conceited of their talent like Périclès'.[5] In short, European people think of the abstract notion of an abstract noun as being constructed only by the universal meaning which is separated from daily experience, so that they represent it in the singular form; on the contrary, the Indians think of the abstract notion as what is included within an experiential fact like an essential principle, so that they often represent it in the plural form. And again, modern European people lay stress on the significance of the individual, so that they can easily classify a man by the type similar to a special person and change a proper noun into a common noun; on the contrary, the Indians neglect the significance of the individual so that such expressions as 'die Goethe' or 'les Périclès' do not appear at all.

According to the way of thinking of Indians, therefore, the essence of the individual or the particular is no more than the universal by which the individual or the particular is supported and realized. The Indians lay stress on the significance of the universal only, and they almost neglect the significance of the individual or the particular. From this a new way of thinking is introduced; i.e., the difference between those who possess an attribute and the attribute itself is not clarified adequately by the Indians, and the difference between those who support a substance and the substance itself is not clarified. In Indian languages there are many examples of 'κατ' ἐξοχήν' (par excellence) which Buddhist called '*Suō ji bié ming,* 總卽別名', i.e., a common noun used as a proper noun; e.g., *Buddha* (Lit. one who has gained the enlightenment) became a proper noun of Śākyamuni, and *Jina* (Lit. one who has won) became a proper name of Vardhamāna. As the result of the same thinking process, the neuter singular form of an adjective sometimes fulfills the function of an abstract noun, e.g., *śuci* (pure, pureness), *sthira* (= solid, solidity = sthairya), *ślāghya* (excellent, excellence); or again the neuter singular form of an adjective sometimes fulfills the function of a collective noun, e.g., *palita* (gray, gray hair).[6] So in Sanskrit there are such cases where the distinction between abstract 'solidity' and a concrete 'solid' thing is not clarified in the actual language, even though it may be clarified by using an abstract noun.

In short, these linguistic phenomena in Indian languages resulted from the Indians being unaware of the significance of the inherent judgment.

Now the characteristic of the way of thinking mentioned above influences the foundations of the Indian languages and results in some important changes. By this way of thinking, the distinction between an attribute and a supporter of that attribute is almost neglected, so that the Indians can not distinguish between Substantiv and Adjectiv which are two kinds of Nomen. In Sanskrit grammar, these two have little difference in regard to declension, composition and derivation. Especially in the Vedic literature, it is very difficult for us to find out which is Substantiv and which is Epithet among many Nomina that indicate the same object. Even in classical Sanskrit, an Adjektiv is used as a Substantiv, e.g., *suhṛd* (good-hearted, a friend), *tapana* (burning, the sun). On the contrary in classical European languages, as is mentioned, regarding the expression of inherent judgment, Substantiv and Adjektiv show a little variation in the special occasions.

The inclination laying stress on the universal was seen to some degree among the ancient Europeans, and in their languages there were some linguistic bases for it. An adjective takes a form corresponding to the gender and number of the noun, which it modifies, both in classical European and Indian languages, and it does not appear in its original form; e.g., ἀὑράγαθός, vir honus (good man), γυνὴἀγαθή, mulier bona (good woman). Such a grammatical rule makes a speaker understand that it is a self-evident truth that the essence of conception,which is expressed by an adjective, is different from the attribute, which is indicated by the adjective and which is attendant on each concrete thing. Plato touched lastly the problem of 'Virtue itself as to cover whole' (καθδλου), after he had examined human virtue (ἀρετή) analyzing the general idea into the virtue of man, of woman, of child, of slave and so on. This thinking process of Plato would have been very natural and rational for the Greek people at that time; the problem, however, of whether it is possible to pursue the abstract 'virtue in general' apart from concrete things becomes a difficult question in modern ethics. But in India the conception, which was represented by an adjective, had more importance than the individual, which was modified by the adjective; and the significance of individual things, which realized the conception represented by the adjective in it, was reduced to almost nothing for the Indians.

---

1) In modern English, the predicative modifier is called 'predicative', e.g., 'He grows *old*,', 'He goes *mad*.', 'The dream will come *true*.' (cf. e.g. O. Jespersen: *The philosophy of grammar*, pp. 131–132).

In Sanskrit this predicative is often expressed by abstract noun.

2) To denote 'as ——' the instrumental is used generally, but sometimes

the dative and the locative are used in Sanskrit; e.g., '*vṛtavān mitratvāya uṛpo nṛpam.*' (*Kathās.*, 38, 153) (= The king chose a king as his friend.), '*patitve vṛtaḥ*'. (*Nala* 5, 16) (= chosen as a groom.) (Speyer: *Vedische und Sanskrit-Syntax*, S. 36)

What is expressed by the dative and locative seems to have purpose-idea.

3) Speyer: *Vedische und Sanskrit-Syntax*, § 24.

4) cf. Small *Sukhāvatīvyūha* ed. by Ryōsaburō Sakaki in his *Bongogaku* (梵語學 "Sanskrit Grammar"), p. 251.

5) Izuru Shimmura 新村出: *Gengogaku Josetsu* (言語學序說 Introduction to Linguistics), Tokyo, Kōbundo, 1923, p. 251.

6) Speyer: *Vedische und Sanskrit-Syntax*, § 2.

(2) The bestowal of substantiality to the abstract conception

As a result of the Indian propensity for the abstract notion, in their thinking process an abstract idea is expressed as if it were a concrete object, i. e., in their thinking process the universal is easily bestowed substantiality. Already in the Brāhmaṇas, explanations on the Vedic sacrifices, abstract ideas are treated being ranked with the concrete things as if they existed in the same demension. This has been stated as follows: "The most remarkable characteristic of this age was that they gave spiritual powers, mysterious powers and the quality of Godness without personification to the concrete elements by which the universe was constructed (the heaven; the sky; the earth; the sun and the moon; stars and directions; soil, water, fire, wind and ether; years and months; seasons; animals, plants and minerals and so on), to the elements which were necessary for their rituals (the apparatus; the rythm, curse and name and so on), to the physical and mental organs, functions, qualities, abstract conceptions, numerals and so on; in other words, to all sorts of phenomena in the natural world and human life, especially in religious ceremony".[1] It seems that Brahmin priests of ancient India engaged no doubt in their speculations in accordance with such a way of thinking. The word '*brahman*', the original meaning of which was the magical power of spells used freely by Brahmins, became at the same time the name of Brahmins themselves only by changing the position of its accent; by the same thinking process '*kṣatriya*', the name of the royal family, came from the word '*kṣatra*', the original meaning of which was the reigning power. Here the essential of a thing is identified with the realizer of its power, and an abstract noun is used as a common noun; i.e., the Indians miss the consciousness of fictionality in the fictionally substantial notion (fiktive Substanzbegriffe).

According to the description in some *Upaniṣads*, the Indians assumed two ways, i.e. the devayāna and the pitṛyāna, along which man goes after his death.[2] One who goes along the devayāna enters successively into the frame of his cremation, the day, a half month while the moon increases, six months while the sun goes to north, the year or the world of gods, the sun, the moon, the thunderbeam and then he enters into the Brahman or the world of Brahman; thus he never returns to this world. On the other hand, one who goes along the pitṛyāna enters successively into the smoke of his cremation, the night, a half month while the moon decreases, six months while the sun goes to south, the world of ancestors' spirits, the sky, the moon where he stays to enjoy the fruit of his good deeds until the transmitted merits of his good deeds remain; and then he begins to descend to this world; he enters successively into the sky, wind, smoke, fog, cloud, rain; and then he enters into some food like rice and barley; he becomes a spermatozoon if he enters happily into a man; and then he enters into a womb of a woman to make rebirth. Out of these steps after death, the smoke of cremation, the world of ancestors' spirits, the sun, the moon and the thunderbeam have some extents in space, so that it is no wonder that a dead man passes through these steps; but the night, a half month while the moon increases or decreases and six months while the sun goes to north or south are not anything in space but something in time, so that these descriptions in the *Upaniṣads* seem very strange, as it tells us a dead man passes through the devayāna or pitṛyāna both in space and in time. This, however, caused little wonder to the Indians at that time, who had inherited the way of thinking in the Brāhmaṇa literature as it had been. Those scholars, who wrote the Brāhmaṇa literature, thought that all the abstract conceptions or the ideas in space had also substantiality, and discussed them putting in the same level as the material things in space. By this way of thinging, the day, the night, a half month and six months etc. *can be expressed as if they were the concrete things.* Some philosophers in the Upaniṣads seemed to be incapable to get rid of such a way of thinking, and the theory of the two ways after death in the *Upaniṣads* has been adopted without change by the later Vedāntic philosophers.

Thereafter, this way of thinking has become popular among the common people in India. In many popular books, e.g., in the *Upamitibhavaprapañca-kathā*, an educational story of Jains, the *Prabodhacandrodaya*, a drama based on the Vedāntic philosophy, many abstract nouns are used as the main characters of them. These stories and dramas would not be welcomed by the European people, but they can excite much interest among the Indians.

Such cases are not a few that this way of thinking has been adopted by Indian philosophers. In the Buddha period, Pakudha Kaccāyana supposed the pain and the pleasure in addition to the earth, water, fire, wind, souls and sky as the eternal, unchangeable, independent elements, by which all things in the universe were composed. Makkhali Gosāla of the Ājīvikas supposed the gain, loss, life and death besides them as the substantial principles. With the Jains the condition of movement (dharma) and the condition of non-movement (adharma) were also the independent substances. The Sarvāstivādins, who became the most prosperous Buddhist school, maintained that all the elements admitted in Buddhism exist really in all time through three periods i.e. the past, the present and the future. The elements (*dharma*) mentioned by them rather belong to the psychological functions or the abstract ideas. And the Vaiśeṣikas supposed the six padārthas (the meanings of words) as the fundamental principles, and they are such abstract ideas that are classified into six groups and admitted as the substantial elements. The philosophy of the Sarvāstivādins and the Vaiśeṣikas are called the 'Conceptional Existentialism' (Begriffsrealismus) by the European scholars. Their systems are similar to the Realism of European philosophy in the medieval age, but the former has more characteristic than the latter.

Hegel clarified the characteristic of Indian philosophy and characterized it as "growing of the mind toward oneself in the most abstract way" (Fürsichwerden der Seele auf die abstrakteste Weise), and he called it 'intellectual substantiality' (intellektuelle Substantialität).[4] This characterization of Hegel is not right in the case of the Vedānta Philosophy, which has been the main flow of Indian philosophy; however the endowment of conceptional substantility can be regarded as a prominent characteristic among the most of Indian philosophy.

---

1) Naoshirō Tsuji 辻直四郎: *Veda oyobi Burāhumana no Shisō* (ヴェーダ及びブラーフマナの思想 Thoughts in the Vedas and Brahmanas, *Iwanami Kōza* 岩波講座 *Tōyō Shisō* 東洋思想), p. 61.

2) *Bṛhad. Up.* VI, 2, 1–16; *Chānd. Up.* V, 3–10; *Jaim. Br.* I, 45–46.

3) Schayer: *Ausgewählte Kapitel aus dem Prasannapadā*, Einlertung, S. XXII. W. Ruben: *Indische und Griechische Metaphysik*, S. 56. usw.

4) Hegel: *Vorlesung über die Geschichte der Philosophie*, herausgegeben von Michelet, S. 162.

Chapter 3. The negative character

(1) Fondness for the negative expression

The Indians become to aim at the non-determinant at last, as the result of their way of thinking by which the universal is aimed at. To say in general, the universal is less limited than the individual, so that on the last point of aiming at the universal they become to think the non-determinant. Thus the negative character of Indian culture comes into existence.

When we pick up the language as our first problem, we cannot help giving attention to why the Indians are so fond of the noun with the negative. For instance, the Indians say 'victory or non victory' (*jayājayau*) instead of to say 'victory or defeat' as in our languages, and they say 'non-one' (*naneka*) instead of to say 'many'. The word composed with the negative has not only negative meaning but also it has positive meaning. In the Indian mind 'non-idleness' (*apramāda*), 'non-grudge' (*avera*),[1] 'non-violence' (*ahiṃsā*) etc. appeal as the more positive morality than 'exertion', 'tolerance', 'peace' etc. To the Europeans such a negative expression of these virtues appeal less than a positive expression as for the practical meaning, but to the Indians these negatively expressed virtues have more power.

A yoga-disciple of the Brahmanic schools must always keep five moral precepts, i.e., non-violence (*ahiṃsā*), sincerity (*satya*), non-theft (*asteya*), chastity (*brahmacarya*) and non-property (*aparigraha*).[2] Thus three of them are expressed in the negative form. And the precepts which must be kept by the layman belonging to Buddhism and Jainism are all shown in the negative form, and the original meaning of which are 'to rest apart from violence', 'to rest apart from theft' and so on.[3] The Sarvāstivādins also enumerate negatively 'non-idleness' (*apramāda*), 'non-attachment' (*anabhidhyā*), 'non-wrath' (*avyāpāda*) and 'non-violence' (*ahṃisā*) in the ten great deeds of mind. In the Brahmanic canons the various precepts are sometimes written by the positive expression; but in the *Vinaya-piṭaka*, in which the precepts for Buddhist monks are set forth they are almost written by the negative form. Thus the Indians are apt to see morality in the negation of the secular human action, so that they lay stress on the negative phase. To other nations showing the moral precepts in the negative form seemed somewhat powerless and unsatisfactory, but to the Indians, who lay stress on the negative phase and pursue the non-determinant, the negative form of expression has more positive and powerful meaning.

Therefore the Indians like to use the negative conceptions even in the ordinary sentences. In the classical and modern European languages the expression of the negative judgment is usually made by adding the negative to the finite verb, e.g., 'Er wird nicht gehen.' On the other hand, in the ancient Indian language the central conception of a sentence is expressed in negative form, e.g., 'One (who attains to the Enlightenment) goes to the non-meeting with the king of Death' (*adassanaṃ maccurājassa gacche* (Dhp, 46) = *mortis regem non videbit.* = never meet with the King of Death.) Thus the Europeans and the Japanese make the negative sentence using the positive and affirmative conception as its material, while the Indians make it using the negative conception.

Again in the classical European languages, the negative form of the participle of a verb is made in the same way as when the negative form of a finite verb is made; on the other hand in the ancient Indian languages it is made in the same way as when the negative form of a noun is made; e. g., *appasaṃ udayavyayaṃ* (Dhp. 113) = *ortum* (rerum) *et interitum non animadvertens.* This is also a linguistic phenomenon which has intimate connection with their fondness for the negative conception.

The Indians think a negative form is not only negative but also positive and affirmative. So in Indian logic the universal negative judgment (E) is not used, and it is discussed after being changed into the universal positive judgment (A); e.g., 'All the speeches are non-eternal.' (*anityaḥ śabdaḥ*).

---

(1) *pamāda=socordia, appamāda=vigirantia, Dhp.* 21 f. : *vera=iracundia, avera=placabilitas, Dhp.* 5.

(2) *Yoga-sūtra* II, 30.
This is taken up in the *Kūrma-purāṇa.* It is also adopted by Vivekānanda as one of the 'rājayoga' practices. cp. Romain Rolland: *La vie de Vivekananda.* II, p. 66.

(3) In Pali, "*paṇatipātā veramṇī, adinnādānā veramaḥī, kāmesu micchācārā, veramaṇī, musāvādā veramaṇī.*"; In Buddhist Sanskrit, "*prāṇātipātād viratiḥ, adattādānād viratiḥ, kāmamithyācārād viratiṇ, musāvādāt prativiratiḥ*". (*Mahāvyutpatti.* XCII); and the Jains say, "*hiṃsā-anṛta-steya-abrahma-parigrahebhyo viratir vratam*". (*Tattvarthādhigamasūtra.* VII, 1).

(2) Negatively grasping the absolute

Being based on the way of thinking of graping anything negatively, the Indians pursue the Infinite or the Negative and heighten the idea of infinity in their philosophical approaches. The Absolute is expressed as the Infinite or the Negative by the Indians.

In the remote ages, philosophical thought about world creation by the poets of the Ṛg-Veda reached its peak when they sang of the universal principle in the hymn called 'Nāsadāsītya' (Then there was neither non-existence nor existence———).[1] According to this hymn, in primordial antiquity there was neither non-existence no rexistence, neither heaven nor space, neither death nor non-death, and there was no distinction between day and night. All the universe was covered with darkness, and all the universe was a rippling water devoid of light. 'That Oneness' (*tad ekam*) appeared there by his own heat, and he gave existence to Desire (kāma). Then he realized all things in the universe using Desire as the motive power. After the creation of the universe many gods appeared too.

According to Yājñavalkya, the greatest philosopher among the wise men in the Upaniṣada, the highest principle in the universe is that which is free from all differential qualification. He says, "This essential being (*ātman*) is no other than the pure wisdom without internality and externality.——— It has a non-destructive and non-perishable quality.——— This Ātman can be expressed only through the negative as 'not so, not so' (*neti neti*). It is incomprehensible for it cannot be perceived. It is non-destructive for it cannot be destroyed. It is non-attachment for it attaches itself to nothing. It has never been restrained, disturbed nor injured".[2] In another passage he calls this highest principle the 'Non-perishable' (*akṣara*), and says, "He is neither large and rough (*sthūla*) nor infinitesimal (*sūkṣma*), neither short nor long, neither burning nor moisty. He has no shade, darkness, wind, space, attachment, taste, smell, eyes, ears, speeches, mind, light, vitality, mouth, quantity, internality and externality. He eats nothing and nothing eats him".[3]

We can see similar expressions in the later Upaniṣads; it says, "There shines neither the sun nor the moon nor the stars. That thunder-beam also never shines. To say nothing of fire on earth!"[4] Light in the phenomenal world is almost nothing when it is compared with the Brahman as the light of the Absolute.

In early Buddhism, the state of enlightenment is explained by the similar expression. "Where there exists no earth, water, fire and wind there shines neither the sun, nor the moon, nor the stars, and there exists no darkness. When a Brahmin becomes possible to perceive this by himself and becomes a saint (*muni*) by silent meditation, he shall be able to be free from materiality and non-materiality (*rūpārūpa*) ; pain and pleasure".[5)]

Negative expression is used very abundantly in the scriptures of Mahāyāna Buddhism. As one of the instances I would like to introduce some passages from the *Prajñāpāramitāhṛdayasūtra*. "Thus, the things (*dharma*) all have the characteristic of voidness (*śūnyatā*) ; therefore they are neither created nor perished, they have neither impurity nor purity, they can neither increase nor decrease. Therefore, in the voidness there is neither materiality (*rūpa*) nor sensation (*vedanā*) nor imagination (*saṃjñā*) nor volition (*saṃskāra*) nor consciousness (*vijñāna*), there is neither eyes nor ears nor nose nor tongue nor tactile organs nor intellect, there is neither color and shape nor sound nor odor nor taste nor tangibles nor non-sensuous objects; there exists neither the sphere of vision, the sphere of intellect, ignorance, the extinction of ignorance, old age and death, the extinction of old age and death, suffering, the cause and extinction and the path foward extinction, wisdom nor the attainment of wisdom, for there is nothing to be attained. Because the bodhisattva relies on the prajñāpāramitā, the mind is unobstructed. Because there is no obstruction, there exists no fear. Abandoning all inverted phantasies, the bodhisattva penetraties to Nirvāṇa".

By Nāgārjuna (ca. A.D. 150–250), who is considered to have established the foundation of Mahāyāna Buddhism, Buddhist philosophy was demonstrated to expound the theory of "the excellent casual origination of things (*pratityasamutpāda*) that is non-destructive, non-productive, non-extinctive, non-eternal, non-uniform, non-diversity, non-coming and non-going, and that causes vain phenomena to cease".[6)] These eight kinds of negative expression enumerated here, referred to as the 'Eight Negations', can also be found in other Mahāyāna scriptures.[7)] Nāgārjuna, his followers thought, had chosen these eight negations because they are the most important and representative of the numerous negations to clarify the real aspect of the voidness of all things.[8)] Thus the ultimate reality shown by Mahāyāna

Buddhists is the absolute voidness (*śūnyatā*) that is devoid of all qualifications and about which no conceptional determination can be formed.

Such negative expressions of Mahāyāna Buddhism exerted a favorable influence upon many schools including the Vedānta. "There is neither extinction nor creation, neither one who has been bound nor one who has practiced austerities, neither one who wish to emancipate nor one who obtained the emancipation. This is the highest truth[9] (*paramārthatā*)".[10] The influence of such expressions can be seen not only in Śaṅkara[11] and his followers[12] but in the schools of later Hinduism.[13]

Jains also state similarly: "(One who has obtained enlightenment is) neither long nor short nor circular nor triangle nor square nor glevbular nor black nor blue nor red nor yellow nor white nor fragrant nor ill-smelling nor bitter nor pungent nor puckery nor sour nor sweet nor rough nor soft nor heavy nor light nor cold nor hot nor coarse nor smooth, he neither has a body nor departs from the body nor remains in the body, he is neither feminine nor masculine nor neuter; he has wisdom (*prajñā*) and intellect (*saṃjñā*). However there is no simile (by which the emancipated soul can be known). The essence of the emancipated soul has no form. One who has no word cannot speak a word. There is neither sound nor color and shape nor smell nor taste nor tactile objects.———"[14]

Let us compare this with the case of the Greek people. In Greek philosophy it was the traditional idea that the universe is a circular and complete globe in itself. This theory perhaps originated in Xenophanēs[15] and advocated by Parmenidēs who maintained that existence (τὸ ἐόν) as the fundamental principle of the world is a complete globe.[16] Pythagoras and his followers thought, 'What is determinate is more excellent than what is not determinate'.[17] Empedoclēs taught that in the beginning of the world the universe was globular when it was in chaos.[18] And this idea of the globular universe was inherited by Platōn[19] and Aristotelēs.[20]

Greek people, who had prominent skill in intuition and sculpture, prefered to see the clear image of all things. Therefore, that which was devoid of boundaries was considered to be indeterminate, without certitude, incomplete, and imperfect. Therefore, even in regard to the super-sensory, they could not divorce themselves from their concrete way of thinking. Even Parmenidē, who seemed to grasp the ultimate principle most abstractly and negatively, discussed existence as the fundamental principle of the world as if it were a material existence, expressing it as a spatial and extensive thing. And, the fact that he thought it a globe shows us that he was influenced by the intuitive and concrete view of things which was general among Greek people. Even Platōn called the non-material substance by the visual name of 'idea' (Lit. figure, form).

In general, the early Greek people adopted a way of thinking concretely. Though they speculated things rationally and conceptionally they could never reach such higher abstractions as voidness.[21] As I will state later, the Chinese people more than the Greek people were fond of expressing themselves concretely and intuitively. On the other hand, generally the Indians disliked grasping the Absolute or the ultimate principle concretely and intuitively. We should not maintain that our conclusion could apply to all Indian peoples, but we can say that those who liked abstract speculation inclined to grasp the notion of the Absolute or ultimate principle in terms of the unlimitted and absolute negative.

Now the Absolute which seemed to have such negative characteristics has been expressed as *a non-personal principle* by the Indians. We can also discover such a representation of the Absolute in some of the mystics in Europe, but they did not forget to call such a non-personal Absolute by the name of 'God'. For instance, Scotus Eriugena maintained, "It is not unreasonable for God to be called Nothing because of His transcendent superiority". Yet he called the Absolute 'Deus' to whom he rejected to give any attribute. On the contrary, Indian philosophers regard the highest God as an inferior existence when compared with the highest principle. According to the Vedānta school, the creation of the world by the highest God was caused by his illusion (*māyā*). They say, "The God that is Ātman discriminates himself with his own powers of phantasy. (illusion, *māyā*)".[22] The God that is Ātman is deceived (*sommohita*) by the powers of phantasy (*māyā*) of this God".[23] There is no *māyā* in God himself, but when he creates the world as a supervisitor *māyā* attaches itself to him. God is in an illusory state. And because this illusion exists, the evolution of the world is possible. Therefore it became the fundamental notion in the followers of Śankara that 'Supervisor (*Iśvara*) = Highest Principle (*brahman*) + Illusion (*māyā*)'. This view that the Absolute causes the world to come into existence through illusion has been inherited by some sects of Hinduism.

Thus the ultimate Absolute presumed by the Indians is not a personal god but a non personal and metaphysical Principle. Here we can see *the non-personal character* of the Absolute in Indian thought.

The inclination of grasping the Absolute negatively necessarily leads to the negation of the negative expression itself. According to some

Upaniṣad, Bādhva, a wise man, answered by silence when he was asked the true nature of Brahman. Some one asked to him, "Please teach me the true nature of Brahman". Bādhva was in silence. The man asked again and he spoke nothing. When he was asked repeatedly he said, "I am teaching now, but you cannot understand it. For this Ātman is tranquil in itself".[24] Vimalakīrti, a wise Buddhist layman, seems to have attained to a more abstruse stage of mind. According to the *Vimalakīrtinirdeśa*, Vimalakīrti asked thirty-two Bodhisattvas, "How can it be possible to attain the unequalled truth of Buddhism?". And he listened to their answers silently. At last they asked to Mañjuśrī, a Bodhisattva, to tell his opinion. He told them, "Where there is neither word nor speech, neither revelation nor consciousness. Such a state of mind is called the attainment of the unequalled truth of Buddhism". Then Mañjuśrī called on Vimalakīrti to express his own views. But Vimalakīrti was in silence. Seeing this Mañjuśrī cried, "Well done! I have spoken of 'non-word', but you have revealed it with your body".

In India the various religions refer to the sages and to the religions aspicant as 'MUNI', which means "he who maintains silence".[25] They believe that truth is equivalent to the state of silence. Moreover, Mahāyāna Buddhism rejects any view attached to the void emphasizing that "the void too must be negated". (*kōng yì fù kōng.* 空亦復空). Here we can also see the logic of negation.

---

1) *Ṛg-veda* V, 129.
2) *Bṛhad. Up.* IV, 5, 15.
3) *Ibid.* III, 8, 8.
4) *Kāṭhaka Up.* V, 14. cp. *Śvet. Up.* VI, 14; *Muṇḍ. Up.* II, 2, 10; *Bhag. G.* XV, 6.
5) *Udāna* I, 10. p. 9.
6) The salutation verse of the *Madhyamaka-kārikā* (cp. *Madhyamaka-vṛtti*, ed by L. de la V. Poussin, pp. 3–4).

Such an expression can also be found in the *Saddharmapuṇḍarīka-sūtra*, "He (who enters into the a wakening of faith) finds that all Dharmas are non-destructive, non-productive, non-restrictive, non-resolutive, non-gloomy and non-bright". (ed. by Wogihara & Tsuchida, p. 127, *l.* 10). cp. *Madhyamaka-kārikā* XVI, 5; *Mahāyānasūtrālaṅkāra* VI, 1.

7) cf. 菩薩瓔珞本業經 pt. 2, 佛母品 (*Taishō* vol. 24, p. 1018C); 大般涅槃經(南本) vol. 25; 金光明經 依空滿願品 (*Taishō* vol. 6, p. 380 b; p. 425 b); 玄奘譯 大般若波羅蜜多經 vol. 165 (*Taishō* vol. 5, p. 888 b); vol. 411 (*Taishō* vol. 6, p. 170 b); vol. 504 (*Taishō* vol. 6, p. 569 b); vol. 296 (*Taishō* vol. 6, p. 505 b); vol. 384 (*Taishō* vol. 6, p. 987 c); 大智度論 vol. 74 (*Taishō* vol. 25, p. 579—580 a);

Śālistamba-sūtra (Poussin: Theorie des douze causes, p. 75; *Madhyamaka-vṛtti*, p. 569) etc.

8) Candrakirti says, "As to Pratītyasamutpāda, though we can express endless negative predicates, here we adopt only eight negations. Because these eight can reject all objections". (*Madhyamaka-vṛtti*, 11, 4 f). Also Piṅgala says the same meaning. (問曰，諸法無量，何故但以二此八事一破。答曰，法雖二無量一，略說二八事一，則爲二總破二一切法一。" *Taishō* vol. 30, p. 1 c).

9) Paramārtha is translated as '*shèng-i* 勝義' in the Chinese translation of Buddhist canons.

10) *Māṇḍūkya-kārikā* II, 32. This verse is often quoted in many books. cp. *Amṛtabindu-Up.* 10; *Tripurātāpini-Up.* 10; *Avadhūta-Up.* 8; *Ātma-Up.* 31; *Vidvanmanorañjanī* ad *Vedāntasāra*, ed. by Jacob, p. 135; *Sāṃkhyapravacanabhaṣya*, ed. by R. Garbe, pp. 22, *l.* 6; 28, *l.* 11; 122, *l.* 7; 159, *l.* 8.

11) "If the oneness of Ātman were grasped, all the expression (*vyavahāra*) like 'bondage', 'emancipation' and so on would come to the end". (Śaṅkara; *Brahma-sūtra-bhāṣya*, 1, 2, 6. vol. 1, p. 181, 1. 4. AnSS).

12) "As to this a learned man says, 'I am the faculty of seeing, purity, unchangeable essence. In me there is no bondage and no emancipation' ". (*Vedāntasāra*, § 210. ed. by Böhtlingk) cf. *Vivekacūḍāmaṇi* 503.

13) baddho mukta iti vyakhyā guṇato me, na vastutaḥ, guṇasya māyāmūlatvān na me mokṣo na bandhanam. (*Bhagavatapurāṇa* XI, 11, 1) na bandho 'sti na mokṣo 'sti nābandho 'sti na bandhanam, aprabodhād idaṃ duḥkhaṃ prabodhāt pravilīyate. (*Yogavāsiṣṭha* IV, 38, 22.)

14) Āyāraṅga 1, 5, 6, 4.

15) E. Zeller: *Die Philosophie der Griechen*, Bd. I, Abt. 1. S. 661; P. Deussen: *AGPh.* II, 1, S. 74.

16) Zeller: *op. cit.* I, 1, S. 695; Deussen: *op. cit.* II, 1, S. 83.

17) Zeller: *op. cit.* I, 1, S. 458. cf S. 521.

18) Zeller: *op. cit.* I, 2, S, 973; Deussen: *op. cit.* II, 1, S. 117.

19) Zeller: *op. cit.* II, 1, S. 808; Deussen: *op. cit.* II, 1, S. 278.

20) Zeller: *op. cit.* II, 2, S. 448; Deussen: *op. cit.* II, 1, S. 354.

21) Takashi Ide 出隆: *Shijin Tetsugakusha* (詩人哲學者 Poet Philosopher), pp. 238, 244.

22) Māṇḍūya-kārikā, II, 12.

23) *Ibid.* II, 19.
cf. *nirguṇo 'pi hy ajo 'vyakto bhagavān prakṛteḥ paraḥ, svamāyāguṇam āviśya bādhyabādhakatāṃ gataḥ.*——*Bhāgavatapurāṇa* VII, 1, 6 (pub. par Burnouf).

24) This story is quoted by Śaṅkara in his *Brahma-sūtra-bhāṣya* III, 2, 17. Its origin seems to be some Upaniṣads which have been lost now.

25) *Dhp.* 268.

(3) Attraction to the Unknown

It is a fact that the Indians tend to pay more attention to the unknown and the undefined than to the known and the defined, as I have pointed out when we considered the way in which the Indians express the subsuming judgment and inferrence. This attraction for the unknown resulted in a fondness for concealing even the obvious; their way of thinking tended to prefer the dark and obscure over that which was clear. As a result of it, the Indians like expressions in the form of a difficult riddle. In the Saṃhitās of the Veda we can find here and there poems presenting for conjecture. a riddle. By the Indians Gods were seen to amuse themselves with a riddle.[1] Even the philosophical problems are expressed in the form of riddle; e.g.,

"A swan never pulls up one leg when getting out of water,
If he did pull one leg up indeed there would be neither today nor tomorrow,
Also there would be neither day nor night,
Also the light at dawn would never shine".[2]

This poem is interpreted as being an expression of the following truth. The Supreme Existence manifests the world through itself, and yet it exists behind the phenomenal world and is immutable. Such a way of expression has been inherited by the *Upaniṣads* and later literature. This method must not be confused with the riddles that exist thereby for amusement.

In contrast to this, from the outset, Buddhism maintained the position that it was an "open" religion. "Obhikkus, the dharma and the precepts revealed by the Tathāgata sends forth clear light. Never are they observed in secrecy".[3] They are as clear and evident 'as the sun-disk or the moon-disk'. Further more, "Regarding the *dharma* of the Tathāgatha, there exists no teacher-fist".[4] i.e., Tathāgata as a teacher has not secret in his teaching These passages, however, mean only that the religion that originated with Gotama would be never hidden from any people and it would never reject any people. Even Buddhists were unable to free themselves from the Indian propensity to express their thoughts through unintelligible riddles.

"Killing his mother and his father,
killing two kings of the Kṣatriya tribe,
Killing the kingdom and its subjects,
a Brāhmin goes on without pains". (*Dhammapada* 294)

"Killing his mother and his father,
killing two kings of the Brāhmin tribe,
Killing a tiger as the fifth,
a Brāhmin goes on without pains". (*ibid.* 295)

It would be impossible for a Buddhist, who would feel it a sin to kill only a little worm, to teach an other of killing his mother and father etc.,

According to the commentary of these sentences, 'his mother' means 'passion' (kāma); 'his father' means 'self-conceit'; 'two kings' means 'two unjust opinions', i.e., to believe that the soul perishes absolutely after one's death and to believe that the soul exists for eternity after one's death; 'the kingdom' means the 'twelve Āyatanas', i.e., the six internal organs (= eyes, ears, nose, tongue, tactile organ, intellect) and the six external objects (= color and shape, sound, odour, taste, tangibles, non-sensuous objects) by which our individual existence is constituted; 'its subjects' means 'attachment to pleasure'; 'a tiger' means 'doubt' and 'the tiger as the fifth' means 'five kinds of obstacle', i.e., covetousness, anger, sleep, evil-doing and doubt. We are unable to understand the meaning until we paraphrase the interpretation of the commentary. Whether or not this interpretation explains the purport of the analogy, remains a problem; however, that there exist some sort of hidden meaning withi nthis analogy cannot be seriously doubted. We can also find many allegorical expressions in the *Kāṭhaka, Śvetaśvatara* and other *Upaniṣads.*

1) M. Winternitz: *A History of Indian literature*, University of Calcutta, I, p. 184.
2) *Atharva-veda* XI, 4, 21.
3) *Aṅguttara-nikāya* III, 129. vol. I, p. 282.
4) *Saṃyutta-nikāya* vol. V, p. 153.

Chapter 4. Disregard for the individual and the particular

(1) Disregard for the individual and the particular appearing in language

To lay stress on the universal, on one hand, is to disregard the individual and the particular. I have already referred to the Indian disregard for the individual and the particular in a previous chapter, so in this chapter I will consider it from a different point of view.

It is necessary to use an article (Artikel) to show where the individual is placed within one proposition. There was, however, no article in ancient Indian languages. Both the definite article and the indefinite article did exist but ouly in a formative state which failed to develop. So the meaning of the word '*mahān*' can be both 'great, gross' as an adjective and 'a great thing or the great, ein Grosser oder der Grosse' as a noun. And a Substantiv can even enter into a compound as if it were a Substantiv, e.g., hinasevā = same with an Adjektiv and Participien used like an Adjektiv. An Adjektiv can even enter into a compound as if it were a Substantiv, e.g., *hīnasevā* = *hinānām sevā, mahadāśrayaḥ* = *mahatsv āśrayaḥ*.[1]

In the European classical languages to say 'someone's descendant' or 'someone's army' is expressed by *two words*, i.e., 'someone' and 'descendant' or 'someone' and 'army'; while in Sanskrit it is often expressed by one word containing possesive connotation and thus having a vague meaning, e.g., *māmakāḥ pāṇḍavāś ca* = υἱοί μου καὶ οἱ τοῦ Πανδοῦ, *nostrates Pānduidaeque*[2] (*Bhag. G.* I. 1) ; *Saumadattḥ* = ὁ τοῦ Σομαδάτα (*ibid.* I. 8). Here we can conclude as following: the Indians, by the same way of thinking as indicated above, express only the attributive prescription as the determinant, avoiding to indicate the substance as the determined, and they lay stress on essentially determining character of a thing which lies in the background or cannot be seen, ignoring any concrete direct perceptivity.

Such a characteristic way of thinking can be also found in the way they express abstract notions. Early Europeans expressed two opposite onconceptions as what was existing independently in each abstraction; on the other hand the Indians thought that these two conceptions really came into existence dependently, so that through the correlation of these two the more profound conception, from which these two conceptions appeared, had to be pursued. By this way of thinking the Indians often express one of the opposite conceptions by the negative form of another, e.g., *'lābhālabhau jayājayau'* (*Bhag. G.* II. 38) (Lit. 'attainment & non-attainment and victory & non-victory = gains & losses and victory & defeat').

To grasp the abstract idea in such a way of thinking appears eminently A.D. 150–250) said, "Impurity (*aśubha*) cannot exist without depending on purity (*śubha*) so that we explain purity by impurity. Therefore purity cannot be attained. Purity cannot exist without depending on impurity, so that we explain impurity by purity. Therefore purity cannot exist".[3] He did not try to grasp them separately. He thought that: 'purity' apart from 'impurity' or 'impurity' apart from 'purity' cannot come into existence, 'purity', however, exists by negation of 'impurity' and 'impurity' exists by negation of 'purity'; thus they are depending on each other and determined by each other. He advocated such a basic thought of causation that, "When there is this, then there is that, just as when there is shortness then there is longness".[4]

On the contrary ancient Europeans did not like such a way of thinking. So their languages expressed two opposite conceptions by two opposite words independantly, as we have seen in the example of 'gains & losses and victory & defeat' (καὶ τὴν ἐπιτυχίον καὶ ἀποτυχίαν, καί τὴν νίκην καὶ ἧτταν, *praemium iacturamve, victoriam clademve*).

As a result of the thinking method laying more stress on the features or essence of the individual than the individual itself, the Indians incline to express more relational meaning of a thing than its fundamental meaning. For instances, *'tri-locana'* means Śiva who was said to have three (*tri*) eyes (*locana*), *'gatabhartṛka'* means a widow whose husband (*bhartṛ*) is dead (*gata*). Such a way of expression, which was called *'bahuvrīhi'* (Possessive Compound, Attributive Compound) by Indian grammarians, has developed eminently in Indian languages; so that the word of *'bahuvrīhi'* is used as a technical term in modern comparative philology.

That the Indians inclined to neglect the individual can be noticed in many respects of their language. The Indian language has no pronoun to represent 'the same', 'derselbe'. So to express 'the same———' an indeclinable *'eva'*, which shows only emphasis, is added after the demonstrative pronoun *'tad'*. To express 'identical' and adjective *'sama'* is used in Sanskrit, but this word means also 'equal' and 'similar'. And a noun *'sāmya'* means 'equality', 'similarity' and 'identity'. Thus the Indians do not distinguish the difference between 'equality', 'similarity' and 'identity' in their ordinary lives. This entirely resulted from their disregard for the individual. Therefore when they need to express 'identical' or 'same', they used to express *'abhinna'* of which literally meaning is 'not different'. Indian philosophers have invented such circuitous expressions as *'ekatva'*, *'tādātmya'*, *'aikātmya'*, *'ekātmatā'* etc. to denote the meaning of 'identity' or 'sameness'.

By the same way of thinking, ancient Indian languages had no pronoun equivalent to 'each' and 'every', which was distinguished from 'all'. So they used the singular form of *'sarva'* (all) to express 'each' and 'every'.[5] The pronoun *'sarva'* means 'all' in its plural form, and in singular form it means 'each' or 'every'. Therefore the Indians thought that the individual is only the limited one by the universal through all things.

There remains the dual form in Sanskrit and it has been never dropped. The dual form can also be seen in ancient Greek as in Homer's epics, Gothic (ancient German language), Irish native tongue etc., which are called collectively Indo-European languages. Latin language has dropped the dual form in its early age, but we can find out the traces of the dual form adhered to some words. The German language has lost it in the thirteenth century, but we can find its traces in Bavarian colloquial. Among Slavic languages it remains only in some meaningless colloquials. Among Finnic-Hungarian languages, the descent of which is different from Indo-European languages, it remains only in Octiyac and Vogul colloquials, whose cultures are most outstripped, and in othe rlanguages it has been dropped already.[6]

It is not the meaning of the dual form that, as it is usually thought, it indicates 'two things' or multiplication by two, but indeed it indicates two things in such a relation that when one of them is expressed the other is necessarily remembered. For example, the Indian god of Heaven Varuṇa is always connected intimately with Mitra, so 'Mitrā' (the dual form of Mitra) means 'Mitra and Varuṇa'; '*pitarau*' (the dual form of *pitṛ* = father) means not 'two fathers' but 'father and mother', i.e., 'parents'. The same expression remains in Finnic-Hungarian languages, where the dual form of both 'father' and 'mother' means 'parents'. As father and mother are connected intimately, so such an expression by dual form becomes possible. In Finnic-Hungarian languages the dual form of both 'father' and 'mother' means 'parents', while in the Indian language only the dual form of 'father' is used. This fact shows us that in India the patriarchal system of paternal rights has come into existence in its early ages, but in the other the ancient notion from its primitive society has been kept.

It was an original rule that the dual form was adapted to two things which were connected intimately or pair, e.g., two hands, two feet, a pair which exists in the natural world and which is made artificially. The Indians, however, did not limit the application of dual form in their practical use. Therefore they generally used the dual form to express two things connected each other. It is a well-known fact that in a primitive man's mind two things connected intimately could not be separated into two units, and they were usually expressed together as one thing. Together with the advance of civilization, however, the idea of unit became so clear that they thought it is unnecessary to distinguish dual from singular and plural, so by and by the dual form has disappeared from the grammatical system.[7] As a concrete example of this general rule, the dual form disappeared from the colloquial Indian languages (Pāli and other Prākrits). But in India Sanskrit has been used by intelligentsia till recent times, so the dual form has been kept strictly by its user. Therefore the thought pattern of Indian intelligentsia has been influenced till recent times by this way of thinking, by which a pair of things is grasped and expressed in a Gestalt not in each unit.

Moreover, the Indians like to express the notion of number by some concrete nouns which come from their historical and social life, e.g., '*ṛṣi*' (sage) is often used to express '7' for seven *ṛṣi* are enumerated as a group in their myths, '*agni*' (fire) is '3' for three kinds of *agni* are used in a large ceremony.[8)] It can be seen also in ancient Egyptian and German to express a certain quantity by a concrete noun, not by a numeral,[9)] but to express cardinal numerals by concrete nouns cannot be seen in other countries. The Indians indeed like to express number concretely and intuitively.

Discussing problems about the ways of thinking of ancient peoples, Max Wertheimer clarified that the number and the notion of number are so much different between ancient peoples and modern Europeans; i.e., ancient peoples generally grasped the number and the notion of number according to their way of thinking of laying stress on Gestalt, while the notion of number of modern Europeans has been reached at the end of abstraction from the notion of number in usual experiences.[10)] Such a way of thinking remains clearly in the ancient Indians, e.g., '19' is expressed 'substract 1 from 20' (*ekonaviṃśati*), '597' is expressed 'substract 3 from 600'.[11)] The same way of expression can also be seen in Greek language, e.g., "Now, Megasthenēs says, there are '120 lacking 2' (= 118) nations in India". ('Εθνεα δὲ 'Ινδικὰ ε'ικοσι ʿεκατον τὰ πάντα λέγει Μεγασθένης, δυοῖν δέο ντα, Arianos, *Indikē* VII)

Why didn't the Indians use the abstract expression only as to number, in spite of their inclination, as I have mentioned on several occations, to lay stress on the universal and to use the abstract expression? We could say the reason for it as follows: the number is an objective form that is valid to the objective natural world; and the Indians, who didn't endeavor to recognize constructively the external natural world, would not be skillful in the analytical reflection about the meaning of number. That the natural sciences could not develop in India seems to have intimate connection with the way of thinking as mentioned above. And, though the Indians had the intensive consciousness for the idea of time, they had no interest in calculating, grasping and describing time quantitatively. This has perhaps some connections with the fact that India has left few books of historical description.

---

1) Speyer: *Vedische und Sanskrit-Syntax*, § 2.

2) Greek trans. of *Bhag. G.* by Dēmētrios Galanos, and Latin trans. of *Bhag. G.* by A. W. von Schlegel. cp. fn. I.–(1).

3) *Madhyamaka-kārikā* XXIII, 10–11.

4) *Madhyamaka-vṛtti*, p. 10, *l.* 7.

5) e.g., *sarvaḥ sarvaṃ na jānāti sarvajño nāsti kaścana.* (*Nala* 20, 6) (=not everybody does know everything, nobody is omniscient.) *naiva sarva iva yaśaḥ śaknoti saṃyaṃtum.* (*ŚBr.* XIV, I, 1, 6) cp. Śaṅkara ad *BS.* I, p. 28, ll. 4–5; p. 275, l. 2; p. 604, *l.* 1. (ĀnSS).

6) Izuru Shimmura 新村出; *Gengogaku Josetsu* (言語學序說 Introduction to Linguistics), pp. 48–149.

7) The same phenomenon and process can be seen in Semitic languages, descendants of Arabian languages. Such pronouns show that the numbers of three or four number in South-Asian and Polynesian languages are inclined to change into the plural form with the numeral three or four. cf. Izuru Shimmura: op. cit. p. 150.

8) cf. G. Bühler: *Indische Paläographie*, S. 80 f.

9) Brugsch Pascha, *Aus dem Morgenlande*, Reclam 3151. In ancient times one-second of certain amount of corns was called 'Malter', one-24th was called 'Scheffel' and one-384th was called 'Metze'. cp. M. Wertheimer: Über das Denken der Naturvölker, I. Zahlen und Zahlgebilde. *Drei Abhandlungen zur Gestalttheorie*, S. 133.

10) Wertheimer: *op. cit.* S. 106 f.

11) Gauḍapāda ad *Sāṃkhya-kārikā* V, 2.

(2) Disregard for the individual and the particular in the speculation in general

Indian thinking inclination to neglect the individuality and particularity appears in many spheres of cultural phenomena.

At first, their disregard for the individual appears in such a fact that local geography and climatology did not develop in India. Ethical books and moralistic stories have been made but such books in which they discussed and criticized individual person's deed have been scarcely written. Also in the discourses of art they usually discussed beauty in general and the works of art had to be such and such, and they scarcely referred to individual work or time-honored masterpieces.

As an interesting example of their disregard for the individuality, I show such a fact that gods in Indian myths have little personality. Indra, a thunder god, received most respect in the *Ṛg-Veda* but the word '*indra*' is only a common noun; i.e., a godly being who occupies that position is called by name of *'Indra'*.[1]

According to the same way of thinking with the disregard for the individual, the particularity by which the particular comes into existence is neglected; i.e., the particularity of the particular is neglected and the universality of the particular is remarked. This way of thinking leads them to the last point to *see the identity of the particular and the universal.* They become to think that the particularity, by which the particular can exist as the particular, is only an illusion, and that only the universality of the particular is a real existence. According to this way of thinking, the analytical judgment is nomore a thinking process to reach from an illusion to the true reality.

The Buddhist logician Dharmakīrti, (ca. A.D. 650) has already investigated the problems about analytical judgment and synthetical judgment. By him, however, in an inference of "This is a tree. Because it is a *śiṃśpaā*." the major premise of "All *śiṃśapās* are the trees." is an analytical judgment, and 'tree' is the essence (*svabhāva*) of *'śiṃśapā'*, so 'tree' is connected with *'śiṃśapā'* by the relation of indentity (*tādātmya*). According to the common sense, 'tree' is the universal and *'śiṃśapā'* is the particular, so they are different conceptions. The Indians, who lay stress on the universal, however, think they are identical in their ultimate essence. With regard to this Dharmottara, a follower of Dharmakīrti, says, " 'Identity' with the predicated fact means that (the mark) represents itself, its essence. Since (in those cases) the essence of a logical reason is contained in the predicate, therefore it is dependent upon the latter (and invariably concomitant with it)". Then he presents an objection, "The question arises, that if they are essentially identical, there will be no difference between reason and predicate, and then the argument will be (a repetition or) a part of the thesis?" And he answers to this question, "These two are identical with reference to what is the ultimately real essence (i.e., the sense datum underlying both facts). But the constructed objects (*vikalpa-viṣayas*), those (conceptions) which have been superimposed (upon reality), are not the same (in the facts constituting) the reason and the consequence".[3]

According to this way of thinking, the universal or the species, basing on which the particularity of the particular is realized, must be said the particular when it is compared with th eupper universal or upper species. If such relation against the upper species were pursued, they would reach at last the 'ultimate existence' (*sattā*), and think only the ultimate existence exists really. It was indeed Bhartṛhari (ca. A.D. 450–500) who manifested such speculation. He maintained that all the species are realized by the ultimate existence in the final analysis, so all the meaning of word are no other than the ultimate existence. Moreover, he thought, only the ultimate existence is the absolute being and what gives existence to the species as the species is not true being; as this relation between the truth and the non-truth can be seen between the subsuming upper species and the subsumed lower species, so any kind of conceptions is non-true against the universal while it is true against the particular. He said, "Now, as it was testified in the sacred book, these two things (*bhāva*), true and non-true, are staying within every thing (*bhāva*); and the true thing is the species, *the individual is non-true*".[4]

1) Śaṅkara ad *BS* I, 3, 28. cf. R. Garbe: *The Philosophy of Ancient India*, p. 36.
2) *Nyāyabindu* II 17. *Śiṃśapā* is the name of a tree.
3) *Nyāyabindu-ṭikā*, p. 26, *ll.* 12 ff.
4) *Vākyapadīya* III, 1, 32.

Chapter 5. The concept of the unity of all things

As a natural result of their inclination to emphasize the Universal Being, neglecting all individuals and particulars, the Indians conceive the idea of the unity of all things. They ignore the changing manifestations of the phenomenal world. According to them, only the Universal Being behind those manifestations is the ultimate source of reality. And the more a being is particularized and individualized, the less it shares in the element of reality. Individuals are no other than limited manifestations of the Universal Being. From a very early age, the Indians held a strong tendency to think that the multifarious phenomena of this world are self-expressions of the one absolute being. The main current of Indian metaphysics is a thoroughgoing monism.

A primitive form of this monistic view was expressed in the hymns of the world-creation in the *Ṛg-Veda*. And it took a more clearly defined form in the Upaniṣads. The Upaniṣads express the Absolute Being in many different ways. They follow the Vedas, assigning the role of the primal principle to things in nature, such as Wind, Water or Ether. Adding to those survivals of the old Vedic ideas, the *Upaniṣads* hold newly as the Absolute Being the principles and the functions of the individual being such as the Spirit, the Understanding (*vijñāna*) or the Soul (*puruṣa*). And before they named it the Brahman or the Ātman, they attempted to express the Absolute Being by various notions like 'the existent', 'the non-existent', 'that which is neither existent nor not existent', 'the undeveloped', 'the controller within' or 'the imperishable'. Though the *Upaniṣads* express the Absolute by such multiple names, we can point out one feature common to these names. All of them suppose the existence of the One Absolute Being, underlying the diversified phases of the phenomenal world. All of the phenomenal phases belong to it, proceed from it, depend upon it and are controlled by it. Furthermore, in the *Upaniṣads*, they conceive that the soul in individual beings is in its ultimate nature identical with the true Self (*Brahman; Ātman*). And this metaphysical monism in the *Upaniṣads* is succeeded in later Hinduism.[1] It is natural, therefore, that the Indian ethics sets as its highest goal the unification and assimilation of the individual self with the Universal Self. Even when one cannot hope to attain this goal in this life, he should continue his efforts to achieve it in the next world. One of the *Upaniṣads* describes the state that a man freed from desires enters after his death as follows "Being *Brahman*, he goes to Brahman".[2] And the sage Śāṇḍilya declares, "When I shall have departed from hence, I shall obtain him (that Self)".[3] When one has got to this final goal, he is one and identical with the Absolute Being. There he bears no longer any personal differentiation. Uddālaka teaches as follows: "As the bees, my son, make honey by collecting the juices of distant trees, and reduce the juice into one form, and as these juices have no discrimination, so that they might say, I am the juice of this tree or that, in the same manner, my son, all these creatures, when they have become merged in the True (either in deep sleep or in death), know not that they are merged in the True".[4]

This monistic view of the *Upaniṣads* was developed further by the Vedantic philosophers. And it forms the core of the theological system of the Hindu religious schools. Throughout the history of philosophy in this country, the monistic view has been accepted by a majority of the thinkers.

The Buddhists, however, rejected the existence of any metaphysical principle as advocated in the *Upaniṣads* and in the Indian orthodox philosophical schools. And they did not engage themselves in metaphysical discussions upon the unity of one with the Absolute, but they emphasized the actual participation for the realization of the absolute virtue in this world. They taught the importance of unity among individuals in the actual society of human beings. Really from its origin, the Buddhist religious movement strongly opposed to class discrimination in any form. A sentence in one of their sūtras reads: "What has been designated as 'name' and 'family' in the world is only a term".[5] Within the early community of the Buddhist monks, this idea of equality of all classes was faithfully carried out. Gotama the Buddha belongs no longer to any particular caste or family (*gotra*). And whoever, having renounced the world, joins the Buddhist community (*saṃgha*) to become a Bhikṣu is called uniformly a Śākya-putra or a son of Śākya-muni the Buddha. Within the Saṃgha, everyone belongs directly to the authority of the Saṃgha without any intermediating agent and he is treated thoroughly equal with others in all his qualifications. The standing order within the Saṃgha fixed according to the number of the years one has passed after he took order. So, one of their Vinaya texts describes as follows: "Just, O Bhikkhus, as the great rivers——that is to say, the Gangā, the Yamunā, the Aciravatī, the Sarabhū, and the Mahī——when they have fallen into the great ocean, renounce their name and lineage and are thenceforth reckoned as the great ocean——just so, O Bhikkhus, do these four castes——the Khattiyas, the Brahmans, the Vessas, and the Suddhas——when they have gone forth from the world under the doctrine and discipline proclaimed by the Tathāgata, renounce their names and lineage, and enter into the number of the Sakyaputtiya Samaṇas".[6] In one of the *Upaniṣads*, we can find a teaching of the similar context. "Just as the flowing rivers disappear in the ocean casting off name and shape, even so the knower, freed from name and shape, attains to the divine person, higher than the high".[7] It can be said here that the metaphysical or ontological concept of the unity of all beings held in the *Upaniṣads* shows itself in Buddhism taking the form of practical ethics.

Buddhist thought was refined remarkably through the hands of the Mahāyāna Buddhists. The idea of *Śūnyatā* or Voidness admits nothing real or substantial, but even in this idea we can notice a feature of the old Indian monism. *Śūnyatā* means the absolute negation and it permits nothing differentiated. The great teacher of Mahāyāna Buddhism, Nāgarjuna, teaches: "the release (*mokṣa*) is the extinction of the action (*karman*) and of the defilement (*kleśa*). The action and the difilement arise from the differentiating notions (*vikalpa*). They come from the concept of diversity (*prapañca*). This concept of diversity, however, is led to an end at the state of Voidness".[8] The release in Nāgarjuna's sense means the attainment of this state of Voidness.

It is wrong to say that all the Indian thinkers hold such a view of unity of all beings. But this is the view maintained at least by a majority of the philosophers in India. For the Indians, to enter into a perfect state of tranquility where the mind is immovable and identical with the Absolute is the highest religious experience that only a man of wisdom can hope to gain. And they attach only a relative and secondary significance to other states of religious experience considering them to be lower states only serving as an intermediating agent to help one attain the highest.

Now, as additional evidence to show that the core of Indian thought is the idea of the unity of all things, we will proceed to study a linguistic phenomenon observed in the Indian languages.

In Sanskrit, they mean 'all the beings' or 'all things in the universe' by the words in the singular number like "idaṃ sarvam", "idam viśvam", or simply 'idam'. And this usage of the words in the singular number can be observed in the old *Upaniṣads*, in the Buddhist books,[9] and in many other Indian works in general.[10] In Japanese, to mean 'the things in the universe', we use "萬有", "萬象" or "もの み な", all of which imply the infinite diversity of the phenomenal world. In contrast to the Japanese way of thinking, the Indians ignore this diversity and the differentiated phases of the phenomenal world and grasp all the beings as one unit. Of course, it is grammartically correct to write in the plural number the Sanskrit pronoun *'sarva'* and its equivalents in other Indian languages. There are some cases of such usage in old Indian scriptures.[11] But, in those cases, we should not overlook the fact that the word *'sarva'* does not mean all things without limitation, but that it implies the whole within a certain boundary. And to mean all things without limitation, the Indians never fail to write *'sarva'* in the singular number.

This Indian usage of the words in the singular number presents a remarkable contrast to the Greek and the Latin usage of the equivalent words. In Greek, though it belongs to the same language origin as Sanskrit, they use the pronoun equivalent to 'sarva' in the neuter plural form to mean 'all things'. There is a fine example of this Greek usage in Heraclitus' well-known proposition "All things flow (πάντα ῥεῖ)". Both Plato[12] and Aristotle[13] represent the universe as a complex body using the word in the plural number. And this usage was accepted by the Greeks for a long time up to comparatively late ages.[14] When they use πᾶς, the Greek equivalent to '*sarva*', in the singular number, it will have the meaning of 'everything' and the meaning of 'all' will not be expressed accurately.[15] There is a very rare case in Greek to mean 'all things in the universe' by the pronoun in the neuter singular "πᾶς".[16] But, in this case, the philosopher who used this expression took a stand very similar to the Indian monistic view of the world and to their pantheism. His view was more likely an Indian one than a Greek one. And such a view like his was rarely held by the Greeks in general. In Latin, too, they use '*omnia*", the word in the neuter plural form, to mean 'all thing'.[17] And to mean 'all things as one unit' or 'the universe', the Romans have another word "universum" so that they have no fear of confusion that the Greeks might have.

In Greece, not only the philosophers but the people in general think that the universe is a complex body consisting of infinite number of individual and particular things. And in contrast to this Greek view, the Indian people maintain that all beings in the universe are limited and particularized manifestations of the sole ultimate reality. Here, without relying upon the methods of comparative philosophy, we can maintain the foregoing conclusions through observation of a linguistic phenomenon.

Now, as the Indians attach little significance to individual phenomena, it is natural that they are inclined to ignore the fixed value of any individual being. And as a natural result of such a way of thinking, in India appears the idea of the oneness of opposite pairs, of good and evil, and of beauty and ugliness. Megasthenes, referring to the features of the Brahmanistic thought, writes as follows: "[According to the Brahmanists], whatever happens in the human life is neither good (ἀγαθόν) nor evil (κακόν). For if the nature of a thing or an act is fixed for good or evil, why is there the dicerence among men, whose notions are all more or less like a dream, of those who are pleased by a thing or act and those who are troubled by the same thing or act?"[18] And in the old Upaniṣads, too, it is repeated that what appears good or bad to our human eyes is not so in the absolute sense and that the difference between the two is only a matter of comparison.[19] For instance, one of the *Upaniṣads* reads as follows: "[The true Self], the controller of all, the lord of all, and the ruler of all, he does not become greater by good works nor smaller by evil works".[20] And in another text, it is said, "As water does not cling to a lotus leaf, so no evil deed clings to one who knows it".[21] And this idea of the oneness of opposite pairs held in the *Upaniṣads* was accepted by the Vedantins, the most influential philosophical school in the India of later ages.[22]

---

1) The monistic view that the Highest Self appears in manifold forms is held also by the Viṣṇu sect of Hinduism. They teach that "Nārāyaṇa, who is the highest Self and the Self of all, reveals himself in multiple ways." ātmanā 'tmānam anekadhā vyūhyāvasthitaḥ, Śaṅkara ad BS. II, 2, 42; *SBE* vol. XXXIV, p. 440.

2) *Bṛhad. Up.* IV, 4, 6; S. Radhakrishnan ed.: *The Principal Upaniṣads* (London, 1953), p. 273.

3) *Chānd. Up.* III, 14, 4; *SBE* vol. I, p. 48.

4) *Chānd. Up.* VI, 9, 1–2; *SBE* vol. I, p. 101. cf. *Maitri-Up.* VI, 22.

5) *Suttanipāta*, 648; *SBE* vol. X, pt. II, p. 115. cf. *Suttanipāta*, 610; 611.

6) *Vinaya*, Culla-vagga, IX, 1, 4; *SBE* vol. XX, p. 304.

7) *Muṇḍ. Up.* III, 2, 8; Radhakrishnan: *op. cit.* p. 691.

8) Madhyamaka-Kārikā 18, 5.

9) E. g. vinābhāvasantam ev 'idam, (*Suttanipāta*, 805); cf. sabbam idaṃ calam iti pekkhāmano, (*Theragāthā*, 1110); idaṃ sarvaṃ vijñaptimātrakam, (*Triṃśikā*, v. 17).

10) E. g. sarvam idam, (*Bhag. G.* II, 17; VII, 7); idam, (*Bhag. G.* III, 38). Schlegel translates the word 'idam' by 'universum.' svapnādivac cedam draṣṭavyam, (Śaṅkara ad *BS.* II, 2, 28).

11) E. g. tāṇi sarvāṇi, (*Bhag. G.* IV, 5. hosce universos, ἀπαξαπάσας). Cf. sabbe, (*Dhammapada*, 129; 130).

12) πάντα χωρεῖ καὶ οὐδὲν μένει, Platon: *Krat.* 402A.

13) ὡς ἁπάντων τῶν αἰσθητῶν ἀεὶ ῥεόντων Aristoteles *Metaph.* I, 6. p. 987 a 33.

14) E. g. τὰ πανθ' ὁρᾶ θεός, αὐτὸς οὐχ ὁρώμενος = (God sees all things, himself unseen.) As this Greek quotation presents the example, it is commonly observed in some of the Indo-European languages that a subject in the nominative neuter plural form takes the verb of the singlular number. In the *Ṛg-Veda*, we can find some cases of this usage. See Harushige Kōzu 高津春繁: *Hikaku Gengogaku* 比較言語學 (Comparative Linguistics) pp. 261–62. As to this usage in the Classical Sanskrit, see Speyer: *op. cit.* S. 75, §243, Anm. 1. In Prakrit, 'atthi (= Skt. *asti*)' can follow the subject of any gender and number and 'āsī (= Skt. *āsī*)', the subject of either the singular or the plural number. See Woolner: *Introduction to Prakrit*, p. 53.

15) E. g. 'Eυ παντὶ εὐχαριστεῖτε (In everything give thanks.)

16) Eν τὸ ὄν καὶ πὰν ...... Ξ ενοφάνην ...... ὑποτίθεσθαί φησιυ ὁ θεο 'φραστος = ('Xenophanes thought that the being is one and all', it is said by Theophrastus.) Simplicius ad *Phys.* 22, 26D.

17) E. g. Omnia, quae sunt, vel in se, vel in alio sunt. (Spinoza: *Ethica*, Axiomata I.)

18) Megasthenēs: *Fragments*, 41.

19) See *Kaus. Up.* I, 4; *Bṛhad. Up.* IV, 3, 22; IV, 4, 23; *Tait. Up.* II, 9.

20) *Bṛhad. Up.* IV, 4, 22; Radhakrishnan: *op. cit.* p. 279; cf. *Kauṣ. Up.* III, 8.

21) *Chānd. Up.* IV, 14, 3; *SBE* vol. I, p. 67.

22) See *Brahmasūtra*, IV, 1, 13–15.

Chapter 6. The static quality

(1) Comprehension of this quality through static aspects of language

It has already been mentioned that the Indians incline to comprehend phenomena statically. This tendency has close relation with the tendency to esteem universality. All existences of this world are always changing and moving. On the contrary, the substance of these existences continues to exist as long as they exist and its nature changes little. Therefore, the tendency to esteem universality generally pays more attention to the nature of things than to the things themselves which are always changing, and again this tendency notes the static aspect of the thing more strongly than its dynamic function.

In such a way of thinking, special characteristic can be found in usage of parts of speech. Firstly, it can be said that the noun (or verbal noun) is more likely to be used than the verb in a Sanskrit sentence, because the noun expresses static and unchanging aspects of the thing. Secondly, the adjective which modifies a noun is mainly used and the adverbial form is seldom used in Sanskrit.

The fomer characteristic will be explained firstly. Although expression by verbs was very complicated in the sentences of the Veda Scripture, it became very simple in classical Sanskrit. And also the verbal nouns became to be mainly used instead of the finite verbs in classical Sanskrit. Especially in prose writings, the nominal predicate is widely used and the finite verb is seldom used. The noun which is used in Sanskrit as the predicate is in some cases a participle and in some cases a verbal noun. For example, the sentence 'due to rain, the food appears' is expressed in the form of 'due to rain, appearance of the food (is possible)' in Sanskrit. (parjanyād annasaṃbhavaḥ, *Bhag. G.* III, 14.=imbre fit frugam proventus, ὁι δὲ καρπὸι ἐκ τοῦ ὄμβρου.) It was the practice from olden times to use the participial form instead of the finite verb to express the past tense, and it became a common expression in colloquialism of the later periods.[2]

The adjectives of which quality is static are used in Sanskrit in place of the finite verbs used in the classical languages of the West. (For example, the sentence "*sarvam anityam* (all existences are impermament)" is used in Sanskrit instead of using the sentence "all existences change and move" (πάντα ῥεῖ)

Thus the 'periphrastic form' was established in Sanskrit. Although it is seldom found in the Veda Scripture, the periphrastic perfect, one of the periphrastic forms, can be frequently found in the literature after the Brāhmaṇas. For example, in order to express the meaning 'he went', the phrase 'gamayāṃ cakāra (he did to go)' is used. And again the form of periphrastic future is used in some cases in order to express future action.[3] For example, the word "gantāsi (you are one who goes)" is used to express the meaning 'you will go'. (*gantāsi* = pervenies ad ...., ἀποστροφὴν ποιήσεις. *Bhag. G.* II, 52).

Again in Sanskrit, the denominative, a special form of verb, which is formed from noun is established. For example, *putrīyati,* a denominative which was formed from a noun *putra* (son), means 'to desire to have a son', and svāmīyati, a denominative formed from a noun *svāmin* (master) means 'to regard as a master'. Generally speaking, denominative is used as the word which connotes the meaning of 'to be ....', 'to work as ....', 'to regard as ....' and 'to desire ....'. Such special categories of verbs as the denominative are not found in the classical grammar of the west.

The following fact can be considered as a similar tendency. Namely, in Sanskrit, *śakya,* an adjective, or *śakyam,* an indeclinable, is used to express the meaning "to be able to ...." which is expressed by using a verb or an auxiliary verb in the Western languages. (For example; "na devāsuraiḥ sarvaiḥ śakyaḥ prasahituṃ yudhi", *Rāmāyaṇa* II, 86, 11 = non potest proelis superari a cunctis dis daemonibusque).[4]

In the Sanskrit language, it is seldom that a verb in the form of the finite verb is used; the verb is mainly used in the form of the verbal noun. Therefore, the general characteristic of Sanskrit construction is that the nominal sentence is more likely used than the verbal sentence. Especially in classical Sanskrit, the finite verb is seldom used.

In connection with the above fact, usage of the infinitive form of the verb is very much limited. It never occurs in Sanskrit that the infinitive form is used as the subject.[5] Nor is the infinitive form ever used as the object. When it is necessary to use the infinitive verb as an object, an abstract noun formed from the root of that verb is used instead of the infinitive form of that verb. Originally, the infinitive form of a verb preserved the case ending of the verbal noun in the *Ṛg Veda.* Namely, it preserved case endings of accusative, dative, genitive and locative cases. However, in classical

Sanskrit, only one form which ends with "-°tum" (one of the above mentioned case endings) is remaining. Moreover, in most cases in classical Sanskrit, the infinitive form is used only when the meaning 'in order to do—' which denotes an object of behavior is expressed. Even in this case, usage of the infinitive form is not necessarily the same. The infinitive form is used in both cases of active and passive voices.[6]

There is a remarkable difference between Sanskrit and the classical languages of the west on this point. For example, there are two kinds of infinitive, the present and the perfect in Latin. The present infinitive expresses continuance, repetition and usage while the perfect infinitive the perfect. The infinitive in Latin can become subject, predicate and also the object of a sentence as a noun, because it possesses both natures of verb and noun.

It can be considered that the reason why there exists such a great difference between Sanskrit and the Western languages is that the Indians did not pay attention to the changing and moving aspects of existences.

Next, the second characteristic of Sanskrit will be considered. Sanskrit does not possess any adverbial suffix which is common to all Western languages. As a general rule, an adjective can become an adverb by adding some suffixes such as -°ως in Greek and -°ment in French, in the Western languages. However, there is no such adverbial suffixes in Sanskrit. Therefore, the accusative case of the adjective (neutral, singular) is used in Sanskrit when it is necessary to modify the verb. Again accusative, abrative and locative cases (singular) of adjective are used adverbially in some cases. In brief, the adverb is not acknowledged to be a part of speech in the system of Sanskrit grammar. And it is very common to use the adjective in the case when the adverb is used in the case of Western languages.

[The same difference between the Indian way of thinking and other ways of thinking can also be found among the modern western languages. Among the modern Western languages German notes the unchanging, static and universal aspects of phenomena. On the contrary, English attaches great importance to changing aspects of things. There exists no special suffix which can distinguish adverb from other parts of speech in German. On the contrary, in English an adverbial suffix is added to the adjective when it modifies a verb.[8]]

This tendency to comprehend through static aspects can also be found elsewhere. For example, a demonstrative pronoun "sa" is used by adding to the subject when it is necessary to connect two sentences to express the meaning of "and" or "then". Namely, the demonstrative pronoun is used in Sanskrit instead of the conjunction.[9] In order to show the process of time, it is necessary to use the conjunction in Western languages. On the contrary, the Indians repeatedly mention the same subject of action which is unchanging through some periods of time. Also on this point, a characteristic of the Indian way of thinking which pays attention to the unchanging aspects of existence can be clearly found.

The subject of action which influences the gerundive, which has passive meaning, or the past participle, which ends with -°ta, is expressed by the instrumental case or genitive case in Sanskrit. The following sentences are its examples: "*bhavatā* (or *bhavataḥ*) *kṛtaḥ kartavyaḥ* (you fulfilled your duty)"; "*rājñāṃ pūjitaḥ* (one was respected by kings)". In these cases, the instrumental case is apt to express the same meaning with a participle while genitive case with an adjective.[10] In the case of Western languages, the subject of action is always expressed with prepositions such as ὑπο, *a, by, von,* or *par.* It can be concluded from the above fact that the Western people comprehend action through its changing aspects, while the Indians comprehend action attributively. Namely, the Indians consider that action is an unchanging aspect or even an attribute of existence. Therefore, it can be said that the Western people regard action as active phenomenon while the Indians look upon it statically.

The above-mentioned characteristic of way of thinking also influenced the construction of the concept. In classical Indian languages, there was no word which corresponded to the word 'to become' or 'werden'. Although the verb formed from root '*bhū*" connotes the meaning of 'to become', this word also connotes the meaning of 'to exist' at the same time. Why did the ancient Indians fail to distinguish the word meaning 'to become' from the word meaning 'to exist' in their daily conversation? It was because to 'become' was one form or aspect of 'to exist' for them. A noun "*bhāva*" formed from root "*bhū*" is understood as the word which means either 'being born' or 'existing'.[11] That is to say, "to become" is 'to be born' in other words for the Indians. Therefore, the Indians had to manage to produce words "*anyathā bhavati*" or "*anyathābhāva*" (being otherwise) in order to express 'to become' or 'to change'.

For the Indians, therefore, "all existences of this world are changing and moving" is not the expression of changing aspect of existences but is expression of static and unchanging state. In the sentence "*sabbe saṅkhārā aniccā* (all existences are impermanent)", a common expression of the Indian Buddhists, "*aniccā*" is an adjective. Namely, change of existence is understood statically. Such a way of expression is fundamentally different from the sentence "πάντα ῥεῖ (all existences flow)" of the western thought in which the predicate is expressed by a verb.

---

1) It has been the practice since the *Ṛg Veda* to use the past participle instead of the finite verb. Even in the oldest Gāthās of the Jain Scripture, this tendency is found. (Jacobi: *SBE*. XXII, p. 72, n.)

2) In the Apabhraṁśa language, perfect, imperfect and aorist are seldom found and the past tense is expressed by past participle.

3) However, there is no such example in the *Ṛg Veda*. It can be firstly found in the Brāhmaṇas. Delbrück: *Altindische Syntax*, S. 295.

4) Speyer: *Vedische und Sanskrit-Syntax*, S. 67.

5) The sentence which begins with "yad" corresponds to such an infinitive form. Speyer: *Vedische und Sanskrit-Syntax*, S. 87 § 279, b.

6) "*vṛṣala, upālabdhuṃ, tarhi vayam āhūtāḥ*". (*Mudrārākṣasa* III (127, 6)) ="——, so bin ich hier befohlen um gescholten zu werden". (Speyer: *op. cit.* S. 67)

7) cf. "*ekā* (zueret) *prasūyate mātā dvitīyā* (zweitens) *vāk prasūyate*". (*Pañcatantra* ed. Jīv. IV, 6) In the case when the word "*īdṛśa* (such)" modifies adjective, this remains as an adjective. (Speyer: *op. cit.* § 148, Anm. cf. § 132)

8) Stenzel mentioned in his book *Die Philosophie der Sprache* (S. 74 f.) that such a difference is based upon the difference of emphasis upon the subjective aspect and the predicative aspect.

9) Speyer: *op. cit.* S. 82–83.

10) Speyer: *op. cit.* § 69.

11) "*bhāva utpattiḥ sattā vā*" (Ratnaprabhā ad *Brahmasūtra* II, 2, 3)

12) For example: Śaṅkara ad *BS*. vol. II. p. 16, *l*. 9. (ĀnSS.); *Chung-lun* (中論) 15, 5. (cf. Commentaries by Candrakīrti on the 13, 3 & 5; 15, 8 of *Chung-lun*.)

(2) The static quality in thought process

Thus, in Indian philosophy the Absolute is generally explained as Being beyond transitory manifestation. According to the Upaniṣads, the Absolute is also expressed as Imperishable (*akṣara*) in the following ways:[1] "Ātman is impeishable for he cannot be destroyed........He is unfettered, he does not suffer, he is not injured".[2] "This is that great unborn Self who is undecaying, undying, immortal, fearless, Brahman".[3] In early Buddhism such a metaphisical principle as the Absolute is not laid down, but it is claimed that the principle of pratītyasamutpāda, whether the Buddha has appeared or whether he has not appeared, is unchanged and eternal.

According to Mahāyāna Buddhism, *śūnyatā* or *dharmatā* (real aspect of things) is the principle of pratītyasamutpāda that nothing can disappear nor can arise. As stated above, the idea of the Absolute which Indian philosophers have conceived is of negative character. Accordingly, the Absolute can only be expressed as being qualified with static state in the realm of the relative in which everything appears and disappears.

We are able to find out the same kind of way of thinking as the above concerning their concept of man. Let's compare it with the Christian concept of man. According to St. Paul, the concept of man is explained as follows: Man is composed of two parts, i. e. body and mind representing the external and internal aspects of man respectively. Mind is that which gives vividness to body or the source of life. He calls this mind '*psychē*', and when he defined it as the subject of consciousness or self, especially distinguishing it from body, he also gives the name '*pneuma*' or soul to mind. However, the term '*pneuma*', which has employed in few cases, generally means the origin of newly-revived life of the awakened man as distinguished from the ordinary man. In other words it denotes the generative power of the newly-rivived, sacred, and eternal life which comes from God or the Savior and which controls man. Accordingly, soul is identified with the Holy Spirit, which is distinctly to be separated from mind of man. On the other hand, the body, which represents the external aspect of man, is expressed to be constituted by sarcous substance (*sarx*). It might be acknowledged that it does not implied to the mere flesh, but to all the elements composing man-in-nature,[4] because of fancying that the sarx is the main element of all constituents of body. On the contrary, according to Indian philosophers, soul is defined as *prāṇa*, *ātman*, or *jīva*, and body as *śarīra* or *deha*, not as māṃsa or flesh. It appears that they considered the bone as the central part of body. *Śarīrāṇi*, the plural form of *śarīra* (body), means the bones or remains. The bone is considered to be the fundamental component of body as known from the following passage of the *Dhammapada*: "Body is formed by the bones together with flesh and blood spreading on it. It contains decaying, death, pride and falsehood".[5] As seen from the above statement, the Christians in the West find the central significance of body on the dynamic element by which body is constituted; Indian philosophers in the East find it on the static element, i.e. bone.

Such being the case, generally in Indian philosophy, the idea of 'becoming' is not fully considered, but the idea of 'being' is under the central consideration. Therefore, Indian philosophers in general explain three aspects of 'being', i.e. appearance, existinction, and continuance or intermediate state of 'being'. Early in the Old Upaniṣads[6] these three are refered to, and they are generally accepted by the orthodox schools of Brahmanism and the Jain schools. However, the idea of 'becoming' is little mentioned in these schools. *Vikāra, vikriyā, pariṇāma, vipariṇāma,* etc. are considered to be equivalent to 'becoming', but they show that the simple is specialized into the complicated, and these words rather mean evolution or development. Vārṣyāyaṇi, an Indian philosopher of language of ancient time, set forth the theory of the sixfold aspect of being (*bhāvavikāra*)[7] in the phenomenal world, i.e. appearance, existing, changing, increasing, discreasing, and extinction, and in later ages it was accepted by the other famous Indian philosopher of language named Bhartṛhari.[8] However, Śaṃkara, the famous Vedantist, refuted this theory as meaningless, and he maintained that appearance, continuance and extinction are only recognized to be the three aspects of 'being', and that all other aspects of being might be included into these three.[9] Also in Buddhism these three aspects are expressed to be those of the conditioned (*saṃskāra*) or phenomenal being.[10] The Sarvāstivāda school, the most eminent of Abhidharma Buddhist schools, maintained the theory of four aspects of being by adding the fourth aspect of being or the conditioned, namely, *jarā* or decaying, which was interpreted as 'changing to other' (*anyathābhāva, anyathātva*).[11] Accordingly, they show the four aspects of the conditioned as appearance, extinction, continuance, and decaying.[12] However, this theory was not accepted by all Buddhist schools.

From the point of view that the idea of 'being' is mainly considered and that the idea of 'becoming' is ignored, Indian thought is considerably similar to Greek thought, and it is in a different way from Modern thought. As pointed out on several occasions, the central problem of the Ancient Greek philosophy was to investigate the reality or 'being', and there the truth was nothing but 'being' and it was to be materialized in the Existence. The truth is to be realized by insight upon the *form* of reality and it denotes the discovery of the essence of 'being'. Accordingly, the science ofgeometry was the typical pattern of science in the ancient times, through which the principle of the fixed form of materialized existence in space was investigated. Only states developed even in the field of physical science. On the contrary, the idea of 'becoming' is highly investigated in Modern thought. Kinetics has developed in the field of physics of Modern age.

Mathematics has developed in the form of analytics and algebra in which the changeable quantity is examined. And for the first time analytical geometry has been organized and studied. Indian thought is similar to Greek thought from the point of view of its difference from Modern thought in which the idea of 'becoming' or movement is regarded as its characteristics; however, comparing with Greek thought, Indian thought can be said to reach its extremity in expressing the reality ontologically.

Thus, the static quality of ways of thinking of the Indian people is distinctively far from the dynamic quality of Modern thought; however, from the very point of view of its contrast with Modern thought, it can afford a certain significance upon Modern civilization. While Modern life is inclined to drive man to unquietness or crazy restlessness, the static quality of Indian thought is capable of giving peacefulness or rest to the mind of modern people. Accordingly, Indian culture is helpful to present rest and joyfulness to modern people who have tired with dynamic movement of their culture.

In introducing the life and activity of Ramakrishna (1834–86), who was one of the most eminent religious teachers of Modern India, Romain Rolland writes as follows: "He was a fruit (gardener) of early autumn of whom European people have never known". And furthermore he writes: "I should like to inform European people who are febrile without peacefulness of this arterial throbbing. I want to wet the European lips with unperishable blood".[13] Even Albert Schweitzer who is known as a devotional Christian teacher, though critisizing all Indian religions, ought to have acknowledged the following merit of them, and saying: "However, there is one significance which we, European people, ought to acknowledge in regard to religious thought of India. It is that which Indian religion teaches us calmness or equanimity of mind....the Indian people comprehend the essential weak-point which exists in faith of Modern Christianity. We, European people, excessively believe that Christianity is only dynamic in its religious activity. There are too less occasions in our reflecting that we are men who think deeply of ourselves. We, European people, are usually devoid of equanimity of mind".[14] From the very point of viewing that Indian thought is a contrast to Modern thought, the former thought is, instead, attractive to the mind of Modern people.

---

1) *Bṛhad. Up.* III, 8, 8–11.
2) *Bṛhad. Up.* III, 9, 26; IV, 2, 4; IV, 4, 22; IV, 5, 15, cf. II, 3, 6.

3) *Bṛhad. Up.* IV, 4, 25.
4) Seiichi Hatano 波多野精一: *Kirisutokyō no Kigen* (基督教の起源 The Origin of Christianity), pp. 199–200.
5) *Dhammapada*, 150.
6) *Tait. Up.* III, 1; *Tattvārthādhigama-sūtra* V, 29.
7) *ṣaḍbhāvavikārā bhavantīti Vārṣyāyaniḥ, jāyate'sti vipariṇamate vardhate' prakṣīyate vinaśyantīti.* (*Nirukta*, I, 2. p. 29, ed. by L. Sarup.)
8) *Vākyap.* III, 1, 36.
9) Śaṅkara ad *BS.* I, 1, 2.
10) In the 7th chapter of the *Madhyamaka-kārika*, the theory which claims *utpāda-sthiti-bhaṅga* is refuted. Formerly, in the *'Tsêng-i-a-han'* (増一阿含), vol. 12 (*Taishō*, vol. 2, p. 607 c), it is explained that there are three characteristics by which the conditioned elements are formed, namely, appearance (従起), changing (遷変), and elimination (滅盡). The *Abhidharma-jñāna-prasthāna*, vol. 3 (*Taishō*, vol. 26, p. 780 c) also explains the same theory.
11) *Madhyamika-kārikā*, XV, 5. Also see the commentary of Candrakīrti upon *MK.* XIII, 3, 5, XV, 8.
12) This is explained in the *Mahāvibhāṣā*, 39, the *Nyāyānuśāsana*, 13, the *Abhidharma-kośa*, 5 (the Chinese translations by Hüan-tsang), etc.
13) Romain Rolland: *La vie de Ramakrishna*, pp. 22–24.
14) Albert Schweitzer: *Das Christentum und die Weltreligionen*, S. 34.

(3) Lack of common sense concepts of time

The thought process through which the existence at the back of phenomenal world has been more regarded as important than phenomenal world itself naturally results in paralysed state of concept of time, especially of concept of difference in time, which is employed in expressing concrete facts of experiences.

Such thought process can be well known from the fact that the mood of Sanskrit language has gradually vanished and it has been simplified, and that various kinds of tense have disappeared, and accordingly their usages have been confused.

In the proto-Indo-European language, the difference of usage of verb is mainly based on mood and, therefore, the verb of this language was used on flimsy ground of concept of time. The present tense of direct speech simply indicates sustaining action, while the imperfect tense denotes the state of action which was momentarily conceived regardless of duration, perfect, etc. It was fairly later ages when the concept of time was emphatically introduced to the usage of verb. The old writings of the Greek language preserved a pretty amount of usage of mood. It was so with the Vedic language. However, in Latin verb is principally used on the basis of concept of time. Even in the present Greek language the mood of verb remains with considerable tenacity and in the Slavic languages it is still preserved[1]. However, generally speaking, the tense of verb came to occupy the important place and the difference of concepts of tenses came to have been realized in later ages. These trends are remarkably noticed especially in Modern languages.

However, though there are five kinds of tense in the Sanskrit language as in Greek,[2] they are not distinctively discriminated. For example, in indicating the past tense, the following five moods are actually used almost without discrimination in usage, i.e. imperfect, perfect, past participle active, past participle active, aorist and historical present.[3] Simply concerning the frequency of which tense was mostly used, there are differences according to periods. At the end of the period of the Brāhmaṇa writings, aorist[4] was frequently used, and in Pāli language it came to be almost a single tense denoting the past time. According to the famous grammarian of ancient India named Pāṇini (c. 4th cent. B. C.), aorist is a single tense which indicates the recent past time.[5] However, after Pāṇini, past participle has been gradually employed as an equivalent to aorist. And finally in classical Sanskrit there is little usage of aorist.

Besides, the Sanskrit language is devoid of subjanctive mood of past perfect, future perfect, and past tense.[6] This fact displays that discrimination between absolute past and relative one is not made in Indian languages.

Furthermore, the present tense of Sanskrit language is also possible to be used in order to indicate recent past and future.[7] For example, in the sentence 'What is the use of it? (It is of no use)', the present tense is used in the Sanskrit language, while the future tense is used in Latin language. (*kim karomi tena* = *quid faciam eo*) the Indian people did not have a clear consciousness of the discrimination of tense. It seems to be a similar linguistic phenomenon that in Hindustani language the same word (*kal*, adverb) has two meanings, namely, yesterday and tomorrow. Similarly, the term '*parson*' means the day after tomorrow and at the same time the day before yesterday, and the term '*atarson*' means three days after and before. Such being the case, the determination of the meaning of these kinds of words is dependent on the context, and the confusion of understanding can be removed. According to Mr. Yosaburo Omomo, such usage remains also in American-Indian languages.

That Indian people are not distinctively aware of the discrimination of tense denotes their inferiority to comprehend the current of time from past to future in the form of quantitative time through which the length of time is capable of measuring. However, it does not mean that the Indian people have no concept of time, but rather the reverse is the case. The law of transiency and its philosophical expression, i.e. view of the uncertainty of life, which are sharply pointed out by the Jains and the Buddhists, can be realized only by those who understand from their heart changing phases of the world.

The Indian people, who have not exerted themselves to grasp the concept of time quantitatively, have never written historical books with the accurate dates. This fact signifies a characteristic feature of Indian culture. It can be said that it results from the characteristic way of thinking as stated above. Presumably, according to the view of world of the Indian people, the universe, world and social order remains eternally; on the contrary, the personal life is nothing but one of succession of lives existing repeatedly in limitless time, and therefore it finally becomes meaningless. The idea of the transition of life which the Indian people have conceived is transmigration, i.e. perpetual self-revolution of rebirth. Such an idea appeared on occassions in Greek philosophy, and on the contrary in India it has always been supported by all people. So far as such a way of thinking is concerned, such passing phenomena as political or social conditions, as a matter of course, does not attract people. Such being the case, it is natural that the historical descriptions have not been made with the accurate dates in India.

---

1) Harushige Kōzu 高津春繁: *Hikaku Gengogaku* (比較言語學 Comparative Linguistics), pp. 256–257.

2) praesens, imperfectum, futurum, perfectum, aoristum. In the Latin language aoristum is lacking, but plusquamperfectum and futurum exactum are added.

3) Speyer: *Vedische und Sanskrit-Syntax*, S. 53–55.

4) It is improper that aorist should be interpreted as indefinite past tense. See H. Kōzu; *op. cit.* p. 263, note, 1.

5) Pāṇini: III, 3, 135.

6) In order to make up for it, the following three conbinations are usually used: p.p.p. + *āsa* (*abhūt*), " + *bhaviṣyati*, and " + *bhavet*. (Speyer: *op. cit.* S. 62) And in order to show the meaning of past perfect, one may use perfect, imperfect, or past participle active. (Speyer: *op. cit.* § 181).

7) Speyer: *op. cit.* S. 51.

(4) Contemplative attitudes

The attitude of viewing the essential universality at the back of a phenomenon beyond the variety of concrete phenomena of our experience can be defined as contemplative or meditative. It means no more than comprehending all progressive phenomena as in the past. Accordingly, in descripting successive events, present participle is only used in Greek and Latin languages. But gerund which shows a kind of past tense is instead used in ancient Indian languages. Here, some examples are stated below: *upasamgamya* = *accedens* (*Bhag.* 1, 2); *paraṃ dṛṣṭvā* = 'επειδὴ θεωρεῖ τὸν θεόν (II,59) (Only in this case ὁρῶν is also permited to be used.); *pallalaṃ hitvā*=*lacum relinquents* (*Dhp.* 91) (having left a pond, the bird ....); *maccu ādāya gacchati* = *mors prehendens abit* (*Dhp.* 46); *kumbhūpamaṃ kāyam imaṃ viditvā/naṅgarūpamaṃ cittam idaṃ ṭhapetvā //yojetha māraṃ paññāyudhena* (*Dhp.* 40) = *Vasi simile corpus hoc agnosscens, arci similem cogitationem hanc sistens, subigat* (*sapiens*) *Māram intellectus armis* (Having known that this body is like a water-pot and having fixed this mind just like a town, you should battle against the Destroyer with a weapon of wisdom). As seen from the above examples, in the Sanskrit language the main and the subordinate actions are expressed in different tenses, expressing the latter action in the past tense, but on the other hand in the Greek language both of them are expressed in the same tense. Furthermore, in pronouncing 'by means of' for the sake of showing the instrument of action, *ādāya* or *upādāya*, which is gerund form relevant to the past is used in the Sanskrit language; however in the Greek language ἔχων or λαβών, which is present participle, is used.

Also the same characteristic is recognized in constructing the compound in the Sanskrit language. In indicating the relation between two notions which are under the causal relation, its compound is formed in the way of tracing back from effect to cause. Accordingly, the expression of 'effect and cause' (*phalahetu*) is made instead of expression of 'cause and effect' as stated in other languages. Instead of expression of 'the relation of cause and effect', the indication of 'the relation of effect and cause' (*kāryakāraṇabhāva*)[1] is used. Likewise, the following expressions are used in the Sanskrit language: relation of the knowable and the knower (*gamyagamakabhāva*)[2]; relation of the generated and the generative (*janyajanakabhāva*); relation of the proved and the prover (*śādhyasādhakabhāva*); relation of the established and the establishing (vyayasthāpyavyavasthāpakabhāva)[3]; relation of the being excited to activity and the instigator (*pravartyapravartayitṛtva*)[4]; relation of that on which anything depends and that which depends on (*āśrayāśrayibhāva*).[5] These expressions of the Sanskrit language are remarkably different from those of other languages. Accordingly, when they translated the Indian original texts into Chinese, they changed the word order of the above expressions and showed, for example, the expression of 'the relation of cause and effect'. The Tibetan people also translated 'effect and cause' (*phalahetu*) into '*rgyu daṅ ḥbras-bu*' (cause and effect), changing its word order. The way of thinking, in which, between two notions which are formed through recognizing the relation of cause and effect existing in two matters, the notion of effect is firstly formed and secondly that of cause comes to be materialized, is retrospective, and from this angle, it is basically different from the way of thinking of other nations in which the notion of cause is firstly formed and then that of effect comes to be presented. (By the way, it is needless to say that such a way of thinking of the Indian people is basically different from the thinking process of natural science through which, with a help of inductive and deductive reasonings, the cause of effect is investigated and is ascertained.)

The Indian people, even if they investigate the relation of two things from cause to effect, are generally wanting in view that a single distinguished effect is caused by a single active movement, while they are marked in viewing that various effects are produced by the combination of various causes. Therefore, the Indian people do not hold the definite technical term which corresponds to *cause efficiens*. It seems that *nimitta-kāraṇa* is equivalent to cause efficiens, however, it is also used in expressing *causa occasionalis* and 'cause of aim'.

The thinking process through which the experiencing action and change are immediately perceived as the passed or past matters, not only restrict thinking process of Indian common people, but exert an influence on the thinking process of Indian philosophers. That which the main Indian philosophies are contemplative is closely related with this thinking process. Greek philosophy is characterized as philosophy of investigating or perceiving the substance of matter and of watching from the point of view of activity, and therefore it is commonly critisized as theōriatic. However, on this point, it may be rightly said that Indian philosophy has been more contemplative. Generally Indian religious teachers have practiced *yoga* by way of which they have contemplated the truth or intrinsic nature of phenomenal matter, however, it appears that such contemplation did not exist in Greek philosophy. It is said *theōria* is most similar to *yoga*,[6] however, *yoga* does not mean merely watching, but it denotes even attaining a state transcending one's own limited self.

1) e.g. *Nyāyabinduṭīkā*, p. 24, *l*, 11. Śaṅkara. ad BS. vol. I, p. 604, *l*. 10 (ĀnSS.)
2) *Ibid.* p. 25, *l*. 11.
3) *Ibid.* p. 15. We do not minimize the fact that there are some exceptions, e.g. *viśeṣaṇa-viśeṣya-bhāva* (*Vedāntasāra*, 168 b.)
4) Śaṅkara: *op. cit.*, I, p. 603, *l*. 3.
5) Śaṅkara: *op. cit.*, I, p. 604, *l*. 8.
6) In Greek translation of the *Bhagavat-gīta* by Demetrios Galanos, *yoga* is translated as *theōria*.

(5) Passive and forbearing attitudes toward behavior

On account of the contemplative attitude, people come to assume rather a passive attitude toward the objective or the natural world than an active attitude. They attempt to adapt themselves to nature without reconstructing nature. When assuming such an attitude, they especially come to speak highly of virtue of self-surrender or forbearance in the moral aspect. Even in the Upaniṣads forbearance is mentioned as follows: "Therefore he who knows it as such, having become calm, self-controlled, withdrawn, patient and collected sees the Self in his own self, sees all in the Self".[1] Also in early Buddhism it is explained as follows: "By virtue of forbearance he should suppress anger".[2] "Indeed in this world if he return evil for evil, he cannot be apart from evil. Give up his own evil and take a rest. This is eternal and unchangeable law".[3] And also according to the Jain school, the true hero (*vīra*) is a man who has ceased hostility (*vaira-uparata*).[4] Also in Mahāyāna Buddhism forbearance is counted as one of six virtues (*pāramitā*). The following passage shows the common view of Indian religion: "By whom can this world be conquered? It can be conquered by the man who is truthful and patient".[5] Here, 'conquest' does not denote controlling all things existing in the natural world by sheer force, but subduing one's own uncontrollable passion deserves to be called 'conquest'.

Accordingly, in regard to human endevour in action, it is praised to hold one's desire and passion in check in the following way: "Who is the hero? He is a man who is not disturbed by arrow of beauty's eyes".[6] The cause of our existence in illusion (*bhava*) is craving (*tṛṣṇā*).[7] We have to take it off. And as its result we can attain emancipation. In every Indian religion the man who eliminates all evil passions is especially extolled.[8]

Such being the case, the attitude of resistance of the Indian people toward the outward oppression is extremely forbearing and passive. In resisting against the king, Brahmins resort to means of fast. It has been believed in India that, if a Brahmin who resorted to means of fast died of starvation, the king sould have sustained a dreadful injury by the force of its miraculous effect. On account of faith in such miraculous strength, the king has been obliged to submit to the resistance of Brahmins, and to grant their request. Even in India of today, those who resist against the power often resort to means of hunger strike.

In the aspect of economical morality, Indian people lay stress on rather the fairness of sharing than that of production, because they do not approach actively toward the natural world. In other words, they lay stress on rather sharing things than producing things. The plains of the Ganges where the ancient Indian culture flourished possesses fertile soil and the climate of this area is very hot and rainy. Accordingly, it is fit for the rich farm production without much artificial effort. On the other hand, when the natural violence comes, the artificial effort is wasted. As far as the primitive industry is concerned, the nature of India has inflicted an overwhelming power on the Indian people. In such natural environment the production is controlled by the power of nature and only its sharing requires the artificial effort. Such being the case, the morality of sharing is brought to be taught and the virtue of the act of giving has become to be emphasized. Early in the *Ṛg-veda,* there appeared about forty poems praising the act of giving (*dānastuti*), in which the Brahmin poets praised kings and lords who had offered them cows, horses, servants, etc. Since then, the virtue of the act of giving has been much regarded commonly in Indian society. This virtue is taught also in the *Upaniṣads.*[9] In early Buddhism, considering from the extant sacred texts, the act of giving to the mendicants and priests is often emphasized, however, the general donation is also taught as a virtue of social morality. The offered things are to be used efficiently and enjoyed both by oneself and by others, and the central point of donation that one should offer what others want is repeatedly asserted with emphasis. The sūtra condemns and rejects the behaviour that only those who are rich in property and full of treasures and foods live on dainty food[10] And moreover, it teaches us that even the poor people should offer what they can in the following way: "Just like a companion of a traveller proceeding on a wild plain, those who offer something in spite of being poor never perish among the dead.

This is the eternal law".[11] In Jain teaching the virtue of the act of giving is alike regarded as important. In Mahāyāna Buddhism the act of giving is the first virtue which is to be practised by Buddhist followers. After that, in India, being guided by this thought, the act of giving which the king and the rich offer to the poor and solitary has been brought to become an almost perpetual convention. Thus, it might be rightly said that the respect for the virtue of the act of giving is really a remarkable character of Indian morality.[12]

The extremity of the contemplative attitude finally results in praising inactivity or 'absence of work as the ideal state'. Jain followers set a value 'on absence of work',[13] and also they claim to cease to act.[14] They aim at wiping away the dust of karma[15] existing from the past time without acting a new karma or action, because the good and bad actions generally effect pleasure and suffering. Also in Brahmanism inactivity or abstinence from acts (*naiṣkarmya*) is regarded as an ultimate ideal. In Buddhism, though slightly different from the above teachings, it is explained that the saint who has attained the highest state achieved what he should have practised, and there is nothing for him to be done.

However, in regard to this view, some objections have been cast by Indian people themselves. For example, Bhāskara, a scholar of the Vedanta school, says, "Properly speaking, it is impossible to do nothing at all. If emancipation could be attained by the virtue of inactivity, the religious mendicant (*parivrājaka*) would not have attained emancipation. Generally speaking, it is impossible for a living person to do nothing".[16] According to him, it is possible to give up attachment to one's action and egoistic self-consciousness, and it is the very ultimate purpose one should aim at. Certainly his criticism is fit for. In spite of that, ordinary people of India have not thought like this. Inactivity remains the ideal at least ideologically. It is the reason why the Indian people were short of activity.

The inactive and contemplative attitude of the Indian people give an influence even on Indian philosophy. Among the four principles, namely, the Cause, the Matter, the End, and the Form, which are ascribed to Aristotle, the cause (*causa efficiens*) corresponds to *nimitta* (*-kāraṇa*), the matter to *upādāna*(*-kāraṇa*), and the end to *prayojana* in Indian philosophy, however, the form does not have its corresponding term in Indian philosophy. (Of course, it can not be said that the form has not been considered. For some Indian philosophers *śabda* is regarded as the form. However, they do not regard the form as the so-called cause.) In other words, the action in order to create the special form has not been fully considered among Indian philosophers.

Someone may consider that the cause of such an inactive attitude of Indian thought is ascribed to the 'state of despondency' which is due to influence of a hot climate. It may be surely accepted as a reasonable cause. However, it again requires reconsideration.

---

1) *Bṛhad. Up.* IV, 4, 23.
2) *Dhammapada* 223. Also see *ibid.* XVII Kodhavagga.
3) *Ibid.* 5.
4) *Āyāraṅga* I, 3, 1, 2.
5) *Praśnottararatnamālikā* 20.
6) *Ibid.* 7.
7) *Ibid.* 6. Such thought is found in the theory of twelve lniks of causality explained in Buddhism.
8) 問答寶鬘 *Praśnottararatnamālikā* 14.
9) *Bṛhad. Up.* V, 2. Such thought process is noticed in the explanation of the theory of 'two paths and five fire-offerings' that those who are devotional to Brahma with offering of religious service and pure practice, are able to proceed to the *pitṛ-yāna* or the path leading to the heaven.
10) *Suttanipāta* 102.
11) *Saṃyutta-Nikāya* I, p. 18 Gāthā.
12) *Praśnottararatnamālikā* 13, 16. 17. 26.
13) *akamma*, *Āyāraṅga* I, 2, 2, 1 (p. 7).
14) *Ibid.* I, 6, 3, 2.
15) *Ibid.* I, 4. 4. 1. (p. 20)
16) Bhāskara: *Brahmasūtrabhāṣya*, pp. 206, 209.

Chapter 7. Subjective comprehension of personality

(1) Subjective comprehension of personality as revealed in language

It has been pointed out in chapter I in examining the form of simple judgment, 'S is P' that, besides the emphasis on universals, the mode of thought which attaches importance to the predicate has tendencies to emphasize subjective functions rather than objective things. This is also one of the eminent characteristics of Indian thought. We shall examine in the following passage the reflections of this way of thinking in language.

What is to be pointed out first of all as a visible example of this tendency is that, in Western languages, an object or person under discussion is mostly expressed in the accusative case, while in Sanskrit, it is often expressed in the nominative case. For example, in a Greek sentence:

πατέρα Ξενοφῶντα ἐκάλουν (= They called Xenophon father.), both 'Xenophon' and 'father' are expressed in the accusative case. Similarly, a Latin verb *'nomino'* governs two accusatives. While in Sanskrit, what is to be defined or termed is expressed in the accusative case as in Greek or Latin, but the new term to be added is expressed by a noun in the nominative case followed by an indeclinable *'iti'*. This kind of expression appeared even in the oldest literature, e.g. *tám āhuḥ suprajā iti, Ṛg-Veda* IX, 114, 1 (= They call him a man having good offspring.) It may be said that in Sanskrit, importance is attached to a new term rather than to what is already known. By using this kind of lingual form, i.e. by the use of an independent nominative case for a new term, the Indians regard a new term as the expression of an independent subjective existence different from what is termed by it.

The same tendency is eminently observed in the use of the gerundive. In cases of Greek and Latin, the object of a transitive verb is expressed in the accusative case even in gerundive construction. But in old Indian languages it is expressed in the nominative case. The Indians never use the accusative case in such a case.

e.g. (Gr.) διωκιέον τοὺς πολεμίους.
(We should seek after the enemy)
(Lat.) *aeternas poenas in morte timendum est.*
(We must be afraid of the eternal punishment after death.)
(Skt) *brāhmaṇo na hantavyaḥ* (A brāhmin should not be killed.)
tāsmāt svādhyāyo 'dhyetavyaḥ', ŚBr. XI, 5,7,3.
(Therefore the daily lesson is to be practiced.)

Indian languages have no form of *'accusativum cum infinitivum'* as in the Western classical languages.[1] Namely they don't use the accusative case to express the subject which takes a verb shown in infinitive as the predicate. It is substituted by an instrumental.[2] It seems to reveal an Indian tendency of avoiding as much as possible the use of the accusative case for expressing the subject of action.

Then what is the significance of the expression in the accusative? All noun cases except the accusative can stand for the nominal predicate of a sentence.[3] Namely, among all noun cases, the accusative alone has no predicative meaning. It has by nature an objective sense and cannot express a subjective sense. In the light of this linguistic rule and for the fact mentioned above, we may be allowed to draw a conclusion that the Westerners are inclined to comprehend an object of observation as an objective matter, while the Indians, disliking such a way of comprehension, try to catch its subjective significance.

In self-reflection, the Indians did not like to comprehend themselves objectively by placing the self at a distance. In the expressions such as 'to think oneself', 'to call oneself', 'self' is expressed in the accusative case in Latin and Greek, but it is expressed in the nominative case in Sanskrit of old stage. e.g. *parābhaviṣyanti manye*, (*Tait. Saṃh.* II, 5, 1, 2). (I think I shall be disappeared.) *kathaṃ so 'nuśiṣṭo bruvita* (*Chānd. Up.* 5,3,1). (How can he say (by himself) that he has completed his study?)[4]

The Indians did not want to reflect upon their own self objectively being the substratum of mental activities. The use of impersonalia, in which the mental substratum, when it is influenced by sentiment, is shown in the accusative, is occasionally observed only in early Sanskrit literature.[5] But it has a fairly good number of examples in Western languages. Similar contrasts between Western languages and Sanskrit are also observed in impersonalia which expresses the idea of duty or necessity.[6] It shows the fact that some characteristics common to the old Indo-European languages have been lost in Classical Sanskrit.

---

1) Speyer: *Vedische und Sanskrit-Syntax*, S. 67.
2) Speyer: *op. cit.* S. 66.
3) Speyer: *op. cit.* S. 75, § 243, Anm. 3.
4) Speyer: *op. cit.* S. 63.
5) Speyer: *op. cit.* S. 74.
6) *na tvaṃ śocituṃ arhasi* (*Bhag. G.* II, 27).
= *no te lugere oportet*, = οὐ δεῖ σοι λιπεῖσ θαι.
= You need not be sad.
Here the subject 'you' is expressed in the nominative case in the sense of *kartṛ* (agent), while it is expressed objectively in Greek and Latin.

(2) Subjective comprehension of personality as revealed in philosophy

Similar to the cases in language, the Indians tried to avoid comprehension of the mental substance objectively in philosophical thinking. The mental substance, which is termed 'νοῦς', *'spiritus'*, *'mens'*, or 'ψυχή', and *'anima'* by Greek and Roman philosophers, is called *'ātman'* by Indian philosophers. The term *ātman* is etymologically relating to German *atmen* (to breathe), but is used as a reflective pronoun in Sanskrit. In Chinese Buddhist scriptures, it is always translated into '我' (I, *ich*). It was probably inevitable for the Indians, who thought of the mental substance mostly in terms of subjective concept, to use a reflective pronoun in order to express such a concept. If a concept is termed by any kind of noun, as in Western philosophy, there must be more or less objective comprehension about it. In Greek, there is no form like 'τὸ σεαυτόν' or 'ὁ σεαυτός', and 'ὁ αὐτός' means 'the same', but has no sense of 'the self'. In modern philosophy, too, the main point of discussion was on '*das Ich*' (I), but not so much on '*das Selbst*' as in Indian philosophy.

One may perhaps object here that there existed a few Indian thinkers who understood the subject of mental activity in terms of the objective world; for example, the Nyāya-Vaiśeṣika school,[1] the Mimāṃsā school, and even some Vedāntists like Bhartṛprapañca[2] held such an objective way of thinking. But even these philosophers called the mental substance '*ātman*'. Thus, so far as the use of such terms is concerned, they were also in accord with the Indian mode of thought. Their natural philosophy was indeed objective, but its significance lies merely in its criticism of the general tendency of the Indian way of thinking, and they were against the orthodox merely for objection. Therefore there can be no objection to the characteristic of Indian mode of thought as defined above.

In the main current of Indian philosophy, viz. from the Upaniṣhads to the Vedānta philosophy and to Hinduism, this 'self', i.e. *ātman* is regarded as identical with the Absolute, the ultimate Ego, and both are equally called *ātman*. Sometimes the latter is called '*paramâtman*' in contrast with the former, *jīvâtman*'. Though both are different in their attributes, *parama* or *jīva,* they are included in one and the same genus of '*ātman*'. Thus the Indians thought of an intimate relation between the self as the substance of individuality and the reality being the ultimate self. On the contrary, such an idea was hardly established among Western philosophers. There was a lack of investigation on 'the real self' in Western philosophy.[3]

The prominent tendency of Indian philosophy is often referred to as 'pantheistic'. For example, according to Śāṇḍilya, a famous Upanishadic thinker, the Absolute Brahman is said to be 'that which is of true thinking', 'that which is of true intention', and 'that whose own thought and mind is realized as they were'. Also it is said that it 'performs all the activities', it is 'endowed with all kinds of desire', and 'manifests whatever is intended by it'; therefore 'it is possessed of all kinds of odour, all kinds of taste', it is limitless in its scale, 'pervades everything', moves 'as quick as mind', and 'governs over all directions'.

Such a kind of comprehension is not unique to Śāṇḍilya, and we find a similar concept of deity in the philosophy of Xenophon. However,

Śāṇḍilya regarded this Absolute as being identical with the real self, whereas Xenophon did not.

One may here naturally recall the Buddhist negation of *ātman* against the orthodox *ātman*-theory, and this would raise the question that the substantial view of *ātman* cannot be regarded as common to the Indians because a major religion such as Buddhism denies of it. But did Buddhism really deny *ātman*?

According to the Non-ātman theory expressed in the scriptures belonging to the oldest phase of early Buddhism, Buddhism denies the concept of 'mine' or 'my possession' (*mama*). Mendicants are first of all requested to remove their affection towards the concept of 'mine'.[4] It means that they should not harbor the idea of possession of 'mine' and 'other's'.[5] Such a concept of renunciation of all things and its practice was held in Brahmanism since the oldest age. Renunciation is described in the Vedic scriptures as a kind of religious observances under the name of *'sarva-medha'*. In the earliest Upanishadic literature, a real Brahmin who realized *ātman* is said to go wandering and begging, casting off desires for sons, wealth and the world.[6] The same idea of the rejection of the 'mine'-concept is also taught in Jainism.[7] And if the so called Non-*ātman* theory is meant by this rejection of 'mine'-concept, Jains are to be said to have kept the idea of 'non-*ātman*' (*nirmamatva*) until later days.[8]

Why then is the concept of 'mine' to be rejected? Referring to the reason, the early Buddhist scriptures tell us the following teaching. Namely, whatever is regarded as one's own possession is always changeable. Therefore it does not belong to the self for ever, and after one's death, all the things possessed by him and all the relatives and subordinates who are regarded to be his possession will be separated from him. Therefore one should not be attached to his own possession.[9] Thus, in early Buddhism, they taught avoidance of the wrong comprehension of what is not *ātman* as the real *ātman*.[10] Of things not to be the self, the misunderstanding of body as *ātman* is especially strongly opposed. Foolish people comprehend their body as their own possession.[11] Even gods are captured by such an infatuation so that they cannot release themselves from suffering due to transmigration.[12] Buddhists of early days called this mis-comprehension "the notion on account of the attachment to the existence of one's body" (*sakkāyadiṭṭhi*) and taught the abandonment of it.[13] Therefore what is taught by early Buddhists is that whatever is not *ātman*, esp. body should not be regarded as one's own. With the establishment of technical terms in Buddhist philosophy, the component elements of a body or individual existence are understood by terms, *'saṃskārāḥ'* (諸行, conditionings), or *'pañca-skandhāḥ* (五蘊, five groups), and using these terms, the scriptures explain the Non-ātman theory in the following way: "*pañcakkhandhā* (or *saṃkhārā*) are to be understood as different things (than *ātman*), and not as *ātman*".[14] And in the scriptures of a little later period, we find the following formulae often repeated: "Form (*rūpa*) (feeling, idea, volition, conscriousness) is impermanent. What is impermanent is of suffering. What is of suffering is non-*ātman*. What is non-*ātman* is not mine, nor it is I, nor it is my *ātman*". Ordinary people and philosophers superimpose the existence of *ātman* and are seeking it. But whichever elements, mental or physical, that compose human existence, these are not to be understood as *ātman*. These elements are always changing, and hence they are unlike *ātman* which is permanent. Also, being accompanied by suffering, they are different from *ātman*, which is the ideal perfect reality. Then how is our *ātman*? It cannot be comprehended objectively. Whichever principle or function that is imagined to be *ātman* by people is in reality neither *ātman* nor that which belongs to *ātman* at all. ...... Such is the outline of the non-*ātman* theory of Buddhism. Therefore early Buddhists did never maintain the non-existence of *ātman*. They merely opposed the substantial or functional view on *ātman*. As for the question whether *ātman* exists or not, early Buddhist kept silence.

On the other hand, they admitted the self (*ātman*) as the moral agent being a premise for the problem of human deeds.[15] Namely they say that one should perform one's own duty,[16] or one should be conscious about his "own profit".[17] Here what is meant by one's own profit (*svattha, svahita*) is neither material nor sensual, but is the realisation of truth. Lord Śākyamuni is said to have asked those youths who indulge themselves in amusement 'to seek after the self (*ātman*)' than 'to seek for women and advised them to become monks. Seeking after *ātman* is emphasized in the *Upaniṣhads*.[19] In early Buddhism, it is said that, being desirable (*priya*),[20] *ātman* is to be loved and be protected.[12] This teaching corresponds to that of Yājñavalkya.[22] Jains, too, call themselves *'ātmavādins'*[23] and teaches the purification[24] and protection[25] of *ātman*.

Thus, in spite of the existence of different opinions among various religions and philosophies with regard to the essence of *ātman* as the metaphysical principle, the significance of *ātman* as the agent of deeds may *be assured of general admittance among the Indians*. For any religion of India, the ultimate goal of emancipation is the recovering of one's self. In Brahmanism, attainment of self-control (*svārājyam adhigacchati*) is generally considered as the state of emancipation.[26] Hell is said to be nothing but 'the state of bondage to others'.[27] Buddhism specially emphasizes 'man is the master of himself'.[28]

---

1) In the Vaiśeṣika philosophy, *ātman* is counted as one of the substances (*dravya*). There is no passage in the *Nyāyasūtra* where *ātman* is defined as the substance (*dravya*). But as it often refers to the qualities (*guṇa*) which are inherent (*samavāya*) to *ātman*, it may be understood that the perception of *ātman* as a substance is recognized by the Sūtra itself.

2) According to Śaṅkara's description, Bhartṛprapañca was of the following opinion about *ātman*:—The substance *ātman* has two characteristics, viz. oneness (*ekatva*) and manifoldness (*nānātva*). For example, oxes have identity through substantiality of being ox (*go-dravyatā*), and at the same time are distinct from each other through different characteristics on account of the hanging flesh of neck, etc. Just as there is oneness and manifoldness within one (sensible) gross thing, similarly it should be known that in the indivisible, formless substance like space, there exist oneness and manifoldness side by side. Because, this (rule) is experienced everywhere without exception. The case is the same with *ātman*, which involves differentiation on account of seeing, etc., on one hand, and the identity on the other hand. (Śaṅkara ad. *Bṛhad. Up.* iv, 3, 24–30. ĀnSS. p. 622.)

This opinion is summarised in syllogism by Ānandajñāna in the following way:

"(Proposition) What is discussed here (= *ātman*) is differentiated and undifferentiated at the same time.

(Reason) Because it is a substance (*vastu*).

(Example) Just like the case of the ox".

(Ānandajñāna ad Śankara's *Bṛhad. Up. Bhāṣya*, p. 622).

This syllogism can be applied to Brahman, too, and hence Brahman is concluded to be one and the same though it is differentiated and undifferentiated at the same time.

3) The intention of the author is not to assert that the investigation of the 'real self' was not launched in Western philosophy. Kant admitted the existence of the real self (*das eigentliche Selbst*). In the visible world, according to Kant, it is nothing but the intellect (*Intelligenz*), and human beings are merely its phenomena (*Erscheinung*). (*Grundlegung zur Metaphysik der Sitten*, herausgegeben von Karl Vorländer, S. 88) Also he distinguishes 'the real self' from simple phenomena in the thought of its being the will (*Wille*) of the intellect. (ibid. S. 91) However, the concept of '*das eigentliche Selbst*' had no further development in Kant's philosophy. As for the comparative lack of discussions on the self as a philosophical concept in Western philosophies, see Eisler: Wörterbuch der philosophischen Begriffe, s. v. Selbst. Also see Hegel: *Enzyklopädie*, § 405 Zusatz, § 408.

4) *Suttanipāta* 225, 367, 466, 469, 777, 809, 922. *Dhammapada* 367. *Theragāthā* 717.

5) "One who has no idea of 'mine' and 'others'—he has no suffering from the notion: 'I have not this and that', because of the absence of 'mineness' (*mamatta*) with him". (*Sn.* 951) (cf. 809).
6) Especially, cf. *Bṛhad. Up.* iii, 5, 1; iv, 4, 22.
7) *mamāiya-maiṃ jahāi* = *mamāyita-matiṃ jahāti.* (*Āyāraṅga* i, 2, 6, 2)
8) *Pravacanasāra* II, 108; Yenshō. Kanakura 金倉圓照: *Indo Seishin-bunka no Kenkyū* (印度精神文化の研究 Studies on Indian Culture), p. 287.
9) *Suttanipāta* 805, 806.
10) "People in the world, inclusive of deities, think what is non-*ātman* as *ātman*, and are attached to its name and form. (*anattani attamānam—niviṭṭhaṃ nāmarupasmiṇ*, *Suttanipāta* 231; 761.)
11) *Theragāthā* 575, 1150. cf. 766.
12) *Saṃyutta-Nikāya* III, p. 86 G.; *AN.* II, p. 34 G; *SN.* I, p. 200 G.
13) *SN.* I, p. 13 G. cf. *Suttanipāta* 231; 761.
14) *Theragāthā* 1160, 1161.
15) *Ibid.* 597.
16) *attano kiccakārī*, *Theragāthā* 729.
17) *Therayāthā* 249, 250, 289, 587, 1097. *SN.* I, p. 34 G, 55 G, 57 G, 70 G, 102 G.
18) *attānaṃ gaveseti*, *Vinaya*, Mahāvagga, I, 13. p. 23. cf. *attaññū*, *AN.* IV, p. 113; *DN.* III, p. 252.
19) *Chānd. Up.* viii, 1, 1. cf. *Mahānārāyaṇa-Up.* x, 7.
20) *SN.* I, p. 6 G.
21) *AN.* II, p. 21 G.; *SN.* I, p. 71 ff; 57 G.; p. 89; 154 G.; *Dhammapada* 66, 157, 327, 355, 379, 653; *Theragāthā* 141, 1005.
22) "O indeed, (a wife) loves her husband not because she loves him, but because she loves *ātman.* (A husband) loves his wife not because he loves her, but because he loves *ātman.* They love their children not because they love them, but because they love *ātman*". (*Bṛhad. Up.* ii, 4; iv, 5).
23) *Āyāraṇga* p. 25, *l.* 27. cf. pp. 13, *l.* 12; 20, *l.* 20 f. (herausgegeben von W. Schubring)
24) *Ibid.* p. 44, *l.* 20.
25) *Ibid.* p. 13, *l.* 26; 15, *l.* 25; 34, l. 30.
26) e. g. *Manusmṛti*, xii, 19.
27) *Praśnottaramālikā*, XX.
28) *Dhammapada* 160.

Chapter 8. Supremacy of the universal self over the individual self

(1) The unobstructed extension of the self as revealed in language

The self which is grasped through the way of thinking as mentioned above is not identified with the numerable individual selves which are conceived as relative and homogeneous ones in objective world. It is the agent or subject of action which is beyond the opposition between the self and the other, because it can not be conceived as something subjective but its predicative phases alone are emphasized. Here, it may be noticed that it brings out in strikingly distinctive contrast the difference of the view of self between the Indian and the Western people. Generally it is claimed that the consciousness of self appeared at the beginning of Modern Age. However, in some senses, previously it came out among the Western people of ancient times. The Romans of old ages were possessed of the thinking attitude, through which they, having conceived that each self with the same capacity was opposed to other selves, weighed all things respectively on the basis of their own selves. In the Latin language, the expression 'ego et tu' (I and you) is used in order to show one's self and others' at the same time.[1] In Japanese, this is very impolite expression toward others or one's opponent, while in the former language it is rather usual expression. The Romans neither accepted the spiritual supremacy of the other's self over one's self, nor set up a distinction of social standing between one's self and the other's. Even gods and superiors were called to only by the pronoun of the second person 'tu'. It is so with the Greek language. Such being the case in the Western languages of ancient times the honorific expression made little progress.

On the other hand, the Indian people are destitute of awareness that others' self is opposed to one's self. Therefore, in India a tencency that others' self is not regarded as an independent subject of action which is opposed to one's self, is rather often acknowledged.

This thinking attitude becomes manifest even in usage of the Sanskrit language. To prove this, they often employ a kind of particular usage of causative mood. For example, *kārayati* (to cause to do), a causative mood of *karoti* (to do), is often employed in any Indian language and in any time. However, in the Western languages of ancient times the usage which corresponds to it does not exist. Therefore, when man wants to indicate the causative meaning in the Latin language, he is obliged to use the formula 'cogo (gactio, dūco, permitto) ut + subjunctive'. Accordingly, in the Sanskrit language the causative mood is often used, in order to express a certain situation, while in the Western languages of ancient times very *complicated expressions* must be required in order to show the same meaning. Here, two examples will be presented: *kathaṃ sa puruṣaḥ .... kaṃ ghātayati hanti kam.* (*Bhag. G.* II, 21)=*quomodo is homo quempiam out aliorum ministerio, aut sua manu occidat?* πῶς, οὗτος οἰηθήσεται, ὡς αὐτὸς ἀναιρει, ἢ αἴτιος γίνεται ἀναιρεθῆναι; *naiva kurvan na kārayan*

(*Bhag. G.* V. 13) = *neque ipse agens, neque aliis agendi auctor,* μήτ' αὐτὸς πράττων, μήι ἄλλοις αἴτιος γινόμενος τοῦ πράττειν.

When the expression 'to cause others to ....' is used in the Greek and Latin languages, various attitudes of others toward one's self are taken into account, and afterwards, the causative expression comes to be used. Therefore, the causative mood 'to cause some one to ....' is formed by using various verbs according to relation between 'someone' or the opponent and one's self, and to its pattern of behavior. And the subjunctive or the infinitive mood of verb which displays the action of other self is often used in these languages, because they were conscious of a distinction of actions between other self which is to be forced or permitted to do and one's self. In the Sanskrit language the action of other self is manifested *as extention of action of one's self.* The Indian people, who often use the causative mood, are unconscious of a distinction of actions between one's self, one who makes another do, and other self, its opponent. Accordingly, in the Sanskrit language, there are even some cases where the meaning of causative mood of a verb is not different from its original. (For example, *dhārayati* (to cause to hold) is actually used as having almost the same meaning as *dharati* (to hold).) These cases become rather striking in the Pāli and Prakrit languages.

Generally in these languages, the opponent, when caused to do something, is expressed by the accusative case; he, when regarded as a means of action, is expressed by the instrumental case.[2] In this case, he is not a man who is possessed of personal value, but only an *instrument* (means). (Just because of being an instrument, it may be denoted by the instrumental case.) And just because it is nothing but an instrument, the casuative mood of a verb is actually identified with its very active mood.

It often happens that the Indian people concern themselves about monotonic and unobstructed *extention of the will or volition of one's self* on the place of human relation. Such being the case, in the Indian languages, the subject or agent is, sometimes, omitted. On describing the process of personal and mental experience, the Indian people do not use a personal pronoun as well as a term which corresponds to 'one' or 'man' in English. The subject is denoted only by using a verb.[3]

In the social circumastance where the will of the unobstructed extention might be materialized, those who are coerced to do by this will are dependent upon one who possesses and delivers it. And this circumstance comes to give a birth to the honorific usage which has not been so highly developed as in Japan. However, there are some honorific words which belongs to pronouns of the second person.[4] On the other hand, Greek and Latin languages do not possess any honorific words (*bhavān* =Σὺ αὐτὸς, *tu ipse*, *Bhag. G.* I, 8). It was provided for in Indian epics that the pronoun of the second person 'you' are permitted to be used to the younger person or one's contemporary but not to the senior or the high-ranked person, and that one should not call the latter by their real names.[5] Likewise in sacred writings of early Buddhism, it proved that those who were lower in their caste never called the Kṣatriyas by pronouns of the second person as well as by their real names.[6]

---

1) As an exceptional case, the expression, '*ego et rex meus*' (I and my lord), which Cardinal Wolsey always used in an official document, is seen as an arrogant one.

2) For example, *tām śvabhiḥ khādayed rājā.* (The king may cause dogs to bite that woman.) In Buddhist writings some examples can be found, e. g. *tadrūpān yajñān na svayaṃ yajati na parair yājayati.* (*Bodhisattvabhūmi*, p. 118, *l.* 4)

3) Mrs. Rhys Davids: *The Will to Peace*, p. 85.

4) Generally, *bhavān, tatrabhavān, bhagavān* are used as honorific words. *Deva* is used for a king, *ārya* for a honorable trader and others, *āryā* for a lady, *āryaputra* for an honorable husband, *āyuṣman* for a master by his driver, etc. (Speyer: *Sanskrit Syntax*, pp. 195–196).

5) *Tvaṃkāraṃ nāmadheyaṃ ca jyeṣṭhānāṃ parivarjayet. MBh.* XII, 193, 25. (W. Hopkins: The social and military position of the ruling caste in ancient India, *Journal of the American Oriental Society*, XIII, 1888, p. 75, n.)

6) Fick: *Die soziale Gliederung im nordöstlichen Indien zu Buddha's Zeit*, S. 54.

(2) The continuity of one's self and other selves

The Indian people concern themselves only about the unobstructed extension of one's self from the point of view of their languages; however, it is an undeniable fact that they never ignore the existence of others' personality. They have a high regard for others. It is often stated in writings of early Buddhism and other teachings that one should pay regard to others, and that one should not neglect others.[1] It can be only admitted that they did not consider others as other selves or the opponents of one's self. In other words, they conceived a view that other selves become one with the self as an extension of the self. The Aphorism: 'Buddha's identification with the self and the self's identification with the Buddha' which is stated in Tantric Buddhism, is based on the view of the continuity of one's self other selves which the Indian people commonly conceive.

It forms a striking contrast with the view of man which was conceived by the Western people of ancient ages. They hold the view that other selves are, as a counterpart of the self, opposed to one's self and that the self is always placed on the opposition to other selves. Considerably good deal of passages which reveal this kind of view can be found in writings of the Western people as follows: "The war is the father of all things" (πόλεμος πατήρ πάντων — Hērakleitos); "Man is a wolf to others" (Home homini lupus.—Pautus); If you wish for peace, prepare for fighting" (si vis pacem, para bellum). Even in Modern ages, the natural condition of human beings is comprehended as 'fighting of human beings against human beings" (bellum omnium contra omnes—Hobbes).

From ancient times, the Westerner's view of life has been rather aggressive. In Western history peace was gained as a result of some struggles. It is not a continual and static peace but a conquest of ravages of war. On the other hand, in India, peace was eternal and quiet calmness. Of course, the wars occured time after time in India, however, on many occasions only the lords and their mercenary soldiers fighted war, while ordinary people did not join them. In some cases, near the battle field farmers cultivated their lands without fear and worring about it.[2] Therefore, at agricultural districts of India, religious ceremonies and customs of thousand years ago have been conveyed to the present time almost without sustaining any changes and damages. Generally speaking, the character of the Indians is obedient and remarkably opposite to be aggressive. Naturally they want and love a calm and peaceful life. As Indian history affords a proof of this view, we are difficult to find instances that Indians invaded countries outside of India.[3]

Generally, the Indians have no idea of detesting other people. The Aryans conquered other Indian peoples and incorporated them into their community as their slaves, however, they did not treat their slaves with much cruelty and drive them very hard. Megasthenēs the Greek, writes down in his record of his personal experience in India that it is a marvellous fact that all men of India are free people and among them the equality (ισότης) are materialized.[4] Śūdra, a man of the lowest of the four castes in ancient society of India, is commonly interpreted as 'slave'; however śūdra denotes a kind of social standing. Accordingly, śūdras are not identified with the 'slaves' of Western society who were treated badly and driven to hard work. It is imagined that some of śūdras were only engaged individually in labors at the Aryan's family. Accordingly, in the eye of a Greek, the slaves did not exist among the ancient society of India.

In the ancient languages of India there is no pronoun which denotes the public or a mass of people in contrast with individual a pronoun which indicates the common subject, as e.g. 'man' in German,[5] because the Indians did not claim positively the individual self in opposition to other self. Therefore, in order to indicate the common subject, generally the active voice of third person singular is used. If necessary, *sa* (he), *nara* (man), *puruṣa* (person) and *loka* (world) are substituted for. Conversely comparing the ancient language of India with Western languages, this fact shows that, for the sentence whose subject is *man,* the active voice of third person singular is commonly substituted in the former language. In India, it is a common instance that in this connection a proposition is enunciated by setting forth the universal as its subject; on the contrary it is rather exceptional that the individual as its subject. This fact exhibits a tendency to attach importance to the universal self which is beyond the individual self or comprehends it.

To cite an example of the ways of thinking of the Indians, people or men as subject of a sentence are, in many cases, stated in the *singular form,* and then its predicate becomes singular. For instance, *ayam pajā*[6] (whose form is singular) means 'these men'. In the ancient language of India, *jana* (its meaning is people) is predicated in the singular form;[7] on the other hand, *people* in English is predicated in the plural form. In the ancient languages of the West, even though a nation or group is stated in the singular form, its predicate is expressed in the plural form.[8] This linguistic mode is inherited even to German.[9] Therefore, in the West not only modern people but also Greeks and Romans had a clear idea that the subject of action was a *conpound body* of individuals, while in India there was a strong tendency regarding the subject of action as a *group or united body.* Thus, in the Western society each individual self is highly esteemed and each individual opinion becomes the object of public attention. Such passages as '*quot homines, tot sententiae*' (there are as many minds as men) or '*vox populi, vox Dei*' (the voice of people is the voice of God) are characteristic of this society. The Indians, on the contrary, emphasize that as a member of the united body, i.e. human beings, each individual is respectable and worthy of love.

The distinctive feature of the Indians that the individual self is not discriminated from the other is acknowledged also from the linguistic phenomenon that the desiderative mood is often used in India. On a few occasions, an independent word which means 'to desire' is used.[10] However, it is common that the desiderative mood is used, when the meaning 'to desire to do ....' is required. The desiderative mood is formed by a special conjugation of verb. (As its derivative, the noun form is also used.) For instance, in order to show the meaning 'he desires to live', two verbs, i.e. 'to desire' and 'to live' are required in the ancient languages of the West as well as in Japanese, while in the Sanskrit language a desiderative conjugation '*jijiviṣati*' is used.[11] In the latter language, 'to desire' is grasped as only a way for action 'to live', just as the future conjugation of verb denotes only a way for action manifested by the verb. Therefore, in the West, the desire for action is comprehended to *be different* from the action itself as it depends upon the free will of the subject of action whether he desires to act or not, while in Indian, the desire for action is seen to be only *an annexed action* of the subject of that action.

Outside of the desiderative mood, in order to show the meaning 'I hope he may ....', for instance, in the Latin language '*rogo ut vivat*' (= *Je demande qu'il vive*) (I hope he may live) is used; in the Sanskrit language, on the contrary, '(*api nāma*) jivet' is simply used.[12]

Even in the ordinary life the idea of non-discrimination between the self and the other comes out. According to Megasthenes, Indians did not ask for the bond when they lent money to others. Among the Japanese, some hold the belief that it is an unfriendly action to receive the bond from intimate friends. For the Western people who are accustomed to the notion of contract, it would have been an unexpected fact.

In brief, the Indians are not possessed of the well conscious reflection upon the fact that the desire of one's self comes to meet with others' reaction on the other side. It is the *idea of indiscrimination* of all men that underlies it.

As to the way of thinking like this, Hegel states as follows: "Intellectual substantiality (of the Indians) is opposite to reflection, reason, and subjective individuality of the Europeans. For us, Western people, it is the important thing that, in accordance with his own basis, the individual (ich) desires for, knows, believes, or considers something as he pleases, and on the ground of it, the immeasurable value is placed. On the contrary, the intellectual substantiality stands on the other pole, and there the subjectivity of the self becomes lost its significance. For this subjectivity, all the objective things came to be meaningless, and moreover there is neither objective truth nor duty nor right. It results that only the subjective falsehood remains".[13] Obviously it is his misunderstanding that Hegel states that the Indians have neither conception of the objective truth nor those of duty and right, Because many writings of science and law were made out in India. However, it is an obvious fact that the Indians seek for their religious and moral ideal on the way of effacing the subjectivity of the self. It is on the basis of the way of thinking as mentioned above that the absolute devotion is unlimitedly emphasized in the Purāṇas of Hinduism and the Jātakas of Buddhism. It has been the ideal of the Indians to attain the *non-discrimination between the self and the other.*

---

1) For instance, see *Suttanipāta* 206.

2) See Fragments of Megasthenēs 33.

3) The Indians of the Maurya Dynasty had an idea that neither Indian people had been invaded by other people, nor they had assailed the latter, except that they had been invaded by Hēraklēs, Dionysos and the Macedonians. (*Fragments of Megasthenēs* 46)

4) According to Megasthenēs there was no slave (δοῦλός), and all were free people in those days. "In Indian land there are following noticeable facts: All Indians are free people; any of them are not slaves; among Lakedaimonians, Helots are slaves and do work as slaves; on the contrary, among the Indian people other nations are not slaves, to say nothing of the slaves of Indians themselves". (Arrianon, Indike, 10 = fr. XXVI) "He (Megasthenēs) states that any Indian does not hire slaves. Onēsikritos explains that it is peculiar to the Indians who live in Mousikanos". (Athenaeus, IV p. 153 = *fr.* xxviii)

5) Speyer; *Vedische und Sanskrit-Syntax*, S. 75, § 246.

6) *Udāna* VI, 6.

7) For instance, *vippaḍiveei appaṇam*; '*kiṃ esa jaṇo karissai? esa se paraārāme, jāo logammi itthio*' (*Sūyagaḍaṃga* I, 5, 4, 4) (I observe for myself, "What do these men do? In this world women are the best pleasure".)

8) For instance, *dṛṣṭvemaṃ svajanaṃ yuyutsum samupasthitaṃ* (Bhag. G. I, 28) = *visa ista cognatorum turba, qui proeliabundi huc progressi sunt*, 'Ιδόντος μον τούτονς τούς σογγενεῖς παρισταμένονς καί πολἐμησείοντας.

9) *Eine Menge Menschen sind getötet.* (Many people are killed.) *Ein Heer Soldaten marschierten nach Frankreich.* (A group of soldiers marched on France.) But, the following expressions are also used: Das Heer ist versammelt; es war viel Volk da, etc.

10) For instance, *etān na hantum icchāmi* (*Bhag. G.* I, 35); *kāmakāmī* (II, 70); *yuddhakāmān* (I, 22).

11) To cite some examples, *yān eva hatvā na jijīviṣāmaḥ* (*Bhag. G.* II, 6) = *quibus caesis vivere nos non iuvat*, οὓς γάρ ἡμεῖς ἀνελόντες οὐκ εφιέμεθα ςωῆς; *cikīrṣur lokasaṃgraham* (III, 25) = *procurans generis humani commodum*, βουλόμενος ὑπόδε γμα γενεσθαι τῶ κοσμῳ; *mumukṣubhiḥ* (IV, 15) =

emancipationem affectantibus, φίλοι τῇ ἀπαδεία; *yogasya jijñāsuḥ*, (VI, 44) = *devotionem cognoscendi studiosus*, ὁ μὲν ιὺν φιλῶν κτήσα δαι τὴν θερίαν.

12) If one address himself to the other, he may also use the expression '*icchāmi jīvet bhavān*' (I hope you may live). (Speyer: *Sanskrit Syntax*, p. 263, cf. Pāṇini 3, 3, 160).

13) Hegel: *Vorlesungen über die Geschichte der Philosophie*, ed. Michelet, S. 162–163.

(3) Consciousness of the existence of the self

Then is it right to say that in India, where the idea of the continuity of one's self and other selves is generally accepted, no attempt has been made by the thinkers to prove the existence of the self? Nay, on the contrary, already in ancient times the thinkers of India were engaged in the study of the consciousness of the self and the demonstration of its existence. But, their way is quite different from methods employed by the modern European philosophers.

Already in the philosophy of the Vaiśeṣika school, it was asserted that the existence of the Ātman or the Self can be known by intuitive perception.[1] And this idea was remarkably refined by Upavarṣa (ca. 450–500 A.D.), an early Vedāntic scholar, and his followers.[2] According to Upavarṣa, the existence of the Ātman cannot be known by inference or demonstration, nor can it 'be accepted on the authority of scriptual statement'. But, the Ātman is known to exist intuitively through the notions that every individual person entertains upon his self. Because anyone can hold the ideas upon his self like 'I get thinner' or 'I perceive this', we cannot deny the existence of the Ātman or the agent which makes him hold such ideas. Really the Ātman is known to exist from the very fact that 'a man is conscious of his self'. In later period, the Kumārila school in the Mīmāṃsā system succeeded this idea of Upavarṣa, claiming immediate perception of the Ātman. And it was on this point that this school was distinguished from the Prabhākara school of the same system.[3] As far as we have observed above, we can say that the assertions concerning the Ātman that the ancient Indian thinkers set forth are very similar to the view on the ego that modern Western philosophers come to hold through their study of the self-consciousness.

It should be noted, however, that in India the Ātman is generally understood to mean not only the individual ego but also the Brahman or the Universal Self. And the thinkers who represent Indian thought are all inclined *to make a big leap in teir reasoning;* they assume that *the existence of the Universal Self is known directly from the existence of the individual self.* For instance, Śaṅkara, a prominent Indian philosopher of the eighth century, makes a following statement in one of his books. "Moreover the existence of Brahman is known on the ground of its being the Self of every one. For every one is conscious of the existence of (his) Self, and never thinks 'I am not'. If the existenece of the Self were not known, every one would think 'I am not'. And this Self (of whose existence all are conscious) is Brahman".[4] And as to the existence of the Self (*ātman*), Śaṅkara writes as follows: "[The existence of the Self cannot be denied]; for of that very person who might deny it it is the Self".[5] In another part, he gives a full explanation about the existence of the Self. "Just because it (the Self) is the Self, it is impossible for us to entertain the idea even of its being capable of refutation. For the (knowledge of the) Self is not, in any person's case, adventitious, not established through the so-called means of right knowledge; it rather is self-established. The Self does indeed employ perception and the other means of right knowledge for the purpose of establishing previously non-established objects of knowledge; for nobody assumes such things as ether and so on to be self-established independently of the means of right knowledge. But the Self, as being the abode of the function that acts through the means of right knowledge, is itself established previously to that function. And to refute such a self-established entity is impossible. An adventitious thing, indeed, may be refuted, but not that which is the essential nature (of him who attempts the refutation); for it is the essential nature of him who refutes. The heat of a fire is not refuted (i.e. sublated) by the fire itself. —Let us further consider the relation expressed in the following clauses: 'I know at the present moment whatever is present; I knew (at former moments) the nearer and the remoter past; I shall know (in the future) the nearer and remoter future'. Here the object of knowledge changes according as it is something past or something future or something present; but the knowing agent does not change, since his nature is eternal presence. And as the nature of the Self is 'eternal presence', it cannot undergo destruction even when the body is reduced to ashes; nay we cannot even conceive that it ever should become something different from what it is".[6] In another part, Śaṅkara also says that "the interior Self (*pratyagātman*) is "the object of the notion of the Ego (*asmaspratyaviṣaya*)" and is well known to exist on account of its "immediate intuitive presentation (*aparokṣa*)".[7]

Apparently Śaṅkara was influenced by the idea of Upavarṣa. But, starting from the latter's standpoint, Śaṅkara developed his unique system of thought. According to him, the demonstration of the existence of the Self only proves the existence of the individual embodied self which is the agent of the consciousness, but the existence of the Highest Self or the Brahman cannot be known directly from this demonstration. The Highest Self is not the object of the notion of the ego, for it surpasses all the elements that the individual self has. What can be perceived by the individual self is limited only to the beings of the phenomenal world. So Śaṅkara says: "It is only this principle of egoity (*ahaṁkartṛ*), the object of the notion of the ego and the agent in all cognition, which accomplishes all actions and enjoys their results".[8] Strictly speaking, the agent that has the power to cause the notion of 'the eog' is the *buddhi* within the individual self. "If the *buddhi* has the power of an agent, it must be admitted that it is also the object of self-consciousness (*ahaṃpratyaya*), since we see that everywhere activity is preceded by self-consciousness, '*I go, I come, I eat, I drink*', etc.".[9] According to Śaṅkara, it is the *buddhi* within the individual self that causes the notion of the ego and effects all action in practical existence. The Highest Self, on the other hand, shares no element of egoity that the individual self has. It is not the object of the notion of the ego, nor is it the agent that causes the notion of the ego. It surpasses all these elements. It is absolute and indivisible. It is so-called *absolutes Wissen*. It is beyond the perception of the ordinary people, but it reveals itself to a Yogic ascetic in the state of self-nullifying concentration (*saṃrādhana*).

"Neither from that part of the Veda which enjoins works (*vidhikāṇḍa*) nor from reasoning, anybody apprehends that soul (*puruṣa*) which, different from the agent that is the object of self-consciousness, merely witnesses it; which is permanent in all transitory beings; uniform; one; eternally unchanging; the Self of everything".[10] As we can observe in this quotation from Śankara, the Highest Self in his sense is beyond the notion of the ego held by the individual self. It should not be overlooked, however, that in his concept, too, the Highest Self is understood to be identical in the ultimate essence with the individual self which is known to exist on the ground that a man has the notion upon his self. Śankara succeeded and relied upon Upavarṣa's idea of the Self, but he went further than his predecessor and established his unique system of thought.

Up to the present day, Śaṅkara's philosophy has been accepted by most of the traditional orthodox scholars (Paṇḍit) of India. And his idea upon the Self can rightly claim to be the representative view of the Indian people. To wit, similar views are observed in the theological assertions of modern Hinduism. The proposition *cogito ergo sum* has its appearance in India in a way quite different from the European one.

The Self or the Ātman in the Indian concept does not simply mean that the individual souls are numerous in this phenomenal world, each one claiming itself to be distinct from others in spite of its substantial homogeneity with others. But, by the Ātman, Indians imply also the Self hidden behind the competing individual souls, or more properly speaking, the Absolute Self shared in every individual soul. In many Indian books of philosophy and religion, they teach that the Self means the Absolute Highest Self as well as the individual self. As the form of the word (*sol-ips-ism*) indicates to us, solipsism in the Western sense is the concept of 'Only I am'. On the other hand, as a result of their unique concept of the Self, the *ātmavāda* or the Indian theory of the Self-only emphasizes the oneness of all beings in the universe.

As we have seen above, Indians acknowledge the Highest Self as being the substratum of the individual soul. It is natural, therefore, that they insist on the oneness and identity of the two. The relation of the individual self and the Highest Self is one of the major problems for philosophers in India, each working out his own conclusions. But, here, we will limit ourselves and only refer to the fact that the idea of the *avatāra* or incarnation is also based on this concept of non-duality between the individual self and the Highest Self. The *avatāra* is the idea that for the salvation of the living creatures the Supreme God emerges in this world in the incarnate form of man or animal. In India, this idea of incarnation is most remarkably expressed in the Purāṇas and subsequent works. In these works, they relate the multiple *avatāras* of Viṣṇu, though the stories of incarnation of other gods like Śiva and Indra are not few. The number of Viṣṇu's manifestations is said to be variously, six, ten, twelve, sixteen, twenty-two or twenty-three and is not definitely fixed. Generally the Hindu religionists count the following ten as the *avatāras* of Viṣṇu: fish, tortoise, boar, man-lion, pigmy, Rāma with the axe, the strong Rāma, Kṛṣṇa, the Buddha and Kalki. Viṣṇu, taking those forms, subjugates evil, saves living beings and stands for Brahmanism. In Buddhism too, the Buddhas and the Bodhisattvas are supposed to have the magical power of revealing themselves in various forms for the salvation of suffering creatures. For instance, they say that the Bodhisattva Avalokiteśvara possessed thirty-three manifestations.

In India, where the people hold such a non-dualistic view, monotheism in the Western sense has never come into being. In the Upaniṣads and in the philosophical assertion of the Vedāntins, the Absolute Being is assumed to be a impersonal spiritual principle without any limiting attribute. But, because such an abstract principle is far from appropriate as an object of worship for the common people, they desired ardently to have an anthropomorphic god in place of the abstract principle. And as Hinduism accomplished its system as a religious order, one of the gods like Viṣṇu, Śiva or Kṛṣṇa came to be worshiped as the Highest Absolute Being. All the gods other than the Supreme One are supposed as His *avatāras*. Thus, the Indian worship of the One Supreme God at the same time retains a coloring of pantheism. Indians hold whole-hearted devotional faith together with mysticism of high intellectual standard. And in their religious system, the element of refined spiritual introspection is mixed with that of primitive vulgar ritual. Indians, however, feel no sense of contradiction to this existence of antagonistic elements in one system. In their concept, these elements can be embraced in one big unity. Here, it can be said that metaphysical monism in their basic way of thinking justifies such a mixture of different elements.

---

1) *Vaiśeṣika-sūtra*, 3, 2, 14 f.

2) Jayanta, a Nyāya scholar in ca. 900 A.D., quotes the following verse to express the idea of the Self held by the Upavarṣa school.

tatra pratyakṣam ātmānam Aupavarṣāḥ prapedire |
ahaṃpratyayagamyatvāt svayūthyā api kecana ||

'Now, the men of the Upavarṣa school understand the Self by immediate perception. For the Self can be known by the notion of the ego. Some men of our school hold the same view". Then, Jayanta proceeds to explain the notion of the ego (*ahaṃpratyaya*) as follows: "This notion of the ego is within us. Some kinds of the notion of the ego are in close connection (*adhikaraṇa*) with the body; e. g. 'I get fat' or 'I get thin'. And some other kinds of it are in close connection with the knowing agent (*jñātṛ*); 'I know' or 'I remember' ". (*Nyāya-mañjarī*, VizSS. X, p. 429.)

3) *Sarvasiddhāntasaṃgraha* VIII, 37; A.B. Keith: *The Karma-Mīṃāṃsā*, p. 71.

4) *Śaṅkara ad BS.* I, 1, 1 (ĀnSS., vol. I, p. 28, *l.* 1 f.); *SBE.* vol. XXXIV, p. 14.

5) *Ibid.* I, 14 (vol. I, p. 75, *l.* 9); *SBE.* vol. XXXIV, p. 37.

6) *Ibid.* II, 3, 7 (Vol. II, pp. 15–16); *SBE.* vol. XXXVIII, pp. 14–15. Cf. *ibid.* III, 2, 22 (Vol. II, p. 224, *l.* 9).
7) *Ibid.* I, 1, 1 (Vol. I, p. 11, *l.* 1); *SBE.* vol. XXXIV, p. 5.
8) *Ibid.* I, 1, 4 (Vol. I, p. 69, *l.* 10); *SBE.* vol. XXXIV, p. 34.
9) *Ibid.* II, 3, 38; *SBE* vol. XXXVIII, p. 51.
10) *Ibid.* I, 1, 4 (Vol. I, p. 75, *l.* 10 f.); *SBE.* vol. XXXIV, p. 37.

(4) Ethics of the non-duality of one's self and other selves

When Indians think that essentially one is identical with others and that the distinction of persons is merely a matter of phenomenal form, it is natural that they look upon the state of non-duality of one's self and other selves as the ideal. In the Upaniṣads they teach, 'All this thou art',[1] or 'I am thou'.[2] And those statements form the core of their ethics. Both Brahmanism and Hinduism are founded on the basis of this view of non-dualism.

Buddhists do not acknowledge the individual soul as a metaphysical entity, so that they attach no importance to the consideration of the relation between a self and other selves. But, as we have already discussed above, in Buddhism too, it is prescribed that men in the Saṃgha live as one body without any personal discrimination. Here, we can say that the Indian view of non-dualism between one and others takes another form of expression in Buddhism. Śāntideva, a Mahāyāna Buddhist, finds the ideal of an ascetic in 'the equal state with others' (*parātmasamatā*) and in the act 'to make others freely move around within himself (*parātmaparicartana*)'.[3] Really the union of one with others is the ideal in the practical ethics of the Mahāyāna Buddhists.

In the Indian religious schools, a man is urged to work for 'the interests of the public as well as of himself',[4] For Indians, truth (*satya*) means nothing other than the good of the living beings (*bhūtahita*).[5] They think that the good of oneself and others can be realized through one's act of love and mercy. They say, "Benevolence (*maitrī*) brings happiness and ease to the beings",[6] or "Even gods make a respectful salutation to the merciful (*dayā*) persons".[7] The virtue of benevolence is especially emphasized by the Buddhists. They teach that we should abandon hatred against others. "For hatred does not cease by hatred at any time: hatred ceases by love, this is an old rule".[8] And they urge us to be compassionate to others, men and all other living beings. "As a mother at the risk of her life watches over her own child, so also let every one cultivate a boundless (friendly) mind towards all beings".[9] In another part, they teach that we should render to other a service greater than that we get from our parents and from our relatives.[10] This idea of benevolence was developed further at the time of the Mahāyāna Buddhists.

The idea of love and mercy forms one of the characteristics of Indian thought. The Westerner of today, however, has not fully realized the true nature of this Indian idea. Consciously or not, they hold biased views. And those Western views are accepted without due consideration by the Japanese. To quote Bergson as an example, he writes as follows: "Not that Buddhism ignored charity. On the contrary it recommended it in the most exalted terms. And it joined example to precept. But it lacked warmth and glow. As a religious historian very justly puts it, it knew nothing 'of the complete and mysterious gift of self'. ...... That enthusiastic charity, that mysticism comparable to the mysticism of Christianity, we find in a Ramakrishna or a Vivekānanda, to take only the most recent examples. But Christianity, and this is just the point, had come into the world in the interval. ......But let us suppose even that the direct action of Christianity, as a dogma, has been practically nil in India. Since it has impregnated the whole of Western civilization, one breathes it like a perfume, in everything which this civilization brings in its wake. Industrialism itself, as we shall try to prove, springs indirectly from it. And it was industrialism, it was our Western civilization, which unloosed the mysticism of a Ramakrishna or a Vivekānanada".[11]

This view of Bergson can be safely taken as one of the common views held among Westerners in general. But, contrary to Bergson's contention, various manuscripts and edicts of ancient India and the records of the foreigners who travelled through the country all present detailed descriptions on the political or social movements of the ancient Indians, all based on the idea of benevolence. Bergson, for the lack of knowledge of historical facts or for the sake of his preoccupation that complete mysticism appeared only among the Christian mystics, is led to his erroneous conclusion about the Indian social movements.

As historical evidences reveal to us and as the historians confirm, the so-called social policy or charity movement began in Asia earlier than in the Western world. Law books of the ancient Brahmanists refer to many social facilities. And the sacred books of the Buddhists of the earliest time tell us that the kings during Buddha's lifetime, under his influence, advocated social policy for the welfare of the general public. King Aśoka promoted social policy on a larger scale. He had strong faith in Buddhism and he made efforts to effect rules in conformity with the teachings of the Buddha. He taught the people that the acts of spell and rites are useless and he persuaded them to have faith in Buddhism. He prohibited the people from killing living creatures in the name of sport and from castrating animals. He built charity houses to relieve the poor and went as far as to establish hospitals even for animals. He encouraged the cultivation of medical plants. He protected the minority tribes in the remote regions. He granted amnesty to the prisoners. And King Aśoka's social policy, based on the teachings of the Buddha, was carried on by the Indian people of later periods, and the tradition lasted for a long time.[12]

The charity movement in the West, began at a later date. In one of his books of history, Vincent A. Smith quotes Sir H. Burdett's statement as follows: "[In the West], no establishments for the relief of the sick were founded until the reign of Constantine (A.D. 306–37). Late in the fourth century Basil founded a leper hospital at Caesarea, and St. Chrysostom established a hospital at Constantinople. A law of Justinian (A.D. 527–62) recognized *nosocomia* or hospitals among the eccelesiastical institutions. The Maison Dieu or Hôtel Dieu of Paris is sometimes alleged to be the oldest European hospital. It dates from the seventh century".[13] In the Greek philosophy, there was no element encouraging the development of the social welfare service and charity movement. Even Christians began their social service comparatively on a late stage of their history. Really Indians are the people who established spiritual and social tradition of the public welfare service first and earliest in the world. (We should not forget, however, the fact that the social movement in India thenceforth has been doomed to stagnation while the Western one has showed a remarkable progress especially in the modern age. This problem will be dealt with on another due occasion.)

The religious leaders in the modern India have been striving to restore the spiritual tradition of their ancestors. Romain Rolland writes as follows: "Usually in European thought 'to serve' implies a feeling of voluntary debasement, of humility. It is the '*Dienen, dienen*' of Kundry in Parsifal. This sentiment is completely absent from the Vedāntism of Vivekānanda. To serve, to love, is to become equal to the one served or loved. Far from abasement, Vivekānanda always regarded it as the fullness of life".[14] The Indian leaders of the national movements like Gandhi manifest this strong religious faith of love and service manifested by Vivekānanda. The tradition of non-dualism of self and other selves continues to exist in the mind of the Indians up to the present.

1) *Kauṣ. Up.* I, 6; *SBE.* vol. 1, p. 279.
2) *Ibid.* I, 2; *SBE.* vol. 1, p. 275.
3) M. Winternitz: *Geschichte der indischen Litteratur,* II, S. 265.
4) *Praśnottararatnamālikā,* 5.
5) *Ibid.,* 12.
6) *Ibid.,* 14. In *ibid.,* 18, '*karuṇā*', '*dākṣiṇpa*' and '*maitrī*' are taught as the most desirable things.
7) *Ibid.,* 21.
8) *Dhammapada,* 5; *SBE.* vol. 10, pt. I, p. 5.
9) *Suttanipāta,* 149; *SBE.* vol. 10, pt. II, p. 25.
10) *Dhammapada,* 43; *SBE.* vol. 10, pt. I, p. 15.
11) Henri Bergson: *The Two Sources of Morality and Religion,* tr. R. Ashley Audra and Cloudesley Brereton, Doubleday Anchor Books, (N. Y., 1954), pp. 225–26.
12) According to the record of travel written by Fa-hien (法顯), a Chinese pilgrim to India at the time of Candragupta of the Gupta dynasty, the tradition of the social policy based on the Buddha's teaching of benevolence was still surviving in the country of Magadha. (See *Kōso Hokken Den* 高僧法顯傳.)
13) Vincent A. Smith: *Early History of India,* p. 313, n. 1.
14) Romain Rolland: *Prophets of the New India,* tr. E. F. Malcolm-Smith, (London, 1930), p. 453.

Chapter 9. Subservience to universals

(1) Subservience to universals as revealed in language

As we have mentioned above, Indians attach greater importance to the universal beings than to individual particular beings and, in respect to action, they hold the view that one's self is immersed in and identical with others. And it naturally follows that Indians are inclined to submit themselves to the universal beings. For Indians, the acts of individuals are not of great importance; they tend to emphasize the power of the universal being which transcends individuals.

This feature of the Indian way of thinking is revealed in their language. In Sanskrit, to describe an act of a person, they are likely to write in the passive as well as in the reflexive form (*Ātmanepada*). In the Vedic language, they prefer to write in the active form as the Westerners do in their writings. But, in the classical Sanskrit, they seek to write in the passive form. And this tendency gets stronger as time passes. In Sanskrit, even intransitive verbs have their passive forms.

In consequence, there are found in Sanskrit a great number of passive sentences used impersonally.[1] i.e. *karmaṇo hy api boddhavyam* (*Bhag. G.* IV, 16) = τί δ' ε'στὶ τὸ πρακτέον......, ἐγὼ οἶδα = *Tum. ad opus omnino est attendum; kair mayā saha yoddhavyam* (*Bhag. G.* I, 22) = τ' σι δετ μοι σομπλακῆναι = *quibuscum mihi pugnandum.* These Sanskrit sentences are written impersonally in passive and the subject is not stated. In the view of the Indians, an act is not performed by a particular subject. More likely, an act is a changing phenomenon caused by many conditioning factors and the subject of the action is only one of such many factors. It can be said, therefore, that the Indian preference for propositions stated impersonally in the passive form shows the feature of their way of thinking which places importance on the unrevealed and hidden power, rather ignoring the spontaneity of the individual action.

1) Speyer: *Vedische und Sanskrit-Syntax*, S. 75; § 169.

(2) The extension of the subject of action

As a result of this characteristic of Indian thought, the ethical idea which refuses to acknowledge a fixed and substantial subject of action has grown in this country. The Buddhist theory of 'non-self (*anātman*)' is one of the oldest of such ideas. Buddhists, as examined above, do not necessarily deny the existence of the Ātman itself. But, they refuse to recognize any fixed substantial subject of action whether it is the Ātman or not. The idea of 'non-self' is generally supposed to be a concept unique to Buddhism, but there are in reality others in India who hold a similar view. A sentence in the *Maitri-Upaniṣad* (3. 2.), for instance, reads as follows: "Like a bird trapped in the net, (the individual ego) binds itself thinking 'It is I (*aham*)' or 'it is Mine (*mama*)' ". And it exhorts man to free himself from all bondage. The *Bhagavadgītā* (2. 71.) also teaches man not to cling to one's ego saying: "The man who casts off all desires and walks without desire, with no thought of a *Mine* (*nirmama*) and of an *I* (*nirahaṅkāra*) comes unto peace".[1] And a theory of 'non-self' is also found in a book of the Sānkhya. According to their view, the individual soul (*puruṣa*) is delivered from attachments when it has come to 'the pure and complete wisdom' that 'I am not; (Nothing) is mine; and (Nothing) is I'.[2] The Sāṅkhya supposes the Puruṣa, which is identical to the Ātman, to be their unique metaphysical principle. And on this point, their doctrine is in essence quite different from the Buddhist theory of 'non-self'. However, as far as the expression of their doctrine is concerned, they are very close to the Buddhists. Bhartṛhari, in his metaphysical study of Word, asserts a kind of 'non-self' theory. According to him, Word is the subject of cognition — the Ātman or the Absolute Being. And as one projects one's image on the wall, Word, which is the subject of cognition, projects itself objectively on the screen in itself and perceives its own image — Word as the object. This is the cognition in Bhartṛhari's sense. What serve as the screen in the case of Word are the internal organ (*antaḥkaraṇa*) which performs the apperceptive function (*buddhi*). The Buddhi is in reality no more than the screen to reflect the image of the Absolute Being and has no active power in itself. In short, cognition is understood to be only one phase of the self-evolving process of the Absolute Being—of Word which divides itself into two parts, one as the subjective knower and the other as the object, and unfolds itself in a process of mutual interrelation. Bhartṛhari explains action in the same way as he explains cognition.[3] This may be considered an expression of the "non-self" theory.

It is erroneous to maintain that the idea of 'non-self' and the ideas similar to it are popular in India. In reality they are far from popular. However, it should be noted that in no other country has the idea of "non-self" developed into such various forms as we see in India. There exists in their national way of thinking the spiritual background for the growth of such ideas.

Because they suppose that the action of an individual is supervised and regulated by an invisible power and that action, having no creative function in itself, is no more than an attribute of the individual, Indians are inclined to take a *submissive* attitude toward their fate and condition. The ideas of Karma and Saṃsāra are still deeply imbedded in the mind of the Indian people. And a man of a lowly family in India is likely to be resigned to his fate, simply expecting to be reborn under more favorable circumstances in the next life. And here it is assumed that the ultimate subject of action is not the individual but the being beyond and above the individual.

Because of their basic emphasis of the super-individual being, Indians assert that the idea or action of a person is universally valid if it conforms to the True and Universal Law. And it does not matter for them whosever idea or action it is.

It is not seldom in India that a book and its commentary are published at the same time; not infrequently, the two are composed by one and the same author. Indians claim that their books, which reveal the eternal truth, deserve to be handed down to posterity for ages without modification. And commentaries are necessary in order to make others understand the truth expounded in their books. For ancient Indian scholars, therefore, it was never strange to write commentaries on their own works.

In India, there are many forged manuscripts. Of course, there are many of them in China and in the Western countries. But to a degree incomparable to the cases in other countries, there are in India a great number of books pretending to be the works of the ancient saints. Almost all the works which mention the name of the authors are spurious documents. This trend of forgery should be understood in connection with the tendency of the Indians toward self-effacement and their philosophy of de-emphasizing the importance of the individual. All the Mahāyāna texts claim unduly to be "the Buddha's discourse". They are forgeries in the sense that they were not expounded directly from the Buddha's own mouth. Even the texts of the Buddhists of earlier days, nearly all of them, were in reality completed after the Buddha's death by his followers. But all of them claim to be "the Buddha's discourse". Then, how could the ancient Buddhists make such claims without damaging their moral conscience?

It is natural for the Buddhist devotees to assume that the Buddha's teachings are absolutely authentic. And King Aśoka stated in one of his Edicts that "whatever the Buddha taught is a good teaching".[4] The Buddhists after the death of the Buddha went further and they asserted that any idea in so far as it is a good and correct is the Buddha's teaching. A quotation from the *Aṅguttara-Nikāya* reads as follows:

> "Imagine, O King, a great heap of grain near some village or market-town, from which country folk carry away corn on poles or in baskets, in lap or hand. And if one should approach the folk and question them saying: 'Whence bring you this corn?' how would those folk, in explaining, best explain?"
>
> "They would best explain the matter, sir, by saying: 'We bring it from that great heap of grain' ".
>
> "Even so, O King, *whatsoever be well spoken, all that is the word of the Exalted One, Arahant, the Fully Awakened One,* wholly based thereon is both what we and others say".[5]

The ancient Buddhists thought that *whatever is true should have been taught by the Buddha.*

As it has been often mentioned in the previous pages, the significance of the individuals is thoroughly ignored by Indians; the ultimate concern for them is the universally valid truth. They are not concerned with the identity of the author; their only concern is whether or not a certain work expounds the truth. And because the Buddha is the man who has realized the truth perfectly, any book containing the truth is rightly assumed to be the Buddha's teaching. Thus, the ancient Indian Buddhists had no feeling of shame claiming the title of 'the Buddha's discourse' for their own works.[6]

In India there are many anonymous books. The authors did not like to record their names on their own works. There is no need, they thought, to attach the name of a particular author so far as the book conveys the universal truth. In fact, the forged documents and the anonymous books in India are both expressions of one basic characteristic of their way of thinking.

In India the life-history of those who expounded the truth is completely ignored. The word *buddha* is not a proper noun. It means the enlightened one in general. Any one who has realized the truth is the Buddha. And Gotama the Buddha, the historical founder of Buddhism, is one of such many enlightened ones. Since the oldest period of their history, Buddhists had faith in the Seven Buddhas of the Past—Gotama Śākyamuni and the six Buddhas preceding him.[7] In later periods, faith in the twenty-four Buddhas was cherished by them. And Mahāyāna Buddhists came to think that there exist numerous Buddhas in all directions and throughout the three time-periods of past, present and future. Together with this idea of the multiplicity of Buddhas, a new idea appeared which, as we see in the *Lotus-sūtra* of the Mahāyāna, asserts that the Buddha had attained enlightenment many Kalpas (aeons) before his awakening under the Bo-Tree of Buddha-gayā. The Jains hold a similar idea. They believe in the twenty-three saints preceding Mahāvīra. Both the Buddhists and the Jains respect men in history, Gotama and Mahāvīra, as the founders of their religions; and at the same time, they claim that their religions have the origin in the past long before the days of their historical founders. This attitude of the Indians toward their religions presents a remarkable contrast to the case of Christianity.

---

1) *Bhagavad-gītā*: *or The Lord's Song*, tr. by L. D. Barnett, (London, 1905), p. 96.

2) *Sāṅkhya-Kārikā* No. 64. Cf. Deussen: *Allgemeine Geschichte der Philosophie*, I 3, S. 462.
3) Cf. *Vākyapadīya* I, 52; 125; 128; *Puṇyarāja's Comm. ad ibid.*
4) *Calcutta-Bairāt Edict.*
5) *Aṅguttara-Nikāya* IV, *p.* 163; PTS.: *The Books of the Gradual Sayings*, vol. IV, p. 111.
6) A Japanese Buddhist scholar, Kai-jyō (1750–1805), who held a critical view of the Mahāyāna Buddhism though he himself was a Mahāyāna Buddhist, pointed out the pretention of "the Buddha's discourse" made by the Indian Buddhists saying: "The so-called 'the Buddha's discourse (佛說)' is not what Śākyamuni taught directly, but nevertheless, it is the teaching of the enlightened one. All of the Buddha's teaching is on morals and it is not on the art of recording. The ancient followers of the enlightened one called what they understood by their own studies 'the Buddha's saying (佛言)'. 'The Buddha's saying' in this case means what was intended to be taught by the Buddha. Because it is in compliance with the Buddha's intention, they label their own works 'the Buddha's saying' or 'the Buddha's discourse'". Kaijō 戒定: *Gokyōshō Chōhiroku* 五教章帳秘錄 quoted in Senshō Murakami 村上專精: *Daijō Busselsuron Hihan* 大乘佛說論批判 Criticism on the advocation that the Mahāyāna is the authentic teaching of the Buddha), p. 116 f.
7) The idea of *the Buddhas in the past* appears in the Gāthās in the *Suttanipāta*. And as we can tell from the *Nigālī-Sāgar Edict*, King Aśoka made extensions twice to the Stūpa of Konakāmana, one of the Seven Buddhas in the Past.

(3) Reverence for universal standards in behavior

As a result of their inclination to submit themselves to the universal being, Indians harbor an ardent desire to have direct relations with the Absolute refusing any intermediate agent. They assert that salvation of one's soul should be attained only by one's own efforts without relying upon others. In the philosophy of Brahmanism, regarding emancipation of the soul, it is taught that a man who has realized the truth of the universe "gets into his Self by dint of his Self".[1] And Buddhists, though they do not make any metaphysical consideration on 'the Self (*ātman*)', acknowledge its practical significance as the subject of action saying that only the Self can save the Self. A quotation from the *Dhammapada* reads as follows: "Sons are no help, nor a father, nor relations; there is no help from kinsfolk for one whom death has seized".[2] Jains, too, admit that all things other than one's self are useless for one's salvation saying: "They cannot help thee or protect thee".[3] They say again: "Man! Thou art thy own friend; why wishest thou for a friend beyond thyself?".[4]

In later periods the Mahāyāna Buddhists hold faith in salvation through the power of the great compassion of the Buddhas and the Bodhisattvas and the schools of Hinduism emphasize salvation by the grace of Viṣṇu and Śiva. But, it should be noted, even in such cases one stands in the face of the absolute pleading directly to them for the salvation of one's soul. And here little significance is attached to the intermediate agents between the absolute and the individual beings.

It is natural that from such views of the Indians on salvation no religious order, which is itself a limited social organization, would take active leadership as the absolute source of authority. In Europe, the monks united themselves and formed their community which had political power sometimes equal to that of the king. In India, on the other hand, the political influence of the religious bodies were very weak. Brahmanists held a consanguineal cultural unity among them. This unity, however, served only to form their particular exclusive class and this body of Brahmanists did not function as a political unit.[5] What is more, they had no leader to rule over the body and an individual Brahmanist could behave at his own will without any check of a supervising authority. It is natural that such a loose organization had no solid financial basis like the Roman Catholic Church. Since the time of its establishment the Buddhist Saṃgha was also without political or economic unity. Even while the Buddha was still alive, his followers lived apart from him and a regulation binding all of these followers was not made. And after the death of the Buddha, they were intent only in the faithful observance of the doctrines and the disciplines set forth by their late teacher and did not choose to have a political leader of their Saṃgha.[6]

Moreover, the Buddhist Saṃgha *did not claim to be a legislative authority* or *an authority on the interpretation of the doctrine.* This assertion can be safely made at least in respect to its attitude toward the important issues. Buddhists attributed the authority of legislation exclusively to the Buddha. They considered that all the rules of the Saṃgha are authorized by claiming the title of 'the Buddha's own discourse'. And they gave the title to all the rules. Even the new rules established after the Buddha's death to meet the changing social situations were also attributed to the Buddha's authority. One of their books of precepts states as follows: "If the time seems to meet the Saṃgha, not ordaining what has not been ordained, and not revoking what has been ordained, let it take upon itself and ever direct itself in the precepts according as they have been laid down. This is the resolution".[7] Interpreting the vague statements in the old texts, Buddhists attributed their own interpretation to the Buddha. And for authority, they referred, not to the Saṃgha but to the Buddha. This is the attitude of the Buddhists, at least the Buddhists of the early days, in their interpretation of the texts.[8)]

The same features as we observe in the early Buddhist Saṃgha are found among Jains. The Mahāyāna Buddhists who appeared later in history assumed the same attitude. And the schools of Hinduism also took a similar stand. Indeed, as it is most distinctly observed in the Sikh religion, some of the Hindu sects kept a systematic unity in their body. But, they were exceptional cases.

Indians, in contrast to their indifferent attitude toward social organizations like the Saṃgha, attach the greatest importance to the authority of the universal law — the law that all the individuals and all the social organizations should follow. And they call the law "*dharma*". This word comes from the root $\sqrt{\text{dhṛ}}$, which means "to hold", "to support", or "to bear". *Dharma* means "what serves as the norm to support the human behavior", or more in short, "the norm of action" or "the rule of conduct". They affirmed that the Dharma differed from the other as found in the natural world. Further, it means "usage", "customary observance", "the thing to be done", or "duty". An old book of rites in Brahmanism prescribes the four Dharmas of the Brahman: to be a man of a Brahman family; to do what deserves the dignity of the Brahman; to maintain the honor; and to lead the lay people. As to the duties that a lay man should observe toward the Brahman, it mentions the four different Dharmas: to pay respect to the Brahman; to make offerings to the Brahman; to protect the Brahman from harm and injury; and to refrain from condemning the Brahman to death.[9)]

The Dharma, which is the norm that *leads* a man to establish and to perform moral acts, is the power that realizes 'Truth' in this present world. Thus, the ancient Indians understood the Dharma to be the truth that works as the creative power, and identified the two. "Thus the Law is what is called the true. And if a man declares what is true, they say he declares the Law; and if he declares the Law, they say he declares what is true. Thus both are the same".[10)]

And in the course of time, this norm of behavior for the realization of morals was raised to the position of the Absolute. Indians came to think that the Dharma is the basis of the whole universe and that all things in the universe rest on the Dharma. "This whole universe is in the Dharma. Nothing is more difficult to do than the Dharma. On this account, they hold the Dharma in high esteem".[11] "The Dharma is the basis of the whole universe. In the world, people wish to approach to a man who keeps the Dharma best. They eliminate the evils by force of the Dharma. All the beings rest in peace in the Dharma. On this account, they say that the Dharma is the highest being".[12] Furthermore it is maintained that the Dharma has a form superior even to that of the creator of the universe (the Brahman).[13] In the Vaiśeṣika, it is assumed that the rise and the deliverance of the soul is attained only on the strength of the Dharma.[14]

And Indians considered that the Dharma exists *eternally*. Already in an old Vedic text, the lying down of a wife is required at the cremation of her husband on the grounds that it is 'the time-honored rule' (*dharmo purāṇaḥ*).[15] As the following quotation tells us, the Dharma is allegorically identified with the eternal absolute being.

> " 'He from whom the sun rises, and into whom it sets' 'Him the Devas made the law, he only is to-day, and he to-morrow also' ".[16]

This idea of the eternal universal law was inherited by the Jains and the Buddhists. Jains, from their very rationalistic standpoint, assert that there exist universal laws (*dharma*) which all mankind should observe at all times and all places. For instance, one of their sacred books teaches as follows: 'All breathing, existing, living, sentient creatures, should not be slain, nor treated with violence, nor abused, nor tormented, nor driven away. This is "the pure, unchangeable, eternal law" .... '[17] The founder of Jainism, Mahāvīra, set forth the philosophy and the practical morality of this religion in accord with what he believed to be the true principle or law.

Buddhists hold a similar view of the law. They consider that the law of causal origination is the unchangeable truth. "Whether there be an appearance or non-appearance of a Tathāgata, this causal law of nature, this orderly fixing of things prevails, ... "[18] A Tathāgata is the one who, having realized this law of nature, endeavors to reveal it to all sentient beings. The enlightened one is not to be considered as a mystic, inspired by a revelation, but only as a man who has fully perceived the true law of nature that exists eternally. Buddhism, or at least Buddhism in its early stage, pays special reverence to the law that is eternally valid. They assume that the authority of the law preceeds that of the Buddha. All the beings, including even the gods, admire the law that the Buddha revealed and accept it.[19] Even the gods are bound to worldly sufferings. And they have to follow the law to free themselves from the sufferings of rebirth.

Here you may find an analogue of this Buddhist idea of the law in Hugo Grotius's *jus naturale* or the natural law. His natural law is supposed to be impartial to any person and unchangeable under any circumstances. Even God cannot alter. But it should be remembered that the natural law is based on the human existence. The law is valid without God's authority as far as there are the human beings in this world. The Buddhist law of nature, on the other hand, is not the law regulating the relations of the individual human beings, but it is the law controlling the relations between the state of ignorance, which is inevitably attached to the human existence and behavior, and the way of deliverance from it. Though Grotius's natural law and the Buddhist law of nature are similar in form, they are quite different in essence.

As Indians put great emphasis on the universal law that stands above the individuals, the significance of the individual personality is thoroughly ignored by them. And even Gotama the Buddha, the man of greatest character, is considered to be only one of many men who realized the universal law in this world. As it was referred to in the foregoing section of this book, Buddhists espouse the idea of the multiplicity of the Buddhas. The Jains, in a similar manner, assume the existence of twenty-three founders preceding the historical founder, Mahāvīra.[20]

In the concept of the Indians, the Buddhas or the founders of religion, however deified they are as the object of worship, are human beings who are not different from the ordinary people. A man can be a Buddha or a founder of religion if he has accomplished the works necessary for enlightenment. We are all in essence one and the same with the absolute beings. This assertion is correct also in the case of the Bhaktic Buddhism. The man saved by the grace of Amitā-Buddha becomes a Buddha equal in all respects to his savior.

The concept of the eternal and universal law prevailed in the nation and took root among people. King Aśoka believed in the eternal law which should be observed by all, regardless of race, religion, nationality, time or place. This law is the norm of human behavior and he called it '*dharma*' or "the time-honored rule". He stated in one of his Edicts that many kings preceding him had intended in vain to rule the people on the basis of the Dharma and that the reign of the Dharma was first realized by him.[21] King Khāravela who ruled over South India in the second century B.C. was called 'the King of Law (Cakravartin)'[22] After Khāravela, the kings of this country sometimes claimed the title of 'the king faithful to the law'.[23] And all the followers of the religious sects in India were taught that to observe the law was the most precious of virtues.[24]

The Indian religion which acknowledges the authority of the eternal universal law is very logical in its character and it offers a striking contrast to the illogical and irrational religion of the West. A. Schopenhauer once said that the Indian religion which has developed from a logical speculation of the world is superior to Christianity.[25] Setting aside the question of whether it is right or wrong, his remark indicates the essential difference of the religions in the East and West.

---

1) *ātmanā' tmānam abhi saṃviveśa,* (*Vāj. Saṃh.* XXXII, 11.) cf. *paramātmānam adhisaṃviveśa praviśati brahmaiva bhabatīty arthaḥ,*(Mahīdhara's Comm. ad *ibid.*); *saṃviśaty ātmanā' tmānaṃ,* (*Māṇḍūkya-Up.* 12.) cf. *ātmaiva snṃviśaty ātmanā svenaiva svaṃ pāramārthikam ātmānam,* (Śaṅkara's Comm. ad *ibid.*)

2) *Dhammapada* 288; *SBE.* vol. X, pt. I, p. 70.

3) *Āyāraṅga* I, 2, 1, 2; *SBE.* vol. XXII, p. 16.

4) *Ibid.* I, 3, 3, 4. (Schubring, S. 16, 1. 11.); *SBE.* vol. XXII, p. 33.

5) There are many sects and schools within Brahmanism. But among the members of a sect or of a school no sufficient sense of unity is held. They are the men belonging to a sect or a school and they themselves claim so, but the members of the sect or the school seldom act as a unit.

6) According to the legends in Ceylon, the first compilation of the Buddhist texts was made at Rājagṛha just after the death of the Buddha. At that time, the texts of precepts were compiled chiefly by Upāli. And from him the collection of the books of precepts (*Vinaya-piṭaka*) was transmitted in turn through the hands of Dāsaka, Soṇaka, Siggava and Moggaliputta Tissa until the time of King Aśoka. Each one of those five transmitters was said to be the head of the Saṃgha of his days. The story corresponding to this one in the legends of Ceylon can be found in some of the Chinese translations of the Buddhist texts. But, it should be noted, those five men were the master of precepts only, and they did not take part in the handing down of the Buddhist doctrines. Besides, they were not the heads to rule over all the Buddhist Saṃghas. They were no more than the heads of the Vibhajya-vādin Saṃgha in the Theravāda school.

7) *Vinaya,* Cullavagga, XI, 1, 9.; *SBE.* vol. XX, p. 378. At the time of the compilation of the Buddhist texts held at Vaiśālī, the Vajjians promulgated the new ten theses. But, their theses were judged unlawful and rejected. cf. *ibid.*, Cullavagga XII.

8) Hakuju Ui 宇井伯壽: *Indo-tetsugaku Kenkyū* (印度哲學研究 Studies in Indian philosophy), vol. II, p. 185 f.

9) Cf. *Śatapathabrāhmaṇa* XI, 5, 7, 1.

10) *Bṛhad. Up.* I, 4, 14; *SBE.* vol. XV, p. 89. There are many cases of the identification of *satya* and *dharma.* cf. *Chānd. Up.* VII, 2, 1,; VII, 7, 1; *Tait. Up.* I, 11, 1.

11) *Mahānārāyaṇa-Up.* XXI, 2.

12) *Ibid.* XXII, 1.

13) *śreyorūpa,* (*Bṛhad. Up.* I, 4, 14.)

14) Cf. *Vaiśeṣika-Sūtra* I, 2. The Vaiśeṣika asserted: As there are good evidences in the Vedas, a man can reach the celestial sphere and receive blessings by the faithful performance of the religious works. (*ibid.* I, 1, 3; X, 2, 9.). But, at this state, the deliverance of his soul is not yet attained. "(It) results from the knowledge of the essence (*tattva-jñāna*) of the Predicables, Substance, Attribute, Action, Genus, Species, and Combination by their resemblances and differences". (*ibid.* I, 1, 4; *The Sacred Books of the Hindus,* vol. VI, p. 9). Ascension of the soul is produced by one kind of the Dharma (*dharmaviśeṣa*) which is the low Dharma (*aparo dharmaḥ*) and the deliverance of the soul is produced by another kind of the Dharma which is the high Dharma (*paro dharmaḥ*). cf. Candrakānta's Comm. ad *ibid.* I, 1, 2.) The Vaiśeṣika called the whole system of their doctrines "the Dharma" and they made the quest of truth in this system. (*ibid.* I, 1, 1.)

15) *Atharva-Veda* XVIII, 3, 1.

16) *Bṛhad.-Up.* I, 5, 23; *SBE.* vol. XV, p. 98.

17) *dhamme suddhe nitie sāsae,* (*Āyāraṅga* I, 4, 1, 1.); *SBE.* vol. 22, p. 36.

18) *AN.* I, p. 286; PTS.: *The Books of the Gradual Sayings,* vol. I, p. 264; cf. 雜阿含經 vol. 30: 有佛無佛性相常然 (法華文句 九下).

19) E.g. *D.N. Mahāpadānasutta.*

20) *supra.* p. 88.

21) *The Pillar Edict* VII.

22) *King Khāravela Inscriptions.*

23) It can be known from the words inscribed on the coins issued by those kings.

24) *pathyatara,* (*Praśnottararatnamālikā* 4).

25) Quoted in Albert Schweitzer: *Das Christentum und die Weltreligionen* (1924), S. 29.

(4) Perceiving the truth: Faith and rationalism

For Indians, it is a matter of the greatest moral and religious importance to know the Universal Law and to submit themselves to it. And this feature of Indian thought can be observed also in their concept of 'faith'. *Śraddhā* is the Sanskrit word that is usually translated in the Western languages by 'fides', 'Graube' or 'faith'. But what Indians mean by the word is not exactly the same as the faith of Western religions. *Śraddhā* means to believe in and rely upon a man of superior wisdom and at the same time, it indicates wholehearted acceptance of the doctrines that the man professes. Indians, refusing to place faith in a particular person or saint, hope to submit themselves to the Universal Law that stands above all individuals.

Already in early Buddhist texts, faith in the Buddha is expressed. But this should not be understood as being a worship of a particular saint, Gotama the Buddha. Gotama is one of the Buddhas—the Enlightened Ones. Buddhist faith in the Buddha means faith in the law that makes the Enlightened One as he is. Jains hold a similar view of faith. Jains in the early stage of their history taught "not to have faith in the illusory power of god".[1] They express true faith by the word *samyagdarśana* or 'right-seeing', and thus true faith in their sense is none other than to see the truth in the right way.[2]

For Indians, faith is not the worship of particular individuals and this nature of their faith can be more clearly observed in the statements of Brahmanists. Psychologically Śaṅkara defines *śraddhā* as "a particular kind of mental state (*pratyayaviśeṣa*)"[3] the nature of which is "delicate (*tanu*)".[4] And as to the active and practical significance of *śraddhā*, two views are given by the Brahmanists: 1) Acccording to the Vedānta, *śraddhā* is not to put faith in a teacher, but "to accept as true the words in the Upaniṣads that the teacher introduces to us".[5] And all other schools of Brahmanism agree with the Vedānta in their view that *śraddhā* means the acceptance of the sacred doctrines.[6] 2) And as a logical consequence of the first view, *śraddhā* is applied to mean the ideology that urges people to do the things generally approved as good in the Hindu community of the days, especially to perform the religious works in a broad sense of the word.[7] It is "the factor which makes all the living beings do good deeds"[8] and it is in essence "the idea of traditionalism".[9]

Since the oldest days of their history, Buddhists use the word *prasāda* to mean faith in their sense. As the Chinese translate this word by "澄淨 (purity)" or "喜 (bliss)", it means the calm and pure state of mind where one feels the bliss of serenity.[10] Buddhist faith is far from fanatic worship.[11] The enthusiastic and fanatic form of reverence which urges ardent devotion (*bhakti*) to the gods was advocated by some Buddhist sects of later development and by the schools of Hinduism. But, this kind of fanaticism failed to win the heart of the whole Indian nation.

For Indians, the essence of faith is *to see* the truth through any means possible. Buddhists, Jains or Brahmanists, the religious adherents in India all agree in their assertion that right wisdom (*samyagjñāna*) is the way for liberation.[12] They say that liberation means the awakening of mind attained by force of right wisdom.[13] And they all pay great respect to a man of wisdom (*vivekin*).[14] They call such a man "the man who climbed the terraced heights of wisdom".[15] Thus, in India, *faith and knowledge is understood to be compatible.* And this is why the Indian religion bears such a strong *tinge of philosophy.* In India, such ideas as "I believe it because it is absurd (*credo quia absurdum*)" is never held. And there is no conflict of religion and philosophy in this country.

In fact, the Indian religion is based on philosophical contemplation and its philosophy stands very close to religion. As Masson-Oursel has pointed out, in India and in China religion is not antagonistic to philosophy or to science.[16] Indians are a religious and, at the same time, philosophical people.

---

1) *divaṃ māyaṃ na saddahe, Āyāraṅga* I, 8, 8, 24; (ed. by Schubring, S. 40, *l.* 5.)

2) *Tattvārthaśraddhānaṃ samyagdarśanam, Tattvārthādhigama-sūtra* I, 2. cf. *Yogaśāstra* I, 17; *Sarvadarśana-saṃgraha* III, 1. 155 f.

3) *Brahmasūtra-bhāṣya,* Vol. II, p. 143, *l.* 9. (ĀnSS.) But this definition is the words of the pūrvapakṣin. In another place, Śaṅkara states as follows: "the mental conception (*pratyaya*) called faith (*śraddhā*) is the attribute (*dharma*) of the mind (*manas*) or soul". cf. *ibid.* II, p. 144, *l.* 4. And it should be noted that in some cases Śaṅkara uses *pratyaya* to mean confidence or trust. e. g. *aśraddadhānāḥ = apratyayavanto,* (Śaṅkara's Comm. ad *Praśna-Up.* II, 3.)

4) *Brahmasūtra-bhāṣya* II, p. 144, *l.* 8.

5) *Vedāntasāra* 23.

6) The faithful observance of the doctrines given by the teachers of the school is called *śraddhā.* cf. Śaṅkara ad *BS.* vol. I, p. 524, *l.* 6.

7) *śraddhā-pūrvakarma,* Śaṅkara ad *BS.* 11, p. 144, *l.* 10; religious works (sacrifices, &c.) which depend on faith, *SBE.* vol. XXXVIII, p. 108.

8) Śaṅkara ad *Praśna-Up. VI,* 4.

9) *āstikyabuddhi, ibid.* I, 2.

10) It is difficult to find in the Western languages the terms exactly equivalent to *prasāda.* Cf. *pasanno buddhasāsane* (*Dhp.* 368).
=*Buddhae praeceptis sedatus* (Fausbøll's translation.)
=who is calm in the doctrine of Buddha (Max Müller's translation.)
Both Fausbøll's and Müller's translations fail to convey the full meaning of *prasāda.*

11) In the *Theragāthā* 390, the man who puts faith in his teacher's words is called *bhattimā.* This is the only case of the reference to *bhakti* that can be found in all the Gāthās of the Buddhists of the early days.

12) Cf. *Praśnottararatnamālikā* 3.

13) Cf. *ibid.* 10.

14) Cf. *ibid.* 4.

15) *Dhammapada* 28; *SBE.* vol. X, pt. I, p. 10. Cf. *Mahābhārata* 12. 151. 11.

16) Masson-Oursel: *La philosophie comparée,* p. 40.

(5) Transcendence of limited ethical systems

Part 1. Transcendence of national and racial consciousness

For the Indians, the Universal Law is the ultimate and the highest authority. They attach little significance to intermediary beings lying between the individual and the absolute Universal Law. It is natural then that they regarded national and racial questions as secondary. We find this tendency already in their earliest history.

The Vedas, the oldest records in India, are collections of ritual recitations and commentaries on the rites. They are compiled chiefly for the purpose of ritualistic practices. The Vedas also preserve many legends and myths in their original forms. But for the Indo-Aryans, myths concerning the origin of their race or the legendary histories of their expansion and the lineage of their dynasties were not matters of importance. What was crucially important for them was the measure of *their direct relationship with the gods.*[1] They were religious people occupied in the consideration of the gods, or more properly speaking, of the absolute Universal Law. On the other hand, they had a rather low sense of national or racial consciousness. Indeed, in ancient India the aristocrats and the intellectual class took pride in their Aryan descent which accounted for the sense of unity among them. But this unity was the result of the conviction they held in common in the faith in one superior religion and not from their awakening in racial oneness.

They regarded religion as preceding all matters and were thoroughly apathetic to the problems of nationality or of race. Buddhism and Jainism, rising later, carried on this outlook. They claimed the abolition of racial discrimination and preached above all things the realization of the law that is universal to all mankind—*dharma.* And even today, Indians are inclined to form a religious unit rather than a national unit. In other words, their political actions are due to associations of co-religionists rather than to groups of men of common political viewpoint. And so the influence of the movement for national unification as one race is weak in India.

Since the oldest time in India the authority of the state and the king has been subordinated to religious authority. A story about a king illustrates the general feeling of the days before the birth of Buddha. The king was blamed as immoral because he placed his teacher (*purohita*) of the Vedas in a seat lower than his. But, later, having recognized his mistake, he came to learn in a seat lower than that of his teacher.[2] Kings were no exceptions to the decree of Brahmanic sacred codes which stressed that "disciples are not allowed to take seats higher than that of their teacher".[3)]

In the days of Buddha, kings showed absolute obedience to religious leaders who preached the Universal Law that all men should follow. For instance, King Ajātaśatru of Magadha, the strongest state at the time, made a round of calls himself to the six leading philosophers of his day.[4)] Another king of Magadha drove his chariot to Mt. Pāṇḍava where Buddha led a secluded life and asked for an audience.[5)] There is a description in a Buddhist sūtra about a scene of a king calling on Buddha: "King Pasenadi of Śrāvastī descended from the chariot, put aside the umbrella, removed the sword and took off his shoes. Folding his arms in token of respect, he stepped toward Buddha, threw himself to the ground, and made a bow in the most profound manner".[6)] The sword, the unmbrella, the crown, the brush of long white hair with jewels set in its handle and the decorated shoes were 'the five adornments of the king' that a king was allowed to wear from the day of his coronation.[7)] Early Buddhist texts tell us that it was an established custom of the day that the kings removed all these five precious adornments before they saw Buddha.[8)]

After the death of Buddha, religious authority continued to hold sway. King Aśoka who reigned over the whole land expressed his whole-hearted devotion to the three treasures of "Buddha, Dharma and Saṃgha".[9)] "King of Magadha, beloved of the gods, salutes before the Saṃgha and expresses his hope for its peaceful and healthy condition". He was the one who actually presided and supported the religious bodies of the day. And still, as the words "beloved of the gods" indicate, Aśoka accepted the superiority of religious authority over the secular.

In the days of the Kuṣāṇa dynasty and thereafter, the sanctification of the king increased remarkably, but still it was emphasized that unforeseen disasters would occur in case the king neglected to be obedient to the Dharma. The Indians believed in the Universal Law as beyond any state power. And thus religious institutions which led the people with the light of the Law were assumed to be above state authority.

The state authority, therefore, seldom intervened with religious activities. And the inner organizations of the religious bodies were seldom influenced by secular powers.[10)] (And this is still true today in India and Ceylon.) For instance, the seating arrangement within the Buddhist Saṃgha was determined solely by the length of service. Any new member, even if he were a king, had to submit to the lowest rank in the Saṃgha hierarchy.[11] This exhibits a striking contrast to the case in Japan where the men of the highest rank in the secular society, members of the royalty or nobility, always occupied the highest position even within religious functions.

Indian religious bodies, in turn, kept themselves aloof of outside authorities. At the earliest stage of Buddhism, it was already forbidden for the monks to associate with the kings.[12] In one of the oldest Buddhist texts, it is stated: "Monks, you should be attentive to keep yourselves away from state affairs".[13] Buddhists took such an attitude partly for fear of the calamities that the connections with the kings might incur. But also it cannot be denied that the Buddhists of the day thought little of the kings' power. They believed that the devotee who renounced the secular world *no longer belonged to the state*; that he was *beyond state jurisdiction.*

Later on, even Mahāyāna Buddhists continued to take the aloof attitude of church beyond the state. Many monks deliberately kept themselves away from the king and tried to detach themselves from any political affairs. "Bodhisattvas do not serve the king, nor do they serve or associate with the princes, the ministers and the officials".[14] "A Buddhist monk should not get familiar with the king. Why so? Because the monk who associates with the king is disliked by all people and will not receive hospitable treatment. The bad monk who associates with the king is greedy for treasures, and at the court, at a village or at a crowded place, he endlessly thirsts for gains. Even if he is not greedy for treasures, the monk who comes in contact with the king is disturbed in his meditation and in his reading. Such a monk is bound to suffer from distractions even if he tries to concentrate on the way of deliverance. These are the reasons why a Buddhist monk should not associate with the king".[15]

As already stated, the earliest Buddhist monks regarded their life superior to that of the king. Of course, they admitted that it was significant to govern the nation well as a king. But a king was bound by the restrictions of the laity while a monk was completely free from all the restrictions of this world.[16] And it was not rare as the following quotation from a Buddhist Sūtra shows that the kings visited Buddhist or Brahmanist monks to ask for their instructions.[17] "The king made a respectful salutation and then advanced the questions: What is virtue and what is vice? What is guilt and what is not? How can one attain the beatitudes and free from all evils? Having received the instructions, the king endeavored to realize what he was taught".[18] Although Indians placed religious authority above the king, it is true that in reality the Buddhist Saṃgha was supported and protected politically and economically by the king. But the Buddhists were too proud of their role as guardians of the Dharma to acknowledge the king's supremacy. "The religious order forbids salutation to the king".[19]

In concert with this attitude of the Buddhists, the Brahmanists told the adherents, "There is no need for praises and salutations. Cast away any notions of good and bad, and go into the woods alone, finding the eatables on the way".[20] In another text, it is stated: "The disciples should not praise anyone, nor bow to anyone, nor worship the ancestors, but live in this ever-shifting world at will and free from all restrictions".[21]

In Greece, the religion of the *polis* required every citizen to sacrifice himself in the interest of 'the thing greater than oneself—in the interest of the aggregation called *polis*'. And it should be noted that this Greek self-sacrifice was done to meet the practical needs of the men in the *polis* as 'a service to the fraternity'.[22] The Indian religion, on the other hand, attached little importance to secular social organizations. Its primary concern was the quest for the Universal Law. Here, the Indian religion differs essentially from the Greek.

A sense of unity as a nation or a race was not nourished among the early Indins. Alexander the Great, during his invasion of India, not resistances of some local lords but was never harassed by a defense put up by the Indian nation as a whole. To wage a war in defense of their own nation and race did not seem to have appealed to the Indians of the day. King Aśoka, even after he succeeded to bring the whole country under his control, continued to call himself 'King of Magadha' and never thought himself as the 'King of India'. Magadha is the place where his Maurya dynasty had its origin. In his opinion, he was *a local* king and, *as a local king of Magadha,* he guided and ruled the other localities and races in India. In some of his Edicts, he referred to the land of India as Jambudvīpa. But in this concept of land, nothing racial or national superiority is implied. King Aśoka had no *racial or national consciousness* as such; he wished to stand *beyond such limitations.* He considered himself the preserver and actualizer of the *dharma,* and he was ever conscious and proud of this. All of his Edicts place emphasis on the realization of the *dharma* in this world.

After the downfall of the Maurya dynasty, India suffered many foreign invasions. But, contrary to our expectations, in the legends and myths of India there appear only a few names of national heroes who did much to defend the nation in such occasions.[23] In the epics of *Mahābhārata* and *Rāmāyaṇa,* there are legends told of many heroes. These are typical heroes of India, but they are not national heroes in so far as they lack, together with their authors, national and racial consciousness. Ancient Indians preached as a virtue the offering of one's properties, even one's life if neccessary, for the sake of others' happiness. But they were never taught self-sacrifice for a particular nation or race. The concept of the national hero in our sense did not appear in Indian history.[24]

Surprisingly, in the ancient Indian languages, there is no term equivalent to 'the Indian people'. Jambudvīpa and Bharatavarṣa mean only the land of India and do not imply the people living there. The Greeks called the inhabitants of this land "Indos" and this was adopted into the European languages in general. Indians themselves had no name to call their own nation. The Indo-Aryans, who formed the main stream of Indian civilization, called themselves *'Ārya'*. It means 'one who is faithful to the religion of the clan', and is the opposite of the word *'mleccha'* — barbarian or, loosely speaking, Non-Aryan. There was no word in India to include both the Aryans and the Non-Aryans together. Indians for a long time did not awake to the sense of unity as "the Indian people".

The Brahmanists thoroughly ignored the state authority. The early Buddhists conceived a social contract theory for the formation of a state while the early Jains insisted that the state power was nothing but the power of the strongest in arms. Neither the Buddhists nor the Jains found any sacred significance in the state. The ancient Indians in general believed in the rule of *dharma* — the Universal Law, and they assumed that state power was subordinate to the *dharma.* With such a frame of mind, there was no room for the growth of an organic theory of the state or society throughout Indian history.

For more than three thousand years since the time of the *Ṛg-Veda* up to the present, the unity of the Indian people has come about through *common religious faiths* rather than from their awakening in national or racial consciousness. Today, despite her independence India is still troubled with religious problems more than with racial or policy matters. Especially, the antagonism between the Hindus and the Mohammedans is a serious political issue. In the present-day, there probably is no other nation where religious antagonism produces such a crucial influence on national politics as in India.

---

1) The cases in Japan are in marked contrast to the Indian. In the *Kojiki* (古事記) and the *Nihonshoki* (日本書紀), both prominent models of ancient Japanese chronicles, the history of the Emperors' dynasty was the central concern and many myths and legends were told to strengthen its authenticity.

2) *Chavaka-Jātaka*, vol. III, p. 27 f.

3) *Āpastamba-Dharma-Sūtra*, 1. 2. 8. 8; *Gautama-Dharma-Sūtra*, 2. 21; *Viṣṇu-smṛti*, 28. 12; *The Laws of Manu*, 2. 198.

4) *Sāmañña-phala-suttanta* 沙門果經 in *Dīgha-Nikāya* and in 長阿含經.

5) It is about King Bimbisāra of Magadha. Cf. *Suttanipāta*, 409.

6) 法句譬喩經 vol. I (*Taishō*, vol. 4, p. 582 b–c).

7) 中阿含經 vol. XI. (*Taishō*, vol. 1, p. 497 b); *Ibid.* vol. LIX, (*Taishō*, vol. I, p. 795 c); 増一阿含經 vol. XLVIII (*Taishō*, vol. 2, p. 808 c).

8) 中阿含經 vol. XI (*Taishō*, vol. 1, p. 497 b); *Ibid.* vol. LIX (*Taishō*, vol. 1, p. 795 c); 長阿含經 vol. XVII (*Taishō*, vol. 1, p. 108 a); 雜阿含經 vol. XXXVIII (*Taishō*, vol. 1, p. 279 a); 増一阿含經 vol. VIII (*Taishō*, vol. 2, p. 609 b); *Ibid.* vol. XV (*Taishō*, vol. 2, p. 624 a); *Ibid.* vol. XXIV (*Taishō*, vol. 2, p. 679 b); 有部毘奈耶雜事 vol. VIII (*Taishō*, vol. 24, p. 237 a).

9) Cf. *Calcutta-Bairāt Edict.*

10) It is true that ancient Indian religious bodies did not have political influence upon the outside world as did the bodies of Christianity and Mohammedanism. But their independent authority was by no means submissive to external power.

11) King Bālāditya of the Gupta dynasty was dissatified with his low position in the Buddhist Saṃgha. But the Buddhists dared not violate the old rule of the Saṃgha to make an exception in his favor. See 大唐西域記 vol. IX.

12) Cf. *Vinaya, suttavibhaṅga*, vol. IV, pp. 159–160; *Aṅguttara-Nikāya*, vol. V, pp. 81–83; 善見律毘婆沙 vol. XVI (*Taishō*, vol. 24, p. 786-c).

13) 増一阿含經 vol. XLII (*Taishō*, vol. 2, p. 777 a–b).

14) The Lotus Sūtra 法華經, Chap. of Sukha-vihāra-parivartaḥ 安樂品行, U. Ogiwara and K. Tsuchida's ed., p. 235.

15) 正法念處經 vol. L (Taishō, vol. 17, pp. 294 c–295 a).

16) Cf. *Buddhacarita*, 9. 19 f; 佛本行集經 vol. XXI (*Taishō*, vol. 3, p. 749 a).

17) "Every fifteenth and last day of a month, the king (of Kucha) discusses the national affairs with the ministers, consults the learned priests and then promulgates the decrees". 大唐西域記 vol. I.

18) 王法正理論 (*Taishō*, vol. 31, p. 858 a–c). Cf. 四十華嚴 vol. XII (*Taishō*, vol. 10, p. 714 b).

19) 梵網經 pt. 2 (*Taishō*, vol. 24, p. 1008 c).

20) *Mahābhārata*, 12. 242. 9.

21) *Māṇḍūkya-Kārikā*, 2. 37. Cf. *Paramahaṃsa-Upaniṣad*; *Paramahaṃsa-parivrājaka-Upaniṣad.*

22) Tetsurō Watsuji 和辻哲郎: *Homērosu-hihan* (ホメーロス批判 Criticism on Homeros) pp. 41–42; Tetsurō Watsuji: "Polisu-no-keisei (ポリスの形成 For-

mation of the Polis)" in *Jo-setsu* (叙説) vol. I, p. 26 f. The Indian religion also differs from the Japanese. As it will be related later, the Japanese lay stress on the individual ethical organizations rather than on the Universal Law.

23) The founder of the Maurya dynasty, King Candragupta, who beat back the Greek forces from north-west India is often referred to in later Indian books. But these do not praise him as the hero who defended the nation against foreign invasions.

24) In India, there remain many records of donations inscribed in monuments. Judging from these, few donations were made to secular state powers while many made to religious bodies. The Indian idea of the nation differs much from the Japanese notion and also from the Roman idea of "patria".

(6) Transcendence of limited ethical systems

Part 2: The problem of caste

The caste system represents a closed and disunited social organization which was highly regarded by the Indians. Our next step is to study the idea that underlies this unique social system of India.

About one thousand B.C. the Aryan invaders advanced to the upper reaches of the Ganges and established an agricultural community. This Aryan society prevailed over the whole country and, in the course of years, went through some modifications until we find it in its present state. The members of the conquered tribes were reduced to servitude and they—the Sūdras—were strictly distinguished from the free people. Then among the Aryans themselves, new classes were formed. The priests and the warriors created their own independent classes. Their professions were transmitted through heredity and, in this process, class stratification grew rigid until finally the caste system was established. Under the major four castes of the Brāhmaṇa, the Kṣatriya, the Vaiśya and the Śūdra, many subcastes have grown.

The class rigidity over marriage and over eating is universally observed among the primitive tribes in the world. But what is remarkable here is that India which has already gone through the process of acculturation still is influenced by the caste system. Indian factory workers will share a bed room only when they are members of the same caste. Once when a public dining hall was planned in a large Indian city, voices were heard that it should be constructed according to caste lines.

The Buddhists completely opposed the caste discrimination and preached the concept of equality among men while the Jains compromised on it. The Buddhists were popular among the city-dwellers but they failed to win the conservative rural peasants. And this is one reason why Buddhism was doomed and vanished from its birthplace. However, the concept of equality gradually seeped into the minds of the Indians and later on they began to emphasize even Buddha's noble birth.[1]

The caste system has undergone complicated changes before taking its present form. It is not easy to explain the origin and growth of the castes in India. Many scholars have introduced various theories concerning this problem but it is a problem to be discussed at another occasion. Here we can only say that the caste system cannot be explained satisfactorily only through the study of productive means or of geographic and climatic conditions. It must be noted that a mode of thinking crystallized from the early thinking process has deep influence on the system.[2]

On studying the castes, we cannot overlook the influence of the Brāhmin class in Indian civilization. This priestly class has always kept the highest position in the social hierarchy and taken the intellectual leadership of India. In a country where military or political consolidation has been rarely achieved, it has done much to bring the people under one sway culturally and socially. Indeed the civilization of India owes much to it which had strongly advocated the caste system.

Religious divinity viewed from the standpoint of Brahmanism decides the standing of a caste in social privilege. In other words, each caste shares an element of *Brahmanic divinity*. Accordingly, because of the large share of divine power, the Brāhmin class enjoys the highest rank, the Kṣatriya class comes next, then the Vaiśya and the Śūdra. Within a caste, every member is treated with *equanimity*. This phenomenon of equality within the same caste rank is governed by the concept of the Universal Law. The Law functions by actualizing itself within the differing castes and at the same time gives meaning and significance to them. The Indian social structure, therefore, is quite different from that of a consanguineal community, such as Japan, where people highly regard blood-relationship, real or fictional.

Caste membership is transmitted through heredity in India too, so that, blood-relationship is still significant. But, Indians consider religion over consanguinity. If a member of a caste violates the Brahmanic decrees of his caste, he is at once turned out of the caste and transfered to a lower caste. Consanguinity is *held in esteem* only in so far as the *religious divinity* serves it. And thus we see that the peculiar Indian way of thinking which submits to the Universal Law functions and underlies the caste system.

1) "I place strong faith in the pure Enlightened One who is born of pure stock". The opening part of the *Mahāvaṃsa.*

2) Max Weber treated this problem by introducing the concept of "Gentilcharisma". His study is worthy of praise, but this concept is not enough to explain the relationship between the way of thinking of a race and the rise of a caste system in India. Cf. Max Weber: *Aufsätze zur Religionssoziologie*, I, S. 268; Max Weber: *Hinduismus und Buddhismus*, S. 129.

(7) Consciousness of living beings: Indian concept of man

When Indians speak of man, they are likely to use such terms as *'prāṇin', 'bhūta', 'sattva', or 'jīva'.*[1] Western scholars translate these words as 'living being' or 'Lebwessen', and the meaning refers not only to man but also beasts and all living creatures.[2] In Sanskrit, there are such words as *'manuṣya', 'puruṣa',* or *'nara',* wihch are equivalent to the English "human being". But Indians do not like to use these words even when they mean man in particular. They think of man more as an instance of the species of "living being" than as one of the human race. This Indian mentality can be traced in the texts of all Indian religions.[3] According to them, the subject of ethical conduct is 'a living being'. The moral rules that regulate the man-to-man relationship are not enough. Ethics should be such that it rules over all the relations among men, beasts and other living beings. This Indian concept of man in relation to other beings is thoroughly different from the Western concept of man.[4]

From this standpoint of ethics it is natural that Indians accentuate the idea of animal protection. Buddhists and Jains in particular both agree on this point. "All living things have deep attachment to life".[5] 'They want bodily comforts. They should not be treated cruelly'.[6] Brahmanists, too, preach loving care of living creatures.[7] As a matter of fact, protection of animals is emphasized in all Indian religious schools, the ideal being that not even an ant on the road should be stamped upon.

There is no essential difference between man and a beast. Like a beast, man is egocentric and eager to satisfy his desires and is distressed by failures. A leading philosopher of India, Śaṅkara, classed man together with the beasts. He stated: "Man's behavior is not different from that of a beast. A stimulus, such as a sound, comes to a sense organ such as the ears of a beast. The beast avoids or runs away from the sound in case it feels it unpleasant, while it makes its way toward it in case it feels it pleasant. When a beast sees a man swinging a club, it thinks, 'This man is going to kill me' and runs away. But when it sees a man with grass in his hands, it approaches the man. And the same can be said of man, an intelligent animal. When he recognizes a terrible-looking man threatening with a sword in hand, he runs away. But when he recognizes a man contrary to the above mentioned, he approaches him. Thus man's actions with respect to cognitive objects and function are in common to the beast. It is generally known that the sensations of a beast result from its confusion in not being able to distinguish between the Ātman and the Non-Ātman. Man is at many points similar to the beast in that his sensations continue to mistake the Non-Ātman for the Ātman."[8] Classifications of creatures in the ancient texts of many Indian religious schools confirm the view that there is no difference between man and beast.

Jains hold an animistic view and maintain that every thing has its proper spirit. Earth, water, fire, wind and plant, have only tactual sensation. A worm has two sensations and an ant has three. A bee has four and only a man enjoys five sensations.[9] According to another text of Jainism, the gods, the men, the beings in hell, elephants, peacocks and fish, are said to have five sensations.[10] It seems that the Jains assume two groups among the beings with five sensations, that is, those with mental faculties (*samanaska*) and those without (*asamanaska*).[11]

From the modes of birth, Jains classify living beings into three groups:

1) Accidental (*upapāta*);	gods and the beings in hell.
2) Viviparous (*garbha*);	beings born with placenta, without placenta, and from eggs (oviparous).
3) Coagulative (*sammūrchana*);	beings not included in the above-mentioned two groups.[12]

The Brahmanists, on the other hand, classify beings into four groups:[13]

1) Viviparous (*jarāyuja*);	beings such as man.
2) Oviparous (*aṇḍaja*);	beings such as bird.
3) Moisture productive (*svedaja*);	beings produced from moisture such as louse.
4) Germinative (*udbhijja*);	beings produced from the buds such as plant.[14]

In another text, Brahmanists classify all the living beings into two; 'the movable (*cara* or *jaṅgana*)' and 'the immovable (*acara* or *sthāvara*)'.[15]

In these Indian systems of classification, we are able to extract two common features: (1) Man is equal to other animals as one of the viviparous beings. This offers a sharp contrast with the Western concept of man before the Medieval Age, and possibly corresponds with the modern scientific classification. The Indian concept is not the result of scientific study on ecological phenomena, but results from their instinctive and natural way of thinking man as one of the *living beings*. (2) Indians acknowledge the spiritual factor in all living creatures. It is often stressed that not only men and beasts but even plants have souls.[16] However, the spirituality of a plant is not so remarkably developed as in a man. All this does not mean that the Indians did not, in some respects, hold that man is superior to other creatures. Man is a 'thinking' animal.[17] In the text of *Āraṇyaka* of the early Brahmanists, it is stated: "The sap runs in a plant and the mind (*citta*) in an animal. And in a man, the *Ātman* is most clearly revealed because man is endowed with intelligence (*prajñāna*). He sees and tells what he cognizes, knows what tomorrow is about, distinguishes between the real and unreal worlds, and tries to attain immortality though being mortal".[18] The Buddhists highly regarded 'the rare state of man'. One should be grateful that he is born a man for it is more difficult to be born a man than for a blind turtle to enter a hole in a floating wood in the ocean.[19] The Buddhists also advocated the abolition of capital punishment. A paragraph in a Buddhist text states thus: "Be obedient to the saintly kings. Do not condemn a man to death. Why so? Because for him to come into this world as a man and not as any other being is the consequence of superior factors or conditions. If you take his life, you will certainly be punished".[20] This means that man's life as such should be revered and no one should destroy it.[21]

In certain circumstances, man was distinguished from other creatures, being endowed with the characteristics of carrying out the dharma—ethical law. It emphasized the ethical and religious significance in human activities, that those who neglect the dharma are no better than the beasts, In a text of the ancient Upaniṣad, it is stated: "Man of good deeds in this world will be reborn into the life of the Brāhmin of the Kṣatriya, or of the Vaiśya. On the contrary, man of evil doings will be born in the womb of a dog, of a pig, or of an outcast woman (*cāṇḍālī*)".[22] The Vaiśeṣika school says: "The Dharma is the excellent quality of the human race (*puruṣa-guṇa*). It is the basis for man's comforts, benefits and liberation. It is beyond human perception, and it ceases to exist when man understands correctly the ultimate peace (*mokṣa*). This comes about from the unity of the human spirit and the inner faculties, for those who practise the rules of their castes and of life-periods.[23]

Thus it is that the early Indians advocated the superiority of man over other beings on the one hand, but in general, they considered man as only equal to beasts and worms in the whole run of living beings.

---

1) In the oldest Gāthās of the early Buddhists, the holy scriptures of Jains and the Aśoka Edicts, '*pāṇa* (*prāṇa*)' is used to mean living being.

2) V. Fausbøll, in his Latin translation of the *Dhammapada*, translated these words as 'animans' or 'animal'.

3) Cf. *Praśnottararatnamālikā*, 22; *the Aśoka Edicts.*

4) In the West, too, some philosophers have held that the subject of ethical conduct is not to be limited to man. But as we see in Kant's idea of 'vernünftige Wesen', they in reality focussed attention on the problem of man and ignored the consideration of living beings. Cf. Kant: *Grundlegung zur Metaphysik der Sitten, herausgegeben von Karl Vorländer*, S. 28 f; 52 f.

5) *Dhammapada*, 130; *Āyāraṅga*, 1. 2. 3. 4.

6) *Dhammapada*, 132, & 405, *Āyāraṅga*, p. 16, & p. 35.

7) *Mahābhārata*, 13. 113. 5.

The great rites as recorded in the ancient Vedas required animal sacrifice. On this account, Buddhists and Jains deplored the feasts of Brahmanism. The idea of animal protection appears in the Brahmanic texts of the last stage of the Vedic age. In the Upaniṣads, it is stated that 'non-harming' is to be praised just as much as offering to the priests. And in another text, it is decreed not to kill a living thing at the place other than the site of rites. Cf. *Chāṇdogya-Upaniṣad*, 3. 17. 4; 8. 15.

8) *Brahma-sūtra-bhāṣya*, 1. 1. 1.

9) *Tattvārthādhigamasūtra*, II, 23–24. The problem of creature—classification is dealt with fully in Śāntisūri's; *Jīvaviyāra*. (Cf. Winternitz: *Gesch. d. ind. Lit.*, II, S. 354.)

10) Hemacandra: *Adhidhānacintāmaṇi*, 21–22.

11) *Davvasaṃgaha*, 12; *Sarvārthasiddhi.*

12) *Tattvārthādhigamasūtra*, II, 32 f.

13) Cf. *Aitareya-Upaniṣad*, 5. 3.; *Brahma-sūtra*, 3. 1. 21.; *Mahābhārata*, 12, 312. 5; *The Laws of Manu*, 1. 43–46. In the *Chāndogya-Upaniṣad*, the creatures are classified into three groups—viviparous, oviparous and germinative; while there is no reference to beings produced out of moisture. The *Brahma-sūtra* interprets this assertion by saying that these latter beings are included in the group of germinative beings.

14) Cf. Many commentary works on the *Brahma-sūtra*, 3. 1. 21. In a medical book, *Suśruta-saṃhitā*, these four groups are recognized for the classification of animals (*jaṅgama*) and as examples of germinative beings, frogs and fireflies are mentioned. (Cf. Guha: *Jīvātman*, p. 55.)

15) *Brahma-sūtra*, 2. 3. 16.

16) *Mahābhārata*, 12. 184. 17.

17) Sanskrit "*manuṣya*", like English "man", is etymologically connected with "$\sqrt{man}$"—to think.
18) *Aitareya-Āraṇyaka*, 2. 3. 2.
19) *Majjhima-Nikāya*, 129.
20) *Butsui-shōkō-tenshi-setsu-ōbō-kyō* 佛爲勝光天子說王法經, (*Taishō*, vol. 15, p. 125b–c).
21) Jains, too, teach that man's life is very precious and that it is highly significant to be born a man. Cf. M. Winternitz: *A History of Indian Literature*, vol. II, p. 466.
22) *Chāndogya-Upaniṣad*, 5. 10. 7–8.
23) Praśastapāda: *Padārthadharmasaṃgraha*, § 39, *dharmalakṣaṇa*.

(8) The conservative character of Indian thinking

Indians, in their retrospective way of thinking, believe that an ideal state existed in the past where the norm of human behavior was faithfully carried out. But as this state is no longer ideally possible, they worship the past and admire the classics.

In the codes of Brahmanism, anything new and modern is severely criticized and rejected. In the *Laws of Manu,* it was stated: "The legends which are not based on the Scriptures (*smṛti*) and the wrong concepts (*kudṛṣṭi*) are false and useless in bringing happiness after man's death. This is *because they are new* (*arvākkālika*)."[1]

Buddha who had originated a new school scarcely thought himself as a founder. He only thought that he had succeeded in grasping the Universal Law which is valid for all time. In reality he aspired to become a true Brahmin or Śramaṇa and never to build up anything new or apart from Brahmanism. The early Buddhists respected and regarded the age-old sages preceding Buddha as men who had lived according to the dharma. "Verily, the dharma is the banner of the sages".[2] "The sages of the past were ascetics who restrained their inner passions, freed themselves from the five desires and did what was truly good for their own sake".[3] The early Buddhists severely criticised the Brahmin priests, saying that they indulged in pleasure-seeking—storing treasures and keeping beautiful mistresses—and were no better than the secular kings.[4]

Historically speaking, however, the criticism is not true. As a matter of fact the earliest Brahmin priests were engaged in prayers and magical rites for the general welfare of the secular. And it was rather in a late period that high sounding Brahmin priests appeared to lead the enclosed and ascetic life. In disregard of this historical fact, the Buddhists never ceased to set the ideal in the golden age of the past and to detest all contemporaneous things.

In the *Thera-Gāthā,* one of the oldest texts of the early Buddhists, it was deplored that the monks of the day are corrupt and degrading compared with the high standard of those in Buddha's time. From the point of view as this, there gradually developed the Buddhist idea of the three stages (*Shō-bō, Zō-hō* and *Map-pō*) of the world's declining evolution which finally took the accomplished form in the texts of Mahāyāna Buddhism.[5] Brahmanists on the other hand maintained the four-stage theory of world history, Kṛta, Tretā, Dvāpara and Kali. According to this view, our present period belongs to the last one, the period of decay and termination, and equivalent to the Buddhist Map-pō. Indians, assuming the ideal age in the past, did not accept new things or what was in existence as good and desirable.

In India, therefore, new thoughts are constantly tied in with old established authorities and from which they take on significance. For instance, the Indian national epic, *Mahābhārata,* differs from the Vedas in content and maintains that it is more important than the four Vedas,[6] and yet, it regarded itself as one of the Vedas.[7] Buddhists, too, rely upon Buddha's great authority to propagate their ideas. Many of 'Buddha's Teachings' in the texts of early Buddhism and Mahāyāna Buddhism are in reality the works of scholars coming later than Buddha but using his authority.[8]

Together with the adherence to established authority, the obedience to the elders (*sthavira* or *thera*) by the Indians is really remarkable. All the religious sects in India unanimously teach the veneration of the elders and prohibit, above all things, definance of the teachers.[9] "Those who pay due courtesy to the elders will greatly enhance their four dharmas—long life, knowledge, peace and strength".[10]

Although scriptural authority was supreme, there were some materialists, and naturalists as the followers of the Vaiśeṣika school or logicians as Dharmakīrti who claimed that scriptures are not absolutely reliable because they were written by man. But these were in the minority in India. Almost all the schools of philosophy in India have accepted the words in the scriptures as the absolute authority of knowledge.

Even the early rationalistic Buddhists maintained that a proposition should be verified in two ways, one by logical demonstration and one by confirmation through scriptual authority.[11] And in present-day India there still survives with tenacity such blind acceptance of the scriptures which the Western world had long left behind with the rise of the Renaissance.[12]

It is true, however, that the Indian obedience to the scriptures often descended to be only nominal. In reality, the ancient Indians were not so restrained in their free thinking. Madhva and others of the Vedānta school developed a dualistic metaphysics incompatible with the monistic standpoint of Upaniṣads. To resolve the contradiction, they strained their interpretation of the holy scriptures. They made use of the written authority in a twisted way to justify their own assertions.

There was a time in early Indian history when free thinking was encouraged. This was about the time of Buddha when materialism, skepticism, sensualism and all the other kinds of liberal ideas flourished. At that time, many city-states were established along the banks of the Ganges. The kings of such city-states, though concerned in philosophical discussions, never persecuted those who did not conform with their own opinion. But all this was a temporal phenomenon. Together with the downfall of the city-states the liberal philosophical tendency in India died out and could not gain a footing again. It can be said that the Indian allegiance to the orthodox authority undeniably checked the development of free thinking in the land.[13]

---

1) *The laws of Manu*, 12. 95–96.
2) *Aṅguttara-Nikāya*, II, p. 51 G.
3) *Suttanipāta*, 284.
4) Cf. *Ibid.*, 299.
5) The Lotus Sūtra and the *Larger Sukhāvatī-vyūha* hold that their teachings are proper for the period of *Mappo*—the days of decadence. Cf. The Lotus Sūtra, Chap. of *Sukha-vihāra-parivartaḥ* (法華經, 安樂行品); *The Larger Sukhāvatī-vyūha* (大無量壽經), finis.
6) *Mahābhārata*, 1. 1. 269.
7) *Ibid.*, 1. 1. 256.
8) The ancient Indians, too, knew full well of this perversion. To a question why *The Laws of Manu* has, contrary to the fact, the name of Manu as the author, an interpreter answered: "Every teacher consciously makes use of this measure to present his own ideas, that is, in the guise of the teachings of the great predecessors". Cf. *Kullūkabhaṭṭa on Manu* I, 4.
9) *Dhammapada*, 260; *The Laws of Manu*, 2. 156; *Praśnottaratnamālikā*, 4.
10) *The Laws of Manu*, 2. 121. Cf. *Dhammapada*, 109.
11) Cf. 攝大乘論釋 (眞諦譯) (*Taishō*, vol. 31, p. 157b.) Vasubandhu's translation does not contain a sentence which corresponds to this part. This sentence therefore is guessed to be added by Paramārthā (眞 諦), the translater.

12) Indians are by no means irrational people. They have developed mathematics and grammar and other studies based on scientific methods. But still it cannot be denied that the blind acceptance of the authority of the scriptures forms a dominant character of Indian way of thinking.

13) City-states as developed in the West did not appear in India. The Indian cities could not act unitedly as a political organization. It had no right either to make treaties with other cities or to exercise proper jurisdiction over the inhabitants. Such a state of the Indian cities is another reason for the extinction of liberal thoughts in India.

(9) The development of nomothetical learning[1]

Subservience to the Universal Law and negligence of individual varieties lead to nomothetic tendencies and, on the other hand, to the loss of idiographic attitudes concerning everyday living of the individual. Ancient Indians left few chronologies, documentary works and personal biographies.[2] And studies of geography and of topography were scarcely achieved,[3] while recording and descriptive studies like natural science hardly developed. Their interests were primarily directed at the quest of the universal norm.[4]

H. Oldenberg analyzes this Indian nomothetical tendency as follows: "For Indians, history was not a true science. Generally speaking, science in their concept was what led man to a certain action suitable to a system of rules. Indeed, no other nation has showed such a strong tenacity to the rules. Grammar handed down the rules of refined speech; philosophy the rules of release from the worldly hardships; and erotic poetry the rules of true galantry. These were the sciences that an earnest speaker, an eager Nirvāṇa-seeker and an intent love-maker of India could not dispose with. Needless to say, politics, a science consisting of many rules, was acknowledged by Indians as one of the true sciences. But the role to express those phenomena that were not yet embodied in the rules but that for the time only could be related in words was transmitted naturally to a more flexible art of accomplishment and presentation (of literature)".[5] On this point, Indians exhibit a striking contrast to the Chinese who attempted to seek universal and normative significance in the aggregation of individual cases.

Many causes are given for the lack of historical works in India. Some of them are the rather late usage of the Indian written language, the inclement weather conditions for the preservation of manuscripts, and the instability of political and military situations. But a more fundamental cause should be traced in the peculiarity of the Indian way of thinking.

1) The *word* 'nomothetical' here does not imply the meaning that Heinrich Rickert attached.
2) Nothing is known even about the philosophers who died recently. Ten years or so after their death, they are treated as incarnations of the gods. In the pamphlets commemorating the founders and published by the religious schools established in the nineteenth and the twentieth centuries, no dates of birth and of death are mentioned.
3) There are some works of topography in the Prāṇa texts.
4) "The religious tendency of the Indian districts where Buddhism spread and secured a strong footing shows a very remarkable features of bent toward the impersonal and the universal, of alienation from the visible and the tangible and of submergence and dissolution into the infinite". H. Oldenberg: *Aus dem alten Indien*, S. 14–15.
5) H. Oldenberg: *ibid.*, S. 99.

Chapter 10. Alienation from the objective natural world

(1) Loss of the notion of order in the objective natural world

In the same manner as in the contrast between of one's self and others, the Indians had very little consciousness of the contrast between the self (agent) and the natural surroundings.

They have never represented the concept of their native land apart from the inhabitants. Names of countries or districts are described using the plural for of *the name of her inhabitants.*[1] A dislike to represent the land as natural surroundings objectively apart from her inhabitants seems to have been strong.

As Indians recognized the existence of the universal reality behind phenomena and represented it as an existence limited in time and space, what may be overlooked is the distinction between two kinds of existence, viz. universal reality and things in the phenomenal world. Also overlooked may be the distinction between things perceived directly and those perceived by means of inference and other secondary means of cognition.

This tendency of thought can be seen also in the lingual form. For example, there is no 'explicative genitive' (der epexegetische Gen.) in Sanskrit. This form, otherwise called the 'definitive genitive', is used in Latin (esp. in later days and in vernaculars) for explaining a noun determined by it. (e.g. *urbs Romae*, the city of Rome; *nomen amoris*, the name of love.) The same form is observed in modern Western languages, Japanese and Tibetan, etc., while in Sanskrit, the same context is expressed by nouns in apposition. (In case indication of determination is specially required, an indeclinable *'iti'* in the sense of 'called' is used. e.g. *Pāṭaliputra iti nagaram; mṛttiketi nāmadheyam.*) When two nouns, the explaining and the one to be explained, are shown appositionally to each other, very little difference of order exists between the determining and the determined.

The expression 'A as B' is also lacking in ancient Indian languages. Namely they have no term equivalent to the *as* in English or *als* in German. To express such a term, an appositional form between A and B is used. Hence the expression can be construed both ways, 'A as B' and 'B as A'. Such a lingual phenomenon seems to be caused by the same way of thinking as observed in the phenomenon mentioned above.[2)]

This Indian characteristic is shown more clearly in the following grammatical construction. The same content usually shown by the subordinate clause in other languages is expressed in apposition to a word in the principal clause in Sanskrit, in order to avoid the use of subordinate clause. (e.g. *pitā vṛddhaḥ.* = the father, when he is old). They do not like to distinguish the primary realm of experience from the content of thought based upon it. They describe both as if they were in the same dimension. The sentence, 'better is the birth of a daughter,' is expressed in the wording: 'better, a daughter, born (p. p. p.)' (*varaṃ kanyaiva janitā*). Therefore, the distinction between the principal clause and the subordinate clause is sometimes obscure. The term *'iti'* equivalent to 'that' or to a quotation mark in such a sentence as 'he said that....' or 'he said: "——"' is often omitted.[3)] In this case, the quotation passage or the subordinate clause is indistinct by its lingual form unless we construe the meaning from the contents. Again a subordinate clause in a sentence is placed before or after the principal clause, but never in between as in most Western languages,[4)] probably because of the confusion that would result due to the loose rules of Sanskrit syntax.

Indians prefer the direct narration to an indirect approach in describing an idea, opinion, thought, intention or doubt in persons other than the speaker himself. There was very little development of the indirect narration in Indian languages. In Sanskrit, it is mostly limited to the accusative *cum participio* and the indirect interrogatory sentence. A few other cases are sentences beginning with *yad* which shows the content, sentences beginning with *yad* which is equal to the infinitive, and the predicate sentences beginning with *yad* or *yathā*.[5)]

Distinction between 'the precative' and 'the conjunctive' as appeared in Greek was preserved in Vedic Sanskrit, but was lost in Classical Sanskrit and united in the precative. It means that those who used Classical Sanskrit vaguely thought of the same sense out of two forms originally distinguished.[6]

In modern languages, the description of assumption is done by means of the periphrastic expression of long sentence in order to distinguish it from the description of actual matters, while in Sanskrit, there is no distinction between them and the same content is expressed by shorter and simple sentences.[7]

The same characteristic style of thought is also observed in the past approach of linguistics by Indians. Their studies of phonetics and grammar are incomparable in their detailed and exact characters not only among ancient countries but even in the modern world up to the 19th century as well. Nevertheless their linguistic studies are rather weak in the field of syntax. Indian grammar was superior to the Greeks in *analysis* of word-construction while the Greek grammar had a superiority in syntax which treats the *synthesis* of words. The Greeks, who were by no means the rival of Indians in the field of phonetics, showed a distinct superiority in the field of syntax. In regards to the reason why syntax remained undeveloped in India, Prof. H. Kōzu ascribed it to the extremely free sentence-construction of Sanskrit.[8] Undoubtedly this was the main cause, but in a further examination, we may find that the Indians were weak in the notion of order in the objective natural world.

Again due to their way of thinking which did not distinguish clear and direct perceptions obtained through the sense organs from knowledge obtained through fantasy or inference, Indians were poor in expressions cognizing order among phenomena. Intellectual people and scholars were not always so, but there certainly was such a tendency among the common people.

First of all this tendency can be seen in the lingual form. Even when a change of phase is observed between two sentences according to the Western concept of language, Indians describe both *plainly* without inserting the term 'but' and the like. For example, "therefore the dumb can speak, but cannot hear" is expressed by the sentence: *tasmād badhirȯ vācá vadati ná śṛṇoti*[9] (Lit. therefore a dumb speaks, not hears.) On the other hand, Indians frequently use conjunctions to denote conclusions drawn, e.g. *tad, tasmāt, tarhi, atas.* These are used even when Westerners feel that there is no necessity to use them.[10] On this point, Indians are rather similar to the Japanese people. Speyer understood this as to be in accordance with the dialectical tendency of the Indian, but actually it seems to show their inability to understand the relation between the reason and conclusion in sentences in spite of their strong tendency to search for and understand the logical or causal relations among phenomena.

In comparison with Westerners who make classifications of various phenomena according to their importance, Indians describe them exhaustively but without order. In the *Brāhmaṇas,* abstract concepts and concrete matters are described side by side as being in the same dimension.

Loss of the notion of order with respect to the objective world causes Indians to describe the symbol of numerals in a row. For example, '163' is usually described in ancient Indian manuscripts as: 100 60 3.

The Indians are generally very fond of simple calculations of important items. This may be based upon the same tendency of thought. The *Arthaśāstra* and the *Kāmasūtra* throughout use this principle. In the philosophy of Sāṃkhya and Nyāya schools, important principles are merely enumerated in a row and the distinctions of dimension are never indicated (viz. the 25 *tattvas* of the Sāṃkhya, the 16 *padārthas* of the Nyāya). This tendency is striking also in Buddhism, which calls those principles or terms arranged in a row 'the calculated doctrines' (法數) (e.g. *tridhātu, ratnatraya, catvāry ārya-satyāni, pañca-skandhāḥ, ṣaṭ-pāramitāḥ, dvādaśâṅgaḥ pratītyasamutpādaḥ,* etc.)

Thus having no liking for summarisation or making rules of phenomena from a recognition of some order among them, Indians used *frequent repetition.* Tiresome repetition of similar sentences is commonly seen in the Upaniṣads, Buddhist and Jain scriptures, etc.[11]

Repetition of the same wording for each item, which makes modern readers quite tired, is said to have been used for strengthening the memory in the absence of letters. If letters had been used for description from the beginning, such repetition would have no value. Another strong reason for such repetition was the poor development of pronoun use in ancient Indian languages. In Sanskrit the same noun is repeated where the Western classical languages would use a pronoun.

In quite an opposite way, Indians sometimes used extremely simple expressions. This is also said to have been used for students to remember the contents easily. If so, repetition of sentences of the same style were probably used for recitation (viz. *infra,* p. 149). This, however, cannot be applied for the cases of repetition of the *Upaniṣads*. (e.g. *Bṛhad. Up.* III, 7). In case of all Buddhist scriptures, as Oldenberg maintained (*Buddha*, 7 Aufl., S. 206–207), this probably relates to the Indian way of thinking.

Another tendency of Indians more or less relating to this is that synonymous words are often used side by side to express a matter or opinion. This was noticed quite early in history by the ancient Chinese people. Shih Tao-an (釋道安, 4th cent. A.D.) referred to the fact that repetitions in Buddhist scriptures were simplified and omitted when translated into Chinese by saying: "Foreign scriptures (胡經) are very detailed in their description. For example, words of admiration are repeated twice, thrice or even four times without being tired of it. In the present translation, these repetitions are all omitted".[12] This same criticism was also made by Japanese who said; "India is a land where people are fond of thoroughness and minuteness in everything. It is her custom to repeatedly mention synonymous words for admiration. In China, people like simplicity and tried to omit repetitions".[13]

Frequent use of compound words in the ancient Indian languages, and especially in Sanskrit, can also be counted as one of the results of the weakness of the notion of order among various phenomena or ideas. In the *Ṛg-veda*, use of long compound words was comparatively rare. After that, frequency of their use gradually increased in the course of time. In verses of *kāvya* style especially, very long compounds were welcomed and intentionally used. This same tendency can be observed among the Prakrit literature.[14] In this case, the relation of each component word of a long compound is rather difficult to understand. The main purpose of the compound is not in the exact expression of meaning, but to originate, in the mind, the impression of the idea expressed by each word one by one without interruption. It, however, often leaves room for many kinds of interpretation of a compound and tends to make the meaning obscure and less understandable. (On this point Sanskrit comes close to the Chinese.)

Therefore Indians themselves tried to avoid the use of compound as much as possible in scholary works, and especially in prose. In the vernacular languages of ancient India, there is also an avoidance of long compounds. Still as a rule, more use of compounds are found than in Western classical languages. Let us mention the following as an example.

Coins of Parthian kings who governed North-West India before the Christian era have the same phrase in Greek script on one side, Indian

Prakrit on the other. Words like 'brother of the king' and 'king of kings' are written separately in Greek while they are combined in compounds in the Indian language.[15]

The same tendency is prominently seen in popular works like the epics. For example, in the *Bhagavadgītā*, the most famous religious work in India, many such examples can be found though the amount of the compounds is comparatively less. For example:

janmabandhavinirmuktās (II, 51) = generationum vinculis exsoluti, καὶ ἀπαλλαγέντες το ὕεδσμοῦ τῆς γεννήσεως, (released from the bondage of birth); (m.pl.Nom.)

Kuruvṛddha (I, 12) = Curuidarum progenitor, ὁ πρεσβύτερος τῶν ἐν τῇ γενεᾷ Κουροῦ, (grown in Kuru);

sarvalokamaheśvaram (acc.) (V, 29) = universi mundi magnum dominum, πάντων τῶν κόσμων μέγαν ἡγεμόνα, (great controller of the whole universe);

samitiṃjayaḥ (I, 8) = bellorum profligator, ὁ νικητὴς ἐν πολέμῳ, (victorious in battle).

In the verse (*gāthā*) sections of the Early Buddhist scriptures, the expressions are generally quite simple and no such complicated and artificial compounds are found as observed in the later literature. Nevertheless, in a comparison with Latin and other Western languages, use of certain long compounds can be seen. For instance the following examples are found in the Pāli *Dhammapada*:

ariyappavedite dhamme (*Dhp.* 79) = a venerandis enarrata lege (doctrines preached by venerables);

saddhammadesanā (*Dhp.* 194) = verae doctrinae institutio (Instruction of the true doctrine);

paradukkhūpadhānena (*Dhp.* 291) = aliis dolorem imponendo (causing others' sufferings);

rājarathūpamam (acc.), (*Dhp.* 171) = currui regali similem (simile of the chariot of a king);

sabbadukkhā pamuccati (*Dhp.* 189f.) = ab omni dolore liberatur (he is liberated from all sufferings)

More remarkable is the case of the Bahuvrīhi compound (possessive comp.) in Sanskrit, which is very much developed and utilized frequently. A compound word of this kind requires a long sentence when translated into Western classical languages.

e.g. paṭhavīsamo (*Dhp.* 79) = qui terrae instar est (one who is like the earth);

yuktasvapnāvabodhasya (*Bhag.* VI, 17) = qui temperans est in dormiendo ac vibilando,........ ei, μετρίως ἱπνοῦντι καὶ μετρίως γρηγοροῦντι, (of one whose mind is in a dream as well as awake);

kapidhvajaḥ (*Bhag.* I, 20) = simiae effigiem in vexillo gestans, ὁ ἔχων ἐν τῇ σημαίᾳ τὸν πίθηκα, (one who is possessed of the sign of monkey, a name for Arjuna).

Some sentences containing Bahuvrīhi compounds require sentences of an entirely different structure in translation.

e.g. manopubbaṅgamā dhammā manoseṭṭhā manomayā (*Dhp.* 1) = naturae a mente principium ducunt, mens est potior pars earum, e mente constant, (phenomena are governed by mind, consisting mainly of mind, and are made by mind.)

When the subordinate clause is required in Western modern languages, or the absolutive, in case of Western classical languages, Sanskrit expresses it often in a compound.

e.g. adharmābhibhavāt (*Bhag.* I, 41) = impietate gliscente, τοῦ θὲ ἀνόμου ἐ πιγενομένου, (because there is arisen immorality).

Sometimes even two contrary ideas are combined in a compound.

e.g. śubhāśubham (acc.) (*Bhag.* II, 57) = faustum vel infaustum, (pure or impure);

puññāpāpapahīnassa (*Dhp.* 39) = bono maloque vacui, (having abandoned both merit and demerit.) (gen.)

Successive mention of various impressive ideas in a long compound gives vast play in fantasic imagery. Therefore Indian compounds cannot be translated into Japanese or Western languages without the loss of a lingual effect. On this point, Oldenberg said: "As our language is far less effective than Indian languages in its power of composition, we are sometimes obliged to replace one word in the Indian language by several words which makes the final effect weak".[16] (*free rendering*)

Obscurity in the meaning of a word is also caused by omissions of syllables within a word in the ancient Indian Prakrits. Single consonants in particular are often omitted between two vowels. This tendency can be seen in the early Mahārāṣṭrian lyrics causing confusion in meaning. For example, Mahārāṣṭrian '*kaï*' is equivalent to either *kati* (some), *kavi* (poet), or *kapi* (monkey) in Sanskrit; in case of *uaa* (=*udaka*, Skt.), only the vowels were retained. This omission was probably due to Indian consonants not being articulated strongly in comparison with those of Western languages.[17] This omission of consonants gives the Prakrit languages a womanly impression in their pronunciation, as has already been recognized and indicated by the ancient Indians.[18] It may correspond to the womanly trend commonly observed in Indian ways of thinking. Prakrits are purely Indian in character in contrast with Sanskrit being of proto-Indo-European characteristic.

In their clear expression of order among the objective world by lingual form, modern Western languages are far more developed than Sanskrit and Western classical languages. In case of sentences of judgment, the latter maintain no distinction between subject and predicate in their grammatical form, while the former maintain it. For example, in sentences like 'mountains are high', 'trees are green', etc., the predicate adjective agrees with the subject in gender, number and case, in Greek and Latin, as is also the case in Sanskrit and other ancient Indian languages. In these languages, the consciousness of assimilation or identification of both ideas contained in the subject and in the predicate is conspicuous. On the other hand, in modern languages the predicate adjective has no declension. (Diese Bäume sind grün; these trees are green, this tree is green.) It signifies that in modern Western languages the subject and predicate are expressed in distinction to each other in their functions, though the concordance of both parts in judgment is recognized on the one hand.

That Indian tendency which tends to alienate the objective natural world and to live in the world of meditation also characterizes the Indian art. Coomaraswamy says in effect that Indian artists had never used models but imagination in making sculptures. This method, which was accepted, no doubt, unconsciously at the beginning, was authorised by rules in a scripture called *Śukranītiśāstra.*[19] Indeed ancient sculptures as seen in Sānchī (3rd-2nd cent. B.C.) are fairly realistic and sensual, but the character of arts gradually changed into fantasy in the course of time.

---

1) *Aṅgāḥ Kaliṅgāḥ, Pañcālā ramaṇīyāḥ* (Kāśikā ad *Pāṇini* I, 2, 52).

2) When a clear expression of 'A as B' is required, they express B in the instrumental case. e.g. "*dautyena gacchati*". (he goes as a messenger.) (*dautya*<*dūta*) Mostly, however, the instrumental case is shown by '*-tvena*' (*-tva*, a suffix making the abstract noun).

3) *Kathaṃ so 'nuśiṣṭo bruvīta* (*Chānd. Up.* V, 3, 4)="wie könnte er sagen, er wäre ausgelernt". Cf. Speyer: *Vedische und Sanskrit-Syntax,* S. 56 §186, S. 94 § 293.

4) Speyer: *op. cit.* S. 84 § 271.

5) Sometimes a sentence starts with an indirect narration but changes into direct narration on the way. Sometimes both kinds of narration are used side by side. Such examples are observed in the *Mahābhārata* and the *Rāmāyaṇa*. (Speyer: *op. cit.* S. 92 § 288.)

6) On this point, Latin is similar to Sanskrit.

7) For example, "*evaṃ mā kánīyāṃsam eva vadhāt kṛtvā*" (*ś. Br.* III, 6, 3, 8) is translated by Speyer into "nachdem er mich kleiner gemacht hatte, als dass ich getroffen werden könnte".

8) Harushige Kōzu 高津春繁: *Hikaku-gengo-gaku* (比較言語學 Comparative *Philology*), p. 308, n. 1.

9) *Maitrāyaṇī-Saṃhitā* 2, 3, 6; Delbrück: *Altindische Syntax* 41; Speyer: *op. cit.* § 258.

10) Speyer: *op. cit.* S. 81–82.

11) Speyer: *op. cit.* § 66; M. Winternitz: *Geschichte der indischen Litteratur* II, S. 52; H. Oldenberg: *Buddha*, S. 211.

12) *Ch'u-san-tsang-chi-chi-hsü* 出三藏記集序, vol. VIII, 摩訶鉢羅若波羅蜜經抄序 (Preface to the Selections from the *Mahāprajnāpāramitāsūtra*). He also says: "(In Indian scriptures) when a subject has been described and another subject is going to be explained, they repeat the same sentences used for the previous subject before entering into the new subject. While (in China) the whole (repetition) is omitted". (*ibid.*)

13) Kogatsuin Jinrei 香月院深厲: *Kyōgyōshinshō Kōgi* 教行信證講義 (Bukkyō Taikei Edition 佛教大系), p. 367.

14) This tendency is prominent in Jain scriptures of a little later days such as '*Ovavāiya*', and in inscriptions of c. 2nd cent. A.D. kept in Buddhist cave temples.

15) Coins of Spalirises, a Parthian king, have the following inscriptions "βασιλεως ἀδελφοῦ Σπαλιρισου" at the head, and "*maharajabhrata dhramiasa Śpaliriśasa*" at the tail, respectively. (Sten Konow: *Kharoṣṭhī Inscriptions*, Introd. p. xli). Likewise, some coins of the King Azēs have the following inscription "βασιλέως βασιλέων μεγάλου Αζου", *maharajasa* (or *rajatirajasa*) *mahatasa Ayasa*". (Sten Konow: *op. cit.* p. xxxix) Coins of King Maues are of a similar inscription to those of Azēs. (Rapson: *Indian Coins*), Plate I. no. 15.

16) H. Oldenberg: *Die Lehre der Upanishaden und die Anfänge des Buddhismus*. S. 49, Anm.

17) A. C. Woolner: *Introduction to Prakrit*, p. 12.

18) At the beginning of the *Karpūramañjarī*, a stage-director asks his assistance why Prakrit and not Sanskrit is used in the drama, and receives the following answer: "Sanskrit verses sound stiff, but Prakrit verses sound smooth. The difference between both languages is like the difference between that of a man and a woman".

19) Ānanda K. Coomaraswamy: *History of Indian and Indonesian Art*; Japanese translation by Chikyō Yamamoto 山本智教: *Indo oyobi Tōnan Ajiya Bijutsu-shi* (印度及東南亜細亜美術史), p. 40.

(2) Imagination which ignores natural law

Divested of the concept of order of his natural world environment, there is a tendency among the Indians not to be fully conscious of differentiating between the actual and the ideal or between the fact and the imagination or fantasy. "If there were a place where the dreams of ideal existence possessed of by mankind since his early life were to be realized on earth, that is India".[1]

To the Westerners, God is believed to exist in the high Heaven, while to the Chinese, the Heaven (天) is a place situated above. However, the Indian Buddhists thought of the Buddhas of the past, present and future to live in all conrners of this universe, including the worlds above and beneath this world. The Buddhas live even beneath the earth. In contrast to the imaginations of other ethnic groups which conceived of a divinity within the limits of a visible world, the Indian imagination transcended the bounds of world concepts.

The extremity of Indian fantasy is found in the concept of numbers. A very long unit of period is called a *kalpa* (eon), whose duration is beyond our ability of expression. It is said that, even if there were a man of longevity who would rub the mountain of 40 square *yojanas* with a smooth cloth once for every 100 years until the mountain exists no more, a *kalpa* period could not be exhausted. Or it is said that if a man of longevity were to take a poppy seed once for every hundred years out of the mass of seed filled in a big castle of 40 square *yojanas, a kalpa* period would not come to an end even though the seeds in the castle are exhausted.[2] They also speak of a practice lasting for 3 *mahā-asaṃkyea-kalpas,* which are a period equivalent to 3 (10^{60}) *kalpas,*[3] for a man to attain Buddhahood. On the other hand, they conceive of *kṣaṇa,* ashort unit of time, which is again divided several times into smaller units.

One of prominent characteristics of Indian ways of thinking is that it is saturated with an extreme abundance of imagination, and often leads them to ignore the limits placed upon our world environment with regards to time and space. This tendency is particularly marked in the Mahāyāna scriptures and the *Purāṇas.* Vimalakīrti in the *Vimalakīrti-nirdeśa* is said to have welcomed 32 thousands of monks to his small room by means of his super-natural power. Once when Buddha Śākyamuni was preaching the *Saddharmapuṇḍarīkā* (the Lotus Sūtra) at Mt. Gṛdhrakūṭa, it is said that a tower, which was 500 *yojanas* high and 250 sq. *yojanas* decorated with jewels and in which the holy relics of the entire Tathāgata Prabhūta were kept, emerged from the earth all at once, and that from it voices praising the sermon of Śākyamuni and recognizing the authority of the *Saddharmapuṇḍarīkā* were heard. In dealing with these fantasies, the Indians never cared of the contradictions which existed with regards to the description of time and space. They ignored the laws of nature and remained unperturbed. That mythology relates matters which are in contradiction to the natural law of time and space is a phenomenon which can be observed in any country; however, in the case of the Indian's it is one of extremity. They carelessly refer to such big numbers as million, billion, 'as many as the number of the sands of the Gangetic river', etc. It transcends the realm of imagination, crushing and paralysing the ability of expression.

Among the Hindu scriptures, the *Purāṇas* are particularly fantasic in its expression. For example, the myth of the miraculous power of the child Kṛṣṇa is typically Indian in character. The whole story is full of fantasies and the heroic feature of Kṛṣṇa is described with qualities which is beyond human imagination. This myth corresponds exactly to the mental atomosphere created in the Indian paintings and sculptures, of which we are astonished to witness their portrayal of the fantasic and illusional qualities. The rich and sensuous illusion that is typically Indian emerges out from this myth and drives us to a state of great astonishment.

Such extreme imagination often sweeps away historic facts. E. Senart, a famous Indologist of France, was of the opinion that the biography of the Buddha was nothing but a kind of solar-myth. Here is well observed the difference between the Indians' fantasic character and the Westerners' realistic character. Indians' fantasic character also checked the development of natural science in India. Even chemistry, which is said to have developed first in India, inevitably changed into a kind of magic.

Furthermore, the Indians never made a conscious effort to check such an extravagant development of fantasy. They are extremely sensitive. They response immediately to all the impulses or impressions, real or illusory, brought on from the outer world, and create fantasies one after another. But they are completely passive towards such impulses or impressions, and never try to force their will on them. It may be said that they have nerves, but no muscles.

Referring to this characteristic of the Indian ways of thinking, Romain Rolland said as follows: "Please don't compare Western 'realism' to Indian 'idealism'! There are two kinds of realism. The Indians are by nature *réalisateurs*. They are difficult to be satisfied with any abstract idea. It is through physical pleasure and alluring charm that they attain realization".[4]

Tominaga Nakamoto referring to this characteristic of the Indian thought the *'gen'* or *'maboroshi'* (Jap.) (=*māyā*, illusion,) said as follows: "The Indians are habitually very fond of hallucination, which can be compared to the Chinese love of *wên* (文) or 'culture'; he who wishes to establish a school and teach must follow its way, without which he will not be able to win the confidence of the masses".[5] He also remarked, "The learnings of the Indians consist in their pursuit of hallucination without which the people will not follow".[6] Many fantastic narrations are found described in the Buddhist scriptures which are means designed to enlighten the mass.[7]

He quotes the following sentences as the words of a venerable personage: "Magic characterizes Buddhism. It corresponds to *'izuna'* (magic) in present Japan. The Indians are fond of it, and unless it is employed in preaching, there would be no followers. Therefore Śākyamuni must have been a great magician. The purpose of his six years of ascetic practices in the mountain was to learn this magic. The supernatural powers (*abhijñā*) described in the scriptures imply magic. For example, the cases of the manifestation of three thousand worlds delivered from the light emitted from between the eyebrows (*ūrṇa-keśa*), of the vast long tongue reaching the Heaven of the Brahman, of Vimalakīrti's ability to create 84 thousand seats in a small room, or of the goddess who transformed Śāriputra into a woman, are nothing but descriptions of the magical powers in the realm of fantasy. Furthermore, the doctrines on transmigration, on moral causality, stories of marvelous events in previous lives and other curious stories, were means of inducing the people to believe in the newly established doctrine. This is the Indian way of teaching, but is not the way necessary for the Japanese".[8] If we were to follow this view, the theory on hell and paradise constitutes but a means.[9] Criticizing this opinion, Tominaga said: "Inspite of the venerable's opinion, *abhijñā* is different from *izuna*. *Izùna* is merely a matter of technique, while *abhijñā* is the result of the practice of meditation. Nevertheless his words stand with reason". Thus Tominaga believed that the miraculous power was attained by practice and it was this aspect which characterized Indian Buddhism.

If we were to examine the views held by the Indian Buddhists on this matter, we find, for example, the following words of Nāgārjuna: "There is a man of evil nature, who, possessed of a jealous mind, slanderously says, 'the Buddha's wisdom is not beyond that of the mortals; he misleads the world by means of magic'. The Buddha manifested the infinite divine power and the infinite wisdom power for the purpose of severing one from such a state of mind".[10] Nāgārjuna further remarked, "A bird without feather cannot fly. Likewise, the Bodhisattvas without the miraculous power cannot lead the people".[11] Thus, Nāgārjuna, himself, was of opinion that the Buddhas and the Bodhisattvas were actually endowed with miraculous faculties far powerful than those of the heretics.

Such a way of thinking naturally met a reaction. The materialists of India strongly opposed the doctrine of miraculous power, while the natural philosophers ignored it completely.

Indian myths and legends of fantastic character were not accepted by the Greeks. Ambassador Megasthenēs who was sent by a Syrian king to the court of Indian Emperor Candragupta at about 300 B.C., wrote the "*Ta Indika*", a record on India of those days based upon his experiences, of which a few fragments are preserved today. These fragments, which are today estimated as valuable materials for the study of ancient India, contain a lot of myths and legends held in India of those days. According to modern studies, these myths and legends are proved to be identical to those described in the *Mahābhārata* and the *Purāṇa* literatures.[12] In his days, however, the Greeks who had read his report did not believe it at all.[13] Not only was his report, but also those descriptions of India by Déimakhos, Onesikritōs, Nearkhos and others were also generally criticized by the historian Strabōn as being unfactual.[14] The Greeks thought of those myths and legends, spoken seriously by Indians, as fantasies and of no value at all.

The same criticism is held by modern Europeans. Hegel said: "Sensual evidence is of no value, because to the Indians, generally speaking, there is no sensual perception. Everything is reformed into fantasic images, and any kind of dream is regarded as truth and reality".[15] Kern, a famous scholar on Buddhism, thought that when an Indian conceives of an image in meditation, he seems to lose distinction between that image and the phenomenon of the objective world. "Buddhists are idealists, they maintain no clear distinction between phenomenal facts based upon observation and the products of fantasy....... The world is created by meditation (*dhyāna*)".[16] It may be dangerous to generalize the Buddhist way of thinking in this way, but it is true that such a tendency did exist among some Buddhists.

Among the later Vedantists, a school developed which held that by realizing the realm of the undifferentiated by means of meditation, the world of the phenomena could be eliminated; that, they conceived, was emancipation (*mokṣa*). This theory was called *'prapañca-vilaya-vāda'*, i.e. the theory of the disappearance of the phenomena. In the Upanishads, frequent command is made in terms of 'the Ātman should be conceived like this'. It is a command to eliminate the realm of the phenomena (*prapañca-vilaya*). In other words the dualistic contradiction indicative of the phenomenal world constitutes 'an obstacle to the realization of the truth (*tattvāvabodha-pratyanīka-bhūta*)'; thus, emancipation is realized only after the obstacle has been eliminated. This theory was often referred to as heterodoxical in the later Vedantic works. Śaṅkara, too, denied it.[17] His criticism is as follows: If the elimination of the phenomena meant the extinction of our natural world, that is a statement of absurdity; if, on the other hand, it meant the extinction of illusion which is a product of our ignorance, it is not a matter which could be realized by a 'command' but through 'understanding'. However, the real intent of those who maintained this theory was to 'command' a series of negation and thereby to enable realization that Ātman is of no-character (*nirguṇa*), e.g., in the scripture, it is commanded, "conceive Ātman as A", "conceive Ātman as B". etc., in which case, by conceiving Ātman as A, Ātman is being negated as B, similarly, by conceiving Ātman as B, Ātman is being negated as A, etc. As can be seen, the theory here expressed was, more or less, similar to that held by Śaṅkara.[18] Of course, such a view was not necessarily held by the Indians in general, but it does reveal that the Indians have had established such a thought pattern, a pattern which can be recognized as one of their characteristics of the ways of thinking.

This pattern of thought is quite significant in that it provides men develling in the darkness of reality with light and hope for the future, but because there is no grasping of the distinction between the real and the ideal, it lacks the forces of rational control of the matters of the world of reality. The Indians maintained an infinite desire for pleasure and profiting, but did not develop a system of capitalistic economy. "An unlimited desire for profiting is not necessarily identical to capitalism, nor is it of the same 'spirit'. On the contrary, capitalism requires the repression of the irrational forces of desire, or at least the controlling of these forces."[19] Of course, it was not only the Indians who lacked the rational forces".[19] Of course, it was not only the Indians who lacked the rational capitalism, but it can be reasoned that it was due to the fact that the Indians did not think much of controlling matters of this world that hindered their development of capitalism.

Not only is there recognized the difference between the social and economic systems of modern India and the West, but also in the ways of thinking in the mediaeval periods of these two areas with regards to social principles. Even European Scholastics who, from the views of modern men, discussed meaningless and uninteresting problems in detail, nevertheless, dealt with matters of 'control' with regards to state and society (e.g. Thomas Aquinas). On the other hand, although the conservative Buddhist scholars of mediaeval India likewise discussed many complex problems as indicated in the Abhidharma literature, nevertheless, did not greatly concern themselves with the problems of state or social structure. They engaged themselves to the discussions pertaining to mental cultivation and sheer fantasy. Both Hīnayāna and Mahāyāna Buddhism discussed in detail the problems pertaining to the rebirth of mankind in which cyclic process was considered possible to accumulate work necessary for salvation. It is felt that men who had engaged themselves to the narration of this process were those who had lived in a world entirely different from ours.

There might be some objection to the above statement in that Mahāyāna Buddhism had dealt in considerable length with the problem of the state.[20] However, it is to be noted that Mahāyāna Buddhism can not be considered to be representative of the thoughts of the Indians in general; it reveals only one characteristic aspect of Indian thoughts. The governing class of India supported the traditionally conservative Buddhism, and the state concept of Mahāyāna Buddhism revealed nothing more than a reaction against it. Realistic ideas of state and government were dealt with by the more secular Brahmins, while the more catholic religions of Buddhism and Jainism tended to escape from secular matters.

---

1) Romain Rolland: *La vie de Ramakrishna*, p. 31.

2) *Ta-chih-tu-lun* (大智度論 *Mahāprajñāpāramitā-śāstra*), vol. 5.

3) *Hua-yen-wu-chiao-chang* (華嚴五教章) of Fa-tsang (法藏) (Kwannō 觀應 Edition), Part b–2, p. 48b.

4) Romain Rolland: *op. cit.* p. 56.

5) Tominaga Nakamoto 富永仲基: *Shutsujō-kōgo* (出定後語), Pt. 1, Chap. 8 Jinzū (神通).

6) *Ibid.*

7) "Heretics of those days, too, preached doctrines by means of fantasy". "In the Tripiṭaka, there are lot of illustrations on fantasy. It is because Indians have many experiences of fantasy in their life and they are fond of it". "Heretics called it illusion (*māyā*), while Buddhist called it miraculous faculty (*abhijñā*). In reality, both are one and the same". "Illustrations such as a poppy-seed and Mt. Sumeru, the net of Indra are also beloved by the people". (*ibid.* Chap. 8).

8) *Okina-no-fumi* 翁の文, Chap. 14.
9) "And those doctrines on moral causality, on Hell and Paradise, were originally of other religions (outside of Buddhism). They were beloved by Indians". (*op. cit.* "*Shutsujō-kōgo*," Chap. 8).
10) "*Ta-chih-tu-lun*" 大智度論, Vol. 1 (*Taishō.* vol. 25, p. 58b.)
11) *Ibid.*, vol. 94 (*Taishō.* vol. 25, p. 717b.) cf. vol. 37 (*Taishō.* vol. 25, p. 332a.)
12) Cf. "Megasthenēs" (by O. Stein), in Pauly-Wissowa's *Realenzyklopädie.*
13) J. W. McCrindle: *Ancient India,* Introd. pp. 18–21.
14) *Ibid.* p. 20.
15) Hegel: *Vorlesungen über die Geschichite der Philosophie,* hrsg. von Michelet, S. 154.
16) Kern: *Manual of Indian Buddhism,* p. 57.
17) Śaṅkara ad *BS.* III, 2, 21 (vol. II, p. 217, *l.* 5 ff.)
18) Cf. Hiriyanna; (*Prapañcavilayavāda,* a Doctrine of Pre-Śaṅkara Vedanta in *Journal of Oriental Research Madras*), vol. I, 1927, p. 109 ff.
19) Max Weber: *Aufsätze zur Religionssoziologie,* I, Vorbemerkung S. 4.
20) The *Pao-hang-wang-chêng-lun* (*Ratnāvali*) 寶行王正論 attributed to Nāgārjuna is a typical one of this kind.

(3) The tendency to resort to extremes

The imagination of Indians ignores the natural limitations of time and space. It is free, boundless and extravagant. And it often goes to extremes.

And as they do not fully realize the distinctions between realities and dreams, they continue to seek after their dreams even within the bounds of reality. Their behavior is thoroughgoing. An Indian epicurean absorbs his whole soul and body in pleasure-seeking. And an ascetic in India leads a very austere life in the woods.[1] The Buddhist advocation of the middle path detached either from enjoyment or from self-affliction is an exceptional case in this country.[2]

The radical conservatives of the Jain monks were called '*Digambara*—the sky-clad'. They went about completely naked, or in other words, 'clothed in space'. They said: 'Our body is a cover of the Ātman. The garments are the outer coverings of that covered Ātman. To lessen the coverings of the Ātman, we do not wear a garment'.[3] And Jains praised as a master of the highest virtue the monk who killed himself observing a fast. One of their sacred books gives a detailed description of the saints' death by starvation.[4]

The Greeks set a high value on the virtue of moderation. They hold, as the words of the sage Solon, a maxim of 'not anything too much (μηδὲν ἄγαν; *ne quid nimis*). In China, too, the middle-of-the-road is one of the essential virtues in their ethics. Indians, on the other hand, are likely to go to extremes. The idea of the golden mean (*aurea mediocritas*) has not developed in this land with only one exception of the Buddhist advocation of *the middle path.*

As a result of this feature of their way of thinking, Indians are inclined to idealize and to consecrate the great men in their history to the utmost. This offers a sharp contrast to the Western trend to avert over-sanctification of their great heroes. In India, as in other countries, there are many biographies of great men. Especially the sagas of the saints are quite numerous. And the stories described in such books are very wild and fantastic. They are myths rather than the life-stories of the heroes. And in India the legendary heroes ,such as Kṛṣṇa, have been deified exceedingly in the course of time. At the origin, the stories of Kṛṣṇa described the hero's human affairs such as his birth, his childhood, his romances, his fights and his victories in a realistic style. But, as the stories were handed down among people, they resorted to the fantastic description and finally, Kṛṣṇa was deified and became the object of enthusiastic savior-worship.

---

1) An ascetic of the Yoga lies on the floor covered with projecting nails. By such hard exercise, he tries to accomplish the subjugation of the body to the control of his will. And further, as for the control of the mind, it is stated: "With such an indefatigable effort as to drain off the ocean scooping up its water with the cusp of a leaf, the control of the mind should be accomplished". *Māṇḍūkyā-Kārikā* III, 41.
2) Judging from the old *gāthās*, Buddhists too in the earliest period of their history encouraged their followers to lead an austere life of mortification.
3) *Sarvasiddhāntasaṃgraha* III, 12.
4) M. Winternitz: *A History of Indian Literature*, vol. II, p. 452.

(4) Fondness for myths and poetry

Indians are very fond of myths and the poetical forms of expression. And this is a natural result of their inclination to idealize the actual phases of human life. Indians try to beautify the realities and to observe the hard facts of reality from a detached standpoint.

From the time of the *Ṛg-Veda* up to present, for more than three thousand years, Indians have never ceased creating new myths. And many myths thus produced come from one source. The gods in the Epics of the *Mahābhārata* and the *Rāmāyaṇa* are the gods of the Vedas. The Vedic myths find continuance in and are revived in the legends of the Epics. The legends of the Epics are in turn assimilated in the *Purāṇas*. And the legends formed in the modern age are based on the myths transmitted in this way. Indians have always been tolerant toward the myths of the older ages. Sometimes the myths of older origin are heterogenous to their own. But, even in that case they have included them in their mythological system.

The Chinese are limited in their development of mythology while their achievements in the historical works are very remarkable. Indians, on the contrary, have produced an abundance of myths, but their documents of history are quite few in number. And the books of history and the sagas written in India are all embellished with mythological overtones. In their works it is difficult to distinguish the historical facts from the outputs of their imagination.

Even in philosophical discourses, mythical explanations and metaphors are frequently used. The philosophers of India follow the rules of methaphysical and logical reasoning within their own particular circle. But in order to afford a better understanding of their theories to the common man, they are willing to resort to mythical ways of explanation. It has been recognized that the philosophers of the Upaniṣads resorted to this means of instruction. Uddālaka Āruṇi, for instance, explains the relation between ultimate entity, which he terms 'being (*sat*)', and all other beings by resorting to various allegories.[1]

And the Greeks noticed this Indian affection for myths and poems. Megasthenēs stated in ca. 300 B.C. as follows: ".... like Plato, they (the Brahmins) weave into the fabric of myths (μύθος) the (philosophical) problems as to the immortality of the soul or the judgment after the death".[2] Thus Megasthenēs found a resemblance to Plato in the figurative explanation of the philosophical issues as found in the Upaniṣads.

The Epics, the Purāṇas and the texts of Mahāyāna Buddhists, all resort to the allegorical method in order to explain their doctrines. The Lotus Sūtra is called 'the king of all the Sūtras' and it is really a representative text of the Mahāyāna. And we wonder what other elements would remain in this Sūtra if we were to remove the elements of allegory and of the stories explaining the past origin of the present events. Indian philosophers consider allegories (*dṛṣṭānta*) to be indispensable in explaining their thought even when they are pursuing their arguments in accordance with rules of logical reasoning.

Indians are a poetry-loving people. Since the ancient period, many poems of a high artistic standard have been composed in this country.

Besides, great works in the diverse fields of religion, philosophy, politics, laws, economics, mathematics and other sciences employ the verse form. And since the oldest days, Indians like to count numerically not by means of numbers but by using names; that is, common nouns. For instance, by "the moon" or 'the earth' they mean 'one' and by 'the eyes' or 'the wings' they mean 'two'. And this manner of counting has grown into a very complicated one. At the most, they have for a certain numerical figure fifty ways of expression by means of various nouns. It is noteworthy that they have adopted this method of counting simply to satisfy the need for a rich vocabulary for rhyming in their literature. This is distinctly one result of the Indian adherence to the verse even in their scientific works.

And Indians are very fond of reciting the verses. At present, at various parts of India, many 'parties of poetry' are held. These many poets gather together to read their poems in front of an enthusiastic audience. And one of the general characteristics of today's Indian periodicals is their custom of devoting a considerable number of pages to poems.

Indians have much in common with the Western Romanticists in their way of thinking. For instance, they hold in common a longing, or more properly speaking, a vague and undefined attraction toward the infinite, distant and supernatural being. It is natural, therefore, that many Romanticists of the West interested themselves in Indian thought and engaged themselves in introducing this new thought to their own world. Geothe spoke in the highest terms Kālidāsa's *Śakuntalā*. August Wilhelm von Schlegel (1765–1845) translated the *Bhagavadgītā* into Latin. Wilhelm von Humboldt read this Latin translation and extolled it highly. He said that it is the most beautiful and the sole philosophical poem ever known in the world literature, and he was thankful for the good luck to see this book.[3] Friedrich von Schlegel, a younger brother of W. v. Schlegel, wrote a book in 1808 which is one of the most significant works in the history of the German Romanticism. (*Über die Sprache und Weisheit der Inder,* 1808). A. Schopenhauer, who was influenced much by the Indian philosophy was one of the philosophers of Romanticism. A successor of his thoughts, Paul Deussen, became absorbed in the study of the philosophies of India. And Graf von Keyserling who was also deeply interested in Indian thought, once stated that "the savior of the spiritual and material disorder of the world after the World War I is the ideal of the Bodhisattva".[4]

Indian thought is a romanticism with both the virtues and the defects inherent to this system of thought.

1) Cf. *Chāndogya-Up.*, VI.
2) Megasthenēs, *The Fragments*, 41.
3) Cf. M. Winternitz: *Geschichte der indischen Litteratur*, I, S. 16; 17; 366.
4) Cf. G. H. Keyserling: *Reisetagebuch eines Philosophen*, finis.

(5) Lack of historical consciousness

All Indian books of history, which are on the whole very few in number, are tinged with a fantastic and lengendary color. They are not products of historical science but rather works of art. Usually they are written in *verse.* Indians are not satisfied with the simple and naïve description of facts, the language of daily use. From the artistic viewpoint, Indians beautify the past and try to idealize it. They ignore precise figures, the sequences of events and other prosaic details relating to the time and the place where the events took place. Furthermore, to give full play to the imagination, they exaggerate the figures astronomically and stretch the truth with their magnificent and brilliant style of hyperbole. Like many of their sculptures, their historical works are far from the reality of things but are the products of their fantasy.

The *Mahāvaṃsa* is the most elaborate and reliable work of history ever accomplished in Ceylon. And even this book is covered with a mysterious and legendary atmosphere. For instance, though Mahānāman, the author of this book, lived in the fifth century—in an age not too distant from the time of King Duṭṭhagāmani's reign, his descriptions of this greatest ruler in the history of the island are full of mythical and legendary elements, and therefore, a careful distinction must be made between myth and that which is historically true. We know that the histories of the monks (Mönschchronik) in Medieval Europe and the biographies of eminent Buddhist monks in China and Japan have a similar element. But, to a degree incomparable to these cases, the *Mahāvaṃsa* goes far beyond the bounds of historical truth.

Kalhaṇa's *Rājataraṅgiṇī* is the chronicle of a Kashmirian dynasty. This is one of the best historical works ever written by Indians. In it, Kalhaṇa details the social situation of his time and the activities of the various characters in it with the accuracy that no other Indian book of history has attained. But, still, the poetic and emotional atmosphere pervades the whole of this historical work. To quote Oldenberg: "If one removes all the poetic elements from Kalhaṇa's story, and compares it with things of the time, he will find that the story is in essence on the level not higher than that of a more or less accurate article in a newspaper or a cartoon in a political comic paper. The process of formation that this story has undergone is not that of the historical thinking but of poetry—poetry in the Indian sense with its brilliant quality and also with its weakness. And Kalhaṇa himself has a very distinct idea on this point; he feels himself as a poet and he is a poet".[1] And Kalhaṇa scarcely pays heed to historical or causal sequence when considering historical events. His mentions of dates are inaccurate and sometimes they are the products of pure imagination.

In all the Indian documents of the past, little significance has been attached to the books of history. Indians are much more interested in religion and in poetry than in historical documentation. For Indians, a minor error in the recitation of the Vedas is a serious matter. But, they are thoroughly indifferent to the erroneous recording of dates or of facts in their books of history.[2] And this unhistorical character of the Indian way of thinking is distinctly observed in the Buddhist attitude to the rules of their order. Buddhists in the period after the death of the Buddha had to establish new precepts for their body in order to meet the changing social conditions. As some of the rules newly established by them were not compatible with the older ones, they hesitated to include their new rules in the old and traditional books of ordination (*pāṭimokkha*), and managed to attach them to the *pāṭimokkhas* as supplements.[3] They, however, dared to claim the authority of the Buddha's own teaching even to these supplementary precepts of their own creation, completely ignoring historical evidence. *Their concern for the proper observance of the precepts and of the rites preceded and was stronger than their regard for historical accuracy.* And here the historical facts were completely ignored.

The Chinese derive their rules of social conduct from the examples of their ancestors as described in their books of history. Indians, on the other hand, gain their principles of behavior from their religious books and, at the same time, *the fables* and *the parables* such as the *Pañcatantra* and the *Hitopadeśa* contribute toward the diffusion of practical morals into the daily life of the Indian people.[4] To quote Oldenberg again on the unhistorical character of the Indians, he states as follows: ". . . . but, should we blame Indians for no other reason that they are Indians? The Indian folk-spirit would not have been what it was without the unhistorical character. For the formation of their folk-spirit, the factors other than the historical value had the decisive power".[5]

---

1) Cf. H. Oldenberg: *Aus dem alten Indien*, S. 93.
2) In India, there is no uniform system of marking historical eras. Their method of determining historical periods differ according to time and place. According to a historian, there are more than twenty ways of marking the eras in India. This fact presents a great contrast to the uniform adoption in the West of the Christian era. Cf. V. A. Smith: *The Early History of India*, p. 20.
3) H. Oldenberg: *Buddha*, S. 385.
4) Cf. *Pañcatantra*, *Hitopadeśa* and Buddhist *Jātaka* tales. Jains also have what they call *Jātakas*.
5) H. Oldenberg: *Aus dem alten Indien*, S. 107.

(6) The concept of truth

The Indian concept of *truth* is different from that of the Westerner. *Satya* is the oldest Sanskrit equivalent for truth. And as we have mentioned above, in the Upaniṣads of the early days *dharma* is considered to be identical with *satya*. From this fact, we become aware of the difference in the concept of *truth* as held by the ancient Indians and the modern people. The ancient Indians did not find truth in the agreement of subjective knowledge with the objective order, nor in the universally valid knowledge, but rather, they sought truth in the practice of ethics; that is in the observance of rules of conduct. In other words, they sought complete accordance or oneness with ethics, and they considered this to be the truth.

Later on, another word *tattva* came in use together with *satya* to mean *truth*. And, in addition to these two words, Buddhists had their unique term *tathatā* also to mean *truth*.[1] The original meaning of *tattva* is "that-ness" and *tathatā*, "such-ness". Truth in the ancient Indian concept is no other than "to be that" or "to be such". They indicated truth by "that" or "such" — the terms of the simplest prescription of the object. In other words, *truth exists where all forms of discrimination have been negated*. And *satya* means "being" or "relating to being". Generally speaking, Indians are inclined to take an ontological view, and not an epistemological view, of truth. Of course, it is wrong to assume that the philosophies of India are all tinged with one color. Nevertheless, it is not incorrect to affirm that the ontological view has been dominant in this country.

In the West, on the other hand, many philosophers have found truth in the agreement of knowledge and its object. Kant, for instance, stated as follows: "If truth consists in the agreement of knowledge with its object, that object must thereby be distinguished from other objects; for knowledge is false, if it does not agree with the object to which it is related, even although it contains something which may be valid of other objects".[2] Although this view of Kant was criticized by Hegel and others, we can safely say that the Kantian view of truth has been always predominant in the West. And this trend can be traced back as far as the ancient Greeks. The Greek equivalent of truth is "ἀλήθεια". The original meaning of this word is "not to be hidden", "to be known as it is" or "to be noticed". It comes from the negative form of the verb "λανθάνω", which means "to escape notice", or "to be unknown". This Greek concept of truth is based on their idea of the relationship between the subjective knower and the known object.

Of course, in the West too, there are some philosophers who have tried to indentify "truth" with "being". At least in their manner of expression, we are able to discern cases of such indentification, unconsciously made. In Greek, "truth (ἀλήθεια)" is sometimes used in the same sense with "being (οὐσία)".[3] And the German word *wahr* is said to have an etymological connection with "Wesen".[4] However, in the history of Western thought such concepts were rarely expressed with clear intention.

---

1) Hsüan-chuang (玄奘) translated *tattva* by the words "眞實" or "眞實義" and *tathatā* by "眞如" or "如". Cf. Hsüan-chuang's translation ad *Bodhisattvabhūmi*, p. 212, *l.* 12; p. 37; p. 39. *Tattva* is used also to mean the order of nature. Cf. *Vākyapadīya* III, 3, 3; *Nala* XVI, 38 (*tattvena hi mamācakṣva*); *Saura-Purāṇa*, a. 4 (in Gonda: *Sanskrit Reader*, p. 65, *l.* 3), *brūhi me tattvataḥ*.

2) *Immanuel Kant's Critique of Pure Reason*, tr. by Norman Kemp Smith, p. 97.

3) This is written by the suggestion of Prof. Kumatarō Kawada 川田熊太郎.

4) Cf. Pinloche: *Etymologisches Wörterbuch*.

(7) Non-development of natural sciences

In India, studies of the natural world have remained underdeveloped. The ancient Greeks were aware of this fact. "As to the nature (φύσις), on the other hand, the statements [of Indians] are very simple and innocent. This is said by him [Megasthenēs]. The reason is that they are skilled in practice (ἔργοι) rather than in argument (λόγοι) and that they accept as true what is said in the myths (μύθος)".[1] Of course, it is an overstatement to state that there is no natural science in this country. The ancient Indians developed their own astronomy chiefly in relation to the Vedic rites. And in their texts of incantations and ceremonies, a remarkable degree of knowledge is revealed in regard to the structure of the human body.[2] Their medical science developed into many branches of specialities. And it is said that chemistry arose in this country earlier than in any other country. In the third century B.C. and thereafter their mathematics, astronomy and chemistry were greatly stimulated by the introduction of the Greek sciences.[3] But, Indians ended in adopting and imitating the Greeks and there was no further development of their own science. The scientific approach to problems failed to develop in this country.

Indians set a high value on learning. But they are not satisfied with the mere knowledge of substances which are in themselves limited in time and space. They emphasize the being existing behind and beyond such substances—the subjective entity or the Universal Being. Greek philosophy started as a study of nature (φύσις). Indian philosophy, on the other hand, from the beginning has sought the being which transcends nature. As G. Misch pointed out, Indian philosophy is *metaphysical* in marked contrast to the Greek concern for the physical world.[4]

Western metaphysics has developed in correspondence with their physical science (*ta physika*). Western metaphysics is, or was at least up to the eighteenth century, the study of or the inquiry into the ultimate principles of 'being'. Thus as the study of the principles innately attributed to 'being', the Western metaphysics established their own field of study clearly distinguished from natural science. And we can see a good example of this in the Scholastic study of 'being'. In India, however, they did not and do not consider metaphysics in contradistinction to physical science. The ultimate goal of Indian philosophy (*darśana*) is to seek the ultimate principles of universal nature and therefore, they do not pay special regard to natural science. The Indians include metaphysics and natural science together in one idea—learning in general (*vidyā*). And they are unwilling to acknowledge natural science as an independent field of study distinguished from metaphysics. Even in the naturalistic philosophy of the Nyāya and the Vaiśeṣika, natural science held no independent position. Uddālaka and the scholars of the Vedānta regarded 'being' as the ultimate source of truth like the Greek philosophers. But it should be noted here that there is an essential difference between the Greeks and Indians in respect to the concept of 'being'. For the Indians, *'being'* is Ātman and essentially it is *identical with the subjective knower.* 'Being' as conceived by the Indians is not objective but subjective; herein, lies the great difference between the Indians and Greeks.

Kauṭilya's *Arthaśāstra* classify knowledge into four groups: 1) philosophy (*ānvīkṣikī*); 2) study of the Vedas (*trayī*); 3) economics (*vārttā*); 4) study of laws (*daṇḍanitī*). In his system, no independent significance is recognized for natural science. Probably he includes the study equivalent to natural science in our sense of the term in the third group *vārttā* because it serves to make our lives easy and comfortable just like economics. And his system of classification has been accepted by the Indian philosophers of later ages.[5] Buddhists classify knowledge into five groups: 1) study of language (*śabda-vidyā*); 2) studies of technology and calendar (*śilpakarmasthāna-vidyā*); 3) medicine, pharmacy and also the study of charm (*cikitsā-vidyā*); 4) logic (*hetu-vidyā*); 5) study of the Buddhist doctrines (*adhyātma-vidyā*).[6] The second and the third groups above mentioned belong to what we call natural science. But, it should be noted that Buddhists established this system of classification only from a practical concern. They had no idea of natural science unique and independent from other fields of studies.[7] In India of later periods, knowledge comes to be classified into more elaborate and smaller groups. And all the systems of classification follow the decrees of the Vedas and give priority to the Vedas. And no endeaver was made to establish natural science as a separate field of study.

The Indian studies regarding nature developed somewhat independently of mathematics. And this fact presents a great and basic difference between the Indian concept of natural science and the Western concept, which as we can see in Kant places mathematics at the base of all natural sciences.

Indian philosophy has developed completely divorced from the natural sciences. And this is one reason why epistemology in the modern sense has not grown in this country. Generally speaking, modern Western philosophers hold a different idea on the problem of knowledge from their predecessors of the ancient and the medieval ages. And the philosophers of the Nyāya, the Vedānta and the Mīmāṃsā in India are the same as the Western philosophers of the ancient and medieval ages in their assertion regarding knowledge that truth is in the agreement of knowledge with the substantial being to which it is related. Together with these philosophers, there were others who refused to acknowledge any substantial being. Buddhists were the representative of the latter. Both in their rejection of the concept of a self-existent substance and in their idea of the opposition of 'the subjective knower' and 'the object', the Buddhist view is common to the epistemological standpoint of the modern Western philosophers. Essentially, however, Western epistemology differs from this ancient Indian theory of knowledge. One of the chief purposes of the modern thinkers of knowledge is to supply a theoretical basis for natural sciences. And to meet this purpose, whether they are conscious or not, they have tried to find a theoretical basis for synthetic *a priori* judgments. It is true that the ancient Indians had a very penetrating insight into the problem of knowledge. Dharmakīrti, for instance, made a clear distinction between synthetic judgments and analytic judgments and he inquired into the functions of these two different types of judgments in actual and concrete cases of inference. But, synthetic judgments in his case are what can be aquired by experience and are not what exist *a priori*. In Dharmakīrti, there existed no factor such as the need for rational sciences which eventually led Kant into his quest for a theoretical basis for synthetic *a priori* judgments. And, though Dhamakīrti is often compared with Kant due to the superficial similarity of their assertions, there is a distinct and essential difference between the two.

A similar characteristic can be observed in logic of Indians. As it is well known, the Greek philosophy originated as a *theōria* on the order of the objective world. And it gradually formed its logic through the study of *logos*. In the case of Indians, on the other hand, it was not the consideration of the nature that led them to the study of logic. Their interest in this study arose from a different source. The need for a correct interpretation of the phrases in the Vedas led the Brahmin scholars to their study on the principles of grammar. And a close examination of the word-forms led them to an analysis of the process of thinking and subsequently, to the study of the categories and to the process of reasoning. Verily, in contrast to the Greeks, Indians became intersted in logic through their study and analysis of language.

Naturally, in India where logic developed for the sake of exegesis, discussion for synthesis between the holders of different opinions could not be expected. And the dialectic in Plato's sense—dialectic which consists of the three processes of discussion between the antagonistic parties, sublation of these different opinions and discovery of a new proposition—was difficult to develop in this country. In the Upaniṣads, the sacred books of the early Buddhists, and the codes of Jains, discussions between a teacher and a disciple, between friends or between a man and his wife are mentioned. In these cases, there is a sharp distinction between he who teaches and he who receives the teachings. The lessons were always one-sided; the teacher taught and the followers accepted his instructions with unthinking obedience. And at this stage there is hardly any interchange of ideas between the two sides. In the books of later periods, controversies between the men of opposing ideas are presented. An old Buddhist sūtra *Pāyāsi-suttanta*,[8] for instance, is a story of a nihilist, Pāyāsi, who was converted to Buddhism by the refutations and persuations of a Buddhist sage, Kumāra Kassapa. And the *Milindapañhā*, which appeared in the second century B.C. or later in the present form bears a strong influence of the Greek 'dialogue'. This is a story of the conversation between Menandoros, a Greek king who reigned over Northern India in the second century B.C., and a Buddhist elder, Nāgasena. It ends with the king's conversion to Buddhism out of respect for the elder. The form of dialogue employed in the *Milindapañhā*, formulated under Greek influence, failed to prevail further in this country. Dialogue was not a form of discussion suitable for the Indian way of thinking.

After the dialogue, a form of debate between two schools came to be employed. In this case, the individual elements of the representative orators were all eliminated. And they did not care who the orators were. At the end of a close and heated battle of words, the victorious party took pride in their victory while the defeated party sank into silence. But, it should be noted, the yielded party continued to hold their former view even after the defeat. And there was in either party no altering of opinion after the debate. Indians, in their stationary view of things, consider truth permanently unchangeable. And they failed to give deep consideration to the process of evolvement or development through dialectics.

The non-development of natural science has determined the economic activities of this country. The natural science of the West with its rationalism based on mathematical calculations has made the growth of modern capitalism technologically possible in the Western world. But, India had no such foundation for its economic development.

1) Megasthenēs, *The Fragments*, 41.
2) Cf. Winterniz: *op. cit.*, III, S. 54.

3) The influence of the Greek sciences upon Indian sciences remains to be clarified by future studies.
4) Cf. G. Misch: *Der Weg in die Philosophie*, passim.
5) Cf. *Yājñavalkya-smṛti* I, 310. The scholars of the Nyāya also accepted as true Kauṭilya's system of classification. Cf. Jacobi: *Sitzungsberichte der Preussischen Akademie*, 1911, S. 733.
6) Cf. 菩薩地持經 vol. III; 菩薩善戒經 vol. IV; 瑜伽師地論 vols. XV, XXXVIII; 大唐西域記 vol. II.
7) It should be remembered here that the Chinese Buddhists in some cases managed to translate these Sanskrit terms by the words, "聲術, *art* of language", "因術, *art* of logic", "内術, *art* of internal doctrines" or like those. In their practical way of thinking, Buddhists understand the learning as the arts. Cf. Hakuju Ui 宇井伯壽: *Indo-tetsugaku Kenkyū* (印度哲學研究) vol. IV, p. 462 f.
8) *Pāyāsi-suttanta*, in *Dīghanikāya* No. 23; 弊宿經 in 長阿含經. The same story can be found in the Jain Sūtra, *Rāyapasenaïjja*; cf. Winternitz: *Geschichte der Indischen Litteratur*, vol. II, S. 307.

Chapter 11. The introspective character of Indian thought: The development of the sciences of inner reflection

As we have examined above, Indians emphasize the universal and also the subjective and personal aspects of the individual being. As a result of such tendencies in their way of thinking, the material-external-objective-sciences are not regarded highly in this country and are doomed to stagnation. The spiritual-introspective-subjective-sciences, on the other hand, are greatly encouraged in this country. Natural sciences and mathematics failed to develop in ancient India.[1] Even later on, although the Greek and the Roman sciences were introduced into this country, these sciences did not take root among the people. On the other hand, subjective and introspective sciences such as linguistics or reflective psychology have made noticeable advancements in India.

Like other primitive tribes, Indians in the early stage of their history believed *language* to be the objective substance. And they identified a word—the name of an object—with the thing it indicates. According to them, there is magical essence in things and language—the names of objects—is endowed with mystic power. Those who know words and have a good command of them are able to control and dominate at will the things themselves. Thus they believed that *knowledge of language* constitutes power. And upon this assumption, they established the elaborate system of the Vedic rites. Some philosophers asserted that language is the ultimate principle of the universe, the master of gods, the ruler of the universe, omnipresent in the universe and unperceivable by the human senses.[2] They did not think *language* merely as a symbolic means for communication of the will, but they acknowledged it as the substantial principle. In this regard, the Indian idea of language in some way corresponds to the Japanese belief in the soul of language.

The Greeks began their study of language chiefly to enhance the beauty of their language. But Indians were led to the study from their belief in the mystic and sacred power in language. In India, therefore, linguistic study started first among the Brahmin scholars. At the earliest stage, they concentrated their efforts on the study of the sentences in the Vedas. But, gradually they extended their study into a systematic analysis of their language, Sanskrit, which was at that time the spoken as well as the literary language. The Sanskrit grammar was first established by Pāṇini in the fourth century B.C. And after the critical modifications added by Kātyāyana, this grammar was completed into the final authoritative form by Patañjali in the second century B.C. The study of the Sanskrit grammar after Patañjali ended in the expatiation of the established doctrines. And except for some growth in the philosophical inquiry of language, they made no advancement from the established grammar.[3]

The ancient Indians in their study of grammar were purely empirical. They analyzed elaborately the forms of the words. This empirical and analytical attitude of the Indian grammarians was due chiefly to the nature of the language with which they dealt. Sanskrit has word-forms more distinct than any of the Western classical languages. The ancient grammarians of India analyzed all the words into three elements: the declensional ending, the stem and the root. And they reduced every word into the corresponding root form. Not all the root forms are proper or correct when re-examined by present methods of comparative grammar. Nevertheless, we are surprised at the thoroughness and consistency of the ancient Indians in their study of grammar. The Western grammarians adopted abstract concepts such as the stem and the root for the analysis of their languages only after the dawn of the Modern Age when they came into contact with the ancient grammar of India.

In the morphological study of language, the ancient Indians had their general and distinct system of various categories. For instance, they made strict distinctions between the primary and the secondary verbal endings. Moreover, they accomplished a very elaborate system of declensions and conjugations. No other ancient nation produced such a detailed system of grammar as we see in India.

In the phonological field they also made a very careful study. They invented a very reasonable and scientific arrangement of the Sanskrit alphabet. They put the vowels first in order and then arranged the consonants. In the West, on the other hand, phonology or the study of sonic elements (τὰ στοιχεία; elementa) never developed sufficiently. Indeed, the Greeks and Romans in some measure inquired into the physiological structure of vocal sounds, but they failed to achieve a clear and distinct view regarding this that equalled the ancient Indians. At best, they classified the sounds into two groups: the vowels (φωνήεντα; vocales) and the consonants (σύμφωνα; consonantes), judging from the degrees of vibration and from the function in a syllable. It is rightly supposed that because their languages are less distinct than Sanskrit the Greeks and Romans fell behind Indians in their study of linguistics.

The ancient grammarians of India arranged their texts chiefly to meet the conveniences of oral teaching and of learning by memory. They made free use of many abbreviations, rhyming words, and other efficient means which would aid memory. And naturally their texts have no such orderly systems such as distinguished parts of phonology, morphology and syntax as found in the modern texts of grammar.

The orthodox Brahmanist scholars of the Mīmāṃsā and of the Vedānta tried to establish logical theories in order to prove the permanent, unchanging nature of words. And the grammarians after Patañjali set up the doctrine of *sphoṭa* to explain metaphysically the essence of the words. Bhartṛhari (ca. 450–500 A.D.) contributed to a further development of this doctrine of *sphoṭa*.

Together with linguistics, *the psychology of reflection* flourished remarkably in India. The ancient Indians set a high value on introspection and they exercised the silent meditation of *Yoga* to attain serenity of mind. And at the same time, they made very careful analyses of the human mental processes from the religious and ethical standpoint. The *Yoga* school, as the name of their school indicates, laid emphasis on the virtue of Yoga. And in their exercise of the concentration of the mind they were engaged in the examination of the mental constitution. The Buddhist ascetics, too, were greatly interested in psychological problems and they arranged and expressed their view on the problems in the Abhidharmas. Maitreyanātha, Asaṅga and Vasubandhu of Mahāyāna succeeded this psychological view of the Abhidharmas and systematized it into the theory of 'Mind-only'. Dharmapāla from his unique standpoint developed this theory further and his system of thought was brought to China, and then to Japan, to flourish in these countries as the Hossō sect (法相宗). As to the psychology of "Mind-only" established chiefly by Dharmapāla, Ryō Kuroda expresses the following view: "The position that the theory of 'Mind-only' deserves in the whole history of psychology remains to be determined by future studies. It is generally accepted that the Asians are excellent in the synthetic approach while their analytical ability is inferior to that of the Westerners. But, at least as far as the theory of 'Mind-only' is concerned, this general assumption is by no means true. Its sharp and minute analysis with a good command of logic (*hetu-vidyā*) exceeds the works of the Western psychologists. .... Moreover, analysis is not the sole function of the theory of 'Mind-only'. In regard to the synthetic function as well as the analytic one, it stands unchallenged".[4] And there is the other system of Buddhist idealism which was originated by Dignāga and brought into completion by Dharmakīrti. This idealism is generally considered to be a logical and epistemological assertion rather than a psychological one. But, in reality, it contains many suggestions noteworthy from the standpoint of modern psychology.

In the West, too, as we can see in Aristotle's *De anima* and in Spinoza's *Ethica,* reflective psychology had been established long before experimental psychology with its usage of the methods of natural sciences arose. And, in a striking contrast to Indian psychology, which was deeply concerned about the ethical or practical value that the human mentalities have, Western studies of psychology made observations of the various states of the human mind without any critical evaluation. This difference in the Western and the Indian sciences of psychology is considered to have resulted from the difference of their approach in the study of the human mental process. The Westerners consider the human mental process to be objectively substantial, while Indians deny its objectivity and understand it only to be attributed to the subject of action.

Indians, in their study of the volitional and the emotional mentalities of the human being, place great importance upon the ethical value that each one of these mentalities has. They evaluate the ethical and practical worth of the mentalities and, according to the judgments, classify them into three groups of the good, the bad and the neutral (*avyākṛta*). Furthermore, they inquire into the origin of each one of the mentalities and finally go into the examination of the relation between a given mental state and the ascetic methods which will serve to check or promote it. To quote Kuroda's comment again on this point, he says as follows; "One of the big defects of empirical psychology is in its undue negligence of the practical aspect of the problems. It is generally assumed that empirical psychology or pure psychology should confine itself to the study of the mind as it is and that the consideration of the practical significance of the mentalities should be left to the hands of the scholars of applied psychology and of pedagogical psychology. But, so far as psychology claims to be the study dealing with all the matters touching upon the mind, it cannot be a deviation from the proper line of the study that the psychologists are engaged not only to observe closely the individual mental phenomena and to anlyze them to build a synthesis, but also to inquire into the practical value of them. As long as this side of the problems remains untouched, psychologists cannot claim to have done their duty properly. .... In its ability of mental analysis, too, the theory of 'Mind-only' can match the theoretical psychology which has a long history of development in the West. And with its proper regard to the practical significance of the mentalities, the theory of 'Mind-only' is akin to the ideal system of psychology".[5]

Indians have made a very elaborate introspective examination of the mentalities, especially of the emotional ones. And they have always placed special emphasis upon the practical significance that the mentalities have. These two points are the remarkable features of Indian psychology.

---

1) The ancient Indians had an advanced skill in numerical calculation. But they made no efforts toward a theoretical understanding of the problems of mathematics. They made no demonstration. For instance, the Pythagorean theorem was required to be understood by the intuitive grasp of the figure without resorting to the demonstration.

2) Cf. *Ṛg-Veda*, 10. 71; 10. 125.

3) In the field of the Prakrit, however, there emerged many grammarians one after another.

4) Ryō Kuroda 黒田亮: *Yuishiki Shinrigaku* (唯識心理學 Psychology of the 'Mind-only'), introduction, 1944.

5) *Ibid.*, p. 253.

Chapter 12. The metaphysical character of Indian thought

(1) The religious character of Indian thought

As a natural result of their ways of thinking with their deep longing for infinity and for the unknown world and with the deep regard for the Universal Being, Indian civilization has a very remarkable religious coloring. The everyday life of Indians is regulated to the most minute details by their religion. In this chapter, we are to take into consideration some of the cases where their religious character is most clearly observed.

The philosophies of India are very religious. To quote Hegel: "The philosophy of India is identical with its religion; so that the interest in religion is the same as what we find in philosophy".[1] Every leading philosopher in the history of Indian thought professed faith in the orthodox Brahmanism, Buddhism or Jainism and he was a member of one of the religious orders. Materialists and sceptics opposed religion, but usually their movements in this country ended in short duration and could not take root in the course of history. Both Buddhism and Jainism had very philosophical systems of thought, but they grew into religious orders rather than into the philosophical schools. Even logicians and scholars of natural sciences, except those who held materialistic views, all had a deep regard for the mystical religious intuition. At least they acknowledged a special significance in it and believed that the release of mind could be achieved by aid of this intuition.

Since the oldest age, philosophy with a strong religious bent held the dominant position in the Indian community. This was noticed by the Greeks. Apollonius of Tyana, a Neo-Pythagorean in the first century, wrote in his book of travel in the East that philosophy (φιλοσοφία) was greatly esteemed in India and that there they governed well under the guidance of the philosophical wisdom.[2] It is clear that what Apollonius described by the word φιλοσοφία was chiefly the one with a ment toward religion and metaphysics.

As the religious character of Indian thought is generally acknowledged, here we will confine ourselves to mention that the inclination toward religion is not a feature merely observed in the thought of individual philosophers, but that it is imbedded in a deeper source—in the way of thinking of the Indian people in general. The languages that they use as the means of expressing their ideas bear remarkable influence of the religious character of their way of thinking.

One of the religious features of the Indian languages can be clearly observed in what the Western logicians call 'impersonal propositions'. In the languages of the Indo-European group, the verbs expressing the natural phenomena are always used impersonally in the form of the third person singular. (e.g., ὕει in Greek; *pluit* in Latin; *it rains* in English; and *es regnet* in German.) All the languages of this language group follow this rule of expression and this rule has been often discussed by the logicians as the problem of 'impersonal propositions'. In the languages of ancient India, however, they preferred to use such forms of expression as 'The god makes the rain fall' or 'The god makes the thunder roll'[3] In many cases 'the god' is only insinuated and not stated clearly in words.[4] But the form of a sentence which sets 'the god' as the subject had been used by the Indians until recently. The ancient Greeks had similar ways of expression. In the epics of Homeros, for instance, the verbs indicating the weather set Zeus as the subject.[5] And in Latin, too, they keep similar forms of expression. So, these ways of expression are not unique products of the Indian languages. But, the fact that these forms of expression were particularly favored by the ancient Indian people at large and the fact that they had been used for centuries indicates the religious character of the Indian people. *The ancient Indians, when they thought of the natural phenomena, always imagined the god who made the phenomena as if they existed behind a curtain.*

In India, they developed a very elaborate idea of god. They have numerous words to mean god. The Sanskrit equivalent to the Greek θεός and the Latin *deus* is *deva.* These three words correspond to each other etymologically and also in their meanings. In Sanskrit, however, there are many other terms to mean god. They call the gods of the lower ranking *devatā,* which the Indologists translate as "divinity" or "deity". In the form of the word, *devatā* has remarkable affinities to German "Gottheit" or to the English "Godhead". But in its meaning, it is nearer to "göttliche Person" or "godlike person". *Brahman* is a neuter noun to mean the ultimate principle of the universe. But when they consider this principle of the universe as the divine power, they use *brahman* specially as a noun of the masculine gender. Besides, they have *ātman* and *paramātman* to mean the Absolute or the innate Self.[6]

All these words indicate divine beings. But each one of them has its unique meaning and is by no means synonymous with others. In Greek such a rich vocabulary for the word "god" does not exist. Galanos in his Greek translation of the *Bhagavadgita* managed to translate all of these words in Sanskrit only by one word "ϑεός".[7] (Cf. Schlegel, in his Latin translation of this Indian sacred book, gave *'deus'* for the equivalent of *deva* and *devatā*; *"numen"* for *brahman*; *"spiritus"* for *ātman*; and *"spiritus summum locum obtinens"* for *paramātman*.)

The languages of ancient India had very rich vocabulary for the idea of god, in contrast to the Western classical languages. It is chiefly because the ancient Indians had a very prolific imagination concerning gods or godlike beings. And it is wrong to assume their rich vocabularies of god to be a result of the polytheistic system of their religion. It should be remembered that the Greek, the Roman as well as the Japanese religions began originally as polytheism.[8]

Indians are inclined to understand every phenomenon from a religious standpoint. Already one of their oldest theological records explains the cosmic phenomena, relating them to the parts of a beast's body in sacrifice. "Verily the dawn is the head of the horse which is fit for sacrifice, the sun its eye, the wind its breath, the mouth the Vaiśvānara fire, the year the body of the sacrificial horse. Heaven is the back, the sky the belly, the earth the chest, ..."[9] And the similar cosmological views are expressed in the *Brāhmaṇas* and in the *Āraṇyakas*. In the North European countries and in China, there are stories equivalent to the Indian myth which explain the creation of the world by the self-splitting of the Cosmic Man.[10] But, the stories to acknowledge the corresponding relation between the elements of the religious rites and the natural phenomena developed exclusively in India.

In India, the Absolute is called *brahman*. Originally this word meant 'the phrases in the Vedas' which were recited in the magical rites. In no other civilized countries, such an idea relating to the ritual as *brahman* rose to the position of the Absolute.

For Brahmanists, it is a matter of great importance to attain the age which would permit performance of the religious rites. For them, to be born in this world is the first life; to get qualified for the performance of the ceremonies is the second life; and to die to be reborn in the Heaven is 'the third life'.[11]

We referred above to the Indian prolix style of writing, saying that it comes from their particular repugnance to arrange matters according to rules. We will add here one more fundamental cause that urges them to cling to this redundant style. It is their religious concern. The ancient Indians *recited by heart* and transmitted the sacred texts of their religion by word of mouth. In the course of time, the form of recitation was established. And they came to suppose a magical power in the act of recitation itself. To keep the magical power at work, it was conceived necessary to follow the established form obediently and to repeat it faithfully in any case of recitation. No arbitrary change of the form was allowed. Thus, the ancient Indians made neither condensations nor abridgements of the established form, however repetitive and wearisome the form may be. Any sentence in the formulae was required to be recited and to be listened to carefully. The omission of a single word in recitation was considered a grave religious error. The ancient Indians followed obediently and patiently, or even without any sense of obedience or patience in their mind, the long and dull form of recitation which is utterly unbearable for the modern people. For an ancient Indian ascetic in a cottage in the depths of the forest or for a monk in a dark cavern, the passage of time seemed really endless and infinite.

Indian natural sciences, too, were strongly influenced by their religious concern. The ancient Indians wrote many books of mathematics, astronomy, medicine and other sciences. And their scientific works were stimulated further after the Greek and the Roman sciences were introduced. Here it is noteworthy that almost all these Indian books of science open with *words of admiration for and faith in the gods.* The Greek sciences made real progress only after they had shaken off the fetters of theology. The Indian sciences, on the contrary, grew as a subsidiary study to aid the study of the Vedas. Among the natural sciences, astronomy was first acknowledged as an independent field of study. From the early time, the orthodox Brahmanists regarded astronomy (*jyotiṣa*) highly as one of the six subsidiary studies for the Vedas. They needed astronomical knowledge to hold the religious ceremonies on the exact dates given in the sacred codes. And for this purpose they began with the observation of the relations among the sun, the moon and the fixed stars; thus, the study of 'the twenty-eight constellations' occupied an essential part of their astronomy. And it is natural that their science of the heavenly bodies had from the beginning a very strong hue of astrology and that its later development was inseparably related with this art of divination. The growth of mathematics in India was paralleled with that of astronomy. Mathematics, too, developed chiefly to meet ritualistic needs. The ancient Indians had their alchemy and this also bore a strong religious coloring.[12] The naturalistic philosophy of the Vaiśeṣika supposed 'the invisible power (*adṛṣṭa*)' to explain the movements of the atoms. And with the lapse of time, they came to attach religious significance to this power.

From ancient times, all Indian scientists were pious devotees of their religions. Even at present some of the scientific research institutes in India hold religious services. This does not mean the distortion of scientific study by religion. In India, religion and science are not necessarily antithetical; rather, it was believed that they exist in harmony and co-operation.

The Indian arts are also deeply connected with religion. Almost all the artistic works are related to the religious structures. And according to some of the old Indian books of discourse on art, the ultimate beauty of art is understood as nothing but the self-unification with the Absolute. As to their music, many of the favorite songs of Indians are religious ones. Even Indian immigrants in foreign countries retain this strong affection to their native religious songs.

Indians are a religious people. After they settled in the ranges of the Ganges, the ancient Indians came to conceive the idea of *Saṃsāra*. And they felt at heart that all beings including man are involved in the circle of transmigration. Some of their verbal ways of expression tell us manifestly that all the conduct of the ancient Indians in their everyday life was strongly influenced by their belief in *Saṃsāra*. For instance, the Sanskrit equivalent to English 'here', *iha* is used in many cases to mean 'in this world'. *The ancient Indians led their life on this side of heaven with the expectation of the life after death.* The belief in the coming kingdom after death was once very widely cherished among the Western people, too. But, in a degree incomparable to the Western cases, the belief of rebirth permeated the mind of the Indian people and strongly influenced their daily life. It is reasonable, therefore, that the Western translators of the ancient Indian languages have managed to translate *iha* only by resorting to circumlocution. E. g.: iha (in *Bhag.* II, 5) = ἐν τούτῳ τῷ βίῳ = quoad vivam; *Idha modati pecca modati katapuñño* (in *Dhp.* 16.) = *In hoc aevo* gaudet, morte obita gaudet qui bonum perfecit.

For Indians who believe in rebirth by *Karma,* there is no eternal grace nor final damnation. Any conduct of a man in this temporal world is in itself temporal and it cannot be the final factor for the fate of the man for all his future lives. The fate of a man in the next world is inevitably determined by the sum of the good deeds and the evil deeds he performed during his life in this world. And when he has lived the fate destined by his deeds in the former life, he will live a new life and thus the transmigration by *Karma* proceeds without end.

---

1) Hegel: *Vorlesungen über die Geschichte der Philosophie,* ed. Michelet. S. 144.

2) F. C. Conybeare: *Philostratus, the life of Apollonius of Tyana,* 1917, vol. I, pp. 196–197.

3) There are the examples also in the Pāli books. e. g.: *atha ce patthayasī, pavassa deva,* (*Suttanipāta* 18–19.); *devo ca vassati, devo ca galagalāyati.* (*Theragāthā* 189.); *deve vassante katamena udakaṃ gaccheya,* (*Milindapañhā,* p. 57.)

4) E. g.: *Manu* IV, 38; *kāle caivaṃ pravarṣati.* (*Suvarṇaprabhāsa* XII, v. 61.)

5) "...... alors que chaque phénomène natural était tenu pour le résultat de l'activité de quelque génie, ὕει signifiait 'le dieut, le génie pleut'; en fait, Homère n'a pas ὕει, mais seulement deux fois M25=ξ 457:

υε δ'ἄραzεύς.

Le latin a *loue tonnate,* etc. L'expression védique *vāto vāti* le vent vente est plus caractéristique encore. Ce ne sont donc pas des impersonnels qui expriment les phénomènes naturels, mais troisièms personnes dont le sujet, qui est un génie plus ou moins vaguement conçu, n'est pas indiqué avec précision. (A. Meillet: Introduction à l'étude comparative des langues indo-européennes, pp. 212–213.) Cf. Shinkichi Sudo 須藤新吉 *Ronrigaku Kōyō* (論理學綱要, Outlines of logic), p. 154.

6) Cf. *supra,* Pt. II, Chap. 7, B.

7) In case he means the Absolute Being, he writes it with a capital lettering, θεōς.

8) From the ancient time, many Indians take the name of gods such as Śaṅkara or Viṣṇu as their family name or their personal name. This custom of naming is not observed either in the West or in China or Japan.

9) *Bṛhad. Up.* I, 1, 1.; *SBE,* vol. XV, p. 74.

10) Cf. Ideishi 出石誠彦: *Jōdai Shina ni okeru Shinwa oyobi Setsuwa* (上代支那に於ける神話及び説話, The Myths and Legends in ancient China) in Iwanami Kōza (岩波講座): *Tōyō Shichō* (東洋思潮, Eastern thoughts), p. 21.

11) H. Oldenberg: *Die Lehre der Upanishaden und die Anfänge des Buddhismus,* S. 25.

12) Cf. Mādhava: *Sarvadarśana-saṃgraha,* Chap. of Raseśvara.

(2) The tendency to transcend this world

The Indian idea of *Saṃsāra* is based on their *view that the life in this world is suffering.* This view of life existed early in the Upaniṣads.

Yājñavalkya thought that a man is happy when he has realized the Ātman and that a man is in torment when he is detached from the Ātman, ignorant of this source of happiness. He explained the essence of the Ātman (the Self) saying: "This is thy Self, the ruler within, the immortal. Everything else is of evil".[1] Gotama renounced the world to seek for the way of deliverance from the pains in this life. Really the first problem that Buddhism took up was the suffering of this life. Wherever he is or whatever refuge he goes to, a man cannot be free from pains.[2] Everybody will get old and die. "Birth is suffering, age is suffering. Grief, lamenting, suffering, sorrow, despair are suffering. Not to get what one wants, also that means suffering. In short, the five *skandhas* (involves) suffering".[3] Man is exposed to the impending crisis of death.[4] "Woe upon life in this world!"[5] And Jains stepped further to expound the miserable state of man in this worldly existence. One of their sūtras says: "Beings torment beings. See the great danger in this world; many pains (are the lot) of creatures".[6] In another place, it says: "Having well considered it, having well looked at it, I say thus: all beings, ... (experience) individually pleasure or displeasure, pain, great terror, and unhappiness. Beings are filled with alarm from all directions and in all directions".[7] In another place, it says: "The (living) world is afflicted, miserable, difficult to instruct, and without discrimination. In this world full of pain, suffering by their different acts, see the benighted ones cause great pain".[8]

The view that the life in this world is suffering is an idea spread all over the land of India. Mādhava, who was learned in all the philosophies of India, wrote in the fourteenth century: "That all transmigratory existence is identical with pain is the common verdict of the founders of all sects and schools; or else they would not be found desirous to put a stop to it and engaging in the method for bringing it to an end. We must, therefore, bear in mind that all is pain, and pain alone".[9] All the thinkers of India taxed their brains to the problem of this suffering life. Even materialists and epicureans were not excepted. They could not hold such optimistic views of life as held by the thinkers of other races. In all the religions of India, the problem was how to find the way of emancipation from this suffering existence of *Saṃsāra*, the way leading to the quiet state of mind, has been always their central concern.[10]

It is natural, therefore, that Indians are inclined to belittle their physical body to the extreme. The ancient Buddhists said in one of their sūtras as follows. "After a stronghold has been made of the bones, it is covered with flesh and blood, and there dwell in it old age and death, pride and deceit".[11] Brahmanists held a similar view on their physical existence.[12] *Mokṣa* in their sense is the deliverance of the Ātman from the body. For Jains, deliverance means no other than 'the decay of the body'.[13] And we can see that Buddhists, too, in the early days of their history regarded 'the cessation of the existing body' as pleasure.[14] The Indian ethics of ascetic mortification is based on these views of the physical body. And here developed no idea such as we see in a Chinese book of morality, *Hsiao-ching* (孝經) which reads, "We get our body, hair and skin from the parents. To keep it from ruin and injury is the beginning of filial piety".

And Indian sages refuse sensual pleasures. They teach us not to stick to the external materials. Buddhists and Jains are all in accord in teaching not to cling to things or thinking 'these are *of my possessions* (*mama*)'.[15]

And every Indian religious thinker seeks to live within nature and there to have direct communion with the Absolute. He renounces the world, lives in the depths of the forest, sits under a tree or on a rock and, keeping himself aloof from all secular affairs, concentrates his thought on the quest for truth. There have been a few thinkers who try to seek for truth while remaining in the secular world and living among people in the street. But, in India, such thinkers have been quite a few in number and not so influential. And the main current of the Indian civilization has been not in the cities but in the woods. It is the civilization of the tranquil life in the forest.

In this country, there developed no city representing its civilization. The ancient Greeks had the center of their civilization in Athens; the ancient Romans in Rome; and the modern Europeans in London, Paris and Berlin. But, in India there was or is no city corresponding to these cities in the West. It is true that the cities of Pāṭaliputra and Kānyakubja once flourished. But the prosperity of these cities was of a short duration. There are no cities prospering throughout the whole history of India to represent its civilization.

For Indians who are inclined to transcend this world and who hold a strong longing for the future existence, it is difficult *to accept a religion that sets a high value on the secular mundane life.*[16] More than four hundred years have passed since the Christians began their missionary works in this country. And at present there are about six millions Christian adherents in India — a number which amounts to only a little more than one-sixtieth of the whole population. Besides, as the results of the national censuses and the reports of the Christian missions indicate, many of the converts to Christianity are living in South India and they consist chiefly of those expelled from the Hindu community, the Śūdras, the vagabonds, and the uncivilized people of the mountains. It is truly significant that the Christian missions have worked much to enlighten the peoples left out of the Hindu society. But in spite of their great effort, the Christian missions failed to capture the minds of the Hindus who are the guiding force in the Indian community. As one of the reasons for the stagnation of the Christian missionary works in India, a Japanese scholar writes as follows: "In India, a religious missionary is considered to be a man free from and by far aloof from secular desires. From the days of Śākyamuni up to present, almost all the religious founders of India are ascetics who lead the very severe life of mortification. But, the life of a Christian missonary, who has a wife and children to accompany him, a fine house to live in, a chariot to drive in and meat to eat, is too secular to be understood by the Hindus as the life proper for a religious man".[17)]

The super-mundane idea of the Indian religions has influenced the ethical ideas of the Indians. In this country, it is urged as a virtue to abandon private property. Buddhists and Jains all teach in accord to give up the idea of 'mine (*mama*)' and encourage the virtue of no-property. They teach the performance of unlimited service to others by surrendering all of one's possessions. This Indian *negation of private property* is very similar to the philosophy of modern socialism and communism. But, it should be noted that the Indian assertion is based on their super-mundane way of thinking. In practice the socialistic reformation of Indian society is far from being accomplished.

Indians, in spite of their pessimistic view of life and of their super-mundane religions, have optimistic tendencies. This contradictory assertion can be safely made on the basis that generally the Indian peoples are free from despair. Their optimism is derived from their belief that although this life is filled with suffering, once one has been united with the Absolute, one will live at ease and without fear. And the Indians never give up this hope of unification with the Absolute. This phase of their way of thinking can be observed also in their dramatic literature; they have no 'tragedy'. Almost all the Indian plays end, after many scenes of thrill and suspense, with 'All lived happily ever after'. And corresponding to this feature of the Indian way of thinking, their religion is optimistic in itself. It promises them that any man, however bad he is, will be saved by his earnest faith or by his practice of hard disciplines.

In a striking contrast to their super-mundane character, Indians have at the same time a yearning for material and sensual pleasures. But, these two different trends in the Indian way of thinking possess one common trait: both tend to neglect and to transcend limited social organizations. Sometimes Indians dare to neglect and violate ethical norms of behavior. And here, in the inclination to transcend limited social institutions, their negligence of the ethical norms in pleasure-seeking has an essential affinity to their religious passion to submit themselves to the Absolute without admitting any intermediary conditioned agent between themselves and the Absolute.

The decisive factor in the idea of *Saṃsāra* is death. All the sufferings of man in this world come from death. Facing death, a man is led to the metaphysical contemplation of the problem. *And the Indian civilization has grown through the contemplation on the phenomenon of death.* Buddhism and Jainism both are religions arising from deep reflection on this inevitable moment of human life. A quotation from the *Dhammapada* reads as follows: "How is there laughter, how is there joy, as this world is always burning? Do you not seek a light, ye who are surrounded by darkness?"[18] And Hinduism holds the similar view on the problem of death.

Megasthenēs, a Greek who visited India at the end of the fourth century B.C. or thereabouts, mentioned as a remarkable inclination of the Brahmins their practice of philosophical speculation on death. He wrote: "Now, among the Brahmins, the problem of death is the issue very many times debated. Usually (they) compare the life in this world to the state of a child quickening in the mother's womb. And they hold that the true life begins verily at the moment of death in this world. And they consider this (life of truth) as the ultimate source of happiness for the philosophers (φιλοσοφήσαντες). And in order to make the mind ready for death, they urge the needs of the severest asceticism (ἀσκήσις)".[19] In Japan, too, Matsumiya Kanzan (1686–1780) commented this feature of the Indian thoughts saying: "In India, ... people are old and feeble in spirit and they like the sombre teachings of Buddhism, which is always talking about the problem of death".[20]

The artistic works of India reflect this feature of the Indian religion. Indian structures and sculptures originated from the decorative works around the *Stūpas*. A *Stūpa* is a hemispherical grave-mound built on the ashes or the remains of a sage. The *Stūpas* of the early periods were rather small in scale, but after the Mauryas they began to build larger ones. And the ancient Greeks called the *Stūpas* "Pyṛamids".[21] Gorgeous artistic works of ancient India were all carved on the gates, pillars and railings of the *Stūpas*. And the temples were built at the origin abound the *Stūpas*. The fine art of the temple architecture grew as one part of the decoratory works of the *Stūpas*. It can be said that grave-worship is the origin of the Indian art. But their artistic expressions, developed thus as the ornaments of the grave, bear no gloomy shade of death. On the contrary, they are bright, lively and beautiful. This bright feature of the Indian artistic works is different from the expressions of the sunny and innocent disposition of the primitive or uncivilized tribes; rather, it reflects the peaceful state of mind of the religious people who challenged and conquered the fear of death. Indians seek eternity through the medium of contemplation on death.

---

1) *Bṛhad. Up.* III, 7; *SBE*, vol. XV, p. 136.
2) Cf. *Dhammapada* 189.
3) There is an elaborate study on this familiar expression of Buddhism in Hakuju Ui 宇井伯壽: *Indo-tetsugaku Kenkyū* (印度哲學研究), vol. III, p. 353.
4) E. g. *Dhammapada* 286–287.
5) *Suttanipāta* 440.; *SBE*, vol. X, pt. II, p. 70.
6) *Āyāraṅga*, herausgegeben von W. Schubring, S. 27, 1. 28.; *SBE*, vol. XXII, p. 54.
7) *SBE*, *ibid.*, p. 11.
8) *Ibid.*, p. 3.
9) Mādhava: *The Sarva-Darśana-Saṁgraha or Review of the Different Systems of Hindu Philosophy*, tr. by E. B. Cowell, p. 22. Especially in Buddhism they assume that 'all is pain and pain (*sarvaṁ duḥkham*)'. Cf. *ibid.*, p. 15.
10) *Praśnottararatnamālikā* 3.
11) *Dhammapada* 150; *SBE*, vol. X, pt. I, p. 42.
12) *The Laws of Manu*, 6. 761.
13) Kāyassa viavāa (= vyavapāda), *Āyāraṅga*, S. 32, *l.*20; dehabheya (=°-bheda), *ibid.*, S. 40, *l.* 2. Cf. *ibid.*, S. 37, *l.* 18.
14) sakkāyass' uparodhana (*Suttanipāta* 761); sakkāyass' nirodha (*SN.* III, p. 86G.)
15) Cf. *Āyāraṅga*, S. 12; *Suttanipāta* 220, 367, 466, 469, 494, 777, 922; *Theragāthā* 717.

16) In contrast to the Chinese Christians, the Indian Christians have a strong inclination to transcend the secular affairs. But this will be treated in later chapters.
17) Jinnosuke Sano 佐野甚之助: *Indo oyobi Indojin* (印度及印度人 India and Indians) p. 253.
18) *Dhammapada* 146; *SBE*, vol. X, pt. I, p. 41.
19) Megasthenēs: *The Fragments*, 41.
20) *Sankyō Yōron* (三教要論, 寳曆十年刻) in *Nihon Jurin Sōsho* (日本儒林叢書, Series of the Japanese Confucianism), Kaisetsubu (解説部), vol. II, p. 7.
21) Pauly-Wissowa: *Realenzyklopädie*, s. v. Megasthenēs, 319–320.
The Chinese "塔" has the etymological origin in *thūpa* or *thuba*, the Prakrit forms of *stūpa*. And what we Japanese mean by "塔 (tower)" at present are the modified forms of the original Indian *Stūpas*.

(3) The tendecy of thought to transcend the gods

As we have seen above, every expression of Indian thought is strongly tinged with religious coloring. It should be noted, however, that their attitude toward religion is by far different from that of the Westerners. In the West, God is the centre of their whole religious system. In the Indian religions, on the other hand, God does not hold such a prominent position as in the West. Indians have their own very richly and elaborately developed idea of god, but they never consider god as the Absolute Being. In the Indian concept, the gods are beings lower than the Absolute and the Absolute *stands high above the gods.*

According to the Brahmanistic point of view, the grace of the gods is the reward given in return for offerings. There is a fixed relation of cause and effect between the ritualistic service to the gods and the grace given back to man. And no free-will on the part of the gods is acknowledged to intervene in this relation. It is natural, therefore, that the idea of the personal god or of the grace given by him has been scarcely conceived among the Brahmanists. And in the course of time, their attention has been focused more exclusively on the permanent law that regulates all the beings including even the gods. Except for some theological assertions of Hinduism of the later periods, almost all the ancient philosophical schools of India regarded the gods as being of no great significance. Buddhists and Jains, for instance, considered the gods to be no more than the beings enjoying super-human powers. And the scholars of the Vedānta school attached little importance to the God presiding the universe; they considered him to be merely an incidental over cause. In short, Indians have a higher regard for the authority of law (*dharma*) than for the gods. The gods, in their concept, are beings to follow what the law decrees. They are not the founders of the law. But, on the contrary, it is the universal and unalterable law that makes the gods as they are.

The gods in the Indian religions, especially the gods of Brahmanism, are loose in morals. Their deeds are not always virtuous. The *Brāhmaṇa* books tell us many stories concerning the gods' indiscreet deeds of envy, jealousy, hostility, infidelity, greed, arrogance, cowardice and adultery. The gods of India are not different from mean creatures. They are by no means the supreme authority of morality. And generally speaking, Indians who worship such gods are little awakened to the sense of morals. In the *Ṛg Veda,* only Varuṇa is the god of morality. But, as the *Brāhmaṇas* and the books of the later periods tell us, even this god gradually changed his character and lost his strict morals. It is natural, therefore, that Indians of the later ages sought the basis of their morals apart from the gods' authority. And they came to conceive that the moral law should be observed not because of the gods' authority but because of the retribution according to *Karma.*[1]

Many gods of Brahmanism were adopted in the Buddhist myths, transformed into Buddhist gods. In the Buddhist concept, these gods, though they possess super-human powers, themselves are bound to a life of ignorance and are waiting to be saved by the teachings of the Buddha. Jains, too, refused to regard the gods as the Absolute Being. The concept of the Supreme Lord had taken a fixed form in India by the time the Christian era began. But, one of the most outstanding philosophical schools of India, the Non-dualist (*advaita*) school in the Vedānta, asserted that the highest God (*īśvara*) is no other than the Absolute, the Brahman, clouded with ignorance (*ajñāna*) and that because of the ignorance he is bound to the world of illusion like other beings. The schools of Hinduism urge to have faith in the Supreme Lord. But, as we see in their myths relating to this Supreme Lord, he is more likely a human being than the absolute and supreme being. And here, we are safe to generalize that Indians have found the authority of their morals in the law which exists independent of the gods. In India, *the law (dhama) is considered to stand above the gods.* This Indian concept of god is in a striking contrast to the Western idea that places the Lord as the sole source of morality.

The ancient Greeks and Romans used their words to mean god, 'theos' and 'deus', in a very loose way. The great men, the philosopher-emperors and all others who were men of superb intelligence, who contributed much to make people happy, to free the people from all the faults and troubles and to lead them nearer to the divine life—those, whether they were the human beings or somewhat mythical beings, who were the saviors of the mankind are the gods (*theos sōter*) in the concept of ancient Greeks and Romans.[2] For Indians, on the other hand, a savior is a master of the universal law. Whether the savior is a human being or a divine existence does not matter. He is a savior by the authority of the Absolute that stands higher than the gods. He is an incarnation of the Absolute, but not necessarily a god or the only son of God. The Indian concept of God has produced an idea of the savior quite different from that of the Western religion.

The difference of the concepts of god in the West and in India is clearly observed also in the ways of description of their literary works. The Greek writers were careful to make their gods speak in a manner decent and proper to the dignity of gods and succeeded to produce satisfactory effects. But, the authors of India, for instance, the authors of the Upaniṣads, could not or more properly speaking did not care for such ways of expression. Everything goes in this actual world. Like the Indian artists in their works of sculpture, the Indian writers scarcely attempted to idealize the gods or to describe them as being more sublime than the human beings.[3]

---

1) Of course, as we see in the Epics, especially in the *Bhagavadgītā*, or in the Mahāyāna texts, some philosophers appeared who in disregard of the Karma's retribution esteemed the value of the good deed for itself and who tried to do good for goodness' sake. They rejected the idea of retribution and encouraged the practical observance of the morals to realize the absolute value in this actual life. But, even in their cases, the morals are not necessarily connected with the concept of God.

2) Seiichi Hatano 波多野精一: *Kirisutokyō no Kigen* (基督教の起源), Origin of Christianity), p. 214.

3) Cf. H. Oldenberg: *Die Lehre der Upanishaden und die Anfänge des Buddhismus*, S. 146.

Chapter 13. The spirit of tolerance and conciliation

Generally speaking, Indian people have a tendency to recognize raison d'être in the fact that there exist many different world-views, philosophies and religions in the world. For they think that these different views which seemingly conflict with each other are based on the Absolute One. Their viewpoint is, objectively, based on the idea that all things in the universe are one, and subjectively on the reflection that all human activities originate from the metaphysical and monistic principle.

The reflection on the fact that there are different philosophies in this world, conflicting with each other, appeared in India when Gotama the Buddha was born and when many towns thrived in the Ganges basin. Sañjaya, a sceptic, suspended judgment on any metaphysical matter. When he was asked to answer, he used to speak ambiguously and offered no definite answer. It was difficult to grasp the true meaning of his answer, for it was *just like attempting to grasp eels by hands.* But Mahāvīra, founder of Jainism, tried to transcend scepticism. He advocated the theory of 'Naya', and proved the possibility of offering judgments on general matters provided that the qualification 'from a certain point of view' was added.

Among these philosophers of ancient India, Gotama the Buddha was the first to reflect thoroughly on this problem. He criticized the philosophers and religious leaders in endless debate as "being attached to their own views".[1] And they were said to have committed moral crime as the result of being involved in discussions which, from the metaphysical point of view, would never be solved. Gotama himself avoided participation in these discussions[2] and regarded them as quite useless for the attainment of Enlightenment.[3]

Gotama the Buddha was said "to have remained aloof from all discusions" and "to have taught ascetics or *bhikkhus* to transcend any *prapañca* (discussions which were useless for the attainment of the religious goal)". Gotama did not insist that his teaching was the only Absolute Truth of the exclusion of all others. Therefore, he remained in harmony with other philosophers. In this way of harmony he attained and realized the Enlightenment — Tranquility of mind. Such being the case Gotama's teachings could never be comparable with other teachings.[4] We can not say that his teachings are 'equal', 'superior', or 'inferior' to other ones. Comparison will be possible only in the case where a common standpoint is seen between two. Buddha's teachings differ from other doctrines in their standpoints and in dimensions. Gotama himself seems to have gone so far as to recognize raison d'être of other philosophies. All philosophers, as far as they adhere to their own views, are fools. But there must be some reason in each opinion as long as they believe it.[5] According to Gotama, those Buddhists who want to keep aloof above the views of any type of philosophy must reflect upon themselves all the time, bearing in mind that they should not be prejudiced.

Such an attitude towards other doctrines can apparently be seen in Mahāyāna Buddhism, especially in the *Saddharmapuṇḍarīkasūtra.*[6] Even the lower doctrines, the Sūtra declares, are the *upāyas* or the means for the Buddhas to teach mankind the right way. Such a way of thinking was carried on in Shingon Mysticism (Esoteric Buddhism). In Shingon even heretical dogmas are regarded as a part of Buddhism. Buddhism is not a special religion which conflicts with other religions, but is, in itself, the Absolute Truth. Heretics are nothing but a manifestation of the ultimate truth. From the absolute point of view here is in the universe only one principle called "Buddhism".

The spirit of tolerance was not maintained in the same manner among the later Buddhists in India. It was a natural tendency of history that in actual society, the Buddhist order had to stand face to face with other religions and philosophies as it became an established religion and created special rites and customs. However, almost all the Buddhists in India, believing that the fundamental standpoint of Buddhism was not contradictory with other heretical views, did not intend to compete with them actively. As a result, Buddhism, in spreading over the Asian countries, caused less frictions among the indigenous faiths of the peoples who had received it. Native and indigenous faiths and customs were scarcely destroyed by Buddhists and could easily survive, as far as they were regarded ethical from the Buddhist point of view; they were able to remain in existence in parallel with newly-arrived Buddhism and sometimes absorbed in Buddhism. In later days Buddhism itself fused into one with native religions giving them philosophical foundations.

As for the fact that there exist many different philosophies and religions in the world, Vedānta philosophers also expressed views similar to the Buddhists. Basing themselves on Absolute Monism, they regarded even heretical doctorines as having their basis in Brahman. According to them, there are many ultimate principles — elements, gods, breath, time, etc., — which are respectively asserted by many schools philosophical to be the Absolute Principle. And this is why there are so many schools with diversified views. From the viewpoint of Vedānta, however, none of them deserves to be regarded as the Absolute Truth. They are only assumed (*vikalpita*) to be the world-principle. The fact is that the Ātman is the Absolute

One. These philosophers misunderstood the real state of matters, adhering to their wrong views on the Absolute.

Their views, however, are of course wrong, but these heretical views are also included in the Ātman-theory of Vedānta. Vedānta philosophers went so far as to say that even these heretical views were manifestations of the Ātman, and were true partly even though they were incomplete in themselves.

Vedānta philosophy can never stand in the same sphere as other doctrines. The standpoint of Vedānta should be quite different from these heretical views in its dimensions. In the *Māṇḍūkyakārikās* we read: "Those who admit duality, adhere to their views and are inconsistent with each other. However, (Vedāntists) are not inconsistent (with such dualists)".[7] According to Śaṅkara, this is likened to limbs that are not inconsistent with their bodies.

In later Jain philosophy the same idea was also expressed. Hemacandra says: "Discussions in other schools produce jealousy because the one insists while the other opposes. But in Jainism they advocate no dogma and no discussions because they admit the teachings of 'Naya' ".[8]

Because of such a way of thinking that in every heretical view some raisons d'être exists, Indian philosophers in mediaeval age tried to establish a 'Comprehensive system of world philosophy', or a 'Systematic conception of the world'.

They are so tolerant as to recognize the raison d'être in each other that different views are taken into the same school as having some positive reason. Other views are regarded as a means (*upāya*) to lead the fool to the right way. Generally speaking in any Indian religion we can *not find the conception* of "heretic" in the sense of Western usage.

Such a thinking method is found not only in religious teachings but in the fundamental principle of administration taken by many kings and rulers throughout the history of India. King Aśoka, for example, being himself an earnest Buddhist layman, never excluded other religions. Far from that he endeavored to protect and assist other religions — Brahmanism, Jainism, Ājīvikas, etc. He "adored both monks and laymen of all religions".[9] His sincere wishes were that "everyone in every religion dwell peacefully side by side", and cooperate each other for promoting the welfare of mankind. Though King Aśoka made Buddhism as a state religion, he did not persecute the non-Buddhist religions in his territory.

King Khāravela, who gained control of southern part of India after the collapse of the Mauryan Dynasty, was a patron of the Jaina order, but he also repaired the shrines and temples of other religions. He was called "*sarvapāṣaṇḍapūjaka* (he who adored all the sects)". Kings of Kaṣāṇa Dynasty, who ruled northern India, also protected many different religions. King Kaniṣka for example cast many coins on which the statues of gods — of Greece, of Zoroastrianism, Hinduism and of Buddha — are engraved. The Gupta Dynasty in the fourth century was tolerant to all the religions.[10] Centuries later, Akbar the Great (1556–1605) ruled almost all India, and intended to establish a new religion by mixing other religions which existed before. He declared that Hindu and Mohammedan should worship the same and single God. But he was rather tolerant not only to Hinduism and Mohammedanism but also to Jainism, Parsism, and Christianity. He also admitted solar-worship. Though not complete, the principle of tolerance was kept by him in his religious policy.

Such an attitude towards other faiths is manifest in the modern religious movements in India. A religious reformer in the nineteenth century, Rām Mohan Rai, organized a religious society called Brāhma-Samāj, and he made it a fundamental principle of the society for the followers to worship the same God irrespective of their race, class, nationality and even their religions. Rāmakṛṣṇa. who was the founder of the Ramakrishna Order declared that "all religions, pursuing different ways, will finally reach the same God".[11] "All the religions that existed are true".[12] Vivekānanda, his disciple, delivered a famous address at the International Religious Conference held in Chicago on Sept. 27, 1893, saying that: "Oh, the Sacred One, called Brahman by the Hindus, Ahura Mazdah by the Zoroastrians, Buddha by the Buddhists, Jehovah by the Hebrews and God in heaven by the Christians! May bestow inspiration upon us! Christians should neither be Buddhists nor Hindus. Buddhists and Hindus should never be Christians. Everyone, however, must grow up in accordance with their own principle, holding their individual character firmly, assimilating others' spiritual merits. ...... This Conference has proved that Holiness, Sereneness and Compassion should not be monopolized by any religious order. And it has also proved that there were no religions in the world which had never produced noble and spiritual personalities. I firmly believe that we will read the following passages on the flags or banners of all the religions in the future — Help each other. Don't struggle each other. Be reconciled with others. Don't destroy others. Keep harmony and peace. Don't compete in useless matters".[13] "I approve of existing of religions in the past. I adore God with them".[14]

These facts mentioned above differ from those in the West. In the history of Europe we often find religious antagonism which inevitably led to political, military conflicts. But we can hardly find such a case of religious war in India. There were, of course, in India a few rulers who oppressed some of the the universal religions produced by Indian people as they were believers of some indigenous religions. But we can not find any rulers who, being Buddhists or Jainists, persecuted other religions.

This fact would be more obvious if we compare it with the facts in the West. Even Christianity or Mohammedanism was the cause of waging religious wars. According to the Calvinists' explanation, hatred against the sinners or heretics is regarded as a virtue.[15] It is not rare that religious leaders in the West were often persecuted and killed. On the contrary, in India there were no religious war. In the Buddhist or Jain order they never executed the heretics. What they treated heretics was only to exclude them from the orders. Religious leaders in India died peacefully in bed attended by their disciples and followers. Tolerance is the most conspicuous characteristics of Indian culture.

Recent statistics on the research of life-ideals show that there are many students in India who think that among many different ways of life the most noble is the recognition and understanding of the existence of varied paths. This fact shows that such a way of thinking of toleration still lives among the Indian students.[16]

What, then, is the reason behind the spirit of tolerance in people's mind in India? H. Oldenberg enumerates the following reasons: Indian climate and circumstance, early and easy invasion of Aryan race, non-existence of great wars, calm atmosphere in the Brahmin class, etc.[17] Wars in India were fought only by mercenary soldiers, and not by ordinary people. This fact contributed much to promote the attitude of toleration by the Indian people. Throughout the centuries of Indian history no military expedition was attempted by Indian rulers. According to Arianos' report, "Megasthenēs says that Indians never attacked other peoples outside the borders, and other peoples never attacked the Indians. Alexandros was the only exception to have attacked the Indian people".[18] "Indians did not conquer other countries because of their spirit of righteousness (*dikaiotēs*)".[19]

Love of peace by Indians is already recognized by the Western scholars. The word "peace" signifies in itself to recognize others or other views besides one. So the peace-loving attitude in Indian people must have come from the unique way of thinking that different philosophies and different conceptions of the world are nothing but the manifestation of the Absolute One.

---

1) *Sutta-nipāta* 891.
2) *Sutta-nipāta* 844–845.
3) *Sutta-nipāta* 837, 845.
4) *Sutta-nipāta* 842f., 855, 860.
5) *Sutta-nipāta* 880–881, 905–906.
6) E.g. 大薩遮尼乾子所說經; 大般涅槃經.
7) ***Māṇḍūkyakārikā*** **3–17.**
8) *Vītarāgastuti* 30 (*SDS.* III, *l.* 409).
9) *Rock Edict.* Chap. 12.
10) Rama Shankar Tripathi: "Religious toleration under the Imperial Guptas" (*IHQ.* 1939, pp. 1–12).
11) Romain Rolland: *La vie de Ramakrishna*, p. 93.
12) *Ibid.* p. 186.
13) Romain Rolland: *La vie de Vivekananda*, I, pp. 47–48.
14) *Ibid.* II, p. 110.
15) Max Weber: *Die protestantische Ethik und der Geist des Kapitalismus*, S. 121.
16) Charles Morris: "Comparative Strength of Life-Ideals in Eastern and Western Cultures." in *Eassays in East-West Philosophy*, ed. by Charles A. Moore, Honolulu 1951, pp. 353–370.
17) H. Oldenberg: *Die Lehre der Upanishaden und die Anfänge des Buddhismus*, S. 3.
18) *Arianos*, V. 4., V. 7.
19) *Ibid.* IX, 12.

PART III. THE WAYS OF THINKING OF THE CHINESE

—Characteristics of the Ways of Thinking as Revealed in Various Cultural Phenomena, Particularly in the Process of Accepting Buddhism—

Chapter 1. Introduction

The Chinese did not accept Buddhism in its Indian form. After it was introduced into China, it was modified under the influence of the traditional ways of thinking of the Chinese. Chinese Buddhism has diverged from Indian Buddhism to a very great degree. The following facts have influenced the nature and extent of these divergencies:

1. The Chinese made complete translations of the Buddhist scriptures into their own language. They did not use Sanskrit or Prakrit as a sacred language of the Buddhist church.
2. In translating, Chinese scholars and exegetes often gave twisted or distorted interpretations of the original. Thus the Indian texts were not always faithfully translated. Interpolations were often added. The sentences were frequently embellished with Chinese literary ornament, thus taking on the appearance of original works of Chinese literature.
3. Later Chinese Buddhist scholars, with few exceptions, were not in a position to refer to or to understand the original Indian texts, and sometimes they failed to understand even the meaning of sentences in earlier Chinese translations.
4. Many texts of Chinese Buddhism developed along lines entirely different from the doctrines of Indian schools.
5. The exegetical techniques of the Chinese Buddhists are entirely different from those of the Indians.

These differences and divergencies are to be understood as occurring under the influence of the persisting indigenous ways of thinking of the Chinese. The purpose of this section is to attempt to describe those persisting traditional ways of thinking by pointing out the ways in which Indian Buddhist thought was altered under their influence.

Chapter 2. Emphasis on the perception of the concrete

(1) Graphic character of the writing

The results of Granet's study of the vocabulary of Chinese coincides with many of the findings of Lévy-Bruhl's study of the languages of American Indians.[1] However, there exists an important difference between Chinese and American Indian languages. Granet says, "Whereas primitive languages are characterized by the extreme variety of verbal forms, Chinese is extremely poor on this point. It uses uninflected monosyllabic words; there is no distinction of parts of speech. However, the flavor of concreteness—provided by various forms in other languages, is shown by the extreme abundance of Chinese words which convey concrete phases of things with unparalleled power ......"[2]

Consequently it is characteristic of Chinese that it is abundant in words expressing bodies and forms, but poor in verbs expressing change and transformation. Whether this is peculiar to Chinese alone or common to primitive languages in general, is still to be investigated. Stenzel writes:[3] "Considering the process of the establishment of syntactical forms, we can say that subjects were in origin mostly words expressing 'things' (Dingwort); for a single word as a unit can reproduce a 'thing' as a unit. When this idea of thing is applied to objects in general, appellations expressing changing phenomena come to be substantiated. This process can be perceived in German; but more conspicuous in Greek. In any language, generally speaking, verbs, adjectives, pronouns, adverbs, etc. were originally nouns expressing 'things', but they have changed to become other parts of speech; losing their independent meaning, they have sometimes become affixes. This process of transformation is said to be most conspicuous in isolating languages, especially in Chinese". It seems clear, in any case, that Chinese thinking has tended to be expressed in concrete terms.

The influence of the language structure on thought can be seen in the way in which the characters are made. Chinese characters are, of course, originally hieroglyphic. The character 日 is derived from a diagram — which symbolizes the sun...... The character 火 symbolizes fire through a representation of flame 火. Later many phonetic characters were also devised, but these were based upon hieroglyphics. The four classic ways of constructing Chinese characters are termed 象形, 指事, 會意, 形聲, while the two modes of transference are termed 轉注 and 假借. Yet the hieroglyphs are fundamental to the characters developed by these six devices.

The Chinese were accustomed to these types of symbols, even when they transcribed foreign words with Chinese characters. The choice of characters for transcription was random. There was no systematic way of consistently transcribing a particular foreign sound by a particular character. Even one and the same translator often adopted different ways of transcribing one and the same sound.[4] They did not go on to invent an analytic and constructive method of consistently using an agreed set of characters equivalent to the sounds of say, Sanskrit. In choosing characters to transcribe foreign sounds, the Chinese were *influenced by the appearance* of the character. For example, the Pali word bhikkhu was always transcribed 比丘 and never as 毘鳩. Characters chosen to transcribe certain key words were invariably so used, regardless of the fact that the same syllables in other words were differently transcribed.

---

1) Lévy-Bruhl: *Les fonctions mentales dans les sociétés inférieures*, deuxième partie, chap. V, p. 187 et suiv.

2) M. Granet: *Quelques particularités de la langue et de la pensée chinoises* (*Revue Philosophique*, 1920, p. 126).

3) Stenzel: *Die Philosophie der Sprache*, S. 50–51.

4) Many Chinese *dhāraṇīs* (陀羅尼) transcribed Sanskrit sounds of the Sanskrit original texts (cf. e.g. 揵稚梵讚 Gaṇḍīstotra). But we cannot find any definite or consistent rules.

(2) The concrete expression of concepts

On the basis of a study of the vocabulary of the *Book of Songs* Granet observed that Chinese concepts are expressed in highly concrete form. Nearly all words express particular ideas, viz. forms of existence perceived in a particular phase. They aim at expressing things by individualization and particularization rather than by analysis. For example, in the *Book of Songs* more than three thousand words are used: this seems a very large number in proportion to the limited number of ideas expressed therein. These words correspond to images of ideas which are complex and particular. In the book there are 18 words which might correspond to one French concept 'montagne' qualified by one or more adjectives. In the same work there are 23 words which mean 'horse'.

On the other hand there is no word which corresponds to a Western word expressing a general and abstract idea. Because of their synthetic and particular character Chinese words are more nearly proper nouns than the common nouns of Western languages. For example, the many words for 'rivers': 河, 江 etc.[1] The vocabulary of the Classics, including the *Book of Songs* has continued in use up to the present day and the observations made above thus have some application to the whole history of the expression of Chinese ideas.

The Chinese way of expressing concepts is concrete. Thus for the notion expressed in Western languages as "epigraphy', 'Inschriftenkunde' the Chinese use the graphically concrete expression 'writing on metal and stone'. (金石文)

In the expression of attributive qualities they tend to use concrete numbers, thus for 'a fast horse' they use 千里馬 'a horse good for a thousand *li*': for a man endowed with clairvoyance they use the expression 千里眼 'thousand *li* vision'. These numbers are not used in a simple quantitative sense but symbolize qualities which are expressed in Western languages in more abstract terms. The two characters 矛盾 ('halberd and shield') is a compound used to mean 'contradiction' and no other compound is used for expressing this concept. The association of the original meaning of these characters is not lost so that it was perfectly natural for the Chinese to create an alternative compound on the same basis 鉾楯.[2]

The same associative process is revealed in the case of the character *li* 理 'reason' which is of key importance in the history of Chinese philosophy. This character originally meant 'well distributed veins on minerals or precious stones'. It eventually came to mean 'Principle' and finally 'universal principle'.[3] This third meaning was developed by 程明道 in the Sung period. Under his interpretation it became the fundamental principle which pervades and makes possible all phenomena. "The development of this abstract meaning is generally attributed to the influence of Buddhist scholars particularly those of the *Hua-yen* sect who set up the distinction and contrast between *li* (理) and *shih* (事)".[4]

The tendency to express abstract philosophical ideas in concrete images is conspicuous in Zen Buddhism. The universe or cosmos is expressed as, 山河大地 'mountains, rivers, and the great earth'. The basic ego of a human being is expressed as 曹源一滴水,[5] 'a drop of water in the source', one's true nature as 本來面目 'original face and eye' or 本地風光 'the wind and light of one's native place'. Words which were used as literal translations of such original Indian words as Bodhi 本覺 or Tathatā 眞如 were not well adapted to Chinese ways of thinking and they thus developed such concrete expressions as those noted above. Zen Buddhism uses highly evocative terms to create the type of concrete image which its teaching requires. Thus for the human body the Zen term is 臭皮袋 "stinking bag of skin". The Zen term for essence is 眼目 'eye' or 眼睛 'the pupil of the eye'. For a monastic community the Indian word is *saṅgha* or *gaṇa* which mean 'group, conglomoration'. Zen on the other hand uses the word 叢林,[6] by which it means to suggest that the harmonious life of a monastic community is analogous to a thicket where trees and grasses grow together. The Zen term for an itinerant monk is 雲水 'clouds and water' which, of course, graphically symbolizes the monks' lack of a fixed abode. This is in striking contrast to the Indian term for mendicant '*parivrājaka*', 'wanderer'.

The tendency suggested by these examples is not confined to Zen Buddhism. The founder of the San-lun sect expounded the fundamental teachings of Buddhism in concrete poetical terms of which the following is an example: "It has been a long time that the sweet drug (= the Buddha-nature) has dwelt in mountains (= the minds and bodies of individuals). A long period has elapsed since the round jewel (= the Buddha-nature) sank in water (= transmigrated) .... May reflections be revealed in mirrors and may faces (= our proper selves) return to their proper places. Lost children (= sinful people) are those who have wandered a little from their native places".[7]

The use of concrete imagery is common not only to Buddhism but to Chinese philosophical writing in general.

---

1) Granet: *op. cit.* pp. 103–104.

2) Cf. *San-lun-hsüan-i* 三論玄義 (ed. by Y. Kanakura in Iwanami Bunko ed. 岩波文庫, p. 19). In other edition 栫楯 instead of 鉾楯.

3) Yoshio Takeuchi 武內義雄: *Shina Shisō-shi* (支那思想史 History of Chinese Thoughts), p. 263.

4) *Ibid.* p. 264.

5) e.g. *Jen-t'ien-yen-mu* (人天眼目), vol. IV (*Taishō.* Vol. 48, p. 323c).

6) A passage in the *Ta-chih-tu-lun* (大智度論 *Mahā-prajñāpāramitā-śāstra*), vol. III is often mentioned as the source. But such an expression was not usual in India.

7) *Ta-ch'eng-hsüan-lun* (大乘玄論), vol. III (*Taishō.* vol. 45, p. 35b).

(3) Explanation by means of perceived symbols

One of the most important characteristics of Chinese psychology is reliance on perception. They are antipathetic to that which is beyond the immediately perceived. In novels, for example, they tend to recreate the tangible world of sense perception. Of course there are exceptions such as the *Hsi-yu-chi* but works of this genre are far fewer and less influential than realistic writing.[1]

For the purposes of instruction and persuasion they resort to images that have the appeal of direct perceptions. For example, in the *Yen-shih chia-hsun* there is the following argument illustrative of this phenomena: there are some who doubt the wonders and miracles accepted by the Buddhists. Such doubt is mistaken because there are things which may not lie within the field of our immediate perception but which may be perceived in the future. When I lived in South China, I could not believe that a tent existed which could cover a thousand people. But when I came to North China, I found such a tent. I, as a southerner, know very well that there are ships which can carry twenty thousand *tan* but northerners do not believe that such vessels can exist. It is the same with wonders and miracles. In conclusion Yen Chih-tui says: "What a man believes is only his ears and his eyes. Everything else is doubted".[2] This is an expression of a typical characteristic of Chinese thought. The Chinese in esteeming what was immediately perceptible—especially visually perceptible — sought intuitive instantaneous understanding through direct perception. This tendency is reflected in the use of characters which convey concrete images to express abstract concepts; it is also revealed in the manner of elucidating philosophical doctrines. Thus, the use of diagrammatic explanation is frequently resorted to. It need hardly be said that the use of the symbols of the *I-ching* as directly perceptible images of a wide range of phenomena is a case in point.

In Chinese perfection is most often expressed as round. It is said, for example, that the heart of a sage is round.[3] In the translation of Buddhist scriptures into Chinese, the Indian word 'perfect' was translated by the 'round and filled'. The Sanskrit word *sampad,* 'equipped with', was translated by the same compound. Parinişpannalakṣaṇa, the ture 'nature of all phenomena', was translated by Hsüan-chuang as 圓成實性, and in this case the word 圓 (= round) was not expressed in the original Sanskrit term.[4] The most perfect doctrine in Buddhism was, in some systems, called 'the round doctrine' (圓教).[5] This equivalence between perfection and the circle, or the quality of roundness was peculiar to the Chinese. It did not have such a meaning for the Indians. On the other hand the wheel (cakra) was highly esteemed as the symbol of the perfect doctrine of the Buddha, or as an attribute of the God Vishnu; while the wheel suggests change, the circle is static. Moreover, the Indians regarded an absolute as without limits and therefore incapable of being represented in concrete symbols.

The Greeks regarded a globe as the highest form of reality, and this attitude persisted through much of Greek philosophy.[6] But whereas the circle—symbol of perfection for the Chinese—is a plane, the Greek symbol is two dimensional. The Vaiśeṣika philosophy conceived an atom to be globular (parimaṇḍala) but the Chinese translator rendered this as 圓體 "circular".[7]

Even in expounding such an elaborate philosophical system as the *Hua-yen* its founder resorted to a visual demonstration of the close interrelationship of all phenomena by the use of ten mirrors facing inward at eight different angles and placed above and below with a Buddha figure in the middle.[8] His purpose was to elicit, through an immediate appeal to visual perception, an intuitive understanding of the nature of phenomena.

---

1) Kōjirō Yoshikawa 吉川幸次郎: *Shinajin no Koten to sono Seikatsu* (支那人の古典とその生活 The Classics of the Chinese and their Way of Life), p. 201.
2) *Chia-hsün-kuei-hsin-pien* (家訓歸心篇) written by 顔之推 (Yen Chih-tui), in the third vol. of *Kuang-hung-ming-chi* (廣弘明集).
3) Kōjirō Yoshikawa: *op. cit.* p. 32.
4) So *Chên-ti San-tsang* (眞諦三藏 Paramārtha) translated the same word as 眞實性.
5) In the system of 三教 delivered by *Kuang-tung, Vinaya Master*, (光統律師) of the Wêi dynasty, the third one, in that of 四教 of the T'ien-t'ai sect, the fourth one, in that of 五教 of the Hua-yen sect, the fifth one is called 圓教.
6) Edward Zeller: *Die Philosophie der Griechen*, Bd. I Abt. 1, S. 661; 695; 458; 521; I, 2, S 973; II, 1, S 808, II, 2, S 448; Deussen: *Allgemeine Geschichte der Philosophie*, II, 1, S 74; 83; 117; 278; 354.
7) 慧月 (Maticandra): 勝宗十句義論 (Dasapadārthaśāstra) translated by Hsüan-chuang. Here 體 does not mean (body), but a Sanskrit suffix -tva, designating a universal or abstractness.
8) *Sung-kao-sêng-chuan* (宋高僧傳), vol. V. (*Taishō*. vol. 50, p. 732a.)

(4) Diagrammatic explanation

In the course of the domestication of Buddhism in China there appeared a tendency to explain Buddhist doctrines by means of diagraming. 峯圭宗密 (780–841), a scholar of the *Hua-yen* sect explained the relation between the pure and the impure aspects of mind by a diagram in which the former was indicated by the sign ○ and the latter with the sign ●.

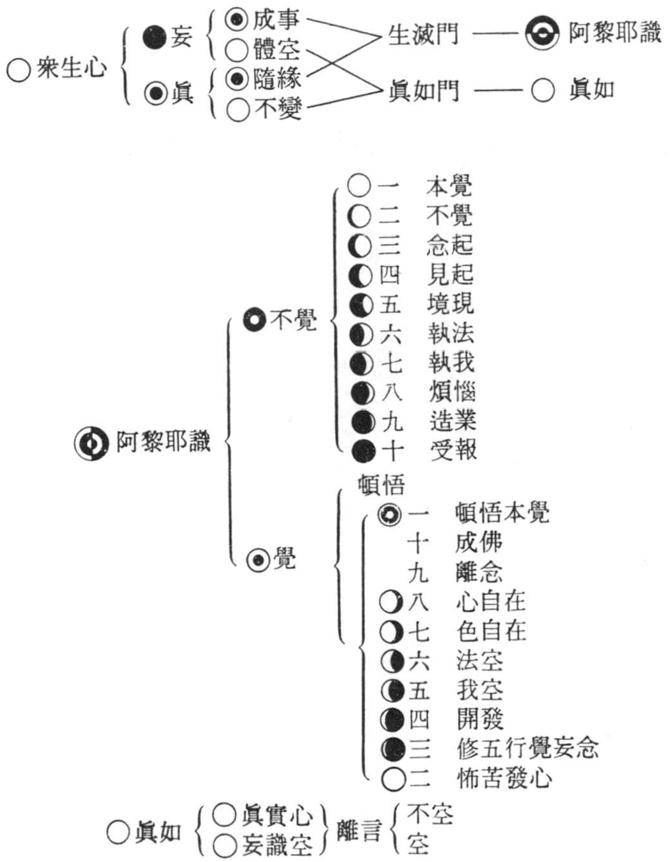

The fundamental essence of existence (ālayavijñāna) consists of pure and impure aspects. The process of development of a mundane creature is shown in ten stages and the means by which this existence is annulled and absorbed into reality is likewise explained in ten stages:[1]

The amalgamation of different kinds of visual arts was also characteristic of Chinese culture. For example, the Chinese custom of writing an appreciation or a panegyric on a painting did not exist in ancient Greece or in India. An example of a series of pictures accompanied with panegyrics in the Chinese Buddhist tradition is the 佛國禪師文殊指南圖讃.[2]

The same tendency manifested itself in Zen Buddhism. Tung-shan (洞山良价 807–869) lectured on the five stages (洞山位五). Behind this scheme there is a type of abstract speculation, but the disciple of this Zen master 曹山本寂 attempted to *explain these five stages with diagrams* and poems relating each stage to *a hierarchical position between monarch and subject.*[3] Here a set of abstract notions was explained by means of readily perceived imagery.[4] Still later this explanatory device was fused with explanations in terms of the symbol of the *I-ching*.[5] [6]

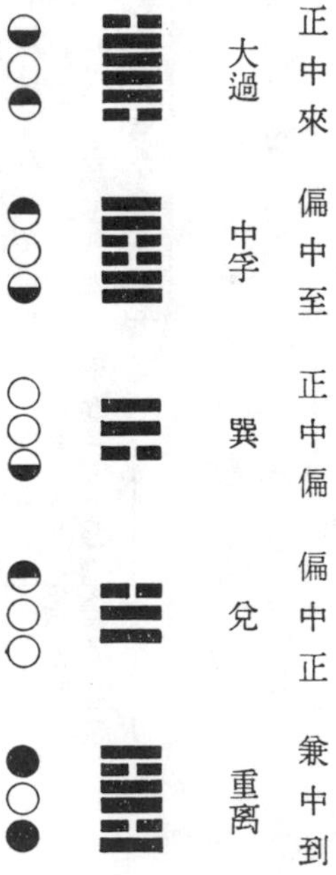

The tendency to resort to diagrammatic explanation tended to be unified with traditional Chinese scholarship tof 'I' (易). In Tung-shan's Pas-ching San-mei-k'o, the Five Stages were explained in terms of "I" scholarship. Finally Hui-hung (寂音慧洪) of the Sun period explained them with the following diagrams.

This tradition of diagrammatic explanation exerted great influence on Sung neo-Confucianism, and was manifested in the 太極圖說 of 周敦頤 (1017–1073). There is no doubt that in his diagram of the gestation of the universe he was influenced by Buddhism. However, in explaining the

genesis of the universe he did not resort to abstractions of the Indian variety but introduced such concrete empirical principles as *'yin* and *yang'* (陰陽) or 'man and woman' (男女).[7] It is interesting to note that the 太極圖 of neo-Confucianism in turn influenced Buddhism and the theory of the five stages was modified and developed by it.[8] [9]

In Zen Buddhism there appeared a diagram called the Poem of Reality (眞性偈). The twenty characters of the diagram are arranged in a circle as follows:[10]

The author advised the practitioner to meditate upon reality by means of these twenty characters. They express, or suggest, a variety of abstract notions but there is no indication of the logical interconnection between them.

Such means of explaining metaphysical theories are not found in Greece or in India where such theories were rather set forth in complicated series of sentences. The same tendency can be observed in the use of diagrammatic genealogies depicting the descent of doctrine from master to pupil,[11] while in India the same material is presented in dry prose.[12]

1) Cf. *Chan-yüan-chu-chüan-chi-tu-hsü* (禪源諸詮集都序), ed. by H. Ui 宇井伯壽, p. 136 f.
2) *Taishō.* vol. 45, p. 793 cf.
3) *Fu-chou-tsao-shan-yüan-chêng-yü-lu* (撫州曹山元證禪師語錄). (*Taishō.* vol. 47, p. 527 a); *Jen-t'ien-yen-mu,* vol. III, (*Taishō.* vol. 48, p. 316 b)
4) *loc. cit.*
5) *Yün-chou-tung-shan-wu-pen-yü-lu* (筠州洞山悟本禪師語錄). (*Taishō.* vol. 47, p. 515 a); *Jen-t'ien-yen-mu,* vol. III (*Taishō.* vol. 48, p. 321 a)
6) *Ho-ku-ch'ê* (合古轍), vol. I. (智證傳, 卍續藏經, Second Series, XVI, fasc. 2).
7) Although the words 'man and woman' (男女) cannot be taken in a literal sense, yet the author preferred them.

8) *Tung-shang-ku-ch'ê* (洞上古徹), vol. I (永覺元賢禪師廣錄, vol. 27, 卍續藏經, Second series, XXX, fasc. 4).
9) 卍續藏經 Second series, XVI, fasc. 2.
10) *Jen-t'ien-yen-mu*, vol. VI.
11) *Chung-hua-chuan-hsin-ti-chan-mên-shih-tzu-ch'eng-hsi-t'u* (中華傳心地禪門師資承襲圖), (禪源諸詮集都序, ed. by H. Ui, p. 188 f.)
12) For example, cf. genealogies transmitted in the monasteries of the Vedānta schools.

Chapter 3. Non-development of abstract thought

(1) Lack of consciousness of universals

We have seen that the Chinese esteemed the data of direct perception, espeically visual perception, and that they were concerned with particular instances. This meant that they were little interested in universals which comprehend or transcend individual or particular instances. They thus seldom created a universal out of particulars. Thus for example there are many words denoting different varieties of mountains while there is no word to designate the universal concept of 'mountain' or 'mountainness'.

In Chinese one finds many different words used to denote subtly shaded variance of the same thing or action. Thus, for example, the following words are used for different shadings of the action word 'to carry': 擔, 持, 任, 運, 搬, 保, 帶, 着. The same phenomenon can be seen in the languages of primitive peoples elsewhere. For example, in Malay there are many different words translatable into German only as 'tragen' but which mean 'to carry by hand', 'to carry on a shoulder', 'to carry on head', 'to carry on the back', 'to carry on the body, as a garment, a weapon, or an ornament', 'to carry a child in the womb', etc.[1] Although one can see the residue of some such variety in Greek, in Greek and English generally, such a range of variant verbs does not exist. It may be said that in these languages, unlike Malay, a degree of universalization and abstraction has been reached, which is higher than that in Chinese or Malay.

Another example. In Chinese there is no word which corresponds to the English 'old'. For sixty years old the Chinese word is 耆; for seventy years old, the Chinese word is 老; for eighty or ninety years old the Chinese character is 耄. Similarly different words were used to express the notions of death and to die. The term varied according to the status of the person concerned. For the Emperor it was 崩, for feudal lords it was 薨, for

大夫, 卒, for 士, 不祿, for the common people 死.[2] We might draw the conclusion from such examples as these that the Chinese did not develop the mental habit of comprehending a group of related phenomena in a universal.

This is not to say that all Chinese philosophers were unconscious of a relationship between universals and particulars. Hsun-tzu had a rather clear idea of this.[3] He distinguished between common or general names (共名) and particular names (別名). But he did not, like Aristotle, attain full consciousness of 'definition'. His lack of this consciousness is symptomatic of the general lack of consciousness of *genus indifferentia* among the Chinese.

Of course efforts were made to express concepts more clearly using compound words. This device aimed at making the meaning of the word clearer by defining the extent of the meaning through a second character. This is quite different from the Greek practice which aimed at making the meaning clearer by limiting the *genus* with *differentia.*

So, generally speaking, the notion of a universal and of the ordering of particulars under universals are not characteristic of Chinese thought.

---

1) Stenzel: *Die Philosophie der Sprache*, S. 76.
2) *Li Chi* (禮記), 典禮 pt. 1 and pt. 2.
3) *Sun Tzu* (筍子), 正名篇. Yoshio Takeuchi 武内義雄: *Shina Shisō-shi* p. 12.

(2) Non-logical character of verbal expression and thought

The non-logical character of the verbal expression of Chinese thought is of course intimately connected with the characteristics of the Chinese language. Words corresponding to the prepositions, conjunctions and relative pronouns of Western languages are very rare. There is no distinction between singular and plural. A single character, 人, can denote 'un homme, des hommes, quelques hommes, or humanité'. There are no fixed and difinite forms for the expression of the tense or mood of verbs. There are no cases. One word can be noun, adjective, or verb. This kind of ambiguity has meant that the exegesis of the classics has produced an immense variety of interpretations, many of which are directly opposite in sense to others.[1] Because of this tendency toward ambiguity the Chinese had the greatest difficulty in understanding the meaning of the Buddhist scriptures which had originally been written in an entirely different type of language. Because of the lack of number, gender, and case in Chinese pronouns, sentences in the Chinese version of Buddhist writings were often understood in a sense different from that of the original. The misinterpretations thus produced were often very important in the dogmatic development of Chinese and Japanese Buddhism.

For example, the famous verse in which Nāgārjuna sets forth the concept of the middle way (*Mādhyamika śāstra* XXIV, 18) as translated from Sanskrit runs as follows: "What do we call dependent origination? We call it the void; that is an assumptional being; that is the middle way". In this Nāgārjuna asserted that the four concepts—dependent origination, the void, an assumptional being, the middle way were synonymous. This verse was translated by Kumārajīva as follows: 衆因緣生法, 我說卽是無, 亦爲是假名, 亦是中道義. Later Chinese scholars altered the wording of the sentences: 因緣所生法, 我說卽是空, 亦爲是假名, 亦是中道義.[2] 慧文[3] explained this verse as follows: Everything has originated from causes. These causes are beings but not definite beings; they are 'void', but not definitely void. It is this situation which is called 'the middle way'. The T'ien-t'ai sect explained the verse as teaching the three truths: all things have originated from causes and are destitute of individual essence, i.e. are void, but even 'the void' is 'assumptional'. We should not substantiate it; the void also should be negated. Thus this sect set up the three truths, the void, the assumptional and the middle.[4] This variety of interpretation—involving misinterpretation—is attributable to the lack of gender, number, or case notation in the demonstrative pronoun.

There are no plural forms of Chinese nouns. Various devices are used to express the plural: adding numerals to nouns, e.g. 五人, 千卷, reduplication e.g. 人人, the addition of a character such as 諸 to nouns, e.g. 諸人. Moreover the character 等 can be used as a suffix expressing the plural, but it can mean et cetera. For example, 牛等 may mean 'oxen' or 'oxen and horses and sheep'. When the Chinese came in contact with Sanskrit they recognized the difference between a plural and et cetera. Chinese Buddhist scholars differentiated the pluralizing *teng* 向內等 from the et cetera *teng* which they called 向外等. However, this distinction did not go beyond Buddhist scholarship. It was never used in secular thought.

Another non-logical characteristic of Chinese is reflected in the frequency of anacolutha or change of subject within a sentence. In Sanskrit this occurs only in such ancient literature as the Brāhmaṇas,[5] whereas in Chinese it is very common because Chinese frequently omits subjects of sentences. In the Chinese versions of Buddhist scriptures anacoluthon is common even though it is rare in the Sanskrit originals from which those versions were translated. It is especially conspicuous in Kumārājīva's translations which are famous for their style, i.e. their appeal to Chinese literary taste and habitual ways of thinking.[6]

The various ambiguities described have meant that the Chinese has been an awkward medium for the expression of abstract thought. Although there is evidence of metaphysical speculation in the Taoist writings there is little of this in the Confucian tradition which long dominated the thinking of the ruling class. In the *Analects* of Confucius there are many separate instances of behavior from which certain lessons are drawn. There are many aphorisms, but there is no dialectic such as one finds in Plato. *I Ching* scholarship was often, in later times, united with metaphysics, but the *I Ching* itself—full of suggestive explanations of human events—did not itself aim at metaphysics. Metaphysical theory which developed in neo-Confucianism for the first time, was, as we have seen, still figurative and intuitive.

The lack of the spirit of dialogue in ancient China is noteworthy. The dialectic—the art of questioning and answering as a device for philosophical analysis—did not develop as it had in Greece. Western Sinologues[7] often assert that the dialectic is present in the rules of discourse given by Mo-tzu,[8] but we have too little data on the application of these rules to establish the existence of a true dialectic.

In India it was long a custom for the assertor and the objector to argue with each other in a public assembly sponsored by a great personage. In China this parctice was relatively rare. It occurred for a short period in the sixth and seventh centuries.[9] Likewise, Chinese court[10] procedure was not characterized by the full development of judicial dialogue between the accused and the accuser. The almost total absence of this type of phenomenon in Chinese society meant that a great deal of Indian logic, which in origin was a logic of dialogue, had no significance for the Chinese. For this reason Indian logic could not be taken over in its original form by the Chinese.

---

1) Cf. Kōjirō Yoshikawa 吉川幸次郎: *Shinajin no Koten to sono Seikatsu*, pp. 73–81.
2) Chi-tsang (嘉祥大師吉藏): *Êrh-ti-i* (二諦義), vol. I. (*Taishō*. vol. 45, p. 82c, p. 83b); *Chung*-*lun*-*su* (中論疏), (*Tashō*, vol. 45, p. 49 a, p. 973.
3) *Fo-tsu-tung-chi* (佛祖統記), vol. 6 (*Taishō*. vol. 49, p. 178 c).
4) Especially in the works of *Chih-i* (天台大師智顗).

5) J. S. Speyer: *Vedische und Sanskrit-Syntax*, S. 91.
6) 觀音經 cf. Giei Honda 本田義英: *Hokekyō Ron* (法華經論), pp. 287–288.
7) H. Maspéro: Notes sur la logique de Mo-tseu et de son école. *Toung-Pao* 1927, p. 29.
8) *Mo-tzu* (墨子), 小取 No. 45.
9) *Hsü-kao-tsêng-chuan* (續高僧傳), 24, 慧乘傳; *ibid.* 11, 吉藏傳. Cf. Hiroshi Yamazaki 山崎宏: *Shina Chūsei Bukkyō no Tenkai* (支那中世佛教の展開 The development of the Chinese Buddhism in the Medieval Age) pp. 721 ff.; 727.
10) Max Weber: *Gesammelte Aufsätze zur Religionssoziologie*, I, S. 416.

(3) Lack of comprehension through conscious use of general laws

It was perhaps a result of some of the non-logical characteristic of Chinese thought which we have described, that the Chinese tradition was weak in the formation of objective laws. The esteem for the individual and particular, lack of interest in universals, aborted the discovery of laws which order many particulars. This parallels the lack of strict laws for linguistic expression. *Indifference to or lack of consciousness of the necessity for rules of language meant that the science of grammar never developed.* Unlike the Greeks and the Indians, the Chinese produced no works on grammar or syntax, although they engaged in elaborate investigations and compilations of characters, phonetics, etymology, etc. Even though some Chinese pilgrim monks became acquainted with the Indian science of grammar, they did not attempt to establish a parallel science of Chinese grammar. Such a science has only developed since the impact of Western civilization.

Similarly, natural science was not highly developed. Up to a point, Chinese investigative study can be called inductive, for the Chinese sought for precedence and facts but induction ceased at a certain point and deduction based on the authority of the classics then took over.[1] This is a partial explanation of the non-development of science in China.

In Sung neo-Confucianism 致知格物 was esteemed, but this was not natural cognition nor particularly objective cognition; it was rather an ordered intuition into the essence of all things.[2]

In the Chinese Buddhist tradition there is no single authoritative interpretation of meaning of a given phrase. Chinese Buddhist scholars produced different and varied interpretations of the same phrase. Zen Buddhism carried this to extremes enunciating the principle "not to set up any words" (不立文字). Similarly, 'if our mind goes astray we are ruled by the *Fa-hua-ching*. If our mind is enlightened, we rule the *Fa-*

hua-ching'.[3] 'Not to set up any words' does not mean 'do not resort to the use of the written word', for there were few sects which used and valued literary expression as much as the Zen sect. The term therefore mean, rather, 'do not set up dogmas in the form of propositions'.

Zen Buddhism, with this attitude, denied the importance of the Buddhist canon. They compare the canon to fingers pointing at the moon; they also use the simile beloved of the Taoists and compare the Buddhist canon to fish nets and rabbit traps.[4] In other words one should concentrate on the content, not place great value on the literary meaning of apprehending that content.

Chinese dislike for canonical formulae can be seen in the process of their acceptance of various Buddhist arts.[5] Although the Chinese built many Buddhist monuments and reliquaries they cannot be classified into canonical types. In the case of Buddhist images there were formulae for making images and such formulae were carefully followed in Japan, but they were not followed in China and one cannot classify surviving Chinese Buddha images according to these type-forms. For example, in China a Buddha image holding a medicine vessel is not always Bhaiṣajyaguru-tathāgata and his image is not always accompanied by this object. Buddha images were made arbitrarily in whatever form the artist desired.

1) Cf. Kōjirō Yoshikawa: *op. cit.*, pp. 136–141.
2) Yoshio Takeuchi: *op. cit.*, p. 292.
3) *Liu-tsu-tan-ching* (六祖壇經).
4) *Ching-tê-chuan-têng-lu* (景德傳燈錄) vol. XXVIII (*Taishō*. vol. 51, p. 443 c.).
5) Daijō Tokiwa 常盤大定: *Shina Bukkyō-no Kenkyū* (支那佛教の研究 A Study on Chinese Buddhism), vol. III, pp. 109–110.

(4) Acceptance of Indian logic in a distorted form

Since nomothetical sciences did not develop in China, it is natural that logic which deals with the laws for the expression of thought did not develop either.

A certain degree of logical consciousness naturally existed among the Chinese, but they did not build upon that consciousness 'a logical science'. Some scholars assert that deductive argumentation — if not logic — was developed by the followers of Mo-tzu being termed 效.[1] In my view, it is doubtful that this term really coincides with what is known in the West as deduction.[2]

In later times Indian logic was introduced into China, but it exerted no significant influence on the ways of thinking of the Chinese. It soon declined and disappeared as a branch of study.

In some Buddhist works translated into Chinese there are passages on logic. For example, the *Upāyahṛdaya* (方便心論) translated by Kiṃkara (吉迦夜), the 如實論 translated by Paramārtha (眞諦),[3] the *Nyāyamukha* (因明正理門論) of Dignāga translated by Hüsan-chuang and the *Nyāya-praveśaka* 因明入正理論 translated by Hsüan-chuang. The commentary upon the last name called the 因明入正理論疏 by a disciple of Hsüan-chuang, Tz'u ên (慈恩大師基), was regarded as the highest authority in this field in China and Japan. After Hsüan-chuang at least thirty works were composed on Buddhist logic.[4]

In the history of the introduction of Buddhist logic into China we can observe several striking phenomena. Firstly, very few logical works were translated into Chinese. If we compare that number with the vastly larger number of such works which were translated into Tibetan, we are bound to conclude that interest in Buddhist logic was very slight among the Chinese. Secondly, only logical works of the simplest kind were translated into Chinese and voluminous works intended to be systematic expositions of the whole science of logic were left untranslated. It would appear that the Chinese translated simple handbooks or compendia, the bare minimum necessary to get a rudimentary knowledge of the logical terminology of Buddhist treatises in general. Thirdly, Indian works on epistemology which attempted to develop a theory of knowledge as a basis of knowledge for logical theory were not translated. Perhaps the ultimate development of Buddhist logic in India was accomplished by Dharmakīrti. He sought the source of human knowledge in perception and reasoning. He differentiated between synthetic and analytical judgments. On this basis he established an elaborate system — a science of knowledge. His system has often been compared to that of Kant. The Tibetans translated and studied Dharmakīrti's works, whereas the Chinese Buddhists made no effort to study or to understand them. Even after Dharmakīrti the Chinese translated earlier works mainly on discipline and ritual. On the basis of this it is perhaps justifiable to say that the Chinese did not seek theory for theory's sake but rather gave their attention to that which was immediately relevant to practical understanding and behavior.

Thus Indian logic was accepted only in part and even the part that was accepted was not understood in the sense of the Indian originals. Even Hsüan-chuang, who introduced Indian logic, seems not to have fully understood it. In a great assembly in India he made the inference that mind alone really exists while objects in the external world do not exist. In developing his argument he violated the rule of Indian logic which holds that the proposition 'reason' should be one which is admitted by both assertor and opponent. Under this heading he set forth a proposition which was only agreed to by the assertor.[5] Tz'u-ên (慈恩)'s work, which was regarded as the highest authority in China and Japan, contains many falacies in philosophical and logical analysis.[6] He apparently did not understand the Indian rule that in syllogisms the middle term should be distributed by the major term. The formula of the new Buddhist logic was called the three-membered syllogism (三支作法) and it consisted of assertion, reason and simile.[7] Some Chinese Buddhist scholars understood this[8] but Tz'u-ên misunderstood it, asserting that it consisted of reason and similes of likeness and unlikeness.[9] This mistake in interpretation became henceforth authoritative in China and Japan.

In Chinese Buddhist scriptures *ratio essendi* (kāraka hetu) is translated as 生因 and *ratio cognoscendi* (jñāpaka hetu) as 了因.[10] But Tz'u-ên failed to understand the distinction and connected both concepts with three concepts of 言, 智, 義.[11] In doing this he simply made a mechanical classification and his explanation is self-contradictory as well as at odds with the original meaning. His application of logical rules in elucidating the idealist philosophy (the mind only theory) was utterly fallacious. This fact was pointed out even by early Japanese Buddhist scholars such as Genshin (源信), Rinjō (林常), and Kaijō (戒定).[12]

There is a further fundamental difference between Indian logicians and Chinese Buddhist scholars. Indian Buddhist scholars of the logical school accepted perception and reasoning as the sole sources of right knowledge; they denied the independent authority to the Canon in this field whereas Chinese scholars of Buddhist logic accepted the authority of the Canon.

Even the sort of limited logical study carried on by the sect of idealism, whose founder was Tz'u-ên, declined when this sect declined. It was only in the T'ang dynasty that logical studies had any vitality.

Logical studies having no basis in traditional Chinese thought never became significant and exerted very little influence on later Chinese thought. It should be noted that this is in striking contrast to the importance and vitality of logical studies in Tibet.

---

1) Henri Maspero: Notes sur la logique de Mo-tseu et de son école. *Toung-Pao*, 1927, p. 12.

2) Hu Shih: *The Development of the Logical Method in Ancient China*, Shanghai, 1922, pp. 83, 95.
3) Cf. Hakuju Ui 宇井伯壽: *Indo Tetsugaku Kenkyū* (印度哲學研究 Studies in Indian Philosophy), vol. VI, p. 72 ff; 94 ff.
4) Cf. Shōkō Watanabe 渡邊照宏: *Inmyō Ronso Myōtōshō Kaidai* (因明論疏明燈抄解題), *Kokuyaku Issaikyō* (國譯一切經, Ronshōbu 論疏部, vol. XVIII).
5) 因明入正理論疏 vol. II (*Taishō*. vol. 44, p. 115 b), 玄奘三藏唯識比量諍過決 vol. II in 唯識分量決 (*Taishō*. vol. 71, p. 451 f) Cf. Hakuju Ui 宇井伯壽: *Bukkyō Ronri Gaku* (佛教論理學 A Study on Buddhist Logic), pp. 323, 321; *Indo Tetsugaku Kenkyū*, vol. V. p. 104 ff.; Senshō Murakami 村上專精: Kōyō Sakaino 境野黄洋: *Bukkyō Ronri Gaku* (佛教論理學 A Study on Buddhist Logic).
6) Cf. his explanation about 同品定有性 (因明入正理論疏 vol. I. *Taishō*. vol. 44, p. 105 a).
7) Cf. Hakuju Ui: *Bukkyō Ronri Gaku*, p. 365.
8) 定賓 was one of them. (cf. Shōkō Watanabe: op. cit. *Kokuyaku Issaikyō*, Ronshōbu, vol. XVIII, p. 4.
9) 「因一喻二, 三爲能立」(「因明入正理論疏」 vol. I. (*Taishō*, vol. 44. p. 106 c)).
10) Hakuju Ui: *Indo Tetsugaku Kenkyū*, vol. II, p. 478 f.; Senshō Murakami: *Bukkyō Ronri Gaku*, pp. 37, 88 f.
11) 窺基: 因明入正理論疏 vol. I. (*Taishō*. vol. 44, p. 101 c). Cf. 因明論疏明燈抄 (*Taishō*. vol. 68, p. 212 a).
12) Hakuju Ui: *Indo Tetsugaku Kenkyū*, vol. V, p. 105; *Bukkyō Ronrigaku* p. 345.

(5) The non-logical character of Zen Buddhism

The non-logical character of Chinese thought is particularly conspicuous in Zen Buddhism which is the most sinicized of Chinese Buddhist sects. Early Zen was not non-logical. The early system of explanation known as 'the two enlightenments and four practices' (二入四行)[1] was quite logical and even later the dialogue of Hui-hai (大珠慧海) is characterized by logical consistency.[2]

However, a non-logical tendency soon manifested itself and eventually prevailed. The monk Huang-po (黄檗) said [3] "....they say that the true universal body of the Buddha is like the sky....but they do not understand that the universal body is sky, and sky is the universal body. The two are not different". Now the Buddha nature or the originally pure mind (自性清淨心) were often compared to the sky in India. But the Indians regarded the sky as an element or principle in the natural world, and distinguished it from the Buddha nature, whereas the Chinese lost sight of this distinction. When the tendency exists to lose sight of the function and significance of a simile theoretical philosophy is unlikely to develop. Moreover, theoretical assertions were neither widely understood nor was their meaning developed. For example, Lin-chi (臨濟義玄)'s four alternatives 四料揀 are philosophically important and allow many different explanations. Their author did not, however, discuss them in an abstract speculative way. He explained them in figurative language: " 'To take away man and not to take away objects' — warm days appear and brocade is laid out on the earth — baby's hairs falling are like white thread. 'To take away objects and not to take away man' — the king's orders are promulgated and circulate over the empire; generals take their ease outside the stronghold. 'To take away both men and objects' — to live in a retreat cut off from all communication. 'Not to take away either men or objects' — a king ascends to a jeweled palace and old peasants sing gaily".[4] The point in this quotation is not that figurative explanations are given but that figurative explanations alone are given. Poetical and emotional phrases take the place of logical exposition. Later explanations of these four alternatives were generally of the same sort.

The non-logical character of Zen is most conspicuous in its dialogues. We have said that the spirit and technique of the dialogue did not develop in China, so it is important to emphasize that so-called dialogues of Zen were utterly different from Greek dialogues. When Chao-chou (趙州) was asked "Does the Buddha nature exist in a dog?" he answered in the affirmative on one occasion and in the negative on another. Ma-tsu(馬祖道一) said on one occasion 'Mind is the Buddha' and on another occasion 'Neither mind nor Buddha'.[5] The reasons for these contradictory answers is to be found in the concrete situations which elicited them. We may compare this to the different advice given by doctors to patients of different physical types suffering from the same disease. There is conspicuous contradiction in the theoretical sense but no contradiction in the practical sense. This is an example of the expediency (方便) aspect of Buddhist thought.

However, in the type of thought which is called expediency (方便), there is a definite connection between the end desired and the means employed. Later Zen Buddhism gradually lost sight of that connection. For example, there is a frequently repeated question in Zen Buddhism: 'For what purpose did Bodhidharma come to China?' It really means something like 'What is the essence of Zen Buddhism?' To this question Zen masters gave a variety of answers:[6]

'I am tired, having been sitting for a long time'.

'Today and tomorrow'.

'A piece of tile and a bit of stone'.

'The wind blows and the sun heats'.

'Frost comes upon clouds'.
'An oak tree in the garden'.
'In daytime I see a mountain'.
'White clouds embrace rocky stone'.
'Ch'ang-an is in the East, Lo-yang is in the West'.
'With a fan of blue silk, I feel cool enough in the wind'.
'A thousand sticks of bamboo outside the gate and a piece of incense before the image of Buddha'.
'There being no water during a long drought, rice plants withered in the fields'.

There are said to be more than a hundred answers to this question. Since no semantic connection between the questions and the answers was required, the answers can be of infinite variety. The question and the answer are given in a moment. There is no sustained development such as characterizes Greek dialogue. The answers seem strange indeed, but it is said that many of those who heard the answers gained enlightenment. Zen masters never answered questions in the form of universal propositions. They believed that philosophical problems could best be solved by evoking intuition through concrete figurative language.

This whole complex of ideas and practices is alien to Indian Buddhism. The *dharmas,* that is, universal religious and moral norms were in China seen not as the content of judgments shared by other people, but as the direct experience of each individual inexpressible in words. Yung-chia (永嘉玄覺) said of himself "Since I was young I have been devoted to scholarship. I investigated sūtras and commentaries. Nothing but ceaseless discrimination of terms! It is like counting the sands in the sea. The Buddha reprimanded me saying 'What is the use of counting the treasures of others?' "[7]

Once they had given up the effort to grasp and to express truths in the form of universal propositions, the Zen Buddhists gradually fell into the habit of non-logical discourse. Chu Hsi pointed out that Zen masters at first engaged in very clear dialogues but later became complacent, enmeshed in nonsensical dialogues.[8] Chu Hsi himself had this in common with the Zen masters: he never gave exact answers. The later Zen masters did not seek to give explanations in rational terms, they sought rather to give them in a figurative and intuitive way.

A commentary by Wan-sung (萬松老人) to an ancient dialogue by Bodhidharma runs as follows: (the comments are given in brackets) "Emperor

Wu of the Liang inquired of Bodhidharma [he got up early and went to market without making any profit.] 'What is the ultimate reality, the sacred truth?' [now ask the second head.] Bodhidharma said 'That where there is no sacredness at all.' [He has split open the abdomen and dug out the heart.] The Emperor said 'Who is talking with me?' [We can perceive a tusk inside the nostril.] Bodhidharma said 'I don't know'. [We can see the jowls behind the brains.] The Emperor could not agree with him. [A square peg cannot go into a round hole.] Finally, Bodhidharma crossed the Yang-tse and went to the Shao-lin temple where he practiced meditation for nine years. [If a family does not have overdue rent it cannot be rich.]"[9]

Though this dialogue itself has a hidden logic of its own, we can see from this bracketed commentary the tendency in later Zen to use explanations made up of concrete images of a suggestive kind.

1) Cf. Hakuju Ui 宇井伯壽: *Zenshū-shi Kenkyū* (禪宗史研究 A Study on the History of Zen Sects), p. 3 ff.
2) 頓悟要門 ed. by Hakuju Ui (in Iwanami Bunko ed. 岩波文庫), pp. 44–47.
3) 傳心法要 ed. by Hakuju Ui (in Iwanami Bunko ed. 岩波文庫), p. 20.
4) 鎮州臨濟慧照禪師語錄 (*Taishō*. vol. 47. p. 497 a); 人天眼目 vol. 1 (*Taishō*. vol. 48, p. 300 f).
5) 景德傳燈錄 vol. VI. (*Taishō*. vol. 51, p. 246 a)
6) Hakugen Ichikawa 市川白弦: *Zen no Kihonteki Seikaku* (禪の基本的性格) The Fundamental Character of Zen), p. 49 f.
7) 證道歌
8) Yoshio Takeuchi: *op. cit. Shina Shisō-shi*, p. 299.
9) 從容錄.

Chapter 4. Emphasis on the particular

(1) Emphasis on particular instances

The tendency to value and to devote attention to the particular rather than the universal is observable in many different aspects of Chinese culture.

The Five Classics which are works of the highest authority regarded as providing the norms for human life contain, for the most part, descriptions of particular incidents and statements of particular facts. They do not state general principles of human behavior.[1] Even the *Analects* of Confucius records mostly the actions of individuals and the dicta of Confucius on the separate incidents; these dicta for the most part have a personal significance. Through the classics and their commentaries the Chinese sought valid behavioral norms through individual instances.

Buddhism which had, in the Indian manner set forth general and universal principles, was often presented to the Chinese through concrete examples and individual instances. The most conspicuous example of this development is the mode of explanation developed by Zen Buddhism. "A priest asked Tung-shan (洞山) 'What is Buddha?' He replied 'Only three pounds of hemp' ". Yuan-wu (悟圜) of the Sung dynasty explained this as follows.[2] "Many people have given different explanations of this. Some say that Tung-shan was weighing hemp when he was asked the question. Others say that he is inclined to answer west when asked about the east. [i.e., he was inclined to answer in an unexpected way.] Others say, 'Originally you yourself are Buddha whereas the questioner sought for Buddha outside himself; in order to tell him how silly he was, Tung-shan answered in an elliptical way'. Other silly people say that the three pounds of hemp themselves are nothing but Buddha. These answers have nothing to do with Tung-shan 's purport". Then what is the true meaning of the answers? Yuan-wu is evasive, saying, "The true way cannot be obtained by words". In these explanations and Yuan-wu's comment we can see a distinctive feature of the Chinese way of thinking, i.e., the true way is not to be obtained by words—not through universal propositions—but only through concrete experience. Thus, one *should not regard the Buddha as something mystical and transcending ordinary life.*

Nāgārjuna had expressed a similar idea. He said that the long sequence of discussions on the essence of the Buddha did not reveal that essence. He said "The Buddha transcends all metaphysical discussions and is indestructible; yet those who discuss it fail to see the Buddha being blinded by their own sophistication".[3] According to him in every experience we experience Buddha. "The true essence of Buddha is nothing but that of this mundane world". This thought coincides in meaning with that of Tung-shan. But the difference between the Indian and the Chinese ways of thinking lies in the difference of the expression of that meaning. Whereas Nāgārjuna taught in the form of universal propositions, the Chinese did not do so but produced the concrete example of the three pounds of hemp.

We can see much the same contrast in the differing answers to questions about the life after death. "A monk asked, 'Where did Nan-ch'üan (南泉) go after he died?' The master replied 'In an eastern house he became an ass, and in a western house he became a horse' ". This answer did not mean that he had been reborn as an ass or a horse. "The monk asked, 'What do you mean by this?' The master said 'If he wants to ride he can ride, if he wants to get off he can get off' ".[4] This means that the deceased had attained the freedom to do what he wanted having transcended life and death. Let us compare this with the answer to a comparable question in early Buddhism. When the Buddha was asked whether the Enlightened One existed after death, he did not give any answer to the question because, as the Sutras say, discussion and speculation about such metaphysical problems could not lead men to enlightenment. Thus, not giving any answer is a kind of definite answer and is logically conceived. Here we can see the difference of ways of thinking between both peoples.

---

1) Kōjirō Yoshikawa *op. cit.* p. 70.
2) 碧巖錄 chap. 12.
3) *Mādhyamaka-śāstra* (中論), XXII, 15.
4) 景德傳燈錄 vol. X. (*Taishō.* vol. 51, p. 274 b.)

(2) Explanation on the basis of particular instances

The way of thinking in which the Chinese think much of the particular and like concrete and intuitive explanations may be seen even in the way of explaining the truth and guiding people, for they endeavor to teach on the basis of particular instances. Therefore, ethics is not understood as part of a universal law, but is grasped on the basis of particular experiences, and is then utilized to realize human truth. Such a mental attitude is readily discernible in *Lun Yü* (論語), and especially in Zen Buddhism. Men are placed in some special circumstances limited by time and space, their experiences changing every moment, which means that no two people can have exactly the same experience. There is a limit to recollective experience. The particular situation wherein the individual is placed is called *"Chi"* (機) by Zen Buddhism. The idea of *"Chi"* (機) is characteristically Chinese, for we cannot find its equivalent in India.[1]

Next, I wish to relate, as a concrete case, of a Kōan the "Chü Chih Shu Chih" (俱胝竪指)—Chü Chih's erected finger. Chü Chih was a disciple of the monk T'ien-lung (天龍). When asked about the most important matters of life and death, he would reply always by showing his finger. Later, a boy who was studying under him imitated his master's manner of showing his finger when he was asked by a stranger about his master's teaching. When Chü Chih heard of his conduct, he cut off the boy's finger. The boy went away crying, unable to endure the pain. He then called back the boy. The boy came back and saw his master unexpectedly show an erect finger. At that instant, the boy attained enlightenment. Chü Chih said at the time of his death, "I was taught 一指頭禪—Zen of a finger tip, by my master and have been unable to exhaust it all during my life-time".

The venerable Hui-k'ai (慧開) made the following criticism: "The enlightenment to which the boy attained does not exist in the finger. If one can understand this, he will realize that he, Chü Chih and the boy are not different".[2]

I think this catechism is an admonition that one should not pretend to have attained to enlightenment if he has not actually done so. I should like to make a comparison here with an Indian case. In the Vinaya-piṭaka of Hīnayāna Buddhism, *uttari-manussa-dhamma* is thought to be one of the four terrible sins for a monk. This means that one who has not attained superior stage, should not pretend that he has.

The Indian liked to express the truth about human beings with a universal proposition, while the Chinese did not like to do so. The Chinese made an effort to realize the universal truth in the human being and revealed in particular instances which cannot be altered by factors of both time and space. When Fa-ch'ang (法常), a famous monk of Zen Buddhism, gathered his disciples at his death, and finished giving his final instructions to them, they heard a flying squirrel cry out, whereupon he said, "That's it! Nothing but it! Retain this well. I am going to die soon".[3]

In Zen Buddhism, they call the particular cases "*Chi*" (機). It is said that an enlightened man knows "*Chi*" and utilizes expedients. It should not be called merely "Chance" or "Contingency", but should be thought of as something containing a motive in which subject and object are in both opposition and response to each other. It freely shows its subtleness according to each situation. Generally speaking, it means that 'one should be the master in every situation'. Thus, Zen Buddhism aims at a suitable mind activity for each situation, i.e., an intuitive action 'correctly manifested'. Therefore, it is said that although the act of ridding oneself of mind and body is rather easy, it is difficult to express in words stage as it is.[4] It is thought that we must remove deep attachment and prejudice, and must be "mindless" in order to take measures suited to the occasion, and must have a "free tension" to have an adequate cognition suitable to the situation and time.

---

1) Its equivalent is not found either in the *Mahāvyutpatti* (Unrai Ogiwara 荻原雲來: *Bonkan Jiten* 梵漢辭典) or in *the Index to the Laṅkāvatāra-sūtra* (Compiled by Daisetz T. Suzuki 鈴木大拙: *Ryōgakyō Sakuin* 楞伽經索引)".
2) 無門關 Chap. 3.
3) 景德傳燈錄 vol. VIII. (*Taishō.* vol. 51, p. 255 a.)
4) 碧巖錄 Chap. 46.

(3) Development of descriptive science in regard to the particular

The Chinese lay stress especially on particular facts in the historical and social spheres, as the result of their emphasis on particulars, namely, they give attention to a phenomenon which is perfectly unique either in time and in space, and of which nothing can take its place.

In the historical sphere, this trend may be observed in the objective and minute compilation of historical works. It is said that the ideal of the compilers of the *Erh Shih Ssu Shih* (二十四史—Twenty-four Dynastic Histories up to the Manchu Dynasty) was the exhaustive entry, as far as possible, of the incidents occuring in each dynasty. Moreover, it is recognized that Chinese historians continuously tried to enlarge and perfect their historical annals, and were always at work on supplements which would include materials omitted from the standard histories. Therefore, they think that the more complex the description is, the more superior the historical work is. Such a method of describing history is just the opposite to the method which aims at simple and concise description. Of course, we can also recognize the trend of summarization and simplification, but it was more usual to take the method of making the historical records more complex through the compilation of histories[1] Therefore, some Westerners criticize such history books and say that they are elaborate, encyclopedic and almost impossible to read through.[2] But even the Western scholar who believes in the superiority of the Greek culture cannot help acknowledging that the Chinese history books are not only minute but also accurate and objective.

"A l'autre bout de notre continent eurasiatique, la Chine offre à notre désir d'information de prestigieuses annales, d'une objectivité hors pair, que pourrait lui jalouser notre propre culture".[3]

The Chinese made an effort to preserve the historical materials which are apt to be destroyed. They collected many kinds of epitaphs and produced such works as the *Chin Shih Ts'ui Pien* (金石萃編) and the *Pa Ch'iung Shih Chin Shih Pu Chêng* (八瓊室金石補正) which is a bulky work of 130 volumes. In India, we cannot find such materials as these.

Moreover, they made every effort to record climatic features and peculiarities, and produced many kinds of book catalogues like the *Ssu K'u Ch'üan Shu Tsung Mu* (四庫全書總目) in 200 volumes. So many catalogues of books have been made that we even find 'catalogues of catalogues'.[4]

Such phenomena are just the opposite of what holds true for India. As mentioned above, there are few historical books, and even these have contents which are largely legendary. Indians have seldom produced topographies, much less catalogues of books. The Indian paid attention only to the universals, neglecting the historical and climatic particularities while the Chinese, on the contrary, attached great importance to these. For this reason the descriptive science of particulars reached a high level of development in China. According to the philosophy of Rickert, the designation "Idiographische Wissenschaft" is applied to that kind of descriptive science which treats non-recurring historical phenomena. If we allow this term to include peculiarities of space and climate, then it is most applicable to the studies of the Chinese.

Such a way of thinking of the descriptive studies of the particulars limited the forms of the acceptance of Indian Buddhism which is contrary to the Chinese attitudes. When accepting Buddhism, the Chinese did not neglect historical reflection and self-examination, and highly valued historical works on Buddhism and biographies of Buddhists, translating them into Chinese. In India also, history books and biographies were made, though their contents were not historically accurate, but these were lost because Indians cared little for them. The *I Pu Tsung Lun Lun* (異部宗輪論), for instance, which describes the process of the formation of sects of Hīnayāna Buddhism in India was translated into Chinese three times. Besides, biographies of King Aśoka, the Buddhist philosophers, Aśvaghoṣa, Nāgārjuna, Āryadeva, Vasubandhu and others, all of which are legendary, were translated into Chinese.[5] The originals of these works have all been lost, and their translations also for the most part do not survive.[6]

As Indian historical works and biographies were few in number, the Chinese themselves tried to write a history of Indian Buddhism. The result of these efforts is the *Fu Fa Tsang Yin Yüan Chuan* (付法藏因緣傳) in three volumes. This is a description of the transmission of the True

Teaching from the first Patriarch Mahākāśyapa (摩訶迦葉) to Buddhasiṃha, the twenty third Patriarch. It is presumed that this work was completed by T'an-yao (曇曜), and is based on the accounts transmitted by Kiṃkara (吉迦夜), a monk from Central Asia, with occasional reference to the Indian "Biographies".[7] Thus, many were produced describing the order of the transmission of the teaching from masters to disciples ranging over India and China. The record of the propagation of the Lotus Sūtra was compiled by Sêng-hsiang (僧祥), a Buddhist monk of the T'ang dynasty, under the title *Fa Hua Ching Chuan Chi* (法華經傳記) in 10 volumes. Similarly Fa-tsang (法藏) of the T'ang dynasty wrote the *Hua Yen Ching Chuan Chi* (華嚴經傳記) in five volumes, and Shih-hêng (士衡) in the Sung dynasty compiled the *T'ien T'ai Chiu Tsu Chuan* (天台九祖傳) in one volume; yet it was Zen Buddhists who turned out history books on the largest scale. *Ching Tê Chuan Têng Lu* (景德傳燈錄) in 30 volumes by Tao-yüan (道原) of the Sung dynasty, *Fo Tsu T'ung Chi* (佛祖統紀) in 54 volumes by Chih-p'an (志盤) of the Sung dynasty, *Chuan Fa Chêng Tsung Chi* (傳法正宗記) in 9 volumes by Hsieh-ch'ung (契嵩) of the Sung dynasty, *Fo Tsu Li Tai T'ung Tsai* (佛祖歷代通載) in 22 volumes by Nien-ch'ang (念常) of the Yüan dynasty, *Shih Shih Chi Ku Lüeh* (釋氏稽古略) in four volumes by Chiao-an (覺岸) of the Ming dynasty; these above-mentioned books are representative ones. Besides, biographies of famous Chinese Buddhist monks were edited separately, and at the same time collected biographies of famous monks were also produced; for instance, *Hsü Kao Sêng Chuan* (續高僧傳) in 30 volumes by Tao-hsüan (道宣) of the T'ang dynasty, *Sung Kao Sêng Chuan* (宋高僧傳) in 30 volumes by Tsan-ning (贊寧) and others of the Sung dynasty, *Ming Kao Sêng Chuan* (明高僧傳) in six volumes by Ju-hsing (如惺) etc. Besides, there appeared such works as the *Ta T'ang Hsi Yü Ch'iu Fa Kao Sêng Chuan* (大唐西域求法高僧傳) in two volumes edited by I-ching (義淨) of the T'ang dynasty, which is a collected biography of famous monks who went to Central Asia or India to study Buddhism.

The Indians, when compiling short treatises into a larger work, were apt to omit their titles and names of their authors. Such works as the *Mahābhārata* and the *Abhidharma-mahā-vibhāṣa-śāstra* are examples of this. In China, however, each title, the authors' names and careers, etc., of the short treatises contained in the larger books were carefully preserved. Books like *Hung Ming Chi* (弘明集), *Kuang Hung Ming Chi* (廣弘明集), *Yao Pang Wên Lei* (樂邦文類) are good examples.

In this way, the Chinese, trying to understand matters historically on the basis of particular individuals, would accept even the founder Śākyamuni as a historical person. That explains the fact that Sêng-yu (僧佑), a Buddhist monk of the Sung dynasty, compiled and arranged many records of biographies of the Buddha under the title *Shih Chia P'u* (釋迦譜) in 5 or 6 volumes, and Tao-hsüan, a Buddhist monk of the T'ang dynasty, edited the *Shih Chia Shih P'u* (譜迦氏釋) in one volume. It was a matter of great importance when, where and to whom Śākyamuni taught the sūtras which were translated into Chinese. Therefore, they tried to relate each sūtra to a period in Śākyamuni's lifetime. The "*Wu Shih Chiao P'an* (五時教判)" devised by the Chinese scholar T'ien-t'ai (天台) is a typical example of this. According to modern textual criticism, we know that sūtras were all produced in a later period, so such efforts are meaningless. Yet, Chinese Buddhist scholars at that time believed that these theories were correct. We can say that the dominant object of their faith was Śākyamuni, which probably was the result of their emphasis on historical matters. Even if there were some statues of Vairocana as an object of their worship, they were exceptions. They made it a rule to enshrine the statue of Amitābha in the west, Maitreya or Yao Shih Ju Lai (藥師如來) in the east, with Śākyamuni as a central figure in the grand hall of the temple.

They usually install statues of Kāśyapa and Ānanda, the two great Arahats, Manjuśrī and Samantabhadra, the two great bodhisattvas, often replace these. Śākyamuni, having these Buddhas as attendants, might be considered as a Sambhoga-kāya (reward-body), i.e., a Buddha endowed with all the virtues of Buddha, by most Buddhists. Thus, we can see the tendency to regard Śākyamuni as a historical person by the fact that they enshrine the two great disciples, Kāśyapa and Ānanda.[8] That is an important difference between Chinese and Japanese Buddhisms. The objects of worship in most of Japanese temples, though they are not all the same, are originally Amitābha, Vairocana, Bhaiṣajyaguru and Śākyamuni. Śākyamuni, however, had already been considered not so much a historical person as a Tathāgata (the truth-revealer) of Original Intelligence, namely as a Sambhoga-kāya Buddha.

There is also a tendency among the Chinese of emphasizing spacial and climatic particularities. *Fo Tsu T'ung Chi*, previously mentioned, contains two volumes entitled *Shih Chieh Ming T'i Chi* (世界名體志). Records of travels written by Buddhist pilgrims who traveled to the Central

Asia and to India from China contain considerable geographical and climatic descriptions. The *Ta T'ang Hsi Yü Chi* (大唐西域記) in 12 volumes by Hsüan Chuang is well known for its accuracy in geographical descriptions, even when compared to modern surveys. Chinese pilgrims tried to hand down detailed topographies of India although the Indians themselves did not.

Another manifestation of the tendency to emphasize particularity seen in the form of the acceptance of Buddhism is the publishing of catalogues of sūtras. In the first stage, the catalogues of sūtras were only very simple lists of the sūtras found in libraries which were owned by Buddhist monks, devotees, scholars and others. In addition, catalogues of sūtras were made to preserve the record of the achievements of Buddhist translators for posterity. Eventually, such catalogues were brought together, the many surviving catalogues of the Buddhist canon being their result. These evolved from the catalogues made for the convenience of individual scholars in their study, and included the contents of the catalogues possessed by each temple at that time. The compilers examined as carefully as possible the titles of sūtras, names of translators, dates of translation etc., and strove to list all sūtras translated into Chinese. *Tsung Li Chung Ching Mu Lu* (綜理衆經目錄) in one volume, which was edited by Tao-an (道安) in 374 A.D., was the first such catalogue. Fifteen kinds of catalogues were compiled by the T'ang dynasty.[9]

---

1) Kōjirō Yoshikawa: *op. cit.* p. 20.
2) Tanaka; Watsuji; Jugaku (田中; 和辻; 壽岳) [tr.]: *Girisha Seishin-no Yōsō* (ギリシア精神の樣相 Characteristics of Greek Spirits), Iwanami Bunko ed., Tokyo, Iwanami, p. 27.
3) Masson-Oursel: *La philosophie comparée*, p. 19.
4) Cf. Kikuya Nagasawa 長澤規矩也 [comp.]: *Shinagaku Nyūmon-sho Ryakukai* (支那學入門書略解 Brief Explanation of Introduction to the Sinology) p. 43 f.
5) 馬鳴菩薩傳, vol. 1; 龍樹菩薩傳, vol. 1; 提婆菩薩傳, vol. 1; 婆藪槃豆法師傳, vol. 1.
6) Only *Aśokāvadāna* (in the *Divyāvadāna*) is remaining at present.
7) 安法欽譯 阿育王傳 vols. VII; 僧伽婆羅譯 阿育王經 vols. X; 失譯 天尊說阿育王譬喩經; 曇摩難提譯 阿育王息壞目因緣經 vol. 1.
8) Daijō Tokiwa 常盤大定: *Shina Bukkyō no Kenkyū* (支那佛教の研究 A Study on Chinese Buddhism), vol. III. p. 76 & p. 81 f.
9) Tomojirō Hayashiya 林屋友次郎: *Kyōroku Kenkyū* (經錄研究 A Study on Catalogue of Sūtras), vol. I, p. 13f. Cf. Daijō Tokiwa: *Yakkyō Sōroku* (譯經總錄 A Study on All the Catalogues of Sūtras in Chinese Translations)

Chapter 5. Conservatism expressed in exaltation of antiquity

(1) Importance attached to past events

It has been already pointed out that there is a tendency in the Chinese ways of thinking to understand phenomena statically in the illustration analyzing the forms of expression of subsumptive judgment and identical judgments. This trend can also be seen in the modes of expression of Chinese language. In Chinese there is no word capable of expressing only the meaning of "werden" or "to become" as seen in modern European languages. The character *"ch'êng"* (成), which is used by Japanese philosophers as an equivalent for "werden" originally meant "accomplish", i.e. "a single phenomenon or thing is brought to a more advanced stage and this has accomplished its object", and, therefore, does not have precisely the same meaning as "werden". The character *"wêi"* (爲) is indeed used with the meaning of "to become", but it was employed as a copulative "to be" (essentia) as well as "do" and "to make". Thus, it may be seen that at least ancient Chinese lacked a common verb (or auxiliary verb) meaning merely "to become". This attitude of static understanding, linked with the way of thinking which emphasizes particulars, produced a trend of thinking which attaches importance to past events.

A nation stressing particulars and concrete perception is inclined to set a basis of law in the past events occurred before, i.e., previous examples. Namely, a precedent, i.e., something experienced by people of an earlier age, arouses in the Chinese mind a sense of validity. It is only natural then that the Chinese would feel a certain uneasiness regarding the method which attempts to fix the laws governing human life by the abstract thinking faculty of the individual. The laws which are determined by abstract thinkink teach what should be in the future, but they leave a sense of uneasiness with the Chinese people who do not trust abstract thinking. For this reason, the conclusion reached by abstract thinking is not relied on to the same extent as the life experience of the past. It is quite understandable then that with such an outlook, the Chinese try to discover in precedents the laws governing life. Thus, for the Chinese, learning implies full knowledge of the precedents of a past age, and is therefore referred to as *"chi-ku"* (稽古), i.e., "searching out the ancient ways".

The Chinese think it better to imitate in their writing the ways of expression used by their predecessors rather than to contrive new styles by their own efforts. Ability in writing was always closely tied to a knowledge of the classics. Therefore, classical Chinese texts consisted of a series of phrases or idioms generally taken from old texts, the foremost of which were the classics styled "*ching*" (經).

As a consequence of this texts abound in literary and historical allusions, which is the result of the Chinese attachment to ways of expression based on historical particularity; for example, "*Ssu-mien Ch'u-ko* (四面楚歌)"—to find oneself surrounded by enemies; "*Hsien Wêi Shih* (先隗始)" — to begin with oneself. In both of these instances, a phrase or a sentence denoting a single historical event is used, to convey a universal, abstract concept. In the arts also artistic effects are hightened and a powerful stimulus is given to the viewer or reader through the medium of historical allusions or quotations from the classics. Such productions as the Yüan drama (*Ch'ü-tzu,* 曲子) as well as the modern *Ching-chü* (京劇) are essentially a series of historical allusions and set literary phrases. Metaphors used in Chinese literature are always linked with historical facts of the past, with the result that Chinese literature has become very extensive and profound.[1] We can see a striking contrast in this respect with the Westerner's use of metaphor which is limited to his own direct experience or at least that of the age to which he belonged as well as with the Indian's use of metaphors which transcended historical experience, or at least, was thought of in such a manner.

Chinese Buddhists did not prove to be an exception to this trend of thinking. Chinese equivalents of Sanskrit terms appearing in the Buddhist canon, when once fixed, were seldom changed thereafter. For this reason Hsüan-tsang (玄奘) writes, "I follow the old usage and do not translate this word anew". Such a trend of thinking was particularly in evidence in Zen Buddhism. Particularly, the Zen sect began to use the *Kōan,* a kind of question-and-answer dialogue by a master and his disciple, with increasing frequency after the Sung dynasty. The original meaning of "*Kung-An*" (*Kōan* 公案) is "records of cases in the public office", and its meaning changed to "pattern" or "previous example" and came to be called "law of ancient times (古則)". They consist of questions-and-answer dialogues, actions and anecdotes taken from the lives of famous monks as well as quotations from sūtras, among which there are not a few creative works made in a later period.

1) Sakae Takeda 竹田復: Hiyu ni Tsuite (譬喩に就いて On Metaphors), *Kangakukai Zasshi* (漢學會雜誌 Journal of the Chinese Classic Studies), vol. 10, No. 1.

(2) Continuity of the identical way of thinking

As long as the Chinese practiced the way of thinking described above, it is quite natural that they should have regarded the writings of their predecessors as having unquestionable authority. The thought and life of the Chinese people must always be examined in relation to the Chinese classics, for the life of the Chinese has been strongly conditioned by the classics. Since ancient times in China, the books which set the pattern of life have been fixed. They are called *Wu Ching* (五經) (the five Chinese Classics), i.e., *I* (易), *Shu* (書), *Shih* (詩), *Li* (禮), and *Ch'un Ch'iu* (春秋). Each of these five classics are equal in status, and are accorded a degree of authority not possessed by any other books. According to tradition, Confucius selected precedents which were to serve as models and based on these compiled the works now known as the Five Chinese Classics. It seems to be true that Confucius held the *Shih* and *Li* in high esteem, and urged people to put the *Li Yüeh* (禮樂) of Chou Kung (周公) into practice. Mencius (孟子) included *Ch'un Ch'iu.* It was Hsün-tzu (荀子) who finally fixed the number of classics at five. Mencius had particularly high regard for *Ch'un Ch'iu,* and thus strengthened the tendency of respecting precedents. Hsün-Tzu, who fixed the number of the classics at five and advocated respect for the doctrines of one's teacher, contributed much toward the formation of the peculiar character of classical learning in the Han dynasty afterwards. Han-fei (韓非) and Li-ssù (李斯), however, strongly urged replacing the laws of past emperors with the law of the new ruler. But this exceptional view held sway only during the reign of Shih-Huang-Ti (始皇帝) of the Ch'in dynasty (秦), and was unable to produce any change in the characteristic way of thinking of the Chinese people.

Thus, the *Five Chinese Classics* was established as a pattern for the life of the Chinese people. It offered the precedents par excellence, ruling over all other precedents, so that in time it came to be considered Truth Itself and Perfection. It was thought that no matter how much human life might change, all the Truth vital to human life was to be sought in these *Five Chinese Classics.* Another word for "Ching (經)" (classics) is "Tien (典)" (law) or "Ch'ang (常)" (eternity), which indicate the eternal aspect of the truth embodied in the Five Chinese Classics.[1] Though dynasties in China have often changed, each dynasty has accepted the Five Chinese Classics as a supreme authority and treated them as the pattern for human life. The *Ch'un-Ch'iu Tso-Shih Chuan* (春秋左氏傳) tells us that by the time of the Chou dynasty that particular attitude which considers the classics as the pattern for human life was already in existence. In the dialogues of the *Ch'un-Ch'iu Tso-Shih Chuan* we find individuals seeking authority for their own thoughts or deeds in the *Shih Ching* or the *Shu Ching*. Thus, by the middle of the Chou dynasty these two classics to some extent enjoyed a comparable position to the one they had in later ages. At that time, however, the status of the *Shih Ching* and the *Shu Ching* was not yet determined. It was Confucius who firmly established their status and laid the foundation for using the classics as the pattern for human life.[2]

Confucius' teaching did not aim at finding new truth by free speculation and originality. He tried to imitate and revive past traditions while at the same time affirming the social organization and family system of his day. He had no desire to alter the system or social organization of his time. He says in his *Analects*, "I do not invent, but merely transmit; I believe in and love antiquity", and "I am not a man born wise. I favor what is ancient and strive to know it well". Therefore, the truth in which he believed was not of his own creation. He had an awareness that he was only amplifying a truth that had been handed down from ancient times. Hereupon, the Way of antiquity, according to Confucius, was, concretely speaking, the Way adopted by Duke Chou Kung, who had laid the foundation of the political and social systems of the Chou dynasty as well as its moral principles. Confucius called the system of Duke Chou Kung "the *Li* (禮) of Chou Kung", and expressed regret that it had declined and was no longer practiced completely in his days. The essence of his teachings was the revival of the "Li" so that they might be practiced once more.

Respect for the classics was not limited to people of the Confucian school only; other schools also held them in high regard, although there was some difference in degree. Mo-tzu (墨子), for example, quotes the *Shu Ching* as a work of considerable authority. The only difference between the Confucian attitude toward the classics and the attitude of the other schools is that the former regarded following the way of the classics as indispensable.[3] The attitude of reverence toward the classics can also be seen in the Chinese translation of the Buddhistic scriptures, wherein we often come across the word "Ching" (classics or sutra) in the title of a Chinese translation of a Sanskrit work, although no such word is found in the Sanskrit original.[4)]

Many peoples besides the Chinese hold their classics in esteem and strive to make their life conform to them, but it does not necessarily follow that their efforts at conformity mean that life in all its everyday details must be in complete accord with the latter. But in the case of China an extraordinary effort was made not only to let the classics set the patterns for life, but also to cause ones everyday life to conform entirely to the classics. Thus, Chinese thought was passed on from generation to generation without any remarkable change or development after its form had become fixed. As Chinese society and culture were fixed, its thought was also fixed in keeping with them. Scholars differ in their opinion as to how far fixed thought controlled the actual life of the Chinese. On this problem, Dr. Sôkichi Tsuda offers the following explanation:

"China has never had a revolution in her world of thought. The reason for this is that Chinese life itself was fixed. Yet, we should not fail to notice a secondary cause, namely, that the thought had authority only as thought and did not necessarily control the actual life, it was not deemed necessary to resist and reform thought which has no authority on the actual life, as both actual society and politics, whatever the doctrines of morality or politics may be, was working independently of them, and yet doctrine itself had an authority as doctrine in China".[5)]

I think that this explanation also contains considerable truth. The degree to which ancient thought controlled the actual life of the Chinese is a question requiring further examination in the future, but at any rate, it is a peculiar phenomenon of culture that the Chinese preserved and esteemed the same form of thought because of its antiquity.

Once Voltaire stated that it was miraculous that there had never been any remarkable change in the legal and administrative system of the Chinese for about four thousands years, i.e., from about 2000 B.C. to his own day, and he considered it a proof that the legal and administrative system of the Chinese was the most excellent in the world.[6)] Such a deep impression on the thinkers of enlightenment, including Voltaire, may not be left now. I think the reason why the same ways and forms of thinking had prevailed for four thousands years can be attributed to the fact that they had considered the legal and administrative system devised by themselves to be the most excellent or natural, so that they dared not resist them.

People who knew China well before the War would often remark that when Chinese were discussing a problem with each other, if a man would quote a passage of the classics, the others would at once express their approval. Since China's turn to Communism, Marx, Lenin and Hao Tse-tung have replaced the Chinese classics. Although this is a great change, we can see how deeply the way of thinking of the nation is rooted that they offer no resistance as long as an authority is cited.

---

1) Kōjirō Yoshikawa: *op. cit.*, p. 27.
2) *Ibid.* pp. 39–40.
3) *Ibid.* p. 46.
4) e.g. 鳩摩羅什譯 中論 13-1: ...... 如佛經所說
Its Original Text: .... *yad Bhagavān ity abhāṣata.*
5) Sōkichi Tsuda 津田左右吉: *Shina Shisō to Nippon* (支那思想と日本 Chinese thoughts and Japan), pp. 29–30.
6) Sueo Gotō 後藤末雄: *Shina Bunka to Shinagaku no Kigen* (支那文化と支那學の起源 Chinese Culture and the Origin of the Chinese Studies), p. 376 f.

(3) Influence on the reception of Buddhism

Then, such classical and conservative ways of thinking regulated the form of the reception of Buddhism. As frequently pointed out previously, Chinese Buddhists, especially the priests took over the doctrine founded and taught by Śākyamuni, and considered it their duty to exalt it, in spite of the fact that Chinese Buddhism differs from Indian Buddhism in some respects. Therefore, they rewrote arbitarily even the sentences of the sūtra; for instance, in spite of the original of *Fa Hua Ching* (法華經) which states that "An enlightened for self (*Pratyekabunddha*) opened his eyes to the Truth *without looking to his master for help* (*anācāryaka*)", the Chinese translation reads "he listened to the Buddha's law and accepted it as being true".[1] This is just the opposite of its original meaning.

The way of thinking that is indicated in a phrase like 'I only state it but don't make it' dominated even Buddhist scholars in China; for instance, the venerable Hui-chao (慧沼) (.....714 A.D.), the second founder of the Fa Hsiang school (法相宗), said that the teaching of the pure consciousness (唯識), the fundamental doctrine of the Fa Hsiang school, was preached by Śākyamuni, and Vasubandhu (世親), who expounded the doctrine of the pure consciousness practically, was a mere explainer.[2] In fact, the historical Śākyamuni expounded no such teaching, but Vasubandhu and other persons expounded this theory for the first time seven or eight hundreds years after Śākyamuni's Death; whereas, Chinese scholars thought the actual and first advocator to be the explainer. Therefore, as the venerable Chi-tsang pointed out, in case an author of a Buddhist treatise denounced the theories of other schools, he would claim that his theory was in accord the teachings of Śākyamuni and he based his arguement on the authority of the Buddha.[3] Zen Buddhists also decided on 古教照心 (the lessons of antiquity enlighten our mind) as their fundamental attitude.[4]

The attitude attaching importance to past events led the Chinese produce a way of thinking that a master is generally superior to his disciples. And the question why Āryadeva, disciple of Nāgārjuna, vehemetly denounced the philosophical theories of other schools in his treatise called the *One Hundred Verse Treatise* (百論), in spite of his master Nāgarjuna having never rejected other schools, the venerable Chi-tsang explained, as the reason for this, that since Nagārjuna had achieved world-wide-fame, none of the heretics and Hīnayāna Buddhists dared argue against him; whereas they argued without restraint against Āryadeva who was only Nāgārjuna's 'disciple'.[5]

The above-mentioned reason explained by Chi-tsang is not understandable to modern people.

This attitude of respect for the transmission of the master's teaching to his disciples led the Chinese Buddhists to be strict with the genealogy of transmission from a master to his disciples. The very venerable Chi-tsang, who liked arguments, examined carefully the history of schools in Indian Buddhism and the distinctions of their languages.[6] The venerable Chih-i (智顗), who had completed a new Buddhist theory, wrote down the transmission of the True Teaching to the disciples amounting to twenty-four Buddhist monks, from Kāśyapa (迦葉), an immediate disciple of Śākyamuni's to Buddhasiṃha (師子覺) in a later age.[7] As for Chinese Buddhism of that day, temples of all over China belonged to the Zen schools who esteem their master in Zen Buddhism so highly that it came to be discussed of the master under whom they practiced austeries and followed his teachings of Buddhism. Such an attitude of thinking led to call the relation between master and disciples in question also as for the age before Bodhidharma, the founder of Zen Buddhism in China, was living.

Thus, they made up unreasonably the genealogy of the twenty-eight founders ranging from the great Kāśyapa, one of Śākyamuni's immediate disciples, to Bodhidharma.[8]

As pointed out previously, many history books on Buddhism were made out especially by Zen Buddhists on the basis of the genealogy of transmission of teaching from master to disciples. The Indians, with their deep respect for universal law or doctrines, don't mention the transmission from master to disciples as seriously and minutely as the Chinese do.

As a result of this high esteem for the master the Chinese Zen sects in some instances attach more importance to their founder than to Śākyamuni or Tathāgata; they went so far as to think the founders' Zen Buddhism to be superior to Tathāgata's Zen Buddhism. As the result of such a way of thinking, the master's sayings and deeds became their golden rule. They became clues to accomplish their object in the practice of Zen meditation. They were finally standardized to form many Kōan of the Zen school.

Then, as the result of the way of thinking on former examples and ancient practices, the founder's analects which denoted the founder's sayings and deeds came to be regarded as more important than the sutras of the schools of Mahāyāna Buddhism which were scanty in historical descriptions: *Kōan* depending on sūtras of the schools of Mahāyāna Buddhism are merely 5% of all the catechisms recorded in the *Pi Yen Lu* (碧巖錄) and the *T'sung Jung Lu* (從容錄), and the rest, 95% of them are depending on the founder's analects.[9]

As a result of this high esteem for the founders' analects, Zen Buddhists in later ages preferred their founders' analects to the Indian sūtras, and began to concentrate more and more on their many catechsms.

As for the origin and the significance of the Chinese manifestation of respecting for the aged, this should be dealt with separately, but I consider it to be closely related with the classical conservatism which is traditional in the Chinese. These words, '*Lao Jen*' (老人), '*Lao Tsêng*' (老僧), '*Lao Han*' (老漢), are spoken by Zen Buddhists containing a sense of respect and intimacy.

Rational thought which would critically examine statements in the sacred books themselves, is not in accordance with the Chinese ways of thinking because their classical conservatism regards the authority of the sacred books to be absolute. This is the reason why rational Indian logic did not take root in China. The school of logic brought to China from India by Hsüan-chuang (玄奘) was the latest one (new *Hetu-vidyā*) in India of those days, which stood on a thoroughly rational standpoint and acknowledged only sense (*pratyakṣa*) and inference (*anumāna*) as the basis for forming knowledge and considered the sacred books of religion, tradition, the sayings of great men and so on as impossible to be a source of knowledge, and disqualified them as a basis of knowledge.[10] In this regard, it has something in common with the natural philosophy of Vaiśeṣika.

Such logic concerning knowledge was brought to China together with the formal logic. But rational logic about knowledge was, somehow, not perfectly in tune with the Chinese who had high regard for the authority of ancient traditions. They wished to qualify traditional knowledge as the basis of knowledge at any rate, and did not permit sense and inference as the basis for knowledge to take root in China. They insisted that the traditional sacred books are more authoritative than knowledge based upon sense and inference, and considered it natural to feel this way.[11]

Bearing in mind this characteristic attitude of Chinese Buddhists, we can easy comprehend how the problem of 'forged sūtras' came about. A thought theoretically explained is not sufficient to convince the ordinary Chinese. To make the Chinese accept it, it is necessary to base it on the authority of books. Thus, many 'forged sūtras' were produced in China, which were always professed to have been made in India. If they came to be suspected of having been produced in China, they would at once be regarded as lacking truth and authority.

The Chinese way of thinking which idealizes and praises the past, naturally came to consider the present and future as degraded and corrupted. Hence, Chinese thought is said to be pessimistic and non-futuristic. Therefore, the pessimistic way of thinking that became predominant in ancient Chinese Buddhism seems to be related to this Chinese way of thinking.

---

1) 法華經, 譬喩品.
2) 慧沼: 成唯識論了義燈 (*Taishō*. vol. 43, p. 671 b). Cf. *Madhyāntavibhāga-ṭīkā*, ed. by S. Yamaguchi 山口益, p. 2f.
3) 三論玄義 (Ed. by E. Kanakura) p. 157.
4) 百丈清規, vol. VI. 亀鏡文. Cf. Dōgen (道元): Shuryō Shingi 衆寮箴規 (in *Eihei Shingi* 永平清規).
5) *Op. cit.* 三論玄義. p. 170.
6) *Ibid.* p. 119 & p. 125 f.
7) 摩訶止觀 vol. I, No. 1, (*Taishō*. vol. 46, p. 1).
8) 六祖壇經. Cf. Hakuju Ui 宇井伯壽: *Daini Zenshū-shi Kenkyū* (第二禪宗史研究. Studies on History of Zen Buddhism, vol. II), p. 164.
9) Tetsubun Miyasaka 宮坂哲文: *Zen ni okeru Ningen Keisei* (禪における人間形成 Formation of Human Character in Zen), p. 148 f.
10) Cf. *Tarkajvālā Madhyamaka-hṛdaya*, VIII, 47.
11) Cf. 禪源諸詮集都序 (Ed. by Hakuju Ui), p. 36.

(4) Non-development of free thought

Of course, it cannot be said that free thought did not appear in China. It is a well-known fact that all the philosophers of the Spring and Autumn Period as well as the Period of the Warring States were advocating their own opinions. Miscellaneous schools of thought which had been disputing with one another disappeared of themselves as the study of Confucianism came to be the official course of study during the Han dynasty and it became the basis for civil service examinations, i.e., the thought of the intellectuals were consolidated by Confucianism. Of course, it cannot be said that all thoughts with the exception of Confucianism disappeared completely, but rather that no independent school of thought could exist in opposition to Confucianism. Once the authority of Confucianism was established, it continued and no resistance to it, nor questioning its authority came about. Consequently, due to this kind of mentality, the Chinese felt no contradiction between their yearning for the social and administrative systems of old times and their efforts to maintain the social and administrative systems of the modern day and age. Conservatism and the principles to maintain the status quo were unanimous. It is often said that the classics like the *Four Books* and *Five Chinese Classics* of Confucianism restrained the Chinese from thinking freely, but in reality, it is their conservative attitude and worship of the past which emphasized the authority of the Classics, that naturally restrained the Chinese.

Thus, free thought never had its best days in China. The real cause for this seems to be connected with the fact that no urban community had never developed in China. Concerning urban community, Max Weber explained the following; "In China, there had never been formed any citizen's defensive and political sworn organization. Cities in China had not the characteristic of religious service organization or sworn organization as seen in the West. Of course, there existed a pre-type of thought. The tutelary deity of cities in China was not a guardian god for union, but merely a guardian spirit for a region, so we might rather say that they were generally deified beings of high excutives of the cities. Cities, the fortresses of the Imperial Government had, in fact, less guaranty of self-government than the village communities. Cities were permitted to have neither the right to conclude a contract nor a jurisdiction, so that they were unable to take united action. At any rate, the village communities, on the contrary, had all of those rights. Now, the reason for this type of city can be attributed to the fact that the cities in the West were formed to be trading cities. whereas in China, they were rational products of the administrative offices. First of all, there was constructed an enclosure or a castle wall around a city, and then a small number of people were often forcibly brought within. Moreover, the very name of the capital city itself or of cities in general was changed whenever one dynasty changed to the next".[1] He added to say as follows;

"Cities in China were not administrative by character, and they had no administrative privilege as seen in the polises in Greece or modern cities in the West. It is true that there were many cases in which the whole city rose to resist the bureaucracy, but their purpose was always limited to mere opposition to a certain government official or a given order, especially to an imposition of a new tax, but not once did they venture to stipulate the political freedom of the city. The reason why the latter could not be accomplished by the way it was in the West can be attributed to the fact that the Chinese could not get rid of their ties with kinship. The settlers in the cities — especially the rich — had never severed their connections with their native places, or their own kinship societies, but they maintained all of their ritual or individual relationships with the village communities where they were born".[2]

In China, private property rights were established, but rights of freedom guaranteed by law did not exist.[3] It is natural, therefore, that free thinking did not appear, and conservative thought and respect for the past was dominant; cities did not develop as independent communities, and right to personal freedom was not recognized and only village communities continued to exist maintaining the same way of life as in ancient times.

1) Max Weber: *Konfuzianismus und Taoismus*, S. 292.
2) *Ibid.* S. 291–292.
3) *Ibid.* S. 436.

(5) Traditional character of scholarship

Within the realm of such a way of thinking, learning is mere acceptance of traditional knowledge handed down from generation to generation without change. The word 'to learn' has no other meaning but 'to imitate'. This is especially obvious in the teachings of Confucius. The most important plea of Confucius was that man should make his norm for living of previous examples and the classics. Therefore, he regarded reading books as most important. "The master said that once he had not taken a meal all day and stayed up all night to meditate, but he found it to be useless, and then he realized that nothing is better than learning".

It means that meditation is useless and inferior to reading books. In other words, our life should be based on thorough knowledge of previous examples rather than meditation. Therefore, he stated in his moral theory that the concrete contents of Jên (仁) as "the way", in other words, the practical model for morality, should be taught by other persons as knowledge. He, however, did not explain how the moral model given as knowledge had relation to Jên and how Jên reacted toward the knowledge. Also in the *Analects* of Confucius, he made no mention of why *'Jên'* was a core or a basis for human morality, and of why it was morality itself.

He also made no explanation of *'I'* (義) as well as of *'T'i'* (悌) which are concrete and practical matters. He, also, did not explain definitely of where the basis for morality should be placed,[1] so that, in China, 'to learn' is nothing but 'to search for ancient ways'. Subsequently, 'things' or 'meaning is, in fact, nothing but 'things which were taught'.[2] This trend then led the study of the school of Confucius to be a study of annotation of the classics mainly. The main achievements of Chêng-hsüan (鄭玄), a representative scholar, in the Later Han dynasty, is the annotation of the classics. Chu-tzu (朱子) is a great philosopher of the Sung dynasty, who completed Confucianism; and yet his works consist largely of annotations of the classics or his own explanations of annotations of the classics. He had no completely independent, systematic statements exist in his works.

This trend also dominated Buddhist scholars. Since Buddhism took its rise in India, Chinese Buddhist scholars were influenced by the Indian ways of thinking so that some of their statements are more systematized and inclusive, but many of them made efforts to annotate sutras and theories, or to explain their chief meaning. The venerable T'ien-t'ai (天台) has written an independent and systematic work in 20 volumes called *Mo Ho Chih Kuan* (摩訶止觀), but most of his works consist of explanations of sutras.

Among the works written by the venerable Chi-tsang (吉藏)—twenty-six kinds of his works are in existence— of which only two books, i.e., *Erh Ti I* (二諦義) in three volumes and *Ta Ch'eng Hsüan Lun* (大乘玄論) in five volumes, are systematically treated, and the rest of them are explanations of sutras or of theories. As for the representative books written by the venerable Fa-tsang (法藏), who completed the doctrine of the Hua Yen school, we should mention his work called *Hua Yen Wu Chiao Chang* (華嚴五教章) in three or four volumes, but most of the rest of his books are explanations of sutras or theories, of books elucidating sutras and theories. Consequently, it may be adaquate to call Chinese Buddhism to be explanatory, though it is referred to as academic.

The way of thinking which esteems explanation brought some very extraordinary phenomena, for instance, Chêng-kuan (澄觀), a famous scholar of the Hua Yen school under the T'ang dynasty, who wrote an explanatory work for *Hua Yen Ching* (華嚴經), i.e., *Ta Fang Kuang Fo Hua Yen Ching Shu* (大方廣佛華嚴經疏) in sixty volumes, and later on, he continued his explanatory work by adding a 90 volume study to it called *Ta Fang Kuang Fo Hua Yen Ching Yen I Ch'ao* (大方廣佛華嚴經演義鈔).

Since the sacred books of Buddhism in China were all translations from the Indian originals it may have been necessary for the Chinese to consult explanatory studies in order to grasp the meaning perfectly, so that those explanatory works themselves came to have the peculiarity of being more meaningful than the original books. The way of thinking which esteems explanations is not only to be seen in the past but also in the present. Once Marxism-Leninism was fixed to be a national policy, the leader comments on it and lower rank leaders add explanations to the comments of the former. Such a way of thinking has been steadfastly maintained to the present in spite of the fact that they often experienced revolutions.

---

1) Sōkichi Tsuda 津田左右吉: *Rongo to Kōshi no Shisō* (論語と孔子の思想 Analects and Thoughts of Confucius), pp. 309–311.
2) Cf. 天台四教儀, vol. I.

Chapter 6. Fondness for complex multiplicity expressed in concrete form

(1) The concrete character of the artistic imagination

The Chinese had high regard for particulars, and presented content concretely in accordance with their way of thinking, and therefore they naturally came to be fond of complex multiplicity expressed in concrete form. Their standpoint which especially relied upon and clung to sensual characteristics made them sensitive to multiplicity not bound by laws in stead of directing them toward grasping the lawful unity of things. Within the realm of sensuality, the phenomena in this world are not similar but multifarious. Consequently, the Chinese who depend upon perceptive presentation and esteem particulars, are naturally sensitive to the multiplicity of things. Therefore, they don't attempt to think about the universal validity of laws which regulate this multiplicity of things.

Tre characteristic trait of this way of thinking has influenced the force of artistic formation in Chinese art. There is a definite limit in the force of artistic imagination of the Chinese. Their attitude of observing only those things that can be concretely experienced, that are grasped specifically through sensory effect and that are directly perceived weakens their power of imagination. This is the reason why in China no epic has been produced, although novels and a kind of drama, which combine concreteness and reality developed on a large scale. This is just the opposite of the Indians who produced the *Mahābhārata,* the world's greatest epic, and the *Rāmāyaṇa,* a beautiful poem of a hero, and the like, but very seldom produced novels. Indeed, the Chinese too, under the T'ang and the Sung dynasties, produced very excellent poems, but most of the ideas of the content were concrete and did not overlook the natural laws of time and space. In the later T'ang dynasty, there were people like Li Chang-chi (李長吉),[1] a poet who was unusually imaginative, but the basic, individual ideas contained in his poetry are not very imaginative. The Indian on the one hand gives play to the power of his imagination filled with huge quantity, while the Chinese on the other gives play to the power of imagination, loving complex multiplicity expressed in concrete form.

Hereupon, the following question may arise: The Chinese are given to exaggeration by their artistic nature, for instance, as seen in an expression of a poem of Li Po (李白), "White hair, 3000 feet long on account of my sorrow". In this expression the laws of nature clearly seem to be disregarded. But, reffecting upon this, we cannot simply dismiss this matter by accepting it as necessarily imaginative. Masaaki Tozaki, a Japanese scholar, offers the following explanation: 'The 3000 feet mentioned in the poem have the same meaning as thousands of feet long, i.e., unfathomably long. Expressions of 'three thousand disciples', 'three thousand court ladies', 'a distance of three thousand ri' are the same".[2] Therefore, both the concepts of "white hair" and "three thousand" are permissible as concrete representations of human experience.

Only the combination of the words, "white hair" and "3000 feet long" ignores the natural laws. This Chinese way of thinking has to be distinguished fundamentally from the Indian way of thinking, which uses huge numbers such as "hundred millions of", "hundred thousand millions of", "as many as the grains of sand in the Ganges river", which are beyond the capacity to express human experience concretely and nonchalantly represent concepts outside of the natural world.

---

1) 李賀, 長吉 (字). His poems are criticized as 怪險危語 and are difficult to understand.

2) 唐詩選 (*Kanbun Taikei* 漢文大系, vol. IV.) p. 6.

(2) Fondness for ornate diction

As mentioned above, Chinese writing developed in accordance with their special characteristic fondness for complex multiplicity in concrete form.

Chinese language consists of various kinds of rhythmical forms, that appeal to our senses. The characters in sentences are often arranged in patterns of four each or seven each. For the sake of form they often sacrifice the meaning and do not reject a sentence because it is vague. This is how the euphemistically antithetic style, '*Ssu Liu P'ien Li T'i*" (四六駢儷體) originated during the Six Dynastics. It can be said that the Chinese language is an artistic one, for it aims at euphony, and that its sentences are full of elegant nuances, that are not based upon universal and abstract concepts but rather on free usage of historical allusions and phrases.

This characteristic of the Chinese way of thinking naturally also transfigured Buddhism. All the schools of Chinese Buddhism which are linked directly with the philosophical systems originating in India, are abstract and speculative; while the Zen sect, a purely Chinese form of Buddhism, is very literary. I have previously indicated how this characteristic is concerned with concreteness in the Chinese way of thinking. The literary character of Zen Buddhism is especially remarkable in the verses attached to catechisms (*Kōan*) of the Zen sect, where they created a certain religious, metaphysical atmosphere in the abstract by an array of persons and things which are concrete and appeal to the eyesight. In those places, no abstract remarks can be recognized.

The trend of fondness for complex multiplicity expressed in concrete form makes efforts to fascinate people by its excessive array of abstract words and sensual representation in writing. Therefore, it tends to use expressions which aim to bring people to be conscious of the meaning by an intertwining of various receptive representations rather than simple and clear expressions, and it thinks much of using complex expressions with elaborate words full of suggestions, even if the meaning is simple. Hereupon, there can be seen the habit of rhetorical devices used by the Chinese. The Japanese scholar, Tominaga Nakamoto alrady pointed this out by stating the following:

"The Chinese scholar of Confucianism likes to use ornate styles, while the Japanese is fond of using concise and pithy expressions". It means that the Japanese love the use of concise and plain expressions and dislike exaggerations, while the Chinese love to use difficult passages which are hard to read.[1] He said, "Buddhists are inclined to use passages too mysterious to understand, while Confucian philosophers like to use passages too ornate to understand. If only they would abandon this habit, they could express their true meaning".[2]

It is also due to this same way of thinking that the Chinese like to discuss and are eloquent. The Chinese explain themselves only in relation to others and such explanation is not based upon theoretical reflection.

They grasp the psychological state of the other person and try to make him conform to their own opinion. This is only due to their skill in eloquence.

The Chinese themselves recognized their mental peculiarity. Tao-an (道安), a famous Chinese monk, recognized an essential difference in the Chinese's fondness for ornate diction, and the writings in the Indian language. He said, "The Sanskrit sutras lay stress on essence, but the Chinese are concerned primarily with style and strive to make the sutras suit the taste of the people".[3] Even though there had been a gorgeous style, the so-called Kāvya style, in the ancient Indian languages, it was hardly used in Buddhist sutras. He felt that a defect of the Buddhist sutras translated into Chinese is the fact that the translated version tried to please popular fancy by aiming at aesthetic effects.

Tsung-mi (宗密), a Chinese monk, felt that the sect taught the attitude of 'No reliance on word or letter' in order to cure Buddhists of this bad habit. He said, "The Chinese cling to ornate styles, and harbor illusion in their minds. Because they settle for name instead of substance, Bodhidharma selected some sentences and transmitted the true meaning of

Buddhism to his disciples by claiming to stand for its name, revealed the substance, for instance, by practicing the meditation facing the wall to break off various kinds of relations with others".[4)]

Yet in spite of this, it is a well-known fact that Zen Buddhism eventually developed a fondness for Zen expressions and turned into a book religion.

China is said to be a country of literature. The Chinese are fond of ornate styles and are skillful in composition. However, the concepts met with in their writings are based on the actual experiences. It is true that the Chinese are a nation who love grandiloquent styles, but such styles are no more than mere exaggeration, and it seems that there are few cases in which they overstep the natural limits. The Chinese have never made any presentation of abstract universal things themselves by enlarging on them freely without any relation to the reality of life as the Indians did. Since the Chinese did not make abstract speculations and ignored the universals, they did not try to transmit the contents of thought exactly, but were content to give only some impression to the reader. Moreover, the Chinese orators thought that the most important thing was eloquence without regard for certain regulations, good or evil, truth or error.

Chinese sophistry was formed on the basis of such a mentality, but even Confucian philosophy, which has occupied the chief position as government-supported scholarship, is not essentially different from this.

Ju philosophy, which is the official name for Confucian philosophy, is a 'Lehre der Literaten'[5)] of people who love style. As Max Weber defined it, Ju philosophy is nothing but a system of class ethics maintained by secular and rational allowance-receivers who have a certain literary culture.[6)]

These literati were meant to be not only intellectuals or well-read people but also leaders for a moral life. Successive officials in China were selected from among such literati. Although the general public could not afford to read books, fundamentally their lives centered around in learning literature and in enjoying literary things.

T'ao Yüan-ming (陶淵明) says in his work, biography of Wu-liu (五柳), "I was fond of reading books, but I didn't always try to understand it thoroughly. Whenever I found any agreeable passage, I would often gladly forget to eat. I always enjoyed myself by composing sentences".

This was the ideal for the Chinese literati.

1) *Shutsujō Kōgo* (出定後語), chap. 8. *Jinzū* 神通.
2) *Ibid.* chap. 24. Sankyō 三教.
3) 出三藏記集序, vol. VIII; 摩訶鉢羅老波羅蜜經抄序, vol. I.
4) 禪源諸詮集都序 (Ed. by Hakuju Ui 宇井伯壽), vol. I. p. 83.
5) Max Weber: *Konfuzianismus und Taoismus,* S. 432.
6) *Ibid.* S. 239.

(3) Exegetical and literary predilections of Chinese

Chinese Buddhism was a religion for the literati in its intellectual aspect. Chinese Buddhism might be called "a religion of documents"[1] because the whole Chinese culture is characterized by an emphasis in documents.

Indeed, there are many schools in Chinese Buddhism. These varieties are based upon theoretical distinction, not upon the administrative or social differences as seen in Japan.

We had better call them schools than sects. We can find at least seven schools which were initially formulated in India: "P'i T'an School" (毗曇宗), "Chü She School" (倶舎宗), "San Lun School" (三論宗), "Ssu Lun School" (四論宗), "Ti Lun School" (地論宗), "She Lun School (攝論宗), "Fa Hsiang School" (法相宗), These schools of Buddhism are linked directly with theories of Indian Buddhism. There are similarly seven schools of Buddhism which arose in China: "Lü School" (律宗), "Nieh P'an School" 涅槃宗), "Ch'ing T'u School" (淨土宗), "Ch'an School" (禪宗), "T'ien T'ai School" (天台宗), "Hua Yen School" (華嚴宗), "Chên Yên School" (眞言宗). The Lü School consists of the "Ssu Fen Lü School" (四分律宗), the "Shih Sung Lü School (十誦律宗), and the "Sêng Chih Lü School" (僧祇律宗), and the Ch'an School is divided into five branches and seven sub-schools. The main reason why so many schools were formed is that there are basic differences among sutras and theoretical works.[2] But these differences apply to theoretical rather than practical matters. In the Sung dynasty a merger took place between the Pure Land school and Ch'an schools, both of which are representative of the practical aspect of Buddhism.

Consequently, generally speaking, it can be said that Chinese Buddhism is divided into many schools theoretically, but they are quite similar in their practical aspect. Chinese Buddhists were largely literati, and consequently had a deep attachment for complex styles of writing. This trend became particularly prominent during the Northern and Southern dynasties, especially during the Southern dynasty. I should like to point out a few interesting examples of this. The *Sheng Man Pao K'u* (勝鬘寶窟), a well-known commentary, was written by Chi-tsang (吉藏). He says in its comment, "I have been studying and appreciating this sutra for many years, and have made reference to many books of all ages. I have examined many sutras and treatises, selecting passages with profound meaning, which I have compiled into a three volume work".[3)]

As he mentioned, we find many passages quoted from a great number of sutras, and many explanations on each word and character. Because he cited such a wide variety of authorities, we soon become weary and bewildered when reading this work, and ironically the main meaning of the book becomes all the more vague. Fujaku, a Japanese monk, commented on this book thus: "We find therein very elaborate explanations. In this book, the author commented on each phrase and sentence minutely to enlarge the beginner's knowledge. There probably is no more elaborate book than this". But this Chi-tsang's commentary does not give us the main meaning of this book. That this book came to be highly prized by scholars, Fujaku observes, shows that the study of Buddhism has been degraded to mere formalism.[4)] The very opposite of this may be seen in the *Shōmangyōgi-sho* (勝鬘經義疏) written by Prince Shōtoku of Japan, which is much more concise and pertinent.

The *Chü She Lun Chi* (俱舍論記) written by Pu-kuang (普光) is said to be the most authoritative book on the *Chü She Lun* (*Abhidharma-Kośaśāstra* 俱舍論), which is an important guide to the doctrines of Hinayana Buddhism. The book is said to include the interpretations of Sarvāstivāda scholars of Western India as related to Pu Kuang by Hsüan Chuang, which are quite accurate. However, because of respect for tradition, Pu Kuang included the different theories found in the *Abhidharma-mahāvibhāṣā-Śāstra,* the largest explanatory work of Sarvāstivāda School, as well as passages from the earlier translation of the *Chü She Lun* and the *Shun Chêng Li Lun* (*Nyāyānusāra-śāstra* 順正理論), so that too many opinions are given and therefore it lacks conciseness.

This tendency is seen in all the commentaries on the *Fa Hua Ching* (*Saddharmapuṇḍarīka-sūtra* 法華經) produced in China, and especially the *Fa Hua Hsüan Tsan* (法華玄贊) written by K'uei-chi (窺基), which contains many ornate phrases. In general, documents written during the first part of the T'ang dynasty are hard to read, but there are few books which contain such munute and needless explanations as the *Fa Hua Ssüan Tsan.* The *Erh Ya* (爾 雅), *Kuang Ya* (廣雅), *Shuo Wen* (說 文) *Yü P'ien*

(玉篇), *Ch'ieh Yün* (切韻) are freely cited, but their value here is little more than decorative.[5]

Therefore, it was no easy task for Chinese Buddhist scholars to explain even the title of a sutra or treatise. The Chi-tsang explained in great detail the title of the *Madhyamaka-śāstra* (中論) (sometimes called 中觀論—*Chung Kuan Lun*—in China) written by Nāgārjuna, on which the school of Chi-tsang (吉藏) was based.

As for the main point of his explanations, he says, "In short, each of these three characters of the *Chung Kuan Lun* has the meaning of *Chung*, of *Kuan* and that of *Lun*". Logically speaking, this is utterly meaningless, and we may not be far wrong to say that he is enjoying himself by playing with words.[6] Judging from the next example, he must have been ignorant of the fact that a title of a book denoted a definite notion. He says, "Each of these three characters of *Chung Kuan Lun* has no definite meaning of its own and therefore, one might say *Kuan Chung Lun* or *Lun Chung Kuan*. The first one is represented by the Theorist, the second one by Insight, the third one by Theory". He added further very complicated explanations to these classifications in an effort to amplify the text.[7]

In short, it may be said that the Chinese scholars were forgetting the fact that a name indicates a certain concept. Even the scholars of Buddhistic logic, who ought to have been able to think matters through logically took no account of this. "Ying Ming" (因明) is the Chinese equivalent for the Sanskrit word of "*hetuvidyā*", which is translated literally the science of reason". Nevertheless, the Chinese Buddhists forgot its original meaning and recognized only the meaning resulting from the linkage of the two characters, "Yin" and "Ming", giving arbitrary explanations. K'uei-chi says, "The character of Yin means a statement made by a debater and serves as the proposition; and the character of Ming represents the wisdom of the opponent, which illuminates meanings and words". He explains again, "It is a cause of Ming, and therefore called Ying Ming, and Ying is the original cause of a word, and Ming means a revealing cause of wisdom". All of these explanations are in error. He merely listed these absurd explanations one after another, and did not offer any conclusion, nor did he try to decide which was right. In addition, he also gave minute explanations for the title *Ying Ming Ju Chêng Li Lun* (因明入正理論) *Nyāyapraveśaka*), listing five kinds of explanations one after another.[8]

Virtually, examples of the extremes to which Chinese commentators went when interpreting a title are not uncommon. The full title of the *Hua Yen Ching* (華嚴經) is *Ta Fang Kuang Fo Hua Yen Ching* (大方廣佛華嚴經). Its original name is "Mahā-vaipulya-buddha-avataṃsaka-sūtra", and therefore, we must be careful to read it "Ta Fang-kuang Fo Hua-yen Ching". Nevertheless, Fa-tsang, whose teachings centered around the *Hua Yen Ching* and is recognized to be the highest authority on it, did not think that the title was composed of certain concepts, but further regarded the title merely as so many characters, and offered an explanation for each separate character; Ta (大) stands for inclusion; Fang (方) for regulation; Kuang (廣) for a state where activity is extended universally and the mental constitution has reached its ultimate; Fo (佛) for a state where the effect is in perfect harmony and the enlightenment is full; Hua (華) for a simile which means a state where all kinds of practices has been accomplished; Yen (嚴) for a simile indicating the ornament of substance; Ching (經) for a state where all forms of existence are linked with one another to reveal the Teaching of Buddha. Following to the Law, using similes with regard to human being, we call it "Ta Fang Kuang Fo Hua Yen Ching".[9] It is only natural that we should grow tired of such complicated explanations, yet his predilection for explanatory expressions does not stop here. He goes on to say, "Ta (大) has ten kinds of meaning", and enumerates the ten kinds of complicated explanations for this character.[10] He then says, "Next, I want to denote ten kinds of explanations of Fa Kuang", and enumerates ten kinds of explanations for this word, etc., giving ten explanations for each of the words. Fa-tsang's passion for enumerating ten kinds of explanations is due to the fact that the *Hua Yen Ching* itself has a tendency to enumerate things in groups of ten. But he did not give any conclusion about which meaning was fundamental and which was of lesser importance. Also we cannot find any trace of his own reflection on these matters.

In general, when translating Buddhist sutras into Chinese, the Chinese aimed at heightening magical and artistic effects; for instance, the Chinese equivalent for "*Prajñā*" in Sanskrit is "Chih Hui" (智慧), which stands for "Wisdom", but the Chinese chose to use the word "Pan Jo" (般若) rather than "Chih Hui" in order to give the word dignity.[11]

Such being the case, exegetical studies developed in China, but there has been no scholasticism as seen during the middle ages in Europe. Exegetics lack the character of rational formalism as seen in Jurisprudence in the Western countries. It is, in addition, said that it had not the

Kasuistik character seen in the Rabbis of Judaism, in the theologians of Islam, and in the Buddhist scholars studying the theory of the Abhidharma.[12)]

In Chinese Buddhism, which is a religion of documents, scripture was highly esteemed, so that as a matter of course the copying of sutras came to be regarded as an act of religious merit, of greater value than executing the practical morality of Buddhism. Chih-i (智顗) says, "The aim of sutra copying lies in enforcing people to practice the Eight-fold Sacred Path so as to awaken them from delusion. There are various ways of carrying out Buddhistic practices, and therefore he who is possessed of insight into the fact that our consciousness is appearing and disappearing incessantly and is impermanent, and he who wants to practice the Eight-fold Sacred Path should copy the collection of sacred books; and he who is possessed of insight into the fact that our consciousness is capable of many kinds of false discrimination which he, the ordinary person, as well as persons of the two vehicles can not realize, although Bodhisattvas who have eyes of the Law can perceive it, and who wants to practice the Eight-fold Sacred Path should copy sutras of the separate doctrines; and he who is possessed of insight into the fact that our consciousness is nothing but Buddha nature, and who wants to practice the Eight-fold Sacred Path should copy sutras of the Middle Path".[13)]

If there had been no way of thinking which emphasized sutra-copying, such statements on sutra-copying would never have been made. Because of this kind of thinking, stone slabs were engraved with Buddhist scriptures. The first persecution of Buddhism occurred during the reign of the Emperor Tao-wu (道武) of the Northern Wei dynasty, resulting in the destruction of Buddhist images and sutras. A great number of monks and nuns were forced back into common society. Buddhists at that time came to have a premonition of another persecution, and therefore they engraved Buddhist sutras in stone, on the face of cliffs, in stone pillars, in stone slabs and walls. We find the *Wei Mo Ching* (維摩經), *Shêng Man Ching* (勝鬘經), *Mi Lê Ching* (彌勒經) engraved on walls of stone caves which were polished as smooth as glass at Mt. Pei Hsiang Tang in Wu An Hsien of Ho Nan Province (河南省武安縣北響堂山). A religious vow, still extant, written by T'ang-yung (唐邕), a distinguished official under the Northern Chi dynasty, tells us that he intended to engrave the entire canon on the walls of famous mountains. Under the Sui dynasty, Ching-wan (靜琬), a Buddhist monk, also made a vow to engrave the canon on stone slabs. Efforts were made during five successive dynasties to have the canon incised in stone, but were at last discontinued as a result of the persecution by the T'ang Emperor Wu-tsung (武宗). Again during the Liao dynasty the work was continued with the support of the government. More than half of the entire Buddhist canon has been carved in rock.[14] It may be said that no other nation could not have achieved so remarkable a feat.

In India, where Buddhism was originated, some sutras may have been engraved on bricks or stone slabs, but we can only find short statements of the "Twelve-linked Chain of Causality" and "the Four Noble Truths". In India, the purpose of engraving a part of a sutra was not mere sutra-copying, but was done for the sake of obtaining religious merit. It would be proper to say that such a difference between India and China is due to the characteristic trend of thinking of the Chinese who place such emphasis on literary style.

---

1) Max Weber (in his book *Hinduismus und Buddhismus*, S. 290) called Chinese Buddhism as "Buchreligion" (Religion of Books).
2) Zen sect also has such characteristic as it esteems highly 楞伽經, 般若心經, 金剛經, 圓覺經 among many sūtras.
3) *Taishō*. vol. 37, p. 1 c.
4) *Shōmangyō Kenshūshō* (勝鬘經 顯宗鈔), vol. I. (*Nihon Daizō Kyō* 日本大藏經 *Hōdōbu* 方等部 vol. V. p. 8)
5) Kōgaku Fuse 布施浩嶽: *Hokke Gensan Kaidai* (法華玄贊解題) (*Kokuyaku Issaikyō* 國譯一切經 *Kyōshobu* 經疏部 vol. IV.) p. 3.
6) 三論玄義 (Ed. by Y. Kanakura), p. 174 f.
7) 大乘玄論 vol. V. (*Taishō*. vol. 45, p. 73 c).
8) 因明大疏 vol. I. (*Taishō*. vol. 44, p. 92 a–b).
9) 華嚴經探玄記 (*Taishō*. vol. 35, p. 107 b).
10) *Taishō*. vol. 35, p. 121 f.
11) Cf. 宋高僧傳 vol. III, 滿月傳.
12) Cf. Max Weber: *Konfuzianismus und Taoismus*, S. 415.
13) 摩訶止觀 vol. III. pt. 2. (*Taishō*. vol. 46, p. 31 c).
14) Daijō Tokiwa 常盤大定: *Shina Bukkyō no Kenkyū*, vol. III. pp. 115–116.

Chapter 7. Formal conformity

(1) Fondness for formal conformity

As mentioned before, the Chinese regarded certain old classics as absolute authorities, and it was only on these that they composed their commentaries and explanations. They never looked at the classics from its historical origins or criticized them, and thought it sufficient if there were no contradictions among the phrases and words. That is to say, they attached great importance to the Formal Conformity. In the following, the characteristics in these Chinese commentaries will be mentioned.

Cheng-hsüan (鄭玄), a representative scholar who commented on the Chinese classics in the Latter Han (後漢) dynasty, studied the Five Chinese Classics with some other similar classics, and composed commentaries on them as a unit. His characteristic style in his commentaries is that he always referred to the other classics and tried to remove the contradictions between them, because he believed that all classics stood on the same basis. In order to have uniformity in the contents of all the classics, he sometimes changed the words and characters because he thought some words or characters of the classics were miscopied.

This tendency continued in the San-kuo (三國) and Liu-ch'ao (六朝) dynasties.[1]

The Chinese Buddhist scholars also commented on the sūtras and abhidharmas in this manner. Buddhism was first introduced into China in the time of Emperor Ming (明) of Latter-Han dynasty, while the translations of Buddhist scriptures first started during the time of Emperors Huan (桓) and Ling (靈). The basic Buddhist sūtras were mainly translated by An Shih-kao (安世高) and the Mahāyāna sūtras by Lokarakṣa. Therefore, sūtras of both Hīnayāna and Mahāyāna coexisted in China since the time right after the first introduction of Buddhism. Afterwards, many sūtras were introduced and translated by many Buddhist monks such as Chih-ch'ien (支謙) of San-kuo dynasty, Dharmarakṣa of Hsi-chin (西晋) dynasty, Kumārajīva, Buddhabhadra and Dharmarakṣa of Tung-chin (東晋) dynasty, and continued on to the later periods by other scholars. Among them, Paramārtha who translated many abhidharma works, Hsüan-chuang (玄奘) who translated many sūtras and abhidharma works, and Amoghavajra who translated many esoteric writings were famous. The contents of these sūtras and abhidharma works were so varied and different that Chinese Buddhists could reach no conclusion as to what the fundamental basis was. Therefore, Chinese Buddhist scholars selected a certain sūtra or abhidharma work as the fundamental text and classified other sūtras and abhidharma works under it. And they also endeavored to show the relations between them and systematized various doctrines of many sūtras under one system. This is so-called "critical classification of the doctrines". It was tried first in Tung-chin dynasty and frequently in the later periods. It is one of the characteristics of Chinese Buddhism that the Chinese classified various doctrines of Buddhism under a certain system. Each one of Chinese Buddhist scholars made his own classification under a certain sūtra or abhidharma work which he regarded as the highest authority. Therefore, many classifications arose in China. Among them, the classification in which the way of thinking of the Chinese is typical is the classification of 'the Five Periods'. The Chinese highly esteemed the individuality of man and interpreted Śākyamuni as a historical personage who preached all the sūtras. Therefore, they tried to apportion the different sūtras to certain periods, e.g. five periods, of his life between the time of his enlightenment and his death. This classification of the five periods was first formed by Hui-kuan (慧観) of Liu-sung (劉宋) dynasty and reorganized by Chi-i (智顗), the founder of T'ien-t'ai (天台) sect of China. According to this classification the five periods are as follows:

The first period is the period of the Avataṃsaka Sūtra. Just after enlightenment, Śākyamuni preached the doctrine of Avataṃsaka Sūtra at Buddhagayā under a bodhi-tree for Boddhisattvas for three weeks. The truth can immediately be realized by hearing this doctrine.

The second period is the period of Deer Park. The average people could not understand the teaching of the Avataṃsaka Sūtra. Therefore, Buddha expediently taught the Hīnayāna doctrine at the Deer Park near Benares in order to lead them. The length of this period is twelve years.

The third period is the period of general Mahāyāna sūtras. For those who understood the teaching of the Hīnayāna doctrine, Buddha taught the doctrine of many Mahāyāna sūtras such as *Vimalakīrti-nirdeśa-sūtra, Viśeṣacintābrahma-paripṛcchā-sūtra, Suvarṇaprabhāsottama-sūtrendrarāja-sūtra* and *Śrīmālā-siṃhanāda-sūtra.* This period continued for eight years.

The fourth period is the period of the *Prajñāpāramita-sūtras.* After the third period, Buddha taught the Prajñāpāramitā-sūtras for twenty-two years in order to let the people understand the doctrine of Śūnyatā (non-substantiality).

The fifth period is the period of the *Saddharma-puṇḍarīka-sūtra* and the *Mahāparinirvāṇa-sūtra.* The Buddha preached the doctrines of the *Saddharmapuṇḍarīka-sūtra* in which he taught that both Hīnayāna and Mahāyāna Buddhists can realize the truth, for the last eight years of his life. At the moment of his death, he taught the *Mahāparinirvāṇa-sūtra* in order to manifest the principle of the Buddha-nature.[2]

The Chinese counted these numbers of the year of each period from fragmentary records concerning the length of preaching mentioned in the above sūtras Actually most of these sūtras were composed in periods after the time of the historical Śākyamuni. Nevertheless, they counted the length of preaching based upon the records of these sūtras. Here, the characteristic of a Chinese way of thinking can be seen very clearly. A question of great importance was whether this sūtra came before or after that sūtra.

This division of years of each period is however most unreasonable. Even at that time, people who studied the sūtras logically became aware of this irrationality.

For example, even thought it was generally believed that the Avataṃsaka Sūtra was preached by the Buddha just after his enlightenment, there are some points in the sūtra which lead to a different conclusion. Even people in those days were doubtful as to whether it was stated immediately after his enlightenment.

It is stated in the sūtra that Śāriputra was at this preaching and listened to this sūtra with his disciples. The other sūtras, however, mentions that Śāriputra lived in a remote country at the time when Śākyamuni realized the enlightenment. Therefore, it was impossible for Śāriputra to attend the teaching of this sūtra taught by the Buddha just after his enlightenment. It is also unreasonable that the Buddha preached this sūtra in the 'Hall of Truth of Universal Light' (普光法堂),[3] as this hall was not yet constructed at the time of Buddha's enlightenment.

Such questions from a detailed study of the text press its weak points. However, Chih-yen (智儼) mentioned concerning this problem as follows:

"According to the doctrine of the Avataṃsaka Sūtra, there worlds of the past, present and future are mutually penetrated and identified. Therefore, it is not unreasonable that there are some contradictions concerning 'before and after' of the time in this sūtra".[4]

From this statement, *Chih-yen did not understand the difference between time in the phenomenal world and that in the metaphysical truth.* If this doctrine of Chih-yen is recognized, *the criticism of the original texts* cannot exist. The Chinese Buddhist scholars classified not only the critical classifications of various doctrines, but also synthesized systematically the thought of the sūtra which they regarded as the absolute authority. It may have been the influence of the Indian way of thinking when Chinese Buddhist scholars of the Sui (隋) and T'ang (唐) dynasties made systematic and methodical explanations in spite of the fact that the average Chinese were not fond of systematic arguments. Among the many systems of Buddhist philosophy which were organized in China, those which possessed the greatest systems are the doctrines of the T'ien-t'ai sect and the Hua-yen (華嚴) sect.

The sūtra which the T'ien-tai sect relies on is the Saddharma-puṇḍarīka *Sūtra* on which a new philosophy was systematized. The second chapter of this sūtra in the Chinese translation states: "Only the Buddha and Buddhas can fully realize the basic realities of all existences which are thus-formed, thus-natured, thus-substantiated, thus-forced, thus-activated, thus-caused, thus-circumstanced, thus-effected, thus-remunerated, and thus-beginning-ending-completion of existences". The Chinese took the ten categories of form, nature, substance, force, activation, cause, circumstance, effect, remuneration, and beginning-ending-completion from this passage, and said that all existences should possess natures of these ten categories and upon it, the doctrine of 'a moment of thought has the whole cosmos immanent in it'. Based upon this doctrine, they again formed different ways of meditative practice. In such ways, they developed the new doctrine based upon and summarizing the thought of the Saddharma-puṇḍarīka Sūtra.

The *Avataṃsaka sūtra* is a collection of sūtras which are of similar type, and consists of 60 volumes in the old translation by Buddhabhadra and 80 volumes in the new translation by Śikṣānanda. This sūtra states various philosophical ideas in the imaginary description beyond human thoughts. Therefore, it is very difficult to systematically grasp and understand the thought itself. Chinese scholars, however, read this sūtra in detail and systematized the doctrines through their own experiences. Thus, the ten profound theory of Tu-shun (杜順) and six-forms theory of Chih-yen (智儼) were organized. It was Fa-tsang (法藏) who combined these two theories together and established 'ten-profound-six-forms' theory. The Chinese endeavored to systematize not only the sūtras, but also the Vinayas. The precepts stated in various Vinaya Piṭakas (scriptures on precepts) which were conveyed from India to China were not always the same. Moreover, the views of Buddhists who practiced precepts were also different. Therefore, it was necessary for the Chinese to arrange and systematize the precepts when they actually followed the precepts in their lives. The most important personage among scholars who studied and systematized the precept-rules was Tao-hsüan (道宣). The Chinese Vinaya sect was founded by systematizing the precepts in the above manner. This sect continued to prosper for a long time in China. Although this sect was introduced into Japan, it never became popular among the people.

Its reason will be mentioned later. As we have seen, it was the important task for Chinese Buddhist scholars[5] to keep the formal conformity by classifying, organizing and systematizing various doctrines and precepts in sūtras and vinayas.

---

1) Kōjirō Yoshikawa 吉川幸次郎: (*Shinajin no Koten to sono Seikatsu*), pp. 89–94.

2) Although the term 'five periods' was not used, Tsung-mi (宗密) also systematized the similar classification. (禪源諸詮集都序, p. 116 f.) Chi-tsang (吉藏) criticized the five-periods theory of Hui-kuan. He, however, did not criticize the method of classification itself, but only criticized his interpretation of each period. (三論玄義 ed. by Y. Kanakura.)

3) It is stated in the third chapter of the Avataṃsaka Sūtra that Buddha preached this sūtra in the Hall of Truth of Universal Light. (六十華嚴經 chap. 3, 如來名號品.)

4) 華嚴孔目章 vol. IV (*Taishō*. vol. 45, p. 584 a).

5) Chi-ts'ang divided all adhidharma into 'general abhidharma' and 'detailed adhidharma'. This also is one example of a classification. (*op. cit.* 三論玄義 p. 133.) He also mentioned the difference of standpoints between the *Chung-lun* (中論) and the *Pai-lun* (百論). (*Ibid.* p. 153.)

(2) External conformity

When the Chinese organized the classifications and systematizations, they did not deeply consider the logical connections of various doctrines, and only tried to match the external and formal conformity. They were not aware of the fact that there were many logical faults in the explanations of their commentaries. They liked to apportion all things under one diagram. A typical example of it can be seen in the theory of five natural elements. They did not investigate the essential character of each thing, but combined all things together by looking for some similarities in their external appearances. Namely, each one of five directions, five sounds, five forms, five tastes, five internal organs and many other things which can be divided into five classes was apportioned to each of the five natural elements each possessing one nature of the five natural elements respectively.[1] Based upon this theory, a new doctrine was made, explaining the change of dynasties. This theory says that each dynasty possessed one nature of the five natural elements such as wood-nature and fire-nature; therefore, the change in dynasty conformed with the change in the order of the natural elements.[2] When a dynasty would not fit satisfactory in their system, *the sequence of lineage of dynasties of the past periods was even reversed.*[3]

In the accesptance of Buddhism, the same kind of logic appeared. Yen Chih-t'ui (顏之推) of Northern Ch'i (北齊) dynasty mentioned that the five precepts taught in Buddhism is the same as the five invariables taught in Confucianism. And he matched each one of five precepts to the five invariables.[4] An interpretation such as this was also adopted by the Buddhist monks. For example, Tsung-mi said that the objectives of the five precepts and the five invariables were the same although their ways of practices were different. He also identified each one of the five precepts with each one of the five invariables.[5] They did so even though this identification was not logical. Furthermore, Chih-i matched each one of the five precepts of Buddhism to each one of the five invariables, the five holy classics, and the five natural elements respectively.[6]

The method of classification and systematization of Chinese Buddhist scholars is to make a certain system and then include all things under it. A great importance was attached to their newly made system which tried to explain all other doctrines relative to their basic doctrine. This tendency runs to an extreme. A typical example of this will be mentioned in the following:

In the fourth chapter of the Saddharma-puṇḍarīka Sūtra, there is a parable in which a father sought his run-away son. The father is similar to the Tathāgata and the son, sentient beings. In one paragraph, the father in seeking the son arrives at a big house where there were abundant treasures and gems such as gold, silver, ruby, amber, coral and chrystal in the storehouse, and many kinds of servants, such as child servants, head-servants, the second servants, the third servants, and general servants. It is true that powerful families in the country of India possessed such a lot of treasures and servants in olden times.

The Chinese, however, did not consider this phrase as a phrase of a mere parable. They thought that there must be some important meanings in this paragraph, because it was a part of their holy scripture, the Saddharma-puṇḍarīka Sūtra. Therefore, they tried to classify the above-mentioned different kinds of servants to each step of discipline in Buddhism. According to Fa-yün's (法雲) opinion,[7] they are divided as follows;

child servants —— commoners, both Buddhist and non-Buddhist, as well as novices in Buddhist study.

head-servants —— Bodhisattvas who are ranked higher than the 8th stage.

the second servants —— Bodhisattvas who are ranked between the 1st and 7th stages.

the third servants —— Pratyekabuddhas.

general servants —— Bodhisattvas of Ten State Grades.

According to Chih-i's identification;[8]

child servants —— Pratyekabuddhas, Śrāvakas and Bodhisattvas of Distinct and Common Vehicles.

head-servants —— Boddhisattvas of Distinct and Perfect Vehicles in ten stages.

the second servants —— Bodhisattvas of Ten Merit-transference Grades.

the third servants —— Bodhisattvas of Ten Practice Grades.

general servants —— Bodhisattvas of Ten Stage Grades.

Again, according to Chi-tsang's interpretation;[9]

child servants —— non-Buddhist commoners.

the third servants and general servants —— Buddhist commoners.

head-servants and the second servants —— Bodhisattvas higher than the first stage.

In the same story, it also mentions that the run-away son who became a laborer happened to come to his father's house and saw his father sitting on the lion's seat surrounded and respected by many Brāhmins, Kṣatriyas and capitalists (*gṛhapati*)

Chinese Buddhist scholars also classified these people in detail.

According to Fa-yün's interpretation;[10]

Brāhmins —— Bodhisattvas higher than the 8th stage.

Kṣatriyas —— Bodhisattvas lower than the 7th stage.

Capitalists —— general people of Mahāyāna Buddhism.

According to Chih-i's apportionment;[11]

Brāhmins —— Bodhisattvas of enlightenment who got rid of all defilements.

Kṣatriyas —— Bodhisattvas between the 9th and the 1st stages.

Capitalists —— Bodhisattvas of the 30 grades under the Ten Stages.

According to Chi-ts'ang's interpretation;[12]

Brāhmins —— Bodhisattvas higher than the 8th stage.

Kṣatriyas —— Bodhisattvas of the 7th stage.

Capitalists —— Bodhisattvas higher than the 1st stage

Although each one of these scholars mentions the reason why he made such a classification it will not be mentioned here.

A great many of such classificational divisions and identification can be found in the commentaries on sūtras written by Chinese scholars.

Almost all of these interpretations are unreasonable and twisted. Therefore, they are useless for comprehension of the true spirit of the *Saddharmapuṇḍarīka-sūtra.* Also in the philosophical and systematic doctrine of the Hua-yen Sect, all things are frequently divided into ten categories and classified into each one of them. In this case also, the Chinese esteemed the formal conformity rather than logical and systematic thinking.

---

1) Sōkichi Tsuda 津田左右吉: *Shina Shisō to Nippon,* 支那思想と日本 p. 25.
2) *Ibid.* p. 10.
3) Shōichi Kuno 久野昇一: *Zenkan-matsu ni Kan-katoku-setsu no Tonaerare-taru Riyū ni tsuite* (前漢末に漢火德說の稱へられたる理由について) (*Tōyō Gakuhō* 東洋學報), vol. XXV. p. 582.
4) 家訓歸心篇 (廣弘明集, vol. III.)
5) 原人論 chap. 2, 斥偏淺.
6) 摩訶止觀 vol. VI. pt., 1. (*Taishō.* vol. 46., p. 77 a–b.)
7) 法華義記 vol. V. (*Taishō.* vol. 33., p. 635 a.)
8) 法華文句 vol. VI. pt., 1. (*Taishō.* vol. 34., p. 81 b.)
9) 法華義疏 vol. VII. (*Taishō.* vol. 34., p. 546 c.)
10) 法華義記 vol. V. (*Taishō.* vol. 33., p. 635 c.)
11) 法華文句 vol. VI. pt. 1. (*Taishō.* vol. 34., p. 82 b.)
12) 法華義疏 vol. VII. (*Taishō.* vol. 34., p. 547 c.)

Chapter 8. The tendency towards practicality

(1) The anthropocentric attitude

The Chinese have the tendency to consider all things from an anthropocentric standpoint. They are apt to understand even abstract ideas in relation to man. The Indians gave expressions to the meaning of "being" by using the term "bhāva", and "existence" by "bhava". The Chinese, however, translated the both bhāva and bhava with the same term "yu (有)" without distinguishing any differences. "Yu" connotes the meaning "man possesses" as well as "to exist". Namely, they considered all things anthropocentrically and did not consider the idea of "existence" as a universal apart from man. In Chinese sentences, the subject is in most cases man even if it does not appeare in the sentence, and the objective is stated in the predicate. Therefore, the Chinese can understand the meaning of the sentences in spite of the fact that case-endings are not used, the order of the words not fixed, and most of phrases consist of the same number of characters. Therefore, there are differences in the way of expression of ideas between the Indian and the Chinese. The Indians, sometimes, make abstract ideas the subject, while the Chinese usually makes man the subject.

For example, the Indians say, "therefore, the sufferings accompany with him (*tato taṃ dukkham anveti*)",[1] while, the Chinese express the same idea as 'therefore, he is suffered by sufferings'.[2]

Moreover, when they express ideas, the Chinese are apt to consider man as the subject. In this way of thinking, it is very difficult to grasp man as a predicative or objective existence. Therefore, the passive voice of the sentence was not well developed in the Chinese language. If there is no objective case following, the transitive verb changes into a passive verb.[3] As the Chinese did not pay attention to the passive voice, they did not understand man objectively in spite of the fact that they considered all things anthropocentrically. Influenced by this way of thinking, the Chinese thought of most subjects anthropocentrically.

This way of thinking of the Chinese is different from that of the modern European in that it is utilitarian and pragmatic. It is a well known fact that the racial nature of the Chinese is commonplace and utilitarian. Therefore, all Chinese learnings are practical. All thoughts which were developed among the Chinese intelligentsia were centered on practical subjects which had direct relations with actual life. Namely, most of the Chinese were interested in morals, politics, worldly ways of life and the way to success. The teaching of Taoism is the art of self-protection, the method to success or the way of governing. Confucianism which occupied the highest position in Chinese thought is also an ethics for the governing class and a way to govern the people

By this reasoning, the Chinese did not develop the study of logic which had no relation with utility. The theory of Category which was mentioned by the Chinese is based on pragmatic views. The Japanese translated 'categoria' into 'Han-chū (範疇)' which derived from the term 'Hung-fan-chiu-ch'ou (洪範九疇)'[4] in the *Shou Ching* (書經). This Hung-fan-chiu-ch'ou, however, is not the grammatical or formal-logical category, but a political, moral and systematic deduction. Chinese historiology also is based upon this pragmatic attitude.

For example, the *Tzu-chih T'ung-chien* (資治通鑑, 'a general history written for the purpose of governing'), which is a history written by Szu-ma Wen-kung (司馬溫公), quoted more than two sources connected with each event of the history in order to have ascertain correct records. Whenever there are some contradictions among the records, he tried to ascertain which one was correct after a detailed collation. Even if the difference was minor and did not greatly influence the event itself, he gave the collation in detail and judged which was correct. In such an attitude it is said that the style of this history is similar to the modern science of positive history.[5] The purpose of histories such as *Tzu-chih T'ung chien* was only to assist the government as has been shown in its title.

Such a realistic thought of the Chinese can be called *'realism'*.[6] This thought, however, can be called realism in so far as it is a study of only those morals and politics needed in actual human life. They did not consider whether or not they could actually be practiced in actual life. Therefore, it can be said that the Chinese thinkers did not observe things objectively in conformity with the order of the natural world.

This tendency of thought also appeared at the time when Indian thought came to be accepted by the Chinese, when they did not accept the natural sciences and mathematics developed in India. It was an exception to the rule that Hsüan-chuang translated the *Sheng-tsung-shih-chu-i-lun* (勝宗十句義論 *Vaiśeṣika-daśapadārtha-śāstra*) of the Vaiśeṣika philosophy which is a kind of natural philosophy in India. Therefore, no one continued the studies on this book after him. In the same light, Indian logic was not accepted by the Chinese.

The method to grasp the objective objects in conformity with daily life of man can be found in the expressions of Zen Buddhism which is the most typical Buddhism in China. For example, Fa-ch'ang (法常) said at the moment of his death, "no one can stop man coming and no one can follow man going".[7] The Indian Buddhist expressed the same idea in a different way as "must not take any thing from it and must not remove any thing from it. One should see truth as truth. Those who see truth are emancipated".[8] The Chinese explained the idea which the Indian grasped in relation between the man and the object, in conformity with human relation in their daily life.

---

1) *Suttanipāta* 770.
2) 義足經 (in Chinese translation).
3) 王力:中國文法學初探 p. 73.
4) 尙書, 周書, chap. 6. 洪範. cf. Shō Saitō 齋藤晌: *Tetsugaku Dokuhon* (哲學讀本 Introduction to Philosophy), pp. 76–77.
5) Kōjirō Yoshikawa 吉川幸次郎: *op. cit.* p. 21.
6) Masson-Oursel: *La philosophie compareé*, p. 118.
7) 景德傳燈錄 vol. III. (*Taishō*. vol. 51, p. 255 a.)

8) *Madhyāntavibhāgaṭīkā*, p. 29; '無ニ一法可ㇾ損、無ニ一法可ㇾ增、應見實如實、見ㇾ實得ニ解脫一。' (佛性論 vol. IV. Chap. 10. 無差別品, *Taishō*. vol. 31, p. 812). The similar expressions can be also found in Mādhyamika-śāstra 25–3; *Catuḥśatikā* XV, 350 (p. 513); *Māṇḍūkya-Kārikā* III, 38.

(2) Worldly tendency of religions

The tendency of thinking which centers on the actual daily life of man and neglects the transcendental universality naturally makes man worldly and materialistic. Such a tendency appeared in various cultural spheres.

Firstly, it can be said that there is very little mythology of the Chinese; especially, in connection with the process of how the sky, earth, sun, moon and human beings were created. Although some mythological explanations exist in collateral records such as *Chun-nan-tzu* (淮南子), the *Shu-i Chi* (述異記) and the *San-wu Li-chi* (三五歷記), such explanations cannot be found in the traditional and authoritative scriptures and records of China. The first record which is described in the *Shih-chi* (史記), a history of ancient China written by Szu-ma-ch'ien (司馬遷), is a record of five Emperors who are regarded as the first human beings. Therefore, supernatural and inconceivable stories are not mentioned in this history. From ancient times, the Chinese who were lacking in mythological imagination have been very materialistic and worldly. A typical example of this tendency can be found in the answer of Confucius when asked by people about death: he answered "I do not know what birth is, then how can I know what death is?"[1] (The same attitude can also be found in other philosophers of China.)

Various folk religions existed in China from ancient times and exerted their influence not only on the common people, but also on the intellectuals who partially followed these religions. Certain supernatural existences beyond human power were relied upon. From ancient times, ancestor worship was the important ceremony in China by which the family and its prosperity was upheld. It was therefore impossible to change this religion into future-worldly and metaphysical religion. There was the idea of 'T'ien' (天, Heaven) which can be identified with the idea of 'God' in other religions. On the one hand, they rationalized this idea by giving the meaning of natural principle to it, while on the other they gave a religious meaning of God to it. Saints were deified and worshipped, and even the scriptures written by them were highly respected by the people, in spite of the fact that a saint is still a human existence. In the Han dynasty, Confucianists taught ways of ridding oneself of disasters and looking for good fortune. Lao-tzu was also worshipped, and his doctrine was combined with the theory of superhuman beings which insisted on the existence of human beings who were immortal, and how one can attain it. Taoism was founded by organizing and systematising the folk faiths centered on this theory of superhuman beings and developed through Buddhist influence. Consequently, the religions of China were nothing but prayers and charms through which people wanted to remove disasters and to receive good fortune. Originally, Confucianism tried to remove spells and charms from its teaching.[2] They, however, could not neglect this religious tendency in the common people. It was not unusual that the teaching of moral and politics combined with these religious teachings, because the fundamental aims of the Chinese were to satisfy the physical and material demands of human beings.[3]

Chinese Buddhism was also influenced by this trend of thinking. Indian Buddhism was generally a metaphysical teaching which taught the past and future worlds of man, and yet *the Buddhism which spread among the common Chinese was a Buddhism of spells and prayers.* In the early period of Buddhism of China, most Buddhists were immigrants from Central Asia who were naturalized as Chinese. All the Buddhist priests who translated the sūtras into Chinese in the early period of Buddhism in China were familiar with spells and charms. For example, it is said that An-shih-kao mastered astronomy, geography, medical science, and even voices of animals and birds.[4] It is also said that Dharmakāla mastered all kinds of studies and sciences;[5] and K'ang-seng-hui (康僧會) mastered astronomy, geography, and the art of Taoism and worked many miracles.[6] There was Fo-t'u-ch'eng (佛圖澄) who came to China in 310 A.D. and spread Buddhism at one time among the people by performing various miracles.[7] He constructed 893 temples and pagodas during his life time. He was respected by the Emperors of the Latter-ch'ao (後趙) dynasty and spread Buddhism through political power. It was in his time that the Chinese people were openly permitted to become priests by the Emperor.[8] Most of Chinese Buddhist priests in later periods also spread and propagated Buddhism among the people in the same way as Fo-t'u-ch'eng. As the Chinese highly esteemed the element of spells and charms, they did not accept the Buddhism which prohibited spells and charms in its doctrine. Therefore, they rejected the traditional and conservative Buddhism which prohibited spells and prayers, and called it "Hīnayāna Buddhism". On the whole, they accepted Mahāyāna Buddhism *which permitted charms and prayers to some extent.*[9] In early Buddhism, any sort of charm, prayer, divination, sacrifice, or the art of devil-subjugation were excluded as superstitions. Not only priests but lay followers as well were forbidden to perform them in early Buddhism. This tendency continued on to the later periods.

Mahāyāna Buddhism, on the contrary, compromised with the faiths of the common people and adopted charms and prayers as expedient methods to teach people, as Mahāyāna Buddhism was originally founded as a religion of common people. It was this Buddhism that was introduced to later flourish in China.[10] Therefore, spells and charms were clearly a part of Chinese Buddhism. For example, there is a spell in the last part of the Chinese-translated *Prajñā-pāramitā-hṛdaya-sūtra* as follows: 羯諦羯諦波羅羯諦波羅僧羯諦菩提薩婆訶. This is the transliteration of "gate gate pāragate pārasaṃgate bodhi svāha" which connotes the meaning "gone, gone, gone to the other shore, enlightenment, gone to the other shore, so may it be!"

The Indians understood this phrase literary, while the Chinese, on the contrary, transliterated it by adopting Chinese characters which could not be understood in order to increase the effect of the spell. Therefore, it can be said that Chinese Buddhism possessed the tendency of Shamanism or superstitious ceremonies very strongly. Even at present, the Chinese people perform prayers to various bodhisattvas, heavenly beings and deities of Buddhism as well as to various gods of folk faiths when they become ill or are destitute. They also possess highly esteemed amulets. Buddhist schools which did not possess this tendency did not spread among the people. Even Chih-i, the founder of T'ien-tai Sect, who was one of the philosophical and systematic Buddhist scholars, taught that "illness is in some cases caused by devils or Māras; therefore, man should chant a certain charm when he is taken ill".[11]

It was the mystical esoteric Buddhism which greatly developed and taught the art of spells and charms. This Buddhism was first introduced in the T'ang dynasty and flourished fairly well. The esoteric Buddhism was prohibited in the Ming dynasty because of its harmful effects. But it has been revived in recent times as it is suited to the racial psychology of the Chinese who were originally very fond of ceremonies to receive good fortune and be relieved disasters.[12]

Influenced by such a tendency among the Chinese, spells and charm came to be accepted in the doctrine of the Chinese Pure Land teachings, which, originally, did not possess magical elements. The Japanese Pure Land teachings, and in particular the Shin Sect, openly opposed such a tendency. Chinese Pure Land teachings, on the contrary, compromised with the tendency of the Chinese. When the Chinese translated the sūtras of the Pure Land teachings, they made use of the special terminology of Taoism. Moreover, they infused the thought of superhuman beings into the Pure Land teachings by adopting Taoistic words and phrases which could not be found in the original Sanskrit texts.[13] Chinese Pure Land teachings since the time of its first introduction from India and Central Asia, has been under the influence of Taoism. Chinese Buddhism today is generally the teaching of the Pure Land. At present, Chinese chant a certain spell to invite the soul of the dead before the corpse is put into the coffin. Next, the sūtra to reject hell is chanted, and finally the names of Amita Buddha, Avalokiteśvara Bodhisattva and Kṣitigarbha Bodhisattva are called three times respectively as a prayer for the dead. And the spell 'Oṃ maṇi padme hūṃ' is chanted after each name of these Buddha and Bodhisattvas.[14] Also in the prayer which is chanted after the corpse is put into the coffin for the dead to be born in the Pure Land, there is a spell 'Oṃ' at the begining and 'Ahūṃ' at the end.[15] The name of 'A-mi-ta-fo (阿彌陀佛, Amita Buddha)' itself which has been in the Chinese Pure Land sects possesses the elements of spells or charms. A-mi-ta-fō is the transliteration of the Sanskrit term Amitāyur Buddha which connotes the meaning "Buddha who possesses infinite life". This Buddha also has another name Amitābha, which means 'the one who possesses infinite light (or wisdom)'. As we can see, the idea of this Buddha is very philosophical. Such a philosophical idea, however, could not spread among the common people of China. Up to the Sui dynasty, the Chinese translated name 'Wu-liang-shou-fo (無量壽佛, Buddha of Infinite Life)' was used.[16] After the T'ang dynasty, however, the Pure Land teachings spread widely, and the transliterated name "A-mi-ta-fo" came to be adopted. One reason was that the tone "Nan-wu-a-mi-ta-fo (Adoration to Amita Buddha!)" sounded better than "Nan-wu-wu-liang-shou-fo (Adoration to the Buddha who possesses the infinite life!)" when chanted, and another is that the transliteration of the Sanskrit term possesses strong power of charms when chanted repeatedly. Moreover, the Sanskrit name which was especially sanctified and could not be understood by the Chinese was easily accepted by the Chinese Buddhists.[17] They felt an exotic and mystical inconceivable connotation in the name which could not be understood. The name "A-mi-ta (阿彌陀)", however, is not the complete transliteration, because it lacks the last part, namely, Shou (life) or Kuang (light). Nevertheless, the Chinese did not pay much attention to this error. (The name of 'Amita' only did not exist in India.) When the Indians say "Amitāyur Buddha", it is always associated with "the Buddha whose life is infinite". On the contrary, the Chinese did not associate this name with its meaning because they transliterated it as "A-mi-ta", instead of Amitāyur or Amitābha. However, the Chinese were fascinated in chanting a word which could not be understood. Tan-luan (曇鸞) thought that the name "A-mi-ta-fo" itself was identified with the actual Buddha just as in the words of Dhāraṇi or a spell. He said that this name possessed inconceivable powers like that of a spell or charm.[18] In this sense, the Pure Land teachings which originally rejected the elements of spells and charms spread in China among the people only through its magical nature.

The tendency which gave great importance to magical power appeared in an unexpected aspect in China. For example, it was frequently performed that a priest cut his arm or burnt his fingers in order to express his gratitude and pleasure in hearing and accepting the teachings of Buddhism from his master. It occured at times that one burnt himself to death in the joy of hearing the teachings. Such priests were highly respected by the people.

The tendency, however, which esteemed incantation prospered only so far as incantation brought worldly and material advantages. Therefore, it did not stemmed from the complicated and illusional imaginations as with the Indian people. Namely, the Chinese are not fond of mysterious, extraordinary imaginations.

> Paramārtha who came to China from India and translated many sūtras into Chinese mentioned "there are two kinds of felicities in China, one is that there is no devil and the other is that there is no heretical thought in this country".[19] Namely, the religions which taught illusional imaginations did not exist.

The Chinese disliked the mysterious, imaginary and illusional atmosphere which covered Buddhism. Therefore, the Chinese who opposed Buddhism often attacked and criticized this point. In Zen Buddhism, these illusional imaginations were clearly disliked. It cannot be said that no mysterious tendency exists in Zen Buddhism. However, they acknowledge mysticism only in the nature or the events of daily life, and seldom referred to inconceivable miracles or illusional and imaginary mysteries. An example of this can be found in the following questions and answers:

> A priest asked his master, "It is said that one who used to chant the *Prajñāpāramitā-sūtras* can become most meritorious. Do you believe this?"
>
> The Master answered, "I do not believe it."
>
> Then the priest again asked, "If so, is it useless to believe in the miraculous stories mentioned in the sūtras?"
>
> The Master then answered, "It would be useless to be dutiful to one's parents who are already dead. The sūtras consist of only words, papers and ink. Therefore, there is no miracle in the sūtras themselves. Miracles exist only in the minds of persons who chant and believe the sūtras; namely, the divine power of the sūtra completely depends on the person who reads it. Place the sūtra on the desk. Does the sūtra possess miraculous power by itself?"[20]

According to the Zen doctrine, therefore, the divine power or the miraculous function taught in Buddhism is none other than the daily activities, such as "fetching water and carrying brushwood".[21] Namely, they are not miraculous experiences. Furthermore, Zen Buddhism in China did not teach that one could be born in the heaven by practicing Zen meditation. It is said that the difference between heretical meditation and Buddhist meditation exists on this point.[22] The fact that the Chinese were generally worldly does not always mean that they regarded this world as the best world from an optimistic standpoint. From ancient times, there were some thoughts in China which highly esteemed quietness standing on the pessimistic basis as well. For example, Lao-tzu mentioned, "The reason why I am suffering is that I have a physical body, If I did not have this physical body, then I would not be suffering". (13th chapter of *Lao-tzu*). Chuang-tzu (莊子) also mentioned similar statements in the *Tai-tsung-shih* (大宗師) chapter of the *Chuang-tzu*, and regarded this world as the world which should be despised as in Buddhism. This similarity was one of the reasons why Buddhism was easily accepted by the Chinese. Nevertheless, Lao-tzu and Chuang-tzu did not consider the past worlds before birth and the future world after death. The Chinese had a very simple idea concerning the destiny of man after death. They thought that death was "the separation of one's soul from the physical body". And again they believed that one's soul was always wandering around the physical body after burial in the tomb. Therefore, they thought it possible to call back one's soul to his physical body by crying and calling his name. For this reason, a religious ceremony where the friends cry and weep for the dead was established several centuries B.C., and it is still held among common people at present in China.[23]

Chinese philosophers also were very indifferent to man's destiny after death. For example, Confucius, being asked about death, answered: "I do not know what birth is, then how can I know what death is?" We see it is useless to ask about the world after death as the present world itself cannot even be understood well. This idea is very different from the ideas of Indian philosophers at large. According to the early Buddhist sūtras, Gotama Buddha was silent in answering this question. In the case of Gotama, however, he did not answer as he realized that the answer to such a question would generally fall into an antinomy. Confucius, on the contrary, answered to the question standing on the worldly and utilitarian standpoint. Zen Buddhism's way of expression concerning this problem is strikingly Chinese in accepting the essential standpoint of Buddhism. For example, Hui-hai (慧海)'s view can be seen in the following question and answer:

> A disciple asked to his master Hui-hai, "Do you know the place from where you were born?"
>
> Hui-hai answered, "As I am not yet dead myself, it is impossible to discuss birth. If you realize that birth is identical with the essence of non-birth, then you will never assert the existence of non-birth apart from the essence of birth".[24]

In the philosophy of Chu-tzu (朱子) also, the soul and spirit are not mentioned. "Even the saint cannot explain what the soul and spirit are. It is, of course, not correct to say that the soul exists. Again it is not correct to say that the soul actually does not exist. Therefore, it is better not to mention anything about the matters which man cannot actually see or clearly understand".[25]

The problem of eschatology which discusses man's destiny after death was discussed very little and hardly existed in China. According to the way of thinking of the Chinese, death is a necessity phenomenon for birth. Therefore, they faced death composedly and did not worry about the life after death. That is to say, "birth is identical with death".[26] Yang-hsiung (楊雄, died in 18 A.D.) taught, "Those who were born will surely die. It is the natural principle that those which have the beginning must have an end".[27] This way of thinking is very different from the conception of death and birth of the Indians. According to the view of the Indians in general, man, as one of the living beings, has to go through repeated transmigration in a cycle of birth and death. Therefore, for the Indians, the ideal state of man is to be born in the heavenly world or to attain the state of absolute existence or absolute joy in the future life by accumulating merits through good deeds and practicing various disciplines in this life. Buddhism of India was not an exception to this idea. After Buddhism was introduced into China, however, a view peculiar to the Chinese concerning the conception of birth and death appeared instead of the original view of Buddhism. For example, Chi-tsang mentioned at the moment of his death as follows:

> Man cherishes birth and fears death as he does not realize the real aspect of birth and death. Death originates from birth. Therefore, man should fear birth instead of death. If I were not born, then I would surely not die. If birth, the beginning, is realized, then death, the end, will surely be known. In this sense, man has to be sad of his birth and need not fear death.[28]

From this statement, it can be understood that Chi-tsang who was a great Buddhist scholar was still actually a Chinese.

Such a tendency concerning the conception of birth and death can be seen most clearly in Zen Buddhism. Namely, it is widely believed that high priests who seriously practiced Zen meditation would be born in the land of death instead of the Heaven where the Europeans and Indians believed such great recluses were born. For example, Ju-ching (如淨) composed a poem at the moment of his death as follows:

> For sixty-six years, I committed a great many sins, and now I am going to the land of death.[29]

Dōgen (道元) of Japan also was in a similar state of mind on his death bed. In India as well as the medieval ages in Europe, the thought that life of this world was a preparation for a better future world was very strong. In China, however, such thought did not manifest itself clearly. Therefore, the Chinese did not practice deep and religious introspection. That is to say, they did not possess a deep consciousness of sin. It is oftenly pointed out that the ideas of 'original sin' (*Erbsünde*) and 'emancipation' were not taught in Confucianism. Buddhism was accepted and spread quickly in China as a religion which fulfiled these deficiencies of the other Chinese religions and had great influence on Chinese culture. Buddhism, however, gradually became harmonized and mixed with popular folk religions or Taoism and again became a worldly religion.

It is an undeniable fact that religion still possesses an important significance in the society of present day China. De Groot mentioned in his book that those who know Chinese religions know the Chinese people because in China as in all half-civilized races, every activity of social life of the Chinese was greatly influenced by religious thoughts and religious customs which were to a great extent the basis of public morality, customs, family system, government system and the legislation of the Chinese.[30]

In the philosophies of the Chinese religions, the deep consciousness of sins and a reliance on, or obedience to, an absolute cannot be found. On this point, the present-day Chinese religions are greatly different from the present-day Indian religions. Therefore, it is said that "most of the rituals and customs which are conducted by the Chinese at present cannot be recognized by people of the world except in uncivilized areas".[31] Thus, again it can be said that the basis of the Chinese religions is incantatory, utilitarian and worldly.

This same characteristic of the traditional Chinese trend of thinking in the acceptance of Buddhism can also be found in the acceptance of Christianity. Generally speaking, the Indian Christians highly esteem the church and the faith, and they are other-worldly, transcendental and mystical. Chinese Christians, on the contrary, are generally this-worldly, humanistic, realistic and pragmatic. They are, furthermore, political and practical. They are, however, destitute of the deep consideration concerning the transcendency of the Gospel or the relation between the God and man. On the contrary, the Indian Christians believe that the practice of Christian Love never exists in politics, and they exclusively pray to God.[32]

Thus, the same differences of the ways of thinking between the Indians and the Chinese also can be found in the case of Christianity just as in the case of Buddhism which was discussed above.

---

1) 論語 11.12.

2) It is said that such thought can be found in the teachings of Confucius. cf. 論語: 先進篇, 雍也篇, 述而篇.

3) Sōkichi Tsuda 津田左右吉: *Shina Shisō to Nippon* pp. 11–12.

4) 高僧傳 vol. 1. (*Taishō*. vol. 50, p. 323 a–b); 出三藏記集 vol. 1. (*Taishō*. vol. 55, p. 95 a.)

5) 高僧傳 vol. 1. (*Taishō*. vol. 50, p. 324 c).

6) *Ibid.* p. 325 a.

7) His miraculous powers are mentioned in 梁高僧傳 vol. IX. (*Taishō.* vol. 50, p. 383 b), and also in 晋書 vol. XCV, which is one of the authoritative historical records of China. It is unusual that a record of a person who is not a Chinese is mentined in the authoritative history of China.

8) Tomojirō Hayashiya 林屋友次郎: *Kyōroku Kenkyū* 經錄研究 pt. 1. p. 338.

9) In the early periods of Chinese Buddhism, missionaries from An-hsi (安息) mainly introduced Hīnayāna Buddhism and missionaries from Yüeh-chih (月支) mainly Mahāyāna Buddhism. However, in later periods, only Mahāyāna Buddhism spread and was followed in China. The following opinion is widely recognized as the reason why Mahāyāna Buddhism spread especially in the northern direction of India.

Aśvaghoṣa was invited by King Kaṇishka and introduced Mahāyāna Buddhism into Yüeh-chih country. It was this Mahāyāna Buddhism that was introduced into China. [Cf. Senshō Murakami 村上專精: *Nazeni Daijō Bukkyō wa Hoppō ni Tsutawarite Nanpō niwa Kore nakika* (何故ニ大乘佛教ハ北方ニ傳ハリテ南方ニハ之ナキ乎), *Tetsugaku Zasshi* (哲學雜誌), 1894, p. 727 f.]

It is proved, however, that Hīnayāna Buddhism, especially Sarvāstivāda, was influential in Yüeh-chih at that time according to modern researches on inscriptions. There is no inscription mentioning Mahāyāna Buddhism among inscriptions discovered in the modern age. (Cf. Sten Konow: *Kharoshthī inscriptions*, passim). It is also recognized by modern studies that Mahāyānistic thought can not be found in the writings of Aśvaghoṣa. (The author of 大乘起信論 must be distinguished from Aśvaghoṣa, the master of King Kaṇishka). According to an original Sanskrit manuscript which was discovered by Rāhula Sāṅkṛtyāyaṇa in Tibet, Aśvaghoṣa was regarded as a Sarvāstivādin (*JBORS.* vol. XXI, 1935, p. 8 n.). Therefore, it must not be understood that Mahāyāna Buddhism was introduced into China because it was influential in Yüeh-chih, but it must be interpreted that the specific tendency of the ways of thinking of the Chinese selected Mahāyāna Buddhism as their religion.

10) Biographies of priests who possessed such mystical and miraculous powers are found in 神異篇, 感通篇, or 習禪篇 in *the Biographies of High Priests* (高僧傳).

11) 摩訶止觀 vol. VIII, pt. 1. (*Taishō.* vol. 46, p. 109 b.)

12) Cf. Taiken Kimura 木村泰賢: *Shina Bukkyō Jijō* (支那佛教事情 Some Informations on Chinese Buddhism), *Shūkyō Kenkyū* (宗教研究 Journal of Religious Studies), 1924, p. 119; Shinyū Kichijō 吉祥眞雄: *Shina Mikkyō no Genjō ni tsuite* (支那密教の現狀について On the Present State of Esoteric Buddhism in China); 法舫: *Chūgoku Bukkyō no Genjō* (中國佛教の現狀 The Present State of Affairs in Chinese Buddhism), *Nikkwa Bukkyō Kenkyūkai Nenpō* (日華佛教研究會年報 Annuals of the Chinese and Japanese Buddhist Research Society, 1st year).

13) In the Chinese versions of the sūtras, there are many technical phrases and words of Taoism which can not be found either in the original Sanskrit texts or in the Tibetan translations. For example, 福德度世長壽泥洹之道 or 福德度世上天泥洹之道 in 大無量壽經; 咸善降化自然之道, 求欲不死, 即可得長壽 in 大阿彌陀經 and 平等覺經; 自然虛無之身無極之體 or 無爲自然 in 無量壽經. (Cf. Sōkichi Tsuda: *Shina Bukkyō no Kenkyū*), pp. 37–40 and p. 85 f.

14) de Groot [tr. by Kinjirō Shimizu & Hakudō Oginome (清水金二郎・荻野目博道): *Chūgoku Shūkyō Seido* (中國宗教制度 Religious Systems in China), vol. 1, p. 69.

15) *Ibid.* p. 116.

16) T'an-luan (曇鸞) prefered the term 如來 (Tathāgata) to 阿彌陀 (Amita) and used it frequently.

17) Zenryū Tsukamoto 塚本善隆: Shina ni okeru Muryōju-butsu to Amida-butsu (支那における無量壽佛と阿彌陀佛) (*Shūkyō Kenkyū* 宗教研究 1940, p. 1047)

18) 無量壽經優婆提舍願生偈註 pt. 2. (*Taishō*. vol. 40, p. 835 c.)

19) 摩訶止觀 vol. X. pt. 1. (*Taishō*. vol. 46, p. 134 b.)

20) 諸方門人參問語錄 (頓悟要門 tr. by Hakuju Ui, p. 110).

21) A praise of 龐 to the 42nd rule of "碧巖錄".

22) Cf. Hakuju Ui: *Zenshū-shi Kenkyū*, preface p. 3.

23) de Groot (tr. by Kinjirō Shimizu & Hakudo Oginome): *op. cit. Chūgoku Shūkyō Seido*, vol. 1, p. 218 f.

24) 頓悟要門 p. 86.

25) 朱子全書 51, (quoted from Forke: *Geschichte der neueren chinesischen Philosophie*, S. 190).

26) This phrase is mentioned in the footnote of "呂氏春秋" as the words of 陳駢. (Yoshio Takeuchi: *Shina Shisō-shi*, p. 83).

27) 法言, 九君子 (*ibid.* p. 175). The following phrase has been conveyed as the words of 楊王孫: "且夫死者終生之化、而物之歸者也。歸者得至、化者得變、是物各反其眞也。" (前漢書 vol. 67.)

28) 續高僧傳 vol. 11. (*Taishō*. vol. 50, p. 514 c~515 a.) Although he was a descendant of a naturalized man, this fact did not influence the form of his thought.

29) Keidō Itō 伊藤慶道: *Dōgen Zenji Kenkyū* (道元禪師研究 A Study on Zen Master Dōgen), vol. I, p. 117.

30) de Groot: *op. cit.* p. 4.

31) *Ibid.* p. 5.

32) Kiyoko Takeda 武田清子: Ajia no Kirisuto-kyō to Kyōsan-shugi (アジアのキリスト教と共產主義 Christianity and Communism in Asia), *Shisō no Kagaku* (思想の科學 Science of Thought), 1949, July.

(3) Non-development of metaphysics

In connection with these tendencies, metaphysics did not develop well in China. Records mentioned in the *Five Classics of China* (Wu Ching. 五經) mostly represent events connected with the actual human world, and are hardly concerned with the transcendental worlds. An example of the latter is the mentioning of the idea of "T'ien (天, Heaven)". According to the view of the Chinese, T'ien is the place where kings, generals and ministers go after death. Sometimes it explains that T'ien rules all existences as well as human beings. This idea of T'ien, however, is not separate from the idea of T'ien as the sky above us. In this sense, this idea either does not transcend this empirical world.[1]

Among the ancient Chinese philosophies, the philosophy which possessed a metaphysical character was Taoism. Taoists thought that the real truth (*Tai-tao,* 大道) exists in the realm where all names and ways of practices of doctrines such as benevolence and justice in Confucianism are abandoned. And the original state of the Universe was an existence of neither form nor name as the symbol of the Truth.[2] We can recognize a germ of the metaphysical character in this consideration. Taoism, however, harmonized and combined with the art of self-protection and cultivation in later periods with a ceasing of its metaphysical system. Aside from this idea of Taoism, there were some other metaphysical ideas in Chinese philosophies. The conception of T'ien in the *Wu Ching,* the doctrine of *T'ai-chi* (太極, first principle) in the *I-ching* (易經) and the principle of *Li* (理, reason) taught by Chu-tzu (朱子) of the Sung dynasty are examples of such ideas. Explanations of these metaphysical principles, however, were scarcely mentioned. Namely, clear definitions of these principles were not shown. The existence of these principles was only insisted. For example, in the philosophy of Chu-tzu, which is the most philosophical study of all, a clear explanation of 'reason' cannot be found. Chu-tzu mentioned frequently that reason ruled all existences in this world. However, he invariably answered the questions of his disciples as to what reason was as follows:

"It will be realized in near future".

Which is to say, he kept silent about the character of reason in spite of his assertion on the existence of it.[3]

In this manner the metaphysical system did not develop in China. Chi-tsang pointed out the fact that the general Chinese philosophies merely affirmed the confrontation of the subjectivity and the objectivity as they stood on the standpoint of relative opposition; namely, they did not transcend common sense.[4] Tsung-mi (宗密) also criticized this same point in the Chinese philosophies.[5] Again some Buddhist priests criticized Chinese philosophies in general because they never set forth the three worlds of the past, the present and the future, or the six divine powers,[6] and moreover they did not understand what the soul or the spirit was.[7] These criticisms can be said to be correct evaluations of Chinese philosophies in general.

It is said that the Chinese philosophical thought attained its summit when the Sung-hsüeh philosophy was completed. Nevertheless, even Chu-tzu, the founder of the Sung-hsüeh philosophy, did not state a systematic explanation of the doctrine at all.[8]

As is pointed out, the Chinese were not quite conscious of the judgements of attribution. Therefore, they could not clearly distinguish the differences between the metaphysical principle and its derivative phenomena.[9] Therefore, after Buddhism was introduced into China, it was greatly influenced by the weakness of constructive thought of the Chinese. For example, the Chinese San-lun (三論) sect was based upon the *Chung-lun* (中論) of Nāgārjuna and other treatises. In the doctrine of Nāgārjuna, it states that worldly truth as the foundation of all existences and the real truth as the essence of the worldly truth are realistically different. In the doctrine of the San-lun Sect, on the contrary, it is thought that the differences between these two truths are only differences in a way of expression. Therefore, they interpreted the worldly truth as an explanation of what existence was and the real truth as an existence of non-substantiality.[10] In such a view-point a constructive metaphysics cannot be established. By this reasoning the philosophy of the Vijñaptimātratā (pure consciousness) which investigated the order of establishment of the existence did not become influential in the world of thought in China in spite of the fact that it was introduced into China by Paramārtha in the Liang (梁) and Ch'en (陳) dynasties. This philosophy again was introduced by Hsüan-chuang (玄奘) in the T'ang dynasty and was protected and supported by the nation. Nevertheless, it soon declined.[11] An analysis of the psychological phenomena in the doctrine of the Abhidharma of Hīnayāna Buddhism also did not develop in China. This kind of thought was not suited for the mentality of the Chinese. The metaphysical tendency can be scarcely found in the doctrine of Zen Buddhism. Tsung-mi acknowledged the fact that the teachings of Zen Buddhism concerning metaphysics were very simple.[12]

It may safely be said that the doctrine of the Hua-yen sect is the greatest system among the various philosophical systems organized by the Chinese. This doctrine transcends the traditional Buddhist philosophy while accepting it at the same time. The philosophical thought in Buddhism as well as in India generally established two ideas of the absolute existence and the phenomenal world. The former is the idea of non-form and non-discrimination, while the latter is an idea of form and discrimination. They are used to explain the relations between them. Namely, they argued about the relations between the noumenon and the phenomenon. The Chinese Hua-yen sect, on the contrary, insisted that every individual phenomenon is mutually penetrating and identifying, and moreover, each one of them possessing the absolute significance in itself. In this theory, the noumenon is not the important subject while the relation between phenomenon and phenomenon is greatly expanded. It is from this standpoint that the basic doctrines are taught, which are that "all phenomena are interdependent without obstructions" and "one is all and spontaneously at the same time all is one". In these theories, the noumenon is understood as something which is included in phenomenon. In the Indian philosophies, the relations between the individual existence and the permanent existence or the one and the many were the central subjects. On the contrary, in the Hua-yen sect of China, the main subjects were relations between one individual existence and another, or between limited existence and another limited existence. Although this tendency can be found in the doctrines of the T'ien-t'ai sect, it is more clearly formulated in the doctrines of the Hua-yen sect. Therefore, it can be said that the Hua-yen sect is a more Chinese and more developed form of Mahāyāna Buddhism. In such a philosophy, the attempt to assume the metaphysical principles was completely abandoned; philosophers dwell only in the shadow of the empirical and phenomenal worlds.

---

1) Kōjirō Yoshikawa 吉川幸次郎: *op. cit.* p. 70.

2) Sōkichi Tsuda 津田左右吉: *Shina Shisō to Nippon*, 支那思想と日本 p. 8.

3) Kōjirō Yoshikawa: *op. cit.* pp. 24–25.

4) 三論玄義 (Ed. by Y. Kanakura, p. 24.): "外存二得失之門一、內冥二二際於絕句之理一。外來二境智兩泯一、內則緣觀俱寂。"

5) 原人論 chap. 1: 斥二迷執一。

6) 三論玄義 (Ed. by Y. Kanakura, p. 24.): cf. *Shōbō Genzō* (正法眼藏), Shizen *Biku* (四禪比丘).

7) 萬善同歸集 pt. 1. (*Taishō*. vol. 48, p. 987 c.)

8) Alfred Forke: *Geshichte der neueren chinesischen Philosophie*, S. 201.

9) Masson-Oursel: *Revue de Métaphysique et de Morale*, 1912, p. 820.

10) 大乘玄論 (*Taishō*. vol. 45, p. 15 a). There are many similar statements mentioned in the writings of Chi-tsang.

11) Daitō Shimaji 島地大等: *Nippon Bukkyō Kyōgaku-shi* (日本佛教教學史 Historical Study of Teachings in Japanese Buddhism), p. 233: According to 護持正法章 written by Ryōhen (良遍), a scholar of the Hossō sect in the Kamakura period, there was only one temple which belonged to the Hossō sect (the school of the Vijñaptimātratā) in China at that time. In modern China, it is remarkable that the philosophy of the Vijñaptimātratā has been revived. This tendency originates from the fact that the necessity for a philosophical study of Buddhism has been recognized.

12) 禪門師資承襲圖 (禪源諸詮集都序 ed. by Hakuju Ui, p. 205).

Chapter 9. Individualism

(1) The tendency towards egoism

As has been stated the ways of thinking of the Chinese is anthropocentric, and spontaneously with it there is the tendency towards egoism. That is to say, the Chinese always considered all subjects centered on the self as an individual existence as well as the family which is the most private human nexus. When morality was thought of, for example, only the morality among individuals was considered with such special relations as between father and son, sovereign and subject, or wife and husband. And they scarcely paid attention to public morality of society or the masses.

The morality taught by Lao-tzu is consequently a morality for self-protection and safety of the individual even in the cases where altruistic virtues were taught. The Buddhists critisized him saying that his teaching pertains only to one's own life and is useless to the people.[1] The view of Yang-chu (楊朱) is "to complete the true nature of man and follow truth"[2] which consequently is none other than to satisfy man's physical desires. Chuang-tzu also insisted that man should not perform good deeds for fame, should not perform evil deeds which would bring about punishment, and should behave in conformity with his physical desires, then, he could realize his true nature and live a long time.[3] The theory of self-cultivation which appeared in the latter part of the Chan-kuo (戰國, the age of wars) period represents an art to protect and keep up one's physical body. The theory of seclusion also sets forth the art to protect one's life by keeping away from worldly and powerful positions where dangers are apt to arise. The theory of superhuman beings also stems from the desire to prolong man's life eternally and to enjoy life endlessly. All these theories are egoistic and can be said a kind of egoism. The teaching of Mo-tzu (墨子) which taught the way to love others is also a form of egoism as he mentioned that to love others is namely to be loved by others.[4]

The altruistic spirit can be found in Confucianism as it teaches the way of statemanship. It, however, teaches the way of statecraft of the governing class. Therefore, this theory was not derived from the spirit that man is saved as man and sentient beings as sentient beings. The moral practice of filial piety also possessed the tendency towards egoism. Dōgen of Japan pointed out this fact very clearly. "Only Buddhas and Bodhisattvas of three worlds possess the virtue of manifestation, while common people cannot change themselves. It is impossible for the general people to change their bodies freely. The theory of this manifestation or even the manifested footprints cannot be found in the doctrine of Confucianism".[5]

That is to say, the teaching that Buddhas and Bodhisattvas can appear in various forms at any place and time in order to save all living beings placing themselves in the same state cannot be found in the teachings of Confucianism.

It is considered that this altruistic and individualistic tendency in Chinese thought has a close relation with the actual livelihood in the Chinese farm-villages. It is said that even at present there is hardly any group consciousness in the Chinese farm-villages. It is very seldom that farmers cultivate and irrigate together. Therefore, the self-government of the farmers are very conservative. It can be thought that these characteristics in the life of the Chinese farm-villages is naturally in conformity with the Chinese way of thinking.

---

1) 萬善同歸集 pt. 2 (*Taishō*. vol. 48, p. 987 c).
2) '全性保身、不以物累形、楊子之所立也。' (淮南子, 氾論訓).
3) Cf. 莊子, 養生主篇; Yoshio Takeuchi 武内義雄: *op. cit. Shina Shisōshi*, p. 97.
4) Cf. Sōkichi Tsuda 津田左右吉: *op. cit. Shina Shisō to Nippon*, pp. 13–15.
5) *Shōbō Genzō* (正法眼藏), *Shizen Biku* (四禪比丘).

(2) The spiritual leadership of Buddhism and its transformation

Mentioned above, Chinese Buddhists criticized the self-centered attitude of the Chinese philosophers in general. After Buddhism was introduced into China, Buddhists practiced a great many altruistic activities in accordance with the ideal of "Compassion". Ever since Shih-le (石勒) of the Latter-chao (後趙) dynasty, who was influenced by the teaching of Fo-t'u-ch'eng (佛圖澄), left the education of his children to the temple, the temple has possessed great importance in education. The social work of Buddhist priests was especially noticeable in medical treatment and in relief of the poor. In the Tun-chin dynasty, Fo-t'u-ch'eng, Fa-k'uang (法曠) K'o-lo-chieh (訶羅竭), An-hui (安慧) of Lo-yang (洛陽), and Tan-tao (單道) of Lo-ching-shan (羅淨山) helped the people by medical treatments. The necessary offerings also were performed in the temples as well. In the T'ang dynasty, the system of the temple hospital was established. Also relief for the poor was frequently practiced as well as institutions for the poor, the sick and the orphaned were built in the T'ang dynasty. In times of famine, Buddhist priests and nuns devoted themselves to the relief of the people. As the organ of monetary circulation for the general people, a pawn house called "Wu-chin-tsang (無盡藏, the limitless storehouse)" was founded in the Nan-pei dynasty. Besides these activities, Buddhist priests endeavored to build bridges, plant trees, dig wells and construct rest-houses. In the Nan-pei dynasty, many temples were built in the center of the city. The people were charmed by the noble images of Buddhas or the ornaments of the temples which gave rise to thoughts of the Pure Land. Thus, temples became comfortable rest places for the people who became interested and familiar with Buddhism.[1]

It is supposed, however, that the Chinese Buddhists were not conscious of the worth of others when they performed these social works. They believed that one could be identified with others by practicing these activities. From ancient times, the Tao religion taught that "the correct way of human morality is the oneness of all existences".[2] Chuang-tzu also esteemed "the equality of nature", and again Chang-tzu (張子) of the Sung philosophy mentioned that "human beings and all other existences are my friends".[3] In the traditional Chinese thought system, it seems that the problem of "confrontation of one and the other" was not logically realized. On the contrary, in the Buddhist doctrines of the Sui and T'ang dynasties, this problem was logically explained. According to the doctrine of the T'ien-t'ai sect, the fundamental principle which makes possible the practical and altruistic activities is the "non-duality of self with the other".[4] Therefore, the doctrine of "helping others in conformity with their capacities" can be established. In the Hua-yen sect, the doctrine that "one is namely all as well as all is one" was taught to be also used by Zen Buddhism.[5] Philosophical arguments such as the demonstration of the existence of the others mentioned by Dharmakīrti of India[6] and the proof of the existence of ego discussed in modern Europe were not set forth in China.

The thought of the altruistic practice based upon the compassion of Buddhism could not change the Chinese racial characteristic which was originally egoistic. Buddhism was accepted and spread in China in ways in which it compromised with the thought of seclusion which was peculiar to Chinese and was conformed to this tendency of the thought. Generally speaking, Chinese Buddhism was transcendent and other-worldly and apart from common society. Most of its temples were situated in forests and mountains.[7] This can be clearly found in the Chinese phraseology that "to build a temple" was called "to open the mountain". The famous and big temples were all built in far-off mountains far away from villages.[8] All Buddhist recluses went to these mountains and observed the precepts, practiced meditation and furthered themselves there living together with their fellow-monks. They believed that truth could be realized only through these practices. Although the followers who chanted the name of Amida Buddha were mainly in contact with the people, many of their famous monks were confined to mountains.[9] Famous Buddhist scholars such as Tsung-mi[10] and Chi-i, the founder of the T'ien-t'ai sect, and also secluded themselves in mountains for study and self-cultivation. It was the ideal of Zen priests to be secluded in mountains to enjoy the quietness. When Dōgen intended to return to his homeland Japan, his Chinese master, Ju-ching (如淨), instructed him as follows:

> "When you will go back to your country, spread the doctrine of Buddhism for the benefit of both men and deities. Do not stay in the center of cities or towns. Do not be friendly with Kings and state ministers. Dwell in the deep mountains and valleies to realize the true nature of man. Do not break the tenets of our Sect!"[11]

Corresponding with this tendency among the Buddhist priests, the Chinese in general also praised and esteemed it as the pure and desirable way of life. For example, Meng-hao-jan (孟浩然) composed the following poem to praise the hermitage of Zen practice of his teacher I (義):

> "Master I (義) practices the quiescence of meditation and built a hermitage in the forest; a mountain is situated near it and shadows of trees cover the hermitage; when the sun sets there is perfect silence around the hermitage. Here, he realized the pure mind of man by observing the pure and beautiful lotus".

There are many poems honoring temples and priests in the *T'ang-shih-hsüan* (唐詩選, a collection of poems composed in the T'ang dynasty). These poems praise the fact that temples were situated in quiet places far from the villages and also praise the priests who sincerely endeavored to purify themselves and practice the Buddhist practices in these quiet places.[12]

Such an attitude of life where one lives in a quiet place and enjoys the state of quiescence is especially prominent in Taoistic teachings. According to Lao-tzu, a return to the root of existence is called quietness and is namely rebirth.[13] And again his follower, Kuan-yin (關尹), said "one should be quiet as mirror and response should be like an echo", and "one becomes pure by quiescence".[14] Lieh-tzu (列子) taught that man should abandon all discrimination and thought and should have quiescence and "emptiness".[15] T'ien-p'ien (田駢), P'eng-meng (彭蒙) and Shen-tao (愼到) also taught that man should abandon discrimination and judgement, that is one should reject judgments of this and that, one or the other and should observe the oneness of all existence.[16] Such thought also can be found in the teaching of Kuan-tzu (管子).[17]

This sort of attitude also influenced Chinese Buddhism. The practice of meditation was highly esteemed in Chinese Buddhism.[18] The important practice for Chih-i (T'ien-t'ai-tai-shih, 天台大師) was that of meditative concentration of the mind. Even the San-lun sect which is regarded as a representative sect of philosophical Buddhism insisted upon the importance of "concentration of mind".[19] Introspective and meditative tendency is especially prominent in Zen Buddhism, in which, the mind is called "the origin of the truth or *Dharma*",[20] and asserts that our mind is namely the Buddha itself.[21] In order to purify and attain mind realization, which is the essence of the truth, one must practice meditative sitting (*zazen*).[22] Meditative sitting is not merely a means to attain the final stage, but meditative sitting in itself is the "fundamental essence"[23] of man. Meditation is the substance of the wisdom.[24]

The wisdom which is emphasized in the Zen sect is one which is absolutely separate from the confrontation of "self and the others". This can be said also in general Buddhism. "The true *Dharma* is to abandon both the mind and its objects".[25] It is when discrimination of form is rejected that the absolute appears. "When thought is stopped and discrimination abandoned, the Buddha spontaneously appears before one".[26] And this state is namely the state of emancipation which can be attained only by realization of the nature of the mind in meditative sitting.[27] This state of emancipation, however, is not always a special state of quiescence. For the enlightended priests of Zen Buddhism, this is an awareness of life in practice. And this is called "one road of furtherance"[28] which must be realized by the man who practices himself.

The teachings of the Pure Land sect were also influenced by this mode of thought in Zen Buddhism. Some of early Pure Land teachings of China possessed characteristics of Indian thought. For example, the Pure Land teaching taught by Shan-tao mentioned that the Pure Land actually exists in the western direction of this very world. It is said, therefore, that many people committed suicide in order to be born in the Pure Land among the followers of Shan-tao who taught the doctrine "Loathe this defiled world and desire to be born in the Pure Land". The way of practice of thinking of Buddha taught by Chih-i was to meditate and observe each one of excellent features of Amida Buddha in one's mind.[29] The Chinese, however, who were worldly, unimaginative and esteemed the quietness of the mind, changed the teachings of the Pure Land. They insisted that the Pure Land of Amida Buddha existed only in the mind of man. There is a paragraph in the Chinese translation of the *Amitāyur-dhyāna-sūtra* which stated that "the Pure Land of Amida Buddha is situated not far distant from this world, and therefore, the features of the Pure Land can be observed by meditative concentration of the mind". Zen monks interpreted this as follows:

> "The ignorant desire to be born in the Pure Land by calling the name of the Buddha. The enlightened one, on the contrary, purifies his own mind. The Buddha therefore, said "In conformity with the purity of the mind, the land of the Buddha also becomes pure". If the mind is purified, the people of the east are sinless. If the mind is not purified, on the contrary, even the people of the west are sinful. The ignorant desire to be born in the land to the west. The lands of the east and the west, however, are situated in the same place. If the mind is pure, the Pure Land exists close to this world. On the contrary, if one awakens impure thoughts in the mind it is difficult to be born in the Pure Land even if one chants the name of the Buddha".[30]

The Zen monks then asserted the teaching which they derived from the passage of the *Vimarakīrti-nirdeśa-sūtra* that "the pure mind is namely identical with the Pure Land".[31] Thus, they insisted "a mind-only *nembutsu*"[32] and finally the teaching came to be taught that "the Pure Land of the pure mind exists in all the directions of the world".[33] After the Sung dynasty, the Chinese Buddhists exclusively followed the above-mentioned thought, and after the Ming dynasty, no contradiction was felt in practicing together meditative sitting and the Pure Land practice.

In Chinese Buddhism, the most important practice was to purify and realize one's own mind as above-mentioned. Therefore, the man who practices had to depend exclusively upon oneself. They did not to rely upon any other power, not even the power of the Buddha. In this connection, Hui-hai (慧海) said;

> "You should realize the fact that man saves himself, and the Buddha cannot redeem man. Practice by oneself and do not rely upon the power of the Buddha. It is set forth in the sūtra; therefore, those who look for the true *dharma* should not rely upon Buddha".[34]

In this theory, each individual has to face the Absolute by himself. Therefore, the authorities of the church, religious organizations or again the deistic existences which are the medium between the individual and the Absolute are not recognized.

---

1) Cf. Ryōshū Michibata 道端良秀: *Gaisetsu Shina Bukkyō-shi* (概說支那佛教史 Introduction to the History of Chinese Buddhism), p. 51 f. & p. 98 f.; *ditto*: *Shina Bukkyō Jiin no Kinyū Jigyō* (支那佛教寺院の金融事業 Monetary Activities of Buddhist Temples in China), *Ōtani Gakuhō* (大谷學報 Journal of Otani Univ.), 14–1; *ditto*: *Tōdai Jiin no Shakai Jigyō* (唐代寺院の社會事業 Social Activities of Temples in the T'ang Dynasty), *Eizan Gakuhō* (叡山學報 Journal of Eizan Coll.), 15; Hiroshi Yamazaki 山崎宏: *Shina Chūsei Bukkyō no Tenkai* (支那中世佛教の展開 Development of Buddhism in the Mediaeval Ages of China), p. 677 f.

2) Yoshio Takeuchi 武内義雄: *Shina Shisōshi*, p. 82.

3) 西銘.

4) This theory is the seventh theory of 十不二門 in T'ien-tai sect. Cf. 湛然: 法華玄義釋籤 vol. 14. (*Taishō*. vol. 33. p. 918 b); 十不二門 (*Taishō*. vol. 46. p. 704); 知禮: 十不二門指要鈔 pt. 1. (*Taishō*. vol. 46. p. 718 a.)

5) For example, this thought can be found in the 信心銘. Again it is mentioned in the 證道歌: "One nature covers completely all natures and one doctrine includes all doctrines. One moon is reflected on the water of any place and all reflections of the moon are namely one moon. True bodies of various Buddhas enter into the body of man and the body of man is identical with that of the Tathāgata".

6) *Santānāntarasiddhi*, ed. by Th. Stcherbatsky. Only the Tibetan translation of this text exists at present. Cf. Stcherbatsky: *Buddhist Logic*, vol. I, p. 521 f.

7) *Eihei Kōroku* (永平廣錄) vol. VIII: Cf. Daijō Tokiwa 常盤大定: *Shina Bukkyō no Kenkyū* (支那佛教の研究, vol. III. pp. 99–100. 世尊言、山林睡眠佛歡喜、聚落精進佛不㆑善。所以鷲嶺・鷄山・嵩山・黃梅・曹谿・南嶽・青原・石頭・藥山・雲巖・洞山・雲居・雲寶・芙蓉・太白・諸大祖師皆以居㆑山而已.

8) Hui-yüan 慧遠, the founder of the Pure Land practice of the White Lotus Society never left Lu-shan mountain during his life time. The eighth patriarch of the same society Lien-ch'ih 蓮池 also confined himself to the mountain.

9) *Op cit.* 禪源諸詮集都序 p. 20. Cf. *ibid.* p. 240.

10) This thought is derived from the words 絕學無憂 in 19th chapter of Lao-tzu (老子).
11) *Kenzeiki* 建撕記 vol. I, *Dai Nippon Bukkyō Zensho* (大日本佛教全書), vol. 115. p. 544. Similar teachings also can be found in the *Hōkyōki* 寶慶記.
12) '題₌玄武禪師屋壁₋' (杜甫, vol. II.); '破山寺後禪院' (常建. vol. III.); '聖果寺' (釋處默, vol. III.); '靈隱寺' (駱賓王, vol. IV.); '漚湖山寺' (張說, vol. V.); '過₌乘如禪師蕭居士嵩丘蘭若₋' (王維, vol. V.); '題₌竹林寺₋' (朱放, vol. VI.) Hui-yüan who lived in the Lu-shan mountain was especially respected and praised by the Chinese intelligentsia of the time. '贈₋錢起秋夜宿₌靈壽寺₋見₊奇' (郎士元, vol. V.); '僧院' (釋靈一, vol. VIII.). It can be also considered that the author of the *T'ang-shih-hsüan* (唐詩選) selected and compiled only this sort of poems. Nevertheless, it can be safely said that such way of thinking was influential during the T'ang and Ming dynasties.
13) 老子 (Lao-tzu) vol. XVI.
14) 莊子 (Chuang-tzu) 天下篇.
15) 列子 (Lieh-tzu) 天端篇.
16) Yoshio Takeuchi: *Shina Shisō-shi*, p. 82.
17) *Ibid.* p. 85 f.
18) In *the Biography of High Priests* (高僧傳), there are many biographies of priests who mastered the practice of meditation.
19) Chi-tsang (吉藏) attached great significance to the fact that the character *Kuan* (觀) is added to the *Chun-lun* written by Nāgārjuna in China. Namely, the Chinese used to call *Chun-lun as Chen-kuan-lun. Kuan* connotes the meaning of observation or insight in meditation. (Cf. *op. cit.* 三論玄義 p. 172 f.)
20) *Op. cit.* 禪源諸詮集都序 p. 156.
21) Cf. 景德傳燈錄 vol. VIII. 法常章. *ibid.* vol. VI. 馬祖章; 碧巖錄 Chap. 44; 宗鏡錄 vol. XXV; 傳心法要 p. 8; 宛陵錄 p. 67.
22) 頓悟要門 p. 8.
23) *Op. cit.* 禪源諸詮集都序 p. 14 f.
24) Cf. 諸方門人參問語錄 pt., 2, 頓悟要門, ed, by Hakuju Ui, p. 131.
25) 傳心法要 p. 20.
26) *Ibid.* p. 8.
27) Cf. 頓悟要門 pt., 1. p. 8.
28) 景德傳燈錄 vol. VII. 盤山寶積の條.
29) Cf. 摩可止觀 vol. II, pt. 1. (*Taishō*. vol. 46. p. 12 b.)
30) 六祖壇經, Hakuju Ui 宇井伯壽: *Daini Zenshū-shi Kenkyū* (第二禪宗史研究 Studies on History of Zen Buddhism, vol. II), pp. 147–148.
31) *Ibid.* p. 125.
32) *e.g.* 萬善同歸集 pt. 1. (*Taishō*. vol. 48. p. 967 a.) This thought also is prominently mentioned in 樂邦文類.
33) 萬善同歸集 pt. 1. (*Taishō*. vol. 48. p. 966 b.)
34) 頓悟要門 p. 60.

(3) Non-formation of religious sects

As mentioned above, the individual looked directly to the Absolute with deistic existences and religious organizations unnecessary in the Chinese religions. On this point, the non-sectarian character of the Chinese religions can be seen. Confucianism which was originally worldly was combined with national power. It did not, however, form a religious organization. Taoism either did not form a religious organization with a central controlled corporation. The same circumstances can be found in the case of Buddhism. There were no monks in China such as the itinerant Śramaṇas of India. All the monks in China stayed and lived in temples, where sectarian distinctions were not found.[1] The individual priest had a right to live in any temple in so far as he observed the Buddhist precepts.

In present day Chinese Buddhist society, there is no organization controlling the temples and they are not interfered politically. Mt. T'ien-t'ai is the sacred place for Chinese T'ien-t'ai priests as it was here that the founder Chih-i lived and founded the doctrine of this sect. Therefore, this place should be the headquarters of the Chinese T'ien-t'ai sect. Nevertheless, there is no relation between this mountain and T'ien-t'ai priests in various districts. There are no relations between an individual priest and another priest as well. Again the Shao-lin-ssu (少林寺) Temple on Mt. Sung (嵩山) is the place where Bodhidharma, the founder of the Zen sect practiced meditative sitting facing the wall for nine years. Therefore, this temple is the most holy temple as well as the incomparable practice-grounds for Zen priests. Nevertheless, it is not the headquarters of the Zen sect and there is no connection between this temple and other Zen temples although some pilgrims come to it. Zen Buddhism originally insisted on the importance of the conveyance of the teachings from teacher to disciple and the relation between master and disciple was very important. In spite of this fact, there is no connection between various temples at present.[2]

Actually the sectarian divisions which control temples and priests do not exist in China. The temple in Chinese Buddhism is a mere structure to accommodate priests. Therefore, priests of various sects are living in the same temple. If the head priest of a temple is a priest of the Pure Land sect, the temple belongs to the Pure Land sect. If the head priest of a temple is a priest of the Zen sect, it is the temple of the Zen sect. By this reason, the sect of one and the same temple is always changing in accordance with the sect of the head priest.[3] In this sense, it can be said that the distinction of sects solely depends on the individual priest. In Japan, on the contrary, a temple always belongs to a certain sect. Namely, the sect of the temple does not change by the sect of the head priests in Japan, as, in China, where the sect of the temple is always changing in conformity with the change of the head priest.[4] This is possible because present day Chinese Buddhism is completely one. Generally speaking, present day Chinese Buddhism is a Buddhism which included and harmonized various sects into the Zen sect.[5] It seems that this tendency of the Chinese Buddhism appeared in the latter part of the Ming dynasty.[6]

Therefore, the Chinese became Buddhist followers only through a reliance on the individual priests. Chinese temples do not possess the fixed followers or believers. Great land owners who supported the temple sometimes contributed land or forests. It was with these contributions that a temple could nurture its disciples and become prosperous. Head priests of great temples considered it a very important mission to train and foster many priests. Therefore, they requested contributions and offerings from their followers, believers or anyone with whom they had relations.[7] On the occasions of religious services and funeral rites, the Buddhist followers usually invited a certain priest to perform them. Or in some cases, they held the ceremonies at a temple they designated. In this connection, many followers of Buddhism gathered at a temple of a famous and virtuous priest whose name was widely known. Therefore, many times a temple was revived or newly built through contributions and offerings which were donated to these virtuous famous priests.

---

1) Cf. R. F. Johnston: *Buddhist China*, London, 1913.
2) Cf. Daijō Tokiwa 常盤大定: *Shina Bukkyō no Kenkyū*, vol. III, p. 108.
3) Of course, there are some exceptions concerning this tendency of the Chinese Buddhist sects. Cf. Daijō Tokiwa: *Shina Bukkyō no Kenkyū*, vol. III. p. 91.
4) *Ibid.* p. 76.
5) For particulars, refer to Enjō Inaba 稻葉圓成: *Shina Bukkyō no Gensei to sono Yurai* (支那佛教の現勢と其由來 The Present State of Affairs in Chinese Buddhism and its Origin), *Mujintō* (無盡燈), vol. XXIII, no. 1.
6) It is mentioned in the *Chikusō Nihitsu* (竹窓二筆) of 雲棲 as follows: "禪講律古號二三宗學者一所居之寺、所服之衣亦各區別、如二吾郡一則淨慈虎跑鐵佛等禪寺也、三天竺、靈隱普福等講寺也、昭慶靈芝菩提六通等律寺也、衣則禪者褐色、講者藍色、律者黑色、豫初出家猶見二三色衣一、今則均成二黑色一矣、諸禪律寺均作二講所一矣。嗟呼吾不レ知二其所レ終矣" (this is quoted from the thesis of Enjō Inaba mentioned above).
7) According to the travel records of Daijō Tokiwa (*Shina Bukkyō no Kenkyū*, vol. III, p. 109); "When I visited famous temples in southern China, many of the head priests were absent. It seems, they went to the South Sea Islands to collect contributions from Chinese merchants overseas".

(4) Universality of Tao (道)

Chinese Buddhists disapproved the authority of the religious organization or church as the medium between the Absolute and the individual as mentioned before. And they exclusively followed the *dharma,* or the *tao* which was considered as the Absolute itself. (Indian people made use of the term dharma in many cases but the Chinese preferred the term *tao.* The word *Tao* possesses more concrete idea than the word *dharma.* The meanings of these two words, however, is essentially the same.) In this sense, the Chinese were fully conscious of the universality of *tao.* Even though the countries differ, the same worldly morals are observed and followed.[1] A certain thought system trancends time and possesses a universal validity true for all ages.[2] The idea of *tao* which can be found in all religions in various forms is also universal truth. Therefore, it is said that *tao* is not abble to realize itself, but can be realized by man. Even though there are various ways to realize it the *tao* itself, however, does not change through the ages. That which changes in time and place are not tao. The theory of the *one principle covers all* of Confucius, the *non-creation* of Lao-tzu, and the *emptiness* of Śākyamuni point up the fact that different men taught the same truth".[3]

The idea of *dharma* is a higher doctrine than the Buddha. The authority of the Buddha is established only so far as it is based upon the authority of the *dharma.* "Those who realized the *dharma* are called Buddha".[4] It is said that Tan-hsia (丹霞), a priest of the Zen sect, burnt a wooden image of the Buddha to admonish people who idolized the Buddha, ignoring the significance of the *dharma* behind it. The Pure Land teachings state that one should meditate on Amida Buddha heart and soul in his mind. The present-day Chinese interpreted this teaching as none other than to meditate on Tathatā (thusness).[5] The Chinese Buddhists also esteemed the authority of the *dharma* more highly than filial piety, as is shown in the statement:

"The obligation to ancestors covers only seven generations, while the obligation of the Buddhist teacher is so great that it covers a great many Kalpas".[6] To respect a Buddhist teacher does not mean to respect the teacher himself as the individual, but it means to respect the person who realized the truth of Buddhism by himself.[7] Tsung-mi taught that only those who were inferior in their spiritual capacities had to depend upon a teacher.[8] This point is directly opposite to the case of Japan where devotion or reliance to an individual teacher is strongly emphasized.[9]

A prominent characteristic of the Indian religions shows in the idea where the *dharma* was highly esteemed, and Chinese Buddhism as well accepted it. The Chinese, however, emphasized only the concrete aspect of this idea of the *dharma*. The universal principle appears in different forms in accord with the time and place. The principle can be universal only by changing its form in conformity with the time and place. The idea of the *dharma* mentioned in Buddhism is not a stagnant one. Therefore, it naturally develops with the lapse of the time. A characteristic of Chinese Buddhism in the later periods can be found on the point where they paid attention to the individual form of principle.

As above mentioned, Chinese Buddhists did not form religious organizations which governed the priests and temples. Nevertheless, they greatly esteemed the observance of the precepts and believed that it was the essential basis of all good deeds to keep the precepts, because they were fully conscious of the importance and sacredness of the *dharma* as the Absolute.[10] Even at present, Chinese priests observe and practice the precepts.[11] It is said that priests who violated the precepts can not be respected by the people. The laymen as well as the priests, observe the precepts very strictly in China.[12] There is no governing religious organization in China. Therefore, Buddhist followers are not punished or expelled even if they do not observe the Buddhist precepts. Nevertheless, they follow them closely. This fact is directly opposite to the case in the Japanese Buddhist society where the precepts are not observed by the followers in spite of the fact that they are strictly controlled politically and economically by the sectarian organization.

To keep the precepts does not merely mean to practice ascetic practices or continue a life of mortification. The great priests of China excluded ascetic practices. This can be seen in the writing by Fa-tsang (法藏) who praised the precepts of a Bodhisattva stated in the Fang-wang-ching (梵網經 Brahmajāla) sūtra as follows:

> "If one does not observe the precepts of the Bodhisattva, he is the same as an animal or a bird even if he does undergo the ascetic practices in the mountains or eats only fruits and vegetables".[13]

In Zen Buddhism, the ascetic practices were also completely excluded.[14] The observance of the precepts was esteemed only so far as it was a help in realizing the *dharma*.

In this connection, there was also no discrimination of social position or status in the monkhood and nobody was refused entrance in the Buddhist organization on this account. Thus, Chinese Buddhism in modern times came strikingly to possess a democratic character. In reaction to this tendency, members of good families or the upper class did not become priests since the time of the "Suppression of Buddhism". That is to say, people from the upper classes used to enter the priesthood in the time before the Sung dynasty. In modern times, only people from the lower classes, on the contrary, entered priesthood. This tendency is still going on at present. In present day China, priests are mostly from the illiterate and ignorant classes and in particular the farmers and common inhabitants.[15] The principle of equality in Buddhism concerning the social position and classes is strongly supported by the general Chinese. However, it could not stop the idea of class morality which was traditionally and strongly rooted in the Chinese society.

---

1) According to Chan-jan 湛然, the way to govern the family and save people is also mentioned in the Veda scriptures. [*Ma-ka-shi-kwan* (摩訶止觀), vol. X, pt. 1. (*Taishō*. vol. 46, p. 134 b); *Shi-kwan-bu-gyō-den-kōketsu* (止觀輔行傳弘決), vol. X, pt. 2. (*Taishō*. vol. 46. p. 440 b)]. Cf. *Shōbō Genzō* (正法眼藏), *Shizenbiku* (四禪比丘).

2) Cf. *op. cit.* 三論玄義 p. 62 f.

3) 無外惟大 (early part of 14th Century, Yüan dynasty): *Kasanete Zengensen wo Kokusuru Jo* (重ねて禪源詮を刻する序). (*op. cit.* 禪源諸詮集都序 p. 161.)

4) *En-ryō-roku* (宛陵錄) (*Den-shin-hō-yō* 傳心法要, ed. by Hakuju Ui 宇井伯壽 p. 65).

5) Present-day Chinese Pure Land teachings regarded the idea of "一心不亂" in the small *Sukhavatīvyūha-sūtra* as 修惠 or 一行三昧, and they also regarded this idea as the same as the idea of 眞如三昧 in *Dai-jō-ki-shin-ron* (大乘起信論 Mahāyāna-śraddhōtpāda-śāstra). [Genmyō Hayashi 林彦明: Shina Genkon no Jōdo Kyōgi (支那現今の淨土教義 Pure Land teaching in Present-day China) (*Nikka Bukkyō Kenkyū-kai Nempō* 日華佛教硏究會年報, 1st year, p. 9)].

6) 道宣: 淨心誡觀法, pt. 2 (*Taishō*. vol. 45. p. 833 b).

7) 禪源諸詮集都序敍, p. 11.

8) op. cit. 禪源諸詮集序都, p. 35.

9) This idea of the Chinese is mentioned in detail in the *Mujintō* (無盡燈) 1918, p. 7 f. written by Enjō Inaba 稻葉圓成. On this point, a striking difference can be seen between the Chinese and the Japanese ways of thinking.

10) Needless to say, this thought can be found in the doctrine of the Lü (律, precepts) sect. Also Fa-tsang 法藏 of the Hua-yen sect mentioned that "excellent behaviors of all Bodhisattvas are based on the pure precepts". (梵網經菩薩戒本疏, (*Taishō*. vol. 22, p. 602 c.)

11) One reason why Chinese Buddhism does not degenerate even at present is based on the fact that most of the temples are situated in mountains or valleys far away from villages or towns. However, it can also be thought that the ways of thinking of the Chinese do not cause the degeneration of Buddhism.

12) Concerning this fact, it is mentioned in detail in Taiken Kimura 木村泰賢: Shina Bukkyō Jijō (支那佛教事情 The State of Affairs in Chinese Buddhism), *Shūkyō Kenkyū* (宗教硏究) 1924, p. 117, and Yūshō Tokushi 禿氏祐祥: Koji Bukkyō ni Tsuite (居士佛教に就て On the Laymen's Buddhism), *Nikka Bukkyō Kenkyū-kai Nempō* (日華佛教硏究會年報) 1st year p. 20.

13) 梵網經菩薩戒本疏 vol. 1. (*Taishō*. vol. 22., p. 602 c.)
14) 傳心法要 p. 44 f. (cf. 宛陵錄 p. 76 f.)
15) Max Weber: *Hinduismus und Buddhismus*, S. 292.

Chapter 10. Esteem for hierarchy

(1) The moral personality

Needless to say, all Chinese philosophies esteemed hierarchy in human relations since ancient times. One characteristic of Chinese thought is its ethical nature.[1] The Chinese regarded learning as ethical studies instead of the sciences connected with nature. However, the contents and the significance of "ethical" in Chinese thoughts are clearly different from that in Western thought or Christianity. In the following, the ethical characteristic in the ways of thinking of the Chinese will be discussed.

It seems that the Chinese were not very conscious of the line between the natural phenomena and the deeds of human beings. They thought that man could exert cosmic power and the universe solely depended upon the behavior of man, and that the natural power and the ideal entity were two aspects of the same one existence.

They again esteemed hierarchy in human relations and included individuals in this hierarchy. As a results of this line of thinking, the discrimination between the individual and the human organization to which the individual belongs was not fully acknowledged. An interesting example concerning the relation between the individual and the human organization can be found in Chinese Buddhism. *Seng* (僧) is the abbreviation of *seng-chia* (僧伽 the transliteration of *saṅgha*) which signifies a Buddhist organization. The individual, on the contrary, who belonged to this organization was called a *pi-ch'iu* (比丘, bhikkhu or bhiksu). These two terms are clearly distinguished in the Buddhist sūtras. In China, however, the individual monk was also called *seng* (僧) which originally meant the organization. In India, the individual monk was never called *saṅgha* (original term of *seng-chia* (僧伽)). I-ching (義浄) who made a pilgrimage to India pointed out this fact,[2] which the Chinese Buddhist scholars in general acknowledged. Nevertheless, they insisted that they were justified in using the term.[3] And this idea of the Chinese also was inherited by the Japanese.

The Chinese highly esteemed hierarchy of man, and therefore, they established the clear discrimination between human beings and other living beings. They thought that man was man only when he observed the right way of man. In this respect, Kan-t'ui-chih (韓退之) excluded barbarians, animals and birds from the concept of man.[4] This way of thinking is remarkably different from that of the Indians. In most cases, the Indians included man and the other living beings as well into one concept which was "being" (*sattva, prāṇin,* or *dehin*), as they thought all beings suffered from defilements and illusions of this world in the same way. Buddhism in China also was influenced by this kind of Chinese thought. According to Tsung-mi (宗密), the human being is the highest being of all existences and is the only living being who can completely harmonize with the spirits and gods.[5] Fa-tsang (法藏) also instructed people by saying, "if an ascetic does not observe the precepts, he is exactly the same as an animal or a bird".[6] Buddhism which originated in India changed its way of thinking in such ways, after it went into China in order to conform to the Chinese concept of man. That is to say, the views of the Chinese and of the Indians concerning man and the other living beings were directly opposite. It can safely be said that the view of the Western people concerning this subject is similar to that of the Chinese.

It can be considered that these two different views were derived from difference in viewpoints in regards to man. As has been pointed out frequently in the above, the Chinese people as well as many other peoples have attached great importance to the individual or the particular. The Indian people, on the contrary, greatly esteemed the universal or permanent. For the Chinese, social nexus possesses the most important significance to human beings. Man is regarded as the most significant and highest existence, and existences transcending man possess little meaning in actual human life. For the Indians, on the contrary, the life of man in this world was impermanent and mortal, with the differences between man and the other living beings being almost nil. Consequently, Chinese thought cannot transcend ethics while the Indians transcends it to possess a religious character. Such features in the ways of thinking are not always peculiar to a certain race, and it is also possible that a certain race can accept different ways of thinking. The Chinese were greatly influenced by Indian thought for long periods since the introduction of Buddhism into China. For example, the idea of compassion taught in Buddhism was widely accepted in the Sung dynasty and many compassionate acts, such as liberating living creatures, abolition of animal sacrifice, and refraining from killing living beings were performed.[7]

1) The *Der Weg in die Philosophie* written by Gerog Misch mentions that Greek philosophy is physical (physisch), Indian philosophy is metaphysical (metaphysisch) and Chinese philosophy is ethical (ethisch).

2) '凡有二書疏往還一 題云二求寂某乙小苾芻某乙住位苾芻某乙一。………… 不レ可レ言二僧某乙一。僧是僧伽目二乎大衆一。寧容二一已輙道二四人一。西方無二此法一也' (南海寄歸傳 vol. III, *Taishō*. vol. 54, p. 221 a).

3) Cf. 大宋僧史略 pt. 2, 對王著稱謂の條. (*Taishō*. vol. 54, p. 251 c.)

4) 原人篇. It cannot be said that such thought cannot be found in Indian. (e.g. *Chānd. Up*. V. 10. 7.) However, the thought of the Indians in the later periods is generally metaphysical and both animals and men were included in the concept of "living beings".

5) 原人論.

6) 梵網經菩薩戒本疏 vol. I. (*Taishō*. vol. 22, p. 602 c.)

7) Chūshō Suzuki 鈴木中正: Bukkyō no Gonsetsu Kairitsu ga Sōdai no Minshū Seikatsu ni Oyoboshitaru Eikyō ni Tsuite (佛教の禁殺戒律が宋代の民衆生活に及ぼしたる影響について *On Influence of the Buddhist Precept 'abstaining from killing' upon the Public Life in the Sung Dynasty*), Shūkyō Kenkyū, III, No. 1).

(2) Elegant attitude on sexual matters

Generally speaking, Indians are indifferent about sexual matters. This tendency is also found in Indian Buddhism. They are plain-spoken in describing sexual affairs. The matter was accepted by the Indians only so far as it was a description of an objective fact, and those which caused indecent feeling in one's mind were disliked. On the contrary, the Chinese, or at least Confucianists, felt disgust in written sexual matters. To be sure, some indecent literatures were written in China. It was however considered unworthy for wise men or gentlemen to mention such sexual affairs. Such a tendency is not peculiar only to the Chinese but to all decent people of the world as well. Nevertheless, it can be said that this tendency was one of remarkable characteristics of the Chinese educated people.

Buddhism was also influenced by this tendency. When the Chinese translated the Buddhist sūtras, for example, they tried to remove the plain-spoken words and phrases on sex. The Chinese version of the *Saddharma-puṇḍarīka-sūtra* (chapter Devadatta) states that "a female dragon suddenly changed her figure to become a male dragon". This phrase is very famous as proof of enlightenment of women in China as well as in Japan. The original text, however, states that "a daughter of the dragon king in the ocean explained the fact that she became a Bodhisattva by concealing her female organ and displaying the male organ".[1] The Chinese removed or abbreviated such expressions of the Indian text when they translated it. Another example: why was it wrong to drink stimulants? This was because various evil mistakes would arise. The original Pāli text says that "those who drink liquor are apt to display their sexual organs" as one of the difilements. The Chinese translator turned this phrase into "those who drink liquor are apt to become angry".[2]

The Chinese version of the *Hua-yen-ching* (華嚴經 *Buddhāvataṃsaka-sūtra*) *sūtra* translated in the Chin (晋) dynasty states as follows:

> Vasumitrā told Sudhana-śreṣṭhi-dāraka: "Those who *A-li-i* (阿梨宜) me surely attain the state of Samādhi where all-beings are saved, and those who *A-chung-pei* (阿衆鞞) me surely attain the state of Samādhi of virtue and mystery".[3]

A-li-i is the transliteration of Āliṅgana which connotes the meaning of *embracement,* while *A-chung-pei* is derived from Paricumbana which means *to kiss.*

The original Sanskrit can be translated as follows:

> Some people can remove all defilements only by *embracing* me and can surely attain the state of the Bodhisattva Samādhi called "the womb which saves all beings of the world" without fail. Again some people can become rid of all defilements only by *kissing* me and can surely attain the state of the Bodhisattva Samādhi called "the state where the womb of virtue of all beings of the world can be realized".[4]

As is seen in the above phrases, the Indian indifferently used terms connected with sex such as 'embracement' or 'kiss'. On the contrary, the Chinese who taught *the correct way* (Tao) of a gentleman could not follow this tendency. For the Chinese, it was a terrible thing to mention sexual words in religious scriptures. They thought that indecent terms desecrated the scriptures' authority and sacredness. Buddhabhadra, therefore, who translated the *Hua-yen-ching* (華嚴經) *sūtra* transliterated these two terms in order to conceal them.

In the other Chinese translation of the *Hua-yen-ching-sūtra* translated in the T'ang dynast, however, these two terms Āliṅgana and Paricumbana are literally translated as embracing and kissing.[5] It is thought that Confucianism was more influential in the Chin (晋) dynasty when this sūtra was first translated than later in the T'ang dynasty.

In this connection, German scholars among the modern Europeans, usually translated the sexual explanations mentioned in the Indian literatures literally. On the contrary, the English scholars, in many cases, used the Latin or euphemistic explanations instead of the literal translation. In this respect, it is considered that there is a similarity between the ideal of Confucianism and the gentlemanship of England.

In another part of the *Hua-yen-ching sūtra,* there is a story of a mother and daughter whose names are Sudarśanā and Suvalitaratiprabhāsaśrī.[6] Both mother and daughter were prostitutes (agragaṇikā). This sort of thing can also be found in modern Indian society and may be one of its characteristics. Most of this story in the Chinese T'ang dynasty version was translated literally.[7] Nevertheless, some differences can be found between the original Sanskrit text and the Chinese translation due to the influence of Confucianism. They are as follows:

1) According to the original text, both mother and daughter are prostitutes, and they talk about the teachings of Buddhism. From a Confucianistic standpoint, such facts were not agreeable. Therefore, the word "prostitute" is removed in the Chinese translation.

2) In the original text it states that "the daughter wishes to marry the prince Tejo'dhipati". According to Confucian thought, however, marriage is none other than the wife serving her husband. Therefore, this part was translated as follows: "If possible, I wish to serve this person".

3) According to the original text, the reason why the mother had her daughter give up this love was that "we prostitutes are the pleasure instruments of all the people; therefore, you cannot become the wife of one person". On the contrary, the Chinese translation says, "we lower people are not suitable for wives of such noble people". That is to say, the reason why the daughter had to give up her love was the difference in the social position. On the contrary, the original text does not mention that the prostitute is a lower class person. In Indian society, some prostitutes were ranked highly in society and were also very rich. Such facts, however, can not be recognized in the Chinese thought.

The older Chinese version[8] of this sūtra translated in the Chin (晋) dynasty states that the prince instead of the daughter fell in love. This explanation is exactly opposite to the explanations of the above two: the original text and the Chinese version of the T'ang dynasty. Of these, it can safely be said that the explanation of the original Sanskrit text and the T'ang version of the Chinese are the original form as there is a contradiction in the Chinese Chin version concerning this explanation. That is to say, the Gāthā (verse) portion mentions the daughter expressing her love for the prince. Moreover, it can usually be said that the verse is older than the prose portions of the same sūtra. Therefore, it is certain that the explanation of part of the Chin version was modified in a later time. Again possibly the translator of the Chin version changed the expression of this part. Perhaps, the translator thought that if this part would be translated literally, the ethics of the social position would be broken.

In connection with sexual ethics, the commentary on the *Adhidharmakośa* written by Yaśomitra mentions: "the man who observes the five precepts marries a wife". The Chinese version of this commentary translated by Hsüan-chuang, on the contrary, translated it as "the man who observes the five precepts marries a wife and concubines" (18th vol., p. 18 left). Buddhism, from its beginning, prohibited sexual relations with women except with one's own wife. Therefore, concubines were not permitted. It is true that it was permissible to have plural wives in India as can be seen in the Brāhmin scriptures or in the Jātaka Buddhist stories (*Jātaka,* IV, p. 99 G.). It was permissible only so far as the women were wives. China, however, permitted concubines without the sanction of marriage. Therefore, Hsüan-chuang who translated this sūtra added the word "concubines" when he translated this part of the sūtra. This idea was also accepted by the Japanese. For example, it is not forbidden to have concubines in the *Jū-zen-hō-go* (十善法語) written by Jiun (慈雲) of Japan, although sexual relations with wives or concubines of others are strictly prohibited. In this respect, a somewhat different ethical idea can be recognized between India on the one hand and China or Japan on the other.[19]

Buddhism seems to have had many followers among the elite, therefore, the words and phrases of the sūtras had to be translated in the above ways, at least up to the T'ang dynasty. However, further investigations are necessary in this field.

Sexual relations in China were strictly prohibited which opposed the human order based on the family system. This thought probably stemmed from the idea esteeming human order in the family. The love affair was regarded as physical and not spiritual. Confucianism did not recognize the spiritual significance in love although some romantic poems can be found in the *Shih Ching* (詩經). This tradition also influenced Buddhism.

Esoteric Buddhism arising in the last stage of Indian Buddhism was influenced by the Śākta school, the folk-faith of that time and included many indecent elements. Mysterious rites and ceremonies which broke public moral were performed under the name of Buddhism. The Chinese, however, did not accept these mysterious rites although the esoteric Buddhist doctrine itself was adopted. Among the esoteric sūtras translated into Chinese in the Sung dynasty were some which described sexual relations symbolically and yet they hardly exerted any influence. Although the Chinese accepted the magic spell element of esoteric Buddhism wholesale, the indecent side connected with the sex was not. Therefore, no sexual esoteric image at all exists among the images of Buddhas and Bodhisattvas which were worshipped by the Chinese. A few among the European scholars see a similarity between the worship of Bodhisattva Avalokiteśvara and that of the Madonna, and tried to find a latent element of Indian Śakti in Kan-yin. Such elements, however, cannot be found in any sūtra stating the worship of Bodhisattva Avalokiteśvara. According to the Chinese view, the physical body of man is ugly and dirty with the clothes as coverings for the ugly body.[10] Therefore, the Chinese neither accepted nor founded any religious customs as are seen in Jainism where clothes are regarded as shackles and the naked image of the Jina is worshipped.

---

1) Sāgara-nāgarāja-duhitā —— tat strīndriyam antarhitaṃ puruṣendriyaṃ ca prādurbhūtaṃ bodhisattvabhūtaṃ c'ātmānaṃ saṃdarśayati. (Saddh. P. p. 227).
2) Hajime Nakamura 中村元: *Shyakuson no Kotoba* (釋尊のことば Words of the Śākyamuni Buddha), p. 198 f.
3) *Hua-yen-ching* (tr. in the Chin dyn.), vol. L. (*Taishō.* vol. 9, p. 717 b.)
4) The *Gandavyūha-sūtra*, ed. by Daisetz T. Suzuki & Hōkei Izumi (鈴木大拙・泉芳璟) p. 204.
5) Hua-yen-ching (tr. by Śikṣānanda), vol. IXVIII. (*Taishō.* vol. 10, p. 366 a.)
6) op. cit. The *Gaṇḍa vyūha-sūtra*, pp. 404–405.
7) *Hua-yen-ching* (tr. by Śikṣānanda), vol. LXXV. (*Taishō.* vol. 10, p. 408 b.)
8) *Hua-yen-ching* (tr. in the Chin dyn.), vol. LVI. (*Taishō.* vol. 9, p. 756 c.)
9) Ye gṛhīta-paṃca-śikṣā-padāḥ saṃto "bhāryāḥ pariṇayanti", vivāhayanti.
10) 摩訶止觀 vol. IV, pt. 1. (*Taishō.* vol. 46, p. 41 c.)

(3) Formalism in behavior

The most important thought of ancient China is the idea of Li (禮) (Rules governing the way of life) which Confucius gave to the whole system of political and social customs which were handed down from an early age. It was the ideal to be performed in actual life. Every behavior of man such as filial piety or obedience to an elder had to be performed in conformity to it. Therefore, the ideal state of the Chinese is where every behavior conforms to the idea of Li. This doctrine was strictly observed by the Confucianists. At the time of the Emperor Wu of the Han dynasty, Confucianism was authorized as the national religion. Thus, the idea of Li became the fundamental moral in Chinese society.

This tendency is likely to change to a formalism in behavior. Buddhism was also influenced in a manner shown above where the Chinese Buddhists in the time observed Buddhist precepts very strictly. The following story will show how strictly the Chinese Buddhists observed the formal precepts.

When Hui-yüan (慧遠) of Lu-shan (廬山) became seriously ill, his disciples asked him to drink alcoholics as a cure. He refused, for it was transgressing on the Vinaya Piṭaka. A disciple then asked him whether he would drink rice porridge. He refused agin as it was already after twelve o'clock. (In India the precepts state that the priest must not partake of food after twelve o'clock noon.) Finally, he was offered honey and told to mix it with water and drink it. Hui-yüan then told his disciples to search the Vinaya Piṭaka in order to find out whether it was admissible to drink honey with water. He died before they finished reading all the Vinaya texts.[1] Tominaga Chūki (富永仲基) of Japan criticized this story saying: "One can say that he observed the precepts very strictly, since he did not break them even when he was dying. However, how eccentric it was that he did not eat the rice potage."[2] The Vinaya sect was founded in a later period influenced by this kind of strictness of behavior. I-ching (義淨) even went to India at a great risk to primarily clarify the rules of the precepts. Although Zen Buddhism has become very loose today in China, the spirit of strict behavior still exists. It is said that the Pure Rules which are the precepts of Zen Buddhism were formed by Huai-hai (懷海, 720–814 A.D.). It is in these Pure Rules that even the minor points of everyday life in a Zen monastery are stated. Among Zen priests in later periods, some have behaved very freely, but the tendency in which even the minor precepts are strictly observed still remains.

1) 高僧傳 vol. VI. (*Taishō*. vol. 50, p. 361 b.)
2) *Shutsujō Kōgo* (出定後語) vol. XIV, *Kai* (戒, precepts).

(4) Esteem for superiority in status

The ethics of Li rules esteemed order in status and social position. The ethics in Confucianism was one for the governing class, namely, for people who were ranked in high positions in society. These people were the governing class politically and the intelligentsia culturally.[1] Superiority in society and status in the governing class was the important thing. A one-sided obedience of the lower class to those of the upper class was emphasized. This phase of Confucianism was also supported by rulers of all dynasties after the Han. The fact was that Confucian morality protected the position and the power of the government and gave it justification. This line of thought was easily accepted by the Chinese, because from ancient times, the Chinese sociey was based on an order constructed upon discrimination in class.

Words and expressions used commonly in everyday life in China were also greatly influenced by this idea of social order. For example, many kinds of personal pronouns directed to others exist, and each of them used in accordance with who the person is, with whom one talks.[2] This is the same in the case of the person doing the talking.[3] In the universal phenomena of human beings in such acts as death, various terms are also used to match the social status of people.[4] Besides these, the Chinese classics[5] state in detail that the different terms expressing the same thing should be used in accordance with the social position of the person. There are also some kinds of adverbs which express respect or humility in China.[6] Furthermore, there are gradations even among children born to the one parent. The children are called *kyōdai* (兄弟) in Japanese, brothers and sisters in English, and *bhaginyaś ca bhrātaraś ca* in Sanskrit. In Chinese, however, they are divided into four kinds, namely *hsiung* (兄, elder brother), *ti* (弟, younger brother), t*zu* (姉, elder sister) and *mei* (妹, younger sister).

Buddhism which was introduced to the Chinese society where discrimination of standing existed and one's social position was a determining factor was revolutionary and taught equality of mankind with disregard for status and class. It seemed almost impossible that Buddhism could concur or even compromise with the thought of Confucianism. Therefore, the Confucianists frequently criticized the Buddhist teaching as one which destroyed human relationship. Some Chinese Buddhists, however, asserted the superiority of the Buddhist doctrine from the standpoint of Chinese ethics. That is to say, they said that the Buddhist doctrine stemmed from Śākyamuni who was from a royal family and therefore was superior to the doctrines of Lao-tzu and Chuang-tzu who were persons from the lower classes. Chih-i (智顗), the founder of the T'ien-t'ai sect, mentioned that "The Buddha was the person from a royal family in India, while Chuang-tzu and Lao-tzu were low government officials. ' Therefore, one cannot compare these teachings on the same level".[7] He again stated that Tathāgata Śākyamuni turned the wheel of the Dharma and became Buddha in spite of the fact that he possessed the possibility of becoming a great King of the World, Lao-tzu, on the contrary, did not give up his position and his land even though he was only a low official and a poor farmer; therefore, it is impossible to say that both teachings possessed the same value and significance.[8] Chi-tsang (吉藏) also stated this.[9] It is also said that the Buddha possessed greatness and magnificence as a spiritual king or ruler, while, Lao-tzu and Chuang-tzu did not. The Chinese Buddhist finally came to a conclusion that a Buddha was expected to surely be born in the family of a King or a Brāhmin, and could not be born in a low class family or a commoner's. Therefore, it is said that all Buddhas will never be born to the two lower classes, the Vaiśy and the Śūdra, and they will surely be born to the upper two classes, the Kṣatriya and the Brāhmin.[10] Thus, we see that Chih-i and Chi-tsang who founded the Buddhist doctrines of China could not but help compromise with the idea of class discrimination. Otherwise, they could not propagate their teachings to the general Chinese.

The Chinese explained even philosophical ideas in the framewark of class discrimination. An example of this will be shown in the following:

> In the doctrine of Hīnayāna Buddhism, the function of the mind is called "caitta" (in Chinese hsin-so, 心所) and the central mind, "citta" (hsin, 心). Hsüan-chuang (玄奘), however, translated the term "citta" into "hsin-wang" (心王), the king of the mind. After Hsüan-chuang, the Chinese scholars were fond of using this term "hsin-wang" instead of mere "hsin". They thought that the mind could not function by itself but had to be accompanied by other actions. This character of the mind is somewhat similar to that of a king who was always accompanied by many soldiers and servants whenever he went out. (In the original Sanskrit text of the *Abhidharmakośa śāstra,* such terms as "cittarāja" which indicates the king of the mind does not appear.)

Generally speaking, Buddhism could not be accepted by the Chinese without compromising with the idea of class discrimination.

For example, the early Buddhist texts state that both the master and his servants have duties to each other. The master had to care (serve) for his servants in the following five ways:

The task had to be given in accordance with the ability of the servant. Board and salary was necessary. Illness had to be cared for. Delicious food had to be shared. Timely rest had to be given.

The servant had to serve his master in the following five ways:

He had to rise earlier and retire later than the master, receive only what he was given, work hard, and also spread the fame and praise of the master.[11]

In all ages and countries, the moral, "the servant should serve his master and the master should love his servant", has been universally taught. The early Buddhist teaching, however, states this differently in that the master should serve the servant. It can be understood that the noble religious spirit of early Buddhism can be recognized on the point that the upper class entertain the lower with a spirit of respect and service.

Such a thought, however, could not be accepted verbatim by the Chinese who thought it a terrible and absurd fact where the master respected and served his servants. Therefore, the Chinese translator changed the words as follows:

"The master has to *teach* his servants in five ways".[12]

Only in such ways by changing into Chinese forms could the thought of equality in Buddhism be introduced into China.

Buddhism, therefore, could not change the idea of class order of the Chinese in spite of the acceptance of Buddhism. Although the Sung (宋) philosophy was greatly influenced by Buddhism, the ethics of Confucianism still remained. Ch'eng I-ch'uan (程伊川) understood the philosophy of the Hua-yen Sūtra deeply and was greatly influenced by it. Nevertheless, his doctrine was based upon only the idea of non-obstruction between noumenon and phenomenon, and he could not realize the idea of the non-obstruction between one phenomenon and another. It is possible to suppose that he considered it is harmful to Confucian moral to teach the idea of non-obstruction between phenomenon and phenomenon.[13]

As the result of the two revolutions in the modern period, the traditional order of status and social class are completely destroyed. However, a new class order was re-established after these two revolutions. In the Communist government, the iron rule is supreme, and demands strict obedience from the people. In this sense, it can be said that esteem for superiority in status still dwells at present in China.

---

1) Sōkichi Tsuda 津田左右吉: *Rongo to Kōshi no Shisō*, p. 297 f.

2) Senkurō Hiroike 廣池千九郎: *Shina Bunten* (支那文典 Chinese grammar), p. 125 f.
3) Cf. *Li Chi* (禮記), vol. II. 曲禮下.
4) The different terms which express death were used in accordance with the social position of the dead.
5) In detail cf. *Li Chi*, 曲禮下.
6) Yang Shu-ta 楊樹達: *Kōtō Kokubunpō* (高等國文法 Advanced Studies of Chinese Grammar), p. 412 f.
7) 摩訶止觀 vol. V, pt. 1. (*Taishō*. vol. 46, p. 68 c.)
8) *lco. cit.*
9) *op. cit.* 三論玄義 p. 27.
10) This phrase was quoted in the *Tendai Shikyōgi Shūchū* (天台四教儀集註) of Tai-kan (諦觀), vol. I, pt. 1, p. 19 a, as the words of Myōraku Tai-shi (妙樂大師).
11) D. N. III, p. 191.
12) *Jō-agon-gyō* (長阿含經). vol. XI. 善生經.
13) Yoshio Takeuchi 武内義雄: *Shina Shisōshi*, p. 268.

(5) The high value placed on patriarchal kinship

The Chinese moral was one which centered on the family as it was the family that was all-important in the life of an individual. Therefore, the moral of human relations between family members was the moral of the Chinese, and filial piety was the most important among them. The moral of Confucianism was, consequently, the moral of the governing class. Therefore, it is said that cultivating oneself and family government was applied and extended to governing the whole nation or to statemanship.

How did this moral affect upon Buddhism introduced from the foreign country of India? The Buddhist organization was symbolized by the *chia* (家, family or home) and was called *fo-chia* (佛家, Buddhist family).[1] Each sect of Buddhism was also called a family (*chia* 家). For example, priests and followers of the T'ien-tai sect called their sect "this family".[2] The rules of Zen Buddhism were generally called *chia-feng* (家風, the customs of the family) and specially formed rules were called *chia-hsün* (家訓, the instructions of the family). These rules had to be observed and practiced because they were the customs and instructions of the Buddha, the founder of Buddhism.[3] Furthermore, the Chinese regarded people who had deep relations with Buddha as his *relatives*. For example, the Chinese regarded the five companions with whom Śākyamuni had undergone various ascetic practices before he attained enlightenment as relatives of Śākyamuni in spite of the fact that the families and classes of these five Bhikkhus were unknown.[4]

It is a very interesting fact that the Chinese even expressed the idea of natural science in the form of kinship relations. According to the Indian atomic theory, in ancient time, a dual-atom body is formed from the union of two atoms, and the natural world is formed by the combination of many "dual-atomic bodies". The Chinese called the simple atom a "parent atom" and the dual-atomic body a "child atom".[5] The Greeks or the Indians did not use such names.

Buddhism was forced to teach filial piety to the common people. The most important virtue in Confucianism was, of course, filial piety which expected a one-sided obedience from children, the younger people, in a family to their parents, who were the venerated ones of the family. This idea, however, did not exist in the Indian Buddhism, as can be seen in the original Sanskrit texts where there is no such term corresponding to the idea of *hsiao* (孝), filial piety, found frequently in Chinese translated sūtras. Thus, the translators must have added this term. The virtue, of course, which corresponds to the idea of filial piety is taught in the original Buddhist sūtras, but only as one of the virtues and not esteemed as the supreme virtue.[6] The Chinese could not be satisfied with the family moral taught in Buddhism. In the Buddhist sūtras, the moral of filial piety in Chinese sense was not taught, so as a last resort, spurious sūtras such as the *Fu-mu-en-chung-ching* (父母恩重經 I vol.) and the *Tai-pao-fu-mu-en-chung-ching* (大報父母恩重經 I vol.) were composed teaching filial piety.[7] The great and deep obligation to the parents was stated as well as an insistence that the children repay it back to their parents. These two sūtras spread widely not only in China but in the neighboring countries and were frequently quoted: commentaries on them were written by famous Buddhist scholars.

The family-centered moral in China attached great importance to the ceremony of ancestor worship which was based upon esteem of the family-line. It possesses an important social and economical significance. In India, there was the worship to the Pitṛ (the soul of the ancestor) and the Preta (the ghost) which was performed in each family. China, however, gave it great importance. Ancient Israel also performed the dead-soul worship (*Totenkult*) which seems to have completely vanished in later periods with the decrease of the social and ceremonial significance of the family-line.[8] Thus, one of the remarkable characteristics of the Chinese religions is this soul and ghost worship (*chthonischer Kult*).[9]

After Buddhism's introduction Confucianist scholars strongly criticized Buddhism as a religion which destroyed the family and its morality. As monks did not marry, no children followed with the line becoming extinct and the ceremony of ancestor worship not performed. Chao-yüng (邵雍,

1011–1077 A.D.), a scholar of Confucianism in the Pei-sung dynasty, criticized Buddhism by saying that it was against natural human relationships. "The Buddha abandoned the relationships between sovereign and subject, parents and children, wife and husband. Then how can it be said that its teaching corresponds to natural reason?"[10] Brāhmanism of India also criticized Buddhism in the same way. The filial piety taught by the Indian Buddhists was "to respect and serve one's living parents in this world". The necessity of a memorial service for the dead parents or the ancestors was not strictly taught, because they believed that parents, after death, would be born either in heaven or hell according to behavior in the past. They performed ancestor worship only to express the feeling of gratitude to their ancestors, and the achievements or the memorial day of the individual ancestor were not esteemed. This fact has close relation with the tendency of Indian thought towards universality. In this sense, it was very difficult for Buddhism to be accepted by the Chinese in its original form.

Therefore, Buddhism could not help but adopt ancestor worship of the general Chinese. This trend is seen in the period of Northern Wei (北魏). A good example of this amalgamation is the *Ullambana* ceremony held on July 15th, the last day of summer retreat period for the sake of forebears for seven generations. On this day, people gave offerings to the monks in order to have the forebears' sufferings cease. Although the idea existed in India that the sufferings and pains of one's dead parents could be removed by offering foods to the monks, it is not clear whether this Ullambana ceremony was observed in India. It was, however, greatly esteemed in China and widely performed by the general Chinese from its start in the time of the Emperor Wu (武帝) of the Liang (梁) dynasty. It is believed that one can attain the highest state of Buddhahood[11] by performing this ceremony. Its significance and method is explained in the *Ullambana-sūtra* (盂蘭盆經). Many commentaries on it were written in spite of the fact that it was not known in India.

Esteem for family has a close relation with the social structure of China where the individual family could live without relationship to the prosperity of the nation. For the same reason, patriotism in the political sense did not develop well in China. Therefore, it was natural that the Chinese who esteemed only the family and relatives was surpassed by the Japanese who possessed a strong sense of nationalism in the modern period. At present the Chinese circumstances and conditions are very different.

As a result of the revolutionary success of Communism, the land owner class lost their position in society. Therefore, the idea of the family will probably be changed drastically.

---

1) Cf. *Kuan-wu-liang-shou-ching-shu* (觀無量壽經疏), pt. 2 (*Taishō*. vol. 37, p. 186 b). Hui-yüan 慧遠 called Buddhism itself as the "Buddhist family" in his commentary.
2) *Tendai Shikyōgi Shucchū*, vol. I, pt. 1, p. 35 b.
3) It seems that the Indian Buddhist did not call the Buddhist organization or school a family. In Jainism, the big school was called *Gotra* (姓) and the small school was called *Kula* (家) or *Śākhā* (枝派). (Cf. *Kalpasūtra* and many Jain inscriptions of the Kśāna dynasty). However, Chia (家) in Chinese Ch'an Buddhism had no relation with the Kula (家) of Jainism.
4) *Tendai Shikyōgi Shucchū*, vol. I, pt. 1, p. 19 b.
5) *Ibid.* vol. II, pt. 1, p. 5 a.
6) In the original Pāli Buddhist text, filial piety is stated in the following texts:
Itivuttaka 106 Gāthā = *AN*. I, p. 132 G.; *SN*. I, p. 178 G. (It also states that one has to respect one's elder brother here); *Dhammapada* 332; *SN*. I, p. 178 G.; *Suttanipāta* vv. 98, 124, 262; *DN*. III. p. 191 f.
In Pāli, one who is in allegiance with his parents is called "assavo putto". In Sanskrit, however, such a term cannot be found. "Metteyyatā" and "petteyatā" in Pāli are rather similar to the idea of Hsiao (孝) in China. These terms do not correspond exactly to Hsiao, because filial piety to the father and the mother is explained in different terms in Pāli. Again these terms are seldom found in the Pāli texts. In the Mahāyāna sūtras translated into Chinese, the gratitudes to the parents is stated in the *Shō-bō-nen-jo-kyō* (正法念處經), vol. LXI, and (Daijō-hon-shō-shin-ji-kan-gyō), vol. II.
7) Besides these, there are some sūtras which state filial piety, such as the *Bussetsu-ko-shi-kyō* (佛說孝子經, *Taishō*. vol. 16, p. 708), and *Bussetsu-fu-bo-on-nan-ho-kyō* (佛說父母恩難報經, *Taishō*. vol. 16, p. 778–779). These sūtras, however, are very short and not well-formed sūtras.
8) Max Weber: *Das antike Yudentum*, S. 150.
9) *Ibid.* S. 158.
10) *Shō-ri-tai-zen* (性理大全) vol. XII. pt. 6. 觀皇極經世書.
11) Tsung-mi 宗密: *Yü-lan-pên-ching-shu* (盂蘭盆經疏), (*Taishō*. vol. 39, p. 512 b.)

(6) Religion's struggle against the state and its defeat

The thought of respecting the Emperor is derived from the thought esteeming order. In China, this thought was established under the name, "the theory of Heaven's command" (天命說) in which the King is the son of the heaven. The power of the King ranked above various divine beings in folk-faith, and his authority existed in the power given by heaven. It was thought that the duty of the king was to organize a moral system and establish social order. "Only the king could discuss moral, virtues and organize the system of the world".[1] Thus, the king was gradually deified, and after the T'ang dynasty came to be regarded as the perfect human being. This thought cannot be found before the T'ang dynasty.[2] This thought greatly influenced the Chinese history thereafter. In China, however, this thought did not develop into the idea that the king was the living god. His power was limited by heaven's command. According to it, the King's throne was given by the command of heaven which the people had to follow. It further states that "when the king possessed little virtue and the people did not obey him, then his throne was given to the person whom the people would follow". The Chinese believed that this change of the throne was caused by the change in heaven's command. In this respect, this theory is also called "the theory of revolution".[3] In this sense, the King was not an absolute autocrat. High officials of the court whenever necessary possessed the right to advise and instruct the king who was thought to be a wise man possessing many virtues. And even the King had to follow and observe the universal moral virtues. The power of the King was limited in this sense, although actually he possessed great authority and power. "The king is the main trunk while the subjects the branches".[4]

The most important study in Chinese ethical thought was the study of the king's rule. Politics and cosmology were not separate studies as is shown in the word "T'ien-hsia (天下)" which connotes the meaning of the world as well as the empire.[5]

It was natural, therefore, that governmental power opposed and suppressed Buddhism whose goals were equality and compassion to all human beings.

Buddhism was regarded as the teaching of the outer world since the time Buddhism was introduced into China. After the Latter Han dynasty, many Buddhist priests came from India or Central Asia to become teachers of Kings and eventually the doctrine of the Buddhism with the other studies was taught to the king as well as the state ministers and other high officials. It was natural for the Chinese, however, to attack this tendency. According to Taoists, as the king is ranked the highest with the *tao* (道) and the *t'ien* (天), and priests are the subjects of the king, it was unreasonable that the king should be taught by a low monk or again to venerate monks, but that they should respect and pay homage to the king. This problem was frequently discussed in the years to follow.

This problem was of great importance during the time of Hui-yüan (慧遠) of the Lu-shan (盧山). He wrote the *Sha-men-pu-ching-wang-che-lun* (沙門不敬王者論, a treatise on Buddhist priests who need not pay homage to the king) and opposed the suppression of Buddhism by King Huan-hsüan (桓玄) who insisted that Buddhist priests as well should attend the Imperial ceremonies together with other government officials. This was opposed by Hui-yüan who tried to separate the Buddhist organization from governmental power. He could oppose to king strongly because he was supported by the aristocrats of South China who cherished his opinion.

However, since the Buddhist organization florished, it was not desirable for the state to have the Buddhists outside of its power. Thus, this attempt by the Buddhists was suppressed in North China. Generally speaking, the power of the state was stronger in North China than in the South. From an early time, many people entered the priesthood in order to evade military service and payment of tax. At times, several hundred young men entered the temple together and became monks. The safety and prosperity of the nation was threatened by the increase of such kind of monks. As a preventive examinations of monks were held often. That is to say, all those who did not possess a monk's ability were forced to return to secular life. Buddhism was finally crushed through such practices. Among the many Emperors who suppressed Buddhism, King Tao-wu (道武帝) of the Northern Wei (北魏) dynasty, King Wu (武帝) of the Northern Chou (北周) dynasty, King Wu (武宗) of the T'ang dynasty and King Shih (世宗) of the Latter Chou (後周) dynasty are famous.

In some cases, Buddhism was persecuted as a danger to the state's economic status in regard to metal currency. A great amount of metal and other materials was used for Buddhist arts, such as Buddha images, vases and other temple treasures. The economical condition of the nation became steadily worse. The state tried various measures to meet the situation which were not really effective in the long run.[6] The real cure was to wipe out the Buddhist organizations.

In this way the Buddhist organizations were gradually taken over and controlled by the nation. A system of officials to control Buddhism was founded in the Eastern Chin (東晋) dynasty. After that, in every district and prefecture, the priest official was appointed as a government officer to control the monk group of the respective district or prefecture.

Because Buddhist society was completely controlled by the state, Buddhists had to compromise with the thought in which the king was deified.

Fa-kuo (法果), the first priest officer in the Northern Wei dynasty, regarded Emperor Tao-wu (道武帝) as a living Tathāgata and said that "all monks must respect him".[7] Many other people such as Wei Yüan-sung (衛元嵩) and Jen Tao1lin (任道林) also stated that the King is a Tathāgata or Bodhisattva. Emperor Wu (武帝) of the Liang (梁) dynasty was a faithful Buddhist and called the 'Bodhisattva King' or 'King Bodhisattva' by his subjects and again he was called a 'real Buddha' by a foreign country. A religious ceremony was held on the birthday of the king since the T'ang dynasty. In the Sung dynasty, the priest of Zen Buddhism prayed for the long life of the King, and finally in the Yüan (元) dynasty, people came to believe that the King must be a Dharma-kāya Buddha (the Buddha of the true body).[8]

During the Yüan dynasty, all of China was conquered by the military might of the Yüan. The Zen Buddhist organization, the representative religion of the time, showed its submissive attitude to the Yüan government stating:

> "The most valuable matter for man is to realize the principle of Tao (道). From ancient times, therefore, the excellent Emperors of China respected the teaching of the Buddha, the saint of the Western country, and for this reason, we Buddhist priests were treated with special hospitality by the Emperors. The Yüan government has especially treated us well. We can endeavor to realize Buddhist truth free from tax and other worldly duties. Our obligation to the Emperor is so vast and great that it cannot be expressed by words. To return this obligation we will surely endeavor to realize Buddha-nature and teach the holy doctrines of Buddhism to the people. We Buddhist priests will never forget his mercy and do our best".

Furthermore, a religious ceremony to honor and pray for the long life of the King was provided.[9] In this respect, the attitude of Chinese Buddhists towards state power was exactly the same as the Japanese. The basic spirit of Buddhism repeatedly taught since its original form which was not to make friends with emperors or kings was completely ignored.

More investigations and study are necessary to realize how this idea of Buddhism changed in the Ming (明) and the Ch'ing (清) dynasties. One fact is that Buddhism was supported and protected by the state. Until the establishment of the Chung-hua-min-kuo (中華民國), the authority of the Emperor ranked higher than the authority of the Buddhist organization.

Although there was no king in the Chung-hua-min-kuo, the authority of the religion was no more influential or powerful in society than the past.

In present day Red China, religion is strongly controlled. Various opinions exist among people who have visited Red China recently concerning the relation between religion and state. Some people report that religious organizations are protected by the state, while others say that they are suppressed. What is common to all opinions is the power and strictness of the state. It is indeed an admirable fact that such a strong Communist government was established in China in such a short period. However, what must be considered is that this was possible because the Chinese by nature have traditionally accepted strong state power since ancient times.

---

1) *Chung Yung* (中庸).
2) Kōjirō Yoshikawa 吉川幸次郎: *op. cit.* pp. 105–106.
3) Sōkichi Tsuda 津田左右吉: *Shina Shisō to Nippon,* pp. 18–19.
4) *Chun-nan-tzu* (淮南子), 繆稱訓.
5) Masson-Oursel: *La philosophie comparée,* p. 118.
6) Max Weber: *Konfuzianismus und Taoismus,* S. 285.
7) Zenryū Tsukamoto 塚本善隆: *Shina Bukkyō-shi Kenkyū* (支那佛教史研究 A Study on the History of Chinese Buddhism), p. 86.
8) Daijō Tokiwa 常盤大定: *Shina Bukkyō- no Kenkyū* vol. III, pp. 97–98; Ryōshū Michibata 道端良秀: *Gaisetsu Shina Bukkyō-shi* (概說支那佛教史 General Outline of the History of Chinese Buddhism), p. 74 f.; Hiroshi Yamazaki 山崎宏: *Shina Chūsei Bukkyō no Tenkai* (支那中世佛教の展開 The Development of Chinese Buddhism in the Medieval Age), p. 129 f. *Cf.* Enichi Ōchō 横超慧日: *Shina Bukkyō no Okeru Kokka Ishiki* (支那佛教に於ける國家意識 National Sentiments in Chinese Buddhism). (*Tōhō Gakuhō* 東方學報), vol. XI, No. 3.
9) *Choku-shū Hyaku-jō-shin-gi* (勅修百丈清規). (*Taishō*. vol. 48, p. 1112 c.)

(7) Racial pride and reverence for lineage

The Chinese who recognized the reign of the king and his deification as the highest ethical significance and ignored the value of individual man, insisted on the superiority and the greatness of their own race. Racial pride and haughtiness of the Chinese were established on this point. They discriminated foreign countries from their own country by calling their land 'Chung-kuo (中國, the central or the superior country)' to believe that other countries belonged to their country 'China'.

However, some people among the Chinese did not recognize the superiority of old Chinese culture, and they did not call their country the central kingdom. To the Chinese monks who traveled to India to look for the doctrines of Buddhism, China was only a 'remote country' before the splendor of Indian culture. Therefore, these priests used the term '*Chung-kuo* (中國)' for India.[1] However, in accordance with the spread of Buddhism in China, Chinese Buddhist also came to call their country '*Chung-hua* (中華)'[2] or '*Chung-hsia* (中夏)'[3] This tendency naturally was connected with nationalism. According to the general opinion of the Chinese, Buddhism was a teaching of a foreign country and not the thought of China. They, therefore, thought that China was occupied and governed by foreign races for a long time because of Buddhism. For this reason, some people such as Fu-i (傅奕)[4] insisted on its suppression. This thought is equivalent to the thought of xenophobia in Europe.

Nevertheless, they had to recognize the worth of foreign culture to some extent. Therefore, the Chinese tried another angle in order to show the superiority of their culture; namely, the advocation that all kinds of studies and true teachings were originally founded in China. When Buddhism was recognized as a teaching which stated truth, the Chinese showed the superiority of traditional Chinese thought by saying that "Buddhism was originally taught by the Chinese", instead of criticizing the doctrine of Buddhism logically. Thus, the *Lao-tzu-hua-hu-ching* (老子化胡經) which was composed by the Taoists in the Western Chin (西晋) dynasty stated that Lao-tzu went to India and became Śākyamuni in order to teach the Indians, or again that he was the teacher of Śākyamuni. Furthermore, Fu-i (傅奕) of the T'ang dynasty insisted that the Buddhists borrowed and used the profound terminology of Lao-tzu and Chuang-tzu in the Buddhist sūtras.[5] In the Eastern Chin (東晋) dynasty, many sūtras showing the relation between Taoism and Buddhism were composed by the Taoists. The Buddhist also composed many spurious sūtras concerning this problem. According to the *Ch'ing-ching-fa-hsing-ching* (清淨法行經), one of sūtras composed by the Buddhists, Buddha dispatched three disciples to China in order to teach the Chinese. It further stated that these three disciples were called 'Confucius', 'Yen-yüan (顏淵)' and 'Lao-tzu' in China. In this arguments, doctrinal truth was not important. They did not give much attention to which doctrine taught the religious truth. Only the problem of which religion was the original was discussed. The Chinese did not recognize that the Indian religion originated earlier than that of China. Therefore, Chih-i (智顗) who organized a Chinese Buddhist doctrine adopted the Chinese theory that the saint of China appeared earlier than that of India. He thought that even the devil could transform his body into a Buddha image, and heretics could show divine power; therefore, it is very possible that Lao-tzu taught the Indians by transforming his body into the Buddha. He further stated that the teaching in India was not the real teaching.[6]

This way of thinking also influenced natural science. Although scholars of the Ch'ing dynasty were interested in and accepted the culture of Europe to some extent, they were still proud of the superiority of Chinese culture in the same way. They accepted the astronomy of Europe but they said: ——— To be sure, European astronomy has become fairly well-developed. However, originally it came from the astronomy of China. It is written in Chinese history that many students of astronomy went to foreign countries in order to escape war in the Chou (周) dynasty. Present-day astronomy of Europe was developed by their descendants. Therefore, it can be said that European astronomy is derived from Chinese astronomy. ——— In spite of the fact that the scholars who accepted the astronomy of Europe were comparatively progressive in the Ch'ing dynasty, they stated and believed this story.[7]

As the result of this esteem in historical lineage, the Chinese Buddhist came to insist that all sciences and studies were originally founded and devedoped by Buddhism and the heretical people adopted these sciences and studies afterwards in their doctrines. This way of thinking can also be found in India. However, it can be said that it was more outstanding in China than in India.[8]

---

1) Tao-hsüan (道宣) called Bodhirūci who came from Indian "中國三藏菩提留支". (*Taishō*. vol. 50, p. 470 b–c.)
2) e.g. 禪源諸詮集都序 pt, 1, p. 29; p. 83.
3) e.g. 禪源諸詮集都序敍 p. 5.
4) Arthur F. Wright: Fu-I and the Rejection of Buddhism. (*Journal of the History of Ideas*), vol. XII, No. I, 1951, p. 42.
5) *Ibid.* p. 44.
6) 摩訶止觀 vol. VI. pt. 2. (*Taishō*. vol. 46, p. 80 a.)
7) Kōjirō Yoshikawa 吉川幸次郎: *op. cit.* pp. 143–144.
8) Hajime Nakamura 中村元: *Shoki no Vedānta Tetsugaku* (初期のヴェーダーンタ哲學 Vedānta Philosophy in early stages), p. 305 f; p. 345 f.

Chapter 11. Esteem for nature

(1) Conformity to nature

The tendency of Chinese thought which paid attention only to concrete and phenomenal objects and considered that all existences could exist only so far as they were in conformity with man, came to esteem the natural principle which exists in mind of man. The idea of T'ien (天) which existed since ancient times in China was thought out by the Chinese in close relation with man.[1] According to a poem composed in the early Chou dynasty, Heaven created man, and therefore, Heaven is the ancestor of man and at the same time it handed down moral precepts which man had to observe.[2] This was inherited by Confucius. He esteemed "acknowledging the order of the Heaven" which meant "one should follow the morality given by Heaven".[3] Some modern Europeans were deeply stirred by the fact that ancient China where Confucianism was recognized as the national ideology and the politics was administrated by its doctrine, followed a law based upon natural law. It is an undoubted fact that some similarities exist between the idea of natural law in Europe and that of ancient China.

The opinion that "man should follow his true-nature" was also stated by other scholars in ancient China, and yet their meanings were different from that of Confucius. Mo-tzu (墨子) taught that the ruler should follow what Heaven wished and not follow what it did not wish. Lao-tzu insisted that the correct way of man is to follow the way of Heaven; therefore, it can be said that the basis of the correct way of man is T'ien-tao (天道, the Way of Heaven). Yang-chu (楊朱) stated, "The original nature of man desires only sex and food. Therefore, it is better for man not to have relations with others but only to satisfy one's own desires". "It is the natural law that man does what he wants".[4] Meng-tzu taught that "the true character of man is good; however, the evil mind arises by temptation of material desires. Therefore, man should cultivate his mind himself and exhibit his own true-character". An exception to Chinese thought was Hsün-tzu who mentioned that the true character of man is evil. Nevertheless, he recognized the possibility of man to become good. Chuang-tzu taught that man should perfect his true character, and his followers came to teach the theory that "man should return to his true character". In the San-kuo (三國) dynasty, Wang-pi (王弼) also asserted the "return to the true character".[5] This thought developed greatly in the Sung philosophy where the central theme was the concept of man's true character. The traditional current of thought in Chinese history is "to return to the true and natural character of man".

Buddhism was also influenced by this current of thought. They did not look for truth in the phenomenal world but the world inside in endeavoring to concentrate their inner mind. In Zen Buddhism, Chinese traditional thought is expressed in a Chinese way of expression which is "if one realizes the truth that all existences are the same, he immediately returns to his true nature".[6] Both illusion and enlightenment of man were understood to be derived from the natural character of man. "The mind is the ground and the nature is the king. Where there is nature there is the king, and where there is no nature, there is no king. Where there is nature, there are the body and mind. Where no nature exists, there is neither body nor mind. Buddha is created by self-nature; therefore, one must not look for the Buddha by the body. If self-nature is a illusion, then the Buddha is namely a sentient being. If self-nature is enlightenment, then the sentient being is namely the Buddha".[7] There was, in India, no such idea of self-nature as the principle which maintains the body and mind or is ignorant or enlightened. Some Chinese scholars recognized a Taoist influence in this conception of self-nature.[8] However, this concept could have appeared from the traditional idea of the Chinese.

Chinese Pure Land teachings also adopted the idea of Taoism. The Chinese Buddhists had to pass through the process of complex reflection and thought before they acknowledged a Chinese naturalism. In this connection, Chi-tsang mentioned;[9] The Chinese philosophical thought, and especially in Lao-tzu and Chuang-tzu, regarded existence as phenomenon and voidness as a substance somewhat other than existence. Therefore, voidness was not in conformity with existence. Buddhism, on the contrary, taught that phenomenon as it is is the manifestation of the Absolute.[10] Therefore, the absolute significance cannot be recognized in actual life of the phenomenal world in the philosophy of Lao-tzu and Chuang-tzu. In Buddhism, however, one can live in this phenomenal world standing on a state of absoluteness, because actual life in this world is identical with absolute existence.[11]———

Although this criticism of Chi-tsang may not be correct, at least he tried to recognize a significance in life in this world. T'ien-tai and Hua-yen sects further expanded on this thought. According to the T'ien-tai sect, phenomenon and noumenon are not different but are mutually the same. Phenomenon as it is is identical with noumenon. Therefore, they taught that "each existence in this world is the middle way". Each of the phenomenal forms of this world is namely absolute existence. The Hua-yen sect even developed this thought further. That is to say, the theory of "mutual penetration and mutual identification between one thing and another is taught in this sect. The supreme meaning exists where phenomenon and phenomenon are perfectly identifying and penetrating mutually without obstruction. Therefore, noumenon does not exist outside of phenomenon. The true nature of phenomenon is to manifest various different forms.

As a result of this tendency, the actual natural world was acknowledged as the absolute existence as it is. In Zen Buddhism, the following answers were given to the question 'what is the absolute existence?' 'It is the cypress tree in the garden' or 'it is three pounds of hemp'. It is also seen in Su-tung-p'o's (蘇東坡) following poem; "the sound of the stream is the teaching or sermon of the Buddha, and the colour of the mountain is the pure Dharma-kāya (true body) of the Buddha". In such ways, this naturalistic tendency came to the conclusion that each one of the existences of this world is just as it is the manifestation of truth.

Zen monks of course opposed and rejected mere superficial naturalism. For example, Hui-hai stated; "ignorant people do not realize the fact that the Dharmakāya manifests its form in accordance with the object although it does not possess any form originally. Therefore, they say that the green bamboo is none other than the Dharmakāya and the chrysanthemum is identical with Prajñā (wisdom).[12] If the chrysanthemum is wisdom, then wisdom is the same as an insentient existence. If the green bamboo is the Dharmakāya, then the Dharmakāya is the same as the grass or the tree. If so, eating the bamboo-shoot carries the meaning of eating the Dharmakāya. Therefore, it is unworthy to think of such things".[13]

Nevertheless, the common Chinese generally believed in the view that nature was the absolute. Finally, the T'ien-tai sect taught the theory that "all existences and even grass, trees, and earth can attain Buddhahood". That is to say, even the physical matter existing in nature can realize enlightenment and become Buddha. Generally speaking, the tendency existed to regard nature as the most beautiful and highest existence with man on an equal plane. It was these tendencies that influenced Buddhist thought in the above manner.

Therefore, the Chinese Buddhists (especially Zen monks) tried to seek the absolute significance in everyday life. "Those who wish to attain the state of Ekayāna must not defile the six sensual objects (form, sound, smell, taste, touch and ideas). If one does not defile the six sensual objects, then he is enlightened".[14] Namely, everyday life is as it is identical with enlightenment. This thought is clearly found in the following questions and answers; "Chao-chou (趙州) asked 'what is Tao?' His master Nan-ch'üan (南泉) answered 'the mind in everyday life is Tao' ".[15] "The priest asked 'what is the mind in everyday life?' His master answered 'it is to sleep whenever necessary and to sit whenever necessary'. The priest said 'I do not understand you'. Then the master said, 'It is to be cool when it is hot and warm when it is cold' ".[16]

The state of enlightenment is therefore none other than this actual world. A poem composed by Su-tung-p'o (蘇東坡), states that Rain is falling at Lu-shan and the tides are full at Che-chiang (浙江).[17]——— Namely, they enjoyed the oneness with nature. In China many other poems exist which expressed nature as it is. "The moon shines and the wind blows. What shall I do in this long and beautiful night?"[18] "Various flowers bloom in the spring, the moon shines in autumn, cool wind blows in summer and snow falls in winter. What nice and pleasant seasons they are for men!"[19] "Everyday is a pleasant and good day for the man"[20]

The state of the enlightenment cannot be distinguished from the ignorant state so far as it is seen from the outside. In the following questions and anewers, this is shown very clearly and impressively———

A priest: "What is Buddha?"

Chao-chou: "He is at Buddha's hall".

A priest: "The Buddha at Buddha's hall is the Buddha image made of mud".

Chao-chou: "Yes, you are right".

A priest: "Then what is the true Buddha?"

Chao-chou: "He is at Buddha's hall".[21]

While the external appearance is not different in the states before and after enlightenment, the spiritual condition must be completely different from the state before enlightenment. When Chih-hsien (智閑) was asked "what is enlightenment?", he answered "it is the flute behind the dead tree" or "it is the eyes behind a skeleton".[22] These things are not lifeless. Those who have realized truth can manifest the absolute light in things which seem unworthy or meaningless.[23] Zen monks, namely, expressed the state of the enlightenment poetically by impressive examples.

As the result of the tendency to regard nature or actuality as the absolute existence, the Chinese came to possess the idea of optimism. Thus, they regarded this world as the good place to live. They finally came to believe that the perfect existence must exist in this world. Here, the idea of the "Sheng-jen (聖人, sage)" was established. He was the perfect person such as the Emperor Chou Kung (周公) or Confucius. The saint is not a god but still a man. However, he himself is principle itself. In art, Wang-i-chih (王羲之) was called 'the sage of writing' and Tu-fu (杜甫) 'the sage of poetry'. They were regarded as the perfect manifestation of principle in art.[24] In the idea of *Wu* (無, nothingness) of the Wei and Chin dynasties, the concept of the creator or the absolute was amalgamated with the concept of the sage or the perfect human being. In this theory of nothingness, the perfect human being realizes the principle of nothingness and is able to manifest every phenomenon and give the correct way of life to every person.[25]

This way of thinking which insisted on perfect existence in this world established the thought that perfect existence existed in the past world. That is to say, the Chinese made what occured in the past world as the rule in present life. As the result, the Chinese came naturally to esteem the life in the past more highly than the life in the present. The thought which acknowledged the natural actuality was also one of the foundations for the establishment of the Chinese classicism, although it was not the sufficient condition for it.

The more important fact is that the long Chinese history has been comparatively peaceful because the Chinese identified nature with man. Undoubtedly there were wars in China. However, Bodde, an American sinologue, states that the typical hero in Chinese literature was the poor but virtuous scholar. The military genius, on the contrary, is praised and appreciated in Western literature. However, Chinese literature seldom praised military heros. Their attitude is shown in the following saying; Good iron cannot be a nail and the good man does not become a military man".[26] The harmony of all existences is necessary in order to harmonize with nature and live in peace. Thus, they asserted the idea of 'moderation'. As the Chinese identified the nature with man whom they regarded as a part of nature or the universe, they did not regard the nature as an existence opposed to man. Therefore, they seldom observed nature experimentally, thus natural science did not develop in China. This fact is the greatest reason why China lagged behind other countries in the modern world. Leaders of the Red China recognized this fact and are trying to improve and develop natural science.

---

1) The ideogram *T'ien* (天) is derived from the letter *Ta* (大) by adding a line on the top. *Tai* is a hieroglyph which originally meant man. Therefore, it can be thought that this ideogram *T'ien* indicates the sky which

is above the man. (Yoshio Takeuchi 武内義雄: *Shina Shisōshi* pp. 4–5.)
2) *Ibid.* p. 9.
3) *Ibid.* p. 18. Cf. P. Masson-Oursel: Etude de logique comparée, *Revue Philosophique,* 1917, p. 67; Sueo Gotō 後藤末雄: *Shina Bunka to Shinagaku no Kigen,* p. 282; p. 467; p. 472.
4) *Lieh-tzu* (列子), 楊朱篇.
5) Yoshio Takeuchi: *op. cit.* p. 187.
6) *Shin-jin-mei* (信心銘).
7) *Roku-so-dan-gyō* 六祖壇經 (Hakuju Ui 宇井伯壽: *Daini Zenshū-shi Kenkyū* 第二禪宗史研究), p. 149.
8) Rousselle asserted this opinion and A. Forke agreed with him. (Alfred Forke: *Geshichte der mittelalterlichen chinesischen Philosophie,* Hamburg, 1934. S. 363).
9) 三論玄義 p. 25.
10) It is stated in the chapter *San-hua-pin* 散華品 of the *Mahā-prajñā-pāramitā-sūtra* "不レ壞ニ假名一、而說ニ諸法相一" and also in the chapter *Shih-chi-pin* 實際品 of the same sūtra, it mentions "以ニ不壞實際法一、立ニ衆生於實際中一". (*Taishō.* vol. 8, p. 277 b; pp. 400–401).
11) This thought is derived from the phrase "不レ動ニ於等覺法一、爲ニ諸法立處一" in the 放光般若經 sūtra. (*Taishō.* vol. 8, p. 140 c).
12) Concerning this poem, Dr. Hakuju Ui mentioned that this poem is quoted in the 荷澤神會語錄 found at Tung-huang (30) as a poem written by 大德. However, its composer is unknown. In the old commentaries, this poem is said to be composed by 道生. This poem also was quoted in the 大乘要語 (*Taishō.* vol. 85, p. 1206 a).
13) 頓悟要門 p. 86. Cf. *ibid.* p. 96.
14) 信心銘.
15) 無門關 ch. 19.
16) 景德傳燈錄 vol. X. 長沙和尙の條 (*Taishō.* vol. 51, p. 275 a).
17) The following poem also expresses the same state of mind; "我來問レ道無ニ餘說一、雲在ニ青天一水在レ瓶". (Cf. Hakuju Ui: *Daini Zenshū-shi Kenkyū* 第二禪宗史研究 p. 450).
18) 證道歌.
19) 無門關 ch. 19.
20) Words of 雲門 (碧巖錄 Chap. 6).
21) 景德傳燈錄 vol. (*Taishō.* vol. 51, p. 277 c).
22) *Ibid.* vol. XI. (*Taishō.* vol. 51, p. 284 b).
23) Cf. 景德傳燈錄 vol. XVII. (*Taishō.* vol. 51, p. 337 a.)
24) Kōjirō Yoshikawa 吉川幸次郎: *op. cit.* p. 28.
25) Masaaki Matsumoto 松本雅明: *Gi Shin ni okeru Mu no Shisō no Seikaku* (魏晋における無の思想の性格 The Character of Concept 'nothingness' in the Wêi and Chin dynasties), *Shigaku Zasshi* 史學雜誌 1940.
26) Derk Bodde: *Dominant Ideas in the Formation of Chinese Culture.* (*Journal of American Oriental Society*), vol. LXII, 1942, p. 299.

(2) Relationship of mutuality between heaven and man

In connection with thought of nature, the theory of 'relationship of mutuality between heaven and man' will be mentioned. In the period of Chan-kuo (戰國), 'scholars of the positive and negative principle' advocated a kind of nature worship which was carried over to the Han dynasty. According to it, natural phenomenon and artificial phenomenon are mutually related, and therefore, if the king, who was the representative of man, reigned the country well, then nature such as weather, wind and rain will be favorable to man. If the reign of the king was poor, on the contrary, then calamities from nature will arise. It was most strongly stressed by Tung-chung-shu (董仲舒) of the Early Han (前漢) dynasty who thought that disasters were sent from heaven in order to admonish the king. The thought of *Ko-ming* (革命, revolution) which literally means 'to change the direction of Heaven' was formed at this point. Its influence held in check or even corrected the tyranny of autocrats.

This thought was also influential in later periods in China. Buddhism, as well had sūtras which stated the theory of disaster and which were highly regarded by the Chinese. A typical example of these sūtras is the *Chin-kuang-ming-ching sūtra* (金光明經) where it states in detail in the 13th chapter that if the king does not protect the *dharma* well, a terrible calamity will arise. That is to say, as the result of maladministration of the king, falsehood and struggle will increase in his country, and the ministers and subjects will arise against the king. Furthermore, the deities will become angry; wars will break out; the enemy will overrun the country; family members will fight each other; nothing will be pleasant or comfortable for man. Natural phenomena as well will become worse.[1] Living beings will lack rigor, plagues will arise and pestilence will sweep the land. Therefore, the king should attempt his best in governing the country by the *dharma*— This sūtra is unusual as a Buddhist sūtra as sūtras seldom teach the theory that "disasters arise through poor governing of the king". The Chinese Buddhists highly esteemed this theory in this sutra as can be seen by the five different Chinese translations as well as many commentaries on this sūtra which were composed in China.

Naturalized Buddhist monks from India propagated Buddhism in conformity with this way of thinking of the Chinese. Guṇavarman, for example, taught Buddhism to Emperor Wen-ti (文帝) of the Sung dynasty in the following way; "The four seas are your land and all existences are your subjects. One pleasant word and all your subjects are happy. One act in good rule brings harmony to the people. If you only punish wrong doers without killing and not impose heavy taxes, then nature will harmonize with man and fruits and crops will ripen well".[2]

More investigation is necessary to know how long this form of thought continued in China. However, it can safely be said that this thought showed one characteristic of the Chinese ways of thinking. It was taught not only in Buddhism but also in other Indian thought as well in that good results generally spring from good deeds and evil comes from evil deeds. Chinese Pure Land teachings also explained this theory in relationship of mutuality between heaven and man.

---

1) *Suvarṇaprabhāsa,* Chap. 13, v. 38.
2) 梁高僧傳 vol. III. (*Taishō.* vol. 50, p. 341 a).

Chapter 12. Reconciling and harmonizing tendencies

(1) The absolute character of existence

If reality of natural phenomenon was absolutely upheld, then nothing could be denied. This way of thinking existed since ancient times in China. For the Chinese, the five holy classics are higher than ethics. They further believed that the other classics or books are also a partial manifestation. As mentioned before, the Chinese thought that perfect existence must exist in this world but the other existences cannot be denied in spite of the fact that they are not perfect. Thus, even a single existence is not denied although there is existence which must be absolutely affirmed.[1]

Therefore, the Chinese lacked the idea of absolute evil. Every form of human life was acknowledged for some reason. It is natural that the Chinese did not explain the origin of evil because they lacked the idea of absolute evil.[2]

Chinese Buddhism was also influenced by this way of thinking, and particularity in the doctrine of 'mutual penetration of the ten worlds' of the T'ien-t'ai sect. These are the worlds of hell, hungry-ghosts, beasts, fighting-demons (Asura), man, heaven, Śrāvaka, Pratyekabuddha, Bodhisattva and Buddha. The first six worlds belong to the illusional world and the last four to the enlightened world. Each one of these ten worlds mutually possesses all the characters of the ten worlds. Therefore, Buddhahood is possible for beings in hell, while at the same time Buddha possesses the possibility to going into the illusional world. In such a world, there is neither an absolutely evil person nor an absolutely good person. There are neither permanent rewards nor retributions.

In Chinese Zen Buddhism, this thought is explained very clearly. "The pure-nature of thusness (*tathatā*) is the actual Buddha and evil thoughts and the three kinds of defilements are the actual demons. Those who possess evil thoughts are the demons and those who have right thoughts are Buddhas. Where there are three kinds of defilements originating from various evil thoughts, there is the king of the demons. On the contrary, where there is right thought, the demon changes its form and can attain Buddhahood".[3] Here, the demon is identical with the Buddha.

Such being the case, not one man exists who is absolutely evil and does not possess the possibility of being saved. This thought greatly influenced the Pure Land teachings introduced from India. The eighteenth Vow of Amitāyus (Amida-Buddha), which is highly esteemed in Japanese Pure Land teachings is as follows: "If the beings of the ten quarters—when I have attained Bodhi—blissfully trust in me with the most sincere mind, wish to be born in my country, and chant the name of Buddha ten times, but are not so born, may I never obtain the State of Enlightenment. Excluded, however, are those who have committed the Five Deadly Sins and who have abused the True *dharma*".

The Chinese could not understand the last part of this Vow, because they believed that all evil persons could be saved by Amida-Buddha. (The Five Deadly Sins are generally to kill one's own father, kill one's own mother, kill an Arhat (one who has attained the enlightenment), to disturb the harmony of the Buddhist organization, and to harm Buddha's person.). Shan-tao (善導) explained it as follows: "The reason why those who committed the five deadly sins or abused the *dharma* are excluded in Amida-Buddha's vow is because these two transgressions are very heavy sins and if one performs them, he will surely be born in the lowest hell and stay there for a long period of time. Therefore, Tathāgata mentioned these words as a means to stop one from committing these sins and does not mean that he does not save such evil men".[4] He further explained why both good and evil men can be born in the Pure Land as follows: "The Amida-Buddha, in compassion, took this Vow before the attainment of Buddhahood. And it is by the power of this Vow that the Five Deadly Sins and Ten Evil Deeds are cut. Therefore, those who have committed these sins can also be born in the Pure Land. Even the Icchantika who has abused the true *dharma* can be born in the Pure Land if he will turn his efforts towards the Pure Land".[5]

Because of this idea of the Chinese, the religious wars or struggles which frequently arose in Europe did not arise in China. It is true that Buddhism was frequently suppressed. But this was not the suppression of Buddhist doctrine but that of the Buddhist organization which menaced and weakened the nation's power politically and economically. In Mohammedan countries fighting sometimes started by causes such as eating pork. On the contrary, religious wars never started in China by such causes. The Emperors of China and India were similar in that they both did not have religious prejudice.

1) Kōjirō Yoshikawa 吉川幸次郎: *op. cit.* pp. 31–32.
2) *Ibid.* p. 33.
3) 六祖壇經 35 (Hakuju Ui 宇井伯壽: *Daini Zenshūshi Kenkyū*), p. 168.
4) 散善義 (*Taishō*. vol. 37, p. 277 a).
5) 法事讃 pt. 1. (*Taishō*. vol. 47, p. 426 a). Cf. *Kyōgyōshinshō* (教行信證), vol. III, pt. 2.

(2) Acknowledgement of all heretical doctrines

As above mentioned, the Chinese acknowledged the significance of existence of every human being. Therefore, they recognized each kind of philosophy as a thought which possessed truth to some extent. This leniency, however, does not exist in the thought of ancient China and is seen in the example where Confucius stated that "it is harmful to study heretical thoughts".[1] Commoners, however, thought, as above mentioned, that all writings as well as the five holy classics revealed truth more or less for some reason, even though their contents were not perfect. As the result study was highly esteemed in China, and it became necessary to read old classics in order to become a more perfect man.[2]

It was natural that foreign thought could not be excluded as they acknowledged truth to some extent in all writings. It was not strange that Buddhism which was introduced into China as one great thought system was discussed and admired by the Chinese to gradually and slowly permeate into their thought. The Chinese in the medieval age did not feel any contradiction in the fact that they followed Buddhism and also esteemed the Confucian classics as manifestations of truth at the same time.

From the very beginning, Buddhist thought was understood by the Chinese in a reconciling and harmonizing way. The method used first was '*Ko-i* (格義)' which means to explain the meaning of Buddhist terms by another philosophy. That is to say, the doctrines of Buddhism were explained by the doctrinal writings of the Chinese philosophies. In the first stage of Chinese Buddhism, sūtras of the Prajñā group were translated and studied. As many similar points between the thought of the *Prajñā-sūtras* and the thought of Lao-tzu and Chuang-tzu existed, Buddhist scholars explained the thought of the *Prajñā-sūtra* in conformity with these Chinese philosophies. They regarded the idea of *K'ung* (空, non-substantiality) of the *Prajñā-sūtras* and the idea of *Wu* (無, nothingness) of the Lao-tzu and Chuang-tzu philosophies as one. They were probably influenced by the general tendency of the time of the Wei and Ching dynasties in which the philosophy of Lao-tzu and Chuang-tzu flourished. Scholars prior to Tao-an (道安) understood Buddhism through this interpretive means.

A few Buddhist scholars started to oppose this way of interpretation. Chi-tsang, for example, rejected Lao-tzu and Chuang-tzu as different from Buddhism. According to his opinion, the philosophy of Lao-tzu and Chuang-tzu were merely heretical philosophies similar to the heretical thoughts which confronted Buddhism in India.[3] Many times the theory of practical morality was the issue between Confucianism and Buddhism giving rise to great disputes.

Chi-tsang and others, however, could not change the traditional mode of the Chinese. A compromise between the theory of Confucianism and Buddhism appeared in that the both are aiming at the same goal. This thought can be recognized in the *Yü-tao-lun* (喩道論) of Sun-ch'o (孫綽, Eastern Ching dynasty) and *Chia-hsün* (家訓) of Yen-chih-t'ui (顏之推, Northern Chai dynasty). Chih-i (智顗) acknowledged the authority and significance of Confucianism and identified the five permanent morals of Confucianism with the five precepts of Buddhism. He again recognized a corresponding relationship between the five precepts of Buddhism and the five holy classics of Confucianism.[4]

Again he compared the three practices of Buddhism (Śīla (precepts), *Samādhi* (meditation) and *Prajñā* (wisdom)) with the virtues of Confucianism.[5]

The similarity of Buddhism with Taoism existed as well as that between Confucianism and Buddhism. In 467 A.D. of the Sung dynasty, Ku-huan (顧歡) wrote a book called '*I-hsia-lun* (夷夏論) in which he rejected Buddhism as Taoistic. Many people opposed his opinion and insisted that both Buddhism and Taoism were the same.[6] Chang-jung (張融), a Taoist in the Southern Chai dynasty, seems to have passed away with the *Lao-ching* (老經) and *Lao-tzu* in one hand and the Chinese-translated *Prajñāpāramitā sūtra* and the *Saddharma-puṇḍarīka-sūtra* in the other.

A syncretism of three religions in which Buddhism was identified with Confucianism and Taoism finally arose from these two relations. This theory was stated by the Buddhists in the T'ang dynasty. Tsung-mi for example stated: "Confucius, Lao-tzu and Śākyamuni all attained Sainthood. They preached the teaching in different ways in accordance with the time and place. However, they mutually helped and benefitted the people by their teachings". He, however, stated that Confucianism and Taoism must ultimately be rejected as they were expedient teachings.[7] On the contrary, other Zen monks at that time said these three religions were the same. When one asked whether these three religions were the same or different teachings, the master answered: "For those of great wisdom, they are the same. On the contrary, for those with little capacity they are different. Enlightenment and illusion depends solely on the capacity of man and not on the difference of teaching".[8] With this idea, Buddhists completely abandoned the idea of the superiority of Buddhism.

In the Wu-tai (五代) and the Sung dynasties, this theory that the three religions were the same was widely believed and supported by the general public. Many scholars of the three religions also backed this theory. Many Zen monks such as Chih-yüan (智圓), Ch'i-sung (契嵩), Tsung-kao (宗杲) and Shih-fan (師範) also believed in it.[9] In the Ming dynasty, many monks asserted the syncretism of Confucianism and Buddhism. Furthermore, when Mohammedanism was introduced in the Yüan dynasty, Chinese Mohammedans identified the God of Allah with the Heaven of Confucianism.[10]

It was possible to advance such a theory because the Chinese regarded the original *tao* or principle of the Universe as one to appear in this world in different forms, such as Buddhism and Confucianism. Therefore, they said that "Buddhism and Confucianism are not two different teachings but their origin is the same with the development different".[11] Hui-lien (懷璉) said: "The four seasons of heaven nourishes and furthers the growth of all things. Like this the teachings of the Sages perfect and teach those under the heavens. However, the original principle or ultimate truth of these teachings is only one".[12] Ch'i-ch'ung (契崇) also stated "All teachings of saints are good. All the ways taught by saints are right.——— The good and right teaching is not only Buddhism, not only Confucianism, not only this, not only that. Buddhism and Confucianism are only offshoots of the original truth".[13] Therefore, they said that every thought system possesses some significances of its existence. "In olden times, there were many holy saints such as Buddha, Confucius and others. Although their teachings differed, the basic doctrine was the same. They all desired to teach people that 'man should do good'. However, this was taught in different ways.——— The teaching of Confucianism is necessary to this world, as are also the other religions, and, therefore, Buddhism is also necessary. If one teaching vanishes, then the evil of this world will surely increase".[14] Li-p'ing-shan (李屏山), a Confucian scholar, also acknowledged the significance of other philosophies.[15]

Such being the case, both Buddhists and Confucianists recognized the same significance in other thought systems as existed in their own thought system. Of course, much opposition existed to this way of thinking which lingered on and was supported by people for a long time.

---

1) 論語 vol. II. 爲政.
2) Cf. Kōjirō Yoshikawa 吉川幸次郎: *op. cit.* pp. 33–36.
3) Cf. 三論玄義 (Ed. by Yenshō Kanakura 金倉圓照 p. 23).
4) 摩訶止觀 vol. VI, pt. 1. (*Taishō.* vol. 46, p. 77 a–b).
5) *Ibid.* (*Taishō.* vol. 46, p. 78 c).
6) 弘明集 vol. VI; vol. VII. (*Taishō.* vol. 52, pp. 41 b–48 a).
7) This is based upon the *Yüan-jen-lun* (原人論). In the *Chan-yüan-chu-chüan-chi-tu-hsü* (禪源諸詮集都序) written by the same author 宗密, Taoism and Confucianism are completely ignored. (Ed. by Hakuju Ui 宇井伯壽 in Iwanami Bunko 岩波文庫 p. 51 f.)
8) 諸方門人參問語錄 (「頓悟要門」 p. 94.).
9) Kyōdō Itō 伊藤慶道: *Dōgen Zenji Kenkyū* (道元禪師研究 Studies on Dōgen Zenji), vol. I. p. 65 f. However, according to Dōgen (道元), his master Ju-ching (如淨) admonished him by saying "those who insist on the oneness of the three religions are those who destroy the holy teaching of the Buddha". (*Shōbō Genzō* 正法眼藏 Shohōjissō 諸法實相). Nevertheless, the analects of Ju-ching, acknowledged the authority of Confucianism and Taoism, and furthermore the phrases and words were quoted from the *Analects of Confucius* and *Lao-tzu-ching* (老子經) in his writings. (Kyōdō Itō: *op. cit.* vol. I. p. 32 f. & p. 69 f.)
10) 王治心 (tr. by Chinken Tomita 富田鎭彥): *Shina Syūkyō Shisō-shi* (支那宗教思想史 History of Religious Thoughts in China), p. 220.
11) 弘明集 vol. VI. (*Taishō.* vol. 52, p. 39 a).
12) Daijō Tokiwa 常盤大定: *Shina ni okeru Bukkyō to Jukyō Dokyō* (支那に於ける佛教と儒教道教 Buddhism, Confucianism and Taoism in China), p. 201.
13) 輔教篇 pt. 2. (*Taishō.* vol. 52, p. 657 a.)
14) *Ibid.* (*Taishō.* vol. 52, p. 660 a.)
15) Daijō Tokiwa: *op. cit.* p. 401.

(3) Syncretism within Buddhism

Since the significance of all philosophical thoughts was recognized, various different thoughts within a certain religion had to be harmonized. The doctrinal classification of all Buddhism by the Chinese must be considered in the light of how the different thoughts within Buddhism were regarded and harmonized.

This classification went through a complicated process of development, but what was common to all of them was the idea of expediency which the Indians used when different opinions existed within the same religious scripture. Therefore, it can be said that classification of doctrine originated from the way of thinking of the Indians. Such being the case, this thought also possessed the characteristics of the Indian conception of the world. For example, history is completely ignored. In China, however, only the doctrines within Buddhism were classified and all other doctrines ignored. This attitude is common to all sects such as the T'ien-t'ai, Hua-yen, San-lun and Fa-hsiang sects.

(It is true that the San-lun sect referred to various philosophies other than Buddhism such as Confucianism and Taoism, because the fundamental standpoint of this sect is "the refutation of erroneous views and the elucidation of right views". However, these thoughts were only refuted as erroneous views and not acknowledged as the right views.)

The Chinese did not like to grasp anything following only one doctrine. Therefore, scholars' task was to criticize and classify the various different thoughts within Buddhism in a good arrangement. General Buddhists however did not like to bother with a complicated classification. Therefore, they threw logic aside to acknowledge all sorts of thought and effect an easy compromise. One example of this is the theory of "oneness of all Buddhist sects" as advocated by Tsung-mi. He deplored the fact that Buddhists insisted on the superiority of their own sect while refuting the doctrine of others,[1] and said it was useless to quarrel over the doctrine among Buddhist sects mutually. He further emphasized all which was superior. "Supreme principle is one and not two. It is unreasonable, therefore, that two types of truth should exist. The highest principle and its meaning also is not one-sided. One should not understand only a part of truth. Therefore, all Buddhist doctrines should be unified into one in order to have a perfect teaching".[2] He stated this in spite of the fact he classified Buddhist sects into doctrinal and practical ones, and further divided them into three kinds of teachings.[3] All doctrines had to ultimately lead to the one truth.[4] Then, how were the dispute and opposition of Buddhist scholars with one another within Buddhism reconciled in his theory? According to his opinion, disputes were not refutations but a mutual establishment of thoughts by both sides, because new standpoints were established by the mutual refutation of prejudices of each side.[5] Namely, he wanted to acknowledge a new philosophy founded on the conclusions of the arguments of the philosophers.[6]

The way of thinking which acknowledges a significance in all Buddhist doctrines is especially striking in Zen Buddhism. For example,[7] someone asked Hui-hai: Who is the superior? The master of precepts, the master of meditation or the master of doctrine?" He answered: "Although the methods of presentation in accordance to the ability lead to superiority in one of the three learnings, they are all ultimately one". The Zen sect according to its followers is not just another sect of Buddhism. "The sect founded by Bodhidharma is the essence of Buddhism".[8] Zen (meditation) is the same as the body of Buddha while it is also the essence of all Samādhis.[9] Its doctrine, therefore, neither contradicts nor opposes doctrines of other sects. One should not be overly attached to one doctrine. "One can not understand based on only one teaching, one ability, or one sentence, because the Buddha never taught any fixed doctrine.———".[10] "It is not difficult to realize the supreme enlightenment. One must not, however, select a fixed doctrine. If one neither likes nor dislikes a set doctrine, then enlightenment can easily be attained".[11]

Such eclecticism or syncretism can also be found in other sects. In the Sung dynasty, those who endeavored solely in the Pure Land teaching did not exist. The famous Pure Land followers were those who practiced T'ien-tai, Vinaya, and Zen sects. The Pure Land teaching especially prospered in the T'ien-t'ai sect. Many priests also practiced both Zen and the Pure Land practice with the rise of the Zen sect. Yün-ch'i-chu-hung (雲棲袾宏 1535–1615 A.D.), a representative Buddhist of the Ming dynasty (1535–1615 A.D.), revived the precepts to harmonize it with the Zen practice and the Pure Land practice of calling the name of Amida-Buddha.

The *Saddharma-puṇḍarīka-sūtra* was highly esteemed as king of all sūtras in China. It seems that this fact also was based upon a syncretic way of thinking.[12] One of the main thoughts in this sūtra is its acknowledgement of the enlightenment of those who practiced Hīnayāna. Even Devadatta who intended to destroy the Buddhist organization, and a female dragon become enlightened in this sūtra. This spirit of tolerance and harmony probably suited the tendency of thought of the Chinese.

1) P'ei-hsiu (裴休): *Chan-yüan-chu-chüan-chi-tu-hsü-hsü* (禪源諸詮集都序敍), p. 4.
2) *Chan-yüan-chu-chüan-chi-tu-hsü* (禪源諸詮集都序), pt. 1. p. 33.
3) Concerning three sects of practical teaching and three sects of doctrinal teaching—Cf. *ibid.* pt. 1.
4) Cf. *ibid.* p. 91 & p. 51.
5) Cf. *ibid.* p. 70 f.
6) Gauḍapāda (*Māṇḍūkya Kārikā,* Chap. 4.) and Bhartṛhari of India advance the same thought. Hegel and W. Dilthey interpreted it from the historical standpoint.
7) *Chu-fang-mên-jen-san-wên-yü-lu* (諸方門人參問語錄), pt. 2. (*Tun-wu-yao-mên* 頓悟要門), p. 94.
8) *Chan-yüan-chu-chüan-chi-tu-hsü,* p. 114.
9) *Ibid.* p. 18.
10) *Chuan-shin-fa-yao* (傳心法要), p. 38 f.
11) *Hsin-hsin-ming* (信心銘).
12) It is said that the *Saddharma-puṇḍarīka-sūtra* was frequently used in examinations for government officials in the Northern Sung dynasty.

(4) Chinese characteristics of reconciling and harmonizing

Although it seems that this way of Chinese thinking is very similar to that of the Indians who acknowledged the authority of various thoughts from the tolerant and harmonic spirit, a great difference exists between them. Most Indians acknowledged the significance of various religions and philosophies and understood them as partial manifestations of truth. Further, they considered that absolute truth was to transcend and at the same time include all religions and philosophies. They did not state however that the doctrine of these religions and philosophies matched and were mutually alike. The Chinese, on the contrary, simply kept asserting that the doctrines were the same.

Yen-chih-t'ui (顏之推) of the Northern Chai dynasty stated that the five permanent morals of Confucianism were the same as the five precepts of Buddhism. In the Sung dynasty as well, Ch'i-sung (契嵩) interpreted that ten good virtues and five precepts of Buddhism were identical with the five permanent morals and the idea of benevolence and justice of Confucianism.[1] Yang-kuei-shan (楊龜山) and Hsieh-shang-ts'ai (謝上蔡) asserted the oneness and conformity between each idea of Buddhism with that of Confucianism.[2] According to their opinion, Buddhism and Confucianism were exactly the same teaching. Therefore, founders of both teachings were the same. "Chou-kung (周公) and K'ung-tzu (孔子) are identical with the Buddha, and the Buddha identical with Chou Kung and K'ung-tzu at the same time. —— the term *Buddha* is Sanskrit while the Chinese use *Chüeh* (覺, enlightenment). Both connote the meaning of realization of truth. ——"[3] The same statements can be asserted in the oneness of Buddhism and Taoism. "Taoism is identical with Buddhism and Buddhism identical with Taoism at the same time. ——".[4] What stands out in this sort of reasoning is the character of the utilitarianism and easy compromise with cold logical consideration completely abandoned.

When the Chinese explained these theories of oneness, they used only the intuitive similes. For example, when they explained by the following simile they concluded that the substance of both Buddhism and Taoism was the same: "Once, a duck was flying in the sky. Someone saw it and said that it was a pigeon, while another said it was a mandarin. A duck is always a duck, however, only men are distinguished from each another".[5]

Such intuitive explanations always satisfied the Chinese. Hui-hung (慧洪) in his poem said, "Buddhism and Confucianism is like the difference between a fist and the palm. There is no difference in the respect that both the palm and the fist are the hand".[6] When Li-shih-ch'ien (李士謙) was asked whether Buddhism, Confucianism or Taoism was the superior teaching, he answered "Buddhism is the sun, Taoism the moon, and Confucianism the five stars". The questioner could not ask any more.[7] Tominaga Chūki of Japan criticized this answer by saying: "His answer seemed excellent to the people of that time. However, this answer is meaningless. I myself cannot understand what it means. Therefore, this is not a wise and excellent answer".[8] As he pointed out, Li-shih-ch'ien's answer was not logical and yet the Chinese were satisfied. As the result of the tendency, these three teachings were harmonized without deep logical reflections.

Attempts were tried to recognize one as the fundamental teaching by giving them different status. Even in this case, basic differences between philosophical systems were not seen. What was emphasiped was which one was older historically based upon the idea that anything older is more correct. For example, Taoists composed spurious ancient classics such as *Lao-tzu-hua-hu-ching* (老子化胡經) and *Lao-tzu-hsi-sheng-ching* (老子西昇經), which stated that Śākyamuni was an incarnation of Lao-tzu. On the other hand, Buddhists also composed spurious sūtras such as *Ch'ing-ching-fa-hsing-ching* (清淨法行經), in which Śākyamuni dispatched three disciples K'ung-tzu (Confucius), Yen-huei (顏回) and Lao-tzu to China to teach people.[9] The origins only were discussed in these cases, without opinions existing whether one religion or philosophy was more fundamental or superior doctrinally than another.

Although the Chinese vaguely pointed to the one way as the basis of the three religions, there were no deep and metaphysical connotations. However, some Buddhists explained *tao* by a theory of two-fold truth which explained that the highest *tao* is real truth and various others are world truth.[10] Or again they explained *tao* by an expedient theory[11] just as in the Lotus Sūtra. Again Buddhism was thought to be a metaphysical explanation, while Confucianism was a practical religious teaching.[12]

The Chinese regarded these three religions not as different in teachings or thought but in ideological influence. Therefore, they did not deal with various types of thought, but with the influential power of the three religions in their society. Philosophical thoughts unpopular to the Chinese society or again Indian ideas stated frequently in Buddhist sūtras were not discussed in spite of the fact they were known. Furthermore, in some cases, Indian philosophy was looked down upon. A typical example of the non-logical and political compromise tendency of the Chinese Buddhists can be found in the following sentences of Chih-i: "When the people follow the non-enlightened currents of thought, evil teachings such as Sāṃkhya, Vaiśeṣika and the 95 others arise. Again good teachings such as positive-negative theory, theory of divination, the study of the five classics and other excellent teachings appear in accordance with the purity of the mind".[13] Why are the metaphysics of the Sāṃkhya and the natural philosophy of the Vaiśeṣika evil teachings? Why are superstitions such as the theory of positive-negative and the theory of divination good teachings? The discrimination here between good and evil is not based upon the logical standard but solely upon one that is political and social. Therefore, very little criticism exists in such a thought, compromising with the social and political powers.

Tominaga Chūki of Japan pointed out this logical weakness of the Chinese as follows: "Good teachings are not confined only to the teachings of the three religions, but include many heretical teachings and doctrines as well. Their basis is one with the differences in manifestation".[14]

Thus, it can be thought that the Chinese, consequently, tried to solve the problem concerning various philosophies in a frame of mind restrained by powerful conventional ideas of society. Therefore, they did not consider this problem from a universal standpoint unlike the Indians who thought of various types of philosophies in their philosophical content to ignore their practical social side. Materialism did not possess the power to become a philosophical school in India. Buddhism disappeared in the 11th century in India. Nevertheless, Indian scholars with a wide world conception[15] always referred to it. In this respect, a great difference can be recognized between the Indian way of thinking and that of the Chinese.

Such being the case, a study of world concept (*Weltanschauungs-lehre*) was not established in China with the exception of the classification of doctrines that was introspective in character.

This aimless syncretism had great influence on the common people. This syncretism is one of the striking characteristics of the modern Chinese religions. Typical of this compromise and syncretic attitude is that seen in a Taoist temple where many images of various deities including a central image of Lao-tzu are enshrined. A Taoistic classic mentions that Śākyamuni, Lao-tzu, Christ, Mohammed and Hsiang-t'o (項槖) were fellow-deities of Lao-tzu, and a follower of any religion can become a Taoist without conversion. Among their various deities in a Taoist temple John of Christianity, Chu-ko-wu-hou (諸葛武侯) and Yüeh-fei (岳飛), images of Avalokiteśvara, and Śākyamuni, the *Prajñā-pāramita-hṛdaya sūtra* and *Kao-shih-kuan-yin-ching* (高世觀音經) (a Kan-yin sūtra) are revered. Taoist wrote three short classics to teach the common people which are the *T'ai-shang-kan-ying-p'ien* (太上感應篇), *Wen-ch'ang-ti-chün-yin-chih-wen* (文昌帝君陰隲文) and *Kuan-sheng-ti-chün-chüeh-shih-chen-ching* (關聖帝君覺世眞經). The three are based upon the idea of retribution and teach that "one must not perform evil, but do good", which if followed would result in one becoming either a heavenly super-human being or an earthly super-human being. This Taoist doctrine came from the ethical theory of Buddhism.

The amalgamation tendency between Buddhism and Taoism started in the period of the Six Dynasties to become very prominent in and after the Ch'ing dynasty. In famous and large Buddhist temples today, Kuan-ti (關帝, the god of war) is enshrined in most cases, with divination and fortune-telling performed. Such being the case, present common Chinese do not discriminate between Buddhism and Taoism.[16]

The compromising and syncretic tendency is especially remarkable in the Buddhist faith of the present Chinese. For example, in Peking, a powerful layman, who is a Pure-Land devotee enshrines not only various images of Buddhas and Bodhisattvas in his place of worship, but Tibetan Buddha images as well. Any standard or fixed pattern of these images does not exist. These images are neither art nor curios, but objects of worship for this layman where reverence and homage are paid to these various images. In Japan, the object of worship is different in accordance with the respective sect. Therefore, followers of a certain sect do not worship Buddhas and Bodhisattva which have no great importance with their sect, but they merely respect them. On the contrary, the Chinese people worship any image of Buddhas and Bodhisattvas. Another example of compromising and sycretic tendency of the Chinese is that another powerful layman in Peking is a follower of the Hung-wan (紅卍) religion as well as a follower of Buddhism, Confucianism and Taoism at the same time. He sincerely believes in all of them together without political or social reasons[17] which a Japanese would suspect him of.

From ancient times, the Chinese governing class acknowledged Confucianism as the correct religion and tried to suppress the other religions in an attempt to maintain the superiority of their class and social position. They tried to make the teaching of Confucianism the literary studies. Nevertheless, they failed to suppress the compromising and syncretic traditional Chinese way of thinking.[18]

---

1) *Fu-chiao-p'ien* (輔教篇), pt. 1. (*Taishō.* vol. 52, p. 649 a–b).
2) Cf. Daijō Tokiwa 常盤大定: *Shina ni okeru Bukkyō to Jukyō Dōkyō,* p. 321 f.
3) *Sun-ch'o* 孫綽: *Yü-tao-lun* (喩道論). (*Hung-ming-chi* 弘明集 vol. III, *Taishō.* vol. 52, p. 17 a).
4) *Hung-ming-chi* (弘明集), vol. VII. (*Taishō.* vol. 52, p. 45 c—p. 46 b).
5) *Ibid.* vol. VI. (*Taishō.* vol. 52, p. 38 c—p. 39 a).
6) *Tan-chin-wên-chi* (鐔津文集), vol. XIX. (*Taishō.* vol. 52, p. 748 a).
7) *San-chiao-p'ing-hsin-lun* (三教平心論), pt. 1. (*Taishō.* vol. 52, p. 781 c).
8) *Shutsujō Kōgo* (出定後語), vol. XXIV. *Sankyō* (三教).
9) *P'o-hsich-lun* (破邪論), pt. 1. (*Taishō.* vol. 32, p. 478 c); *Fo-tsu-t'ung-chi* (佛祖統記), vol. IV. (*Taishō.* vol. 49, p. 166 c); *ibid.* vol. XXXV. (*Taishō* vol. 49, p. 333 b—c).
10) Cf. *Hung-ming-chi* (弘明集), vol. VI. (*Taishō.* vol. 52, p. 42 c).
11) Cf. *ibid.* vol. VII. (*Taishō.* vol. 52, p. 46 a).
12) Cf. ibid. vol. III. (*Taishō.* vol. 52, p. 17 a).
13) *Mo-ho-chih-kuan* (摩訶止觀), vol. III. pt. 2. (*Taishō..* vol. 46, p. 31 b).
14) *Shutsujō Kyōgo,* Chap. XXIV. *Sankyō.*
15) *Sarvadarśanasaṃgraha*; *Sarvasiddhāntasaṃgraha* and etc.
16) Present common Chinese called both Taoist temple and Buddhist temple "Miao (廟, temple shrine)". Cf. A Report by Enjō Inaba 稻葉圓成 (*Mujintō* 無盡燈, 1918, p. 11).
17) Daijō Tokiwa: *Shina Bukkyō no Kenkyū,* vol. III. p. 110 f.
18) Cf. *op. cit.* A Report by E. Inaba. (*Mujintō* 無盡燈 1918, p. 10).

The various tendencies of Chinese thought indicated in previous several chapters are the outstanding and important ones only. Others of course exist. A conclusion can be drawn that these characteristics mentioned above are those peculiar to the Chinese. When a characteristic seldom seen in Indian Buddhism is outstanding in Chinese Buddhism, we cannot help but conclude that is a peculiar and distinctive characteristic of the Chinese.

PART IV
THE WAYS OF THINKING OF THE JAPANESE

—Characteristics of Japanese Ways of Thinking, as Revealed in Various Cultural Phenomena, Particularly in the Process of Accepting Buddhism—

Chapter 1. Introduction

We are now ready to examine some outstanding features of Japanese thinking as they reveal themselves in various phases of Japanese culture especially as revealed in the assimilation of foreign culture. We note, first, that the Japanese of the past were in the habit of expressing abstract notions through the medium of the Chinese script. That is, the Japanese, while they never abandoned the native language, had to resort almost without exception to the Chinese script whenever they wished to convey abstract ideas in writing. The influence of the Chinese script upon Japanese patterns of thought was therefore tremendous. It will be remembered that it was through the sutras written in Chinese that the Japanese first came in contact with Buddhism and Indian thought.[1]

Chinese writing was introduced into Japan in a very remote period. Up to the Suiko period, however, Chinese had been used only by a small group of specialists, and its influence on the native tongue had been but slight. With the beginning of direct contact with China and the introduction of Sui and T'ang civilization, the number of those who read and spoke Chinese increased greatly; we may well assume that Chinese words were used quite frequently in the daily conversations of the ruling class.[2] At this early time, however, the first Chinese words adopted in Japanese, were, for the most part, nouns. In the Heian period (897–1185) verbs and adverbs, such as, *nenzu* (meditate), *gusu* (to be equipped), *kechienni* (conspicuously), *yūni* (elegantly), *sechini* (acutely), and later *shiuneshi* (to be exquisite) and *sōzoku* (to dress oneself) came in use with the Japanese inflections. The tendency to adopt Chinese words grew stronger as time passed. In the late Heian and the Kamakura period (1185–1393) which was the age of popular Buddhism, imported Chinese words were passed down orally from monks to the common fold, and even the uneducated began using them.[3] In the Tokugawa period (1603–1867) the number of Chinese in the spoken language increased more than ever before,[4] but it was in the period following the Meiji Restoration, when Western civilization was introduced and progress was made in education, that the use of Chinese words became truly great. A large number of entirely new Chinese words were coined as equivalents of terms used in Western sciences, techniques and inventions.

In the world of thought, the educated Japanese of early times, Buddhist monks and Confucian scholars, published their works in the Chinese language. Only in the Kamakura period did books on thought begin to appear in the native language. And even such original thinkers as Tominaga Chūki and Miura Baien of the Tokugawa period left works that are written in Chinese. As specialists have recognized, even Japanese Buddhism, which was practically national religion was, "when viewed from the larger standpoint of Buddhist history, a mere branch Buddhism growing out of the Buddhism of China".[5] Many Buddhists of the past had regarded Japanese Buddhism as one with Chinese Buddhism and the multifarious sects in Japan were thought to be but offshoots of Chinese sects of Buddhism.

The Buddhism of Japan, on the other hand, exercised little or no influence upon Chinese Buddhism. In 988 A.D., Buddhist monk Eshin (Genshin) made an attempt with some success to introduce his belief into China; his book *Ōjō-yōshū* (Compendium of Teachings Concerning Paradise and Purgatory), which "called upon all persons, believers and unbelievers alike, to join hands with him for the purpose of attaining a rebirth in the Land of Extreme Happiness" caused some temporary stir among the Buddhists of the Sung Dynasty. This, however, was one of few instances in which the Japanese were able to have any influence on Chinese Buddhism.

The Buddhism of this country, then, grew up under the dominance of Chinese Buddhism. There was ever the conscious effort on the part of Japanese Buddhists to identify their religion with that of China.

How are we to explain this prevalence of Chinese culture in Japan of the past? Shall we say it was the outcome of an urge to imitate slavishly the superior culture of China?

As histories of peoples illustrate, it is not always the case that a backward people willingly accepts culture from an advanced people. There must be such conditions in the recipient people as will make acceptance of foreign culture possible. As we can point out in discussing Japanese statements of reasoning and judgment, there existed a marked similarity of features between Japanese and Chinese ways of thinking. And we find, aside from certain similarities of the social structures and industrial techniques of the two countries, a ground in Japanese thinking itself which favored adoption of Chinese thought in this country. We may ascribe the formation of this ground to similarities in the social life of the two peoples in similar climate.

Matsumiya Kanzan, a Confucian scholar of the Tokugawa period, was aware of this when he said, "China is not far from our land. Nor do Chinese and Japanese manners and customs differ greatly. Confucianism and Shintoism have therefore much in common".[6] Matsumiya in this case is speaking of the similarity of Chinese 'customs and manners' as compared with the Indian. Although scholars of Japanese Classics in the feudal period were wont to stress the difference between the Japanese and Chinese minds and their ways of thinking, we should find, if we take a broader world view, more points of similarity than points of difference.

In spite of its overwhelming influence, however, Chinese thought was not received by the Japanese in its original form. Chinese thought was not to determine the life and thought of the Japanese in the way it did for the Chinese. The same can be said of Buddhist thought. Though Japanese Confucian scholars and Buddhist monks had a considerable reading knowledge of Chinese, their interpretations of original texts were not necessarily faithful. The reasons for this are: 1) misunderstanding of original texts through lack of reading ability and 2) misrepresentation on purpose for some reason or other.

The Chinese language differs from the Japanese language in its origin and structure. It was a task of considerable difficulty for the Japanese to master the Chinese language which employed as the means of expression elaborately developed characters. It apprears that even the official students sent to China by the court of the Heian period were not able to understand Chinese fully.

The eight celebrated monks sent to China by the court of the early Heian period, Saichō, Kūkai, Engyō, Jōgyō, Ennin, Eun, Enchin and Shūei, had no facilities for studying the Chinese language before their departure for China; moreover, their stays in China were generally too brief for them to learn to speak Chinese. They talked with the Chinese with the help of writing. Consequently, they had to emphasize the collection of Buddhist documents and the acquisition of Buddhist ceremonial articles rather than attending lectures in Buddhology. Saichō took with him an interpreter, but others did not. They had to admit their inability to converse orally; one of them says, "I could write Chinese, but not talk. Therefore, when I had a question to ask, I wrote it out", and another says, "I could not speak the Chinese language, but could write it. I had a pad brought to me (whenever I wanted to ask a question) and wrote on it".[7]

Firstly, it is plain that the Japanese were confronted by considerable difficulty in understanding Chinese thought.

Secondly, we frequently find that the Japanese have misinterpreted original Chinese texts. Misinterpretation of Chinese texts, we may note, as one of the most significant phenomena in the history of Japanese thought. The Japanese acquired much in the way of culture and particularly in thought, but it seems that they did not feel necessarily obliged to conform strictly to the Chinese ways of thinking. The translators of those Chinese writings by the Chinese would, knowing that the Chinese language has no rigid grammar, make quite free interpretations of Chinese texts, adding to these ideas of their own for their own purposes. The Buddhist scholars in Nara and Mt. Hiei[8] were able to read and write Chinese with accuracy in the sense they conformed to the Chinese ways of thinking. This, however, was not so with the religionists who were propagators of Buddhism for the Japanese public. We note that the more genuinely native the thought of a religionist was, the greather was his deviation from Chinese texts. Shinran,[9] for example, was, as scholars of the orthodox Jōdo Shin sect which upholds the traditional doctrines recognize,[10] frequently inaccurate in his reading of Chinese texts. Dōgen,[11] too, construed interpretations that betray disregard of the Chinese grammar. Distortions and devious interpretation are frequent in scholars working with the common masses, such as Ninomiya Sontoku. But we must note here that the practice of intentional misinterpretation is found among well-educated scholars, and that interpretations of this type were sometimes even commended and officially accepted by the Imperial Court, as seen in the case of the Religious Debates of Owa.[12] (963 A.D.). Chinese texts, then, were seldom understood correctly by the Japanese.

Now, what were the factors which brought about such a practice of arbitrary misinterpretation? It cannot be ignorance alone, for scholars versed in Chinese were sometimes guilty of it. Nor could it be a persistence in the Japanese of certain particular viewpoints, as distortions and deviations are found in passages which could not be strategically important enough to necessitate them. We are compelled to believe that in such cases it must have been the psychological discrepancies which existed between the linguistic forms of the Chinese and the Japanese process of thinking.

There are a number of cases which indicate such discrepancies between the Chinese way and form of thinking and that of the Japanese Confucian and Buddhist scholars who were accomplished writers in Chinese. Where and why do these discrepancies manifest themselves? This will be one of our questions in this chapter.

Since Chinese texts were often misinterpreted, it follows that the elements of Buddhist and Confucian thought which were transmitted through Chinese books, were not always adopted in their original form.

Buddhism in particular underwent vast changes after it was introduced into this country. To the minds of Buddhists, however, the doctrines which various Japanese sects hold are of true lineage from the sects of Indian and Chinese Buddhism.[13] Nevertheless, it is apparent that Japanese Buddhist thought took on a number of new individual features. Are their new features merely *developments* as Japanese scholars in general assert? Or should they not, in certain cases, be regarded *degeneration*? Could not the general opinion of the Japanese Buddhists that 'only in Japan was the true message Śākyamuni manifested' possibly be a case of self-conceit? I should like to give careful consideration to these matters.

---

1) Owing to the wide practice of Buddhism, Sanskrit terms also found their way into Japanese. In the *Manyō-shū* (萬葉集), for example, such terms as *tō* (塔 pagoda) and Baramon (婆羅門 Brahmin) are found, and the word Shaka (釋迦 Śākya) appears in the *Bussokuseki* (*Buddha-paduka*) poems. Others gradually came to be employed, but their number is never considerable.

2) Shinkichi Hashimoto 橋本進吉: *Kokugogaku Gairon* 國語學概論 (*Hashimoto Shinkichi Hakase Chosaku-shū* 橋本進吉博士著作集 vol. 1) p. 91. Such words as *goroku* (五六) *sugoroku* (雙六 a dice game) *sai* (采 dice) *kō* (香 perfume) *kasho* (過所 custom pass) *e* (繪 picture) and *hōshi* (法師 priest) appear in the *Manyō-shū*. (*ibid.*)

3) *Ibid.* p. 98.

4) *Ibid.* p. 101.

5) Daitō Shimaji 島地大等: *Nihon Bukkyō Kyōgaku-shi,* (日本佛教教學史 The History of Doctrines of Japanese Buddhism), p. 2.

6) Matsumiya Kanzan 松宮觀山: *Sankyō Yōron* 三教要論 (published in 1760) (in *Nihon Jurin Sōsho,* 日本儒林叢書 Kaisetsubu 解説部 vol. 2 p. 7).

7) *San Tendai Godaisan-ki* 參天台五臺山記 Taijō Tamamuro 圭室諦成: *Nihon Bukkyō-shi Gaisetsu* 日本佛教史概說 An Outline of the History of Japanese Buddhism p. 41.

8) *Tannishō* 歎異鈔.

9) cf. *Kyōgyō shinshō* 教行信證 *Bukkyō Taikei* 佛教大系 edition, p. 2322. There are also misreadings in the *Ching-t'u lun-chu* 淨土論註 of T'an-luan 曇鸞 annotated by Shinran (Teikichi Kida 喜田貞吉: *Rekishi-chiri* 歷史地理 vol. 41, no. 1 pp. 14–16).

Teikichi Kida once asserted that the postface of the Hōon-ji manuscript of the *Kyōgyōshinshō* is not in Shinran's hand (*Rekishi-chiri* vol. 40, no. 2, p. 96 ff.). In any case, it is clear that there are far-fetched misinterpretations in it. Besides, Shinran's wilful misinterpretations were made in response to his own personal philosophical point of view. I shall speak more of this later.

10) "All texts cited by our founder are commented upon immediately by him. He adds reading marks to suit his own convenience and reads in such a way that it fits the circumstances". (Kōgatsuin Jinrei 香月院深厲 (1749–1817): *Kyōgyōshinshō Kōgi* 教行信證講義 (*Bukkyō Taikei* edition, p. 1334)).

11) For example in the *Nehangyō* (Nirvāṇa Sūtra) vol. 25 (Siṃhanāda Bodhisattva section, 1), there is a sentence normally construed as meaning "All sentient beings have the Buddha-nature". That is to say, 'all sentient beings which are caught up in the afflictions of this world, have the capacity to be released from them and become Buddha in a future world'. However Dōgen explains it thus: "'All-existence' is the Buddha-nature. One part of 'all-existence' is made up of sentient beings. At this very moment 'all-existence', whether sentient or not, is the Buddha-nature" (*Shōbō Genzō,* 正法眼藏, Buddha-nature 佛性). Here Dōgen takes the phrase 'all have' as a noun meaning an 'absolute one'. That is, "one who exists universally. (Tetsurō Watsuji 和辻哲郎: *Nihon Seishin-shi Kenkyū* 日本精神史研究, pp. 348–349).

12) Ten learned monks each from the Tendai and Hossō sects took part in the religious debates held in the Seiryōden in the palace ground during the eighth month of the third year of Ōwa (963 A.D.) in the time of the Emperor Murakami. The last to debate were Jie (Ryōgen) of the Tendai sect and Chūsan of the Hossō sect. The title selected for debate was the phrase 無一不成佛 from the *Hokke-kyō* (*Saddharmapuṇḍarīka-sūtra*). The Tendai sect reads 'there is not one who does not achieve buddhahood', that is, all sentient beings can become Buddha. They even attempted to include the possibility of Buddhahood for grass, and countries. However, the Hossō sect read the text as 'The one of non-existence does not achieve buddhahood'. In other words the Hossō sect maintained that there were five distinct natures among sentient beings, one of which was never to achieve buddhahood. Both from the general tenor of the *Saddharma-puṇḍarīka-sūtra* and from the contruction of this particular sentence, it is evident that the interpretation of the Hossō sect is erroneous. (*Ōwa Shūron-ki* 應和宗論記, in *Dai Nihon Bukkyō Zensho* 大日本佛教全書 vol. 124, p. 87 ff. Cf. also the account of the *Ōwa Shūron-ki* in the

Bussho Kaisetsu Daijiten 佛書解説大辭典). Both the Tendai and the Hossō sects traditionally claim to have gained the victory in this debate. However, in *Honchō Kōsō Den* vol. 9, the Hossō tralition is accepted: "When the debate was over, the emperor called Chūsan to his room, where he expressed his gratitude and rewarded him. Thereafter, the Hossō was made the chief of the six sects".

13) Ryōjin Soga, the famous Shinshū priest, said on the doctrines of the Jōdo Shin sect in the following way. "In the case of the teaching of the Jōdo Shin sect, one should not consult the *Daimuryōju-kyō* (*Sukhāvatīvyūha-sūtra*) to find out whether the *Kyōgyōshinshō* is wrong. Once the *Kyōgyōshinshō* was completed, there was no necessity of consulting the *Sukhāvativyūha-sūtra*. The Holy Shinran went through the [Ching-t'uwang-sheng] lun-chu (of T'an-luan) and read the *Ching-t'u lun* (of Vasubandhu). If you have the [*Ching-t'u wang-sheng*] *lun-chu*, there is no need of the *Ching-t'u lun*. Further, if you read the *Ching-t'u lun* there is no need of the *Sukhāvatīvyūha-sūtra*". (In *Kyōgaku* 教學, 1947, vol. 1 no. 1, p. 12) It must be said that those who are standing on the Shin-shū standpoints hold this view. However, in these various texts there do exist successive historical developments and changes.

Chapter 2. The tendency to emphasize particular social nexus

(1) Overstressing of human relations

I have already pointed out that there is in the Japanese a tendency to respect the natural feelings of man. This tendency in their character leads to another of their tendencies, that of attaching much importance to the rules of propriety which are based upon human relationships. This latter tendency of thought can be noted in the usage of their language.

It is to be noted here that today, having with them the introduction of Western thought, the uses of the passive voice and the inanimate subject have come to be seen increasingly in Japanese writing. Originally, however, with some rare exceptions, the subject was confined to living things, especially, animals with rather advanced mental operation.[1] Furthermore an foreign word used as a verb in Japanese would be suffixed with the native verb *'su,'* which originally indicated an action of some kind. We thus find that the operation indicated by a verb was then represented as an active operation originating from a living being rather than something belonging to an objective existence.

The recent trend in philosophical writings of Japan to regard the individual thing as nothing but man, we may note in passing, might have come from this tendency of thinking inherent in the Japanese.

A reply to interrogation in Japanese is often the converse of a Western reply. The proper negative reply to the question "Aren't you going?" would be in Japanese "Yes, I am not", much the same as the Sanskrit reply "Evam, tathā" ("That is so" or "Yes") in such a case. English reply here would be "no, I am not". The Japanese reply is a reply to the opinion and intention of the interrogator, whereas the Western reply is a reply to the objective fact involved in the interrogation. In short, a Japanese answers to his interrogator, not to the fact involved. This may account for the ambiguity of reply of which the Japanese are generally accused.

The habits of attaching importance to human relations is manifested outwardly in their practice of the rules of propriety. Generally speaking, exchange of greetings in the West is simple. Japanese greetings are, on the contrary, highly elaborate. Politeness is observed not only among strangers but even among family members. This habit gave rise to elaboration of honorifics in their language. It is said that if all the honorifics were to be taken out of Lady Murasaki's *Tale of Genji,* the book would be reduced to one half in thickness.

The Japanese habit of stressing proprieties determined the way of assimilating Chinese thoughts. Confucianism, which was adopted with especial enthusiasm, deals largely with concepts of propriety. Proprieties are stipulated in great detail in accordance with social rank in such books as the *Book of Rites* etc.

These Confucian concepts of propriety were much appreciated as soon as they were imported with Mainland civilization, as one may well gather from Prince Shōtoku's Injunctions (604 A.D.), Article 4 of which states that if the duty of the inferior is obedience, the duty of the superior is decorum. This does not mean, however, that the concepts of propriety were practical in Japan as they were laid down by Confucianism in China. The practical rules in this country were to differ considerably from the Chinese rules. It was as concepts—and as a means of keeping social order and the clan system—that Confucian proprieties were appreciated, and as concepts the Japanese and Chinese proprieties had much in common. And it was such points of similarity that made it easy for the Japanese ruling class to enforce the rules of propriety upon the people without undue resistance and friction; Confucian concepts would not have spread as widely among the populace as they did, had these been adopted only as a means of government.

Stressing of proprieties again was to determine the course of assimilation of Buddhism. We find this tendency clearly manifested in Dōgen, the founder of a sect most characteristically Japanese of all the Zen sects of this country, who laid down strict rules regarding even such minutiae of daily conduct as ablution, eating, evacuation, etc. Many of these detailed rules are considered to have been Dōgen's own creation. Now, let us compare Dōgen with his teacher Tendō Nyojō. We find Nyojō saying, in the fashion of the Zen priests of the Sung Dynasty of China, things that seem eccentric to us modern men, as for example, in the following passage which reads: "Squatting in his private room, he gouged out the eyes of the statue of Bodhidharma. Making balls of mud, he struck people with them. In a loud voice he cried, 'Behold, the sea has dried up, the bottom can be seen. Waves rise up so high that they strike Heaven!' "[2] Yet, we find nothing which we may call eccentric in Dōgen's private life. Rather his daily conducts were strictly in keeping with the decorous manners of the Zen school. Many others beside Dōgen were responsible for the importation of Chinese Zen Buddhism, but the eccentricities of the Chinese Zen sects did not come into general vogue in the religious circles of this country.

---

1) Izuru Shimmura 新村出: *Gengogaku Josetsu* (言語學序說 Introduction to Linguistics), Tokyo, Kōbundō 弘文堂, 1923, p. 172

2) *Nyojō Zenji Goroku* 如淨禪師語錄 (Analects of Zen Master Nyojō) vol. I, (*Taishō*, vol. 48 p. 121 c.)

(2) Superseding of human relationships takes precedence over the individual

To lay stress upon human relationships is to place heavy regard upon the relations of many individuals rather than upon the individual as an independent entity.

The elaboration of honorifics in the Japanese language has already been mentioned as one of the phenomena ascribable to such a trait. Honorifics, it is true, are found in Korean, but not to the great extent as in Japanese; honorifics as such do not exist in other Asian or Western languages, though in the latter languages, the feeling of respect may be expressed by the uses of certain special words and the third person plural.[1] Honorifics are thus something quite peculiar to the Japanese language.

Further, *personal pronouns* are much more *complicated* in Japanese than in other languages. The choice of the proper pronoun to fit the particular situation is an ever recurring problem in speaking Japanese. Special pronouns are required for superiors, equals, inferiors, for intimates and strangers. If one should confuse them, difficulties would ensue. The Japanese, therefore, must bear in mind such human relationships as rank and intimacy every time he uses a personal pronoun.

Such restricted use of personal pronouns are related to the use of nouns and verbs as well. A distinction is made, for example, between words used in addressing persons of superior rank and those used in addressing persons of inferior rank. Such a custom of differentiating parlance in accordance with the persons addressed,[2] we may call a "ritual in conversation". The same sort of "ritual" is to be found in other Asian tongues, under feudal reigns, but nowhere is this as pronounced as in the Japanese language.

When this type of thinking is predominant, consciousness of the individual as an entity is apt to be less explicit; the recognition of the equal value of the individual is lessened.

The fact that the first person or the second person is often omitted as the subject in a Japanese sentence seems to be an indication of this type of thinking. Generally in such a case the subject is implied in the whole sentence structure, but frequently a sentence may completely lack the subject. This indicates that there is in the Japanese no full awareness of the individual or of an independent performer of actions as an objective being; the Japanese have no inclination to state, or to attribute actions to, a specific performer of actions.

Further, we note that number is not made explicit in Japanese sentences. Not always is a distinction drawn between the singular and plural numbers (as also in Chinese and the languages of the South Sea Islanders),[3] and reduplication in the Japanese language cannot be said strictly to indicate plurality, as reduplication requires the individuality of signification. Thus, the forms *Kuni-guni* ("nation-nation") and *hito-bito* ("person-person") are not strictly the equivalents of the English plural forms "nations" and "persons" or "people", but they are actually like English "every nation" and "every person", or as the case may be, "several nations" and "several persons". Furthermore, not all nouns can be made plural forms. The plural suffixes *-ra, -tachi* and *-domo* cannot, as a rule, be affixed to words indicating inanimate objects, such as, book or stone, though the reduplicated forms *ie-ie* ("house-house") and *yama-yama* ("mountain-mountain") are permissible. Hence, we do not say *hon-ra* (*hon* "book"/*ra*) or *ishi-ra* (ishi "stone"/*ra*). Nor could we affix the plural suffixes to worse meaning animals of lower orders, such as insects, fish, birds, though we sometimes hear *kemonora* ("beasts") or *inudomo* ("dogs"). Plurality, however, becomes better indicated as we proceed higher from domestic animals to servants. Several kinds of plural suffixes are variously used to suit different occasions. *Domo* and *tachi* are used for persons of equal or inferior status of for intimates, as for example, *funabitodomo* or *funabitotachi* ("boatmen"), *hitotachi* ("people"), *tomodachi* ("friends"). When respect must be shown, the suffix *kata,* which originally meant place, is used, as for example, *anatagata* ("you") and *senseigata* ("teachers"). In the past, *hara,* a word for field, was used as a plural suffix; thus we have *tonobara* ("lords") and *yakkobara* ("footmen").[4] In short, the use of plural suffixes was determined by the relationship of ranks and the feeling (intimacy, hate, respect, disrespect) the speaker entertains for the persons of whom he is speaking. This clearly evidences the Japanese trait to think of things in terms of human relationship rather than as objectively existing facts. These plural forms are, therefore, not strict equivalents of Western plural forms, though in modern times owing to the influence of Western logic number has come to be expressed in nearly the same way as in Western languages.

The individual, then, is not clearly conceived as the unit of society. Consequently, it sometimes happens that a plural suffix attached to a noun loses its own meaning, becoming simply a blank, meaningless component of a compound, and the compound may indicate the singular number, as in the case of the word *wakaishū,* which is made up of *wakai* ("young") plus *shū* (plural suffix "people"). This word may mean both 'youngsters' and 'a youngster'. Words *heitai* (regiment of soldiers) and *sōryo* (monks) may mean also 'a soldier' and 'a monk'. In order to make plurality more explicit, there were created already in the Heian period such a peculiar plural form as *wakashūdomo* (young persons/plural suffix) or *kodomotachi* (child/plural suffix/plural suffix).[5]

The Japanese prefer not to represent as objectively existing but when two people are conversing, they are clearly aware of the distinction between singular and plural. As we have seen, one of the most distinguishing features of the Japanese language is the lack of clear indication of number. This is not so, however, with regard to personal pronouns, particularly, the first and second person. The first and second person are clearly distinguished; the pronouns *ware* or *watakushi* ("I") could only be the first person singular, and could by no means be confused with *warera* or *watakushitachi* ("we"). It is to be noted that the plural forms here are made from the singular forms. We note here, in passing, that in the languages of the South Sea Islanders number is rather distinctly indicated in nouns, although it is vague in other respects.

We have the converse of this in modern Western languages where number, though explicit in the case of nouns, is ambiguous in the case of personal pronouns. The second person singular, *'Sie, vous,* or *you'* are etymologically plurals. The speaker at a lecture, or the author of a book, in the West, customarily refers to himself as "we", when the actual number is singular. Speaker and audience are brought closer to each other by identification. Contemporary Japanese has a similar usage, probably a Western influence.

This phenomenon in their language indicates that the Japanese who are disinclined to measure the objective world with a certain established unit are quite sensitive to the distinction between "I" and "you" in human relations.

This tendency in their thinking may be found also in their assimilation of Buddhism. In the course of assimilation of Buddhism the problem of the contrariety of one ego with another ego was never given serious consideration.[6] The general view then held is represented by that of Dōgen who, in advocating identification of the self with other selves, taught that: "oneself and others should be benefited at the same time". While Tenkei (Japanese), his pupil, said: "If you alone comprehend your own mind, then it is evident that all other beings, animate and inanimate, in all directions should partake of the wisdom of the Buddha at the same time". Ryōnin, the founder of Yuzū-nembutsu sect, is said to have seen, while meditating deeply in May, 1117 A.D., Amida Buddha appear and presented a poem to him, saying, "one person is all persons; all person are one persons; one meritorious deed is all meritorious deeds; all meritorious deeds are one meritorious deed. This is called deliverance to the Pure Land by the grace of Amida". These views upheld by the Kegon sects in China and Japan have their origin in the Indian Kegon Sūtra. (*Buddha-avataṃsaka-sūtra*). More than we realize, the Japanese mind was affected by the views of the Kegon Sūtra. And the problem of 'proving the existence of others' such as Dharmakīrti, Indian logical and philosopher, was interested in was never given attention either in China or Japan.

But while such features of the Japanese way of thinking are manifested in the linguistic phenomena of the race, good instances of their manifestation in the course of assimilation of Buddhism cannot easily be found.

Presumably, this is due to the fact that Buddhism which contained from the first the idea of identification of the self with others had little to be influenced by the traditional Japanese thought.

The lack of a clear distinction between the individual and the collective to which it belongs has, however, brought about a number of interesting phenomena. For example, individual monks training in a Buddhist order are known by the term '*sō*' (derived from the Sanskrit *saṅgha*) which is itself a term for a Buddhist order. Such a linguistic phenomenon is seen also in China. This type of thinking is apparent in Dōgen where he says: "One should be more intimate with brethren in a Buddhist order than with oneself".[7] In contrast, the primitive Buddhism of India teaches: "Sons are no help, [nor] a father, [nor] relations; there is no help from kinsfolk for one whom death has seized". and "The self is the master of the self".[9] Thus, self-reliance is taught.[10] And primitive Jainism teaches: "Friend, thou art a friend of theyself. Why seekest thou friends beside thyself?"[11] When we compare Dōgen's views with those of the Indian we cannot help being amazed by the great difference lying between them. Lack of individual consciousness, is a phenomenon common in feudal societies of all countries, but nowhere is the sense of human affinity as predominant as in this country.

As the objective causes which brought about such a tendency in the Japanese people, we may cite the social life peculiar to their land and climate. The primitive Indo-Europeans, being nomadic and living chiefly by hunting, were in constant contact with alien peoples. Here, human relations were marked by fierce rivalry. Peoples were in great migrations; one race conquered another only to be conquered, by still another. In such a society struggles for existence were based not on mutual trust but on rational plan and stratagem.

Japanese society, on the other hand, developed from small localized farming communities. The Japanese early did away with nomadic life, and settled down to cultivate rice fields. People living on rice are made inevitably to settle permanently in one place. In such a society *families* continue on generation after generation. Genealogies and kinships of families through long years become so well known by its members that the society as a whole takes on the appearance of a family. In such a society individuals are closely bound to each other and they form an exclusive human nexus. Here an individual who asserts himself will hurt feelings of others and thereby do harm to himself. The Japanese learned to adjust themselves to this type of familistic society, and created forms of expression suitable to life in such a society. And here grew the worship of tutelary gods and local deities. Even today there is a strong tendency in Japanese social structure to settle closely around such tutelary gods and local deities. This tendency is deeply rooted in the people and it has led to their stressing of human relations. The Japanese have learned to attach unduly heavy importance to their human nexus in disregard of the individual. This question will be discussed in the next section.

---

1) This can be seen in Sanskrit and German, for example.

2) In his novel, *Deutsche Liebe*, Max Müller relates the story of the pure love of a noble youth for a princess. The princess speaks to the youth as follows:

"We were close friend as children; and surely this relation between us has not changed. Then, I can not say 'Sie' when I speak to you, as to a stranger. But it's not right for me to use the familiar word 'du', so the only thing we can do is to talk in English.
(In English) Do you understand me?"
—Prof. Morimine Sagara, trans. *Ai wa Eien ni* (Love is everlasting) p. 33.
This is the same problem we have in Japanese.

3) *Transactions of the Asiatic society of Japan*, 1925 pp. 78–79.

4) A very similar phenomenon occurs in languages structurally close to Japanese, such as Mongolian and Manchu (Izuru Shimmura, 新村出: op. cit. *Gengogaku Josetsu* pp. 133–134.)

5) Cf. *Makura-no-sōshi* 枕草紙 21, in which the plural form *kodomo-domo* (children) is used.

6) Is there not some relevance to this in the dialectical Japanese usage of *ware* ("I") in the sense of "you"? I wish specialists would instruct me on this point.

7) Dōshū Ōkubo 大久保道舟 ed.: *Dōgen Zenji Shingi* (*Iwanami Bunko* series) p. 95.

8) *Dhammapada* in Pali, No. 288.

9) *Ibid.* No. 160.

10) *Ibid.* Nos. 380, 236, 238.

11) *Āyāraṅga*, 1. 3. 3. 4.

12) See above, pp. 68–84.

(3) Unconditional belief in a limited human nexus

The Indians regard man as the subjective maker of actions, and the peoples of the Western Hemisphere have, from ancient times, inclined to regard him as the objective being possessing potentialities of universal significance. The Japanese, on the other hand, look upon man as a being subordinated to a specific and limited human nexus; they conceive him in terms of human relations.

Thus a human event, in this way of thinking, is not a purely personal event but an event having some value and emotional significance to the broader sphere of human relations. This characteristic way of thinking seems to manifest itself in the Japanese use of an intransitive verb in the passive voice—a form expressing the subject as being indirectly affected by some event or act; for example, '*Kare wa tsuma ni shinareta*' (lit. "It happened to him that his wife died") or '*Kare wa kodomo ni nakareta*' (lit. "It happened to him that his child wept"). An objective event—a wife's death or a child's weeping—is here stated in its relation to one's interests and feelings. Such a statement of the event contains an entirely different significance from that contained in the Indo-European statement 'His wif edied', or 'His child wept'.

The people to whom a human nexus is important place great moral emphasis upon complete and willing dedication of the self to others in a specific human collective. This attitude, though it may be a basic moral requirement in all peoples, occupies a dominant position in Japanese social life. Self-dedication to a specific human nexus has been one of the most powerful factors in Japanese history.

In the moral sense of the early Japanese good and evil were considered as a matter of morality and not as a matter of fortune, as they are generally regarded in a primitive civilization. Good was not something that profits the self but something that profits others in a collective. Evil was not something that harms the self but something harmful to others or the welfare of the whole. Good and evil concern not the interests of the individual but those of others or the whole.[1] Later the highest virtue was considered to be sacrifice of the self for the sake of the sovereign, the family (especially the parents), or the community. This feudal morality assumed enlarged or extended applications after the Meiji era when it came to be expressed in the form of sacrifice of one's life for the state or the emperor. Attachment to one's native place and to those from the same place are the variations of this attitude.

In contrast to this we find only a few cases in which sacrifices of life were made by the Japanese for the sake of something universal, something that transcends particular human nexus, such as academic truth or the arts. And if we exclude the persecutions of the True Pure Land sect, the Hokke sect and Christianity, cases of dying for religious faith are exceptional phenomena. Sacrifice of all for the sake of truth, when it went contrary to the intentions of the ruler, was even regarded as evil.

Such a tendency of thinking was an influential factor in the assimilation of foreign thoughts. A good deal of Chinese thought was adopted by the Japanese, but not, for instance, were digestible to the Japanese. Though Confucianism which laid particular stress upon the proper order of human proprieties was enthusiastically accepted, the liberalism of some Chinese heterodox thinkers was entirely ignored: Taoism of Lao Tzu and Chuang Tzu which valued the welfare of individual man never spread widely among the people at large. Christianity with its persistent teaching of belief in God met the fate of persecution, and was finally uprooted, when it came to be feared that its teachings might result in the neglect of duties to feudal lords and parents. In the Satsuma Clan the followers of the True Pure Land sect were put to death because of the fear that they would be disobedient to the clan lord.

Religion, particularly universal religion, advocates transcending of specific human relations. This facet of religion, however, is scarcely seen in Japanese religions. A feature common in various Japanese religions is their emphasis on human propriety. From ancient days the importance of an established, limited human nexus has been in the consciousness of the Japanese. As the psychological example parallel to it, we may cite the fact that the Japanese statement of judgment (or reasoning) is severely limited to the environment which includes the speaker and listener. Universal religions from abroad had to be transformed to suit such a tendency of thought.

In spite of the various Western modern thoughts introduced after the Meiji Restoration, the individual as a social entity has not come to be fully grasped by the general public. While the Japanese are keenly conscious of their membership in their small, closed nexus, they are hardly fully aware of themselves as individuals, or as social beings, to the extent the Western peoples are.

In the light of such a way of thinking, it is easy to understand why Japanese Buddhists have tended to disregard the Buddhist Precepts. The traditional, conservative Precepts of Hīnayāna Buddhism which had been observed among the clergy until the Nara period were abandoned by Saichō (Dengyō) who adopted instead the Precepts of Mahāyāna Buddhism. The so-called *Endonkai,* the Mahāyāna Precepts adopted by Saichō, stipulated that Buddhist novices needed not comply with the Hīnayāna Precepts. It was in this way that Buddhism came to have its practicability in Japan. This tendency to ignore the Precepts became stronger in Japanese

Buddhist Sects, especially, in the Pure Land Buddhism. In the True Pure Land sect founded by Shinran, it was thought that even the breakers of the Precepts could be saved by the boundless mercy of Amitāyus Buddha. Buddhism, we note, has thus transformed itself completely for the sake of practicability. Japanese society as the ground of Buddhist practice had rejected the religious practices of India and China. Japanese society was too tightly formed; the restrictive power of its secular community was too great over the religious circles to permit religionists to continue with their imported practices.

This hardly means, however, that Japanese Buddhism was *immoral* or *amoral.* Monks and faithful alike observed assiduously the requirements of their limited human nexus; they were highly moral in this respect. They were devoted to their parents and loyal to their sovereign. They were in every respect quite different from the monks and novices of India and China. Moreover, Japanese monks were devoted workers for the interests of the order to which they belonged. If the followers of one sect founder are divided into a number of different orders, monks in one of the orders become so devoted to his particular order to the point of boycotting the other orders. To them the welfares of their small separate orders are their main concern and the doctrine to which they all adhere is reduced to a secondary concern. Here again they are moral in the sense that they are devoted to their limited human nexus. The Precepts to be kept by an individual as an individual in relation to the Absolute, by an individual in relation to another individual qua individual tend thus to become neglected. The interests of their own small limited nexus become the factors determining their actions.

The antiquarianism so strong in the Japanese may also be said to be the historical, temporal aspect of their attachment to a limited human nexus. The Japanese cherish families and institutions that have long history. One of the national prides of the Japanese people was the length of their history. Japanese poetry is abundant in examples of their antiquarianism; old poetic expressions, obsolete in ordinary conversation, maintain a great role in Japanese poetry. The merits of *waka* poetry have been thought to lie in the use of the words used by poets of the past.[2] This practice continues today. In the Tokugawa period writing of archaic style was prevalent.

How did Japanese antiquarianism affect importations of Continental culture? The Japanese antiquarianism is apparent, rather, in the fact that no liberal thoughts of the Continent took root in this country. (The question of Japanese unconditional subordination to established authorities will be discussed in detail later).

The antiquarianism of Japanese Buddhists was quite different in character from that of the Indians or Chinese. The Zen Priest Tōrei, for instance, idealizes ancient Japan in his *Shūmon Mujintō-ron,* and says:

"In the pure ancient age of Japan, people were honest and upright; so it was easy for them to attain to the Great Way in accordance with their ability. Gods and men were unified in the primeval chaos. What need will be there of Buddhism? In later corrupted age, however, people have gradually lost their own mind. They are addict to the outer (sensual) objects, being lost in them. They have got in transmigration through evil ways. Without the exquisite doctrine of the Enlightened One (= the Buddha), who could be saved out of transmigration in these days?"

It would have been more to our expectation, had the Buddhists regarded pre-Buddhist Japan as a benighted nation. But here we find a Buddhist himself giving us a statement to the contrary.

---

1) Tetsurō Watsuji 和辻哲郎: *Sonnō Shisō To Sono Dentō* (尊皇思想とその傳統 Reverence for the Emperor and its tradition), p. 64.

2) Fujiwara Teika in his *Eika Taigai* says: "There is no master of *waka* (Japanese poetry). We learn from older poems alone. Who, having steeped himself in the old style and learned words from our prėdecessors, will not be able to write poetry?"

(4) Observance of the family morals

The prevailing atmosphere in Japanese social life, we may say, is that of close intimacy and alliance, and this atmosphere of intimacy and alliance is perhaps most manifest in the family, the first and most important of their closed nexus. Under the ancient clan system, the early Japanese were devout ancestor-worshippers and diligent observers of family devotions which were conducted in compliance with Shintoism, their racial religion. Large and small clans, related by blood, having common ancestors and occupations, set up a deity which the entire clan members worshipped as their tutelary deity or *ujigami.*[1] On fixed days clan members would gather and the clan head would offer prayers of thanksgiving and petition for blessings before their protector deity. This religious custom survives today in rural districts. Festivals of tutelary deities are held today by rural villagers after good hervesting; festival carts are pulled out from the barn and travelling players come to present their plays. Thanksgiving for good harvest is thus shown. The precincts of tutelary deities were regarded as the most hallowed place, and the treasures of the clan were stored there to be guarded by all the clansmen. Thus the clan head in charge of religious affairs possessed absolute dictatorship.[2]

According to the beliefs of the early Japanese, multifarious deities were thought to be related by blood, and these deities were also related to the imperial ancestors. Blood-relationship, it is thus apparent, was considered to be the main force for communal unity. We must note here that the actuality of blood-relationship was not essential. It was not the actual ancestors who were deified for worship; it was that the deities worshipped were regarded *as their common ancestors.*[3]

Even after the collapse of the clan system, reverence for the family (although the meaning of family had changed) continued to be rooted in the social eye of the Japanese and the family became the unit of social organism, and from earliest times to the present has been dominant. It was the family, not the individual, which was the determining factor in Japanese life of the past. Professor Yaichi Haga, for instance, says: "The unit of Western society is the individual and groups of individuals make up the State. In Japan, the State is an aggregation of families. Therein lies the basic difference". Prof. Haga asserted that Japanese ancestor worship and reverence for the family name are based on the following facts.[4] In ancient times, one who counterfeited a surname was made to submit to the ordeal of boiling water before the shrine of the gods. The early genealogical work *Shinsen Shōji-roku* which lists many family names, scrupulously indicates the origin of each as Imperial, divine or foreign. Then, too, there is the poem of Ōtomo no Yakamochi, which reads, in part: "I ponder more deeply than ever how to the Ōtomo clan belongs a great office. In which served our far-off divine ancestor who bare the title of Ōkume-nushi"[5] The *samurai* of the middle ages, prior to engaging in combat, would first call out his lineage. For example, "He called out, 'I am Wada Shōjirō Yoshishige, 17 years old, grandson of Miura Taisuke Yoshiaki, not far removed from a princely house, the eleventh generation from Prince Takamochi, descendant of the Emperor Kammu, let anyone come, be he general or be he retainer, I am his man' ".[6] Upstart *daimyō* would often attempt to acquire prestige by falsifying their genealogies. In the *Kyōgenki,* we find the so-called 'genealogical disputes'.[7]

Hence it was natural the religions and thoughts of the Continent would have been assimilated by the Japanese in such a way as to fit them to their institution of ancestor worship.

In the assimilation of Confucianism it was filial piety which was most stressed. Confucian students were made to study, with especial thoroughness, the *Analects of Confucius* and the *Treatise on Filial Piety.* In the fourth month 757 A.D. an Imperial Edict was issued which reads: "In ancient times ruling over people was generally done by means of the instruction of filial piety. Nothing is more important than this, which is the basis of all good conduct. Every house in this country should keep one copy of the *Treatise on Filial Piety.* People should study it diligently. Officials should edify them with it". The *Treatise on Filial Piety* was held to be the "book of examples for a hundred sovereigns", as it was believed that the "basic precept of a philosopher sovereign was filial piety".[8] After February 860 A.D. when the *Treatise on Filial Piety* was presented to the Emperor for his first reading of the year, it became a custom long thereafter for Emperors to read this *Treatise* as his first book of the year. Filial piety came to receive particular emphasis during the Tokugawa period when Confucianism greatly flourished. Filial piety was given religious color by the scholars of the Wang Yang-ming school; it was developed into a metaphysics by Nakae Tōju. The aboriginal institution of ancestor worship was thus further solidified when it acquired from Confucianism a theoretical basis. The Japanese, however, rejected other Chinese thoughts which ran counter to their traditional customs.

But ancestor worship and the family system, we must remember, are not exclusively Japanese, are but the two most potent unifying factors in Chinese social organization. Here arises the question as to the difference between the Japanese institution of ancestor worship and their family system and those of the Chinese. This, however, is a subject matter which calls for separate investigation, and could hardly be discussed here in detail. It will suffice merely to mention here two or three points concerning the transformations which the Chinese family morals underwent when they were introduced into this country.

Scholars have pointed out that the Japanese family system was from old patriarchal while that of China was based upon the principle of joint ownership.

This point will become clearer when we compare the prescriptions of house registration of the T'ang Code with that of the Japanese Yōrō

Code, which was promulgated in the Nara period. In China joint ownership of family property had since the Chou Dynasty been in wide practice; the typical family system as stipulated by the T'ang Penal and Administrative Codes was founded upon a basis called 'joint living and joint ownership of property'. Each family had its family head, assumed by the eldest patrilineal member of the family. The family head (unless he be an ancestor) had as his authority only the custody of the family property and not the parental powers. The jointly-owned property of the family may be partitioned under certain circumstances. When the ancestor was the family head (this situation is called 'father-children ownership') the family property was partitioned as and when he wished, and his descendants were not allowed to object to the way in which it was partitioned. In case, however, the family head were other than the ancestor, that is, if it were a patrilineal member of the family except ancestors, partitioning had to be done by him in conformity with the provisions of the Code, pending approval from the family. The Japanese Code, while based upon the T'ang Code, was altered to suit the native institutions. While the underlying principle in the T'ang Code here had been fair partitioning among the brothers, the Japanese Code provided that the property, in the event of the death of the *pater familias,* shall be partitioned at a certain proportion among the legitimate and illegitimate offspring. In short, the object of partitioning was changed from the jointly-owned property as defined in the T'ang Code to the property left by the head *pater familias.* The patriarchal family system was so deeply rooted in the Japanese that even the radical legislators of the time, who were bent upon imitating the Chinese system, were not able to alter it.

We may add further that one of the miscellaneous provisions of the T'ang Code stipulates that in case a descendant sell or pawn part of the family property without the approval of the family head, the action (selling or pawning) is considered null and void. A provision to the same effect is found in the Japanese Yōrō Code. But it is interesting to note that the officially compiled annotations of the T'ang Code *Li-su-i* uses in this case the phrase 'the property of the family', while the official commentary of the Japanese Yōrō, Code, *Ryo no gige* uses the phrase 'the propertly of the family head'.[9]

We thus become aware of a very important difference which exists between Japanese and Chinese family systems. It does not mean, however, that the head of the Japanese family, who was solely responsible for the custody of the family property, ruled the members with absolute authority in other family matters. Even in days of feudalism, the power to make actions was vested both in the head and the members. Absolute obedience of his wife and children was never enforced. This, as scholars of the civil law point out, differs considerably from the Roman patriarchal family.[10]

The Chinese moral code, which has often been said to be founded upon familism, puts great stress upon *lineage*. In Japan, on the controry, stress was laid upon the 'family' as the unifying force of a tight human nexus rather than upon lineage. Hence, adoption of an heir from a non-related family, often lower in social status, was possible. Confucianism in China, however, placed so great importance upon lineage that adoption from a family of alien stock was impossible, though recent field surveys indicate that this is sometimes done out of necessity. The professed rule, however, prohibits this event today.[11]

It was 'family name' which was most highly priced in Japanese society. Non-consanguinity was not a prohibitive matter. Adoption was given approval by such Japanese Confucian scholars of the Tokugawa period as Kumazawa Banzan in *Gaisho* and Miwa Shūsai in *Yōshi-Benben*. The views of their opponents, Asami Kensai (author of *Yōshibenshō*) and Miyake Shōsai (author of *Dōseiigoshōkosetsu*) did not spread widely enough to exercise restrictive power over the practice of adoption of non-consanguineous heirs.[12]

Moreover, sociologists and ethnographists have pointed out that Japanese familism allowed elements of non-consanguineous, that is, pseudo-parent-children relations to enter into it. However, detailed investigations as to their historical changes and evolution are yet to be made.[13] Nevertheless, it is true that the Japanese familism is predominent in the ruler-ruled relationship, and there is actually little consciousness of opposition between the ruler and the ruled; the ruler considers the ruled equal members of his family and the ruled also consider themselves as such. Outwardly it appears as though the feudal ruler principle did not exist. The whole Japanese nation has been regarded as an extended family; the ideal basis for society has been such familism.

Then how was Indian Buddhism to change when it was brought into such society? Buddhist Mercy, as a practical ideal, takes into consideration not only man but also even creeping creatures of the earth, and extends equally to all living beings. Yet Prince Shōtoku, who tried systematically to introduce Buddhism to the Japanese, mostly spoke of mercy as something existing between father and child, and preached it as such. "Falsity is not employed between father and son", he said, "Precisely because there exists the relationship of father and son (between the Buddha and living being), the Buddha can engage in the work of saving them through many, many aeons". The Mercy of the Perfect One (Nyorai, Tathāgata) is not taken here as the universal virtue of an idealized being but as a realistic, worldly virtue—the mercy of the father in the family.[14)]

We have already pointed out that Japanese Buddhism placed great emphasis upon the attainment of *satori,* or spiritual awakening, through bodily experience. The body, however, was regarded as originating from the parents; respect for one's body thus meant respect for one's parents. Zen priest Bankei called the absolute in the individual "the Unborn Buddhahood passed from parents to child". He further declared, "To change the Unborn Buddhahood passed from parents to us into a vile one is an extreme filial impiety". Now in Indian thought in general the body born of parents is regarded as merely the fetters for the Soul, and the world of the absolute is believed to begin when these fetters are discarded. But, in contrast to this, Japanese Zen Buddhists, Priest Bankei in particular, hold that the world of the absolute is handed from parents. Buddhahood, in him, is identified with filial devotion. "There is nothing more gracious than the kindness of parents. They have brought us up, who were completely ignorant, till we become intelligent and hear Buddhist sermons. It is solely due to the benevolence of parents. You should respect them. This is filial piety. To follow the way of filial piety is the Buddhahood. Filial piety and the Buddhahood are not different".

(As we have pointed out previously), in China Buddhism had to become amalgamated with the tradition of filial piety to be able to spread among the general public. Much the same situation existed in Japan. The Chinese wrote imitation pseudo-sūtras that would preach filial piety; and the Japanese spread among the public these very sūtras with commentaries and annotations, the *Bumoonjū-kyō* ("Sūtra of Parental Benefits") being a typical example of such.

It will be supposed from this that Buddhism whose teachings transcend nation and family would have come to clash with the familistic morals of the Japanese. It was precisely this element incompatible with the familistic morals that Japanese historians and Confucians took up as the target in their criticisms of Buddhism. The Buddhists, on the other hand, asserted that 'true filial piety' may sometimes run contrary to the worldly morals of the family. Nichiren, for instance, declared, "Generally speaking, we should obey our parents. However, as for the way to become a Buddha, not to obey them would be the fundamental filial piety. Therefore in the Shin-ji-kwan-sūtra it is stated: 'To get into the Trans-mundane Way, without repaying others' kindness, is to repay it truely'. That is, to get out of the family, without obeying the wish of one's parents and to become a Buddha is to repay their kindness truely. Even in worldly life, not to obey one's parents when they want to plot a rebellion and so on, is the true filial piety. It is stated in a Confucian canon called "The Book of Filial Piety". When Tendai Daishi was practising the meditation of the Hokke Sūtra, his parents sat on his lap and wanted to disturb his performing Buddhist practice. This was the Evil Ones in the figures of his parents who disturbed him.[15] Nichiren, a believer of the Lotus Sūtra, unequivocally taught that one may turn his back on his parents in order to believe in the Sūtra.[16] Nichiren distinguished filial piety into two kinds, 'Low filial piety' and 'high filial piety'. *He made it plain that he upheld filial piety as the absolute virtue,* but at the same time insisted upon the validity of Buddhist universalism.

In Japan of the past, the reverence for parents was the same thing as the reverence for the family. Japanese reverence for the family affected the assimilation of all foreign religions introduced into this country. Japanese Buddhists resembled Chinese Buddhists in that both tended to regard their religious orders as their "families".[17]

With lineage occupying so important a place in the Japanese mind, it was natural that Buddhist monks or *shukke* (lit. "Those who have forsaken their worldly families"), should have instituted for themselves what we may call 'quasiblood relation'. We recall the Chinese custom in general vogue among Zen Buddhists toward the end of the Northern Sung Dynasty in which a document called "Shisho" (lit. "A document of inheritance") was issued to disciples from masters at certain stages of training. This appeared to the Japanese mind to symbolize blood succession, or establishment of blood relation, and accordingly, when this custom was adopted, the Japanese came to write this document in cinnabar ink which represented blood. Thus, it was natural, again, that in Buddhist orders that approved of the secular forms of living persons actually related by blood to the founder should have come to be regarded with special respect. The Honganji which was originally the mere keeper of the grave of

Shinran came to receive inordinate respect and favors, and assumed the leading position it had among the numerous branches of the Shin sect, simply because it had as its heads the descendants of Shinran.

Japanese Buddhism was able to broaden its sphere of influence as a popular religion when it linked up with the native custom of ancestor worship. It is recorded that as early as the 2nd year of the reign of Emperor Suiko (593) higher officers of the Court dedicated temples to their Emperor and parents; the Rescript of Emperor Temmu (3rd month 686 A.D.) commands: "Every family in every Province should possess a temple, and with the Sūtras and the image of the Buddha services should be conducted". This was the origin of *butsudan,* or Buddhist shrine, found in every Japanese home. It is not known to what extent this rescript was enforced but, later, after the prohibition of Christianity during the reign of Tokugawa Shogunate Buddhist service became family routine of the Japanese.[18] Chapels with Buddhist images have been built in homes of other Asiatic nations in the past and present, but these, unlike the case of the Japanese, have had nothing to do with ancestor worship;[19] and we remember that Chinese ancestor worship was associated with Taoism rather than Buddhism. In Japan, significantly, mortuary tablets of ancestors were placed in home Buddhist shrines. The Japanese, thus, were made ever aware of the spirits of their ancestors, of those of immediate ancestors through the Buddhist mortuary tablets and of those of more distant ancestors through the presence of the Shinto shrine. (The family Shintō shrine, however, is connected with ancestor-worship to a much less degree. Shrine Shintō does not in general practice ancestor-worship. The co-existence of the two kinds of shrine in Japanese homes cannot, therefore, be regarded merely as the result of the mixing of Shintoism and Buddhism.)

Buddhism, when brought to the Japanese soil, thus became linked up with a kind of clan-consciousness. It became a vogue with aristocracies to have family temples built; the Kōfukuji, for example, was the temple of the Fujiwara clan. Heads of these temples were assumed by the members of the owner-families who had renounced secular life to become priests. (Temples similar to the Japanese family temple seem to have existed in India of the later periods). It is interesting to note that Buddhism which had aimed at breaking down the clan system should come to be accociated with clan consciousness in Japan.

Amida Pure Land Buddhism, for instance, took root in the soil of Japan by virtue of a doctrine which preached, not the individual's future happiness and peace of mind, but rather the peaceful repose of the dead. The Sūtra of Infinite Life (*Sukhāvatīvyūha-sūtra*) was explained to the people at the lecture meetings held in the third year of Hakuchi (652 A.D.), Amida's Paradise came to be depicted in the mural paintings of the Hōryūji's Gold Hall, the well-known maṇḍala of the Taima-dera showing Paradise was completed; and all of these were expressions of the Amida Pure Land Buddhism of the time. Amida Pure Land Buddhism flourished more and more in the subsequent Nara and Heian periods.

Yet, of course, there were those who rejoiced at the Wonderful Vow of Amida and who, quite free of any customs of ancestor worship, found individual salvation in the teachings of Amida Buddhism. Shinran, for example, reflected: "The vow of Amida (Amitābha) who meditated for five aeons is, when I consider it well, meant for me alone. Gracious, indeed, is the previous vow of Amida, who wanted to save me from many fetters of Karmas". He also has said: "I have never performed invocation to Amida even once for the peaceful repose and benefit of my dead parents. Why? All living beings are parents and brothers to each other in the long process of transmigration. All should be saved and become Buddhas in future life. If I could actually accumulate some merit by my own power, I would help my dead parents by the merit of Invocation to Amida. (But it is not I who save me, but Amida himself.) So I should give up self-conceited attitude of hoping to save myself and others by the merit of religious practice (and I should rely on the grace of Amida). After I have been saved and become a Buddha I would save beings who will come to be in contact with me".[20] But the Jōdo Shin sect could not spread among the common people with this teaching. To become the largest religious sect in Japan that it did, it had to adopt into itself the traditional customs of ancestor worship. And today many who have lost the true faith of the Pure Land sect are still associated with it on the strength of this one facet of it which has to do with ancestor worship.

The Bon Festival was instituted in the Suiko era (592–628 A.D.). Records have it that the Bon Festival was held in the third year of Emperor Saimei (657 A.D.), and in 650 A.D. the "Sūtra of Bon" was preached in temples in Kyoto as memorial services for expressing gratitude to the ancestors of the seven preceding generations. The Bon Festival with this new meaning added became widely practiced after this time, and is still practiced today, commonly known as *'O-bon'*

The system of memorial days and anniversaries was not a feature proper to Buddhism. Indian Brahminism, we know, teaches a form of ancestor worship, and the Brahmins conduct on new moon and full moon nights what is known as Ancestor Festival, but these festivals differ widely from the memorial days and anniversaries observed in memory of any specific ancestors. Buddhism does occasionally encourage ancestor worship, but it has never instituted a system of memorial days and anniversaries; it was devised by the Chinese. In China memorial services were held on the 49th Day, 100th Day, 1st Anniversary, and 3rd Anniversary. Immediately after the introduction of this system the Japanese, of the remote past observed the 49th Day, 100th Day and 1st Anniversary, leaving out the 3rd Anniversary. Many more anniversaries, however, were added later in the Middle Ages; namely, 3rd, 7th, 13th, 17th, 25th, 33rd, 60th, 100th, and 300th Anniversaries. This was essentially the same as the system of memorial days commonly observed today, viz. 49th day, 100th day, 1st, 3rd, 7th, 13th, 17th, 25th, 33rd and 50th Anniversaries.[21] Thus we may say that the system of memorial days and anniversaries was elaborated in Japan, the fact of which seems to attest to the dominance of ancestor worship among the Japanese.

We have already made mention of funeral service. Funerals and memorial services are the two most important functions of Buddhism in Japan of today. How much will be left of the activities of the Buddhist temple, if these are taken away?

---

1) The 'pillow-word' (*makura-kotoba*) '*chihayaburu*' ("greatly powerful") was prefixed, both to *kami* ("god") and *uji* ("clan"). This may be because the *uji no kami* ("clan head") was originally a god. There are a good many questions concerning the *ujigami* ("clan deity") which should be disccssed further, but I cannot go into them here.

2) Cf. Naoichi Miyachi 宮地直一: *Jingishi Taikei* 神祇史大系 (p. 24) "There are cases where the *ujigami* is not an ancestral god, as for example, the Isonokami Shrine of the Mononobe clan. Then, too, there are *ujigami* who were ancestral gods, two important examples of which are the worship of Amenokoyane-no-mikoto by the Nakatomi clan at the Hiraoka shrine in Kawachi province, and the worship of Futotama-no-mikoto by the Imibe clan at the Futotama shrine in Yamato province" (*ibid.* p. 25). Many points in connection with the clan system must unfortunately be omitted.

3) Tetsurō Watsuji 和辻哲郎: *op. cit. Sonnō Shisō To Sono Dentō* (pp. 46–47).

4) *Kokuminsei Jūron* 國民性十論 (pp. 51 ff.)

5) *Manyō-shū* 萬葉集 18

6) *Gempei Seisuiki* 源平盛衰記 21

7) *Ushiuma* 牛馬: *Suhajikami* 酢薑

8) *Sandai Jitsuroku* 三代實錄, under 16th day of the 10th month of the 2nd year of Jōkan (860 A.D.).

9) Kaoru Nakada 中田薰: "*Waga Taiko ni Tochi no Sonraku Kyōyūsei ya Kazoku Kyōsansei ga atta ka*" 我太古に土地の村落共有制や家族共產制があつたか in *Hōritsu Shimpō* 法律新報 No. 737, July 1947.

10) Based on a lecture delivered by Prof. Takeyoshi Kawashima at the first conference of the Oriental Culture Institute (Tōyō Bunka Kenkyūkai), November 8, 1947.

11) I am indebted to Prof. Noboru Niida for facts on the adoption of children in present day China.

12) Masatomo Manba 萬羽正朋: *Nihon Jukyō-ron* (日本儒教論 A Study on the Confucianism in Japan) p. 134, 188.

13) For example, the custom of *kaneoya* practiced in the vicinity of the city of Mishima in Shizuoka prefecture and in part of the Izu peninsula. *Kaneoya* (also known as *kanaoya*) means "the tooth-blackening parent". The name takes its origin from the fact that, at a wedding, someone was named *kaneoya* and presented the new bride with a tooth-blackening implement (Takeyoshi Kawashima 川島武宜, Toshitaka Shiomi 潮見俊隆: "Kaneoya ni tsuite" カネオヤについて in *Minzokugaku Kenkyū* 民族學研究, vol. 12, no. 1 p. 33 ff.)

14) One also finds such sentiments as "although the Perfect One desires to enter Nirvāṇa, a father cannot bear to cost his son into the flames and turn his back on him". (Shinshō Hanayama 花山信勝: *Hokke Gisho no Kenkyū* 法華義疏の研究 p. 480).

15) *Kyōdaishō* 兄弟鈔.

16) Hyōeshi-dono Gohenji 兵衛志殿御返事.

17) "One forgets his own body and soul, placing himself in the home of Buddha; one relies on the Buddha and follows him. Then, one uses no bodily strength, nor exercises power of mind, but separates from birth and death, becomes a Buddha."—*Shōbō Genzō* by Dōgen—

18) "With the Christian persecution of the Tokugawa period, the home Buddhist shrine spread throughout the country. Ikkō Believers call it the *naibutsu* (interior Buddha), which they worship in a thorough going manner. At the morning and the evening services, the religious sentiments of the children are nurtured, and their character trained. In the Ikkō sect in particular the image of Buddha or the Holy Name is central and the ceremonies honoring ancestral spirits are *an accretion due to the racial characteristics of the faith of Japan*". as quoted from Daijō Tokiwa 常盤大定: *Shina Bukkyō no Kenkyū* (支那佛教の研究 A Study on Chinese Buddhism) No. 3 p. 80.

19) "Home Buddhist chapels (*butsudan*) are peculiar to Japan, and are generally not found in China or Korea. They are an expression of the ancestor-worship of the Japanese race. ....I have not investigated in every part of China, but, from my own casual observation, I never saw a home chapel centered about the Buddha. From late reports we learn that there are Buddhist altars in the gardens of middle and upper class homes in Shansi and Meng-chiang. Whether these have the same significance as the Japanese *butsudan* is got to be investigated. I believe that the home Buddhist chapel centering about the Buddha may be a peculiarly Japanese phenomenon". (Daijō Tokiwa: *Nihon Bukkyō no Kenkyū* 日本佛教の研究 pp. 61–62). "Since there is nothing corresponding to them in Korea, it is probably safe to

assert that they are absent from the Korean tradition. [In China] in the homes of the gentry there are of course rooms in which the ancestors are worshiped, the question is whether such places are centered about the statue of the Buddha. Wherever you go, for instance, in niches at entrances, there are Taoist images, and there are also statues of Kuan-jin at appropriate spots in the house; but are there not quite apart from the worship of ancestral spirits?" (Daijō Tokiwa, op. cit. *Shina Bukkyō no Kenkyū* No. 3, pp. 80–81) The Chinese '*butsudan*' is a home alter, above which hangs a large colored triptych of the Buddha, the Law, and the Priesthood on a table in front are offered cakes, fruit and vegetables, but meat and fish are strictly prohibited. Here altars are adorned with a *dōban* (a part of banner used in Buddhist ceremonies). (de Groot: *Chūgoku Shūkyō Seido* 中國宗教制度, trans. by Kinzaburō Shimizu and Hakudō Oginome, vol. 1 p. 123). "In Tibet, even the poorest household, have *bustudan,* which are the center of the religious ceremonies of the family. *Butsudan* are placed in guest-rooms". (Tōkan Tada 多田等観: *Chibetto* チベット in Iwanami Shinsho, p. 59). However, in Tibet too they appear to have no special connection with ancestor worship.

20) *Tannishō* 歎異鈔.

21) Cf. Taijō Tamamuro 圭室諦成: *Nihon Bukkyō-shi Gaisetsu* 日本佛教史概説 p. 194.

(5) Emphasis on rank and social position

As we have already seen in the section dealing with the 'superseding of human relations over the individual', there is a tendency in the Japanese to lay emphasis upon rank and relations of master and servant, and this, we may say, is an inherent tendency in Japanese culture.

The language of the people, to begin with, evidences this tendency. The basic tenet of Buddhism—equality of man—was so changed as to fit with their tendency of thought.

The basic concept of social good is thought by Buddhism to be *to give* (or *dāna*). (This word *dāna* when translated into Chinese became *fuse* (or to serve widely)). Now, it was most difficult to find an equivalent of this word in Japanese. The Japanese words *ataeru* (to give) and *hodokosu* (to give in charity) denoted a giving action from a man of superior rank to a man of inferior rank. The words *sasageru* (to offer) and *tatematsuru* (to present), on the other hand, denoted the giving action in the reverse direction. In short, the Japanese were able to translate what is implied in *dāna* only in relation to social status.

Anukampā, another basic concept in Buddhism, was also difficult to translate. *Awaremi* (pity, compassion) would perhaps be the closest equivalent, but the word also implies a downward action from one superior to another inferior. The original meaning is no more than "to tremble in sympathy with another person", "sympathy". Here again, the hierarchal emphasis inherent in the language prevented the proper rendering of one of the basic concepts of Buddhism.

It seems that similar instances of Japanese emphasis of rank could be found in the earliest myths of the people. If we are to compare Japanese mythology with that of the Finnish people, we should be struck by the great difference existing between them. The first outstanding feature of Finnish mythology is the equality of social status of its various characters. In the tales of *Kalevala* we find that heroes have their slaves; but kings and priests do not appear as representatives of the ruling classes; gods are treated more or less on an equal plane, and heroes appear on an equal social level. Some of these heroes are fishermen, farmers, or smiths. Japanese mythology, in contrast, is, we may say, aristocratic, for deities and heroes appearing in the *Kojiki* and *Nihonshoki* are rulers of the masses; classes are seen already established.

The second feature we note in Finnish mythology is its lack of concern for lineage. The Finnish people have not, as the Japanese have done, made family ancestors of their mythical gods and heroes, however greatly they may have looked up to them. In contrast Japanese myths, the *Kojiki* and *Nihonshoki,* center around the Emperor, the Imperial family and the nobility as heroes, and these myths serve only to give prestige at the lineages of these families. We may suppose that Japanese myth is only a reflection of the social behavior of the ancient Japanese.

It was thus natural enough that Confucianism which laid stress upon a social order based on rank should have been widely accepted by the Japanese and it was natural also that other Chinese ideas that tended either to be individualistic or democratic should have been rejected by them.

It was probably after the time of Prince Shōtoku that Japan came to have what we may call culture; and it is interesting to note that the most important tenet in Prince Shōtoku's moral views was loyalty to the Emperor and to one's parents.[1] Judging from the Edict of Emperor Kōtoku (646 A.D.), the political ideals of the Taika Reform claimed to be based largely upon Confucianism.

Before Confucianism was adopted by the ruling class of the Tokugawa period as their official philosophy, its utility as the philosophical basis of politics had already been recognized by warrior-generals of the Civil War period. We might cite, for instance, General Oda Nobunaga's moral rule issued to the citizens of Kyoto in 1573 (4th year of Genki): "Those who are diligent in Confucian study in order to rectify the affairs of the state and those who are of loyalty and of filial piety should be esteemed and treated in distinction to others in all important matters such as gifts and the like".[2]

Thus in this time of national upheaval, Nobunaga accepted Confucianism as the guiding political philosophy. Continuing this tradition, the Tokugawa Shogunate Government publicly recognized Confucianism as the philosophical ground of centralized feudalism.

Yet, not all Confucians approved of the rank system existing in the feudal society of the Tokugawa period. Confucian Minowa Shūsai (1669–1744) of the Wang Yang-ming school, for instance, preached the complete equality of man. He said: "From the Emperor down to the petty warriors, Eta (pariah) and beggars, they are all men. From Sages down to men of mediocrity and outcastes, they are all men. The way of True Man is called the Way of Ancient Sage-King's Yao and Shun". At the same time, however, it is apparent from the following quotations from him that he did not completely object to the existing rank system: "Even beggars who are *not fit for* the Way of Man must not be neglected", or (concerning relief work) "We will not take a single man from villages where there are many beggars and outcastes".[3] No Confucianists ever raised strong objections to the feudal rank system.

Buddhists, we find, were not different from Confucians; they kept silence on, or even were not aware of, the basic doctrine of Buddhism, i.e. equality of the castes, denial of social disparity, which had been advocated since its origin. The substance of Buddhist thought was so transformed upon introduction from India as to suit the native stress of subordination. We note that it was in the spirit of repaying for Imperial and parental love that Buddhism came to be observed by the Japanese of the Suiko period. The following passage from *Nihonshoki* seems to endorse this fact: "The Emperor called in the Prince and the Ministers, and commanded them to promote Buddhism. Now court people and local chiefs vied with one another to erect the Houses of the Buddha, that is, temples, in order to reward the benevolence of Emperors and parents".[4] 'Loyalty to the Emperor and devotion to the parents', two concepts essentially alien to Buddhism, had to be attached to Buddhism so as to make it mean something to the Japanese.

This attitude persisted down the ages. We find Nichiren saying, at the beginning of his *Kaimokusho* ("A treatise to enlighten people"), "There are three persons everybody must respect, master, teacher, parent". This, we note, is the same as the Confucian idea of piety. However, if one abide strictly by the Confucian idea of piety, he cannot at the same time fulfill to satisfaction his piety toward all three. "One who does not know the past and the future will not be able to help the future life of his father and mother, his sovereign and his masters, and will be called an ungrateful wretch", said Nichiren, and asserted that one's piety toward the three superiors could only be accomplished by believing in the Lotus Sutra. Here Nichiren was attempting to explain Buddhism from the standpoint of a Confucian, or native, concept.[5] Further, we find him saying, "The Second volume of the Lotus Sūtra deals with the three important matters, the Sovereign, parents and masters. This is the heart of the Sūtra".[6] But contrary to Nichiren's explanation, we find no mention of piety toward the three superiors in the Second Volume of the Lotus Sūtra. What is figuratively explained there is that the merciful Buddha delivers the masses of people as parent brings up their children. (Parable of carts drawn by Sheep, Deer and Ox: Parable of the Rich Man's Stray Son). Neither Nichiren nor later scholars of the Nichiren sect have been able to cite exact words from the Lotus Sūtra that would serve to endorse a morality stressing class and rank distinction. What Nichiren and his followers had done was to *assume* that a book of Truth, such as the Lotus Sūtra, would advocate this kind of morality.

Now, let us here take up the question of 'sovereign' (*Kimi*).

As stated previously, Buddhism originally advocated caste equality, or equality of people. In books of early Buddhism little or no mention of the sovereign, whether it be a feudal lord or the king of a nation, is found. As a matter of fact in a great many Buddhist writings, kings are associated with robbers that harass the people with their brute force. It is easy to see therefore that the concept of equality in Buddhism would not only be incompatible with, but also threaten, the very existence of the Japanese national structure based upon the class and rank system. The government of Prince Shōtoku which made the fervent recommendation of Buddhism not only closely guarded the class and rank system in the Injunctions, but also introduced into their version of Buddhism a class and rank morality. A new idea of respect for a sovereign was created in their annotations of the Lotus Sūtra. While Chia-hsiang Ta-shih Chi-ta'ang or Kajō Daishi Kichizō (Sui Dynasty), listed under the heading of 'the Superiors' (in the Shōman Sūtra) master, father, elder brother and sister, Prince Shōtoku added to these categories *kimi* ("sovereign").[7]

Now what is meant by 'sovereign'? It is a ruler of subjects, or the chief of a limited, closed human nexus wherever subjugation by power prevails; it could therefore be an emperor. Reverence for a 'sovereign', therefore, could at once turn into rank-consciousness in a feudal society and emperor-worship in a nationalistic state.

The attitude of absolute devotion to the master wielded influence even upon doctrines of Japanese Buddhism. Nichiren taught that there must be only one master in a state, as in a family. Similarly, he said, there must be one sutra which is the master of all other Sūtras. His choice of the Lotus Sūtra rested upon the following reasoning: "In the world there are many who want to become powerful. But the sovereign of a country is only one. If there should be two, the land would not be peaceful. If there should be two masters in one family, it would certainly deteriorate. Concerning the complete canon of scripture, things should be the same. Only one sūtra, whatever it may be, would be the great sovereign of all the sūtras".[8]

Absolute devotion to a sovereign has constituted the basis of morality throughout Japanese history. The struggles of the Genji and Heike clans were not always motivated by hatred, or differences of interests or religious beliefs, but by devotion to the lord. In India the warrior's gallant death in the battle field was a source of admiration only in a religious sense. Valour in the minds of Japanese warriors was different. The exemplary attitude of the warrior is given in this quotation: "Besides this bond between lord and subject, we need nothing. We will not waver at all even by the advice of Sākyamuni, Confucius or the Sun God of Japan (Tenshō-Daijin) appearing before us. Let me fall into a hell, or let me be punished by gods; we will need nothing else than to be faithful to our lord".[9] Bushidō (the Way of the Warrior) with its most important motivation in the complete subordination to the lord was, as is well-known, largely endorsed by Buddhism, particularly Zen Buddhism. The ultimate aim of Zen practice became, among the warriors, devotion to the lord.

The Buddhist idea of the transmigration of the soul was also to be revised for the sake of the Japanese stress on the master-servant relationship. The common proverb, 'The parents-children relationship is good for one generation; the man-wife relationship for two generations; and the master-servant relationship for three generations' was a later creation in Japan. It was rather natural that Japanese Buddhist orders themselves came to be organized after the fashion of secular society; a complex system of rank was established in the orders. But, as already stated before, early Buddhism conceived all men to be equal. These ranks of monks were determined by the numbers of years of service; important affairs of the order were decided by majority (*yebhuyyasikā*). To realize the great difference existing between the Buddhisms of early India and Japan, we have only to recall that, before the introduction of Western civilization into this country, such a democratic procedure as decision by majority was something entirely undreamt of in Japanese Buddhist orders.

The most significant thing about the Japanese assimilation of Buddhism, however, was the fact that original Buddhist concepts tended to be altered, in the process of translation into simple Japanese made for infiltration among the common folk, to satisfy the native fondness of the rank system. The Japanese word *akirameru* (to resign oneself to . . . ; to give up) was derived, so it is explained, from the form *akirakani miru* (to see clearly) under the influence of Buddhist thought. The word, however, is used when one gives up one's desire that happens to run counter to the wishes of his superior. The Buddhist expression *inga wo fukumeru* (to elucidate the cause and effect of a thing) is used when one advises another to give up his desire and aspiration for the sake of his superior. What the phrase actually means is "to explain the wishes of the superior". Causal relation came to be explained in terms of the rank system. This rank system, however, the Japanese accepted as a "Divine Gift", and they were aware that their society greatly differed even from the society of ancient China. We find Nishikawa Joken (1658–1724) saying "In China customs are such that even sons of farmers and merchants can ascend to government positions. They may become premier and conduct the affairs of the state. They may rule the nation in such a way that the people are made happy. There is no piety greater than this. Sons of farmers and merchants thus apply themselves diligently to studies, and aspire to obtain government positions, and rise in the world. In our country, however, things are different. Although there have been many scholars since antiquity, none has risen from the common folk, none from the common folk has managed the affairs of the state".

With such a tendency of thinking prevailing, it was natural that the individual as a free and independent agent should never have been conceived by the Japanese till modern times. And it must be said that the retarded development of their cities was in part responsible for this. For there never came to exist in feudal Japan cities that were autonomous, possessing their own judicial powers. Unlike cities in China, Japanese cities were not residences of emperors; nor had they the import of a fort city controlled by a feudal baron; they were without administrative organizations of bureaucrats. Japanese cities were rather nothing more than densely populated areas controlled by warriors. Even after the Meiji Restoration, when cities expanded rapidly, their citizens did not come to possess the self-consciousness of European citizenry. And particularly noteworthy here was the fact that there was a constant flow of farming population in and out of the cities. This farming population continued to be bound by blood relation and economy to the farming village during its residence in the city; it was free to go back to the country if its subsistence in the city became difficult. This situation prevented the growth of public morals as well as the morals of the individual in the Japanese.

The retarded development of cities allowed the social order based upon feudal rank to continue. Any movement toward equalization arising from the masses would by and by be transformed into something else by the prevailing rank system. Take for example the cult of tea. The cult of tea had its place originally in the life of the great merchants of newly-risen cities of near-modern times as a canon of conduct, an ideal basis of living. It aimed to create the relation of host and guest, free of the rank system, in the current society, as we find it stated, "...not based on rank as in ordinary life". Before long, however, the ideal of the tea cult was transformed through a series of compromises and made to conform with the prevailing pattern of feudal society. We find the following words of tea masters: "By the practice of Tea-Ceremony morality beginning with that between lord and subject will be naturally carried to its highest expression" or "Warriors will conform to their own ways. City people will keep their families safe. Noble and low will be of use (in their own positions) and they will not hate the hierarchical order".[10] (Sekishū school)

The Zen Priest Suzuki Shōsan and his followers tried, through euphemistically publicizing anti-feudalistic views, to oppose the feudal morality based on rank, but their campaign had to wither away. Even the modernistic, rational thinker Miura Baien had to approve feudal morality; we find him saying: "There are many vocations—warrior, farmer, artisan, and merchant. All from the Emperor down to the masses aim to obey and realize Divine Providence. What one aims at should be the peace of the family and the state; *what one discriminates should be the relation of noble and low, intimate and remote*".[11] Baien's ethics was in the last analysis the ideal of the Wise Man.

It is then easy to understand why Christianity which condemned subservience to the monarch and parents had to confront persecution in this country; Christianity was thought to destroy the very foundations of social order. Christianity, or more specifically Catholicism in this case, contained within itself, no doubt, a number of elements of feudalism, being a religion that prospered during the feudal ages of Europe. But unlike Europe where monarchs themselves were Christians of Catholic faith, feudal lords in Japan had had almost nothing to do with Catholicism or Christianity. It was the incompatibility of Christianity and the native morality of self-dedication which resulted in the persecution of Christianity.

In this connection we note with interest the comments on the Christian Ten Commandments by Fabian, or "Apostate Brother (iruman)" in his book *Hadeusu* (Contra Deum): He says that with the exception of the First Commandment ("I am the Lord thy God...Thou shalt have none other gods before me"), the Commandments are the same as the Buddhist Five Commandments. Only the First Commandment is objectionable. For it tells one to defy one's lord and father in order to adore the Deus. It must be for the purpose of usurping our nation to spread such teachings.[12] Thus, in order to undermine Christianity, he adapts this point of view. "If one lives in this Land of the Rising Sun, one must follow the proper way, that is, to obey the Shōgun, the ruler of the country".[13]

And we also find the following criticism upon Christianity by Arai Hakuseki, one of the most progressive thinkers of the Tokugawa period: "It is the office of the Monarch to worship the Heaven. It is therefore immoral for all people, from nobles down to the common folk, to worship the Heaven, when each class has its own gods to worship".[14] Confucianism had ascended to dominance as the philosophical basis for the political structure of the society established by the warrior rulers. It was natural that Christianity which threatened the social order based on the rank system should meet the fate of persecution.

To the average Japanese accustomed to stressing rank the tests of a great religionist were his high birth and rank, not the truths he may reveal in his teachings and deeds. Modern historical research has shown that Shinran was not necessarily a member of the aristocracy, but an ordinary monk at Mt. Hiei whose family origin is obscure,[15] and we detect in his writings no proud consciousness of his origin. We have come to know that it was his followers who dressed him up to be of aristocratic origin. We thus find in *Shinran Den'e* ("Biography of Shinran") published in 1295 A.D., 34 years after his death, the following account regarding Shinran's origin:

"His secular name was Fujiwara. He, the son of Arinori, a court minister of the Dowager Empress, who was the fifth descendant of Arikuni, a Vice-Minister, who was the sixth descendant of Duke Uchimaro, a Vice-Premier, who was the grandson of the grandson of Kamatari the Premier, who was the twenty-first descendant of Amanokoyanenomikoto. Therefore he could have grown old in the service of the court, the peak of the priestly Emperor and lived a life of luxury. However, (he took orders...)". A text called *Gozokushō* by Rennyo in which Shinran's lineage is still more exaggerated is regularly recited at certain "thanksgiving service" held on the anniversary of Shinran's death.

As a matter of fact most biographies of Shinran written by the followers of the Honganji are characterized by this tendency to glorify his birth and we are again led to believe that Shinran's religion could not have spread among the Japanese had not his followers distorted the facts of his origin in order to appeal to the peculiar tendency of Japanese thought.

A similar situation exists, in an even more pronounced form, for Nichiren. Nichiren, as he himself humbly, or to be more exact, proudly, declared that he was "the son of a *Sendara* (Skrt. Caṇḍāla. despised outcaste)*",[16] "a son born of the lowly people living on a rocky strand of the out-of-the-way sea", "the son of a sea-diver*".[17] *Nichiren was proud of his lowly birth.*[18] The Nichiren sect, however, had to fabricate a noble lineage for him in order to attract more adherents from the common folk. We thus find in Nitchō's *Nichiren Daishōnin Chūgasan*[19] (published in the early Tokugawa period) the following passage about Nichiren's lineage: "Saint Nichiren's family name is Mikuni. His father was the second son Shigetada of Nukina no Shigezane, Lord of Tōtōmi Province. The Saint was the fourth son. *He was a descendant of Emperor Shōmu.* The Saint's father was exiled from Tōtōmi Province to the lonely sea-shore at Kominato, village of Ichikawa, Tōjō district, Nagasa country, in the province of Awa where he became a fisherman. The Saint's mother came from the (famous noble) Family of Kiyohara". The true import of Nichiren's advocacy that he was imparting the True Way in spite of his lowly birth—

and this was consistent with the traditional spirit of Buddhism—was thus forever lost. Today most biographies of Nichiren we find in circulation speak of him as descending from an aristocratic family, and indeed all representative and popular religious figures have thus been made up to be sons of the aristocracy or descendants of emperors.

One may, however, defend such practice by saying: "Is it not after all, only natural that religion tries to conform to some extent to the prevailing pattern of thought? Was it not natural that these things were so, since most feudal societies do place emphasis upon lineage and hereditary rank?" But let us remember that in the feudal society of India in the Middle Ages, Āḷvārs, Hindu revolutionary religionists, were sons of the lowliest folk, and people, nevertheless, looked up to them. In India religious authority out-weighed rank or lineage of the secular life; the caste system was in fact based upon religious belief. Likewise, the rank system of the Lama priesthood in Tibet, has nothing to do with secular rank and birth. Overstress of rank and lineage, therefore, is a feature, not unique to, but most pronounced, in Japanese thinking.

---

1) The first article of the Injunctions reads as follows: "Harmony is precious; obedience is most honored. Men all have their particular interests, and there are few enlightened ones among them. Consequently they may disobey their lords and parents, and quarrel with the neighboring villages. But when those above are harmonious and those below are well disposed, and there is accord in their discussions, then matters progress spontaneously. If this is the case, what is there which will not succeed?"

2) Masatomo Mamba 萬羽正朋; *op. cit.* p. 83.

3) *Ibid.*, pp. 226–227.

4) Under first day, *hinoe tora* of the 2nd month, spring, 2nd year of the reign of the Emperor Suiko (594 A.D.).

5) "In the *Kaimokushō* it is said: 'Those of all sentient beings who must be respected are three, such as master, teacher and parent'. I say, these three occur in Confucianism, both orthodox and heterodox. The purpose of this book *Kaimokushō* is to reveal the master-parent-teacher doctrine in Buddhism. Although the teaching of master-parent-teacher indeed does appear among Confucians and pagans, yet, when the Buddhist doctrine of master-parent-teacher is revealed, all these become as retainers, pupils and children. Therefore it is proper that the highest expression of the master-parent-teacher doctrine be found among Buddhists. It may be asked, what is the nature of this Buddhist doctrine of master-parent-teacher that you talk about: I answer, that is a further question, which I propose to deal with in due course". (Nitchō 日朝: *Kaimokushō Shikemmon* 開目抄私見聞, No. 1, in *Nichirenshū Shūgaku Zensho* 日蓮宗宗學全書 *Chōshi Gosho Kemmonshū* 朝師御書見聞集 no. 1, p. 191). There is also a work by Nichiren called *Shushishin Gosho* (Writings on Master-teacher-parent). On the question of the master-teacher-parent

doctrine in the Nichiren sect, see, for example, Chiō Yamakawa 山川智應: *Hokke Shisōshijō no Nichiren Shōnin* 法華思想史上の日蓮聖人 p. 643 ff.

6) *Shimoyama Goshōsoku* 下山御消息. He further says: "In my opinion, there are three authorities for the Japanese from the Emperor down to the masses of the people. These are first, parents, second, teachers, third, service of the lord". (*Shimoyama Goshōsoku*)

7) In the *jūdaijushō* of the Shōman Sūtra, there is this text: "From today until enlightenment, in the various situations where veneration and respects are due, do not be arrogant". The *Shōman-gyō Hōkutsu* comments, "Parents and teachers are to be venerated, elder brothers and sisters are to be respected". (*Taishō* vol. 37, p. 22 a). However, Prince Shōtoku in his commentary *Shōman-gyō Gisho* (vol. 1, p. 14 b) says, "three categories are to be venerated, those of the rank of elder brother are to be respected". In other words, whereas the *Shōman-gyō Hōkutsu* lists only 'parents and teachers' among those to be venerated, Prince Shōtoku mentions three, adding 'sovereign' to the traditional two. (Shinshō Hanayama 花山信勝: *Shōman-gyō Gisho no Kenkyū* 勝鬘經義疏の研究 p. 431).

Myōkū comments " 'Three caterogies are to be venerated' means sovereign, parent and teacher ...." (*Nihon Bukkyō Zensho* 日本佛教全書 edition, p. 11 b).

Gyōnen, citing the text of Myōkū, says "The sovereign and the other two categories are all to be venerated; all those of the rank of elder brother are to be respected" (*Shōgenki* 詳玄記 vol. 6, in *Nihon Bukkyō Zensho* 日本佛教全書 edition, p. 6 b). (Shinshō Hanayama: *op. cit.* p. 468, note 217).

8) *Hōonjō* 報恩抄

9) *Hagakurekikigaki* 葉隱聞書, no. 2 (*Iwanami Bunko* edition, p. 114).

10) Tetsubun Miyazaka 宮坂哲文: *Zen ni okeru Ningen Keisei* 禪に於ける人間形成 pp. 210, 221.

11) Hakuon Saigusa, 三枝博音: *Miura Baien no Tetsugaku* 三浦梅園の哲學 p. 530. See also pp. 301, 517.

12) Masaharu Anesaki, 姉崎正治 *Kirishitan Hakugaishichū no Jimbutsu Jiseki* 切支丹迫害史中の人物事蹟 p. 479. Also *Kirishitan Dendō no Kōhai* 切支丹傳道の興廢 p. 789 ff.

13) Masaharu Anesaki, 姉崎正治 *Kirishitan Dendō no Kōhai* p. 778.

14) *Ibid.*, pp. 782 ff. However, not all apostates from Christianity took their stand on the basis of the morality of rank. For example the *Hakirishitan* of Suzuki Shōsan does not bring up morality of rank but criticizes Christianity in a rational manner. However, such an attitude is quite exceptional in the Tokugawa period. (See also *Seiyō Kibun* 西洋紀聞 vol. 3).

15) Kemmyo Nakazawa 中澤見明: *Shijō no Shinran* 史上の親鸞. This work of pure scholarship has been refuted by Bunshō Yamada in his *Shinshūshikō* 眞宗史稿, but the fact remains that there are no materials which constitute positive proof that Shinran was the son of Hino Arinori.

16) *Sado Gokanki Shō* 佐渡御勘氣鈔

17) *Honzon Mondō Shō* 本尊問答鈔

18) Similar assertions are found elsewhere in the works of Nichiren. "Nichiren, in this incarnation, was born a poor and lowly man; he came forth from a family of Caṇḍāla" (*Sado Gosho*). "He who is born of a poor and lowly family' (prophesied in the Hatsunaion Sūtra) is I" (*Kaimokushō* 開目鈔 vol. 2).

19) *Kokubun Tōhō Bukkyō Sōsho* 國文東方佛教叢書; *Denkibu* 傳記部 pt. 1, p. 432.

(6) Problems of ultra-nationalism

The ultimate form in which the Japanese concept of emphasis upon a specific limited human nexus manifested itself was ultra-nationalism. Japanese ultra-nationalism did not suddenly appear in the post-Meiji period. Its beginnings can be traced to the very remote past.

The boast that Japan was the best country in the world has existed from very early times. It, no doubt, began at first in a love of the native country, pure and simple, without ambitions for expansion and conquest. Probably the earliest use of the word *'Dai Nippon'*, ("Great Nippon"), is found in some writings by St. Dengyō.[1] Dengyō, who had studied in China, was more keenly aware than his contemporaries of the fact that Japan's territories were smaller and her wealth and resources much more limited than China's. What Dengyō actually meant by "Great Nippon" was that Japan was a land most suitable to Mahāyāna Buddhism (Buddhism of the Greater Vehicle). Many Buddhists of later dates believed that Japan was the most superior land of the world, as we can see clearly in the following line from a poem by Ean, a Kamakura Zen monk:

> "To the end of the end of the ending generation will
> This land of Ours surpass all other lands."

The notion of Japanese superiority is most boldly expressed in the concept of Divine Nation. We find the following statement in the introductory manifesto of the *Jinnō Shōtō-ki* by Kitabatake Chikafusa, a Shintoist writer: "Our Great Nippon is a Divine Nation. Our Divine Ancestors founded it; the Sun God(dess) let her descendants reign over it for a long time. This is unique to Our Nation; no other nation has the like of it. This is the reason why Our Nation is called 'Divine Nation' " This concept of 'Divine Nation' is accepted in the Nō plays,[2] and Buddhists such as Nichiren adopted it. We find the following statements by Nichiren: "Japan is a Divine Nation",[3] "This Nation is a Divine Nation. Deities respond not to those lacking respect. Seven generations of Heavenly Deities, five generations of Earthly Deities, and a multitude of Good Deities support the Buddha's All-embracing Teachings".[4] A concept similar to this is found in Zen Buddhists. "Though Our Land is situated out of the Way, everlasting is its Imperial Rule, noble are its people. Thus Our Land surpasses others by far... This Land of Ours is pure and divine". This shows us that Hakuin, the Zen master respected Shinto concepts.

Confucianism, however, was the best system to provide a theoretical basis for the theory of ultra-nationalism. It will be remembered that Confucianism which the Chinese had earlier adopted as their official theory of state government was accepted by the Japanese with hardly any trouble. (The only controversial point, however, was the problem of 'changing unsuitable emperors'; even this, however, caused no special friction. This point will be discussed in the chapter dealing with 'emperor-worship'). When Confucianism was introduced into Japan, the ruling class took to studying it so that they could "become government officials and Confucians, and serve the country".[5] This attitude toward Confucianism was to persist among the ruling classes, and in the Tokugawa period Confucianism was taught with special reference to the concept of the state (*Kokutai*) by almost all the schools and individual scholars of Confucianism including Itō Jinsai, Yamaga Sokō, Yamazaki Ansai, and the Mito school.

We further note that Japanese Confucianism, associated with the ultra-nationalism or the authority-consciousness of the Japanese people, asserted its own superiority over foreign systems of thought. Kan Sazan, for example, declared:

"It is only because Confucianism exists that Buddhism is practiced here. If there had been no sovereign, those saints could not have acted independently. As it is said that Buddhism avoids countries with wicked monarchs, and as it is moreover said that the Benefit of the State is one of the Four Benefits, it is obvious that it (Buddhism) could not have been founded here if it were not for the influence of Confucianism... The Catholics, it is said, would willingly give their lives for their Deus. This is most outrageous. It is only because the Sovereign rules our land that we would go through fire and water in an emergency. Besides this, there are religions of many different kinds, called by various names, in different countries and generations. They may have different names, but they are all alike in practising the trick of setting up a master above the lord. It is most apparent that this is harmful to our political ideology".[6]

But, since the Confucian concept of the state was formulated in accordance with the needs of Chinese society, it naturally contained a number of points with which the more thorough-going of the Japanese nationalists could not agree. The state conceived by Chinese philosophers was an idealistic model state; on the other hand, the state that the Japanese nationalists had in mind was the actual Japanese state. This was the reason why Japanese nationalism nurtured, so to speak, by Confucianism had ultimately to deny the authority of Confucianism. Yoshida Shōin, the most influencial leader of the movement to establish the modern state of Japan, declares in his criticism of Confucius and Mencius: "It was wrong of Confucius and Mencius to have left their native states and to have served to other countries. For a sovereign and a father are essentially the same. To call one's sovereign unwise and dull, and forsake one's native state in order to find another sovereign in another state is like calling one's father foolish and moving from one's house to the next house to become the son of the neighbor. That Confucius and Mencius lost sight of this truth can never be justified".[7]

A similar tendency can easily be discerned in the process of assimilation of Buddhism; Japanese Buddhists carefully picked out such doctrines as would be convenient for, or not inconsistent with, their nationalism.

The attitude which Indian Buddhism assumed toward the State was, from the time of its origination, one of cautiousness. For instance, it placed monarchs in the same category with robbers, both were thought to endanger people's welfare, and it taught the people to avoid their dangers as much as possible. Indian Buddhists strived to realize, through their spiritual unity, an ideal society free of the authority of monarchs, and this was but the logical conclusion derived from their idea of Compassion. The *Saṅgha,* the collective body or brotherhood of followers, was the main agent for this cause.

Such a way of thinking was unacceptable to the Japanese according to whose realistic, nationalistic view the Japanese state was absolute, its sovereign, the emperor, was sacred. The traditional and conservative Buddhism of the primitive type came hence to be called the 'Lesser Vehicle' in Japan and looked upon with contempt; and the Buddhism which came to be called the 'Greater Vehicle' and which allowed the Japanese to pursue their religious ideals in conformity with their view of the state was adopted by them.

Nor did the Japanese accept the view of the traditional, conservative Buddhism of the early type that the State originates in a social contract. The concept of state as held by early Buddhists was as follows:[8] Farmland was divided among individuals in remote antiquity, but there still existed individuals who encroached upon the properties of others. To prevent this sort of thing, the people elected a common head ("an equal leader") who would see to it that the people are protected, good people rewarded, evil people punished. The sovereign originated from this. A tax was "something that was paid" to the sovereign by the people; the sovereign was "employed" by the people.[9] The sovereign thus was "the selected master of the people". This concept of sovereignty was afterwards held persistently by the traditional and conservative schools of Buddhism.

It is to be noted that scriptures of primitive Buddhism tell of the Buddha Śākyamuni praising the republic of the Vajjis as the ideal state form.[10]

But the Japanese who accepted Buddhism on a large scale refused nevertheless to adopt its concept of the state which to them appear to run counter to the native idea of 'state structure' (*Kokutai*). We thus have a writer like Kitabatake Chikafusa who was ready on the one hand to accept Buddhism in general but was eager on the other to emphasize the importance of the Japanese Imperial Family in the following way: The Buddhist theory (of state) is merely an "Indian theory"; Indian monarchs may have been "the descendants of a monarch selected for the people's welfare", but "Our Imperial Family is the only continuous and unending line of family descending from its Heavenly Ancestors".[11] Hirata Atsutane on the other hand discredits the whole Indian theory of the origin of the state as mere explanation of the origin of "Indian chieftains".[12]

The Sūtra *Konkōmyō-kyō* (*Suvarṇaprabhāsa-sūtra*) and some later scriptures of Mahāyāna Buddhism, unlike those of early Buddhism, advance a theory that a monarch is 'a son of divine beings' (*Tenshi, devaputra*) to whom has been given a mandate of Heaven, and whom Heaven will protect. This theory which came greatly to be cherished had had its origin in the Brahmin law-books which regulated the feudal society of mediaeval India. Later Buddhists came to mention this theory merely as a prevailing notion of society. It was not characteristic of Buddhism. However, this idea came especially to be stressed by the Japanese.

Buddhism thus was accepted by the Japanese as significant for the support of the state. The spread of Buddhism in this country began, as is well known, with the presentation by a Korean monarch (of Paikche) Seimei to the Japanese Emperor Kimmei in 552 of a gilded bronze image of Śākyamuni, several religious flags, umbrellas and several volumes of the sūtras. It is particularly notable here that the adoption of Buddhism was begun in the diplomatic relations between nations, or more specifically, in the relations between the Imperial Family and a foreign country. The situation here differs widely from the acceptance of Buddhism by Later Han Emperor Ming-ti from the Yüeh-chih. In Japan a state-to-state relation brought about adoption of a universal religion. According to the *Hihonshoki*, King Seimei, King of Paikche, attached to his gifts a letter, a passage from which reads as follows:

"The doctrine (of the Buddha) is the most excellent of all the various doctrines. It is difficult of comprehending and entering. Even Chou Prince and Confucius were not able to know it. This doctrine brings about boundless virtue and happiness, thus, giving the highest salvation".

"When the Emperor learned of it, His joy was great. Summoning the Ambassador, He said: 'We have never heard to this day a doctrine as wonderful as this". These passages in the *Nihonshoki* are in fact, as scholars[13] have pointed out, a fabrication based upon passages from the Sūtra *Konkōmyō Saishō-Ō-kyō* translated by I-ching and the Sūtra *Konkōmyō-kyō* translated by Dharmarakṣa. I-ching translated this Sūtra into Chinese in 703, some 151 years after the 13th year of Kimmei (552). The above-mentioned letter of Paikche's King is in fact a pure fabrication by the author of the *Nihonshoki* based upon the *Konkōmyō-kyō,* and it is quite uncertain to what degree it conveys the true content of the letter of King Seimei. But what interests us here is the fact that significance of the adoption of Buddhism was understood by the Japanese, or, at least, by such court scholars as the author of the *Nihonshoki,* in accordance with the thought expressed in the *Konkōmyō-kyō.*

The Sūtra *Konkōmyō-kyō* as distinguished from other scriptures of Mahāyāna Buddhism contains considerations for protection of the State and references to earthly Shamanistic practices. Shamanism will be discussed later; we shall therefore examine here its ideas regarding the protection of the State. It is evident from the preceding references to the purpose of adoption of Buddhism that considerations for protection of the State constituted a factor dominant in Japanese Buddhism from the very beginning.

The memorial tablet of the Sakas, north-Western Indians, tells us that the Sakas cherished already in the first century B.C. the view that Buddhism manifests its divine influence for the welfare and prosperity of a monarch or state. A certain Patika, a relative of the chieftain (Kṣatrapa), it is said, erected in Taxila in the heart of North-Western India a stūpa, and a building for a religious order (*Saṅghārāma*) "for all the Buddhas, and in memory of my parents and for the long life and power of the Kṣatrapa, his wife and children". The lion-bearing capital discovered at Mathurā also tells us in inscription that the column is dedicated to the Three Precious Things (The Buddha, the Law and the Priesthood), as well as the Saka state (Sakastana=Śakasthāna). The inscription found on the small stūpa erected by a lady Buddhist, by the name of Bhadravala, in the 134th year of the Azes era also states, "This is dedicated to all sentient beings and the City-State (raṭhanikama=rāṣṭranigama)".[14] Such a view regarding the state came to be theorized in numerous scriptures of Mahāyāna Buddhism, and it was from these that Japanese came to have their ideas concerning state protection.

In Japan Buddhism came to be propagated as a national religion during the reign of the Empress Suiko in accordance with Article II of Prince Shōtoku's Injunctions which enjoins "reverence to the Three Precious Things". With the political and economic aids from the state Japanese Buddhism became very active. After the Political Reform of Taika, the state's control over religions became gradually solidified. With the decline in influence of the clan aristocrats, now made bureaucrats, the government abandoned its vague protection of Buddhism as a whole and the attempt to convert it to a State religion. Instead, it adopted as a basic religious policy the positive protection of pure State Buddhism alone which would cooperate in the overall task of government. Thus the protection of Buddhism was strengthened and the government not only furnished emergency building funds, but did not hesitate even to provide vast sums for running expenses.[15]

Most Japanese monasteries in those early days were thus state-operated places of worship. As it is clear in the Rescript of the Emperor Shōmu (first day of the fourth month, 749 A.D.) which states, "Now, We, hearing that of all the various doctrines the Great Word of the Buddha is the most excellent for protecting the State...",[16] Buddhism was adopted by the Court with the first regard for the protection of the State, and indeed, the most profound and difficult doctrines of Buddhism were studied for this purpose. In the Nara period the Kegon Sect which put forward a philosophy regarded as the highest of Buddhist philosophies came to be given the position of a national religion. A Rescript of the Emperor Shōmu (749 A.D.) states, 'We consider the Kegon Sūtra to be the most authoritative Scripture'. The Tōdaiji, the Kokubunji of the Capital, was also known as the Dai-Kegonji, or Great Kegon Temple. Then, what in the Kegon Sect appealed so to the Japanese as to win for it the position of a state religion? According to the scriptures of the Kegon sect, each petal of the thousand-petalled lotus flower upon which the Vairocana Buddha dwells represents a universe, and in each universe there are millions of *jambudvīpa* (these actual human worlds). In each universe of a lotus petal is a Śākya-Buddha which is a manifestatio nof the Variocana Buddha, and in each of the millions of *jambudvīpa* is a small preaching Buddha which is, in turn, a manifestation of Sākya. Such symbolism was most suitable for the requirements of the State. For it was thought that the officials of the government should be manifestations of the state, as Śākya-Buddhas on the petals are manifestations of Vairocana, and the people should be manifestations of the government official, just as Small Buddha of *jambudvīpa* are manifestations of Śākya-Buddha. As long as there is harmony among the state, the government officials and the people, as in the cosmology of Kegon, there will be peace in the land, and the nation will be safe.[17]

The minds of the Buddhists of the time were adjusted to the government religious policies based upon this cosmology. Zenju, great and celebrated scholar, of Akishino Temple in the Nara Period, asks in the Introduction of his *Hongan Yakushi-Kyō* Sho ("Commentary upon the *Bhaiṣajya-guru-vaiḍūrya-tathāgata-sūtra*"), "Unless it be by repenting one's sins with a holy heart and seeking the Commandments with sincerity, how else ought one to repay for the benevolence of the sovereign and express thanks for his goodness?" And he hopes ceremonies of repentance and reception of the commandments will be conducted in order to "abide by the Great Desire of the Sovereign, and compensate for the favors of the State". And he further hopes that through these good deeds all kinds of calamities will be eliminated; "The Imperial body will be as steady as Heaven and Earth; the Imperial life be as everlasting as the sun and moon; the Imperial Family will prosper for a thousand and myriad generation; next, peace will reign in the land; all government officials will be loyal to the throne; the people of all walks of life will be happy; all merits accumulated by sincere actions in body, speech and mind would be turned over to that effect".[18] Here, beyond doubt, the first object of Buddhist prayer, i.e., 'happiness of all sentient beings', has now been 'supplanted' by 'prosperity of the Imperial Family'; Buddhist thought *has been altered to suit the rank system prevailing in Japan.*

'Protection of the state', one of the most dominant concerns in the Japanese mind, was thus firmly established in religion. Buan of the Ritsu sect, a staunch believer in discipline and the precepts of Buddhism, declares: "The Precepts are the basic and most important thing which promises attainment of Nirvāṇa and Salvation". "Therefore, Precepts (*śīla*) make up a small ship for crossing the sea of sufferings; discipline (*Vinaya*) is the only vehicle for attaining the Other Side. It is clear, therefore, that discipline is most important for the protection of the State".[19]

The situation was similar in the case of the Tendai sect and Shingon sect, which are known as the Buddhism of the Heian period. Saichō or Dengyō Daishi, in founding the Enryakuji Monastry, selected the site on Mt. Hiei which was in the Ox-Tiger direction (Northeastern direction) from the Palace. This was done with the idea of protecting the Palace. Here his efforts were exerted to the training of monks who were sincere seekers of the truth, and he called these sincere novices 'treasures of the nation'. His purpose in training these young Buddhist scholars was to 'uphold the Buddhist Doctrine and protect the State'.[20] We find in his works, say, *Kenkairon* ("Elucidation of Discipline") or *Shugokokkaishō* ("Treatise for Protecting the Domain of the Country"), such phrases as 'Shugokokkai' (Protection of the Country), 'Gokoku' (Protection of the nation) 'Gokoku Rimin' (Protection of the state and benefiting people), 'Kokka Yōko' (State Forever), 'Kokka Annei' (Peace and prosperity for the State), etc. Kūkai, or Kōbō Daishi, who frequently practiced prayers at the Court, said he was doing this for the benefit of the State. Kūkai, moreover, had his special names for temples; for example, 'Kyō-ō Gokokuji' (The temple to teach kings how to protect the nation) for the Tōji and 'Jingokokuso Shingonji' (The Temple of Esoteric Buddhism to protect the national fortune by grace of gods) for the Takaosanji.

'Protection of the State' was not the slogan only of the early Buddhist sects, merely in an attempt to curry favor with the state authorities. For we find the same concern in the official documents record of the state which constitute the authoritative history of Japan. Kūkai propagated Buddhism under the slogan, "Practice virtue for the State, and thus benefit man and gods".[21] Shinnen said that Kūkai built the Kongōbuji 'to safeguard the nation and protect the Law of Buddha'.[22] In the Rescript of the Emperor Nimmyō we find it said: "The Buddhist Doctrine is the foremost and the most excellent for protecting the state and benefitting the people".[23] It was in order to "compensate for the August Goodness and protect the State" that Shinshō Risshi erected the images of the

Vairocana and the Buddhas of the Four Directions.[24] The *raison d'etre* of the Enryakuji lay in the "Protection of the Imperial Family".[25] It was also to "protect the State and promote the August Throne" that the monks of the Anjōji adopted the *tendoku* (skip) method of reading the Sūtras of various sects.[26] In his address to the Throne Ennin says, "With all our efforts we will propagate it, thereby protecting the State, benefiting the masses and repaying for the favors of our teachers".[27] Jōan Risshi is said to have said: "The work of copying Sūtras will be done in order to protect the State".

Concerns for protection of the state are seen also in newly-risen sects of the Kamakura period. In the field of newly imported Zen Buddhism we find Eisai writing his *Kōzengokokuron* (A Treatise on Protecting the Nation by Spreading Zen Buddhism).[28] There were at that time the Six sects of Nara, the Tendai and Shingon sects already established as state-authorized religious schools, and for a rising sect it was necessary to stress its concern for protection of the state in order to be made one of them. Such a motive is apparent in such works as *Nihon Bukkyō Chūkō Ganmon* ("A prayer to make Japanese Buddhism prosper again") or *Kōzen Gokokuron.* The full names of the Nanzenji in Kyoto and the Kenchōji in Kamakura are respectively, 'Zuiryūzan Taiheikōkoku Nanzenzenji' (A Temple to make the country peaceful and prosperous) and 'Kofukusan Kenchō Kōkokuzenji'. Kōshōji in Uji which Dōgen founded upon his return from China was called 'Kannon Dōri-in Kōshōgokokuji' (A Temple to protect a nation by propagating the Holy Practice)[29] Soseki erected the Ankokujis (Temples to make the nation peaceful) in different provinces, and, there are the Gokokujis (Temples to protect the nation) throughout his country.

Now, in China, it was the rise of the Mongols that stirred state consciousness in Zen schools of the Southern Sung Dynasty, and this attitude of Chinese Zen schools was, no doubt, reflected in the Japanese Buddhism of the Kamakura period. But significant here is the fact that while in China state consciousness was soon to wither away, it persisted in Japan down to recent times.

The concern for the state, as an idea, however, did not belong logically to the doctrines of most sects. It was with the Nichiren Sect that it came to constitute an essential motive. To understand this situation we have only to observe what position it is given in Nichiren's work, *Risshō Ankokuron* ("A treatise to establish righteousness and to make the country peaceful"). Religion, according to Nichiren, must serve the state. He said: "Thirteen Thousand Thirty-seven Buddhist temples and three thousand one hundred thirty-two Shintō shrines are revered for the sake of the safety of the state".[30] To him the existence of the state was the prerequisite for the flourishing of Buddhism. He says, again: "The Nation prospers because of Buddhism; and Buddhism becomes precious because people revere it. If the Nation perish and people disappear, who will revere Buddhism? Therefore, say prayers first for thy State, then presently Buddhism will be established". Again: "If there be no fall of the State and no destruction on Earth, thy body will be safe, thy mind will be at ease".[31]

And his first and last concern was Japan. In his Commentary on the Lotus Sūtra, (in the 5th chapter, *yakusōyubon*) he cites the passage, "The Buddha appears in the world", and says, "By 'world' Japan is meant". He also cites a passage which reads: "And this personage came to the world", and comments, "This personage is the Bodhisattva Jōgyō (Viśiṣṭacāritra). The 'world' is Japan..... It is a person like Nichiren of the present". He, again, interprets the passage in the commentary by Myōraku Daishi, "When the son propagates the teachings of his father, it is beneficial to the world", in the following way: "By the 'son' are meant the Bodhisattvas who are said to have appeared from the earth when the Hokke Sūtra was preached; By the 'father' is meant Buddha Śākyamuni. By *the world is meant Japan.* The 'benefit' was becoming a Buddha".[32] Now, what Indian Buddhists meant by the word 'World' (or *lokadhātu*) was the area on which the light of the sun and moon shines, i.e., the four Continents around Mt. Sumeru. But Nichiren narrowed this 'world'—the world that is eventually to attain salvation on the strength of the Lotus Sūtra—to Japan.

In the case of the Pure Land (Jōdo) Sect, however, there was comparatively less state-consciousness. Since Hōnen, for instance, was not concerned with state structure (*kokutai*) the Pure Land doctrines were therefore disapproved until recently by a group of ultra-nationalist philosophers. Indeed, the state was not a thing of great concern in the minds of Hōnen or Shinran. But as the Jōdo Sect broadened its sphere of influence, it became necessary, in order to protect itself from the onslaughts from without, to compromise with ultra-nationalists. In the sequel we shall briefly examine the case of the Pure Land (Jōdo) sect,

Shinran, the founder of the True Pure Land (Jōdo Shin) sect held no particular view regarding the state. His only concern was the relation between the sinful mortal, such as he himself was, and Amida Buddha who is the Saviour. Shinran apparently had no thought of compromising with secular authority. But as the True Pure Land (Jōdo Shin) sect spread among the people through the efforts of such a man as Rennyo, its attitude toward the contemporary feudal authority became one of compromise. We see Rennyo saying: "Now you should in no wise neglect your duties to Constables (*shugo*), of provinces or Stewards (*jitō*) of local communities on the grounds that you revere the Law of Buddha and are believers. Indeed you should all the more devote yourselves to public affairs. Thus you will be pointed out as men who know what you are about, and will be the basis of the conduct of the *nembutsu* believer who had faith and who prays for future happiness. That is to say, you will be looked up to as men who make a point of keeping both the Law of Buddha and the Law of the Sovereign".[33] Ren'nyo also admonishes: "Bear in thy head the Law of the Sovereign; bear deep in thy heart the Law of the Buddha".[34] The True Pure Land (Jōdo Shin) Sect developed this idea, and brought out the dualistic theory of Truth. Originally the Buddhist *paramārtha-satya* (Jap. *shintai*) meant Absolate Truth, whereas samvṛti-satya (Jap. *zokutai*) mean a lower order of truth. The meaning of these terms were altered by the Shin sect, so that *shintai* represented the Law of Buddha and *zokutai* the Law of the Sovereign. This gave the solution to the problem of the two conflicting authorities.

In the Meiji era after feudatories had collapsed and the central authority had been established, great stress came to be placed upon the sanctity of the Emperor, and the Honganji Order came to adopt the ethics of nationalism. And we find the following passage in Kōnyo's *Goikun Shōsoku* (A letter written by the late chief abbot") dated the Fourth Year of Meiji (1871) and made public by Myōnyo in the following year:

"There is no man born in this Empire who has not benefit from the Imperial Favor. At this time especially, when His majesty devotes himself night and day to the furtherance of good government and the safety of his people at home and to holding his own with countries abroad, who among us, whether priest or layman, will not aid the spread of his kingly rule and cause the Imperial authority to shine with its true brilliance? What is more, since the spread of Buddhism in the world is due solely to the protection of the Sovereign and his ministers, how can the faithful Buddhist neglect the prohibitions of the Law of the Sovereign? Therefore in our sect it has already been resolved that the Law of the Sovereign would be fundamental, that benevolence and justice would be foremost, that the gods would be revered and morality observed".

Buddhist scholars, upon mentioning Shinran, are wont to argue that Shinran did have concern for the state, and they invariably cite the one single passage as evidence. That is the letter that Shinran wrote to Shōshimbō. Shinran writes:

"It would be a happy thing if all the people who recite the *nembutsu,* recite it not for the sake of their own welfare but for the Sovereign and the people. But those who are uncertain of reaching Paradise, let them recite the *nembutsu* for their own rebirth in Paradise. But I think people who are certain of attaining Paradise should bear in mind the Buddha's mercy, and, in order to repay their mercy, with all their heart recite the *nembutsu* for peace among the people and the propagation of Buddhism".

Now obviously this is not a logical piece of writing. If we were to examine it objectively, we find that the first and second sentences are related to each other antonymously in form and ironically in content. What Shinran is saying here is that happy are the people who are able to say the *nembutsu* for the Sovereign and the people, for their attainment of Paradise has been assured, and so let them do so. But, he says, those who in their self-reflection are uncertain of attainment of Paradise—that is, those who are Shinran's followers—should recite the *nembutsu* in order to attain their own salvation. I think that what Shinran is advocating here is not that the Sovereign be considered as the paramount concern but rather that faith be considered most important.[35]

Surprising enough, however, this passage by Shinran was hitherto grossly misinterpreted. Japanese scholars in most cases believed that Shinran was here *teaching nationalism.* Through misinterpreting the words of the very founder, the present leaders of the sect compromised ultra-nationalism and its leaders of the military clique and were thus, able to mitigate their attacks. (In the case of Hōnen not a single reference to the state is found; this was the ground for ultra-nationalists' criticisms of Hōnen.)

We note with interest here that of the numerous scriptures that exist in Buddhism those which were thought to have state-protecting efficacy were especially favored, the Lotus Sūtra, the *Konkōmyokyō* and the *Ninnō hannyakyō* being just such. The Lotus Sūtra itself, however, embodies no thought for 'state-safety'; on the contrary, it teaches that the true devotee of Buddhism 'remains at a distance from monarchs and state ministers'.[36]

But if we were to look for the part in the Sūtra which led the Japanese to link their concern for state-safety with the Lotus Sūtra, we shall find it to be the part in which it is stated that if things are carried out in accordance with the Lotus Sūtra, there shall be peace and happiness in the world.

As an example, Kusunoki Masashige was a believer in the Lotus Sūtra. In the colophon of a Lotus Sūtra (in the library of the Minatogawa Shrine), copied by his own hand, he says:

"The Hokke Sūtra is the essence of all the doctrines preached by the Buddha, and the heart of the One Vehicle. Therefore all spiritual leaders in the past, present and future, regard it as the true purport of their birth, and eight kinds of divine beings regard it as the authority for protection of the country. Especially, the capacity of this country for the fullness of the Mahāyāna doctrine is great and the august of the Ise Shrine will protect us and answer our prayers. This fact is fully written down in clerical histories. I, who have been ordered by the Emperor to destroy the rebels, have made this vow; if peace come to the world and what is my heart be granted, one chapter of this sūtra will be read every day before the god in this shrine. So I have made a copy of it by myself and fulfilled my long-cherished desire. On the 25th of the 8th month of the 2nd year of Kemmu (1335 A.D.).

(Signed) Kusunoki Ason Masashige, Major General of the Left Palace Guard and Governor of Kawachi.[37]

We are also told in the *Taiheiki* that Emperor Godaigo passed away "with the fifth scroll of the Lotus Sūtra in his left hand and a sword in his right".[38]

The same attitude is noticeable in the way the teachings of the *Avataṃsaka* (*Kegon*) *Sūtra* are observed by the Japanese. The Sūtra describes the ideal monarchical government. It contains, at the same time, a number of passages where it is admonished that monarchs and princes should forsake their states and become Buddhist ascetics.[39] Nevertheless, in Japan of the Nara period the Sūtra was considered to be a philosophy that promised the prosperity of the state. Behind the great efforts exerted for the casting of the Colossal Buddha of Nara was this understanding. And although there is clear evidence of state-consciousness in the Sūtras *Konkōmyō-kyō and Ninnō Hannya-kyō*, this is not an ultra-nationalistic state-consciousness. According to these Sūtras, the eternal and universal *dharma* is the only way upon which we may rely; this is the doctrine of the Perfect Wisdom (*prajñāpāramitā, Hannyaharamitsu*) which enlightens us on the true human conduct, and only through the application of the Perfect Wisdom doctrine to the activities of the state, will the state be protected and prosperous. Thus the state is not regarded as absolute. On the contrary it is emphasized that a state wherein the Law is not observed will perish. But the Japanese, inclined to nationalism, found these sūtras particularly agreeable and adaptable.

The notion that Buddhism protects the state spread eventually among the warriors and the common people. In the period, known as the Age of Northern and Southern Dynasties, when Kyushu rose to assist Ashikaga Takauji, the clan of Kikuchi Taketoki alone sided with the Southern Court. When Kikuchi Taketoki erected a temple in Tamana-gun, Province of Higo, and received the Zen Monk Daichi Zenji as head of the temple, he presented a dedicatory adress of which the following is the final part; "If the principles contained in this address are carried out, and the True Law observed with pure faith we shall receive the unseen protection of the Three Treasures and various Deities; our descendants for generations to come shall live up to the warrior ideals of our family, and be able *to protect the prosperity of our State.* I therefore shed my own blood, mix it with cinnabar ink, and present this address sealed therewith to admonish my descendants".[40)]

Emphasis upon the state is noticeable even among Buddhists who were in close touch with the common folk. For example, we find in Jiun's *Regulations of the Kōkiji* an article which enjoins "Sincerity and diligence in praying for the State".[41)]

We find the case of a state assuming the character of a religious order in ancient Greece, and we also know that the religious order of Sikhism in India took on the character of a state. In Japan, however, religion was thought to constitute the foundation of the state, and the state would be protected by it. Just as Buddhism was thought to contribute to the government of the state, so, at the lower level, it was regarded as contributing to the government of the *feudatory* fief. As has been frequently pointed out, the world-outlook of Zen Buddhism underlies the spirit of the so-called 'Hagakure' warriors of the Saga clan in Kyūshū. The intention to assist clan politics with Buddhism is expressed in the *Gohōshijiron* (five or ten volumes) by Mori Shōken of the Mito clan.

As we have pointed before, there was hardly any political coloring or emphasis on the state, in religions in India. And in ancient China, too, it was observed that "A monk will not respect the monarch". But in the Liu Sung dynasty (420–478) monks did come to "respect the monarch". And although in the end Chinese religion became subordinated to the state, state-consciousness was never stressed by Buddhists themselves. In Japan, however, Buddhism, which is a universal religion, was adopted and spread as a religion serving the interests of the state.

We are now ready to draw some conclusions from the above examination of Japanese nationalism, and this we must do with some reservations. For religion, with which we have mainly been dealing, is merely one of many facets of culture. The outstanding features of Japaneese nationalism, however, may be summed up as follows:

The Japanese people of the past dedicated a large and important part of their individual life to their state. In this respect, the Japanese went to the extent to which no other Eastern peoples have ever gone. The size of such dedication is itself the first feature of Japanese nationalism.

The second feature is that Japanese nationalism was developed from the concern for the particular state of Japan. Now, there are different ways in which nationalism is applied to practice. We know that nationalism has a number of times been expounded by thinkers in India and China, as well as in the West. But their nationalism was theoretically concerned with the state in general, not with their particular states. Now, nationalism tends, from its very nature, to be applied to a state in particular, but nationalism and a particular state are thought separately. In India and China nationalism is theoretical. In Japanese nationalism, on the other hand, the particular state of Japan came to be the sole standard upon which all judgments were based. This, without doubt, has close relation to the general tendency in Japanese thinking, especially in the past, to overlook the universal and to lay stress upon an exclusive human nexus. The natural basis for Japan's exclusive concern for herself is, I believe, the insular position of Japan, isolated from the Continent by water. The Japanese have only rarely experienced the real fear of alien peoples; they have known the existence of foreign nations only indirectly, except in the cases of the Mongolian Invasion and the World War II.

The dominance of the state over individual life was, in a sense, a condition extremely favorable for Japan's making a start as a modern state, if only in form, in the Meiji era. One imagines that it would have been difficult for her to become the modern state that she is today so quickly, were it not for the strong consciousness its people has had for the state. As the modern history of the West has shown, the formation of the state is a necessary condition for the active progress of races.

Japan, in this sense, may be said to have been more favorably conditioned for modernization than other nations of the East which were not so unified.

Certain apprehension may here be felt by some. They may ask: Is not Japanese state-consciousness already a thing of the past? Is she not being rapidly modernized? Has not the experience of defeat in the World War II brought the Japanese people to consider themselves as individuals that make up their society, and who participate in the sovereignty of the State, rather than are 'subjects' of the emperor? We are, however, inclined to give only a 'tentative' yes to these questions. For although it is true that changes are being made in that direction, it is also true that it is no easy task for the Japanese to do away with their inherent thinking. We must remember that the country is overflowing with people. *The network of tightly-formed village communities cover the land.* The nation's economy is such that the state must still exercise controls over a large portion of individual life. Above all, from great antiquity the nation's progress has always had its motivation in the Imperial Family, although it is now not so powerful as before. Furthermore, we may say that the Japanese sentiment toward the Imperial House has been friendly rather than hostile, as in some foreign countries and the ruling class were often quite benevolent in their dealings with the people.[42] All in all we may say that an atmosphere of family-like intimacy pervaded the country. (Such a term as 'family state', for instance, would have been rejected by the Westerners, and even by the Indians, or the Chinese, as self-contradictory. The Japanese, however, felt no inconsistency in the term, but found it good and valid.) Now, in view of these, would it really be possible to put an end to the Japanese way of thinking about the State? This is not something we can take pride in before other nations. But, just as religion was the basis of the ethical thinking of the Indians, family the basis of the practical morals of the Chinese, so the state was the basis of all thought in the Japanese. The Indians will be Indians; the Chinese will be Chinese, and we do not look down upon them or criticize them for it. The Japanese way of thinking is undergoing a change, but their thinking is an inheritance; it is a tradition. We feel that it is our part to see to it that this tradition never again gives rise to an inhuman ultra-nationalism.

---

1) Zennosuke Tsuji 辻善之助: *Nihon Bunka to Bukkyō* (日本文化と佛教 Japanese Culture and Buddhism) p. 56; Shōson Miyamoto 宮本正尊: *Chūdō Shisō*

oyobi sono Hattatsu (中道思想及びその發達 The thought of the Middle Path and its development) p. 904.

2) "New, Great Nippon is the land of the gods. The gods come out from Paradise and assume the form of local manifestations of the Buddha. Naturally this should be the land where the Law of Buddha is most wide spread". (Sakahoko 逆矛).

3) *Gassui Gosho* 月水御書.

4) *Hōjō Tokimune ni Atōru Sho* 與二北條時宗一書.

5) *Kanke Bunsō* 菅家文草 vol. 3 (*Kitano Bunsō* 北野文叢 vol. 2, p. 24 in *Kitano-shi* 北野誌)

6) Kan Sazan 菅茶山, *Fuyu no Hikage* 冬の日影 1 (in *Nihon Jurin Sōsho* 日本儒林叢書, *Kaisetsu-bu* 解說部 vol. 2, pp. 9–10).

7) *Kōmō Tōki* 講孟劄記 vol. 1 (in *Yoshida Shōin Zenshū* 吉田松陰全集 vol. 2, p. 263).

8) This account is based principally on the *Jōagon-kyō* 長阿含經 vol. XXII. (*Seki-kyō* 世記經, *Honen-bon* 本緣品 vol. 12). But similar notices are scattered through various scriptural texts. *Jōagon-kyō* vol. VI. *Shōen-kyō* 小緣經 (*Taishō* vol. 1, pp. 37 38); Pāli *Digha-Nikāya* vol. III, pp. 91–94; *Dairutan-kyō* 大樓炭經 vol. VI. (*Taishō* vol. 1, p. 308); *Kise-kyō* 起世經 vol. X. (*Taishō* vol. 1, pp. 362–363); *Kise Inpon-kyō* 起世因本經 vol. X (*Taishō* vol. 1, p. 417); *Butsuhongyōju-kyō* 佛本行集經 vol. IV (*Taishō* vol. 3, p. 672 c); *Shibunritsu* 四分律 vol. XXXI (*Taishō* vol. 22, p. 779); *Shōshochiron* 彰所知論 (*Taishō* vol. 32, p. 231 a); *Shukomakadai-kyō* 衆許摩訶帝經 (*Taishō* vol. 3, p. 933).

9) Kusha-ron 倶舍論 vol. 12, 14a.

10) Cf. The *Mahā-parinibbāna suttanta* (*Mahā-parinirvāṇa-sūtra*) and the various Chinese scriptures corresponding to it.

11) *Jinnō Shōtō-ki* 神皇正統記.

12) *Shutsujō-shōgo* 出定笑語.

13) Cf. *Konkōmyō Saishō-ō-kyō* 金光明最勝王經 vol. 1 (*Taishō* vol. 16, p. 406 a); vol. 6 (*Taishō* vol. 16, p. 432 b). Cf. Also *Konkōmyō-kyō* 金光明經 vol. 2 (*Taishō* vol. 16, p. 344 b, c). The correspondence between the *Nihon shoki* 日本書紀 and these sūtras was pointed out by Kenkō Fujii ("*Kimmei-ki no Bukkyō Denrai no Kiji ni tsuite*" 欽明紀の佛教傳來の記事について in *Shigaku Zasshi* 史學雜誌 vol. XXXVI., no. 8. pp. 653–656). In passing, it should be noted that the passage of the *Kimmei-ki* (6th year, 9th month) which relates that Paikche built a 16 foot statue of the Buddha and presented it to the Emperor is a reproduction of the text of the *Kudara Hongi* (Hiroshi Ikeuchi 池內宏: *Nihon Jōdaishi no Ichi Kenkyū* 日本上代史の一硏究 p. 325).

14) Sten Konow; *Kharoṣṭhī inscriptions.*

15) T. Tamamuro: op. cit. p. 4.

16) *Shoku Nihongi* 續日本紀 17.

17) T. Tamamuro: *op. cit. p.* 17.

18) *Nihon Daizō-kyō* 日本大藏經, *Hōdōbushōsho* 方等部章疏, 3, pp. 2–4.

19) *Kairitsu Denraiki* 戒律傳來記 (A.D. 830), in *Dai Nihon Bukkyō Zensho* 大日本佛教全書 105.

20) The eight rules among the *Sange Gakushō Shiki* (山家學生式) *Rules for Students of Mt. Hiei*). Further, in the *Kenkairon Engi* 顯戒論緣起 we find the phrase "exalt Buddhism and protect the state", and in the *Rokusho Hōtō Gammon* (六所寶塔願文), "establish and held firmly to Buddhism and safeguard of the state".

21) *Shoku Nihon-kōki* 續日本後記 4, 2nd year of *Shōwa* (A.D. 835), 1st month, letter of Kūkai to the Emperor.
22) *Sandai Jitsuroku* 三代實錄 vol. 41, Reign of Emperor Yōzei, 6th year of *Genkei* (A.D. 882), 5th month, 14th day.
23) *Shoku Nihon-kōki* vol. 12, 9th year of Shōwa (A.D. 842), 12th month, 17th day.
24) *Sandai Jitsuroku* vol. 7, Reign of Emperor Seiwa, 5th year of *Jōkan* (A.D. 863), 9th month, 6th day.
25) *Sandai Jitsuroku* vol. 7, Reign of Emperor Seiwa, 5th year of *Jōkan* (A.D. 866), 6th month, 21st day.
26) *Sandai Jitsuroku* vol. 11, Reign of Emperor Seiwa, 7th year of *Jōkan* (A.D. 865), 7th month, 19th day.
27) *Sandai Jitsuroku* vol. 12, Reign of Emperor Seiwa, 8th year of *Jōkan* (A.D. 866), 5th month, 29th day. Further, the following passage occurs in a letter addressed to the emperor by Henjō Sōjō: When the sun of Buddhism is again at its height, the Imperial dignity will be safeguarded, the virtue of the Imperial House long endure, and the State will be peaceful and safe. (*Sandai Jitsuroku* vol. 47, 1st year of Ninna (A.D. 885), 3rd month)
28) The pagoda of Eisai in the Kenninji, Higashiyama, Kyoto is called *Kōzen gokoku-in* ("Exalt Zen, protect the nation".)
29) Kyodō Itō 伊藤慶道: *Dōgen Zenji Kenkyū* 道元禪師研究 vol. 1, p. 303.
30) *Kangyō Hachiman Shō* 諫曉八幡鈔.
31) *Risshō Ankoku Ron* 立正安國論. However, the first of these quotes appears as the words of a guest addressed to the host.
32) *Ongikuden* 御義口傳, at the end.
33) *Ofumi* 御文 2:10 Cf. also 2:6, 3:10, 3:13, 4:1 and *Jōgai Ofumi* 帖外御文 (Yūshō Tokushi, 禿氏祐祥 *Rennyo Shōnin Ofumi Zenshū* 蓮如上人御文全集 pp. 48, 72).
34) *Rennyo Shōnin Goichidaiki Kikigaki* 蓮如上人御一代記聞書, at the end.
35) This has been pointed out by Yukifusa Hattori. (*Kokudo*· 國土 vol. 1, no 1, p. 91). (*Shinran nōto* 親鸞ノート 32, p. 211).
36) *Hokke-kyō* 法華經, Anrakugyō section 安樂行品. A similar view is expressed in the *Shōbōnenjo-kyō* 正法念處經 vol. 50 (*Taishō* pp. 294 c–295 a).
37) Based on Kazuo Higo 肥後和男: *Nihon Kokka Shisō* (日本國家思想 The thought of the "State" in Japan) pp. 78–79.
38) Taiheiki 太平記 vol. 21.
39) The Eighty Volume Kegon 八十華嚴, vol. XXVIII. (*Taishō* vol. 10, p. 152 a–c), vol. 59 (*ibid.* p. 312 a).
40) Based on Yasusada Hiyane 比屋根安定: *Nihon Shūkyō-shi* (日本宗教史 The History of Japanese Religions), p. 648. Moreover, Takeshige, son of Kikuchi Taketoki is said to have had the same concept. (*ibid.* pp. 648–649).
41) But Jiun did not necessarily attempt to have Buddhists accept intact all the social rank of Japanese society. Thus, in the same *Kōkiji kitei* he warns that "the adopted sons of the nobility should not seek public office". (Cf. Daijō Tokiwa 常盤大定: *Nihon Bukkyō no Kenkyū*, pp. 526 ff.)
42) When Chinese political thought was brought to ancient Japan, the Japanese ruling class, in order to govern the land, established the Taihō code in imitation of the T'ang system. This code, however, differed from the T'ang Model, in that it embodied considerations of social policy. In China land was

destributed to each family in proportion to the labor capacity of each. In accordance with the Taihō code, however, equal shares of land were allotted to boys of no labor capacity and even to girls. The huge income of the national treasury were spent for the welfare of the people and their cultural institutions. (Cf. Tetsurō Watsuji 和辻哲郎: "Asuka Nara Jidai no Seijiteki Risō 飛鳥寧樂時代の政治的理想" in his *Nihon Seishinshi Kenkyū* 日本精神史研究).

(7) Absolute devotion to a specific individual

The tendency to esteem a limited human nexus reveals itself in Japan in absolute devotion to a specific individual. The Japanese, unlike the Indians and Chinese prefer not to conceive of a human nexus in an abstract way. They are apt rather to follow an individual, living representative of that nexus. As I have previously indicated, the 'family' in ancient Japan was not an abstract concept, but was embodied in the person of the living family head. There is also a tendency to identify the *shōgun* with the *bakufu*, the Emperor with the State. In the feudalism of the West, relations between lord and vassal were extremely complex, and the notion of contract played an important part in such relations. In feudal Japan, however, this relationship was a simple one; the vassal tended to devote his entire existence to his lord. This gave rise to the motto 'a loyal vassal does not know two masters'. This way of thinking, characteristic of Japanese society in general, manifests itself among Japanese thinkers as an attitude of absolute devotion and obedience to a specific individual.

Most Japanese thinkers of the past were either Buddhists or Confucianists. Now of course religion is apt to base itself upon some authority. However, Indian and Chinese thinkers do not rely on a specific individual, but tend rather to establish and follow universal laws. Japanese thinkers on the contrary were likely to disregard universal laws in favor of the authority of a specific individual.

For some 700 years after the adoption of Buddhism, it was customary for Buddhists to explain the doctrine and expound their theories in the Chinese language. Japanese Buddhism, therefore, was in a sense an extension of Chinese Buddhism. This does not mean, however, that the Japanese merely took over the universal teachings of Buddhism as it was practiced in China at the time of adoption. Japanese scholar-monks received their doctrines from one specific Chinese teacher, and that is precisely what they wanted to do. Dengyō Daishi (767–882), for example, wished to travel to China so that he might discover the true significance of the

Lotus Sūtra. (*Hokekyō*) In his letter requesting admittance to China, he writes as follows: "I have long regretted the absence of a commentary which would explain the profound import of the Lotus Sūtra. By good fortune I have procured a copy of the excellent discourse of the T'ien t'ai sect. I have studied it a number of years, but errors and ommissions in the text make it impossible to grasp the fine points. If I do not receive instruction from a master, then, even if I were to get (the meaning), I should be unable to believe in it".[1] Thus, he went to China and studied under Tao-sui (c. 800), and returned to Japan.

The attitude of absolute devotion to a specific individual became still more pronounced in Kamakura Buddhism, which is especially representative of Japanese Buddhism. The Pure Land doctrine of Hōnen (1133–1212) was based exclusively upon one master, Shan-tao (613–681). At the same time Hōnen exalted the authority of the teacher. He says, "To view the doctrine of the Pure Land without the aid of oral tradition is to lose sight of one's share in the rebirth".[2] Shinran (1173–1262), too, was absolutely devoted to his master, Hōnen. "As far as I, Shinran, am concerned, the sole reason I have faith is that a good man explained to me that in order to be saved by Amida I had only to recite the invocations (*nembutsu*). I do not know whether the *nembutsu* is actually the means to rebirth in the Pure Land, or whether perhaps it is the road to Hell. Even though, having been persuaded by Hōnen Shōnin, I should go to Hell through the *nembutsu,* I should not regret it".[3]

Wishing to establish rationally the authority of his personal interpretation of Buddhism, Shinran makes the major premise of his reasoning of the absolute authority of the teacher. "If the original view of Amida is true, then the teachings of Śākyamuni are true, and the commentaries of Shan-tao can not be false; if the commentaries of Shan-tao are true, the teachings of Hōnen cannot be false; if the teachings of Hōnen are true, how would it be possible for me, Shinran, to utter a falsehood".[4]

This is cast in the form of a complex syllogism, but in each of the component syllogisms there is a hidden premise, namely, "the word of a disciple faithful to his teacher is as true as that of the teacher". Such a proposition is very questionable. The Japanese, however, consider it perfectly natural. They even pass over it in silence as not requiring overt explanation.

The watchword here is absolute docility before authority. This sort of reasoning is substantially the same as that which produced the notion, a few years back, that "the command of a superior is the command of the Emperor".

Apparently this opinion of which we have just spoken is found in other oriental countries. Scholars and students of religion pretend that they have inherited the orthodox doctrine from ancient time, and cite the genealogy of their teachers to prove it. It appears, however, that in the other oriental countries these thoughts were not expressed in the form of a sorites.

At any rate, Shinran himself had not the slightest thought of originating a new sect. His proposed aim was merely to elucidate the true purport of his master Hōnen's teachings. "My master Genkū (Hōnen), being well versed in Buddhism, took pity on common people, both good and bad. He began to teach the doctrine of the true religion (*shinshū*) in the provinces, and spread the chosen original vow (of Amida) throughout this corrupt world".[5] By 'true religion' Shinran refers to the Pure Land sect (*jōdo-shū*) of Hōnen, and not to the so-called True Pure Land sect (*jōdo-shinshū*).[6] The attitude of dependence upon the master was also influential among the followers of Shinran. "When I take council with myself and consider in my fumbling way the past and the present, I must regret the differences (that have sprung up) in the true faith as taught orally by our master. I fear that future students will fall into an unbroken series of errors, for, unless one is fortunate enough to be grounded upon knowledge derived from the original source, how can he possibly gain entrance to the Easy Way (*Amidian nembutsu*)?[7] One's own insight of one's own private views should in no wise be confounded with the doctrine of Another's Strength (*tariki*). Therefore I shall note down here the gist of the sayings of the late Shinran Shōnin, which remain in my mind. I hope thereby to dissipate the doubts of my coreligionists".[8]

This tendency is also apparent in Nichiren (1222–1282), who attacked the Pure Land teachings. At the end of the scriptures of Mahāyāna Buddhism, it is mentioned that Śākyamuni entrusted the scriptures to various persons, but according to Nichiren the true transmission of the Lotus Sūtra depended on blood relationship.[9] Thus the true spirit of the Lotus Sūtra is revealed only by the specific person who had received its guardianship. It is for this reason that Nichiren called himself the reincarnation of the Bodhisattva Jgyō to whom the Lotus Sūtra had been entrusted.[10]

It is especially his conviction that he is a reincarnation of Buddha which distinguishes Nichiren from the other Chinese and Japanese who studied the Lotus Sūtra. "I, Nichiren", he says, "am like the messenger of the Bodhisattva Jōgyō...Indeed I teach this doctrine...I feel that I must be a reincarnation of the Bodhisattva Jōgyō".[11]

This differs considerably from the interpretation of the Lotus Sūtra by Chinese Buddhist commentators. T'ien-t'ai Da-shih, for example, has this to say on the subject: "Thus entrusting the sūtras to innumerable Bodhisattvas of the thousand universes, he had the sūtra propagated in the sphere of the cosmic body of Buddha. Is not this teaching far superior to that which would have the sūtras spread here and there by humble mortals? May the substance of the Ten Spheres[12] penetrate the different countries of the earth, and may there be obtained the double advantage of darkness and light".[13]

Elsewhere Chia-hsiang Da-shih (549–623), at the beginning of his interpretation of the 14th chapter of the Lotus Sūtra, says: "This chapter, like the 11th, indicates that the ensemble of the Boddhisattvas emanate from the earth, and together are an expression of the cosmic body of the Buddha".[14]

Whereas Chinese commentators gave absolute value to the absolute taken as a basic principle, in Japan, Nichiren attributed this absolute authority to a specific person in certain particular circumstances.

Thus, to believe Nichiren, he himself actually received, two thousand years before, the deposit of the wisdom of the Buddha, which he now in turn transmits to mankind. "On the 25th day of the second month of the eleventh year of Bunei, on Mount Ryōzen (Gṛdhrakūṭa) of the Pure Land, Nichiren, to whom Buddha entrusted the deposit of the essential verities, respectfully received priestly ordination".[15] "More that 2000 years ago Nichiren, as chief of the Boddhisattvas of the thousand worlds who appeared out of the earth, received from the very mouth of the Buddha the three great secret doctrines".[16] In the Zen sect, too, Dōgen (1200–1253), for example, teaches absolute devotion to the master. "In order to embrace Buddhism, one must abandon his own judgements of good and evil. Rather must one follow the words and examples of our Buddhist predecessors, regardless of good or evil. What one regards as good, either in his own opinion or in that of other men is not necessarily good. Therefore, heedless of the world's gaze, and oblivious of one's own opinions, one should follow the teachings of the Buddha".[17] "We recognize immediately and instinctively that such persons as Śākyamuni and Amida are Buddhas, for their features are endowed with radiance and they are remarkable for their preaching and their grace. If however, a learned priest says that a toad or a worm is the Buddha, then one must abandon ordinary knowledge and believe that a toad or a worm is the Buddha. But if one seeks in the worm the radiance of countenance or the various virtues with which the Buddha is endowed, then one still has not modified his prejudices. One must recognize as the Buddha only that which can be seen at a given moment. Thus if one goes along modifying his prejudices in accordance with the words of the master, one will naturally reach agreement. The scholars of recent days, on the contrary, cling to their own prejudices and think that the Buddha must be such and such, according to their private opinions. If anything should differ from their opinion, they say that it cannot be so, but wonder if it may be something similar to their own preconceived notions. Thus in the main they are not devoted to the way of the Buddha".[18]

Then he explains that one should conform absolutely to the various ascetic practices, precepts and rules of the Zen sect, merely because they represent the continuous tradition of the past. "It is false to insist upon ascetic practice as essential, believing thereby that one may reach enlightenment, on the grounds that one should keep commandments and observe the fasts. One observes such things merely because they are the routine of a monk and the customs of the house of the sons of Buddha. One should not necessarily say that such things are essential because they are useful".[19]

For this reason, Dōzen planned to establish rationally each of the rules and doctrines of the Zen sect. However, he abandoned his plan before completing it, and gave precedence to authority over rational thought. For example, Buddhism recognizes four attitudes among the various daily activities of mankind, namely, walking, standing, sitting, and reclining. One speaks of "Zen", however, only in connection with the sitting position. Explaining the reason for this, Dozen says: "It may be asked, 'Why do the priests speak of meditation and enlightenment only in connection with the sitting position?', and I answer, "It is difficult to know the way by which all the various Buddhas achieved enlightenment. If you seek the reason, you must knew that it is just because the priests employed (this way). You should not question further. Our masters before us praised sitting in meditation (*zazen*) as the gateway to bliss. This is why we know that of the four attitudes (sitting) is the way to bliss. What is more, it was not the practice of one or two Buddhas, but of all the Buddhas before us".[20]

Because of his devedence for tradition, Dōgen teaches that the ascetic should practice under the direction of an eminent teacher. "By practising asceticism in a group, one attains the Way. It is like boarding a boat without knowing how to row. Since one trusts a good boatman, it makes no difference whether one knows how to row, one gets to the other side. Thus one should follow a good teacher and practise in a group. Then, since one is not relying on one's own resources, one naturally attains to the Way".[21]

However, the one who decides who is an 'eminent teacher' is the ascetic himself. The basis of this value judgement is the consciousness or experience of universal law within the ascetic himself. It is a rational consideration within the subjectivity of the ascetic which operates here. Thus, when we analyse Dōgen's advice to follow a good teacher without regard for rational consideration, one ends up in a vicious circle. Dōgen, however, never touched upon this question. He simply ordered that one was to devote himself absolutely to a venerated person.

It may be objected at this point that absolute devotion to a teacher is merely one of the social phenomena of a feudal society and that we see here the feudal character of Dōgen. While such is perhaps a plausible explanation, I hesitate to dispose of the question so simply. One hardly finds, in the feudal societies of India or China, this advocacy of absolute devotion to a specific person. One does, to be sure, often come across the phrase 'become intimate with a *zenchishiki*' in the scriptures composed in India, but here *zenchishiki* is a translation of *kalyāṇamitra* which means 'good friend' or 'intimate friend'. In Japan, on the contrary, *zenchishiki* is taken in the sense of 'religious teacher'. *It is the Japanese way of thinking which brings about the change in interpretation.* For the Indians (and for most Chinese Buddhists) the 'law' in the religious sense was not something transmitted to the pupil by the teacher as a specific individual, but rather something which *the ascetic himself mastered.* Indians would never dream of making such a statement as 'I would not mind being cast into hell if lead astray by St. Hōnen'. Thus this characteristic of the thought of Shinran and Dōgen is not attributed to traditional Buddhism and it is furthermore difficult to attribute this attitude to feudalism in general.

In the case of Dōgen, one cannot say that he acquired the characteristic in question from his Chinese master Ju-ching. The latter, in fact, teaches the opposite of Dōgen. Ju-ching was very prone to trample upon authority.

He called Yuima (Vimalakīrti-gṛhapati) a "bandit" and Lin-chi an "ass"; of Boddhidharma's expression "Nothing can be called holy" he says, "*he himself created it, he himself destroyed it*". He even goes so far as to say, "To practice true Zen, one does not think about the masters".[22] Moreover, in keeping with the general tendency of Chinese Zen Buddhism, he denies the authority of specific doctrines. For example, he says, "Atop Mt. Gṛdhrakūta, there are no words of the Master; at the foot of Mt. Shaolin no mysteries are transmitted".[23] (Mt. Gṛdhrakūta is the place where the Buddha explained the Lotus Sūtra; Mt. Shaolin is the place where Boddhidharma sat for nine years in meditation, facing a wall.) Dōgen himself claims to have transmitted very faithfully the teachings of his master Ju-ching, but the fact is that Dōgen opposes him when it comes to the question of the authority of tradition.

One result of this absolute devotion to a specific person is that the faithful of the various Japanese sects are extreme in the veneration accorded to the founder of the sect and have religious ceremonies of which the founder is the nucleus. One has absolute faith in the master as well as in the Buddha, without feeling that this implies the slightest contradiction. It is not that one pays less attention to the Buddha, but the idea is perhaps that a profound faith in the master and devotion to the Buddha have the same significance.[24]

The Japanese then exhibit an attitude of complete devotion to a specific person—the emperor, the feudal lord, the superior, the boss. In the field of religion this attitude appears in the manner we have just outlined. One may say that a similar religious attitude is present in other countries. The attitude of the medieval Catholics toward the saints or that of the Hindu toward the *guru* are two instances. In these cases, however, the religious qualities of the various saints are revered; the question of genealogy barely comes up. Japan differs from these other countries in the great importance attached to genealogy.

This attitude, aided by the Japanese tendency to emphasize blood relationship, is responsible for the veneration of the founder in the True Pure Land sect. As this sect develops, this attitude becomes more and more conspicuous. Already in the *Gaijashō* of Kakunyo (1270–1351), there appears the tendency to venerate a living monk as if he were Amitābha. He himself appears to call himself "the pure stream of Buddha's incarnation".[25] The tendency becomes still stronger and there develops an intense veneration of the chief abbot as a concrete individual who was the leader of the Honganji order. Indeed the order maintains itself and develops around this veneration of the abbot. Intellectual comprehension of doctrine is neglected. Thus the Honganji order itself prohibited the faithful from reading the *Tannisho,* that frank and clear exposition of the essence of the True Pure Land faith. The order openly preached faith in the chief abbot as the principal consideration.

Not only is there no relation between the teachings of Shinran as they affect the conscience of the ordinary mortal and this devotion to the abbot which makes of a specific person an absolute, but indeed the two are logically contradictory. Although Luther preached a faith very similar to that of Shinran, nobody in Germany has thought to venerate the descendents of Luther. In Japan, however, such a religious peculiarity did develop. This tendency, moreover, still persists in modern times. It can be seen in certain divisions of sectarian Shinto which have flourished since the beginning of the Meiji era.

We must recognize that we are dealing with an attitude which is deeply rooted in the soul of the Japanese people. This sort of socio-religious phenomenon did not appear in India or China. Sectarianism does occur in India and China, but the sects for the most part emphasize some universal law. The consciousness of the founder of the sect is often vague, and veneration of the founder hardly existed in antiquity. Needless to say, nothing comparable to the veneration of the chief abbot has ever arisen.

The attitude of absolute devotion to a specific real person manifests itself as an attitude of complete devotion to the Buddha as an ideal person, and thus faith in Buddha is emphasized.

In this connection the Japanese Pure Land sect shows a remarkable development and lays much stress on the purity of faith. This sect esteems the 18th of the 48 vows of Amitābha, which it teaches must be *believed* with all one's heart. Hōnen did not believe with traditional Buddhism that the individual ascetic could obtain salvation through his own practices; but maintained that one would be delivered through faith in Amitābha and reliance on his vow. Among the disciples of Hōnen, Jōkakubō Kōsai, although regarded as a heretic for having preached the efficacy of a single *nembutsu,* placed special emphasis upon faith in Buddha. "The believer is reborn there (the Pure Land) only by virtue of the vow (of Amida), and not through his own efforts. The reason is that the sinful mortal, burdened as he is by worldly distraction, is separated by an abyss from the Pure Land. But, relying on the vow of Buddha, he will at once succeed".[26]

Then with the evolution of the True Pure Land sect, the significance of faith came more and more to be stressed. "To be reborn in the Pure Land, one must have faith above all and not concern himself with anything else. A matter of such magnitude as rebirth in paradise cannot be arranged by the ordinary mortal. He must yield absolutely to the Buddha".[27)]

In the Chinese T'ien-t'ai sect, Buddhism was generally considered under three aspects: doctrine, practice, and illumination.[28)] The Tendai sect in Japan also accepted this point of view.[29)] The doctrine of the True Pure Land sect is an off-shoot of this essential Tendai doctrine. For this reason the basic scripture of the True Pure Land sect is called *Kenjōdoshinjitsu Kyōgyōshō monrui* (abbreviated title *Kyōgyōshinshō*)[30)] (Kyōgyōshō= doctrine, practice, illumination). In the short title the word *shin,* "faith", is added.) That the word faith is absent from the complete title is due to the relationship with the old Tendai doctrine. However, in the book itself, faith is the principal matter considered. In Buddhism as a whole, after "faith" has been affirmed, one devotes himself to "practice"; while in the True Pure Land sect, the two are identical. (Faith accompanied by practice, and practice accompanied by faith.) The believing heart is the "ture heart". In this way faith comes to stand at the very center of Buddhism. Shinran, consequently, tends to regard a skeptic or one who relies upon his own resources as more despicable than a great sinner. Rennyo, who popularized the True Pure Land sect, expresses absolute devotion to Amitābha in terms which still more call to mind human relationships. The use of such expressions as 'rely upon' and 'help me!' seem to date from Rennyo. Such expressions appeal to popular sentiment.

That the Japanese Pure Land sect emphasizes faith and esteems the 18th of the 48 vows of Amida, i.e. the vow which exalts faith, is a peculiarly Japanese phenomenon, completely different from the case of the Pure Land sect in China.

Yang Jen-shan, the promoter of the Buddhist revival in modern China, criticized the exclusive emphasis on the 18th vow characteristic of the Japanese True Pure Land sect. He maintains that this is an affront to Amitābha, for each and every one of the 48 vows is true.[31)]

Here a problem arises. It is natural that the Pure Land sects, which preach absolute dependence upon another's strength, should emphasize faith in a specific individual or in Buddha. However, this should not be true of the Zen sect, which maintains a contrary (doctrinal) position.

Nonetheless, Dōgen does emphasize the significance of faith just as do the partisans of Pure Land Buddhism. The very name, Dōgen, comes from vol. 14 of the Chinese translation of the *Avataṃsaka-sūtra,* which reads: "Faith is the origin of the Way (dōgen), the mother of virtue; it nourishes all the various good practices".[32] Faith, this is the "origin of the Way". "Therefore it is said, 'Faith permits us to enter into the great sea of the Buddha-law'. The actuality of faith is the actuality of the Buddha himself".[33] Without faith it is difficult to achieve perfection in the practice of Buddhism. "One may teach a man who has not faith, but it is difficult for such a one to accept the teaching".[34] According to Dōgen, rather that to achieve the enlightenment through one's ascetic practices, one should, in the final analysis, have absolute devotion to the Buddha as an ideal person, and *be saved by him.* It is better to rely upon "another's strength" than upon one's own. "One detaches himself from his body and mind and flings himself into the house of the Buddha, there to be activated by the Buddha and follow in his footsteps. Then, without effort, physical or mental, of one's own, one escapes the cycle of rebirth and becomes a buddha".[35]

Dōgen's teaching in this regard is the exact opposite of that of the Zen sect in China (or at least of its principal representatives). Chinese Zen priests are continually pointing out that illumination is achieved through one's own efforts. Hui-hai (550–686) says: "This you should know: sentient beings save themselves; Buddha cannot save them. Make efforts! Make efforts! Perfect yourselves, and depend not upon the Buddha. In scripture it says, he who seeks the law does not seek it in the Buddha".[36] In other words, one must not rely even upon the Buddha. Nonetheless, Dōgen fervently depends upon Buddha's strength. The following is Dōgen's praper: "Even if my past sins are piled high and there are obstacles to my enlightenment, I beg all the Buddhas and Boddhisattvas who have achieved perfection through the way of Buddha to take pity on me, deliver me from the chains of Karma, remove the impediments to my enlightenment. May their virtue fill and embrace the infinite world of the Buddha-law. May they extend to me their pity".[37]

In the Chinese Zen sect, faith is merely the portal of Buddhism. Therefore one must not become attached to the Buddha. Thus, the Chinese Zen monk Tan-hsia, in order to combat the deplorable tendency to become over-attached to an image of Buddha and regard it as the Buddha himself, burned a wooden statue of the Buddha as firewood.[38] This story is highly lauded by Chinese devotees of Zen. To the Japanese, however, it is outrageous. Dōgen teaches, "A clay, wood, or plaster image of Buddha, however poorly done, should be venerated. A scroll of scripture, no matter how battered, should be respected. A priest, even if he be a hardened sinner, should be respected for his sacerdotal character. If one respects these with faith in his heart, he is surely blessed. If one is disrespectful of a priest because he is a hardened sinner, a statue because it is poorly done, a copy of the sūtras because it is battered, then he certainly commits a sin. For according to the Buddha's teaching, the statue, the scroll of scripture, and the priest contribute to the happiness of men and gods. Therefore, one certainly profits by respecting them. One who treats them without faith is guilty of sin".[39] Yet when Dōgen is asked why Tan-hsia burned the wooden Buddha, he explains, "That was a common means of preaching the Law". Even Suzuki Shōsan (1579–1655), a Zen priest who had many ideas worthy of comparison with those of modern Western thought, condemns as "the height of immorality" the notion that "A wooden statue is nothing but wood, and an icon is merely a few strokes of the brush; there is nothing respectable about them".[40] He teaches: "Being born among men and hearing the teaching of the Buddha, one should be happy to represent the sacred form in painting and in sculpture and place them in a pagoda or temple to worship. Then, with the thought that the Buddha is actually in the world among us, we should offer our lives in homage. If our faith is not strong enough to make us willing to offer our lives, then there is no merit in it".[41]

There is also a strong emphasis on faith in the Nichiren sect. According to Nichiren, philosophical comprehension is not necessary for salvation. A robust faith is sufficient. "The Buddha, setting aside the keeping of the commandments and contemplation, addressed himself to the intelligence alone. If intelligence is lacking, faith makes up for it. The single word 'faith' is a pillar of truth. Lack of faith is the root of disrespect for the Law; faith is the cause of intelligence..."[42] "For the man of superior gifts, study and contemplation are suitable. For the less gifted, faith alone is important". "He who understands the doctrines yet does not believe cannot become a buddha. He who believes, although he does not comprehend, can become a buddha".[43] "The root of the Law of Buddha is faith".[44] Thus we can say that Nichiren, in this regard, is in agreement with the views of Shinran and Dōgen. We likewise recognize here one of the characteristics which differentiates the Nichiren sect from the Tendai sect to which it owes its origin.

It is not only the new Kamakura sects which place this emphasis upon faith. The Indian or Chinese sects transplanted to Japan also preached faith in the Buddha. The Ritsu sect, for example, attempted to observe in Japan the precepts of traditional, conservative Indian Buddhism. In these precepts, there is no mention of a cult of the image of the Buddha, yet in the Ritsu temples in Japan, images of the Buddha were erected and sūtras recited before them.[45] Even the Tendai and Kegon philosophies, high points of Chinese Mahāyāna philosophy, had to accept faith as their basis, once they became acclimatized in Japan. Thus, in the Tendai sect, Ennin (792–862), emphasizing the importance of faith, says: "To enter into the sacred mysteries, one must go by the direct road of faith. He who has not faith is like a man without hands who, though he gain entry to the treasure room, can take nothing".[46] This emphasis on faith is one of the criteria by which Japanese Esoteric Tendai (*Taimitsu*) can be distinguished from the Chinese T'ien-t'ai sect. And a similar change in the concept of faith can be observed, though it is not so remarkable in this case, in the Shingon sect. Kōgyō Daishi (1095–1143) emphasized "the innocent acceptance of faith" saying that it is by far superior to the preparatory practice following with the intellectual power what the scriptures teach.

Further, as regards the Kegon sect, Myōe Shōnin (alias Kōben, 1173–1232) says: "Knowledge without faith is not only not in accordance with the Law of Buddha, but is actually inimical to it. Wisdom will be founded upon faith".[47] This is a complete reversal of the rationalist position of Kegon philosophy.

In general, Indian religions and Chinese Buddhism are contemplative, focused on the vision of truth. In such religions, faith is merely the first step toward entering the innermost recesses of the religion. It is simply preparatory. However, when these sects were introduced into Japan, faith came to be recognized as the very essence of the religion. Therefore, Japanese Buddhism is above all a Buddhism centering around faith. The Japanese emphasize purity of faith (Even the Zen sect, in which faith is comparatively less esteemed, exhibits this trend in Japan). This faith is of two kinds: (1) faith in a certain real person (founder, teacher); (2) faith in an ideal person (a specific Buddha or Bodhisattva). In practice, however, both appear so commingled that it is difficult to differentiate them. In either case the focus is on a specific individual.

The following criticism is offered by Enjō Inaba apropos of these differences between Chinese and Japanese Buddhism: "The defect of Chinese Buddhist thought is the acceptance as the guiding principle of religion an abstract 'law' such as a truth, a law which was divorced from the concrete 'person'. Buddhism, as a religion which is the life and strength of all men, certainly cannot center around such a law of truth. Only when this law is embodied in a person of flesh and blood can it be beneficial to us human beings... It is nonsensical that a religion whose worship is directed to a law should demand religious fervor. Only by absolute devotion to a person can one savor the joy of prostrating oneself in reverent worship and of praying with all one's heart".[48)]

Ryōtai Hatani has the following to say on the characteristics of Japanese Buddhism: "In India and China, the speculative and practical sides of Buddhism were fully developed. However, the aspect of faith, which is the life of a religion, was never completely developed in India and China. Only in Japan has this aspect of Buddhism been fully explored. Japan had nothing particularly new to add to the speculative and practical aspects of Buddhism as developed in India and China. Japan's special contributions were in the field of faith".[49)]

Japanese Buddhism does indeed exhibit the characteristics pointed out by Inaba and Hatani. However, the assertion that the 'very soul of Buddhism' appears for the first time in Japan, and not in China and India, requires some further comment. Faith as it is understood by the Japanese is not a complete faith in the view of Indian Buddhists, but merely the gateway to faith. Compare, for example, the following passage of a sūtra: "Oh, good man! There are two kinds of faith. The first is 'simple faith' (reliance), the second is 'seeking'. A man may have simple faith, yet be unable to aspire; therefore his is insufficient faith. There are two further categories of faith. The first arises from hearing the teaching, the second from contemplation. A man whose faith is based on hearing the teaching, not on contemplation, has insufficient faith".[50)]

The Indian concept of faith is extremely intellectual. Therefore, simple faith is of little significance, but an intelligent faith is of great value. Thus the criterion of value as applied to faith changed completely in the passage of Buddhism from India to Japan.

Faith in Japanese Buddhism, then, is essentially faith in a specific person, ideal or real. In Indian Buddhism, on the contrary, it is devotion to a universal law. The traditional view of Indian Buddhism was 'depend upon the law, not upon man'.[51] In Japan, however, the exact opposite was followed. Related to this view is the Indian and Chinese veneration of the Buddha as eternal law, whereas the Japanese tend to worship the Buddha as the person who achieved all the ideal virtues through his ascetic practices.

Broadly speaking, emphasis on faith appeared even in Indian Buddhism shortly before the Christian era, as it did also successively in Hinduism and Jainism in roughly the same period. Thus they developed along with the Western religion which emphasizes faith. It is a Japanese peculiarity that a specific person should be made the object of faith. With reference to this last point, there is some resemblance between Japanese faith and the faith of the Western religion. For example, the faith of Shinran and that of Saint Paul appear very similar. In Saint Paul, however, there is an absolute distinction between God and man. Man always assumes a pious and prayerful attitude toward God, and begs his forgiveness. For Shinran, however, there is no gulf between Amida and the ordinary mortal. The sinful mortal will be saved through the mercy of Amida. If he repeats *nembutsu,* it is an expression of his joy and gratitude that he is saved by the great mercy of this Buddha. And an authentic master who understands the true meaning of *nembutsu* never utters it as a prayer. Whether it is about a secular matter or a religious one, he rejects any supplicating attitude toward him for the reason that supplication is not what this Buddha of the great vows wishes.

Generally speaking, the Japanese who devote themselves wholeheartedly to their religious masters are inclined to express total submission to authority in other forms. In the first place, it can be clearly observed in their attitude to the scriptures. The Chinese Buddhists claim that it is not sufficient only to accept blindly what is said in the scriptures unless one tries to seek after truth by oneself by the help of those holy books.[52] The Japanese Buddhists, on the other hand, hold the authority of the scriptures as absolute and inviolable. And in the case of China, the number of the Kyō-shū (the sects established on the authority of specific sūtras) is almost equal to that of the Ron-shū (the sects based on particular Abhidharma treatises). But, in Japan especially after the Heian period, almost all the Buddhist sects, except for the Zen sect which claims not to rely upon any particular canon, are the Kyō-shū in the sense that each one of them regards a particular sūtra as the absolute authority to depend upon.

When he introduced the doctrines of the Chinese T'ien-t'ai sect to Japan, Dengyō Daishi (Saichō), whom we can properly call the actual founder of the Japanese Buddhism, strongly emphasized the fact that the sect pays special regards to the Lotus Sūtra. Such an emphasis on scriptural authority is one of the unique features of Dengyō that distinguished him from the masters of the Chinese T'ien-t'ai sect like T'ien-t'ai Ta-shih 天台大師 or Miao-lo Ta-shih 妙樂大師.[53]

In the Kamakura period, Shinran wrote his chief work *Kyōgyōshinshō*. The full title of this work is "*Ken-jōdo-shinjitsu-kyō-gyō-shō-monrui*" or 'an anthology of the scriptural passages teaching the true doctrine, practice and illustration of the Pure Land'. As the title of this book indicates to us, Shinran claimed authencity for his teaching for the reason that his faith is based on the authority of the scriptural statements.

In the case of Nichiren, too, he tried in his abundant works to demonstrate theologically, on the basis of numerous scriptural statements, that the diffusion of the Lotus Sūtra in Japan at the very time that Nichiren lived concurs with the true intention of the Buddha. The philosophical system of Nichiren's theology is founded solely upon the Tendai doctrine of *Ichinen-sanzen* (the doctrine that teaches all the three thousand spheres of existence of the living creatures are embraced in one thought). And as to another important doctrine of the Tendai theology which Nichiren relied upon to establish his own, 'kyō-gyō-shō' or 'doctrine, practice and illustration', the following is asserted among his followers and is approved as authentic by the doctrinal authority of the Nichiren sect. "While the Chinese master T'ien-t'ai Ta-shih and his Japanese successor Dengyō Daishi both paid special regards to 'practice' and 'illustration' encouraging the exercise of meditation with a pacified and concentrated mind, Nichiren emphasized the importance of 'doctrine' preceding the other two".[54] Generally speaking, the Japanese Buddhist were busy in the demonstration of their authencity on the basis of scriptural authority and seldom sought to establish a grand philosophical system of their own creation.

Even the Zen sect, which had claimed itself in its origin to be free from any fixed traditional doctrine, was transformed in this country into one that is sensitive to authority. It is worthy of note that Eisai, the introducer of the Rinzai Zen to Japan, thought that the inauguration of the Zen sect in Japan would cause no infringement upon the faithful observance of "the ancestral way of Mt. Hiei" or of the traditional theology of the Tendai sect.[55] In his masterpiece *Kōzen-gokoku-ron*, he made many quotations from various Mahāyāna sūtras. Especially the *Yuima-kyō* (the *Vimalakīrtinirdeśa-sūtra*) and the *Kongō-kyō* (the *Vajracchedikā-prajñāpāramitā-sūtra*) were his favorite scriptures. In the final analysis, Eisai was not an exception. He, too, recognized scriptural statement to be the absolute authority, and for verification he went to the scriptures.

The attitude of reliance on scriptural authority is more manifestly observed in the case of Dōgen. At the time of the Sung Dynasty, almost all Chinese Buddhists were adherents of the Zen teaching. And they attached little significance to the sūtras claiming themselves not to be slaves to books. Dōgen, however, called those Chinese Buddhists "the followers of the masters who missed the right course" and denounced them. He said as follows: "Recently in Sung [China], there are many who assume themselves as the Ch'an-shih 禪師 or the masters of Zen. ... Those people are too stupid to take in the profound meaning of the sūtras. Ignoring their own faults, they abuse unduly the sūtras and never study them".[56) Dōgen emphasized the absolute value of the scriptures. According to him, the true intention of the Buddha can be found *only in the sūtras*. Since the earliest time, it was held among the Indian Buddhists that the teaching of the Buddha consists of twelve portions. Succeeding this view, Dōgen expounded as follows: "One who sees the Doctrine of the Twelve Portions is a man who finds the Buddhist masters. One who accepts the Buddhist masters is a man who accepts the Doctrine of the Twelve Portions". Or in another part of the same work, he said, "The Three Vehicles and the Doctrine of the Twelve Portions form the core of the teaching of the Buddhist masters. Without understanding them, who can rightly call himself the descendant of the Buddhist masters? Without their transmission, how can the transmission of the true essence of the teaching of the Buddhist masters be properly made from one master to another?"[57) It is natural that Dōgen encouraged the study of the sūtras. He said, "An ascetic, whether he is an independent ascetic or only a beginner, should never fail to keep the sūtras with the intention of becoming a son of the Buddha"[58) or "An uninitiated ascetic, whether he has any distinct intention to follow the Buddha or not, should read and study the scriptures with good care".[59) The Chinese Zen monks paid so little regards to the scriptures that one of them dared to say, "The sūtras are good as toilet paper".[60) This Chinese attitude toward the scriptures presents a sharp contrast to the attitude of Dōgen.

From of old, '*kyō-ge-betsu-den* 教外別傳' is one of the fundamental principles of the Zen sect. It means that the essence of the Zen doctrine introduced to China by Bodhidharma should be transmitted intuitively from the heart of the master to that of the initiated without relying upon speech or writing. And its meaning is the same as what is signified by the expression 'non-reliance on the letters 不立文字'. Dōgen's advocation that we have seen above is undeniably inconsistent with this orthodox standpoint of the Zen sect. He, who showed the absolute obedience to traditional authority, never dreamt of ignoring the old principle of '*kyō-ge-betsu-den*'. And as a desperate measure, he made a perverted interpretation of the principle.[61] According to him, the word '*kyo* (doctrine)' designates the Buddhist teaching introduced by Kāśyapa Mātaṅga and Dharmarakṣa to China for the first time in 67 A.D. in the days of the Later Han Dynasty. And '*betsu-den* (different transmission)' means the Buddhist teaching bought newly by Bodhidharma apart from ("*ge*") the former one. The principle originally meant the impossibility of expressing the absolute religious truth by means of speeches or writings. But this old principle was thoroughly transformed by the hands of Dōgen to mean that the absolute truth is transmittable only by oral or literal teaching based on the authority of the authentic tradition. Thus, the principle established primarily in China of refusing acceptance of the authority of any specific doctrine was brought to Japan and changed *to mean absolute obedience to it.*

As a result of his special regard for authority, Dōgen sometimes went to extremes to repulse the rationalism that forms one of the unique characteristics of the Chinese Zen sect. One of the traditional principles of the Zen sect teaches 'kenshō-jyōbutsu (見性成佛)'. It means that a man can achieve Nirvāṇa with penetrating insight into the innate nature of his existence. Dōgen made a frontal attack upon this traditional view. He said: "The essence of Buddhism is not in *kenshō* or the intuitive grasp of innate human nature. Among the Seven Buddhas and the Twenty-eight Master of the Zen sect in India and the Central Asia, who advocated such a view? Indeed, in the *Dan-gyō* 壇經 (which claims itself unduly to be the work of the sixth patriarch of the Zen Buddhism) the word *kenshō* is found. But, this work is a forgery. None of the five Indian successors of the Buddha's teaching wrote this sūtra, nor did the sixth patriarch. None of the followers of the Buddha's teaching have regarded it as a suitable authority to rely upon".[62]

While Dōgen respected the authority of the masters as well as of the scriptures, Nichiren did not pay particular regard to the authority of the masters. He was a man who concerned himself with the selection of the reliable doctrine from the various teachings of the diversified and at times contradictory Buddhist sects which existed at that time. He called himself "one who has sought the Buddha's teaching without the aid of parents or masters". What ruled his selection finally was not a philosophical consideration but his belief in *the authority of a sūtra.* Having found in the fifth volume of the Lotus Sūtra the following statement: "This Lotus Sūtra, the secret treasury of all the Buddhas and the Tathāgatas, stands the highest of all among the sūtras", Nichiren believed it and developed his unique theology on the authority of this sūtra.[63] Thus, Nichiren submitted himself unconditionally to scriptural authority. In one of his letters, he wrote: "It is of no use to try to menace me with worldly authority; just show me the proper scriptural statement to verify your point".[64]

In India, many sūtras were forged with the title of "the Buddha's own teaching". The number of such spurious writings is by no means less in China. But, in Japan, few of such works were made. One of the probable reasons for this is that special honor is paid in this country to the authority of the sūtras. This respect to the scriptures, however, did not necessarily lead the Japanese to the ardent study of what those sūtras teach. On the contrary, the Japanese condensed the sūtras into some simple symbolic representations and regarded those symbolic formulae as absolute and inviolable.

The obedient Japanese attitude toward the regulations that tradition imposes upon it can also be observed in the field of their Buddhistic art. The Chinese sculptors, disregarding the iconographic prescriptions established by the Indians, made the statues of the Buddhas freely following their own imagination. The Japanese artists, on the other hand, adhered faithfully to the Indian prescriptions that they came to know through the books imported from China at the time of the T'ang Dynasty.

Those features that we have referred to in our study of the Japanese way of adopting Buddhism can be observed similarly in their reaction to Confucianism or Chinese thought in general.

The Japanese were very much surprised to know for the first time that the Chinese civilization was far superior to their own one. Every thing imported from China was an object of their admiration. They were overwhelmed by the splendor of the Chinese civilization to such a degree as to accept all things Chinese without due criticism. Their inferior cultural standard did not allow them to assume a critical attitude toward the Chinese civilization. They believed any statement contained in the Chinese books to be absolutely true, authentic and infallible. They adopted the Chinese letters and concepts and tried to interpret the realities in their own country by following these Chinese principles. They did not consider whether or not these Chinese principles would be appropriate for the explanation of the social realities of Japan or of their own thought and life. And as a result, adopting the Chinese classification of the divinities into two groups; gods of heaven and gods of earth, the Japanese sorted out their own objects of cult, *kamis,* into the same two categories. In another case, regarding their *tennō* (lit. Heaven-Emperor) in the same light as the Chinese emperor, they borrowed from the Chinese the idea that the imperial dignity is conferred by the heaven.[65]

As a result of such a blind acceptance of the Chinese civilization, it is natural that 'the way of the ancient sages' played the role of absolute authority among the Japanese Confucianists. Though the critical studies on the classical works of Confucianism were started in Japan in the early years of the modern age, even the most radical part in this field, Ogyū Sorai (1666–1718) advocated "the way of the ancient sage-kings" as the highest moral principle. In one of his books, he wrote as follows: "To say nothing of the ancient sage-kings, those who would work for the benefit of the people and save them from miseries should also be called 'good'. For they do what the people long for. The way of the ancient sage-kings is the highest good. Under the sun, there is no principle more excellent than this one. 'The highest good' is, therefore, the word to praise the way of the ancient sage-kings".[66]

And we can find the Japanese inclination of total submission to specific masters also in the case of the Confucianists. For instance, Yamazaki Ansai (1618–1682) was so enthusiastic an admirer of Chu-hsi (朱熹) that he tried to propagate the latter's teaching with a missionary zeal. He went to such an extreme to declare, "If I fall into error studying Chu Hsi, I will be in error with Chu Hsi and will have nothing to regret".[67] These words of Ansai remind us of Shinran's wholehearted devotion to Hōnen.

The attitude of absolute devotion to authority can be observed even among the nationalistic scholars of the Japanese classics who rejected both Buddhism and Confucianism. For Motoori Norinaga (1730–1801), science is nothing other than the study of "the way of the past". He said: "A scholar should confine himself in the field of study only to reveal the way. He should not try to carry it into practice at his own discretion. But, he should study well the way of the past, teach the result of his study to others, take notes of it in book form, and wait for the opportunity, though it is not known whether such an opportunity is given five hundred years or a thousand years later, when the authorities adopt it in their principle of reign and carry it out throughout the country".[68] Though the study of the national classics in the Tokugawa period was a field of science newly risen at that time, still it was not free from the trend of over-attachment to the authority of the specific masters. It will be enough for this account only to mention the naive devotion of Motoori Norinaga to his master Kamo Mabuchi or the case of Hirata Atsutane (1776–1843) who on every occasion claimed himself to be a disciple of Norinaga. (It is doubtful whether Atsutane actually received the instruction of Norinaga.)

The attitude of absolute submission to a specific person is one of the distinct features of the way of thinking that can be commonly observed among the Japanese of the past. And, as we can see in the warrior's motto "a loyal vassal does not know two masters" or in the code of "morals" among the gamblers, the actual social ethics of the Japanese people reflect this feature of their way of thinking. As we have studied above, this can be by no means treated simply as a social phenomena of a feudal society.

The attitude of total submission to a specific authority is not a phenomenon found only among the Japanese of the past, but it can still be clearly observed among the present-day Japanese. Even in those self-styled "progressives" who are very severe toward conventional ideas, this trend is tenaciously adhered to. One reason for this is that the Japanese are always sensitive in their efforts to establish compact relations among the individuals within a small closed community. And this endeavor for mutual relationship serves to create a sense of unity and sympathy among the Japanese. But, at the same time, it sometimes leads them to accept blindly the principle of authority at the expense of individuality. We should make a further and closer examination upon the specific inclination that is consistently surviving in the way of thinking of all the members of a nation.[69] In general, the attitude corresponds to their custom in society which is well represented by sayings such as "A faithful retainer does not serve two masters". As pointed out already, it is not necessarily a feudal relationship.

Such an attitude is not restricted to the Japanese in the past. We notice it is remaining even at present deeply rooted among the contemporary Japanese. It is, therefore, necessary more fully to analyze the tendency of thinking which has been so dominant throughout the history of Japan. Although not an exhaustive study, this discussion opens a way to a deeper understanding of the great influence which leaders, especially religious leaders, had on the Japanese people in the past and are having still in the present. The figure of the *kyōso* (founder or foundress) of the modern religious movements is one instance of the fascination which a certain type of men or women can have for the masses.

---

1) *Dengyō Daishi Zenshū* 傳教大師全集, vol. IV. p. 719.
2) *Tōshūyō* 東宗要, in *Hōnen Shōnin Zenshū* 法然上人全集, (ed. by S. Mochizuki) p. 528.
3) *Tannishō* 歎異鈔
4) *Tannishō.*
5) *Shōshinge* 正信偈
6) With the term *shinshū* he means the tradition of Pure Land Buddhism from Indian masters up to Hōnen, both in the *Kōsōwasan* (高僧和讃) and the *Jōdo-monruiju-shō* (淨土文類聚鈔).
7) The Easy Way is the teaching of *Shinshū.*
8) In the beginning of the *Tannishō.*
9) Chiō Yamakawa 山川智應: *Hokke-shisō-shi-jō no Nichiren Shōnin* (法華思想史上の日蓮上人 Saint Nichiren in the history of Hokke Philosophy), p. 551.
10) Viśiṣṭacāritra Bodhisattva, to whom Śākyamuni entrusted with the propagation of the Lotus Sūtra.
11) In a letter of the year 1278.
12) According to T'ien-t'ai, all living beings, including holy persons, are divided into ten groups, each of them having its own sphere.
13) *Fa-hua-hsüan-i* 法華玄義, VII, (*Taishō*, vol. 33, p. 771.)
14) *Fa-hua-i-shu* 法華義疏 X, (*Taishō*, vol. 34, p. 599.)
15) *Jushiki-kanjō-kuden-shō* 授職灌頂口傳鈔
16) Nichiren's Letter to Ōta Kingo 太田金吾, *San-dai-hihō-rinshō no Koto* 三大祕法稟承の事
17) *Shōbō Genzō Zuimonki* 正法眼藏隨聞記, vol. II, ed. by T. Watsuji. Tokyo, Iwanami, p. 34.
18) *Ibid.* vol. I, p. 20.
19) *Ibid.* vol. I, p. 12.
20) *Shōbō Genzō* 正法眼藏, Bendōwa 辨道話, the sixth disputation.
21) *Shōbō Genzō Zuimonki*, vol. VI, p. 104.
22) *Ju-ching-ho-shang-yü lu* 如淨和尚語錄, (*Taishō*, vol. 48, pp. 130–131.)
23) *Ju-ching-ch'an-shih-hsü-yü-lu* 如淨禪師續語錄, (*Taishō*, vol. 48, p. 135 a.)

24) Daijō Tokiwa 常盤大定: *Shina-bukkyō no Kenkyū* (支那佛教の研究 A Study of Chinese Buddhism), vol. III, p. 82.
25) At the end of the *Gaijashō* 改邪鈔.
26) *Jōdo-hōmon-genryū-shō* 淨土法門源流章, in *Jōdo-shū Zensho*, 淨土宗全書 pp. 15; 594.
27) Shinran: *Shūjishō* 執持鈔.
28) e.g. *Mo-ho-chih-kuan* 摩訶止觀, (*Taishō*, vol. 46, p. 33.) doctrine (chiao 教), practice (hsing 行) and illumination (chêng 證),
29) Daitō Shimaji 島地大等: *Tendai-kyōgaku-shi* (天台教學史 A History of Tendai Philosophy), p. 468.
30) According to D. Shimaji, Shinran wrote the *Kyōgyōshinshō* in the province of Hitachi under the influence of Buddhism of the Kantō District which had established the special tradition of the doctrine, practice and illumination. Shinran added faith to the above-mentioned three.
31) *Nikka-Bukkyō-Kenkyūkai-Nempo* 日華佛教研究會年報, the first year, p. 9.
32) This sentence is also cited in the *Kyōgyōshinshō*, vol. III, pt. 1.
33) *Shōbō Genzō*, Sanjūshichi-hon Bodaibunpō. 三十七品菩提分法.
34) *Shōbō Genzō*, Bendōwa, 辦道話.
35) *Shōbō Genzō*, Shoji 生死.
36) *Tun-yü-yao-mên* 頓悟要門, ed. by H. Ui, Tokyo, Iwanami, p. 61.
37) *Shōbō Genzō*, Keisei-sanshoku 溪聲山色. This passage is often recited as the *Vow of Jōyō Daishi* (*Dōgen*) 承陽大師 發願文.
38) *Ching-tê-chuang-têng-lu* 景德傳燈錄, vol. XIV.
39) *Shōbō Genzō Zuimonki*, vol. III.
40) *Roankyō*, vol. II, § 70.
41) *Fumoto no Kusawake* 麓草分 in *Zenmon-hōgo-shū* 禪門法語集, vol. II. p. 545.
42) *Shishin-gohon-shō* 四信五品鈔.
43) *Niike-gosho* 新池御書.
44) *Himegoze Gohenji* 日女御前御返事.
45) Daito Shimaji: *Nihon-bukkyō Kyōgaku-shi* 日本佛教教學史, p. 6.
46) *Soshitsujikyō-sho* 蘇悉地經疏, in *Dainihon Bukkyō Zensho* 大日本佛教全書 vol. 43, p. 268.
47) *Kyakuhaibōki* 却廢忘記, in Taizo Ebara 穎原退藏, *Myōe Shōnin* 明恵上人 p. 25.
48) *Mujintō* 無盡燈, 1918, pp. 7 f.
49) *Rokujō Gakuhō* 六條學報, 1917, p. 166.
50) The Chinese version of the *Mahāparinirvāṇa-sūtra*, vol. XXXVI. (*Taishō*, vol. 12, p. 575 c.)
51) Shōson Miyamoto 宮本正尊: *Chūdo Shisō oyobi sono Hattatsu* (中道思想及びその發達 The concept of the Middle Path and its Development) p. 68.
52) "When a man is satisfied only believing the words of the Buddha and neglecting his own efforts to seek after truth, his faith is superficial and of no avail for him". *Zengenshosenshūtojo* 禪源諸詮集都序, ed. Hakuju Ui, p. 35.
53) Chiō Yamakawa: *op. cit.*, p. 355.
54) *Ibid.*, p. 652.
55) *Kōzen Gokoku Ron* 興禪護國論, the preface.
56) *Shōbō Genzō*, the section of Kenbutsu 見佛.
57) *Ibid.*, the section of Bukkyō 佛教.

58) *Ibid.*, the section of Bukkyō 佛敎.
59) *Shōbō Genzō Zuimonki*, vol. IV.
60) See In the above, p. 180 f.
61) In the *Hōkyōki* (寶慶記), it is noted as the words of Dōgen's master Ju-ching 如淨 as follows: "Besides Kāśyapa Mātaṅga, our master Bodhidharma came from the west to China to initiate us in the doctrines and the practices of Buddhism. This is the reason why it is said 'kyō-ge-betsu-den'. There cannot be two different teachings of the Buddha. Before our master came to this country of the East, there had been only the practice and no proper teacher to control it. The advent of our master to this country is comparable to the coronation of a king in a certain country. All the land, all the treasures and all the people are under the command of the king". This may not be, however, a faithful quotation of the words of Ju-ching. In the record of his sayings 如淨禪師語錄, there is no sentence expressing such an idea. On the controry, we can find in it the words like "to practice true Zen, one does not think about the masters". And we should be reminded of the fact that he criticized severely the proposition of the founding master Bodhidharma, "Nothing can be called holy" saying "He [Bodhidharma] created it only to volate it himself". It is very probable, therefore, that the above quotation the authority of which Dōgen atributed to his master would be the words of Dōgen himself. Even if it is a faithful quotation of the words of his master Ju-ching, it is very significant exhibiting the Japanese inclination to worship the authority that Dōgen selected this paragraph among many other sayings of his master attaching particular importance to it.
62) *Shōbō Genzō*, the section of Shizenbiku 四禪比丘.
63) *Hō-on Jō* 報恩鈔.
64) *Myōichime Gohenji* 妙一女御返事.
65) *Sōkichi Tsuda* 津田左右吉: *Shina Shisō to Nihon* (支那思想と日本 Chinese Philosophies and Japan), pp. 43–55.
66) *Benmei* 辨名, vol. 1, the section of 善良三則.
67) Tetsurō Watsuji 和辻哲郎: *Sonnō Shisō to sono Dentō* (尊皇思想とその傳統, Reverence for the Emperor and its tradition) p. 230.
68) Uiyamabumi うひやまぶみ, (in *Motoori Norinaga Zenshū* 本居宣長全集, ed. Hōei Motoori 本居豊穎, vol. 4, p. 607.)
69) It is wrong to assume that none of the Japanese in the past took a critical attitude to the established authority. I treated this subject in my recent work *Kinsei Nihon ni okeru Hihanteki Seishin no Ichikōsatsu* 近世日本における批判的精神の一考察. Here, at least we can say that the Japanese in the past were wanting in the spirit of criticism. See Saburō Ienaga 家永三郎: "*Nihon ni okeru Kindaiteki Seishin* (日本に於ける近代的精神) in *Nihon Shisō-shi no Shomondai* (日本思想史の諸問題).

(8) Emperor worship

That way of thinking which pays the highest respect to some particular living person, and at the same time reverences the distinctions of social status, comes to regard as the very highest, and to ascribe absolutely divine attributes to, that individual who stands at the top of the *hierarchy* of Japanese society.[1] Thus is Emperor worship established. Emperor worship, however, is not the only product of this tendency of thought. At times *shoguns* or their ancestors were recognized as having a claim to divine authority. For example, in the Tokugawa period, Tokugawa Ieyasu, the founder of the Shogunate Government, was given the appellation *tōshō daigongen* (literally, 'great incarnate Buddha of the eastern light'), and one referred to Ieyasu as 'Gongen-sama'. At the same time the Dutch referred to the Tokugawa Shōgun as the 'Kaiser'. Therefore we ought to treat Emperor worship and Shōgun worship as a single tendency, examining it first as ruler worship (Kaiserkultus) and subsequently examining it in the special sense of Emperor worship. But while an account following such a course would be logically most satisfactory, because of limitations of space we shall now merely make a few remarks about Emperor worship itself.

When the attitude of absolute loyalty to a particular person, which we have already described is directed toward the head of the state, it becomes Emperor worship. After the Meiji Restoration and until the defeat in the recent war, the attitude of absolute self-sacrifice which in the feudal era had been directed toward the feudal lords was redirected toward the Emperor. "The spirit of *bushido*, which has been developed by the warrior class over a long time",[2] as Yaichi Haga said rightly in 1907, "has now come to be directed solely toward the imperial throne".

The comment has even been made on Louis XIV's remark, "I am the state", that "This is a statement which could most appropriately have been uttered by the Emperor of our own country".[3] The statement, "The kingdom is nothing but the king",[4] is to be found in the most famous of ancient Indian political treatises; but among the Indians no such custom as Emperor worship ever arose. It goes without saying that ultranationalism developed in close relation with a worship of the Emperor as a living god. In fact, Emperor worship has been the most influential form of belief in Japan up to 1945; and even today after the defeat, the Emperor holds his position in virtue of his significance as a symbol of the unity of the Japanese nation. The Japanese like to see in the Emperor as a living individual a condensed representation of the Japanese nation. Although this is not a phenomenon which is unknown to other nationalities, it has a special significance in Japan. In this matter Yaichi Haga has remarked as follows: "There is a golden image of the goddess Germania at the top of a triumphal tower many feet high at the end of the Siegesallee in Berlin. The goddess was intentionally created as an imaginary person and designated 'Germania' to represent the German state. And in England in like manner an imaginary person called 'Britannia' has been fashioned, and in France one called 'Gallia'. In foreign countries where the form of gevernment has often changed, or where one royal house frequently succeeds another, such artificial symbols are naturally devised from the need to cause people to think of their past history and to cultivate the concept of the nation. Only in our country have soil of the nation and the Imperial House been inseparable since the age of the gods. The expressions 'for country' and 'for ruler' are to be understood as having the same meaning". Whether the Emperor is to be thought of as simply equivalent to the state, or is to be interpreted as a symbol of national unity, the Emperor-institution is a thing unique to Japan. It must be noted that it is not to be found among other peoples. Not concerning myself here with the problem of the political and economic basis of the Emperor institution, I should like to examine here the question how emperor worship has directly molded the way of thinking of the entire Japanese people.

Such a tendency of thought did not appear suddenly after the Meiji restoration; on the contrary, an incipient tendency of this kind has existed since ancient times.

According to the tales of the gods in the *Kojiki*, after the heavens and the earth were separated, the two divinities Izanami and Izanagi descended to the island of Onokoro, and then gave birth to the various islands of Ōyashima (i.e. the territory of Japan). After that they gave birth to various other divinities; the gods of the wind, of trees and mountains were born, and at the end the goddess (Izanami) died from burns, because she gave birth to the god of fire. Thereupon, the god (Izanagi) wanted to meet his spouse, and went to the land of night and saw her. Then, after returning to this world, when he washed the filth (of the land of death from himself), from his eyes and nose were born the three divinities Amaterasu Ōmikami, Tsukiyomi no Mikoto, and Susanō no Mikoto. It is said that this Amaterasu Ōmikami was the ancestor of the Imperial House.[5] *In this way the legend of the ancestors of the royal house is connected with the legend of the creation of the universe.* This is probably something without parallel among other nationalities. At least among other civilized people of the Orient, these two types of legends are separated. Thus, the divine authority of the Imperial House is enhanced by the fact that its lineage is connected with the legend of the creation of heaven and earth.

Further, in the older language, the word *ōyake* ('public') originally had the sense of 'the principal family',[6] which meant the Imperial House. In contradistinction, all the people were called *koyake* (minor families). Thus the Imperial House came to be regarded as the principal of ancestral family of all the Japanese.[7] Consequently, in Japan there was originally no conception corresponding to 'public', or 'öffentlich'. Among the Japanese, *public affairs consisted in nothing but relations with the Imperial Family.*

It would seem that the tendency to regard the emperor as divine has existed in Japan since most ancient times. When one looks at the many legends related in the *Kojiki* and the *Nihonshoki,* one finds that stories of the gods are not told for the purpose of demonstrating the greatness of the divinities believed in by the ancients; on the contrary, it is only for the purpose of showing the divine character of the Emperor that accounts are given of the gods which are its basis and of the historical blood relations of these gods. For such a phenomenon to obtain with regard to the legends of a people is completely without parallel elsewhere in the world. To be sure, in the Occident it is a historical fact that Alexander the Great and the Roman emperors were deified, but this was a matter of the deification of these men as individuals; this is quite a different thing from a national legend rooted in the primitive faith of a people. The theory of the divine right of kings in modern Europe has as its premise the Christian conception of God, and aimed at giving a basis to the power of princes in the will of this god.[8] And the theory of divine right in medieval India is to be understood in the same way. Thus, in archaic Japanese religion, the living totality of the nation is comprehended in the Imperial ancestor goddess and in the divine authority deriving traditionally from her. Here is to be found the unifying idea in the stories of the history of the age of the gods. Consequently, the people, united into one nation from various familial or political groups, give concrete expression to their corporate will through the Emperor or the divine Imperial ancestor who directs the government.[9] Therefore, in the society of that time bound together by ritual, the distinction between submitting to or opposing the authority of the totality of society is a distinction between submitting to or refusing to submit to the ruler who is the concrete manifestation of that authority—and this in the last analysis is reducible to submission or non-submission to the authority of the Imperial ancestor goddess. Therefore, it has been felt the distinction between goodness and wickedness is nothing but the distinction between submission or non-submission to the divine authority of the corporate whole, and consequently this means the distinction between submission and non-submission to the emperor.[10] Therefore the Japanese people have generally felt that the rule of Japan by the Imperial House generation after generation has been carried on the basis of the general will of their ancestors since antiquity.[11]

Since the Imperial House was originally conceived as having the position or ruling the entire Japanese people, the Imperial House *has no surname*. Consequently there has almost never appeared anyone aiming at becoming the highest ruler in place of the Imperial House. Of course, in Japan's long history, it is not the case that there have been no persons at all who have undertaken to rebel against the Imperial House. Taira no Masakado, Minamoto no Yoshitomo and Minamoto no Yoshinaka are generally regarded as rebels. However, even these men did not attempt to supplant the Imperial House. They desired to have some position at court, and raised rebellions through dissatisfaction at being unable to obtain it. Thus it is said that even rebels have recognized the Imprial authority. Perhaps the only exception is the case of Yuge no Dōkyō, the priest-premier. Even Ashikaga Takauji was able to establish his regime only by installing the Emperor of the northern court.

Subsequently, also, the concept of the divinity of the Emperor has become a religious tradition. In an edict issued immediately after the Taika reform, the Emperor is called the "bright god" (明神, *akitsumikami*). When the Emperor's power became stronger, there even appeared in an Imperial edict the following sentence: "We are the possessor of the wealth of the world; we are the possessor of the power of the world".[12] The divine-nation-concept and the principle of ultra-nationalism have a close connection with Emperor worship. On the point that Japan has been ruled by Emperors belonging to a line unbroken for countless generations, there has been an attempt to recognize a unique characteristic of the Japanese state.

Although in the past the Japanese have adopted Chinese thought and culture on a large scale, still they have exercised particular care not to injure the distinctive characteristics of the Japanese state. The law codes which formed the basis of administration and justice in ancient Japan were for the most part imitations of Chinese models; however, the traditional Chinese idea of revolution was rejected.[13] In regard to the government of the state, although reference was made to the twenty one

Chinese dynastic histories, the political practices of abdication and righteous rebellion were not initiated. There is a tradition that when the book of Mencius was brought in a ship to be introduced into Japan, the ship was wrecked in a storm on the sea, and consequently *the Mencius* was transmitted to Japan only with great difficulty.[14] What this means is that, because the concept of the ruler involving the notion of abdication and righteous rebellion as expressed in the *Mencius* is incompatible with the Japanese concept of the Emperor and the traditional Japanese pattern of government. This legend has been produced by the fear of men who have not wanted *the Mencius* to be popularized or who were afraid of this.

"Also, I have heard it said that the book of Mencius contains the following argument: at the beginning of the Chou, King Wu with one burst of anger gave response to the people of the world; he is not to be spoken of as a subject murdering his ruler; rather he executed the villain Chou (-hsin) who was a desecrator of benevolence and righteousness. Consequently, although Chinese classics, histories, and even books of literature have all been brought over to this country, only that book of Mencius has not yet been brought to Japan; for, it is said, the ship which carries it is always sunk by a storm. If we ask why, the reason given is that, while there has been no break in the Imperial line since our country was founded and ruled by Amaterasu Ōmikami, if such a clever teaching be transmitted there might appear in future time an adversary who would despoil the descendants of the gods and claim to be blameless; and detesting this possibility, all the gods raise up a divine wind (*kamikaze*) and overturn the ship. Thus, even among the sagely teachings of that country, there is not a little which is inappropriate for this land". (*Ugetsu Monogatari*)

The introduction of Chinese Confucianism into Japan caused almost no friction or disharmony; only the doctrine of abdication and rebellion presented some amount of problems. This doctrine holds that while the Emperor holds his position of Emperor so long as he receives the mandate of Heaven, if he should lose the confidence of Heaven he will inevitably lose his position; such a doctrine is under any circumstances hard to reconcile with the traditional Japanese concept of the Emperor. Therefore, this point became a problem for scholars. The following admonition to posterity is ascribed to Sugawara Michizane: "The mystery of the eternal existence of our divine country is something we dare not try to understand. Although we study the Chinese classics of the three royal dynasties, of Chou Kung and Confucius, the Chinese national tendency of revolution is something we should be deeply concerned about".[15]

Thus, even Confucianism has definitely not been introduced in to Japan uncritically. Fujita Tōko, a Confucianist of the Mito school, argued that among the doctrines of Confucianism, there are two which are "definitely not applicable" to Japan, "namely, the doctrines of abdication and of righteous rebellion. The gaining of the throne by abdication is exemplified by Shin and Yü, while the attaining of the throne by rebellion is instanced by T'ang of Yin and Wu of Chou. Since the Ch'in and Han Dynasties, those who arrogated the throne by deceiving the Emperor's orphans and widows always based their arguments on the examples of the sage-emperors Shun and Yü, while those who usurped the throne by destroying their royal houses and murdering their rulers always pretended to be following the examples of T'ang and Wu. There have been more than twenty dynasties in Chinese history, and not only have those in high and low position changed places, but even the distinction between Chinese and barbarian has been lost". In China, if the Emperor loses the virtue requisite of an Emperor, he must lose his throne; but in Japan, the Imperial throne has been for ages eternal, available only to those in the same blood lineage. Consequently here the Emperor's possession of virtue has been irrelevant. "In our bright divine land, the unbroken Imperial succession has been transmitted without end, ever since the heavenly ancestor gave the heavenly descendants the commission to rule, the augustness of the heavenly throne is just as unsurpassable as the sun and moon. Even if there were in the world someone comparable to Shun or Yü in virtue or equal to T'ang or Wu in knowledge, still the only thing he could do would be to support the Emperor with complete devotion and assist the work of the throne. If it should chance that someone should proclaim the theory of abdication, it would be quite justifiable for any of the people of Ōyashima (Japan) to rise in indignation and attack him".[16]

Of course, most Confucianists did not express themselves so clearly. Even these were aware that there was a contradiction between the ancient Japanese form of government and Confucian theory, *but they kept silence and avoided coming to grips with this contradiction.* Once this contradiction was taken up and became a problem, there was no other course than to interpret it as did Fujita Tōko.

To be sure, among Confucianists there were people who were extremely absorbed in Chinese culture. Nevertheless, even Ogiu Sorai who called himself a 'barbarian' and 'one of the Eastern barbarians' still after all had an attitude of reverence for the throne.[17]

If we reason from the way of thinking which has been described above, we come to the conclusion that Imperial authority is not something derived from separate abstract principles which exist above him, but that it is to be regarded as inhering in his very person. For example, Kumazawa Banzan emphasizes the divinity of the Japanese Emperor. "It is not to be doubted that the Japanese Emperor is the august descendent of the heavenly god". "Only in Japan has the imperia lhouse continued without change. Even in the age of the *samurai*, a man who conquered the country could not become ruler. This is because divine authority is naturally inherent in the three sacred treasures".[18] Again, Yamazaki Ansai, in spite of his profound understanding of Confucianism, did not try to understand Shintō from a Confucian standpoint, but, even while using various Confucian concepts, endeavored to understand Shintō in its own terms. According to him, the god of creation is a divinity with a human body—that is to say, he is the ancestor of the Imperial Family.

The phrase *shinsei* (divine sage) (as applied to this god) means that in him the divine and human are combined. He is the venerable god of the primordial universe; *he is revered as the ancestor of the Emperors, and as the source of their body and blood.* The concept of 'Emperor' (*tennō*' in Japan is different from the Chinese concept of the 'son of Heaven'. "In foreign countries (sc. China), above the chief ruler there is the heavenly sovereign; above the edicts of the Emperor there is the mandate of high Heaven. In our country, however, the ruler is himself this 'heavenly sovereign'; and the edicts of the Emperor must be regarded as the 'heavenly mandate' itself".[19] The Emperor is not the "son of Heaven" who receives the "mandate of Heaven", but is himself taken to be the heavenly sovereign who issues the mandate.

And so, while enthusiastic proponents of reverence for the throne study Confucian doctrines, still there are cases where they completely turn these doctrines around. It is a problem whether or not there actually is in Mencius democratic thought, but at any rate Mencius did refer to the ruler of the state as the 'people's ruler' and took the position that he should be concerned with the circumstances of the people. But Yoshida Shōin in lecturing on Confucianism, attacked the statements in Mencius which yield a democratic nuance. In considering the passage in Mencius that "The people are most valuable, the altars of the land and grain come next, and the ruler is least" (*Mencius, Chin hsin p'ien* II, ch. 14), Yoshida would not accept Mencius' thought as it stood. He interpreted this passage in Mencius as meaning that "the people are most valuable from the point of view of the ruler". Thus he attacked Western democracy, and aimed at a complete overturn of Chinese thought.

"If we read this passage without understanding this meaning, we will utter, in imitation of the Western barbarians, the evil notions that the world is not the property of one man, but belongs to itself, and will come to forget the idea of *kokutai*. This is greatly to be abominated. It has recently been reported that students at Meirinkan school were asked to write an essay on the theory that the world is not the property of one man. Therefore, I reflect that, while this theory that the world does not belong to an individual appears[20] in the *Liutaosanlüeh,* it does not necessarily come from the classical scriptures. It is not a general notion in China. It would seem to be held in connection with the idea of abdication and justified rebellion. But the proverb, 'throughout the world there is no land which is not the king's; throughout the world, there is no one who is not the king's subject', clearly assumes that the world belongs to one person".[21]

The Chinese idea that "the world is not one man's has now been changed contrary-wise to the thesis that "the world is one man's (viz. the Emperor's)".

Hence, in spite of the wide-spread acceptance of Confucianism, Chinese Confusianism and Japanese Confucianism have differed in their emphasis. The basis of Chinese Confucianism was the virtue of filial piety. Thus, since a basic element in their thought was the idea of the change of dynasties, the idea of loyalty could not occupy the central place in their ethical scheme. However, in Japan, due to the hierarchical structure of society, the particular virtue of loyalty occupied the highest place among all virtues.

This difference in ways of thinking between China and Japan on the matter of the authority of the Emperor was manifested in *a difference in ways of compiling histories.* In China, the practical motivation for the compilation of most histories, especially "standard histories", was to check the power of the ruler mildly in advance, and not to let it out of control. Therefore, the official historian recorded both the good and the bad actions of the Emperor, in order to make the reader, whether he be the Emperor or an official, voluntarily criticize and reflect. In Japan, however, this kind of intention is lacking. If we examine the motives for the work of compiling histories in Japan, the reason for comiling the *Kojiki* and *Nihonshoki* was to make clear 'the rule of the Imperial Family and the broad basis of its royal influence'.[22] In other words, the intention was to record selectively, on the basis of Japan's consciousness of itself as a state distinct from the rest of the world, the facts of Japanese history, emphasizing as central the geneology of the Imperial House. Consequently, a critical spirit was not apparent in these books.

The absence of a critical spirit based on human reason, as has already been considered, is a conspicuous characteristic of the Japanese way of thinking, but this defect appears sharply revealed in the way of thinking which reveres the living Emperor as divine.

If this be the case, what may have been the influence exerted upon the form of adoption of Buddhism by the idea of Emperor worship which has had a firmly rooted existence throughout the Japanese nation since antiquity. In the case of Buddhism, in spite of the fact that it is theoretically difficult to join it to Emperor worship, in Japan a union between the two was ultimately achieved.

The idea of emphasizing the prestige and benevolence of the ruler appears in India in the Brahmanistic legal codes, but Buddhists universally rejected it. Only in a few cases, in later Mahāyāna Buddhism, has this Brahmanistic idea been picked up. Nevertheless, the Japanese have particularly noticed these exceptional ideas in the Buddhist sacred texts. In book two of the *Daijō Honshō Shinji-kangyō,* the 'four benevolences' viz. of 'parents', 'all sentient beings', 'the ruler' and 'the Three Treasures' are explained one by one. In the passage on 'the benevolence of the ruler', the scripture teaches that "the happiness of the people depends on the ruler, mountains and rivers, the earth within the state, all are the possessions of the ruler. The ruler's authority is the same as that of the Buddha. He enjoys the special protection of the gods (the celestial beings of the thirty-three heavens). Therefore we ought not to try to rebel against the ruler". Such a concept of the ruler is quite exceptional in the Buddhist texts.[23] King Aśoka, who devoted himself body and mind to the realization in political activity of Buddhist ideals, even went so far as publicly to declare in his edicts that *the ruler receives benevolence of the people.* Yet this doctrine of four benevolences, which is exceptional in Buddhism, was regarded as especially important by the Japanese. Although in the Buddhist sacred texts these four benevolences are only dealt with together, and although as regards their content, the benevolence of the Three Treasures is recognized as having paramount significance, in Japan the benevolence of the ruler is especially emphasized, and is accorded the highest position. For instance, on the seventh day of the tenth month of 862, under the Emperor Seiwa, Tomonosukune Yoshio, who was Chūnagon (n.b.—court rank) and concurrently minister of the bureau of the populace and grand officer in the palace of the Imperial mother-in-law, submitted a memorial expressing a desire to contribute a villa near Fukakusa to a temple. In this document, after citing the doctrine of four benevolences in the *Daijō Honshō Shinji-kangyō,* he concluded by saying, "we ought first to repay the benevolence of the holy ruler in protecting and sustaining us, and second, to requite the virtue of the sphere of Truth for favoring us".[24] Again, in Taira no Shigemori's admonitions to his father, Taira no Kiyomori, there is the passage "I have recently read in the *Shinji-kangyō* that the first benevolence is that of heaven and earth, the second that of the king, the third that of parents, and the fourth that of all sentient creatures. By knowing this we are human beings; by not knowing it, demons and animals. Among them the most important is the benevolence of the king".[25] But the idea that the "benevolence of the king " is most important is not a doctrine of the *Shinji-kangyō,* but is something which the Japanese have asserted using this text. Following this common point of view, later Zen masters also, for example Takuan, emphasized that "No one ought to slight the benevolence of the ruler". (*Takuan Zenshu* book 5 *Tōkaiyawa,* last part)

The national Japanese thought tendency of Emperor worship has, contrary to what one would expect, exerted an influence on Buddhists. A religionist like Shinran who advocated absolute devotion to the Amida Buddh, did not have at all in mind such a thing as Emperor worship. Nonetheless, he calls the Amida Buddha's compassionate summons of living creatures, in order to save them, an "Imperia lorder".[26] Nichiren also, referring to the pronouncements of the Buddha, used the phrases "edict of the Buddha" and "Imperial declaration".[27] Probably these sectarian Buddhists preferred to use such expressions as an appropriate way to express themselves to the Japanese. (In recent years Buddhists were forbidden to use such expressions by the militarist government.)

In the case of Nichiren, in particular, the concept of Emperor worship seems to have influenced inconspicuously the structure of his religious ideas.[28] He related that when he was young he harbored a doubt as to whether the retired Emperor at Oki or the Hōjō regent was the true ruling authority in Japan; and the same sort of doubt caused him to select the Lotus Sūtra from among the many Buddhist sacred texts. "Even though when one looks about the land, one finds that each man says, I am the ruler, yet the ruler of the country is but one man. If there were two, the land would not be calm. If a family were to have two heads, that family would surely be torn apart. Isn't the Buddhist canon also just like this? Whatever Sūtra it may be, surely it is just one Sūtra that is the "great king" of the canon! But if seven out of ten sects struggle with one another without coming to agreement, this would be as bad as for there to be seven or ten kings in a country—the people would not be at peace. What could be done then?"[29] In such a frame of mind he proceeded to evaluate and compare Buddhist texts, and finding in the Lotus Sūtra the statement, "This Lotus Sūtra is by far the greatest of all Sūtras", he finally declared his utter devotion to the Lotus Sūtra.

While Buddhism was being propagated in Japan, Emperor wroship likewise shortly come to be generally recognized as common sense even among Buddhists. Even the *Tsurezuregusa* by the priest Kenko (兼好) says "The great position of the Emperor is awesome indeed. Even the last leaves growing in the bamboo garden (i.e. all members of the Imperial Family, to the end of time) are not of the race of ordinary men; they are noble!" We have already noted the fact that Japan-minded Confucianists have recognized a special excellence of the Japanese nation in the unbroken continuity of the Imperial line; but a number of Buddhists have mentioned the same thing. Kokan Shiren, the author of the *Kenkō Shakusho,* which is the most important history of Buddhism in early Japan, recognized in the tradition of the transmission of the three sacred treasures to Japan, the reason for the superiority of the Japanese state over other countries. "Although China is called a great country and its territories are vast, still the seals of authority there are all human artifacts and are not made by Heaven. Although our country is small, it was founded by gods and has been given the sacred treasures by spirits. China is not even to be compared with it". (book 17) Again, Kōsen (洪川) said, "In our state there is the Way of the Emperor. This is the great way of the heavenly ancestor Gods, and is the orthodox way of the ruler. Its continuity has been endless, for divine descendants have continued in one line and have not mixed with other families..... Although it has been almost three thousand years since the Emperor Jimmu succeeded to the rule, no one yet has ever dared to usurp the heavenly throne and break the divine line of succession. The majestic virtue of the Imperial House is vast. This is why our Kingly Way is unique among all countries". (*Zenkai Ichiran* ("one wave in the sea of Zen")). These men constantly looked up to the authority of the Imperial House.

When this idea was reached, soon the theory was advanced that "The Emperor actually is the state". Tōrei says "Although heaven and earth are vast, there are only one sun and one moon. Likewise the fortunes of the state depend upon one man, the Emperor" (*Shūmon Mujintō-ron* (treatise on the undying light of the (Zen) sect)). We have already noted the tendency toward naturalism among the Japanese, and this is closely connected with the concept of esteem for lineage and with Emperor worship. Even Buddhists have made the strange statement that the word "nature", in its ultimate sense, means the everlasting continuity of the Imperial line. Kokan Shiren says,

"Japan is a pure, pure entity.

The basis of the state is rooted in nature. No Chinese dynasty has ever been like this. This is why we praise our country. This 'nature' is the three sacred treasures. The three treasures are the sacred mirror, the sacred sword, and the sacred jewel. These three are all natural, heaven-made products. The fact that our country has one Imperial line which reaches far back in time and is unbroken over the ages is surely due to these treasures, which are natural and heaven-made. Therefore, even after countless generations, there is no danger that the throne will be menaced. Surely, these heaven-produced sacred treasures will not become the playthings of another clan or of foreign arms".

This point of view corresponds exactly to that urged by Yamazaki Ansai, mentioned earlier, but such a concept of nature is absolutely not to be found among Indian or Chinese Buddhists, and would perhaps seem strange to Westerners as well. Reasoning along a line identical with that just illustrated, Buddhists themselves came to advocate the thesis that the Imperial ancestor, "Amaterasu Ōmikami" denotes the absolute. Master Tōrei says, "The general meaning of 'shin' (god, spirit) is shin (mind). When all dirt is cleaned from the mind, and it becomes as clear as a mirror, then it is called 'spirit'. For this reason, the vehicle of spirit is symbolized by the mirror..... The mirror of the mind is always round and clear, and reflects all things whatsoever. This is called 'Amaterasu Ōmikami' (*Mujintō*, Ruzū No. 10). Herein there is not the slightest trace of a conception of a pagan god. Nonetheless, Emperor worship has introduced a subtle modification and twisting of various Buddhist conceptions.

Among the Five Injunctions of Buddhism there is an injunction against stealing. The original meaning of this in India was, 'do not take things that have not been given you by someone else'. However, among Japanese Buddhists, a tendency appeared to interpret even this in connection with Emperor worship. Jiun-sonja Onkō interpreted it as follows: "There are boundaries between countries just as mountains and rivers are distinct from each other. ....the line of the Emperor of our country has been unbroken since the age of the gods. This signifies that the injunction against stealing has a natural basis. In China, the lines of Emperors are in disorder, and in the course of time even a man of lowest estate can become ruler of the world".[30)]

The idea that the Emperor is divine has brought about a modification of old Buddhist conceptions regarding the relation between the 'ten virtues' and the ruler. The laws which are to be especially observed by all men have since early Buddhism been called the 'ten goods' or the 'ten injunctions to goodness'. These are the virtues which are the opposites of ten evils, namely, not killing, not stealing, non-licence, not talking idly, not breaking faith, not backbiting, not using lascivious language, not being greedy, not to be angry, not to seek vain amusements. It is frequently stressed in Buddhist texts that the ruler must realize these ten goods in the people. In regard to the true law of the ten goods which was expounded by the Tathāgata, the ruler ought to uphold and practice them, and by means of this law to govern the world.[31)] In addition to diligently practising the Ten Goods himself,[32)] the ruler must put them into practice among all the people. "If the ruler causes (the people) to cultivate the Ten Goods, he will be called a blessed and virtuous ruler; but if he does not do so, he will be called an evil ruler".[33)] "The ruler ought, like the sage king Cakravarti of antiquity, to educate the people in the way of the Ten Goods". King Muensoku, under whom the youth Sudhana studied, is said to have "forever put an end to murder, robbery, and licence, to have forbidded idle talk, faithlessness, slander and lascivious language, and banished avarice, anger and idle pleasure".[35)] This conception has exerted a conspicuous influence upon the general conception of the Emperor among the Japanese. In old Japanese books, the Emperor is often called, "master of the Ten Virtues" (*Masukagami, Fujigoromo*). "The ruler in whom the

Ten Virtues are unlimited" (*Eiga Monogatari, Hikage no Katsura*); and the imperial throne is called "The seat of the Ten Virtues" (*Masu Kagami, Kusa-makura*), or "the imperial throne of ten-thousand charriots of the ten virtues" (i.e. the throne of boundless virtue) (*Heike Monogatari*); and the Emperor is thought of as one who ought to realize the Ten Virtues in human relationships. "He rules the land putting into effect the correct law of the Ten Virtues" (*Jinnō Shōtōki,* 1).[36] Such concepts presuppose the Buddhist political theories already explained.

When these came to Japan, they brought about still other interpretations. The Japanese, coming into contact with Chinese thought, identified the *tennō* (Emperor) with the *t'ien-tzu* (Emperor) as conceived by the Chinese, and accordingly thought of him as the 'son of heaven'; but in Buddhist texts it is taught that all men will be born in heaven if they practise goodness; these two conceptions being combined, the Emperor came to be thought of as having kept the rules of the Ten Virtues in past existences and consequently having been born in this life as Emperor, as a result of merit. Thus, e.g. "By the grace of the Ten Virtues he has become Emperor (*tenshi*)" (*Jinnō Shōtōki* 4). The theory that the Emperor is born ruler of the land because of a practice of the Ten Virtues is probably without authority in the Buddhist sacred texts.[37] The general tendency to regard the Emperor as divine has produced this sort of conception. Although according to Buddhism the ruler must realize the Ten Virtues, and the true significance of the ruler is realized just in this way, in the Japanese view the Emperor has *already done this.* While according to Buddhism the divine nature of the ruler is to be realized in *the future* as a moral 'ought', in the Japanese view this is reinterpreted as already given to him, and as being an accomplished fact. We can detect, in the tradition of Prince Shōtoku, a characteristic of a way of thinking similar to this. Prince Shōtoku, in the general conception of later Japanese, was a reincarnation of the Bodhisattva Avalokiteśvara.[38] But this sort of tradition has not appeared in India.[39] The patronage of Buddhism by King Aśoka was, as to the point of its influence on world history, so great that he is not to be compared with Prince Shōtoku; but in the many traditions transmitted among the Indians about King Aśoka, he is merely made out as having acquired virtue through having presented sand to the Buddha, as a child in a former life. And likewise among other kings and Emperors in India who have protected Buddhism, we cannot discover any such traditions. Beneath the way in which Prince Shōtoku is venerated lies the particularly Japanese tendency to Emperor worship.

The Authority of the Emperor has been supposed by people at large to be superior to that of the Buddha. In fact Y. Haga declared: "It is a universally believed proverb that the Buddha is of nine virtues, while the Emperor is of ten virtues". Moreover, prayers are said in Buddhist temples for the longevity and good health of the emperor, while tablets are usually enshrined therein to the same effect.

Since old days the nationalistic tendency for Emperor worship has been prevalent among the Japanese at large, and various religions in Japan have made conscious and unconscious attempts to adapt themselves to such a tendency. It is to be noticed, however, that on the part of the members of the Imperial Family, efforts have not always been made to sanctify themselves. Those who became devout believers in Buddhism, in particular, were least interested in such a tendency. Emperor Shōmu declared himself to be 'a slave of the three treasures of Buddhism' (the Buddha, the law, and the priest). Upon finding a passage in Volume 16 of *Daijū-Kyō*" which read, "We are allowed to take neither family nor property nor throne with us when we die. Only commandments, alms-giving and no licentiousness are to be our companions in our present as well as our future lives". Emperor Kazan left his throne and became a devout believer of Buddhism, "because he understood that even the Imperial throne and the treasures of the state were nothing but illusions".[40] He was aware of the austere fact that even the monarch must die alone, just as commoners do. Some members of the Imperial Family expressed their feeling of *equality before the judgment of Hell.* They, therefore, thought it necessary to become devout believers of Buddhism in order to prepare themselves for the judgment. Emperor Daigo is said to have composed the following thirty-one-syllable ode: "At the abysm there is no difference whatsoever between the members of the Imperial Family and slaves".[41] This is a statement, as a believer, of the equality of men. There are also fairly many odes to the same effect composed by other emperors.[42] In April, 859, owing to a supplication of the empress dowager, three pensionaries were instituted at the Anshōji Temple. The petition reads: "Even those in heavens cannot escape their decline, not to speak of ordinary men on the earth. Crossing the bourn before Hell, we cannot take property with us. Dragged into Yama's judgment-hall, there is no difference between the ruler and the ruled. We have come into the world alone to die alone".[43]

There are many poems composed by emperors which express their sin-consciousness as well as their delight in the vow of Amitābha.

"How many sins of my body reflected in the mirror might be,
I only wish my mind to look toward the Pure Land".

(Emperor Gokashiwabara)

Each of the following poems well expresses an Emperor's consciousness of sin and worldly concerns as well as his joy in the vow of Amitābha that evil men are entitled to be saved.

"The most sinful of all sinners are we who commit sins, knowing that we shall certainly be saved.
How should Amitābha leave us out of this gracious vow!"

(Emperor Gotsuchimikado)

"Afflicted as I am, I will not complain,
Since I trust the marvellous vow of Amitābha".

(Emperor Tsuchimikado)

In these poems the emperors are well aware of being ordinary men.

Motivated by such a consciousness, these Emperors and members of the Imperial Family were led to enter priesthood. After the death of Emperor Junwa, his bones were smashed to pieces to be scattered on the summit of Nishiyama at Ōharano[44] in accordance with his will. There were fairly many Emperors who made their wills not to have any tombs made for them. One of the Imperial edicts issued in the name of Emperor Seiwa at the time of a drought reads, "It's my fault, not the people's. My clothings and provisions should be curtailed". At the end of the Kamakura period, Ex-emperor Kameyama entered priesthood himself prepared meals at the kitchen for those priests who visited the temple on the occasion.[45]

In these cases we cannot discern any intention on the part of the Imperial Family to present themselves as living gods. Such was the general attitude of the Imperial Family toward religion before the Meiji Restoration. At the time of the Meiji Restoration, Emperor worship was instituted by force under the influence of the movement for 'reverence for the Emperor and expulsion of foreigners'. In recent years, it has come to be the only and absolute form of religion in Japan. It is not true, therefore, that Emperor worship was motivated by a subjective intention on the part of the Imperial Family itself. On the contrary, it represents a way of thinking peculiar to the Japanese which assumed an extraordinary form of expression at a certain period of Japanese history. As has been pointed out already, this way of thinking has modified the introduction and development of Buddhism in Japan. There is almost no analogue of such a tendency in India or in China. Indeed it is sure that such a form of living-god-worship is a result neither of the various conditions peculiar to the Eastern societies in general nor of 'feudalism' at large. In fact there remain still various problems to be studied in connection with Emperor worship in the ancient Orient and in the Roman Empire.

---

1) In the article of the *Goseibai Shikimoku,* customary law which had been established prior to Yoritomo is frequently referred to as "established at the time of the great Shōgun (i.e. Yoritomo)", this would seem to be an example of the same situation. Seijirō Takigawa 滝川政次郎: "Nihon Hōritsu Shisō no Tokushitsu" (日本法律思想の特質 Special Characteristics of Japanese Legal Thought) (*Iwanami Kōza, Tōyō Shichō*) pp. 48–49.

2) Kokuminsei Jūron (國民性十論"Ten Essays on the National Characters") pp. 31–32.

3) *Ibid.,* p. 34.

4) "*Rāyā rājyam*" (Kauṭilya, *Arthaśāstra,* ed. by R. Shama Sastry. 2nd ed. p. 325)

5) *Ibid.,* pp. 33–34.

6) *Kojiki* 古事記, ch. 1.

7) *Ibid.,* p. 21.

8) Tetsurō Watsuji 和辻哲郎: *Sonnō Shisō to sono Dentō* (尊皇思想とその伝統) p. 59 ff. For comparable ideas in India, cf. my book: *Shūkyō to Shakai Rinri* (宗教と社会倫理 Religions and Social Ethics), Tokyo, Iwanami, 1959, pp. 286–326.

9) *Ibid.,* pp. 49–51.

10) *Ibid.,* p. 67.

11) Cf. *Nakatomi-barai* 中臣祓

12) Emperor Shōmu, Edict on the construction of the Great Buddha, 10th month, 743.

13) However, in the very understanding of the content of the term "revolution (*kakumei,* ko-*ruing,*) there appears to have been a change a period of time. For example, in the Kakumei Kammon of Miyoshi Kiyoyuki (*Gunsho ruijū, zatsu*) etc., the sense of *Kakumei* appears to be understood merely as "great change" (Suggested by Prof. Masao Maruyama)

14) See various *Zuihitsu* by Japanese writers (refer to the *Nihon Zuihitsu Sakuin* 日本随筆索引) and the *Un tsa tsu* 五雑俎 by a Ming author, etc. (Moku Kondō, 近藤杢; *Shina Gakugei-daijiten* 支那學藝大辭典)

15) *Kanke Ikai* (菅家遺誡 Family Administrations of Sugawara Michizane) But, as this passage does not occur in old manuscripts of this work, it would seem to be later interpolation. (Cf. vol. 8, p. 138 of *Kitano Bunsō* 北野文叢, in *Kitano shi* 北野誌 edited by the curator of the Kitano shrine)

16) *Kōdōkan ki Jutsugi* (弘道館記述義 Commentary on the chronicle of the Kōdōkan [school of Mito]). Contrary to general supposition, there were Confucianists who recognized and advocated the doctrines of "change of surname" (viz. dynasty) and "overturning of the mandate"; one, for example was Ōhashi Totsuan (Shigeki Tōyama 遠山茂樹, *Ōsei Fukko no Imi* (王政復古の意味 Significance of the restoration of imperial government) *Shisō,* 思想 vol. V, (1947) p. 33. However, he was exceptional.

17) Yukinari Iwahashi 岩橋遵成 *Sorai Kenkyū* 徂來研究 p. 444 ff.

18) *Miwa Monogatari* 三輪物語 pt. 1 (*Banzan Zenshū* 蕃山全集 vol. V. pp. 218 and 222.)

19) Tetsurō Watsuji 和辻哲郎: *op. cit. ibid.*, pp. 235236.
20) Tō Yamada suggested that the oldest example is from the *Lü-shih ch'un-chiu* 呂氏春秋.
21) *Kōmōsakki* 講孟箚記, vol. IV. (vol. II, p. 462 of *Yoshida Shōin Zenshū*)
22) *Kojiki*, 古事記 Preface.
23) In vol. 61 of *Shōbō Nenjo Kyō* 正法念處經, there is a discussion of the four benevolences of one's mother, one's father, the Tathagāta, and teachers of the dharma, but the benevolence of the ruler is not mentioned.
24) *Sandai Jitsuroku* 三代實錄 vol. VI. Moreover, in the text under the date 865, 7th month, 19th day, there is the phrase, "the world of the four benevolences is the whole of mankind" (*ibid.* vol. XI.)
25) *Gempei Seisuiki* (源平盛衰記 Records of the rise and fall of the Minamoto and Taira Clans) vol. VI. Cf. also vol. 2 of Heike Monogatari 平家物語.
26) Shinran said (*Kyōgyōshinshō* pt. 2) that "the doctrine of devotion is the imperial order of the call in the original vow", again, (*ibid.* pt. 3) he says the expression "a desire for birth" (in the *Daimuryōju kyō.*) i.e. the desire for rebirth in the pure land, means the imperial order of the Tathāgata calling all sentient beings". Probably his use of the expression "Imperial edict" enabled the Japanese to understand better.
27) Cf. *Kaimokushō* (開目鈔) "An account of various doings of the master", vol. II.
28) However, Nichiren did not regard the emperor as absolutely divine becaus of his secular rank. In his view, religious authority stood above the authority of the emperor. Even the emperor, if he transgressed the law, would go to hell. "Because of the bad karma of having despised the Buddha Śākyamuni and having neglected the Lotus Sūtra, ... the retired emperor of Oki in the 82nd generation and also the retired emperor of Sado ...... ended their lives in these islands. Because their spirits were wicked, they went down to hell". (Reply to the Sister Myōhō)
29) *Hōonshō* 報恩鈔.
30) *Sōryū Daiwajō Suiji* 雙龍大和上垂示 pt. 2. *Jiunsonja Zenshū* 慈雲尊者全集 vol. 13, p. 655)
31) *Shohō Shūyō-kyō* 諸法集要經, (*Taishō*. vol. 17, p. 516 a).
32) *Shōbō Nenjo-kyō* 正法念處經 vol. LV (*Taishō*. vol. 17, p. 324 a).
33) *Daijō Honshō Shinji kan-gyō* 大乘本生心地觀經 vol. II. (*Taishō*. vol. 3, p. 298 a).
34) *Zatsuhōzōkyō* 雜寶藏經 vol. VIII, (*Taishō*. vol. 4, p. 485 b–c).
35) Tang translation of the *Kegon* (*Avataṃsaka*) *sūtra* vol. 66, (*Taishō* vol. 10, p. 355 b); vol. XI of the *Shijū Kegon* has the following passage: "He commanded that all should desist from the Ten Evil Ways, and perfect themselves—the practice of the ten Goods, just as did King Cakravarti" (*Taishō*. vol. 10, p. 712 c).
36) Also, "His birth falling on a sacred day, he was molded by the influence of the Ten Virtues"—*Sandai Jitsuroku*, vol. 6, paragraph under the date 862, 10th month of the reign of emperor Seiwa.
37) Many former Japanese classical scholars explained such conceptions as "the emperor (non of heroine) of the Ten Virtues" as being applied to the emperor on the basis of the Buddhist conception that a man who has kept the commandments of the Ten Virtues in a past life is reborn in present life

as ruler of the land. Probably, Japanese classical scholars have interpreted the matter in the following way. Tokunō Oda (*Bukkyō Daijiten* p. 922 a; *Kokubungaku Jūnishu Butsugo Kaishaku* [explanation of Buddhist terms in 12 books in Japanese literature] p. 85). But literal expressions of this thesis are not to be found in Buddhist texts. Indeed, it is very often maintained in Buddhist texts that if a man does good he will be reborn in heaven; and also there appears, although rarely, the thesis that one is born as ruler in this life because of merit accumulated in a past life. The Rev. Oda cites only the following examples, one quoted from the Judaikakyō in vol. 52 of *Hōen Shūrin.* "How can one be reborn in heaven? By practicing the ten virtues one is reborn in heaven. How can one assume the human state? By observing the Five Injunctions one assumes the human state"; and another, quoted *from Make-bikuni-kyō* in part 1 of *Benshōron*: The five injunctions are the root of the human; the ten virtues are the root of the heaven. In these it is not stated that through a cultivation of the ten virtues one is born an emperor. The foregoing interpretation is developed by the Japanese conception of the emperor which identifies the notion of *tennō* with that of *tenshi,* and further is influenced by the Chinese idea that the emperor (tenshi) is the "son of heaven".

38) Cf. Shinran's *Kōtaishi Shōtoku Hōsan* (a eulogy of the imperial prince Shōtoku)

39) Y. Haga: *op. cit.* p. 42.

40) *Jikkinshō* 十訓抄, ch. 6. cf. *Eiga Monogatari* 榮華物語, ch. 花山.

41) Cited in *Genpei Seisuiki* 源平盛衰記, vol. VIII as a poem by the Lord of the Engi period, whereas in *Jikkinshō,* ch. 5 as one by Prince Takaoka, Cf. *Yōkyoku,* Hachi-no-ki 鉢木.

42) Various poems of the like by Emperors are collected in Mizumaro Ishida 石田瑞麿; *Rekidai Tenno Gyosei ni Haisuru Goshinkō* 歴代天皇御製に拜する御信仰 ("Nihon Kyōgaku Kenkyūjo Kenkyū Hōkoku 日本教學研究所研究報告", No. 8)

43) *Sandai Jitsuroku* 三代實錄, vol. II.

44) *Shoku Nihon Kōki* 續日本後記, vol. IX, S. v. the 9th year of the Shōya 承和 period, in the reign of Emperor Ninmei 仁明.

45) *Monnō Kōtei Gaiki* 文應皇帝外記, in *Zoku Gunsho Ruijū* 續群書類從, pt. VIII, Ch. 1. vol. 190, p. 44. cf. *Nanzen-ji-shi* 南禪寺史, p. 41.

(9) Sectarian and factional closedness

In Japan there exists a strong tendency toward sectarianism and factionalism, which is another manifestation of the trend to regard as absolute any limited and specific human nexus. It is a fact generally observed today that this tendency is still conspicuous, even in Japan at the present time. Yet it is not a phenomenon of recent origin, but it has been deeply-rooted among the Japanese since ancient times.

I should like to dwell upon this tendency first in reference to the constitutional make-up of the Buddhist order and the mode of worship among the believers. In Japanese Buddhisms, it is not the universal creed that is counted as most important. But rather, the emphasis has been placed upon the specific religious order itself as a limited and concrete human nexus.

In the process of the establishment of the Honganji-order, which has become the largest order in Japan, we can find historical evidence of this sectarian factionalism which is conspicuous among the Japanese. Shinran himself, the founder of Jōdo-shin-shū, never had any thought of establishing a new sect of his own. He firmly believed, as has already been pointed out in the preceding chapters, that it was his mission to follow faithfully the teachings of his master, Hōnen, and to reveal the true essence of them. Besides, Shinran recognized the universality of religious doctrine. "The teaching of the Tathāgata is something that permeates everywhere".[1] It was just upon the basis of this belief that he could make the outright assertion that "I, Shinran, have no disciples to be called mine".[2] And he believed that "every one of them is a disciple of the Tathāgata" and "we are all fellow-disciples practicing religion together".[3] It was otherwise, however, with the Buddhist priests of his time. They would say 'this is my disciple", or "that is someone else's disciple", and they vied with one another for the acquisition of more disciples of their own.[4] In spite of Shinran's strenuous effort to warn against such sectarian conflict, it became a strong tendency even within the Shinshū order, until at last the entire followers of Shinshū were transformed into "those who are called to be the disciples of the Saint of the Honganji Temple".[5] Since then the Honganji order has developed into a large organization on a nation-wide scale, not as a free and open association of the believers, but rather as a closed order with the "pope" as its central authority. It came to be a life-and-death problem for the followers whether they are admitted into or expelled from the order. Rennyo, in his effort to avoid an insurrection, warned the followers: "It has been rumoured that the disciples are up to some evil deeds. That would be preposterous. From now on, one who would contrive such an intrigue should certainly be *excommunicated* forever *from the followers of the gate of the saint*".[6] The disciples of this order, as the quotation shows, were called *'monto'* (followers of the gate), and henceforth this appellation has come to suggest the rigidity with which the close door policy of the order was maintained. Each temple then came to function as a 'mediating temple' for the followers.

It has been generally accepted that Shinran advocated that *Buddhism should be practiced under the lay condition.* But, 'neither ecclesiastical nor secular'[7] is his standpoint, in which he permits a priest to marry and raise a family. Thus he was not advocating a lay religious movement in which the priesthood would not be recognized at all. In this respect, it is not quite the same as the religious movement of the Quakers in the West, in spite of their close resemblance. The Shinshū order has centered around the hereditary professional priests. It is to be admitted, however, that in its rudimentary form it resembled most closely a movement for secularization of religion. There even seemed to be no such things as temples at its earliest stage of development.[8] But in spite of this, this order gradually acquired a form pre-eminently sectarian, and in this we can perceive a tendency of thinking characteristic to the Japanese at large.

Such intolerant and exclusive tendencies are also conspicuous among other sects of Kamakura Buddhism said to be characteristically Japanese. It is widely known that the most violently sect-conscious of all is the Nichiren sect, as is indicated by the four-point maxim of its founder, Nichiren. Viz: "Those who practise invocation to Amitābha are due to suffer continuous punishment in hell; the Zen sect is the devil; the Shingon sect is the ruiner of the country; the Ritsu sect is the enemy of the country". Originally the "*Hokke Sūtra*" taught that even the most ignorant and the stupid, should they practice Buddhism faithfully, would all attain the status of absolute perfection. That was a most generous expression of the spirit of tolerance and magnanimity, which used to be the characteristic attitudes of almost all the devotees of the Hokke Scripture. When it came to Japan, however, the Nichiren sect, which took the attitude of placing absolute reliance on the Hokke Sūtra, unfailingly became sectarian and closed, and one faction of it even displayed a tendency toward extreme exclusionism. In the case of "the non-alms-giving-or-taking faction" of this sect the giving, or taking of alms to and from non-believers of the Hokke Sūtra was prohibited.

If we go from Kamakura to Ashikaga, a great majority of the followers of the Jōdo sect had, not respect, but contempt for various Buddhas, Bodhisattvas, or gods and goddesses other than Amitābha.[9] Such a trend also appeared conspicuously in the Jōdo-shin sect. That was precisely why Rennyo repeatedly warned his followers against contempting various Buddhas and gods, though to them they might not owe any special obligation of respect.[10] Such a tendency is relatively slight in the Zen sect. Such a person as Dōgen, however, displayed an attitude of extreme aversion to other ideas of sects. Being confident that he himself was the faithful propagator of the gospel of his master, Ju-ching (Nyojō), he loathed to adopt or compromise with ideas other than his own.[11] When we look at Nyojō's own teachings, nevertheless, we find that he is to some extent close to the theory of the compatibility of Confusianism, Taoism and Buddhism, which has generally been accepted in China.[12] It can be rightly stated, therefore, that it was Dōgen's own version of his master's teachings based upon his own method of selection, which might have very well been unconscious, but which was apparently quite contrary to his avowed and conscious assertion that he was the faithful spokesman for his continental master. It amounts to this: that in Japan there has never been established any religious doctrine like the doctrinc of three stages of the Sui and Tang periods in China that preached universality of the Buddha and the religious doctrine without discrimination.

It was thc Japanesc traits to emphasize the human nexus rather than religious faith that gave rise to the segmentation of quite a number of religious sects, each of which is exclusive and closed to one another. This has also to do with the Japanese propensity for cliquism in general. Among the Zen sect, as an example, it is not the difference in the religious faith or doctrine but *such mere factors of human relationship* as the inheritance of the master's "endowments" that account for the split of the religious school into multitudinous sects and factions.[13] The Master-and-disciple relationship is jealously maintained. It is one of the characteristic of Japanese Buddhism to make much of the inheritance of the lineage of religious doctrines.[14] Today the communication media are so well developed that any single individual is susceptible to the influence of various ideas of many individuals. Should one insist, under such circumstances, on maintaining the absolute authority of *just one* master toward his disciples, that would inevitably foster the sectarian relationship. And nothing is so far removed as this situation from the original Buddhist stand: "Do not depend upon men, but upon the law".

The emphasis upon the inheritance of the master's endowments naturally gives rise to the system of secret and oral instructions.

The Tendai sect, after being transplanted into Japan, introduced a secret oral instruction, called '*Sanjū-shichika no Hōmon* 三重七箇の法門' or the 'three-fold-seven-point gates to the Law' which is a secret oral instruction transmitted from the master to his disciples. It was conceived to have been established during the period before Tōyō Chūjin (1065—1138) and after Kakuchō (960—1034), and it is of a great significance in the Japanese Tendai theology.

"Some of the so-called orally instructed gates to the Law are", according to Daitō Shimaji, "unknown in respect to their origins, authors, and the date of formulation. Nevertheless, herein lie the essence and the rudiments of the Tendai theology in medieval Japan".[15] The fact that their authors are unknown shows that their genesis was in no way connected with the authority of any particular individual, but rather that it was the Japanese inclination of thinking itself that was responsible for such a formulation.

This trend is also present among the Zen sect. According to the Rinzai sect, one is expected to contemplate upon a great number of catechetic questions for mediation, which requires the mastery of innumerable phrases and precedents, in the language other than the native tongue of the Japanese Zen priests. This meant a tremendous effort on their part. Those who were not up to the task were apt to confine themselves to the intensive reading of just one particular book out of many, and to contrive some comments of their own, which were then regarded to be "family inheritance" to be instructed in secret.

This trend for emphasizing secret oral instructions became particularly distinctive among the Zen sect. "Inka", the master's recognition of his disciple's attainment of enlightenment, certainly existed in China, where it meant merely a practice exercised at the moment of having attained enlightenment. In Japan, however, it came to be stressed according to the idea of inheritance. The Myōshin Temple sect reveals its inclination for secret instruction in the form of a certificate for having entered enlightenment. Moreover, all the factions of the Zen sect attached special importance to the forms of comments or foot-notes given to catechetic questions for meditation, and these forms were transmitted in an oral and secret way.

In any sect they make much of the relationships between the central and peripheral temples, all of which are ultimately subordinated to the head temple. Such a system of hierarchy was also introduced into the newly-risen Buddhist sects and Shintō orders. There also existed political factors that gave rise to the split among sects. The divide-and-rule policy of the Tokugawa government was, for instance, responsible for the separation of the Honganji Temple into eastern and western sections, whose differences in doctrine was later evolved and of little significance.

Splits among sects in this sense of the word never occurred either in India or in China. Indeed, there are a number of different schools of Buddhism in India, which may correspond to what we call sects in Japan. But the situation is vastly different from what exists in Japan. There, the distinction among different schools stands for the difference in the doctrines of respective schools. After the Maurya Dynasty (about 317—180 B.C.), each temple or monastery came to be affiliated to this or that school for the purpose of effective management. Even then the essential function of those buildings, namely 'to lodge priests from all the four directions' was maintained, and no priest from other schools was ever refused accommodation. It often happened that people of different schools lived under the same roof. The same thing seems to have happened in China also.[16] Almost all the temples in modern China belong to the Zen sect, where the invocation of Amitābha is also practiced. Within the same temple a person may sit in religious meditation and at the same time practice invocation of Amitābha (with the hope of entering the Pure Land). The practice of meditation and that of invocation of Amitābha are therein compatible.

Contrary to those situations in India and China, a great number of sects in Japan are segregated, exclusive and closed from one another. For illustration the Zen school and the Jōdo school, which in China are in complete harmony without any sense of conflict, form themselves in Japan into separate sects, which are incompatible with each other.[17] (Incidentally, these two schools were not clearly distinguished from each other in India.) In Japan also a person like Dōgen, for instance, violently disliked sect-names and refused to call his own sect the Zen sect. In reality, however, the Zen sect brought forth segmentation of factions and sub-factions.

It follows that in China, if distinction among sects be required, it is made according to the person in charge. In Japan, in contrast, each temple has its own denomination. In China, the denomination of a temple depends upon the resident priest and is consequently submitted to change from time to time, but in Japan the denomination of a temple never changes according to the person in charge.[18]

Such denominational distinction as exists in Buddhism in Japan, might very well be attributed to the religious policy of Tokugawa government with the situation still persisting today. But it can also be suggested that had it not been for the existence of the Japanese way of thinking to serve as a basis for the establishment of such social institutions, the enforcement of such a system would not have been possible.

Buddhist orders with their characteristics of sectarian closedness on one hand, and the followers in general with their family system firmly established on the other, together gave rise to the system of alotting families to each temple. That system means a relationship, stabilized into an institution, between the temples and the families of their followers. The latter would entrust a particular temple with the performance of the funeral and other Buddhist services of their families and the management of their family cemeteries on one hand, and on the other hand, the former would take it for granted to ask, in return for those services, not only for the remuneration for those services but for the donation of money to cover the building, reconstructing, repairing and other maintenance expenses of the temples. Such a system emerged voluntarily toward the end of the medieval age, and was later adopted and enforced by the Tokugawa government. Moreover, during the Tokugawa period, a system was established in which each individuals' religious faith had to be guaranteed by his temple. Those who were confirmed not to be pagan were registered in "the denominational census-register".

Thereupon the Japanese men and women, with their family as a unit, came to be affiliated to one or another temple, and accordingly they submitted to this or that denomination. It follows that, in Japan of the past, it was not the individual but the *family* which determined religious faith. The individual faith of a person is indistinguishable from that of his or her *family*. The relationship between the temple and its parishioners was not always established according to the choice of a religious faith on the part of the parishioners. Mostly their relationship was purely customary and was not usually accompanied by the sense of joy ensuing conversion or redemption. The lack of religious faith prevalent among the Japanese today has its socio-historical roots in this fact.

The attitudes of exclusiveness and closedness were the characteristics not only of the Buddhist orders. A similar situation existed among various Shintō sects. Such has been admitted by the Japanese themselves. "Those who advocate Shintoism", criticized Matsumiya Kanzan, "mostly boast of their own secret teachings, occult instructions and conceited bigotry, and do not wish to impart their knowledge to the people in general. They are all concerned only with trifles ...."[19] The fact that such an attitude prevails not only in Shintoism but also pervades into various arts and crafts was pointed out by Tominaga Nakamoto as follows:

"The habits of Shintoism, to begin with, are occultism and secret-instructionism, which are tantamount merely to hiding everything. Hiding is the beginning of lying and stealing. Witchcraft and figures of speech may be permissible as being interesting to look at and listen to. But those habits alone are extremely inferior. In the olden days when people were honest they must have been less harmful as means for teaching and guiding them. But today is the age of corruption by liars and robbers. So it is wrong on the part of the teachers of Shintoism to defend those evil doings. Even those ignoble businesses like *Sarugaku* (a medieval Noh-dance) and tea-ceremony, all following the example of those habits of Shintoism, fabricate secret instructions and certificates for having attained enlightenment and even set price to sell them for profit-making. This certainly is deplorable. When one asks why such things came about, they answer that it is because of the fact that their instructions are not easily to be transmitted to those who are not ripe for them. That appears to be somewhat reasonable. But one needs to be reminded that a way, which is to be kept in secret, which is not to be readily transmitted, and for which a price is set for instruction, cannot in any sense be called genuine".[20]

A sectarianism not quite so closed but still exclusive was pushed to its extreme in Hirata Shintoism.

After the Meiji Restoration sectarian Shintoism spread with enormous rapidity. In spite of the fact that there was no more state interference or guidance exerted upon Shintoism, curiously enough, there appeared symptoms almost identical to those of Buddhist orders under the control of the Tokugawa government. Moreover, it should be noted in particular that the Honganji Temple order and newly-emerging Shintō orders were once organized according to the prototype of the emperor-system.

Such a tendency as exists in the religious sense of the Japanese cannot be defended as a taken of respect for the purity of faith. It is attributable rather to the social inclination of the Japanese in general for the establishment of some form of limited and closed human nexus. To say the least, the segmentation of religious sects exclusive and closed to one another cannot be ascribed to a difference of religious convictions in respective sects, since the Japanese at large are so markedly indifferent to religion.

Then a question should be raised as to why the tendency toward sectarian cliquism is conspicuous among the Japanese at large. It might be tied up with the Japanese inclination to love and enjoy the small-scaled and closed way of communal living. In search of the existential bases of the exclusive tendency among such small-scaled communities, we have to take into consideration the factor of a social mode of living adapted to the topographical elements of the environment. The density of population of the narrow island since ancient days might be taken as a proof that life here used to be comparatively easy and peaceful. On the other hand the same fact may account for the formation of the traits of exclusiveness. Such problems ought to be discussed independently. Suffice it to point out that these characteristics are distinct among the Japanese in general.

As it has been pointed out in the preceding sections, the Japanese attach great importance to limited specific human nexus, and as the family, lord-and-vassal relationship, the coterie or the state (or the emperor); and even universal world religions, once transplanted into this country, were transformed to fit their propensity. Scarcely any thought has been put to the eternal law which any man should follow beyond the confines of these human nexus. Generally speaking, the Japanese mode of adopting a foreign religion was confined to those cases when it was considered to do no damage to but to promote and develop some concrete human relationship which the Japanese regarded as absolute. For those individuals who took religious faith seriously, it might have implied 'devotion and obedience', but for the Japanese society as a whole it only meant 'absorption and adoption'. Consequently, although Buddhism has been the flesh and blood of Japanese culture for more than the past ten centuries, the people at large still regard it as 'an imported thought'. In this respect, our attitude fundamentally differs from those of the Western nations in regard to Christianity or those of the southern Asiatic nations in regard to Buddhism. As for those nations these universal world religions are conceived to be such integral parts of their own culture as to be responsible for the formation of the respective nations themselves. As for the Japanese, in contrast, such a conception is totally absent. What is called the non-religious character of the Japanese partly consists of over estimation on the one hand of limited concrete human nexus and of the conscious or unconscious indifference on the other to the principles of the universal religion.

In order to interpret those social phenomena above mentioned, one might refer to the underdevelopment of modern bourgeois society. Indeed, that is also one of the causes. But an economic interpretation is not enough to explain away all the characteristics mentioned above. An oversimplified ascription of these phenomena to the facts of immaturity of capitalism, its unbalanced developments and the lag of feudal social institutions is far from satisfactory, since those socio-economic factors are commonly shared by other Asiatic countries and not the unique properties of Japan alone. With respect to the mode of production in agriculture also there exists distinct similarity among Asiatic countries. In regard to religious thoughts, however, there exist some characteristics unique with Japan, which are rather absent among other Asiatic peoples.

One could not but attribute these characteristics, therefore, to the mental propensities latent in the minds of the Japanese. And without subjecting these mental propensities to thorough-going examination, and radical criticism, and without taking strong measures to do something about them, it would be difficult, as I take it, to foresee an overall change of outlook of the Japanese in the future.

---

1) *Kudenshō* 口傳鈔 (by Kakunyo 覺如 (1270– 1351)), Kyoto, *Shinshū Shōgyō Zensho* 眞宗聖教全書, vol. III. Kōkyō Shoin. 4th erd. Showa 16 (1941), p. 9.

2) *Tannishō* 歎異鈔 (traditionally ascribed to Yuien [disciple of Shinran]) *ibid.*, (same edition), vol. II. p. 776.

3) *Kudenshō*, p. 9.

4) Cf. *Tannishō*, *Kudenshō* and *Gaijashō* 改邪鈔 (by Kakunyo).

5) Gaijashō (same ed. vol. 3), p. 84.

6) *Senkōji monjo* 專光寺文書 (T. Tamamuro: *op. cit.*, p. 321) (n.b. the book is *Nihon Bukkyōshi Gaisetsu*—of p. 79, note 22)

7) Cf. *Kyōgyōshinshō* 教行信證.

8) "In Akao, situated on the upper readers of the Shō-gawa in Etchū (Toyama pref.) there remains an organization of a group of faithful which suggests the times of Rennyo." "In this village, a matter which has greatly infrigned me is the fact that in each community there is a *dōjō* (sacred hall). Whereover there are as many as 20 households, there is a stately *dōjō*. A *dōjō* is not a temple. Although the eaves are higher than those of ordinary houses, and the interior is entirely in the style of a temple, yet there is no professional priest. Middle and upper class families of this village take charge in turn, and when necessary hold memorial services without a priest, and also perform funerals. Sometimes priests are invited to preach, but ordinarily there is none there; it is merely a place of worship for the community. In winter, since it is impossible to communicate with other settlements, the people of the community like to assemble here and talk together about their religion. This is the 'meeting in the dōjō' frequently mentioned in the *Ofumi* of Rennyo." (Daijō Tokiwa 常盤大定: *Nihon Bukkyō no Kenkyū*, p. 229.)

9) Cf. *Shaseki-shū* 沙石集 (by Mujū, 無住, also called 圓國師, or according to one source, 大圓國師 1226–1312) 1, b "The followers of Jōdo thinking lightly

of the Shintō gods". But as a contrary example there is the fact that Japan and others also showed respect for various gods and Buddhas.

10) Cf. Rennyo 蓮如: *Ofumi* 御文 (*Shinshū Shōgyō Zensho*, vol. III, pp. 402–518).

11) Dōgen maintained that such an attitude was derived from his teacher, Ju-ching (Nyojō); "The sentence, 'the Three Religions have one end', is inferior to the talk of a little boy. (People who talk this way) are a group who would destroy Buddhism. Each people alone are numerous. They either appear as religious leaders of men and demi-gods, or become teachers of emperors. The present time (the Sung Dyn.) is a time of decline of Buddhism. Religious teachers and Buddhas of old warned". (Dōgen 道元, [1200–1250]: *Shōbōgenzō* 正法眼藏, "Shohōjissō", 諸法實相 Iwanami Bunko ed., vol. II, p. 240).

12) When we look at the collected sayings of Ju-ching, we find that he recognizes the authority of Confucianism and Taoism also and quotes from the *Lun Yü*, the *Lao Tzu*, etc. (Keidō Itō, 伊藤慶道 *Dōgen Zenji Kenkyū* ch. 1, p. 32 ff., p. 69 ff.)

13) It is commonly considered that Dogen's religion is a faithful continuation of its Chinese counterpart. But the fact that the thought of the *Shōbōgenzō* coincides with the teachings of Ju-ching, as recorded in the *Hōkyōki** does not justify this opinion. [*No. 1796 of Iwanami Bunko] The *Hōkyōki* is a work by *Dōgen*, not by Ju-ching. Hence, it is to be feared that in the sayings of Ju-ching quoted there, Dōgen's wishful interpretation have probably been added. If we are to understand the thought of Ju-ching, we must in any case study his own collected sayings; but it is to be regretted that there is yet no study of the content of his thought, going beyond the bibliographical study of the collected sayings by Keidō Itō.

14) The emphasis on doctrinal lineage appears also in the Tang Dynasty, China, and becomes strong with the Sung. But it is a much stronger tendency in Japan than in China.

15) Daitō Shimaji 島地大等: *Tendai Kyōgakushi*, (天台教學史 A History of Tendai theology) p. 466.

16) "In ancient India also, *sūtras* and *śāstras* were studied together; and in early times in China, the three schools were not separated, hence they must have had deep understanding". Accordingly, the priest Eisai of the Kenninji "studied religious law and observed ceremonial rules, studies and practical Tendai, Shingon and Zen alike, and also recommended to others the practise of Nembutsu" .(*Shaseki-shū* vol. X pt. 2 *Kenninji Hongan Sōjō no Koto*".) Many examples can be found in the *Kao-seng-chuan* (高僧傳) of monks of different sects living together in one and the same temple in China".

17) The Jōdo sect usually called Zen the "School of the sacred way (Shōdōmon)" on the other hand, *Hakuin* vigorously attacked the Jōdo sect (N. B. Hakuin was a Zen master, full name Hakuin Ekaku (1685–1768)

18) Daijō Tokiwa 常盤大定: *Shina-bukkyō no Kenkyū* (支那佛教の研究 A Study of Chinese Buddhism) vol. III. p. 76.

19) Matsumiya Kanzan 松宮觀山 (1686–1780): *Sankyō Yōron* 三教要論 (in *Nihon Jurin Sōshō*), p. 3.

20) *Okina no Fumi* 翁の文 by Tominaga Nakamoto (1715–1746) (written in 1738), section 16.

(10) Defense of a human nexus by force

The view that specific and concrete system of human relationship is absolute tends to carry with it the notion that the defense and development of the system is also an absolute. When the existence of the system of human relationships to which one belongs is endangered, one is apt to defend it even with recourse to force. In the Japanese way of thinking, the use of force is not generally regarded as ethically good or evil, or as justified or not under each particular condition. One is inclined, instead, to seek a sacred cause in the mere act of defending a specific human nexus. High esteem for arms had a very important place among the thought-tendencies in Japan at least in the past.

Such a tendency was already obvious in the ancient mythology. This land was then called 'the country of one thousand fine halberds', the name suggestive of the fact that the Japanese were the nation of military prowess from ancient days. A comparison of the Japanese myths with those of other nations reveals some characteristics of the Japanese people. For instance, Finnish mythology, as represented in the Kalevala, is said to be rather lacking in the concept of respect for military power. In Japanese mythology, however, instances of conquest by arms are definitely traceable, and the concept of respect for military power is consistently followed. It is noteworthy as archaeological remains prove to us, that no violent inter-racial conflicts seem to have occurred on Japanese soil. Nevertheless, on the conceptual level there is a strong tendency toward respect for military power, which constitutes a distinct characteristic of Japanese mythology.

In later periods other nations admitted and the Japanese themselves boasted that they were brave and superior in military matters. Matsumiya Kanzan writes: "The Japanese are high-spirited and fond of arms. Valour and dauntlessness make up their distinctive style".[1] Hirata Atsutane also comments as follows:

"The Japanese are endowed with extraordinarily courageous spirit, which one may as well call either fearlessness or heroism. What is it? Being defeated by their enemy or having a grudge against their enemy, and yet having failed to take their revenge, they calmly commit *harakiri* without flinch. Such is the way of the Japanese who, faced with an emergency, are never afraid of death".[2]

The underlying motivation for such prowess is an absolute devotion to one's lord.

"I will not from to-day
Turn back toward home....
I who have set out to serve
As Her Majesty's humble shield".[3]

Either in devotion to one's feudal lord or in that to the Emperor, the identical way of thinking is present. It is vastly different from the case of the Indians. The Indians, indeed, also have their own epics of wars. But they always use religious teachings to encourage their heroes. They are taught that those brave soldiers fallen on the battle-field will be reborn in *the Heaven of Indra*[4] or that they will dwell with the god Vishṇu.[5] It would be totally inconceivable to the Indians that one should march to the battle-field with the conviction that: "To hell may I fall; the punishment of God may be upon me. I pray nothing but to serve my lord, with utmost loyalty".[6]

A question may be raised here. We have already mentioned that among the Japanese there is an obvious inclination to esteem affection. Is it not incompatible with the propensity for the respect of prowess? Kumazawa Banzan was already conscious of this problem: "An old friend asked: 'Japan is a land of military prowess. Why is it then that she is also called to be the land of benevolence?' I answered: 'It is exactly because she is the land of benevolence that she is the land of military prowess. Is it not obvious that the benevolent are always brave?'"

The fact that the Japanese of the past esteemed military force does not imply that they used violence merely for the sake of destruction. In so far as they had to maintain and defend the interests of a specific system of human relationship—a feudal clan, the state, a group of gangsters, or whatever—, they appealed to force. In combat they were brave. The virtue of self-sacrifice was always manifested. But if the leader of the system to which one belongs should ever order to cease fire, at once they would stop using force. Instantaneously peace is established. The reason is that their objective is not to kill men and destory things but to defend the human nexus by force.

If such a way of thinking among the Japanese be understood, it would also be possible to comprehend the fact that the dauntless generals of old Japan were at the same time refined gentlemen of gracious heart, who composed poems, appreciated the beauties of nature, and who were well-versed in the tea-ceremony and were considerate to other people. In almost all the books on the way of *samurai,* the virtue of 'benevolence' is recommended. It was possible for daring brave generals and soldiers to be followers of Buddhism, which ordained not to kill even a single insect without cause. Herein lies, as I take it, the key to solve the secret that the Japanese are by nature peaceful, but brave in combat.

In order to be brave on the battlefield, soldiers were expected to get rid of their fears and worldly concerns. For that purpose, Buddhism, Zen in particular, was observed as a guiding doctrine.

The fact that among the attitudes of the Japanese as warriors such traits were preeminent might very well be attributed to the way of thinking prevalent to the Japanese at large. If such had been the thinking pattern transmitted and maintained only among the *samurai*-class, it would not have been possible that among the chivalrous outlaws, coming from the common people, and among the rank-and-file soldiers after the Meiji Restoration, the same traits should appear just in the same fashion as in the case of *samurai* of the earlier days. These attitudes cannot be interpreted merely by means of the theories of class-ethics or of the mode of production.

The effort to maintain and defend the human nexus even with recourse to power naturally increased the influence of the soldier in Japanese society and made them the ruling class.

Japanese society has never seen firmly established a class comparable to the literati in China or to the caste of Brahmin-priests in India. It cannot be said that the socio-economic situation in Japan prevented such a class from emerging. It was rather the Japanese inclination to emphasize the order of human nexus that enabled the soldiers, whose essential function was the use of power, to rise to the supreme position as the rulers of the society. This tendency persisted from antiquity up to very recent days. Men of letters were, generally speaking, given only minor positions as aides and advisers. These characteristics made Japan vastly different from other Asiatic countries. In reference to this point Max Weber explains:[7] "The contrast of Japan with China, consisted of those parts that were in the closest contact with the feudal Japan, appears particularly in the following aspects. In Japan it was not the 'unmilitärische Literaten-Schicht' but the class of professional soldiers that were most influential socially. As in the Medieval West, it was the custom and culture of the knight that regulated practical conduct, not the certificate of passing the examination or scholarly refinement as in China. It was also 'innerweltlich' culture that regulated practical conduct as in the antique West, not the philosophy of deliverance as in India". As far as this aspect is concerned, the comment of this German sociologist seems to be valid.

Within Japanese society a pattern of conduct has thus been established, in which the soldiers take pride in their position as soldiers, and pledge loyalty under any circumstances to their lords and readily die for them.

Readiness to defend the human nexus even by force, and the consequent dominance of the soldier, also determined modes of acculturation. In transplanting Confucianism, the Japanese ruling class equated the Confucian bureaucracy and the 'samurai' class in Japan. The two, however, were different in substance: therefore, the way of the high officials was not immediately identified with the way of the *samurai*. Consequently, they had to wait until a scholar like Yamaga Soko appeared and formulated the theory of the way of "samurai" availing himself of Confucian theory. Most of the books on the way of *'samurai'* were written in the spirit seemingly independent from Confucian theory.

What changes did Buddhism suffer in this regard? Buddhism originally abhorred control by force and aimed at the achievement of an ideal society not based upon the relationship of dominance-submission-by-power. Consequently, both in India and in China, followers of Buddhism regarded benevolance and forbearance as particularly important virtues. Laymen might resort to violence, but never the clergy. In any order of any world religion in the past history, one could never find men so far-removed from military power as the Buddhist believers in India and China. Even after the advent of Buddhism to Japan, among the earliest Buddhist orders such virtues were still kept intact.

It is impossible, however, that a religious order alone is untouched by the general way of thinking prevalent among the Japanese. After the Heian period, various large temples, which were owners of large estates, supported priest-soldiers, whose force was utilized to achieve the temples' demands. There were also armed conflicts between temples and shrines. At the time of the feud between the Genji and Heike clans, old shrine families affiliated themselves to one or the other clan and fought. The fleet of the Kumano Shrine, for instance, assisted Genji, while the head priest of the Usa Shrine belonged to Heike. Originally the ideal of shrines and temples was to stand aloof from political conflicts and to keep their estates intact as the sacred neutral zones, from invasion of all directions. But the attitude that men of religion are justified to use armed force naturally led the priests of temples and shrines to take up arms for self-defense. According to the reports of Christian missionaries on Japan, the monasteries at Negoro always supported a host of priest-soldiers and let them train themselves in military affairs. Once a giant bell was rung, it was told, 30,000 soldiers could be summoned in just three or four hours.[8] In the 15th and 16th centuries and the Age of Civil Wars, the followers of the Ikkō sect and the Nichiren sect rose to arms against the pressure of feudal lords. At the time the chief abbot Rennyo was in Yoshizaki, he summoned the priests and their families, belonging to the central cathedral, and forced them to decide a few days in advance "Our destiny is predetermined by the deeds in our previous lives, *so you should not be afraid of death. You should fight*".[9]

No precedent has ever been recognized in India or in China that a Buddhist order should use armed force. In India the Sikhs and Nāga ascetics were once armed but those were rather exceptional cases. In Japan at the early stage of the modern period there occurred a war based upon the conflict of religions as in the case of the insurrection at Shimabara. Compared with the *War of Religion* in the West, this insurrection is hardly worthy of mention. But it is noteworthy that such a phenomenon appeared at considerably early days solely in Japan and not in other Asiatic countries.

This is a manifestation of the effort of devotion to defend one's own religious order even when recourse to power was necessary. This is why once the security of the religious order being assured, the order instantly ceased to fight. Since the national unification brought about by Toyotomi Hideyoshi, all the Buddhist orders have abandoned arms. Even thereafter, however, the inclination to maintain and expand Buddhist orders by force persisted. This is, according to my view, mainly based upon the 'sectarian-factional tendency' already discussed.

The Japanese respect for arms in the past influenced the mode of acceptance of Buddhist *thought*. An illustration of it is the fact that the worship of Acalanātha is considerably popular among the Japanese people. Acalanātha, wearing the features of indignation, living in the midst of blazing flame, with a sharp-edged sword in his right hand and a rope in his left hand, burns out all the troubles and disturbances both internal and external and defeats and annihilates devils. Acalanātha is a divine being which made its first appearance toward the last stage of Buddhism when esoteric Buddhism was founded and popular religion for common men was adopted. It scarcely appears in the extant Sanskrit Buddhist Scriptures.[10]

Its place in Indian Buddhism was therefore dubious. In China it was hardly respected either.[11] There are, of course, five great Buddhas in the Kongō-kai and Taizō-kai maṇḍalas, and which were introduced by Kōbō, and thereafter in Japan Acalanātha and other Myōōs (*Vidyārāja*) were very often represented in painting and sculpture. So in the T'ang dynasty in China Acalanātha and other Myōōs must have been worshiped. But the fact that they ceased to be worshiped later seems to be a proof that the idea of the conquest of devils with swords, which is the intrinsic nature of Acalanātha, was not congenial to Chinese view of religion. Benevolence characterized by Avalokiteśvara Bodhisattva was the religious ideal of the Chinese. In contrast, the features of defeating enemies and conquering devils incarnated by Acalanātha was better suited to the minds of the Japanese. For the same reason the worship of the great commander (*Āṭavika*) was widely practiced in Japan. Even Amitābha, who is benevolence itself, was supposed to use armed force. The expression, "the sharp-edged sword of Amitābha", is often used in Japanese literature. It was originally derived from a phrase in the *Hanju Panegyric,* written by Shan-tao of the T'ang period in China; "The sharp-edged sword is another name for Amitābha. An invocation of the name absolves from all sin". The sharp-edged sword in this case, however, is a mere figure of speech. The Japanese took it as if Amitābha had used the real sword to punish the wicked.[12] And they sought in this interpretation of Amitābha for the justification of using armed force in war.

The Japanese respect for arms is manifested in the rigor and relentlessness with which Zen priests trained their disciples. Tsūgen Jakurei (1322–1391), whose teaching was most widely inherited in the Sōtō sect, is famous for his 'pit of burying-alive'. When an itinerant priest came to him in order to receive training, it was told, he tested the new-comer and if he perceives in the latter impurity of motivation, he then simply knocked him down into the pit.[13] In India there were many who performed religious austerities upon themselves, but no such atrocity was perpetrated upon others. Suzuki Shōsan (1579–1655), a *samurai* by origin, advocated what is called the Zen of the two kings. The gist of his teaching is to practice Zen with the spirit of the two kings, fierce and brave. "In these days", he preaches, "it has been overlooked that the Buddhist Law is saturated with great strength of prowess and solidity. It has come to be soft, gentle, disinterested and good-natured, but none has trained oneself to bring forth the spirit of a vengeful Ghost. Everyone should be trained to be brave, and to become a vengeful Ghost of Buddhism".[14] He taught to practice religion, face to face with high-spirited images of Buddha. "Observing the features of the construction of Buddhist images, one would see at the gate an image of Vajra Sattva, in the parlour, twelve divinities, sixteen good gods, eight attendants of Vajrasattva, the four kings of gods and five great Buddhas, all displaying their strength, dressed in suits of armour, and armed with halberds, swords, sticks, and bows and arrows. Those who do not grasp the meaning of such display would be unable to heal the six afflictions which should be regarded as enemies. Pray, observe Buddhist images well and practice religion".[15] Such a violent way of preaching as quoted above seems to have never occurred among the Buddhist followers either in India or in China. That was the way in which Buddhism, particularly the Zen sect, was made to bestow upon swordsmanship its spiritual basis. A Zen priest, Takuan, preached to a swordman, Yagiu Tajima-no-Kami: "What is called the flash of striking fire with stones means to be as quick as a lightning. If one's name is called out, 'Emon!' (like 'Jack!' in English), he answers, 'Aye'. That is intelligence. But if he is called out 'Emon' and asks back, 'What do you want?' after stopping to think what the caller wants, that is afflictions which persist. It is the mind of a mediocrity, which stops to be moved by things and to go astray. That is called afflictions that are made to stay. To answer 'Aye', at the moment he is called 'Emon!', is the wisdom of Buddhas. Buddhas and living beings are not two different things; gods and men are not two different things. Such a mind as described above may be called either god or Buddha. Though there are many ways such as the way of Shintoism, the way of poetry, or the way of Confucianism, all amount to the lucidity of such a mind". The act of killing in combat is here justified by Buddhism. It is the distinctive feature probably of Japanese Buddhism alone to aim at the vindication of Buddhism in war.

---

1) *Sankyō Yōron* 三教要論 (*Nihon Jurin Sōsho* 日本儒林叢書), p. 2.

2) *Kodō Taii* 古道大意 (*Hirata Atsutane Zenshū* 平田篤胤全集 vol. VII. p. 62 a).

3) A poem by Sakimori included in vol. XX of the *Manyōshū* 萬葉集 (Sakimori—a soldier defending the frontier).

4) This idea appears particularly in the epic poem *Mahābhārata* and in inscriptions on stone.

5) Cf. for example the *Bhagavadgītā*.

6) *Hagakure* 葉隠 (Iwanami Bunko ed. p. 114), sometimes....called Hagakure *Kikigaki*, a book or way of the *samurai*, is a book dictated by Tsunemoto Yamamoto (1649–1716) and written down by his disciple Tsuramoto Tashiro

(1710–1716) and edited and annotated by Tetsuro Watsuji and Tesshi Furukawa.

7) Max Weber: *Hinduismus und Buddhismus,* S. 300.

8) *Nihon Saikyōshi* 日本西教史 (Taishōdo ed.) p. 37.

9) *Jōgai Ofumi* 帖外御文 (by Rennyo—a supplementary group of his collection of letters etc.) (p. 30 of *Rennyo Shōnin Ofumi Zenshū* ed. by Yūshō Tokushi). However there is some doubt as to whether Rennyo himself wrote this letter.

10) The Fudō Myōō (—the god of fire—) is mentioned in the Sanskrit Buddhist scriptures only in the *Śikṣāsamuccaya* and the *Guhyasamājatantra,* by the name *acala.* (s.v. acala in *Kanyaku Taishō Bonwa Daijiten* ed. by Unrai Ogiwara)

11) Daijō Tokiwa 常盤大定: *Shina Bukkyō no Kenkyū* vol. III. p. 83: "I want to add, that in spite of the fact that the Bodhisattva Kuan-yin is worshipped everywhere even in Taoist *Kuan* and *Miao,* one can nowhere find images of the god of fire (Fudō Myōō) .... Since I do not recall seeing one example, in spite of the fact that I investigated relatively widely on foot, I assume that the worship of this god did not occur".

12) Chikamatsu Monzaemon 近松門左衛門: *Kaheiji Osaga Ikutama Shinjū* 嘉平次おさが生玉心中 "When we hear the phrase, 'The name of Amida is actually a sharp sword', we understand that even the dagger of death (viz. suicide) is Amida's means (of helping us enter the Pure Land)."

13) Cf. *Tsūgen Zenji Zenshū* 通幻禪師全集 vol. III. p. 55 ff.; Keidō Itō 伊藤慶道 *Dōgen Zenji Kenkyū* 道元禪師研究. vol. 1, p. 363 ff.

14) *Roankyō* 驢鞍橋 pt. 1, (in *Zemmon Hōgo Shū* 禪門法語集 [collection of holy sayings of the Zen sect] vol. 1, p. 289).

15) *Bammin Tokuyū* 萬民德用 (*Zemmon Hōgo Shū,* vol. III. p. 526).

(11) Emphasis upon human activities

The emergent and fluid way of thinking, i.e. the way of thinking that asserts that reality is becoming in flux, as previously explained, is compatible with the inclination of thinking that emphasizes particular human nexus. These two factors are combined to bring about an emphasis upon activities within a concrete human nexus.

It is a well-known fact that primitive Shintoism was closely tied up with agricultural rituals in agrarian villages, and that Shintoist gods have been symbolized, even today, as gods of production.

Coming into contact with foreign cultures and getting acquainted with Chinese religions, the Japanese selected Confucianism in particular, although they were somewhat influenced by the thoughts both of Lao-tsu and Chuang-tsu. In other words, out of diverse Chinese philosophies, they adopted and absorbed Confucianism, in particular, which instructs the way of conduct within a concrete human nexus. The thoughts of Lao-tsu and Chuang-tsu are inclined to a life of seclusion in which one escapes from a particular human nexus and seeks tranquility in solitude. Such was not to the taste of most of the Japanese. In contrast, Confucianism is essentially a doctrine whose worldliness makes it sometimes hard to call it a religion. It principally determines the rules of conduct according to a system of human relationship. In this respect, Confucianism never caused conflict with the existing Japanese thinking-pattern at the time of implantation.

In case of Buddhism, however, there arose many problems. Buddhism declares itself to be a teaching transcending worldliness. According to Buddhist philosophy, the positive state of 'transcending worldliness' is arrived at after one has transcended 'this world'. The central figures in Buddhist orders were all priests, who had freed themselves not only from their families but from any specific human nexus. In China, Buddhism was severely critisized by Confucians that by commending priesthood it destroyed human nexus.[1] In the same manner, it was condemned in Japan in the modern period by scholars of Japanese and Chinese classical literature. It is a well-known fact that at the time of the advent of Buddhism there arose various conflicts. Nevertheless Buddhism rushed in like a torrent and before the Meiji Restoration Japan appeared to be entirely a country of Buddhism. How was it then that the Japanese, who had a high esteem for concrete human nexus, accepted Buddhism, which was condemned for tending to destroy these nexus. Let us dwell upon this question.

In early Buddhism the central figures of the orders were *bhikshus* (monks) and *bhikshuṇīs* (nuns). The lay followers assisted and protected the monks and nuns and devoted themselves to their spiritual guidance and education. Not only in Buddhism but in the religious orders of the time in general, except for Brahmins, the central figures were monks (ascetics). Early Buddhism merely followed the modes of the day. The monks of early Buddhism at first formed exclusively among themselves *Saṁgha* (the ideal society), keeping themselves aloof from the impurities of the secular world; and then they tried to guide laymen with their religious and moral influence. So it is too rash to conclude that to become monks is to destroy human nexus. Not only that, in those days there existed some social reasons that made it necessary for a great many people to become monks.

The topographical characteristics of Japan, vastly different from India, required men to serve humanity within a specific human nexus.

The doctrine of early Buddhism is not quite compatible with such requirements. So it came about that early Buddhism together with traditional conservative Buddhism which inherited the former teachings was despised and rejected under the name of '*Hīnayāna*' (Forsaken Vehicle)[2] and *Mahāyāna* Buddhism was particularly favoured and adopted. Mahāyāna Buddhism was a popular religion that came to the fore after the Christian era, after the period when the Kushana people were in power in Northern India. Some schools of Mahāyāna Buddhism, if not all, advocate comprehending the absolute truth *within secular life*. In accepting Buddhism, the Japanese selected in particular one of such a nature. And even in accepting those doctrines originally devoid of such a nature, they deliberately bestowed such a character upon them. The stereotyped phrase, "Japan is the country where *Mahāyāna* Buddhism is in practice",[3] would be understood solely in reference to these basic facts.

This attitude of accepting Buddhism is clearly shown in the case of Prince Shōtoku, "His Commentaries upon Three Sūtras" are those upon "the Shōman Sūtra", "the Yuima Sūtra", and "the Hokke Sūtra". The selection of these three Sūtras out of a multitude was entirely based upon the Japanese way of thinking. "The Shōman Sūtra" was preached, in compliance to Buddha's command, by Shōman, who was a queen and a lay believer. "The Yuima Sūtra" has a dramatic composition, in which Yuima, a lay believer, gives a sermon to *monks and ascetics*, reversing the usual order. This commends grasping the truth in secular life. And according to "the Hokke Sūtra" all the laymen who faithfully follow the teachings of the Buddha are expected to be delivered. The Crown Prince himself, all through his life, remained a lay believer. It is told that he called himself "*Shōman, a Child of the Buddha*".[4] The intention of Prince Shōtoku was to put emphasis upon the realization of Buddhist ideals within concrete human nexus and himself remaining in secular life.[5]

All through the "Commentaries" by Prince Shōtoku, the author seeks absolute significance within each instance of practical conduct in everyday life. He asserts: "Reality is no more than today's occurence of cause and effect". And he interprets: "The ten thousand virtues are all contained in today's effect".[6] Such an interpretation has something in common with the doctrines of the Tendai and Kegon sects, but the particularistic expression "today's" makes it distinctly Japanese. Since it attaches great importance to action in the human nexus, for those who have gone through Buddhist reflection, this world of impurities and sufferings in itself turns out to be a place of blessings. "Since a sage wishes to enlighten mankind, he regards life and death as a garden".[7] All the good deeds practiced in the world of life and death are eventually turned into the causes that lead men to the rank of a Buddha. *"Uncountable ten thousand good deeds* equally lead to becoming a Buddha".[8] It is worth noting that the ultimate state of religion is not bestowed upon men by divine entities that transcend them, but it is realized through practice within the human nexus. "The result of becoming a Buddha is originated from ten thousand good deeds".[9]

Mahāyāna Buddhism stressed altruistic deeds. Prince Shōtoku put a special emphasis upon them and considered that Buddhas and Bodhisattvas should serve all mankind (or living beings). That is the reason for distorted interpretations given to phrases in the Buddhist scriptures.[10] According to the "Hokke Sūtra" it is advised to sit always in religious meditation. This sentence was revised by Prince Shōtoku to mean: "Do not approach a person who always sits in religious meditation".[11] The meaning is that unintermittent sitting in meditation disables a man from practicing altruistic deeds.

A similar idea underlies the later teachings of Japanese Buddhism. According to Saichō (Dengyō Daishi), both priests and laymen should achieve the self-same ideal (the consistency of priesthood and laity). According to Kūkai (Kōbō Daishi), absolute reason should be realized through actuality (Reality is revealed in accordance with things).

That famous poem of the alphabet (*Iroha-uta*) is said to have been written by Kōbō, but in fact it is a Japanese version of a Chinese poem, which is a translation of a Sanskrit poem.

(The Japanese version)

Although fragrant in hue,
(blossoms) are scattered
For everyone, life is impermanent.
This morning I crossed the uttermost limit.
A shallow dream I will not dream, and I am not intoxicated.

(The Chinese poetry)

Whatever is phenomenal is impermanent; Their essential quality is appearance and disappearance; When these appearances and disappearances come to repose, the tranquility is comfort.

In the poetry quoted above, the Indians said, *"Tranquility is comfort"* (*Vūpasamo sukho*); the Chinese translated it: *"Tranquility is comfort"*. But the Japanese, not being satisfied with these expressions that give impressions of passivity and negation, revised it:

"A shallow dream I will not dream, nor shall I get intoxicated". In this translation there is an expression of positive determination. (It is to be noted that while the original Indian poem is a display of extremely abstract concepts only, the Japanese, devoid of aptitude for abstract symbolizing, revised them into concrete and intuitive symbols.)

Some people might argue that the Pure Land (Jōdo) sects advised their believers to abandon this world and induced them gladly to seek the other world. But that is a serious misconception of the essence of the Pure Land teachings. According to the Pure Land Buddhism, this world is subordinate to the other world. It follows that the other world reveals itself in this world, the land of impurity. The practice of the most pious among the believers is to realize what is beyond this world within this very world. "The Larger Sukhāvatī Sūtra" (*Daimuryō-ju kyō*) praises the splendor and grandeur of the heavenly world (*Sukhāvatī-lokadhātu*), and at the same time it puts emphasis upon the noble meaning of moral deeds in this world.

The maintenance of abstention and purification of oneself with sincerity and determination in this world even for a day and night would excel a hundred years of good deeds in the heavenly world. The reason is, it is taught, that this world abounds with evils and men suffer from afflictions.

The idea that he who believes in the true wish of Amitābha would be delivered even though he remained a layman, persisted all through the Heian period as an influential current of thought. From court nobles, warriors, hunters to prostitutes and robbers, they all expected, even if they remained laymen, to be born again in the Pure Land.[12] It was Hōnen who gave a theoretical basis to such a tendency of thinking. And this idea of becoming a Buddha, although one was a layman, was handed down to Nichiren.[13]

It was Shinran who pushed this point to its extreme. He completely denied the life of an ascetic. He advocated becoming a Buddhist as a layman, and put it into practice himself. He worshipped Prince Shōtoku, who was a layman, as "the founder of the religion of Japan". And he maintains that the absolute state commended by the Pure Land Buddhism can be attained in the secular life. Let us compare his idea with that of the Chinese Pure Land Buddhism. The Chinese Pure Land teachings attach great importance to the significance of the moment of death. According to Tao-ch'uo of China, at the moment of death, a man's whole existence is revealed in a way of overall settlement of the accounts of his conduct not only in this world but also in former existences. "Should a streak of evil thought come up to one's mind at the moment of death, that being by far the most evil of all evils, one should certainly fall into the roads of agony (hell, the inferno of starvation, and the world of beasts), making nil all his blessings in the three worlds (past, present and future)".[14] Such a view was inherited by Hōnen.

According to Shinran, however, one puts an end to this life of delusion at the moment of the attainment of faith, and a new life begins thereupon. In his view, therefore, the moment of death does not count much. "The true believer of the Buddha, since the Buddha accepts and never abandons those genuinely devoted to *nembutsu* prayers, is to stay in the rank of those already destined to be saved. Such a one, therefore, does not need to wait until the moment of death. Such a one does not need to pray for the welcome of the Buddha at the time of death. When one's faith is settled, one's birth in the Pure Land is also determined".[15] At the moment when one attains religious belief even in an everyday situation, he preaches, the cause for one to be reborn into the Pure Land has already been established.

Right along with such a point of view, Shinran, following the writings of Shan-tao of China, gives a somewhat different interpretation to them. Shan-tao says in his "Praise of Birth in the Pure Land"[16] as follows: "Those who wish to be reborn into the Pure Land now ought constantly to exercise self-denial and ought not to cease to do so even for a moment till the end of their lives. Should they keep practising *nembutsu* all through their lives, somewhat hard as it might be, if at one moment their life comes to an end, then in the next moment they will be reborn into the Pure Land. And they would receive celestial blessing that would never come to an end". These lines mean that one who practises the nembutsu prayer can be reborn, the next moment after his death, into the Pure Land. But according to the Jōdo-shin sect, which maintains that one is saved at the time when one establishes one's belief, without waiting until the moment of death, the former moment is interpreted to be the moment when one attains belief, and the latter to be the next moment after one is saved.[17] "What is called Rebirth in the Pure Land does *not necessarily designate the moment when life ends,* but it means that the delusive causes in the six roads, where the soul are transmigrating from the beginningless time, are annihilated by the power of the vow (grace) of the Buddha on which one relies by once invoking his name, '*Namu-amida-butsu*'. And it means that the true cause, which inevitably brings forth Nirvāṇa, for the first time begins to emanate. This is exactly what is to be interpreted from being reborn into the Pure Land and not regressing into the realm of the transmigration of the soul".[18)]

In similar fashion, the Jōdo thought of Tao-ch'uo underwent transformation when it was accepted. He says: "If one is able to be reborn into the Pure Land, the cause-and-effect linkage of the three worlds comes to its end. This is nothing but attaining the status of Nirvāṇa, without being delivered from afflictions. Why could we speculate it?"[19)] This means that after one is reborn into the Pure Land, and then one is to be entitled to enter Nirvāṇa. Basing himself upon this sentence, Shinran asserts: "Without being delivered from afflictions, one attains Nirvāṇa".[20)] According to the doctrine of the Jōdo-shin sect, to be reborn into the Pure Land is itself Nirvāṇa, to be entitled to enter Nirvāṇa is a divine favor given to one in this world.[21)] Rennyo is said to have stated as follows: "When one once comes to rely upon the Buddha, one is placed in the status of being reborn into the Pure Land. This is the secret favor of rebirth into the Pure Land. This is what is called the preliminary status of getting into Nirvāṇa".[22)]

According to the Jōdo-shin sect, it is emphasized not only that all the living creatures are saved on account of their religious faith (the turning towards the Pure Land), but also that the Great Benevolence saves all those who are lost (the returning from the Pure Land).[23)] Pure Land Buddhism was originally full of justifications for realistic and practical activities, which were particularly accentuated in Japan. During the Tokugawa period, the merchants of Ōmi province, who peddled their wares assiduously all around the country, were mostly devoted followers of the Jōdo-shin sect and travelled around in a spirit of service to others.[24)]

A similar tendency is also present in the Zen sect. Eisai who inherited the Zen of the Rinzai school somewhat compromised and fused with other sects. But Dōgen who inherited the Zen of the Sōtō school emphasized: "Concentrate on sitting in meditation". This concentration on sitting in meditation was spread among the people not as a method for each monk to attain tranquility of mind, but rather as a method for warriors and other laymen to acquire their mental trainings.

Among the Japanese Zen advocators, in contrast to the Indian and Chinese Zen masters, there arose an opinion that even monks should perform religious practices in the midst of the tumult of the secular life. A didactic poem by Myōchō (Daito Kokushi) says:

"Sit in meditation, and behold the pedestrians,
On the Shijō Bridge, on the Gojō Bridge,
Emerging like trees on the mountain ridge".[25]

The Zen monks traditionally lived in seclusion in the steep mountains and dark valleys and concentrated upon their ascetic practices, severing the cords of the secular world. But here it is preached that one should attain the mental atmosphere of Zen practice in the midst of secular life, amidst the clamour of the city. It was inconceivable for the Chinese Zen priests to make such a statement.

Suzuki Shōsan, a Zen priest of modernistic learning, pushed this point still further, and advocated sitting in meditation just as though one had been on the battle-field. "Once I told a certain warrior that it was good to train oneself from the very beginning to sit in meditation in a whirl of business. Warriors especially ought to practise sitting in meditation, which means to be fit for use in the midst of a battlecry. It should mean fitness for sudden use amidst the clamour and tumult of the roaring of guns, the exchange of fights with spear-heads, and battle-cries. How could the kind of sitting in meditation that is only fit for tranquility be of any use under such circumstances? However excellent a Buddhist doctrine may be, you had better leave it, if it be of no use amidst the battle-cry. You should always try to live up to none other than the two Deva kings".[26]

According to the regulations of the order of the monks of early Buddhism, the monks who have taken orders are not allowed to look upon soldiers on march to the battle-field. They may sojourn a few nights with the army, if there be some special reasons to do so, but even then their sojourn with the army ought not to be prolonged any further. While they are staying with the army, as the regulation goes, they are prohibited from viewing the line-up, arrangement and inspection of the troops.[27] "A battle-cry sitting in meditation", as advocated by Suzuki Shōsan, is completely against the tradition of the Zen practice as handed down from early Buddhism.

He approached Zen through the experience of a warrior, and he was not satisfied with the attitude of the Chinese Zen priests. He criticized them as being half-way Zennists. "To-hui showed that one should put the two characters, *Life* and *Death,* on the point of one's nose and should not forget about them. Po-shan taught that everyone should paste on the forehead the one character, *Death*. These teachings do not have strength. To preach putting the words on the point of one's nose, or to paste them on one's forehead is a borrowed thought and not one's own thought. Persons like Ta-hui and Po-shan do not seem to have mastered the matters of life and death, driving home to their own hearts the importance of these matters. What they say is too weak. On my part I would teach to hold on to these matters, making this one word *Death* the lord of your mind and placing it above everything else".[28)]

Buddhist morals were also metamorphosed. The Indians considered alms-giving a virtue of principal importance for Buddhists, as something to be strictly observed. Most of the Buddhist scriptures extol the deeds of those who abandoned not only their country, castles, wives and children, but also their own bodies and gave them most generously to other human beings (or animals).[29)] Such a life of abandoning everything and possessing nothing was an ideal life for the Indian ascetics. Recourse to such a drastic measure, however, was not allowed for the Japanese, who attached more importance to the concrete human nexus. Prince Shōtoku, therefore, confined the meaning of "alms-giving" to "the abandonment of properties other than one's own body".[30)] In this manner, the inclination of the Indians going beyond the ethics of the mundane human relationship underwent a revision when Buddhism was accepted by the Japanese.

The emphasis upon the human nexus ran parallel to the stress upon all the *productive activities* of men. In a country like India where the intensity of heat, the abundance of rain-fall, and the fertility of the soil together bring forth a rich harvest, without much human labor exerted on the land, the ethics of distribution rather than that of production is naturally emphasized. That is a reason why alms-giving comes to be considered most important. In the country like Japan, by contrast, production is of vital importance, hence stress is placed upon the ethics of labor in various professions.

The Hokke Sūtra, the most important of all the Japanese Buddhist scriptures, was accepted by the Japanese as something that gives a theoretical basis for such a demand.

The nineteenth chapter of *Hōshi Kudoku-bon* of the Hokke Sūtra says as follows: If one preaches with the comprehension of the true meaning of the Hokke Sūtra, "when one preaches the laws of various teachings, they all coincide with the true meaning and nothing shall contradict the

True Aspect. When one preaches the scriptures that are secularized, the words of this-worldly government, or the deeds of production, they all accord with the True Law".[31] This sentence was interpreted by the Japanese to mean that everything is true as long as it comes from a man who has once comprehended the truth of the Hokke Sūtra. The same sentence was interpreted by the Chinese, however, to mean that all activities in the fields of politics and economics were to be subjected to the Absolute One. Ch'ang-shui Tsu-hsüan says: "The One Mind, the Eternal Truth, and the aspect of appearance and disappearance are not separate things. That they are one is revealed in accordance with the fact that they are three; that they are three is discussed in accordance with the fact that they are one. Government and production, therefore, are not in contradiction with the True Aspect".[32] This idea of Ch'ang-shui came to be taken by the Japanese as the original idea of the Hokke Sūtra.[33]

Some of the Japanese Buddhists were thus led to recognize the particularly sacred significance of physical labor. And the Hokke Sūtra came to be accepted as a scripture to commend physical labor. The following poem, known to have been composed by Gyōki, says:

"That I have attained the Hokke Sūtra
Was attainable only through
Making firewood, gathering herbs,
Drawing water, and laboring thus".[34]

This was referred to in the tale of the Hokke Sūtra, which relates the story that in the past world the Buddha *entered priesthood and lived in seclusion,* practising asceticism under a hermit. "I followed a hermit, supplying daily necessities, gathering fruits, drawing water, picking up firewood, cooking meals and making my own body a place of repose, but I never felt tired".[35] This story, which is only slightly touched upon in the Hokke Sūtra, appeared to Gyōki as something very important, and gave him the impetus to carry out his meritorious works of social welfare.

It is a historically well-known fact that the Buddhists endeavored to go directly to the people through various works of social welfare. To illustrate, during the Nara period, Dōshō (629–700) spent his last years in travelling around the country, providing ferry-boats, building bridges and doing many other things for the good of the people. The social welfare works of Gyōki (668–749) are said to have resulted in the construction of "six bridges, three water-tanks, nine charity houses, two ferry depots, fifteen ponds, seven canals, four conduits and one straight road".[36] It is also well-known that Kūkai had a reservoir constructed and built the university Shugei Shuchiin. After that a tremendous number of roads, harbors and lodging places were built by priests and productive activities were carried out by them. During the Kamakura period, the Ritsu sect was particularly popular among common men and women on account of their endeavors in social welfare works. Eison of the Saidaiji Temple and Ninshō of the Gokurakuji Temple had roads opened up, bridges constructed, wells dug, rice-fields cultivated, bath-rooms, hospitals and homes for beggars built, not to speak of the construction of temples and towers, giving commandments to men and women ecclesiastical and secular, copying scriptures and drawing the images of Buddhas. That some Buddhists are enthusiasts in social welfare works is a phenemenon common to India and China. So it might be too rash to conclude that it is a manifestation of the characteristics only of the Japanese. It is noteworthy, however, that the Ritsu sect which originally belongs to Hīnayāna Buddhism should plunge into such practical and positive activities. It was particularly against the traditional disciplines that Ninshō carried out public works which were deeds of altruism. But it was not considered to be a breach of disciplines either by himself or by his contemporaries. Japanese Buddhists came to uphold that one should repudiate disciplines *in the name of the disciplines* for the promotion of productive activities. According to the traditional discipline of early Buddhism, monks are not allowed to accumulate gold and silver, but on this point Tainin of the Yagotozan Temple says:

"It is an infringement of discipline not to receive or accumulate gold and silver, being satisfied with small things, small deeds and small ambitions, and coveting the fame of petty complacency. Now that you are already a priest who observes the three disciplines of the Mahāyāna Bodhisattva, you should live in the vow of boundless altruism and receive and accumulate gold and silver, in order to make the Three Precious Ones (The Buddha, Dharma, and Saṁgha) prosper and to benefit mankind".[37]

Such a way of thinking as mentioned above leads one to esteem highly the common-place everyday life of men. It is a matter of course that the Pure Land and Nichiren sects, which are closely connected with people's life, should be strongly imbued with such a tendency. But it is noteworthy that even Dōgen and his order are tinged with the same characteristics. Dōgen says that people commonly believe that an occult power is nothing more than exhaling water and fire from the body or inhaling the water from the ocean into the pores. These may be called "small occult powers" but they are not worthy of the name of the true occult powers. The true occult powers, that is to say, "great occult powers", exist within and only within simple everyday occurrences of "drinking tea, eating rice, drawing water and carrying faggots". This "great occult power" is called "the Buddha's occult power" or "the occult power that aspires to be a Buddha", and one who practices the Buddha's occult power will eventually become "an occult-power Buddha". "The occult power" is, therefore, nothing but what is experienced in everyday life. On the contrary, it is nothing but living righteously one's own daily life. It is the wonderless life that emanates the wonder of all wonders. If one lives up to this truly enough, one should be able to become a Buddha (an occult-power Buddha), immediately in his own mundane existence.[38]

Dōgen also thought that Buddhism could be realized within the vocational lives of the secular society. "One who thinks that mundane affairs hinder the law of Buddhism knows only that there is no law of Buddhism within mundane affairs, but knows not that there is no law of mundane affairs within Buddhism".[39] Being asked whether or not a man in the lay condition obsessed with daily business would be able to become a Buddha, and should practice asceticism, Dōgen replies; "In the great Sung country, there are no king, ministers, warriors, commoners, and men and women who did not take note of the way of the founders. Warriors and men of letters alike aspired to Zen practice and learning. Those who aspired mostly attained enlightenment. This naturally proves that mundane affairs are no hinderance to Buddhist laws".[40]

Thereafter Dōgen discarded this view-point and came to emphasize entrance into priesthood as a necessary condition for practicing Buddhism. It is noteworthy, however, that there was once a time, temporary as it was, when he held such a view.

Tettsū Gikai, the third chief priest of the Eiheji Temple says: "The dignity of a Buddha today lies within the daily movements of one's arms and legs. There is no law or profound reason without them".[41] The way is realized when and only when the chief priest and rank-and-file priests "are in one mind to perform actions".

The principal characteristic of *Eihei Shingi,* the regulations of life at the Eiheiji Temple Order (ordained by Dōgen), lies in that they are not only a collection of prohibitory articles of conduct as the disciplinary regulations of Indian Buddhism (*pāṭimokkha*) are, but in that they are the clear statements of the positive forms of action through which one may participate in the activities of a community.

At Zen temples, the daily jobs such as cleaning, weeding, mending and carpentery are generally called *samu* (doing service), in which is found the significance of the reason discussed above. That Buddhism is the foundation for secular life was a necessary conclusion for Nichiren, to be deduced from the theory, in the Hokke Sūtra, of the True Aspect of All Existences. Nichiren says: "When the heaven clears, the earth is distinct. The man who knows the Hokke attains the law of this world, does he not?"[42] According to him, the secular society where men live may in itself become the Pure Land. "These days of degeneration, the place where the Hokke Sūtra lies, the place where the ascetic lives, and the place where people, lay or priestly, male or female, and rich or poor, may live—these are the very elements of what is none other than the Pure Land. Where these things are there the Pure Land is. Then could it be possible that the one who lives there should not be a Buddha?"[43]

Such a view is upheld also by the imperial family. Emperor Hanazono writes in 1310 as follows:

"Among good deeds, not to inflict evil upon people is the most superior. One should not seek the reason of Buddhism outside of this. To reign over the country and to feed the people are the acts of redemption of the warrior clan. Why should one practice the affairs of the Buddha outside of all these? It is a corrupt custom of the time to practice the affairs of the Buddha outside of the affairs of the king. On my part, I do not seek the law of the Buddha except for what is within my own mind. One should not necessarily wait for the scripture which is fitting to the law.... What is called the law of the mundane world and what is called the Law of the Buddha are not separate things. The Hokke says that all the words of the government of the mundane world accord with the True Law. ... Since medieval times they have made it the principal business to build temples and to make them beauteous. This is completely against the law of the Buddha. Emperor Mu of Lian, having had temples constructed, asked Bodhidharma whether it would beget merit. Bodhidharma said in reply: 'No merit'. ... This is exactly what I mean".[44]

Emperor Wu of Lian in China was a devoted follower of Buddhism, who endeavored to govern the country with Buddhism. Having had many temples built, he came across Bodhidharma and asked him whether such good deeds of his were meritorious. He expected praise from him. Bodhidharma's reply was contrary to his expectation. He answered that no merits could come forth therefrom. Bodhidharma is then said to have gone to the Chao-lin-ssu Temple of Sung-shan mountain and is said to have continued sitting on the floor, facing the wall, for nine years. It is needless now to go into a discussion as to the credibility of this story. But herein we recognize the religious ideal of the Chinese Zen priests. By contrast to their ideal, Emperor Hanazono of Japan asserted, that Buddhism was nothing but practical and secular activities.

Toward the modern period there came to appear a theory that if a man put his heart and soul in his own secular profession, then he was practicing nothing but the ascetic practice of Buddhism. The Zen priest, Takuan, teaches: "The law of the Buddha, well observed, is identical with the Law of mundane existence. The law of mundane existance, well observed, is identical with the law of the Buddha. The Way is practical only. Except for being practical, there is no Way". (*Ketsujō-shū*) This point was especially stressed by a Zen priest, Suzuki Shōsan, who says: "Many are the ascetics, lay and priestly, from olden times, who are well versed only in the law of the Buddha; but there is none who advocates applying it to matters of the mundane existence. Am I the *first to advocate* this?"[45] He writes a book called "*The Significance of Everyman's Activities*" (*Banmin Tokuyō*), in which he discusses the problems of vocational ethics. He has found the absolute significance in the pursuit of any profession, be one a warrior, a farmer, a craftsman, a merchant, a doctor, an actor, a hunter, or a priest. Because it is the essence of Buddhism, according to him, to rely upon the original self or upon "the true Buddha of one's own", and because every vocation is the function of this "one Buddha", it amounts to this, that to pursue one's own vocation is to obey the Absolute One. So he preaches to farmers, "Farming is nothing but the doings of a Buddha".[46] To merchants he teaches, "Renounce desires and pursue profits single-heartedly. But you should never enjoy profits of your own. You should, instead, work for the good of all others". Since the afflictions of this world, it is said, are predetermined in former worlds, one should torture oneself by working hard at one's own vocation, in order to redeem the sins of the past.[47] It is noteworthy that immediately after the death of Calvin, an idea similar to his appeared almost contemporaneously in Japan. The fact, however, that it never grew into a religious movement of great consequence ought to be studied in relation to the under-development of a modern *bourgeois* society in Japan.

Thereafter, similar ideas appeared from time to time from among the Zen sect. Hakuin, who revived the Rinsai-zen sect in the modern period, maintained that Zen ought to be lived even in secular life.[48] Nishiari Bokuzan, a high priest and superintendent priest of the Sōtō sect says as follows: "There is nothing of the law of mundane existence within the law of the Buddha. In governing a country as a ruler, in taking part in governance as a subject, in engaging in business, in tilling the land as a farmer, and even in the falling of the rain and in the blowing of the wind, if one opens up one's eyes wide enough and sees through them, there is nothing that is not the law of the Buddha. So to say that this is a matter of the Buddhist law or that is a matter of secular life is the saying of those who have not yet attained the law of the Buddha. In the world of the Law, there is no otiose piece of furniture. Even the otiose piece of furniture is the law of the Buddha".[49]

Such a theory of religion also lends itself to religious movements outside of this particular sect. One instance of those is the Hōtoku-sha movement of Ninomiya Sontoku, the main current of whose philosophical background seems to consist of the Tendai doctrine and the doctrine of Sung Neo-Confucianism. It is worth noting that, while all the monistic philosophies of the past and the present, of the East and West, tend to assume the attitude of a resigned and indifferent spectator, his philosophy of the One Round Aspect inclines to be practical and *activistic*. Sectarian Shintoisms also assume the similar tendency. The founder of the Tenri religion teaches, "Keep your heart pure, busy yourself with your vocation, and be true to the mind of God".[50] The other sectarian Shintō movements mostly fall into a similar pattern.

A vocational ethical theory such as this naturally transforms the concept of freedom. To use the word "freedom" and to aspire to the state of freedom are parts of the tradition of Zen Buddhism from olden days. The concept of freedom, however, was metamorphosed by some of the Japanese Zen priests. Suzuki Shōsan was an admirer of P'u-hua of China. He had something in common with P'u-hua, in respect to his aspiration to the state of freedom, rampant and unmolested. P'u-hua was a free man, and Shōsan also thought freely. A difference lies, however, in that P'u-hua sought the state of freedom by *delivering himself from the human nexus,* always acting like a madman, constantly ringing his bell; whereas Shōsan sought his "freedom" *in compliance with the human nexus,* busying himself with his secular vocation.[51]

Respect for labor in vocational life resulted in the high esteem of things produced as the fruits of labor. Reverence for foodstuff is especially manifest. Dōgen, for instance, recognizes the sacred significance of food and says that each item of foodstuff should be called with honorifics. "So-called rice-gruel (*kayu*) ought to be called honourable gruel (*o-kayu*) or you may call it morning gruel, but just gruel, never. You should say honourable offerings or you may say the time of the offering, but just offering, never. You should say, 'honourably *whiten* rice', but 'polish rice', never. You should say, 'honourably *purify* rice', but 'rinse rice', never. You ought to say, 'Honourably select something of the honourable material of an honourable side-dish', but 'choose a side-dish', never. You should say, 'Honourably prepare some honourable soup', but 'Boil some soup', never. You should say, 'Honourably prepare some honourable broth', but 'Prepare broth', never. The honourable offerings and the honourable gruel ought to be said to be most honourably taken". Indeed, Dōgen intended to "prepare offerings of steamed and grueled rice, revering them with the use of utmost politeness and supremely august wordings".[52] The regulation that one should call the names of foodstuff with honorifics has never been found either in any Indian monastery or in any Chinese temple. Menzan Zuihō, one of the revivers of the Sōtō theology during the Tokugawa period, wrote a book called *"Instructions on The Five Views of Receiving Food"*, in order to teach how to take good care of food. "You should calculate and measure how much of the hard work and toil have been put into this food before it comes to you, in order to comprehend the Reason".[53]

A way of thinking to take good care of all the products of labor, however, trivial they may be, is also manifest among the Jōdo-shin sect, which is diametrically opposed, in other aspects, to the Zen sect. Let me refer to the following anecdote. "Rennyo, passing through the corridor, found a piece of paper thereupon. Murmuring why one should waste a thing of the Buddha's possession, he took it into his hands and raised it above his head, etc. It was said that even such a trifling thing as a piece of paper was considered by Rennyo as a property of the Buddha, and that was why he did not waste it".[54]

The teaching to take good care of things, the fruits of human labor, is not necessarily confined to Japanese religions only, but it seems to be common to most of the universal religions. But in India or South Asiatic countries, where men are not required to labor too hard in order to produce daily necessaries, relatively little has been preached not to waste things. The fact that it is particularly emphasized should be considered in the light of the topographical peculiarities of Japan.

Japanese Buddhism, which tends to recognize religious significance in secular professional life or rather in every-day life in general, is apt to spread among the common people. Indian Buddhism, by contrast, never was able to become a religion of the whole nation. Besides Buddhism, there was Jainism as its rival, and stronger and more deep-rooted than either of them was Brahmanism. It is also doubtful how prevalent Chinese Buddhism was among the people. Chinese Buddhism had a strong tendency of being a religion of literati and a religion of hermits. That Buddhism penetrated into people's lives was also true with Tibet and with South Asiatic countries, just as it was in Japan, but the secularization of it was something unique with Japan.

The inclination to recognize religious significance in secular life gave rise to the tendency to seek the same in everyday arts and crafts. Hence emerged the appellations like the way of tea-ceremony, the way of flower-arrangement, the way of calligraphy, the way of painting, the way of military arts, the way of fencing, the way of *jūjutsu* (i.e. *jūdō*), the way of archery and the way of medicine. Their origins seem to be in an age between Muromachi and Tokugawa periods. Such appellations as these can not find their correlates in the West. In this respect, there seem to be some affinity between the Japanese and the Indians, who developed the theory of art and the theory of technology with religious justifications. But even then, for the Indians, art was a media for deliverance, and fo rthe Japanese it was hardly conceived as such.

The Japanese thought that to propagate Buddhism was to profit the human nexus. Tetsugen says: "That is why it (Buddhism) turns out to be prayer for the state, service to the gods of the heaven and earth, repayment of one's debt to one's lord and father, and compensation for the subjects' services".[55] "All phenomenal things will end up with tranquility; all the doctrines will have their proper status; heaven and earth will be in their places; everything will grow; peace will reign; and heaven and earth and the order of the state will long be secured".[56]

As long as religion in Japan tends to realize itself within secular life, it will naturally lend itself to the practical and active. Among the various Buddhist sects, the Nichiren sect is the most pronounced in such a tendency. In spite of the fact that the Hokke Sūtra itself commends ascetics to live tranquilly in a life of contemplation, the Nichiren sect which subscribes to it tends towards action. Nichiren, at the inauguration of his sect, recited "*Nammyōhōrengekyō*" sonorously toward the rising sun in the forest of Asahi on Kiyosumi mountain. The 'sun' is a fovorite character of the Nichiren sect, which often uses it for priests' names. The Nichiren followers long for the effulgent sun. The religious custom of making a procession, while repeating the Nichiren prayer and beating drums would never have taken shape among the Buddhist orders of India or China. (The only thing which may possibly be comparable to this is the religious movement of Caitanya in modern India.)

For a supplementary remark, the form of the acceptance of Chinese thought also was tinged with an activistic tendency in interpreting the Way of human beings. Itō Jinsai, in particular, understands what is called the Way as being active and as representing the principle of growth and development, and on that basis he rejects the nihilism of Lao-tzu. He says: 'Lao-tsu thinks that everything emerges out of nothing. But heaven and earth cover all from time immemorial; and the sun and moon always shine from time immemorial. The four seasons constantly shift out of nothing. But heaven and earth cover all from time immemorial; and the sun and moon always shine from time immemorial. The four seasons constantly shift from time immemorial; what changes with form always changes with form from time immemorial, and what changes with material always changes with material from time immemorial. Things inherit and ferment one another, and things go on living endlessly. How can one see what is called emptiness?"[57] For him the universe is one big living thing, and its incessant living is what the essence of the universe actually is. And he sought the basis for such a view of looking at the universe as a living thing in the phrase, 'The great virtue of the heaven and earth is called life', in '*The Book of Change*'.[58]

In this manner he bestows a characteristically Japanese interpretation even upon the words of Confucius. Confucius says in '*the Analects*'——"On the river, the master says, 'what passes away passes thus. It never ceases day or night' ". The medieval Chinese interpreted them as the words of lamentation that "what passes away is like the water of a river, which, once gone, never returns". According to Chu-hsi, they are words of observation of an objective spectator in which the water of the river is made to symbolize everything that is in incessant motion and flow. A Japanese scholar, Itō Jinsai, however, gives these words an interpretation entirely different from the Chinese. According to him, the river stands for "the virtue of the wise man that is everyday made new, and never becomes stagnant", and the whole sentence is the expression of the exuberence of human vitality.[59] In contrast to the negative, resigned, and indifferent character of the Chinese interpretation, Jinsai's is positive, active, and full of hopes. He has great confidence in human activity itself.

Ogiu Sorai, diametrically opposed to Itō Jinsai in everything else, extols Jinsai as far as this ethics of activism is concerned. He says, "Master Jinsai's theory of things alive and dead is indeed a supreme wisdom of a thousand years".[60] He positively advocates activism, and rejects the static tendency of the Confucianists of the Sung period in China. "Heaven and earth are living things, and so is man. Those who regard as though they were tied up with a rope are only snubs poisoned by useless learning".[61] Quiet sitting and having reverential love in one's heart are the methods of mental training made by the most of Confucianists of the Sung period; these are ridiculed by Sorai: "As I look at them, even gambling appears superior to quiet sitting and having reverential love in one's heart".[62] (This corresponds to the view of Suzuki Shōsan, who, a Zen priest though he was, rejected the ascetic practice of sitting in meditation, and, instead, recommended labour in secular professional life.) A necessary conclusion drawn from such an attitude was the recommendation, as was made by Sorai, of practical learning, useful in practical life. And such was the mental climate which nurtured the economic theory of Dazai Shundai and the legal philosophy of Miura Chikukei, both of whom were Sorai's disciples.

It is one of the pronounced characteristics of Japanese Confucianism to commend activist ethics on the one hand and to reject the thoughts of passive quietism on the other. Most distinctively Japanese scholars stand for the monism of the material, repudiating the dualism of reason and the material. Yamaga Sokō, Itō Jinsai and Kaibara Ekiken are all monists, believing in the material to be the first principle of existence. The second characteristic, running parallel to the first, is that Japanese Confucianism directs its attention to politics, economics and law, the practical aspects of human life. Although Chinese Confucianism surpasses the Japanese in thinking upon metaphysical problems, Japanese Confucianism is superior in practical matter.[63]

The characteristics of Japanese thinking, as revealed in the form of the acceptance of Confucianism, exactly correspond to those revealed in the form of the acceptance of Buddhism.

That Japan alone was rapid in the process of modernization in recent years, while the other Asiatic countries were generally slow in the process, may partly be attributed to the emphasis laid by the Japanese upon practical activities within the human nexus.

A great danger lies, however, in the fact that the religious view of the Japanese, as discussed above, may easily degenerate into the sheer utilitarianism of profit-seeking activities, in case it loses sight of the significance of the absolute, which underlies the productive life of the vocations. It is especially true with a people like the Japanese, who have but only slight interest in religious matters. But at the same time credit should be given to the tendency to esteem the human nexus. If the religion of Japan be enhanced to such a height where religious truth may be realized in accordance with the human nexus which is at once universal and particular, transcending all the specific human nexus and at the same time embracing all of them, then and only then will it beget a universal significance.

---

1) In regard to this problem the *Hung Ming Chi* 弘明集 provides excellent material. See p. 181–2. Tetsurō Watsuji 和辻哲郎: *Nihon Rinri Shisō-shi* (日本倫理思想史 A History of Ethical Thoughts in Japan), Iwanami Shoten, 1952, 2 vols.

2) The term *shōjō* (小乗 lesser vehicle) is a translation of the Sanskrit *Hīnayāna*. Sometimes the word is translated *geretsujō* (ignoble vehicle), *gejō* (lower vehicle), *gejōhō* (the doctrine of the lower vehicle). (Cf. *Bodhisattvalhūmi*, p. 223, line 2 (*Taishō* vol. 30, p. 531 b); *Madhyānta-vibhāgaṭīkā* pp. 216, line 8; 255, line 18 [*Kanzō-taishō-bon*, i.e., Chinese-Tibetan parallel edition, pp. 104, 128; *Mahāvyutpatti*, (Sasaki edition, pp. 186, 1253). The term *Hīnayāna* is very seldom used in Sanskrit original texts now in existence; nevertheless, Chinese and Japanese Buddhists are fond of using the invidious term *shōjō* to refer to traditionalistic, conservative Buddhism.

3) "Japan is a pure Mahāyānist country, and is the country which has realized the Mahāyāna most perfectly" (Nichiren 日蓮, *Jisshō-shō* 十章鈔) Also, according to tradition, Shinran in his 19th year went to the Mausoleum of Prince Shōtoku in Kawachi no Kuni (N. B. the Ōsaka area) to worship, and in a dream Prince Shōtoku appeared to him, pronouncing a *gāthā* containing the line, "Japan is the country most suited to Mahāyāna" (Goten Ryōkū 五天良空: *Takada Shinran Shōnin Shōtōden* 高田親鸞聖人正統傳, ch. 1, *Shinaga Shōtoku-taishi-byō Mukoku Rokku Kimon* (*Shinshū Zensho* 眞宗全書 *Shidenbu* 史傳部 p. 337.). Again in Hōkū: *Jōgū-taishi shūiki* (上宮太子拾遺記 *Anecdotes of Shōtokutaishi*) vol. 5, the eulogy "*Hiketsu ni iwaku, Gobyō Sekimei no koto* (Account of the mausoleum inscription, according to the Hiketsu*)" contains the line "the virtuous country most suited to the Mahāyāna" (*Dainihon Bukkyō Zensho* 大日本佛教全書 vol. 112, p. 142)—
*Hiketsu: prob. Daibara (-sha) hiketsu (D. Nivison).

4) Shōson Miyamoto, 宮本正尊: *Chūdō Shisō oyobi sono Hattatsu* (中道思想及びその發達 the Idea of the "Middle Way" and its Development) pp. 888–889.

5) Prince Shōtoku has at times used for the word "*bosatsu*" (bodhisattva) the modified translation "*Gishi*". (Shinshō Hanayama, 花山信勝: *Shōmangyō Gisho no Kenkyū* [Research on the commentary on *Śrīmālādevīsiṁhanāda-sūtra*] pp. 432–433). In spite of the fact that the usual translation for the term *bosatsu* is *taishi* (大士 or *kaiji* 開士), he used the translation *gishi* (義士 lit. "man of righteousness"); this is probably to be understood as due to his interest in emphasizing especially the idea that the conduct of the Bodhisattva is to be realized throughout man's concrete moral life.

6) Shinshō Hanayama, *Hokke Gisho no Kenkyū* (法華義疏の硏究 Research on the Commentary on the *Saddharma-puṇḍarīka-sūtra*) p. 469.

7) *Yuimagyō Gisho* 維摩經義疏, (Commentary on the *Vimalakīrti-nirdeśa-sūtra Dai Nihon Bukkyō Zensho* ed., p. 141 a.

8) *Hokkye Gisho* 法華義疏, *Dai Nihon Bukkyō Zensho* ed. p. 4 b.

9) *Ibid*, p. 28 a. Further, similar expressions may be found at random in many places. "Every good action in the Six Spheres can lead man to become Buddha". (*ibid*. p. 5 a) "Every [good] action is a cause leading to the effect of Buddhahood (becoming buddha) (*ibid*. p. 34 a). "Even those good actions which are of a purely secular mode occupy the religious status of the One Vehicle (viz. are on the highest religious plane)" (*ibid*. p. 28 b). (cf. Shinshō Hanayama: *Hokke Gisho no Kenkyū*, pp. 469, 489).

10) The clause, 得一切衆生殊勝供養 which appears in the *Shōmangyō* (*Śrīmālādevīsiṁhanāda-sūtra*) has the sense, "[The Buddhas and Bodhisattvas] enjoy especially distinguished reverence and support from all living beings". But Prince Shōtoku insisted that the word order should be changed to read, 得供養殊勝一切衆生. Moreover he takes 得 in the sense of 令得, and holds that the clause should be read, "[The Buddhas and Bodhisattvas] are caused to offer reverence and support for all especially distinguished living beings" (Shinshō Hanayama: *Shōmangyō Gisho no Jōgū-ō-sen ni kansuru Kenkyū* (勝鬘經義疏の上宮王撰に關する硏究) Tokyo, 1944, pp. 434–437)—It goes without saying that this is an unjustified interpretation in this context. He has read into the passage his idea of altruism toword all living beings.

11) In regard to the clause in the *Sukhavihāraparivarta* (XIII of Skt ed.) of the *Hoke-kyō*, "always fond of *zazen* (sitting in meditation)", he makes the criticism, "If one is always fond of *zazen*, leaving this world to go and stay in the mountains, how will one have any time to propagate this sūtra throughout the world"; and he explains the meaning of the sūtra as being that "one should not associate with Hīnayāna Zen masters who are always fond of *zazen*" (Shinshō Hanayama, *op. cit.* p. 437; Shinshō Hanayama; *Shōtoku Taishi Gyosei Hokke Gisho no Kenkyū*, pp. 386–387). Also cf. Shinshō Hanayama, *Nippon Bukkyō no Engen* (日本佛教の淵源 Sources of Japanese Buddhism) pp. 917–935 in *Bukkyōgaku no Shomondai* (Problems of Buddhist Studies) Iwanami, 1935.

12) Saburō Ienaga, 家永三郎: *Chūsei Bukkyō Shinsōshi Kenkyū* (中世佛教思想史硏究 Studies in the History of Medieval Buddhist Thought, Kyōto, Hōzōkan, 1947) pp. 23–27.

13) *Ibid*. p. 78.

14) *Anrakushū* 安樂集 (NB. by Sui Buddhist of Jōdo School, Tao-ch'ue, (Dōshaku 道綽 6, 天嘉 3, i.e. 562 A.D.—貞觀 19, i.e. 645 A.D.) part 1.

15) *Mattōshō* 末燈鈔, Cf. beginning of *Shūjishō* 執持鈔 (*Mattōshō* is by Shinran; *Shūjishō* is by Kakunyo 覺如).

16) This sentence is also quoted in vol. 3, part 2 of *Kyōgyōshinshō* (Shinran).

17) In the *Gutokushō*, part 1 (Shinran: p. 460 of *Shinshū Shōgyō Zenshū* 眞宗聖教全集 II, Shūso-bu 宗祖部), there is the passage, "*The moment of* the whole-hearted belief in the original vow is the ending of [the ordinary] life [which is the terminal point] of the former invocation [of Amida., that which is proper to this earlier, ordinary life]. [The principle that] one obtains right now a rebirth [in the Pure Land] is [what is meant by] the immediate rebirth [which is the beginning point] of the later invocation [of Amida-viz. the *nembutsu* practiced in the new, recreated religious life]. This passage is quoted in book III B of the *Rokuyōshō*, (by Zonkaku 存覺, great-great grandson of Shinran, (1290–1373); a commentary on Shinran's *Kyōgyōshinshō* (*Shinshū Shōgyō Zenshū*, same vol. p. 301) with the remark, "In regard to the principle of the realization of the true result (life) in the ordinary life, this passage makes evident the effect of [the principle that] the horizontal enlightenment is sudden". NB.—Shinran argues that for the religious man who has attained salvation by achieving *nembutsu* with utterly sincere faith in the original vow—at which point his ordinary mind is cut away by the power of the vow, emptied, so that his calling upon Amida is identical with Amida's own continual calling of his own name, whereupon Amida's Pure Land life enters into him—for such a man the ordinary life in this world and the life in the pure land are not two but one, and further that this pure life is not an other-worldly existence here and now but identical with this life. * NB. It is Shinran in principle that the *zennen* and the *gonen* (note the special senses of 前 and 後) constitute one identical point in the individual's psychological and religious life. The metaphor describing enlightenment as Shinran conceives it is here geometrical [just as his notion of the identity of *zennen* and *gonen* is mathematical—a limiting point of two series, D. Nivision]:

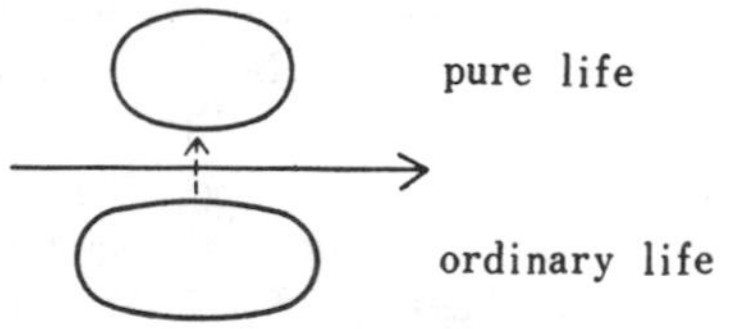

The vertical arrow—called *Jin-chō* 豎超 is gradual, difficult, a dependence on one's own strength (自力) which supposes the pure life to be separate whereas the horizontal arrow called *Ōchō* 横超 "horizontal enlightenment" is obliquely opposite from the foregoing, easy, resting on faith (他力), sudden, in which the two "lives" are identical. Shinran calls these "two kinds of truth". ** Abe here objects that if this were true as stated there would be no difference between Zen and Shin Buddhism—actually for Shinran, from the point of view of Amida the two lives are one; but from the point of view of man, they are utterly separate; he is hopelessly sinful—and just because he has an extreme consciousness of his sinfulness, Amida's love can help him, hence Shinran uses the expression 二卽一, 一卽二. Also the phrase *bonnō*

soku bodai 煩惱卽菩提 "Bad feelings are identical with bodhi" and *fudan bonnō toku nehan* 不斷煩惱得涅槃—"Without stopping bad feelings one is given nirvāṇa"—this doctrine is called *Shōjōju no kurai* 正定聚の位*. This is the position from which *Sokutokuōjō* 卽得往生 is possible—also called 必至滅度 (Metsudo:nirvāṇa). Shinran says, Amida promises to help even good men, how much more so bad men!—also called 不退の位—the point at which, due to Amida's promise and faith in it, one is guaranteed rebirth. In this sense one has it already and at the same time not yet.

18) Zonkaku 存覺 *Shinyō Shō* 眞要鈔 (*Jōdo Shinyōshō*) pt. I, (*Taishō* vol. 83 p. 761 b).

19) *Ōjōronshū* 往生論註 (*Muryōju Kyō Upadaisha Ganshōge Chū*, 無量壽經優婆提舍願生偈註 by Donran 曇鸞 (476–542), *Shinshū Shōgyō Zensho* 1, *Sangyō Shichi-so Bu*, 三經七祖部 p. 319).

20) Shōshinge 正信偈 (: *Shōshin Nembutsuge*, *Kyōgyōshinshō* (*Shinshū Shōgyō Zensho* 2, *Shūso Bu* 宗祖部 p. 44)).

21) *Shōshin-nembutsuge Kikigaki* 正信念佛偈聞書 pt. I (*Shinshū Zensho* 眞宗全書 Supplement, vol. 8, p. 247); *Shōshin Nembutsuge Karohen* 正信念佛偈夏爐篇 pt. II (*Ibid.*, p. 119); *Shōshin Nembutsuge Hoeiki* 正信念佛偈捕影記 pt. II (*Ibid.*, p. 25).

22) *Goichidaiki Kikigaki* 御一代記聞書 (by Rennyo 蓮如) (*Shinshū Shōgyō Zensho* 3, *Ressobu* 列祖部 p. 582)

23) *Kyōgyōshinshō* 教行信證 Pt. I (*Shinshū Shōgyō Zensho* 2, *Shūsobu* 宗祖部 p. 2). Cf. also *Jōdoron* 淨土論, quoted in Part III of *Kyōgyōshinshō* (*Ibid.*, p. 66). The two *ekō* (廻向 Parināmanā—"merit-transference") are also referred to in *Gutokushō* 愚禿鈔, Part II, (*Shinshū Shōgyō Zensho, Ibid.*, p. 475 by Shinran)

24) e.g. Cf. Kanji Naitō 內藤莞爾 "*Shūkyo to Keizai Rinri* 宗教と經濟倫理—*Jodō Shin-shū to Ōmi Shōnin* 淨土眞宗と近江商人" (Religion and Economic Ethics—Jōdo-shin sect and the Ōmi merchants) (Cf. *Shakai Gaku* 社會學 (the annual report of the Japan Sociological Association) 8, (1941) pp. 243–286).

25) But perhaps we cannot say that Daitō Kokushi emphasized a life within the bonds of social morality. Hayashi Razan bitterly criticized Daitō's mode of monkhood as destructive of social morality. (Tetsujirō Inoue 井上哲次郎: *Nihon Shushi-gakuha no Tetsugaku* 日本朱子學派の哲學 p. 73 ff.). But it seems that his way of living together with beggars and other unattached elements was different from the way of life of Zen monks in China.

26) *Roankyō* 驢鞍橋 (Shōsan Suzuki 鈴木正三 —cf. note 14 p. 79) Part I, p. 107, in *Zenmon-hōgoshū* 禅門法語集.

27) *Pāṭimokkha* 48–51. in the *Vinaya*.

28) *Roankyō* Part I, p. 101.

29) A typical example of this way is the famous story of self-sacrifice of Prince Vessantara transmitted in Southern Buddhist countries (*Jātaka* 547).

30) The phrase *shazai* 捨財 which occurs in the chapter "Shōju shōbō" 攝受正法 of the *Shōmangyō* is interpreted by the chia-hisang ta-shich Chi-tsang in the *Shōmangyō hōkutsu* as meaning "to give to others everything except one's own body and life, viz. country, castle, wife and children" (*Taishō*. vol. 37, p. 36 b–c); but Shōtoku Taishi's commentary interprets it as "things other than one's

own body" (pt. 1, p. 36 b), deleting the phrase "to give country, castle, wife and children to others". (Shinshō Hanayama: *Shōmangyō Gisho no Kenkyū* p. 432.) Probably the interpretation of the *Hōkutsu* transmits the Indian idea faithfully.

31) "No teaching of *dharma*, when understood according to the proper sense, is at variance with the *jissō* (實相 true way of being of every thing). When popular books of secular thought, and political proverbs, and precepts about daily work are taught, all are in accord with the true *dharma*". This text is famous, and has been highly esteemed in Japan and China, but the original text is merely as follows:

"He should remain mindful and not forget the *dharma* which he will preach. Popular secular utterances—whether proverbs or mystic formulas, ought all to be explained in accordance with the true meaning of *dharma*".

In this phrase "precepts about daily work" does not occur. (Kern-Nanjō ed. p. 372, Ogiwara-Tsuchida ed. p. 315).

32) *Ryōgon-kyō Chōsuisho* 楞嚴經長水疏 (Commentary on the Suraingama-Sūtra, by Ch'ang-shui 長水) vol. 1, last part. (*Taishō* vol. 39. Shui died in *Taihei* 9 (A.D. 1029), was a Kegon buddhist of the Sung dynasty.)

33) For example, in the *Muchū-mondō-shū* 夢中問答集 of Musō Kokushi 夢窓國師 we read; "This (i.e. Shiei's thought) has the same sense as the argument in the *Hoke-kyō* that daily vocations also are all in accord with the *jissō*" (answer to the second question). (Musō 1275–1351 A. D. Brother of Ashikaga Takauji, Tadayoshi 直義 asked him questions—this book is his answers—93 questions and answers—p. 19 of Iwanami Bunko edition)

34) *Shūishū* 拾遺集 vol. 20 (*Shūi Waka Shū* 拾遺和歌集) This poem is also quoted in Nichiren's *Minobusan Gosho* (*Nichiren-shōnin Zenshū* 日蓮聖人全集 vol. II, 1931, p. 840 Heirakuji Shoten.)

35) *Daibadattahon* 提婆達多品 (*Devadatta-parivarta*) ch. 12.

36) *Gyōki-bosatsu-den* 行基菩薩傳 (Gyōki bosatsu was a monk in Nara. 668–749 A. D.) (*Zoku Gunsho ruijū* vol. 204, ch. 8, the last part.)

37) *Ritsuon Gyōji-monben* 律苑行事問辨 vol. 8. (*Nihon Daizōkyō,* 日本大藏經 *Kairitsu-shōsho.* 戒律章疏 3, p. 493.)

38) *Shōbōgenzō* 正法眼藏 (by Dōgen 道元) Jinzū 神通 (chap. 25)

39) *Ibid., Bendōwa* 辯道話 (chap. 1)

40) loc. cit.

41) *Eihei Shitsuchū Kikigaki* 永平室中聞書 (cf. Hanji Akiyama, 秋山範二: *Dōgen no Kenkyū,* 道元の研究 p. 281)

42) *Kanjin Honzon Shō* 觀心本尊鈔 (by Nichiren 日蓮) (*Nichiren Shōnin Zenshū,* vol. 1 p. 342).

43) *Hokke-shū nai Buppō Ketsumyaku* 法華宗內佛法血脈 (*Nichiren-Shōnin-zenshū* vol. 6 p. 2728).

44) *Ressei Zenshū* 列聖全集 (Collected Writings of Japanese Emperors) *Shinkishū* 宸記集 last part, p. 430.

45) *Ketsujō-shū.*

46) *Roankyō,* last part, p. 41 (by Shōsan Suzuki). Moreover in the *Banmin Tokuyō* 萬民德用 by Suzuki Shōsan, we read as follows: "In Buddhist scripture we are told that if we enter deeply into the secular world there will be nothing lacking in our withdrawal from the world. This passage mean that through the secular law one may become a buddha. Thus, then, the secular law is

the Buddhist law. In the Kegon doctrine we are told that 'The Buddhist law is not different from the secular law; the secular law is not different from the Buddhist law'. If one does not accept the truth that in the secular law itself one may attain buddhahood, then he is not one who fully understands the meaning of Buddhism. It is my prayer that the secular law and the Buddhist law be made one". (*Zenmon Hōgo-shū* 禪門法語集 last part, p. 526)

47) Suzuki Shōsan, *Roankyō* (*Zemmon Hōgo-shū* last part p. 337); *Bammin Tokuyō 5* (*ibid.* p. 536 ff.)

48) *Yasen-kanwa* 夜船閑話; *Orategama* 遠羅天釜.

49) *Shōbōgenzō Keiteki* (NB. one of the best commentaries on *Shōbō Genzō* of Dōgen, by Soei Fusan 富山祖英, following lectures of Bokuzan Nishiari 西有穆山 Date of the lectures is Meiji 32. *Bendōwa* (1st chap.) p. 153.

50) Yasusada Hiyane 比尾根安定: *Nihon Shūkyōshi* (日本宗教史 A History of Japanese Religions) p. 825.

51) H. Nakamura 中村元 *Kinsei Nihon ni okeru Hihan-teki Seishin no Ichikōsatsu* 近世日本に於ける批判的精神の一考察 Tokyo, Sanseido, pp. 58 f.

52) *Shōbōgenzō, "Jikuimbun"* 示庫院文 (p. 119 in Iwanami edition)

53) Menzan Zuihō 面山瑞方 (d. 1769): *Jujiki Gokan Kummō* 受食五觀訓蒙 p. 3.

54) *Rennyo Shōnin Goichidaiki Kikigaki* 蓮如上人御一代記聞書 pt. 2. (*Shinshū Shōgyō Zensho*, vol. 3, *Ressobu* p. 611.)

55) Tetsugen Zenji 鐵眼禪師: *"Ke-en no Sho"* 化緣の疏 (in *Tetsugen Zenji Keji Hōgo* 鐵眼禪師假字法語 Iwanami Bunko ed. p. 50 (N.B.—of the Ōbaku 黃檗 sect —full name Tetsugen Dōkō 鐵眼道光, 1630–1682).

56) "*Kurushima Kō ni taisuru Tetsugen no Kyūmei Konseisho*". (A letter of Tetsugen to the daimyō Kurushima asking him to save men's lives) *ibid.* p. 77.

57) *Gomōjigi* 語孟字義 (by Itō Jinsai 1627–1705), vol. 1, p. 15.

58) *Ibid.*, vol. I, p. 3.

59) *Rongo Kogi* 論語古義 (Itō Jinsai) vol. 5. Also cf. Kōjirō Yoshikawa 吉川幸次郎 *Shinajin no Koten to sono Seikatsu* 支那人の古典とその生活 p. 154.

60) Ogiu Sorai 荻生徂來 (1666–1728): *Bemmei* 辨名 last part, "*Sei Jō Sai Shichisoku*" (性情歳七則 the seven principles of Nature, Feeling and Talent).

61) Ogiu Sorai: *Tōmonsho* 答問書, part 1 (in *Nihon Rinri Ihen* 日本倫理彙編 compendium of Japanese ethics vol. VI, p. 153).

62) Ogiu Sorai: *Rongo Chō* 論語徵 (Junsei Iwahashi 岩橋遵成: *Sorai Kenkyū* 徂來研究, p. 300.)

63) *Ibid.*, p. 446 ff.

(12) Acuteness of moral self-reflection

The emphasis put upon practice within the actual human nexus and the stress laid upon the relationship between individuals rather than upon the existence of the individual person increase the sensitivity of man to his relationship with other men. First of all, given a way of thinking which emphasizes the social cooperative structure as the ground of the individual life, it becomes a matter of vital importance for man what others in the group may think of him. We should not fail to consider, for example, the keen sense of prestige of the Japanese. In the sixteenth century, European missionaries came to Japan and reported that the Japanese placed prestige before wealth, a trait not found among the Europeans.[1] What influence this tendency exerted upon Japanese Buddhism is an interesting question to pose. It would seem that the keen sense of honour of the Japanese is closely tied up, externally, with the high esteem for the hierarchical order. And internally, in some cases, it invigorates the moral faculty of self-reflection. It posits before man the ideal of the endless good that he should strive for, it induces him to reflect in contrast upon the sorry fact that he himself is too weak and helpless to refrain from doing evil; and thus it awakens within him the consciousness of man's sinfulness.

That the operation of moral self-reflection is stronger among the Japanese than among other peoples is highly uncertain. Such a question cannot be settled until a comparative study of the moralities of various peoples has been made, and as comparison is a difficult problem, we wish here to limit our subject to the forms of the acceptance of Buddhism.

The Jōdo sect, introduced from China, reached the zenith of its development with Shinran, in whom the working of moral self-reflection was extremely acute.

"Truly I have come to realize, and it is deplorable, that I am idiotic vulture, drowned in the boundless sea of carnal desires, lost in the enormous mountains of worldly ambitions, not being pleased with becoming entitled to be saved, and taking no pleasure in approaching the True Evidence. Shame on me; woe is me!"[2]

By these sentences it ought not to be understood that it was because Shinran was a monk under the lay condition, getting married and eating meat, that he made such a confession. There are instances, in the Indian[3] as well as in the Chinese[4] Buddhist scriptures, of monks who were married and ate meat. But moral self-reflection as acute as Shinran's seems not to be indicated in the Buddhist literature of other countries. Monks who broke their vows in India appear to have held the notion that sins could be expiated by reciting magical formulae (dhāraṇī).[5] Little has been said about the pangs of conscience of renegade monks in China either. Shinran, on the contrary, could not but face the shameful reality of man. Shinran, who looked into the deeper self of man, turned to the Buddha, the Absolute One. He was thus led to advocate "the discipline of non-discipline", which was underlined by self-reflection of great moral intensity.

(It is a pity that "the discipline of non-discipline" should now come to be interpreted by most of the Shin-sect followers as to do without discipline, and that thus it should now be identified with the lack of moral self-reflection.)

The motivation for the ascetics of India and China to enter priesthood was, in most cases, the realization of the impermanence of the phenomenal world rather than the realization of man's sinfulness. In the case of Shinran, in contrast, little is said about the impermanence of this world. The controlling motivation for Shinran is the sense of sinfulness of man. It is not that man is simply changeful. A more fundamental thing about man is that he is a sinner, obsessed with afflictions, yielding to evils. Realizing as he does that things are impermanent, he still clutches at these impermanent things. Man is so deeply immersed in sins that he could never be saved but for the miraculous power of the vow of Amitābha. Such was what Shinran preached. In his writings, he reflected upon the nature of evils and went so far as to classify the categories of evil.

The Jōdo doctrine of China was transformed by these factors of moral self-reflection into the Jōdo doctrine of Shinran. Shan-tao, in explaining "the heart of sincerity" which the ascetic should always observe, says: "You should not assume outwardly the appearance of wisdom, goodness and religious abstinence, while embracing illusions inwardly".[6] According to Shinran, the illusions such as "avarice, anger, injustice, falsehood, mischief, fraudulence and a hundred others" make for "the evil nature" of man, which is so intrinsic to man that ascetic practice even of the utmost austerity could not possibly purify him of these evils. Such a belief of Shinran led him to read Shan-tao's words differently from the way they originally stood: "You could not assume outwardly the appearance of wisdom, goodness and religious abstinence, since you embrace illusions inwardly".[7] Shinran, whose profound moral self-reflection made him cry, "There is no end of evil nature, Man's mind is abominable like a viper";[8] could not accept the teaching of Shan-tao without the transformation of its meaning into what he himself thought fit.

Herein established is a theory of the redeemability of man of evil nature. Man is by nature evil, and because he is evil, according to that theory, he is entitled to be saved by the great benevolence of Amitābha. He is not expected to be saved through any other doctrine. Although this theory of the redeemability of man of evil nature is generally recognized to have been originated by Shinran, similar views were upheld by others.

The book, *Verbatim notes on the Tales of the Future Life* says: "Since the so-called Original Vow of Amitābha, it ought to be remembered, exists solely *for the sake of sinners and men of evil dispositions and not for the sake of saints and sages,* it is the meaning of faith to believe, without any shadow of doubt, (in the redeemability of oneself) even if one finds oneself to be of evil dispositions". A statement, presumably of Hōnen, is as follows: "Even a good man is reborn into the Pure Land, and how much more so with a wicked man![9] This is an oral instruction transmitted to me". These two instances have much in common with the following assertion of Shinran: "Even a good man is reborn into the Pure Land, and how much more so with a wicked man! But people generally think that even a wicked man is reborn into the Pure Land, and how much more so with a good man! Though this latter way of thinking appears at first sight reasonable, yet it is not in accord with the purport of the Original Vow, the faith in the Other Power".[10] Not only that, the vehement demand for the redemption of the wicked was a consistent under-current all through the Heian period, and the tales of death and various other stories of the period recorded instances that heinous criminals and those who made slaughter as a trade constantly practiced *nembutsu* prayers. By the latter half of the Heian period, at least, the idea of the salvation of the wicked was firmly established in theory, and was socially acknowledged, by believers in the doctrine that *nembutsu* practice enabled one to be reborn into the Pure Land.[11] At that time the systematization of the idea was not yet complete, but such a current of thought gradually developed, with theoretical refinements , into an intrinsic part of the Jōdo-shin doctrine.

This is not to say that all the Jōdo sects of Japan held to this view. But it is significant that this assertion of the right of the wicked to be reborn into the Pure Land came to be explicitly stated in Japan only. The Jōdo sects of India and China, broadly speaking, with due allowances for exceptions, took a view similar to that of Hōnen, namely, "Even sinners are reborn (into the Pure Land), and how much more so with good men!"[12]

It is noteworthy that profound religious self-reflection, based upon the Jōdo doctrine, was professed by some of the emperors.

"Though the mind's moon shines,
To show the way to the Pure Land,
Woe be to the clouds still uncleared". (By Emperor Gotoba)

The poem means that ardent as my desire is to be reborn into the Pure Land trusting and relying upon the vow of Amitābha, the sins I have committed weigh so heavily upon my heart that they make me haunted by doubts about the vow; and how far beyond, how far beyond comprehension, the poem laments, is the state of true salvation.

"I wish to be awakened from a dream,
Only to enter another dream;
Beyond my vision, lies the world of Reality".

That one wishes to be awakened from a dream is a proof that one is still in the dream, the poem asserts, and to be really awakened from the dream is the state that lies still far beyond one's experience.

The idea that the wicked are eligible to become Buddhas was accepted by Nichiren and was incorporated into his religious doctrine. He recognized himself to be one of "the ordinary men as idiotic, ignorant and unenlightened",[13)] and he reflected that "we are fools and dullards unworthy to become disciples of the Buddha, who have fallen into evil deeds in the age of corruption".[14)] Unworthy as a man like himself was, he still believed man would be saved through and only through the Hokke sūtra. "Even he who has committed ten evils and five heavy sins, as long as he does not violate the Hokke sūtra, shall without doubt be reborn into the Pure Land and become a Buddha".[15)]

Is it not, however, that religious and moral self-reflection as profound as stated above is confined only to the Jōdo sect? Is it not that so-called enlightenment in the Zen sect has nothing to do with moral considerations? Such questions may naturally occur to readers' minds. The question about the relationship between Zen and morality requires a chapter of its own. Suffice it to state here that the form of accepting the Zen doctrine in Japan, as in the case of Dōgen, reveals a profound moral self-reflection. He attaches great importance to the act of making a confession. "Should you confess in this manner, the assistance of the Buddha would assuredly be yours. Make a confession to the Buddha with your soul and body, and the power of the confession will eradicate all the roots of your sins".[16)] He commends good deeds and preaches that one will be able to become a Buddha through one's good doings. "Quite an easy way there is to become a Buddha. Not to do evil deeds, not to be obsessed with the matter of life and death, but to take pity upon mankind, to revere one's superior, to be considerate to one's inferior, and to keep one's mind free from hatred, desires, afflictions and anxieties is exactly what is called being a Buddha. One should not seek Buddhahood anywhere else".[17] He emphasizes the observance of injunctions.[18] Let us compare his attitude with that of his Chinese master, Ju-ching. As far as the records of Ju-ching's teachings are concerned, there is no evidence of sin-consciousness in him of any profundity. On the contrary, he keeps himself aloof from the distinction between good and evil, to which he assumes an attitude of nonchalance and lamentation. "I have heard that all good deeds are like a fly eyeing blood. I have heard that all wicked deeds are like a crab falling into boiling water".[19] In the records of his teaching one finds the characteristics of the Chinese Zen priests of the latter-day periods who used to make nonsensical utterances.

The emphasis upon introspection among Japanese priests, is apparent also among laymen. Minamoto Sanetomo says:

"There's no way out
Of this agonizing hell,
Whose empty vault
Only flames can fill."

(A poem reflecting upon one's sins.)

"The founder of a temple,
The erector of a tower,
For their acts get credit;
But none gets merits,
So rewarding as a repentant sinner."

(A song of confession)[20]

On the whole, when and only when one reflects upon one's deeds sincerely enough, is one awakened to one's own sinfulness.

(The consciousness of man's sinfulness is also a distinctive feature of Christianity, and a comparison between Christianity and Buddhism in this respect opens a new theme which cannot be dealt with here).

It may be argued that the psychological unrest caused by the social disturbances during the medieval period, together with the introduction of Buddhism, gave rise to the consciousness of man's sinfulness; and that the Japanese were originally lacking in such a consciousness. It is true that the Japanese of antiquity regarded sin as a kind of material entity, which could easily be purged by means of a ritual of purification. (In this respect, the Japanese have much in common with the Brahmanists of ancient India). The lack of sin-consciousness is also distinctive among the present-day Japanese. It may be rightly asserted that, generally speaking, the Japanese are not wholly sin-conscious and that this fact is closely tied up with the this-worldly tendency of the Japanese, which will be pointed out in a later chapter. And there are features in the history of thought in Japan which disprove the points we have just made. Take, for instance, the case of the acceptance of Confucianism. Ogiu Sorai, a Confusianist with characteristically Japanese attitudes in some respects, supported the theory that the good or evil of a deed is judged by its results as against the theory, as held by the Chinese Confucianists of the Sung period, that it is judged by the motives of the doer.[21]

Whether or not the Japanese in general were acute in religious and moral self-reflection is difficult to decide. But one thing at least is clear, that in accepting the Buddhist thought of China, such transformations as have been discussed above were effected by some of the Japanese Buddhists. It was also reported by the European missionaries, who came to Japan in the sixteenth century, that crimes were relatively few and reason reigned among the Japanese.[22] In any case, although they are weak in sin-consciousness in its religious sense, they are sensitive in shame-consciousness in its practical and moral sense. For the Japanese, whether or not one infringes religious disciplines is a matter of little consequence. A matter of vital importance for them is whether or not one conforms to the mores of a particular human nexus to which one belongs. A question may be raised as to whether the presence of moral consciousness, as just mentioned, may be inconsistent with the lack of the spirit of criticism, as discussed earlier. But the inconsistency ceases to be inconsistency when one understands 'the moral consciousness' to be applicable only to those acts within one's own immediate group.

Let us now consider how the Japanese themselves think of this repudiating of Buddhist discipline in general on the one hand and the observation of moral practice within a particular human nexus on the other.

Onkō was the most prominent among the high priests of the Shingon sect of the past who instructed and enlightened common people without recourse to magical practices but by means of preaching only. And it was the discipline of ten good deeds which was ordained as follows; love and save all the living creatures with a heart of benevolance; do not deprive anyone, from the highest officials down to common men, of his proper due but let him be in his proper place; observe decorum in man-to-woman relationships; do not utter a falsehood; do not use flowery words, which impair the virtues of adults and go against the way of heaven and earth;

do not insult others, or do not put others to shame; do not use double-tongued speech; do not be avaricious; do not yield to anger, which makes nil all good deeds; not have a "wrong view"–i.e., believe in the Buddha, in the Law and that the virtuous power of gods is not futile.[23] He wrote many books on the subject of the ten good deeds, and often preached about them at various places.[24] He was interested neither in the abstract thinking of Indian Buddhism nor in the doctrines contained in the labored commentaries of Chinese Buddhism, but he was mainly concerned with the direct approach of preaching practical virtues. Surprisingly erudite as he was, remarkably well versed as he was in Buddhist philosophy, and especially, forerunner though he was in the modern method of studying Sanskrit, he thought that the discipline of the ten good deeds was enough as far as the enlightenment of the common people was concerned. Those who wished to listen to Onkō's preachings—from the emperor to the common people—were not interested in metaphysical discussions, but interested solely in the moral teachings that would be of immediate use to concrete acts of everyday life. (That was why his philosophical and doctrinal dissertations only were written exclusively in *Chinese*).

Onkō followed the tradition of Indian Buddhism when he tried to realize Buddhism within everyday acts through the discipline of the ten good deeds. The listing of virtues after the fashion of Indian Buddhism, however, was not to the liking of the Japanese in general, who looked for the one central virtue directly posited. It is the virtue of "*honesty*", which was originally adopted from Buddhism, that emerged from such a demand and came to be generally recognized as the central virtue by the Japanese.

The word 'honesty' has come into use since the Nara period.[25] The Imperial rescripts, issued at their several enthronements, of the emperors Ninmei, Montoku, Seiwa, and Yōzei during the Heian period unanimously state "an honest heart" to be the virtue that all the subjects should observe.[26] Probably influenced by them was the doctrine of the Ise Shrine instituted by the *Five Books of Shintoism* during the Kamakura period, according to which the Sun Goddess was supposed to have said: "Divine protection is based upon honesty". During the Muromachi period, the virtue of "honesty" as the doctrine of the Ise Shrine came to prevail among the entire country. According to Kitabatake Chikafusa, the three divine treasures of the Japanese Imperial family symbolize the virtues of "honesty", "benevolence", and "wisdom" respectively.

Although a concept corresponding to the virtue of "honesty" may very well have existed since primitive Shintoism, the term itself was adopted from Buddhism. The word "honesty" may come also from the Confusian classics,[27] but it appears in Buddhist scriptures as well.[28] It was generally recognized by the Japanese of those days that the virtue of "honesty" in Shintoism originated from Buddhism.[29]

The Jōdo doctrine esteems, in particular, the three states of mind, namely, sincerity, believing and praying, and wishing to be reborn into the Pure Land, which are supposed to be the mental attitudes requisite for rebirth in paradise. It was Shinran who made these three states of mind converge upon the one, which is "a heart of truthfulness, not mingled with illusion; a heart of honesty, not adulterated with falsehood".[30] According to Shinran, a religious faith ultimately amounts to honesty. Many other priests also, extol the virtue of honesty.[31]

The virtue of honesty was especially emphasized by Nichiren, who considered that it was with honesty of heart that the Hokke Sūtra preaches the Truth, and therein he recognized the ultimate significance of the Sūtra. "The Hokke Sūtra teaches 'to be honest and to avoid trickery, and talks about those who are 'completely truthful', 'straight-forward in nature and flexible in intention' or 'gentle and straight-forward'. It is the sūtra for those to believe who are as honest as an arrow shot straight from a bow-string, and as a string drawn straight by a carpenter".[32] Thus he traces the authentic source of the virtue, "honesty", to the Hokke Sūtra. He then divides "honesty" into two categories, i.e., "the honesty of this world" and "the honesty beyond this-world",[33] and maintains, "Nichiren is the only individual in Japan who is honest both in this-world and beyond this-world".[34]

At the beginning of the Tokugawa period, a Zen priest, Suzuki Shōsan, developed a theory of professional ethics of his own in his book, "*Rules for Conduct for Every Citizen*", in which he urged that Buddhism put into practice was nothing but the virtue of "honesty" acted upon.[35] Neither in India nor in China was an assertion made explicit that Buddhism was nothing but honesty put into practice, although Buddhist teachings in these countries had similar implications.

Thus, both Shintoists and Buddhists in Japan attached great importance to the word, "honesty", which appeared only sporadically in Buddhist scriptures, and finally according it the position of the central virtue in the general scheme of Japanese ethics.[36]

The virtue of honesty seems to be well fitted for the moral propensities of the Japanese.[37] Such a moral consciousness probably emerged from the tendencies of the Japanese to make much of human relationships, their fondness for fashioning a closed social nexus, and the tendency to demand complete mutual trust among those who belong to that nexus.

These characteristics seem to be manifest also in the forms of acceptance of Chinese thought. Chinese learning was accepted by the Japanese in the past as ethical teaching. From among various Chinese types of thought, the Japanese selected, in particular, Confucianism, strongly imbued with a moralism appropriate to a closed social nexus. This Confucianism itself was then interpreted in terms of "loyalty and fidelity", by Itō Jinsai, who made these notions the two central virtues of his doctrine, while virtue of "sincerity" was stressed in the Kaitokudō school; and this line of interpretation was carried out thoroughly by the Mito school.[38] All of these three schools of Japanese Confucianism aimed at "no falsehood, no deception", as their ideal. Herein lies one of the characteristics of Japanese Confucian doctrine.

A tendency such as this also characterizes the Japanese acceptance of Christianity. It is pointed out that Christianity during the Meiji period was fundamentaly ethical and cultural in nature. Different systems of thought—Buddhism, Chinese ideas and Western religions—met with different forms of adaptation in Japan, and each of these forms has distinct significance. But at the same time the common denominators among all of these forms of adaptation ought not to be overlooked.

Those who observe the moral chaos and decadence of the Japanese in these days may be led to doubt the proposition that the Japanese in the past were moralistically inclined. As far as the observance of honesty within a closed social nexus is concerned, however, little difference seems to exist between the Japanese of the past and the Japanese of the present. The difference seems to lie rather in the fact that what was considered to be morally tenable in the past becomes untenable in changing social conditions. The traditional concept of honesty is applicable only to the conduct of man as a member of the particular and limited human nexus to which he belongs and not applicable to the conduct of man as a member of human society as a whole. Such a shortcoming of the traditional moral concept suddenly proves itself to be a fatal weakness at a time of social confusion such as we are in now.

The following question may still be asked: is it not a contradiction to say that the Japanese put emphasis upon the human nexus rather than upon the individual self-consciousness, on the one hand, and to say that the Japanese are morally acute in self-reflection, on the other? Let us assume (1) that moral conduct in general aims at the unity of oneself and other selves, and (2) that whenever such an ideal unity fails to be attained, as often is the case, one suffers from a moral conflict and is awakened to the problem of one's own conscience. If these two assumptions be true, we are led to conclude that these seemingly discrepant characteristics may not be mutually opposed.

---

1) Tetsurō Watsuji 和辻哲郎: *Sakoku* (鎖國Seclusion) p. 341.

2) *Kyōgyōshinshō*, part III, end. (p. 80 of *Shinshū Shōgyō Zensho* vol. II *Shūsobu*) (Bandōbon 51 J left=51 b)

3) Cf. Prophesies about monks in the final period of the *dharma* in various Buddhist sacred texts.

4) Cf. the works of Kumārajīva. and various entries in the *Hungmingchi.*

5) *Daibucchōnyorai Mitsuin Shushō Ryōgi Shobosatsu Mangyō-shuryōgonkyō* 大佛頂如來密因修證義諸了菩薩萬行首楞嚴經 vol. VII (*Taishō* vol. 19 p. 134 ff.) Sengen Sempi *Kanzeonbosatsu Darani jinjugyō* 千眼千臂觀世音菩薩陀羅尼神呪經 (no Skt. title—(*Beppon, Taisho Nilakanthā-tharani* 1057 vol. 20, p. 94 a.)—Also, there is an Essay on Magic ("呪術篇" in vol. 60 of *Hōon Jurin* 法苑珠林.)

In this essay there is a spell for purging oneself of the sins of 犯欲 (indulging the passions) and of the "Five spicy things" (五辛). The idea here on atonement being effected through magical cult is not essentially different from Brahmanism.

6) *San-shan-yi* 散善義 p. 2 (*More precisely, Kangyō Shōshū Bun Sanzengi* vol. IV; *Taishō* vol. 37, p. 270 c). In the *Hōnen-shōnin Gyōjō Ezu* (法然上人行狀畫圖 portraits illustrating the Career of St. Hōnen) ch. 22; We have, "Do not maintain a saintly external appearance while keeping a deceitful mind within. Rather, regardless of what is external or internal, manifest or hidden, always maintain true sincerity". (Shinkō Mochizuki 望月信亨: *Hōnen-shōnin Zenshū* 法然上人全集 p. 897).

7) *Kyōgyoshinshō* vol. 3 part 2 (*Taishō* vol. 83, p. 601 c.)
Gutokushō (Shinran) part 2 (*Shinshū Shōgyō Zensho* vol. II. *Shūsobu*, p. 464). The phrase "a saintly appearance" is discussed in detail is Shinran's *Yuishin-shomon-i*, p. 25 ff. (p. 635 in *Shinshū Shōgyō Zensho* vol. 2 *Shūsobu*). The phrase is interpreted by Hōnen, in the section entitled "*San-shin Shaku*" of his *Senjaku-hongan-nembutsu-shū* (選擇本願念佛集) *Shinshū Shōgyō Zensho* vol. 1. *Sangyō Shichisobu* 三經七祖部 p. 957, as recommending that we maintain saintliness both within and without.

8) *Hitan Jukkai Wasan* 悲歎述懷和讃 (Shinran) (*Taishō* vol. 83 p. 667 c.)

9) "*The Biography of Hōnen Shōnin*", in the Daigoji Temple edition.

10) *Tannishō* (*Yuien*) ch. 3 (*Shinshū Shōgyō Zensho* vol. 2. 775); also, *Kudenshō* 口傳鈔 (Kakunyo) ch. 19. (*Shinshū Shōgyō Zensho* vol. 3 *Ressobu* p. 32).

11) Saburō Ienaga 家永三郎: *Chūsei-bukkyō Shisō-shi Kenkyū*, 中世佛教思想史研究 pp. 67; 13–22.

12) *Wago Tōroku* 和語燈錄 (Hōnen) vol. 4 (*Taishō* vol. 83) p. 218 c. "Since we have heard that the original vow rejects not even a bad man, we should understand then how much more [Amida] rejoices in a good man". (*ibid.* p. 227 b).

13) *Tōtaigishō* 當體義鈔 (Nichiren) (*Nichiren Shōnin Zenshū* vol. 2, p. 1102). Further, in regard to the fact that Nichiren called himself "*mukai no sō*" (the monk who recognizes no law), cf. Saburō Ienaga: *op. cit.* p. 75.

14) *Shō-hokke-daimoku Shō* 唱法華題目鈔 (Nichiren) *Nichiren Shōnin Zenshū* vol. I, p. 489.

15) *Gessui no Gosho* 月水御書 (Nichiren) *Nichiren Shōnin Zenshū* vol. II, p. 871.

16) *Shōbō Genzō* (*Dōgen*) ch. 9. "*Keisei Sanshoku*" 溪聲山色 (the sound of books and the hue of mountains) (Iwanami Bunko ed. I, 145). The same phrase is used also in the *Jōyō Daishi* (i.e. Dōgen) *Hotsugan-mon.* 承陽大師發願文. cf. also ch. 2 of *Sōtō-kyōkai Shushōgi* 曹洞教會修證義 (in vol. III of *Jōyō Daishi Shōgyō Zenshū* 承陽大師聖教全集)

17) *Shōbō Genzō*, ch. 92 "shōji" 生死 (life and death) (Iwanami ed. III p. 240).

18) Cf. *Sōtō-kyōkai Shushōgi* ch. 3.

19) *Ju-ching Ho-shang* (*Chinese Zen monk, teacher of Dōgen*) *yü-lu* 如淨和尚語錄 last part (*Taishō* vol. 48. p. 131 c)

20) *Kinkaiwaka-shū* 金槐和歌集, zatsu 雜 (A waka-shū is ordinarily divided into sections for the seasons—zatsu section contains those not thus classifiable).

21) Junsei Iwahashi: *op. cit. Sorai Kenkyū* p. 280.

22) TetsurōWatsuji: *op. cit. Sakoku* pp. 341, 353, 474, 477.

23) Here I quote Jiun Sonja's own explanations as they appear—the *Jūzen Kaisō* (also called *Jūzen Kana Hōgo*). This book was dedicated by Jiun Sonja to Emperor Go-momozono in the 28th day of the 1st month of 1774. In other books of Jiun Sonja also, there appear almost the same explanations. (Jiun Sonja 1718—1804 A.O., buddhist scholar, wrote a Sanskrit grammar—using *shittan* 悉曇 or Skt. letters—included in his *Bongaku Shinryō* 梵學津梁.)

24) The following writings exist by Jiun Sonja himself, which deal solely with the Ten Admonitions: *Jūzen Kaisō* (Aspects of the Ten Admonitions) (otherwise called: *Jūzen-kai Kana Hōgo*, Religious teachings in *kana* or the ten admonitions.) *Jūzen-ryaku hōgo* (Informal [i.e. kana] teachings on the 10 admonitions) *Jūzenkai Gohōgo* (Religious teachings on the 10 Admonitions) *Hitotonaru Michi* vol. I (The way of character: The way to become a fine man). *Hitotonaru Michi* vol. 2. *Hitotonaru Michi* vol. 3.

Also, there exists the *Hitotonaru Michi Zuikōki* (Records of followers), a record by Jiun Sonja's disciples of his religious teachings. (All of these are collected in vol. XIII of the *Jiun Sonja Zenshū* 慈雲尊者全集). In his other writings also, Jiun Sonja always emphasizes the 10 Admonitions.

25) Genchi Katō 加藤玄智: *Shintō no Shūkyō-hattatsushi-teki Kenkyū* (神道の宗教發達史的研究 Study of Shintō from the point of view of the history of religious development) p. 874.

26) T. Watsuji 和辻哲郎: *Sonnō-shisō to sono Dentō* (尊皇思想とその傳統 The idea of reverence for the emperor (*sonnō jōi* 攘夷, one of the slogans of the restoration—expel foreigners) and its tradition) p. 103.

27) Genchi Katō: *op. cit.*, p. 1295.

28) *Jōdoronchū* 淨土論註 (T'an-luan 曇鸞. *Jōdoron* was written by Vasubandhu —the "*Chū*" (commentary) is more important for Japanese Buddhism, "Honesty is called uprightness through honesty is engendered a mind capable of compassion for all living creatures". Also in the chapter on "expedients" in the *Hokekyō*, "Among the many Bodhisattvas (the Buddha) is honest and discards expedients, teaching only the highest truth" (i.e. among *bosatsu* as opposed to *shōmon* (聲聞 those who emphasize orthodox teaching) to *engaku* (緣覺 those who emphasize practical teaching)—the *bosatsu* synthesizes both.)

29) The mind of good, which has an included resolve to maintain honesty and discard expediency, is essentially upright, and since this is so, things are as they are". (*Yōkyōku* 謠曲) (Kentarō Sanari, 卷絹 *Makiginu* 佐成謙太郎: *Yōkyoku Taikan* 謠曲大觀 vol. IV, p. 2808, Meiji Shoin, 1931.)

30) *Kyōgyōshinsō* vol. 3, part I.

31) Dōgen: "The word *ko* 古 in the term *kobutsu* (古佛 ancient or eternal Buddha) is identical with *ko* in *shin ko* (新古 new and old); and yet also it transcends time. [The kobutsu] is pure and upright eternally" (*Shōbō Genzō* ch. 44 "*kobutsu shin*" 古佛心 (Iwanami Bunko ed. vol. II, p. 177). *Shōjiki* (正直 "honesty") here differs from "the virtue of *shōjiki*" in meaning, yet there is some connection between the usages.

32) *Nichimyō Shōnin Gosho* 日妙上人御書 (by Nichiren) (*Nichiren Shōnin Zenshū* vol. 2 p. 952 ff.)

33) *Kangyō-hachiman-shō* 諫曉八幡鈔 (Nichiren: *Nichiren-shōnin Zenshū* vol. III p. 1328).

34) *Hōmon Mōsarubekiyōno Koto* 法門可被申樣之事 (Nichiren).

35) "In the notion *shōjiki* (正直 honesty) there is what is superficial and what is profound. If we do not pervent true principles, maintain our duty, stand correctly in the way of the Five Social Virtues, accord with the natural order of things and have no selfish heart, this is the secular notion of *shōjiki*. This is the way to advance from the superficial into the profound. But also, from the standpoint of Buddhism the notion of *shōjiki* is this, if all ordinary phenomenal law is recognized as illusory artificiality, and the essential true *dharmakāya* (法身) is accepted as given by the natural true self, this is the genuine *shōjiki*—". (*Bammin tokuyō* 萬民德用 by Suzuki Shōsan.)

36) The expression 'In an honest head a god resides' (i.e. God defends the right) appears to be a rather ancient proverb.—It has been accepted also by Buddhists—"In the vow of Hachiman there are the words 'I will make the head of an honest man my home and I will not reside in the heart of a sycophant', etc." (Nichiren, *Kangyō-hachiman-shō, Nichiren Shōnin Zenshū* vol. III. p. 1328.) "Among all people, high and low, it is said that 'The great bodhisattva Hachiman resides in an honest head. But he does not make his home elsewhere', etc." (*Hōmon mōsarubekiyō no Koto*)

37) But there is the proverb, "A lie is sometimes expedient". (cf. white bie) This matter needs more study.

38) Yoshio Takeuchi 武內義雄: *Eki to Chūyō no Kenkyū* 易と中庸の研究 p. 325 ff.

(13) The lack of awareness of religious values

The Japanese people's attention is by and large absorbed in the affairs of the human nexus. Their thinking tends not to go beyond this bound.

There was no distinct concept of god among the primitive Japanese. As to the origin of the word '*kami*' (God), there are conflicting views among scholars, and none of them has yet produced any conclusive evidence. '*Kami*' in Japanese may mean 'aboveness', 'one's superior', or 'the hair', and the political ruler was once called '*okami*' (the one that is above us). All that are placed above one both in terms of space and of the hierarchical order are called '*kami*'. Even if the etymologica lorigin of each '*kami*' might have been different, the difference is not discernible in the daily use of people. For the Japanese, therefore, God was not a distinct entity complete in itself, but it was diffused in all that is above ordinary human beings. It was the custom of Shintoism from antiquity to deify those persons who rendered distinguished services to the particular human nexus such as a family, a village or a native community.

"On the whole, *kami* designates first, all the gods of heaven and earth that appear in ancient scriptures, and the spirits that dwell in the shrines where those gods are enshrined; then it also includes man, of course, and all kinds of birds, animals, grass and trees, seas and mountains and everything else that is extraordinary highly virtuous or worthy of reverence. (Not only that which excels in nobleness, goodness or in merits is a god but that which excels in wickedness or in hideousness also is a god. That the godly among men are the emperors, who are gods from generation to generation, is so obvious that it needs no mention. They are also called distant gods, since they are so far above ordinary men and so august and highly revered by them. Then there are godly persons both in the past and in the present. There are also those minor gods, not universally known to the whole world, but known only to one country, one village, or to one family. Even the gods of 'the age of gods' were mostly men in those days, and since men of their time were all godly, their days are now called "the age of gods")"[1)]

This interpretation, which is that of Motoori Norinaga, was accepted also by Hirata Atsutane.[2)]

As long as such a view of gods is held, the conception of God, whether transcendental or immanent, which sets down a categorical imperative, transcending the limitation of any particular human nexus, is impossible. That was why even after the introduction of Buddhism into Japan, the Japanese never discarded their traditional standard of evaluation, that of judging things in terms of a particular human nexus. They regarded as absolute the authority of ancestors, parents, lords, the state and the emperor, to whom religion was subjected and made to serve. It follows that a religious order in a proper sense was never firmly established in Japan. Shrine Shintoism never gave rise to a closely knit religious order, neither did Confucianism. The same was true even in the case of Buddhism, which claims to be a universal religion.

The ecclesiastical authorities of Buddhist orders and sects in Japan were subjected to the secular authorities of the state and feudal lords, and the former assumed an attitude of compromise to the latter, to the point of subservience. The Indian Buddhist tradition that "the ascetic never pays homage to the king"[3] was neither put into practice, nor even given any attention. The Buddhists in Japan regarded honour bestowed by them from the imperial family or by feudal lords as of supreme value. Under these circumstances the Buddhist orders in Japan even in the medieval period never wielded a power comparable to that of the religious orders in medieval Europe.[4] They were even less respected than the Buddhist orders in South Asiatic countries.

The orders were often placed under the control of political powers. The hierarchical structure of secular society was brought directly into the orders. In India, on the contrary, the hierarchical structure of secular society never penetrated into the religious orders, and the ranking of ascetics was determined solely according to the number of years of priesthood. Even the king of a great country, once having entered priesthood, had to accept the lowest rank.[5] Such a tradition appears to have been observed also in China. Even a rich man's son, once having entered priesthood, put on a plain raiment. It was with some surprise that Dōgen recounted the story of a rich man's son in China, who, being asked why he was dressed so plainly, answered simply "because I have become a monk".[6] By contrast, a son of aristocracy in Japan, after having entered priesthood, was given a privileged status. This fact is proved by the existence of a great number of temples which the 'monk-princes' made their places of residence. The status of the 'monk-Emperor' or of the 'monk-prince' has never been recognized in any other country than Japan. If one studied from what families the successive chief abbots of the Tendai sect came, one would be near to understanding the close interconnection established between the secular and ecclesiastical authorities. The Honganji Temple order, which originally aimed at a religion of and for people, finally acquired the privileged status of a temple of a monk-prince. The head-temples of various branches of the Jōdo-shin sect succeeded in establishing a close connection both economically and in kinship relation with the imperial family and aristocracy. The popes of the head-temples of the various Jōdō-shin sects exercised their authority as aristocracy and as the heads of the orders over common believers. Although their status within the hierarchy of the secular aristocracy was not high, still they enjoyed the privilege of being members of the aristocracy, however low their status might be. This is not to deny the existence of those, and their number is by no means negligible, who kept their pride as men of religion impeccable, standing aloof from worldly privileges. Dōgen, for instance, never put on the purple robe, saying that even the monkey and the stork would laugh at him, should he have worn it.[7] The Sōtō sect, however, which continued his teachings, took to the custom of receiving the title of Zen master from the emperor for the chief abbot of its head temples.

The transplanting of the hierarchical system of the secular world transformed the religious order into a secular community. Many of the priests of the Heian period entered temples not in search for the truth but in quest for worldly riches and privileges. "Gorō is a scholar and great high priest of the Tendai sect. He is a great master in Indian logic and Buddhist philosophy. He is also well versed in the Buddhist scriptures and the canons of other schools. He has the *Abhidharmakośa* and Buddhist idealism at the tip of his tongue, and keeps the profound teaching of the Tendai doctrine at the depth of his heart..... No clerical position, high or low, is good enough for him. He aspires only to be chief abbot of the Tendai order".[8]

The surest way to acquire riches and honours as a priest was to become intimate with the aristocracy, who concentrated the greatest power and wealth of society in their hands. Consequently, priests availed themselves of all means and opportunities to gain access to the aristocracy.

With the decline of the power of the Fujiwara clan, an increasing number of their members entered temples and became priests, since high official positions in the secular world were no more guaranteed for them. When the migration of the Fujiwara members into Buddhist temples took place, practically all the key positions within the temples came to be monopolized by the clan. In those days most promising students went into temples and worked hard in order to attain high positions therein. But they were ousted now that those positions were reserved only for the members of the Fujiwara clan. All but the kind of the Fujiwara could not advance to the ranks of "*Ajari*" and "*Sōgō*", unless he was endowed with prodigious learning and extraordinary longevity. On the other hand, even a man of mediocre ability, if he be connected to the Fujiwara family, could rise, immediately after he entered priesthood, to the rank of *'Gondaisōzu'* at best, or to that of *'Gonshōsōzu'* at second best, or at least to the rank of *'Hōgen'*.[9] For the key positions of the religious orders to be monopolized by the royal family and the members of the aristocracy would never have been possible in Buddhist countries other than Japan.

Such a sacrilege wrought by the secular powers upon the Buddhist orders up to the Heian period seems to have its origin in the process with which those orders were instituted. The Buddhist orders of those days in Japan were not necessarily generated from intense religious and spiritual demands of the people. On the contrary, they were instituted to meet the demands of the imperial family and aristocracy, and developed under their protection. So it seems only natural that they were desecrated by their own originators.

The religious orders after the Kamakura period, in contrast, came out of genuine religious demands of the people, and were developed, for the time being, independently of secular authorities. But even those orders were placed under the control of the secular authorities with the inception of the centralized government of the feudal regime at the beginning of the modern period. Even the Honganji Temple, once the stronghold of resistance against the secular power of feudalism, submitted to interference by Toyotomi Hideyoshi, who succeeded in unifying the country.[10] Finally the Temple was divided into the West and the East Honganji Temples by the astute policy of Tokugawa Ieyasu.

When religious orders finally yielded to the secular authority, the feudal political power established overall religious control. In the Tokugawa period, the Office of the Administration of Shrines and Temples (*Shaji Bugyō*) was established within the central government, and similar offices were established within the governments of the various *daimyō*; Office of Issuing Order (*huregashira*) was instituted within the central government. The function of the latter office was to convey the orders of the central government to the temples under control, and to transmit to the government petitions from the subordinate temples. To this office, priests were appointed. But the Office of the Administration of Shrines and Temples was open only to the vassals of the shogunate or to the feudal lords in hereditary vassalage to the shogunate. In medieval China also, overall religious control was set up by the government. But in medieval China, priests were appointed to the office of religious administration. In Japan, in contrast, the secular warriors, *qua* warriors, were appointed to the office and administered religious matters. It was not a religious order itself, but the secular authority, that settled controversy over a religious doctrine within the order. (It was the Tokugawa Government, for example, that worked out the final settlement on the controversy on the three kinds of deeds—mind, body and mouth—the most important of all the doctrinal controversies in the Jodo-shin sect.)

The gradual formation of the relationship between the main temple and sub-temple, based upon the principles of the lineage of teachings and of master-disciple relationship, corresponded to the development of the feudal hierarchical relationship within secular society at the beginning of the Tokugawa period. The Tokugawa Government, when it came to power, enforced this main-and-sub-temple relationship, making it a fixed system of hierarchy. It determined the control-and-submission relationships among the head quarters of main temples, main temples, midmain-temples, immediate-sub-temples, and mediated-sub-temples. In the religious ordinances, strict adherence to the regulations about main-temple-sub-temple relationship was ordained, and it was stipulated that the infringement of the regulations was to be severely punished. For those temples which did not belong to any main temple, the succession of the resident-priesthood was not allowed and the temples were even confiscated.

The history of religion in Japan shows, just as Max Weber rightly pointed out, that the state functioned not as a patron (Schutz-patronat) but as a religious police (Religionspolizei) of Buddhism.[11] And only on such a historical basis was the government after the Meiji Restoration able to realize complete religious control, and to push it to such an extreme that no parallel could be found in any other modern nation. Buddhists during the Meiji period resisted the tendency to destroy Buddhism with violence, by arguing that Buddhism was not in contradiction with Nipponism, and that in the West freedom of religion was guaranteed. The pressure of the state, however, was too great for them to cope with. "Freedom of religion" is now proclaimed by the Potsdam Declaration, and it reminds us of the solitary outcries of our forebears.

Under these circumstances, religious orders in Japan neither had enough authority, nor were the men of religion respected as they were in the West. This is not a phenomenon of recent origin. "*The Buddhist hymns on the reminiscences of grief*", by Shinran, deplores as follows:

"Tokens are these, that Buddhism they despise:
Nuns and Monks are made their slaves,
The names of priests are given to knaves".

Such was the situation even in the medieval period when religion was supposed to have flourished. Kenkō writes: "There are perhaps none less to be envied than monks. Seishōnagon rightly says, 'People regard them as trifling as a chip' ".[12] In this, we find a man who was a priest himself deprecating the priesthood. Such attitudes were those of the Japanese in general and have continued up to the present.[13] Such attitudes would have been inconceivable to the Buddhists of either India or of China.

To illustrate this point, Fujiwara Yorinaga, the Minister of the Left who was exceptionally well versed for a layman in Indian logic, invited Egyō and Zōshun, priests of the Kōfukuji Temple, to teach him Indian logic. The case is exactly reversed in India, where kings drove their cars by themselves to pay homage to men of religion, and graciously asked them to teach them their teachings. In Japan, the status of the Minister of the Left was placed far above the learned priests of the time.

The reason why nuns and monks were despised may be attributed to the fact that in antiquity, even outcastes were able to become nuns and monks, and to the fact that since nuns and monks were exempted from taxes, there were many who secretly entered the priesthood, despite the laws to prohibit such a practice. But in India, where religious ascetics were highly respected, priests even of outcaste origin were never looked down upon, at least among the believers of the same sect. So we are led to conclude that this tendency to ridicule nuns and monks originated from the Japanese inclination to lay greater emphasis upon mundane affairs.

Throughout the feudal age in Japan, the class of warriors preserved their pride and power as the ruling class, and consequently they never submitted themselves to the guidance of Buddhist priests with absolute obedience, to say nothing of Shintoist priests. Nothing like the spiritual guidance of the Guru of India ever prevailed. Although the number of Buddhist temples increased during the Tokugawa period, the social influence of Buddhism decreased. Temples degenerated into organs simply for issuing certificates to their followers to prove that 'they were not Christians'. The ruling class did not wish to recognize in the temples any greater social significance. Since the Buddhist ideal of non-discrimination of classes was not compatible with the hierarchical order of feudal society, it was against the intention of the ruling class to have this ideal pushed too far. When the country was opened to foreign intercourse after the Meiji Restoration, the non-Christian certificates formerly issued from the temples were no more necessary. Henceforward, funeral and memorial services came to be almost the only function of the Buddhist temples.

The Japanese were not devoted to Buddhism from the bottom of their hearts, recognizing its intrinsic value, but they simply followed it, even travestying a Buddha quite frequently. In the common saying, "Not knowing is the state of Buddhahood" (Ignorance is bliss), or "Even the face of a Buddha changes (shows anger) after three times" (There are limits to one's endurance). A Buddha is represented as something extremely close and familiar to man. Still another saying goes: "Borrowing with a *Jizō*-face, repaying with an *Emma*-face" (*Jizō* is the guardian deity of children while *Emma, Yama* is the King of Hell). A children's toy (which is contrived so as to recover its upright position when thrown down) has the figure of Bodhidharma, and a lottery is named after Amitābha.[14] Buddhist terminology is quite commonly travestied in vernacular expressions of everyday language.

Degenerative as these characteristics are, Buddhists after the Meiji Restoration misconceived them as merits and virtues of Japanese Buddhism. They emphasized the peculiarly Japanese characteristics of Buddhism, which essentially is a universal religion. They even went so far as to assert that the true essence of Buddhism for the first time came into actual fruition in Japan.

It was within the framework of their own peculiar standpoint and orientation that the Japanese accepted Buddhism. They were inclined to utilize it as a means and an instrument to realize a certain socio-political end. They were not converted to Buddhism. They converted Buddhism to their own tribalism.

One cannot deny, of course, that there were some instances, when the Japanese paid unqualified respect to a foreign culture and earnestly tried to accept it as it was. It is especially true with the intellectuals in Japan that they are apt to become vehement admirers of foreign cultures, despising their own in every respect. It is said to be a tradition with the Japanese completely to abandon their own tradition in their enthusiasm for a foreign culture newly adopted. The Japanese are acutely susceptible to the excellence of the foreign culture, and once inspired by it, they bocome extremely humble and self-effacing in learning what they believe to be fine and good. Had it not been for such an attitude, the Japanese would not have been able to absorb the diverse cultures of Asiatic countries and to cultivate them on their own soil, despite the fact that the range of actual foreign intercourse, for geographical reasons, was so limited, and the period when such intercourse was allowed, for historical reasons, was so brief.[15] Yet, so great a faculty of assimilating cultures other than their own constituted merely a subjective phenomenon in the Japanese, in the sphere of conscious choice. Objectively speaking, the Japanese never assimilated other cultures in such a way that all their values and their entire outlook might attain a new configuration. They always adamantly kept to their own traditional values and outlook.

These facts being taken into consideration, it is easy to understand how Buddhism was so quickly accepted. Such modern nations as Germany, France or England accepted Christianity in such a way that it has become the soul and blood of their own cultures. In Japan, in contrast, Buddhist thought is still an alien thought. Buddhism is so basic and prevailing a factor in Japanese culture of the past that this culture may very well be called a Buddhist culture; nevertheless Buddhism, in fact, is still regarded by the Japanese as an imported religion. This is vastly different from the attitude of Westerners in regarding Christianity as their own religion. The Japanese accepted Buddhism without changing their own original standpoint an iota. That was why Buddhism spread with such speed.[16] The same applies to the form of accepting Christianity after the Meiji Restoration. For most of the Japanese, Christianity as a religion was a matter of no consequence. They were concerned solely with the Japanization of Christianity, as they once succeeded in the Japanization of Buddhism.

Since the Japanese accepted Buddhism from the standpoint of Japan as a state and of the Japanese as a tribe, it naturally follows that hardly any conscious attempt has been made to propagate Buddhism as a universal religion, transcending the interests of Japan as a particular state. Even after the Meiji Restoration when the country was opened to international intercourse, a universal religious movement of any consequence never took form. Let us compare this with the case of China, our neighbour. In China, a group was formed in 1922 under the leadership of T'ai-hsü, to establish in Wuchang 'The School of World Buddhism' and to promote a 'World Buddhist Movement'. Their aim was to launch a Buddhist movement on an international basis, to renovate the world, and to create a new world culture. Although the realization of their intentions was blocked by internal and international wars in following years, the historical significance of their movement, which inspired a great number of people inside and outside of their own country, is very great. In Japan, supposedly the vanguard of modernization in Asia, Buddhist leaders were engrossed in arguing the superiority and uniqueness of 'Japanese Buddhism', in order to win the favor of the authorities, such as the Imperial Family and the military clique. There was virtually no appearance of such a vision as a 'World Buddhist Movement' in modern Japan.

The lack of the religion-consciousness of the Japanese has moulded most of the Japanese into philistine materialists. They are, generally speaking, lacking in the ability for profound confession and severe compunction. Religion, in the true sense of the word, never deeply took root on Japanese soil. From this fact arises the weakness of religious orders.

Thus, as religion had no strength, materialism and anti-religious movements which aim at the overthrow of religion are almost not to be found. Let us ask ourselves, how many conscious materialists were there, before the Meiji Restoration, except for such a person as Yamagata Bantō. In spite of the fact that the intellectual climate of the Japanese was extremely materialistic, materialism never had a lucid and conscious formulation. In India, not to speak of the West, materialism was developed in such a way as to rival religion. In Japan, the fact that true religious thinking was not fertile kept materialism from becoming evident.

The tendencies of the Japanese, as discussed above from various angles, to emphasize the human nexus, seem to be attributable to the social mode of living, peculiarly adapted to Japanese topography. Japanese mythology, for instance, clearly shows that collaboration among farmers was generally practiced in irrigation and the cultivation of the soil. To disturb cooperation in cultivation (such as 'destroying the foot-path between rice-fields', 'destroying the ditch', or 'sowing the soil already sown') was a serious crime. In Indian mythology, there is no suggestion of this. The topographical conditions of India do not require such strenuous human labor as was required in Japan. In India, one can leave the crops alone and they will yield harvest. Irrigation is hardly necessary. Farmers can reap a harvest of the same kind of crops twice a year. This is vastly different from the farming conditions of Japan. In India, collaboration in farming is not practiced to such an extent as is the case in Japan.

For these reasons, the Indians can afford to live in isolation and they enjoy it. Since their conditions of living are mostly under the influence of nature, they tend to attach importance to magical rituals with which they believe they can influence nature. That was why Brahminism came to exert strong influence upon the whole society. In Japan, however, the topographical conditions are such as to require human effort to combat the conditions of nature, hence the social nexus is made to play an important role in agricultural labor, and consequently the pressure of the social nexus weighs heavily upon individuals. This would seem to be the origin of the principal characteristic of the Japanese, nemely the high esteem of the social nexus, and other characteristics seem to be derived from it.

---

1) *Kojikiden* 古事記傳, ch. 2 (edited by Toyonogi Motoori 本居豐穎, vol. 1, p. 150 ff. in *Motoori Norinaga Zenshū*).

2) "Let us inquire what is the meaning of the word '*kami*' 加美 as used of old in the language of our country: First of all, the various gods of heaven and earth which appear in the *Kojiki* and the *Nihonshoki* were called *kami* and also the spirits residing in the shrines dedicated to these deities. Further, it was the ancient usage to apply the word to men, needless to say, and to birds, beasts, plants, trees, seas, mountains and anything else whatever, if that thing were out of the ordinary and had some distinctive virtue, or was to be revered or feared. The criterion of distinction was not that the thing or person should be honorable or good or meritorious; anything particularly august and dreadful, even something bad or strange, was called *kami*.

Among those *kami* which are human, it goes without saying that the most august emperors of each generation, are all *kami;* thus in the *Manyōshū* and other ancient poetry, they are called, most high gods, for they are far removed from, more honored by and against the ordinary people. So, in every successive age from antiquity to the present there have been human beings who are *kami*. Also, although they are not widely popular, each state, each province, each village and each family has its respective human *kami*, now many, even of the *kami* of "the Age of Gods", were men of that time; that age is called the "Age of the Gods" because the men of that age were all god-like". (*Kodō Daii* 古道大意, *Hirata Atsutane Zenshū* 平田篤胤全集 vol. VII, p. 37.

3) For example, such a phrase in the *Bommō-kyō* (梵網經 *Brahma-jāla-sūtra.*) is quoted by Shinran in vol. 6 pt. 2 of the *Kyōgyōshinshō* 教行信證, but of course it was never practiced.

4) The political power of the religious organization in Japan did not by any means extend as far as that of the Roman Pope in the Middle Ages.

5) According to vol. 9 of the *Ta T'ang Hsiyü-chi* (大唐西域記 *Daitō Saiiki-ki*), King Bālāditya in *Magadha*, when he became a monk, was obliged to occupy the last seat among the monks, and for this reason was highly

dissatisfied. But the Buddhist church did not go as far as to break the traditional rules by giving him special honor. His seat was occupied only higher than that of young man who had not received their vows.

6) *Shōbōgenzō Zuimonki* 正法眼藏隨聞記 (Notes on Dōgen's teachings promotive to time, by his disciple *Ejō*) vol. 5 (section, 2, p. 81 in Iwanami Bunko ed.)

7) In the year 1250 A.D., the retired emperor *Gosaga*, hearing of Dōgen's honorable character, presented him with a purple robe. Dōgen declined the gift two or three times, but when the imperial messenger had come third time to the Eiheiji Temple (in Echizen—Fukui pref.), there was nothing he could do but accept it. Nevertheless, to the end of his life he never used it. The following poem is said to have been written by him on this occasion:

Though the valley below the Eiheiji is not deep.
I am profoundly honored to receive the emperor's command.
But I would be laughed out by monkeys and cranes.
If I, a mere old man, were to wear this purple robe. (*Dōgenzenji Gyōjō Zensho* 道元禪師行狀全書 vol. 115, p. 555.)

From this also we can see that he had no interest in riches and honor.

8) *Shin Sarugaku-ki* 新猿樂記, (By Fujiwara Akihira (Latter Heian-reigns of Goichijō, Gosujaku, Goreizei: 1016–1068 A.D.)—in *Gunshoruijū* 群書類從).

9) T. Tamamuro: *Nippon Bukkyō Shi Gaisetsu* pp. 87–88.

10) Toyotomi Hideyoshi, in collusion with the widow (*Nyoshunni*) of Kōsa (i.e. Kennyo), abbot of the Honganji, deposed his eldest son (Kyōnyo or Kōju) and installed the widow's own son (Junnyo or Kōsho) as an abbot. (N.B.—Ieyasu Tokugawa subsequently re-established Kyōnyo as an abbot of a temple—the Higashi Honganji—splitting the sect)

11) Max Weber: *Aufsätze zur Religionssozioligie*, II, S. 288.

12) *Tsurezuregusa* 徒然草, pt. 1 by Yoshida Kenkō (1283–1350 A.D.)—of a family which hereditarily served in the Yoshida Shrine.

13) "There are countless comical varieties of *daruma* (the figure of Bud-hidharma, the founder of Zen Buddhism): figures moulded or carved in almost every kind of material, and ranging in size from the tiny metal *daruma*, half-an-inch long, designed for a pouch-clasp, to the big wooden *daruma*, two or three feet high, which the Japanese tobacconist has adopted for a shop-sign. Thus profanely does popular art deride the holy legend of the nine years' meditation". (Lafcadio Hearn: *A Japanese Miscellany*. Little Brown, 1901. *Studies Here and There, Otokichi's Daruma*.) People of Southern Asia highly blame the attitude of some Japanese who use the figure of the Great Buddha for a profanely commercial purpose.

14) Y. Haga: *Kokumin-sei Jūron* p. 140 ff.

15) Cf. Tetsurō Watsuji 和辻哲郎: *Zoku Nihon Seishin-shi Kenkyū* (續日本精神史研究 *A Study on the history of Japanese Spirits* pt. 2.) p. 47, pp. 49–50.

16) Christianity under the Goths in the 4th century, had already penetrated among the Germans. But Christianity as transplanted into the German world did not subsequently, in the 5th and 6th centuries, flourish very vigorously. In Japan, on the contrary, in the two and a half centuries after the introduction of Buddhism, such scholars appeared as Saichō and Kūkai. (*ibid.* pp. 76–78.)

Chapter 3. Irrationalistic tendencies

(1) The tendency to be illogical (to neglect logical rules)

We have already pointed out the characteristic that among the Japanese at large, mutual 'subjective' relationships are given special attention, and actions are taken on the basis of mutual understanding and trust among 'subjects'. Upon this basis, there is little intention to make each man's understanding and expression logical and measurable, but rather these tend to be intuitive and emotional. This problem I should now like to discuss.

As a preliminary step for discussing the main problem, we should call attention to some logical characteristics perceived in common Japanese linguistic usages which provide insight into the daily thinking of the Japanese.

As is often pointed out by scholars, the expressive forms of Japanese sentences put more emphasis upon emotive factors than on cognitive factors.

The forms of expression of the Japanese language are more sensitive and emotive than directed toward logical exactness. The Japanese language does not tend to express precisely and accurately the various modes of being, but is satisfied merely with vague, typological expressions. As for nouns, we have no clear distinction between singular and plural nor is there a distinction between genders, and no articles are used. For verbs, either, there are no distinctions of person and number. In these respects, Japanese resembles Chinese. But what is different from classical Chinese, giving Japanese its distinctive atmosphere, is the so-called *'te-ni-o-ha'*, or the postpositional particles. This part of speech corresponds to case declensions or prepositions in other languages, and has the characteristic not only of expressing cognitive, logical relations, but also of expressing to some degree various delicate shades of emotion. Thus this auxiliary part of speech, making its appearance amidst all kinds of words and sentences, plays the role of emphasizing some specific meanings, evoking attention to some aspects of things, distinguishing delicate variations of emotion, and leaves rich overtones of meaning just because of this ambiguity. Moreover, the abundance of auxiliary verbs and their complex usages show that the Japanese language is peculiarly sensitive in its grasp of emotion.

The original Japanese language, as clearly revealed in Japanese classical literature, has a rich vocabulary of words denoting aesthetic or emotional states of mind. On the other hand, words denoting intellectual, inferential processes of active thought are notably lacking. In the original Japanese language, where words were for the most part concrete and intuitive, the construction of abstract nouns was deficient. Hence it is extremely difficult to express abstract concepts solely in words of the original Japanese. When Buddhism and Confucianism were later introduced to Japan and philosophical thinking developed, the vocabulary which was the means of expressing these philosophical thoughts was entirely Chinese, used just as it was. Although Buddhism was so widely propagated among the people, its scriptures *were never translated* into the Japanese language. "In our country, there is no attempt to translate [Chinese versions of Buddhist scriptures]",[1] said Kokan Shiren (1287–1346) in his *Genkō Shakusho* (a history of Japanese Buddhism), and he cited this fact as a characteristic of the Japanese Buddhism. Furthermore, we hardly had before the Kamakura period any original writing by Buddhists in Japanese. Even after the beginning of Kamakura, in the overwhelming majority of cases, Buddhist works were written in the Chinese language. Although the Japanese Confucians began to write some of their works in Japanese from the Tokugawa era onward, such writings never ceased to be viewed as merely an avocation of the Confucians, and even in such works, they followed the Chinese language as far as technical terms were concerned. Now, Western philosophical ideas widely prevail in our country, but the linguistic means by which they are expressed, are, in most cases, words coined by properly connecting two Chinese characters, which are, by convention, made to correspond to the traditional Occidental concepts. The words *gainen* and *risei,* for instance, are the present-day Japanese terms for 'concept' (Begriff) and 'reason' (Vernunft) respectively. Sometimes such words are constructions of three or four characters. The pure original Japanese has never been able to serve as a means of expressing philosophical concepts.

In this connection, it might be said that, as philosophical thinking gradually was beginning to develop among the Japanese people, suddenly foreign philosophical thought came in, with the result that the opportunity to train the Japanese language philosophically was lost; and that this is why, to the present time, Japanese has remained unable to form philosophical concepts.[2] Yet in the case of the German people, although clerics in medieval times carried on their philosophical thinking in Latin, in modern times, the Germans came to build up philosophical systems by means of the pure German language. And such attempts can even be traced back to Eckhart in the Middle Ages. On the other hand, even in very recent times, no philosophy has so far been developed in Japan, which is expressed in terms of the purely original Japanese words. We are, therefore, forced to conclude that this language of ours is not fit for philosophical thinking, as German clearly is.

The greatest obstacle seems to lie in the fact that the Japanese language does not have any fully established method of composing abstract nouns. The language does not have the infinitive form of the verb, the special character which is to express is an indefinite situation, a 'relation' itself rather than 'thing'. Although we do have what is called the 'nominal use' corresponding to the infinitive, this is completely identical in form with a verbal form which, in conjunction with temporal verb endings, indicates the past, or which, when joined to another verb, a noun or an adjective, forms a compound word. For example, the so-called nominal form *warai,* which is completely identical in form with the form of the verb *warau* ('to laugh') appearing in *waraitari* ('laughed'), *waraite* ('laughed and ....'), *waraigoto* ('laughing matter'), etc., signifies the act or fact of 'laughing'. Moreover, this verb form in time has tended to lose its special significance as an expression with a compounding function, and has also come to be used as a noun. For instance, *warai* has the senses both of *warau koto* (the act or fact of laughing) and of *warai to yū mono* ("laughter"); consequently the distinction between 'die Lache' and 'das Lachen' is not made.[3]

Furthermore, we have no established method of turning adjectives into corresponding abstract nouns. As may be seen in such examples as *fukasa* ('depth'), or *fukami* ('deepness'), the suffixes *-sa* or *-mi* make abstract nouns out of adjectives to some extent. But this manner of transformation or noun-building is available for only a limited range of adjectives. In Greek, for example, Plato coined the noun *poiotēs* out of the adjective *poion,* which means *donoyō-na* or *ika-naru* ('of what sort'). And Cicero, in attempting to translate the Greek, coined the abstract noun *qualitas* out of Latin *qualis,* meaning 'of what sort'. Both *poiotēs* and *qualitas* are invented words meaning the quality of a thing, or a thing's 'of-what-sortness'. Literally translated into Japanese, these words would give [the unnatural sounding expression] *dono-yō-na-sa.* This Latin translation term was current in the Middle Ages, and in modern Europe was used without change, as in the words *Qualität, quality, qualité.* But the Japanese, in translating this concept, have made use of the two Chinese characters *sei-shitsu.* This is because in the Japanese language the translation term *dono-yō-na-sa* conveys a somehow inappropriate, unnatural feeling.[4]

In short, the Japanese language has a structure unfit for expressing logical conceptions. Consequently, when we adopted the already highly advanced conceptual knowledge of Buddhism and Confucianism, we made no attempt to express it in the original Japanese language, but used Chinese technical terms without modification. Again, in translating the concepts of Western learning, we used Chinese characters and did not render these concepts into Japanese directly. Consequently, even today, any marked tendency to logical expression is hardly apparent in the Japanese language.

Some abstract concepts which have been introduced from India, have been unable to take root intact among the Japanese people at large. The words *'anyatara'* (one between two) and *'anyatama'* (one among many) were translated into Chinese as *sui-i* (隨一). The ancient Japanese intellectuals used this concept in its original meaning, whereas common people since the Tokugawa period[5] have taken the word *'zuiichi'* to mean 'the first' or 'the most excellent'. There has been no single native Japanese word representing 'one between two' or 'one among many'.

When we step into the realm of syntax from that of word-construction, the Japanese language manifests its illogical character all the more clearly. The language lacks the relative pronoun, 'which', stanling for the antecedent, that helps develop the process of thought. We find it, therefore, inconvenient to advance closely knit thinking in Japanese.[6] It is difficult to tell what modifies what, when several adjectives or adverbs are juxtaposed. Because of these defects, Japanese presents difficulties for scientific expression which has to be exact, and, as is generally pointed out, its illogical, unscientific character naturally handicaps the development of ability in logical, scientific thinking among the Japanese people, and has actually brought about grave inconveniences in their practical lives. Indian books of Buddhistic philosophy were originally written with logical accuracy, but, as was already pointed out, Chinese versions of them became remarkably illogical. Thereafter, the Japanese continued the ambiguous and obscure interpretations of the Chinese withtout change, and as a result, they did not attempt to analyse them logically.[7]

The same ambiguity can be observed in Japanese expressions of sequences or inferences made up of successively related judgments. For instance, the following is one of the well-known examples of such a chain-syllogism: "When wind blows, it becomes dusty. If it becomes dusty, it becomes injurious to eyes. If it becomes injurious to eyes, many people become blind. If many people become blind, there appear many *samisen* players. If there appear many *samisen* players, *samisens* are in great demand. If *samisens* are in great demand, cats are killed (for the stuff of this musical instrument). If cats are killed, rats increase in number. If rats increse in number, boxes are bitten; they are in great demand. Therefore, boxmakers become prosperous".[7]

Although special phraseologies have been worked out in legal jargon, etc., for technical considerations, to avoid ambiguity, such a practice is by no means universal.

Again, complicated expressions of Indo-European languages can hardly be translated, in corresponding forms, into Japanese. For instance, causative passive constructions like *prāpitaś cārthaḥ*[8] ("[by some means, either person or thing, an individual] has been made to reach an object") can only with great difficulty be put into Japanese in like form.

In the same way, Japanese frequently omits the subject, and this too has something to do with the illogical character of the Japanese people. In such a case, even though the subject is omitted, we usually find it naturally suggested or can easily infer what it is by referring to linguistic context, or by looking at the situation in which the utterance is made. But it cannot be denied that at times, when the situation is not completely clear, the omission of the subject makes the meaning ambiguous and causes misunderstanding. This short-coming can, of course, be overcome if the Japanese would try to make their expression logical, by constructing sentences always accompanied by subjects. Nevertheless, up to the present at least, actual Japanese usage is still very inaccurate in this respect.

In connection with the omission of subjects, we must note that anacoluthon very freqently occurs in Japanese sentences. While it is to be found also in Indo-European languages, examples are few;[9] whereas the Japanese not only has abundant examples of it, but also even the fact that the subject has changed within a single sentence is not clearly noticed. For example, in literary works of the Heian period, instances of anacoluthon are very frequent. And this characteristic of the Japanese way of thinking appears also in the annotations to Chinese Buddhist texts.[10] That the Japanese people can dispense with the subject in their linguistic expression is, I think, due to the fact that the intuitive understanding of the scene referred to in their discourse is usually beforehand attained by the close bonds and nexus with others. Therefore, the necessity of clearly indicating the subject occurs only in those cases where some doubt about the intuitive understanding of the subject arises. (In other words, logically correct assertion of the 'obvious' sounds harsh to the Japanese people).

Generally speaking, logical consciousness begins with consciousness of the relation between the particular and the universal; and the Japanese on the whole have not been fully aware of this relation, or have been poor in understanding a concept apart from particular instances. This exactly corresponds to the tendency, characteristic in the Japanese way of thinking, not to make a sharp contrast between subject and predicate in the expression of judgment.

Hio Keizan (1789–1859), in his two volume work *Kunten Fukko* ("Restoration of Kunten"), criticized the usages of *kunten* (marks used in paraphrasing Chinese into Japanese) prevalent in the Tokugawa period. According to his view, for example, scholars at that time misread the Chinese passage Yen Hui che, which means "a man called Yen Hui i.e. Gankai", *as Gankai naru Mono,* which is an abridged form of *Gankai ni aru Mono* (strictly, "the man exemplified in Gankai").[11] In so doing, he argued, they committed an error in the indication of the meaning. However this may be, such a distinction is generally not recognized by the Japanese, and this confusion continues to the present time. Whether or not Hio's theory is right is a question to be entrusted to experts, but in any case one could say that there was no method fully established in Japanese for expressing universals by the universal concept.

Therefore, the Japanese people are not inclined to present the universal concept as a predicate in a judgement, so as to make the expression of it concise. They are not usually content until they have presented a set of particular instances. Dōgen (1200–53), who has been called one of the greatest philosophers Japan ever had, for example, wrote:

> "The Acting Buddha is neither a Buddha in the perfect figure nor a transformation-Buddha. It is neither a Buddha in itself nor a Buddha in other selves. It is neither the initial enlightenment nor the ultimate enlightenment. It is neither the realization of one's own nature, nor the realization of nothing. All these Buddhas together are not equal to the Acting Buddha".[12]

Where an Indian philosopher formulated an idea simply and definitely in a universal proposition, e.g., "The Three Worlds are but one Mind",[13] Dōgen explained the thought by *enumerating various particulars.* Thus:

"The mind is neither one nor two. It is neither in the Three Worlds nor beyond the Three Worlds. It is infallible. It is an enlightenment through contemplation, and it is an enlightenment without contemplation. It is walls and pebbles; it is mountains, rivers, and the earth. The mind is but the skin, flesh, bones, and marrow; the mind is but the communication of enlightenment through the Buddha's smile. There is a mind, and there is no mind. There is a mind with a body; there is a mind without a body. There is a mind prior to a body; there is a mind posterior to a body. A body is generated from any of the womb, the egg, moisture, or fermentation. The mind is generated from any of the womb, the egg, moisture, or fermentation. Blue, yellow, red, and white are nothing but the mind. Long, short, square, and round are nothing but the mind. Life and death are nothing but the mind. Years, months, days, and hours are nothing but the mind. Dreams, illusions, and mirages are nothing but the mind. The bubbles of water and the flames of fire are nothing but the mind. The flowers of the spring and the moon of the autumn are nothing but the mind. Confusions and dangers are nothing but the mind"[14]

Although Dōgen ardently admired Bodhidarma, he never referred to the systematic doctrine of "two entrances and four practices"[15] which was the central theme of Bodhidarma's thought.

A similar way of thinking may be noticed in Japanese Confucianists. Ogiu Sorai (1666–1728), for example, did not like the sort of abstract speculation found in the Sung school; he made more of particular 'things' (*wu*) than of universal 'principles' (*li*):

"The great sage kings of the past taught by means of 'things' and not by means of 'principles'. Those who teach by means of 'things' always have work to which they devote themselves; those who teach by means of 'principles' merely expatiate with words. In 'things' all 'principles' are brought together, hence all who have long devoted themselves to work come to have a genuine intuitive understanding of them. Why should they appeal to words?"[16]

Therefore, learning consists, to him, in knowing as many particular things as possible: "Learning consists in widening one's information, absorbing extensively anything and everything one comes upon".[17] But because Ogiu ignored the science of nature, learning which is to amass a knowledge of particular facts culminates, for him, in the study of history—a preference which is closely related to the ethical character of his 'learning': "Since learning is to have wide information and to have experience with realities, it culminates in history".[18]

Even the scholars of the Japanese classics, who tried to repudiate Buddhism and Confucianism, exhibited the same way of thinking. Hirata Atsutane (1776–1843), for example, rejected the concept of abstract, universal 'principles', and declared that we only had to know 'actual things', or concrete particulars:

> "In fact, that which is called the 'true way' is given in actual things, whereas conventional scholars are erroneously inclined to think that the 'way' can not be found out except by reading doctrinal books. For if we can appreciate actual things, doctrines are dispensed with; and it is only when actual things, in which the 'way' is given, are lacking, that doctrines arise. Therefore, doctrines are far less valuable than actual things. Lao Tzu fully recognized this fact when he said, 'When the Way decays, the doctrines of humanity and justice arise' ".[19]

As is shown by the historical development of Japanese thought—although so far only several representative thinkers have been considered—the ability to think in terms of abstract universals has not fully developed among the Japanese people. They have been very poor in ordering various phenomena on the basis of a universal pattern.

[There might be set forth a question how to reconcile this alleged Japanese preference for *the particular* with the commonly observed modern preference of Japanese scholarship for theoretical learning rather than pragmatic approaches. Among present-day Japanese intellectuals there is conspicuous tendency for German abstract philosophy. Why the change? We would answer: this is not a real change. Such a tendency among high-brow people is not so much due to fondness for theoretical thinking as fondness for things, abstruse which effect imaginative impression upon them. Their alleged fondness for theoretical learning is not always based upon the process of induction and deduction in logical sense.]

Of course, the Japanese do sometimes criticize themselves in such a way as to contradict what we have just said. In these days, moreover, we hear it said among the Japanese themselves that "It is bad for the Japanese habitually to concern themselves with plans on paper and deal with abstract theories". Such criticism, however, confuses abstraction with fantasy (unreality), and the prevalence of such criticism in fact points up the absense in the Japanese of self-criticism on the matter of abstract thinking.

---

1) *Genkō-Shakusho* (元亨釋書), vol. 30.

2) Izuru Shinmura 新村出: *Gengo-gaku Josetsu* (言語學序說 Introduction to Linguistics) p. 182.

3) Tetsurō Watsuji 和辻哲郎: *Zoku Nihon Seishin-shi Kenkyū* (續日本精神史研究) Supplement to Research in Japanese Intellectual History), p. 397.

4) Takashi Ide 出隆: *Shijin Tetsugakusha* (詩人哲學者 Poet-Philosophers), p. 317.

5) Yoshio Yamada 山田孝雄: *Inmyō yori idetaru Tsūyōgo* (因明より出でたる通用語 Popular words originated from Inmyō, in the Journal *Geirin* (藝林) vol. III, No. 2), pp. 22 f.

6) Nevertheless Dr. Kanae Sakuma 佐久間鼎 maintains that the Japanese language contains words performing the function of the relative pronoun, by the suitable manipulation of which the lack of the relative pronoun may be compensated for. ("*Kyūchakugo no Mondai*" The problem of agglutinative languages, *Kokugo-Kokubun* 國語國文 Oct. 1938.)

7) *Tōkaidōchū Hizakurige* (東海道中膝栗毛 上, 第二編下), *Nippon Meicho Zenshū* 日本名著全集 vol. 22. p. 101.

8) *Nyāyabindu-ṭīka*, p. 3, *l.* 11. Stcherbatsky translated this as follows: "[The act of cognition] has made him [=man] reach the object, (i. e. reach it by his cognition)."

9) J. S. Speyer: *Vedische und Sanskrit-Syntax*, § 287.

10) In the sentence "諸有衆生, 聞其名號, 信心歡喜, 乃至一念, 至心廻向, 願生彼國, 卽得往生, 住不退轉, of the 大無量壽經(下), it is obvious that the subject of 至心廻向 is 衆生 (living being), (cf. *Sukhāvatīvyūha-sūtra* 26.—ye kecit sattvās tasya bhagavato 'mitābhasya nāmadheyaṃ śṛṇvanti śrutvā cāntaśa ekacittotpādam apy adhyāśayena prasādasahagatena cittam utpādayanti te sarve vaivartikatāyām santy anuttarāyāḥ samyaksaṃbodheḥ.) but Shinran took the subject of the phrase 至心廻向 for Amitābha Buddha(!), cf. his works 淨土文類聚鈔, 一念多念證文, 教行信證 (Rev. Kusaka 日下無倫 阪東眞本敎行聚鈔, p. 103).

11) Chikurō Hiroike (廣池千九郎): *Shina Bunten* (支那文典) p. 67.

12) *Shōbōgenzō* (正法眼藏), Gyōbutsu Igi 行佛威儀

13) "cittamātram idam yad-idaṃ traidhātukam". (*Daśabhūmika-sūtra* ed. by J. Rahder, p. 49.)
ci vijñaptimātram evedam. (*Trṃśikā*, ed. by S. Lévi, 27, p. 42.)

14) *Shōbōgenzō* (正法眼藏) *Sangai Yuishin* 三界唯心.

15) Two entrances and four practices: the two entrances (*ni nyū* 二入) are the two courses of entry into enlightenment (viz. the priet hood), i.e. through contemplation (*ri* 理) and practice (*gyō* 行). The course of practice is further subdivided into four 'practices' (1) the righting of wrongs (2) the acceptance of the given or resignation (3) seeking nothing (4) following the *dharma* (性淨之理). (1) 報怨行 (2) 隨緣行 (3) 無所求行 (4) 稱法行.

16) *Bendō* (辨道.)

17) *Tōmonsho*, book 1, (答問書 上) in *Nihon Rinri Ihen*, (日本倫理彙編, vol. VI, p. 153).
18) ("答問書" 上) (*ibid.* p. 156).
19) *Nyūgaku Mondō* "入學問答".

(2) Lack of the ability to think with logical coherence

The illogical character of the Japanese people naturally prevent them from thinking with logical coherence or consistency.

Even in ancient times, Kakinomoto no Hitomaro composed a famous poem, said: "In our land covered with reed and rice-ears, they haven't argued since the time of the gods". Out of such a point of view, the technique of constructing universal laws reducing individuals to order is not likely to develop. Motoori Norinaga (1730–1801), phenomenon who claimed to have made clear the spirit of ancient Japan, said: "In ancient times, we had no talk at all even about the Way. The classic declares that in our land covered with reed and rice-ears, they haven't argued since the time of gods.——Not to argue means not to expatiate or have much talk, as the custom in foreign countries".[1]

"In ancient times in our land, even the 'Way' was not talked about at all and we had only ways directly leading to things themselves, while in foreign countries it is the custom to entertain and to talk about many different doctrines, about principles of things, this 'Way' or that 'Way'. The Emperors' land in ancient times had not such theories or doctrines whatever, but we enjoyed peace and order then, and the descendants of the Sun-goddess have consecutively succeeded to the throne".[2]

What was the situation, then, after philosophical theories were introduced from the Chinese continent? It seems that Japanese scholars who first acquainted themselves with the theories were so hard pressed merely in learning to use Chinese ideographs that they did not get to the point of understanding the thought and assimilating the thought expressed therein. The *Keikoku-shū*, ("Anthology on the Arts of Governing the State",) which was compiled in the early Heian period, records several sets of examination questions and answers given to students around the Nara period, the questions are e.g.: of loyalty and filial piety which should take precedence? What is the difference between the doctrine of Confucius and those of the Taoists and Buddhists? Which of them is true? Discuss the merits and demerits of Confucianism that declares the heaven and earth have a beginning but no end, and Buddhism that preaches the cycle of worldly events in the order of emergence, subsistence, destruction and emptiness. The answers entered in the work, however, are merely fraught with flowerly words, and the points of arguments are so superficial and vague that consistency is hardly found. A certain answer even asserts that the two doctrines can not be distinguished from each other, and the truth and falsity of the two cannot be judged. We are surprised at the contrast expressed between superb knowledge and skill to marshall flowery words and the miserably poor ability to think.[3]

The way of thinking on the part of the Japanese in general could not easily be changed by the introduction and dissemination of Buddhism. It is true that great efforts were made to understand and assimilate the philosophy of Buddhism as well as its artistic byproducts. Those who made the efforts, however, were confined to learned monks, and the Japanese at large were indifferent to philosophical argument. Works by the monks, having nearly all been written in Chinese, made no contact with the people at large. Although the founders of various Buddhistic sects which arose in Kamakura period wrote also in the native Japanese language, their central works which deal with the essentials of their doctrines were all in Chinese. Some Buddhists keenly felt the necessity of disseminating Buddhistic thought among the people and, especially for that purpose, produced writings in the original Japanese, but such cases were remarkably few in number and small in scope.[4]

It is commonly said that Japanese Buddhism reached its maturity in the Kamakura period. The 'Kamakura Buddhism', however, did not make in any way systematic philosophical thinking. As we have already learned, such prominent figures as Hōnen, Shinran and Nichiren chiefly concentrated their efforts upon demonstrating the orthodoxy or validity of their own interpretations of Buddhist Sacred texts. To cite an extreme instance, Chishin (1239–1289), who is also called Sage Ippen 一遍上人, declared on his death-bed that the people of this world should be content with the one phrase, "Pay homage to Amitābha Buddha", (Namu Amida Butsu) and ordered his books destroyed by fire.

On the other hand, some of contemporary philosophers in our country have tried to see in Dōgen, who continued to write philosophical works throughout his life-time, the pioneer of Japanese philosophy. Though it is doubtless true that Dōgen was a distinguished thinker as well as a high minded spiritual leader, he was not the sort of thinker who developed a logically coherent system of thought. In spite of the fact that he cherished deep philosophical ideas which were gem-like character, he was not inclined to elabborate the thoughts he apprehended—his '*dōtoku*'—to the pure logical system.

Dōgen commented upon a passage "Inhabitants of Ling-nan not having Buddhahood" as follows:

"This passage means neither that inhabitants of Ling-nan peak do not possess Buddhahood nor that they possess Buddhahood. It just means inhabitants of Ling-nan not having Buddhahood".[5] Probably Dōgen thought that the judgment either that they have Buddhahood or that they have not is based upon abstract or discriminating intellect, which is foreign to Buddhahood, the realm of absoluteness, as all-being or nothing, is opened up where being and non-being are transcended. Dōgen, however, did not like to expound such a principle in abstract, universal propositions, and was satisfied with the concise expression, "Inhabitants of Ling-nan not having Buddhahood".

In another place, Dōgen opined as follows, referring to the problem of life and death: "Life and death matter little because the Buddha exists therein. And one is not perplexed by life and death because the Buddha does not exist therein".[6] As far as the expression is concerned, we have here two formally contradictory propositions. But the gist of what he meant by the two sentences was quite the same.

The teacher Musō (Soseki 1275–1351) declares, very clearly, that he does not aim at fixed logical coherency: "Clear-sighted masters of the Zen sect do not have a fixed doctrine as something to be cherished for all time. They present any doctrines as occasion demands, and preach as their tongues happen to dictate. They all do not have a fixed source to rely upon. If one asks them what Zen is, they sometimes answer in terms of the sayings of Confucius, Mencius, Lao-Tzu or Chang-tzu, Non-Zen Buddhist teachers, and sometimes with popular proverbs, or sometimes they explain what Zen teaches, point out a particular situation, in front of them they simply swing their mace or shout in a loud voice. Or they simply raise their fingers or fists. All these are means used by the masters, and called 'the vivacious ways of the Zen sect' ".[7]

Buddhism originally embraced the idea of expediency, and among the expediencies Buddhists were allowed to use as their means of preaching, a certain system of successive ranking was thought to exist. In case of the Zen Buddhists, however, no consideration is paid to the logical relations among expediencies. Musō's saying quoted above indicates the ways of instruction employed in the Zen sect since its foundation in China, and it was through the appreciation of this aspect of it that Japan welcomed the Zen sect.

From the Tokugawa period, schools of Chu-hsi and Wang Yang-ming came to be energetically studied in Japan, but it is a question how far Japanese scholars understood them. In this connection, some examples will be given to show that Japanese Confucianists did not like metaphysical speculation.

The Chu-hsi school made a distinction between *li* 理 (principle) or *tao* (way) which held to be 'above form' and '*chi*' (氣 matter) or *chi* (器 receptacle) which was 'under form'. Western students on the school sometimes translate the former as 'form', and the latter as 'material'. Roughly speaking, the world 'above form' and the world 'under form' as expressed in the Sung school correspond to the world of ideas and the world of phenomena respectively. This is the reason why the Japanese in modern times have translated 'metaphysics' as '*keijijō-gaku*' (the study of what is above form). However, Kaibara Ekiken (1630–1714), having tried to understand Confucianism from the viewpoint of Japanese practical life, did not understand the distinction between the realms 'above form' and 'under form'. He was disposed to understand the two as belonging both to the realm of the senses and the concrete: "In my opinion", he said "the 'form' means to be corporeal, 'over' means to be in the heavens, and 'under' to be on the earth". Referring to what the 'heaven' and the earth are, he continues: "Those things which 'form shapes in the heaven' are simply the sun, moon, the stars and constellations"[8] "The phrase 'under form' refers to those things which form shapes on the earth, and all that have any shapes whatever such as mountains, rivers, the ground, and men, are 'receptacles (*ch'i*)' ". Thus Kaibara was never inclined to recognize the realm which transcends and underlies the natural world of the senses. Such a way of thinking quite naturally makes it impossible to develop the conception of the intelligible world, of the world of ideas. This is the reason why he could not understand the philosophical significance of the Kegon doctrine, for he, in many places, charged the Sung school of being influenced by the Kegon view of *Dharma-dhātu* (the view of super-mundane law, interdependence of things).

As another instance, Ogiu Sorai, who made much of the will of Heaven, could not grasp the idea of Heaven as an abstract concept. He could not conceive of it as distinct from the visible heaven of the natural world.

Thus, he said: "We need not wait to understand Heaven. We all know it. When we look at Heaven, it seems blue and boundless, and beyond any means of measuring it. It embraces the sun, moon, stars and constellations and is the source of rain, wind, and cold and hot weather. Heaven is the place where all things receive their destinies, and it is the god of gods, holy beyond any comparison, and nothing can rise to its height".[9]

In theoretically denouncing the doctrines of Christianity, most Japanese did so on the ground of no particular philosophy. Habiyan (Fabian), for example, became a priest of the Nichiren-sect after he forsook the Christian faith but he did not make use of the doctrine or philosophy of the Nichiren sect in criticising his former faith. All he had to do, as he saw it, was to point out weak spots of the Christian doctrine and repudiate it in any way whatever. Hence no logical consistency can be found in his attitude. He said he had never witnessed a Christian miracle, and then praised most highly, as a genuine miracle, Nichiren's escape from death. Controversies between a Christian[10] *iruman* and Hayashi Razan (1583–1657), the Confucianist, descended also to a mere exchange of contemptuous shouts, "you blighter!" and "you idiot!".[11]

Absense of the theoretical and systematic thinking is equally characteristic of former scholars of Japanese classics. Motoori Norinaga, for example, had no concrete conception of method in his learning: "In final conclusion, to make strenuous efforts consecutively for long years is most essential to those who are engaged in learning, and it does not matter how they learn. The how is the question about which they need not worry so much".[12] Motoori exhorted his disciples just to be diligent in their study, and did not develop any thinking constructive as to the learning itself.[13]

Of course, we don't deny the possibility that one actually can express one's self as clearly in Japanese as in any other language, if one has the mental clarity and habits of thought to do so. It is said that there is one school of thought which stresses the cultural conditioning of thought patterns more than the limitation of a language concerned. At least the Japanese *esprit* should not be overlooked. However the credit of ways of Japanese expression lies more in esthetic aspects than in exactly logical ones.

Moreover, we don't want to advocate any sort of linguistic determinism. We admit the working influences of other factors. We just point out with regard to logical aspects, some features of expressing thoughts by the

Japanese in older days, for these features are not irrelevant to those in present days.

---

1) *Naobi no Mitama* (直毘靈).
2) *Ibid.*
3) Sōkichi Tsuda 津田左右吉: *Shina Shisō to Nihon* (支那思想と日本 Chinese Thought and Japan), p. 37.
4) *In the Tetsugen Zenji Kajihōgo* (鐵眼禪師假字法語 Discourse of doctrine in phonetic writing by the Zen master Tetsugen), his disciple has written a post-face in which he says, "Since the Zen sect was introduced into this country, there have been few other men who have in this fashion presented the essense of it in the Japanese language. The *Shaseki-shū* 沙石集 by the Zen master Mujū 無住 and the *Muchū Mondō-shū* 夢中問答集 (Dialogue in a dream) by the master Musō are about the only good books there are; although there are many others, some of them are ever worth mentioning".
5) *Shōbōgenzō*, (正法眼藏 Subtleties of the True Doctrine), Busshō 佛性.
6) *Ibid.*, 生死 (Life and Death).
7) *Muchū Mondō-shū*, 夢中問答集
8) *Daigi-roku*, (大疑錄 Record of Great Doubts), pt. 2. *Ekiken Zenshū* (益軒全集), vol. II. pp. 156 f.
9) *Bemmei*, 辯名 (Critical Study of Terms) 下, 天命帝鬼神十七則 (17 paragraphs on Heaven, destiny, God and spirits)
10) He was mentioned as *iruman*, not actually the man's name, from the Portuguese irmão, a lay borner.
11) *Razan Sensei Bunshū* 羅山先生文集 (Collected Writings of Hayashi Razan) ch. 56.
12) *Uiyamabumi* (*Motoori Norinaga Zenshū* 本居宣長全集) vol. IV, p. 601.
13) Eiichi, Matsushima, *Kinsei Nihon no Gakumonron no Ichi-seikaku* (近世日本の學問論の一性格. A Characteristic of Discussions about Learning in Early Modern Japan), *Shisō* 思想 No. 276.

(3) Immaturity of logic in Japan

The logic of Buddhism, *Inmyō*, was introduced into Japan at a very early date. In 653 A.D. during the reign of Emperor Kōtoku, Dōshō went to study in China, and, together with the monk Jion (Tz'u-ên), he personally studied under Hsüang-chuang, the doctrine of idealism (*weishih* 唯識 *vijñāptimātratā*), which was the newest philosophy of the time, and also schooled himself in logic (*inmyō*). In 661, during the reign of Saimei, he returned to Japan and introduced Buddhist logic to our country.

As he disseminated his newly acquired knowledge at the Gangōji Temple, the scholarship originating from him is generally referred to as 'the tradition of the Southern Temple', and also, as 'the Asuka tradition'. It was only sixteen years after the Buddhistic logic was introduced to China that it was further conveyed to Japan. Later on in 716, Genbō went to

China to study the Buddhistic logic under Chishū (Chih-chou), the third patriarch of the Hossō sect. After he came back to Japan, he propagated the learning at the Kōfukuji Temple; this is referred to as 'the tradition of the Northern Temple', and also as the 'tradition of Kasayama'. Since that time, this system of logic came to be studied in the Hossō sect as a discipline supplementing Buddhistic idealism (*vijñaptimātratāsiddhi*), and the *Abhidharmakośa-śāstra*. The number of books written in Japan on Buddhistic logic amounts to a considerable figure, and even the bibliography entered in the end of the *Inmyō Zuigenki* ("The Origin of the Buddhistic Logic") written by Hōtan at the middle of the Tokugawa period, comprises eighty-four Japanese works of the kind.

In looking into the characteristic way in which the Buddhist logic was disseminated in Japan, we find in the first place that this logic was employed as a technique of expression in questions and answers at Buddhist meetings. Logic was then likely to be studied not as a subject matter in itself but as a technique of oral expression.

At the very beginning, in such situation as the Yuima (*Vimalakīrti*) meetings in the Kōfukuji Temple where the essential doctrine of that one sect was propounded, a "confirmer", an "assertor" and a "questioner" were designated, and argument was conducted according to the forms of Buddhist Logic (*inmyō*).

Later it was employed at the Jion-meeting, where the use of logic came to be ritualized.[1] Still later, the Enryakuji Temple and the Onjōji Temple held regular Hokke-meetings in which the catechism of the Hokke Sūtra was discussed, and those who did not know the Buddhist logic were not allowed to join such meetings. Buddhist logic was at that time considered a common subject to be mastered by monks of any sect. Further in such situation as the Great-transmission-meetings (*Dai-denbō-e*), in the Kongōbuji Temple in the Muromachi period, and in the Chishakuin Temple, the Hase Temple and other places in the Tokugawa period, the subjects of Commentaries were discussed according to the forms of Buddhist logic, and ultimately even the Jōdo and Zen sects came to hold such meetings. These were called "discussion" (*rongi*), and in the Zen sect, because of their special form, they were called "questions and answers" (*mondō*). In these uses the *inmyō* deteriorated to the point of extreme formalism.

In the Tendai sect the periodic examinations of state supported student priests were conducted according to this form of argumentation. The official gazette of the Enryaku period informs us that the five questions and ten problems were put and all of them were answered aloud. This was the first step toward ritualization of logical argument. Further, it is held that this is the origin of the argument in the Noh-drama.

In this situation it goes without saying that the forms of *Immyō*, the styles of *rongi*, were used, and further both questions and answers were *recited*, and moreover were accompanied by a certain gracious rythm. And finally outside of Buddhism, the practice of holding public discussions of lyric verse and of *the Tale of Genji* developed in various places; also there came into being the *utaawase*, or form of poetry discussion, in which poems were discussed with any question and answer. Moreover, the ritualized debate continues to be held at Mt. Kōya, even to this day. In this ritual, the answerers (*Rissha*), the questioners (*Monja*), the judge (*Tandai*), the stenographer (*Chūki*), and the manager (*Gyōji*) sit in pious attitude around the statue of the Buddha, according to fixed rule, Buddhist hymns are sung and the sūtras are read. Thus, in Japan, logical debate has been reduced to a mere Buddhist meeting, a decorum of the most pious form. Further, the form of the ritual was extended without change to the poetic debate or *utaawase*.[2] Therefore, the meeting of debate, in which was applied the logic to concrete cases, was completely transformed into a formalized ceremony, then to arts, peculiar to the Japanese culture. Surely, we may say that this phenomenon reveals the artistic, as well as illogical, character of the Japanese people.

It is relevant that the formula of reasoning or syllogism of Indian logic was introduced into Japan in a modified form.

One of the original Indian formulae runs as follows:

(1)	the proposition:	Words are impermanent.
(2)	the reason:	Because they have been made.
(3)	the explanatory example:	It is experienced that whatever has been made is impermanent, like jars etc. It is experienced that whatever is permanent has not been made, like space.[3]

In the above-mentioned formula, the proposition was not regarded by the Japanese as an assertive sentence, but was interpreted as an assertion for persuading others. Therefore it has been usually read in Japanese:

"*Koe wa mujō naru beshi*" (Words are to be impermanent).

In other words, the Japanese understood the assertion as one to be made in debating. Like this, the Japanese have never been interested in abstracting the subject of the debate from surrounding social environments. Further the statement of the example is usually read:

若所作見彼無常——モシ所作ナルハ彼レ無常ト見ヨ。

Regard whatever has been made as impermanent!

若是其常見非所作——モシ常ナルハ所作ニ非ズト見ヨ。(4)

Regard whatever is permanent as not having been made!

Nevertheless the letter "見" which has been translated as the imperative "Regard!" does not have any meaning of imperative in the Chinese translation. Moreover, according to the Sanskrit original, it means "by experience (*dṛṣṭam*)"). Therefore, the statements in question originally mean "Everything which has been made is known to be not permanent by our experience. For instance, it is similar to a thing like a vase", and "what is permanent is by experience known to be that which has not been made, for instance, it is like space".

As is seen here, the Japanese have not been interested in abstracting universally valid sentences from their social relations. As scholars of Buddhist logic always thought of meetings where debates took place, they made much of the *practical* side of Buddhist logic, especially deliberation on fallacies. Such works as *"the Treatise on Thirty-three Fallacies"* (*Sanjūsan-kahon-sahō*) were composed. They have always been considered to be useful for discussion among scholarly clergymen.[5]

In the second place, Indian logic, ever since it was introduced from China, has been studied in a dogmatic spirit. The interpretation of logical scriptures given by Jion (Tz'u-ên), the founder of the Hossō sect, was respected as the highest and absolute authority, which should be studied with the spirit of a defender of the faith. Under Gembō, the importer of logic, Zen-shu, of the Akishino Temple, studied various commentaries on logic and wrote his own commentary of twelve volumes, *"Immyō Ronsho Myōtōshō"*. Not only was this work written in form of an annotation to Jion's commentary, *Nisshōri-ron-sho,* but also logic was studied from Jion's viewpoint, defending his comments and denouncing those of others. This book is the best example of those books which were written with the spirit of a defender of the faith. Thus, as a whole, logic, in Japan, was traditionally studied as one of the auxiliary disciplines of the study of the doctrines of the Hossō sect (idealism). This was presumably due to the fact that the Buddhist logic was the essential preparatory discipline for understanding the texts of the Indian idealistic philosophy. The other sects of the Nara period, for example, the Kegon and Sanron sects, also studied logic. They were influenced by the Hossō sect's keen interest in it, though it was not indispensable to the understanding of their own doctrines. But this tendency did not permeate into all sects of Japanese Buddhism. Especially, Dengyō (767–822) resisted this tendency, owing to his hostility toward the Hossō sect, the strongest enemy of his new religious movement. He declared that logic was necessary to preach the doctrine of "Three Vehicles" of the Hossō sect, but this sect was, after all, nothing but a second-rate Buddhism. The system of logic has no value for the doctrine of "One Vehicle" (*eka-yāna*) of the Tendai sect, which is the highest type of Buddhism. Ever since, the followers of Dengyō on Mt. Hiei attached no importance to logic.

Of course, there existed exceptions. For example, Genshin (Eshin 942–1017), though he had the same views in all respects as Dengyō, was well versed in logic and wrote a book to comment in detail on one of its most difficult problems, the doctrine of Four Contradictions (*Shi-sō-i*). Though this was one of the most important events in the history of logic in Japan,[6] it was an exceptional phenomenon in the Tendai sect itself. In a word, the study of logic has never been extended to the whole Buddhist world of Japan. This was because of the fact that logic, defended by the Hossō sect as its essential discipline, was ignored by other sects[7] just because they, too, had this same dogmatic sectarian spirit.

In the third place, we must mention the tendency of the study to be an *esoteric* tradition. This tendency was conspicuous especially at the zenith of prosperity of logic, that is, from the end of the Heian period to the middle of the Kamakura period. In Nara of those days the study of logic centered in the Kōfukuji Temple of the Hossō sect, and extended to the other two big temples, Tōdaiji and Hōryūji. The Gangōji Temple, called Nan-ji (the Temple of South), had already decayed. Only the school of the Kōfukuji Temple, called Hoku-ji (the Temple of North), prospered, because it was protected politically and financially by the Fujiwaras, the ruling clan at that period. The study of logic, however, gradually showed a tendency to decline after the middle of Kamakura period, just as did the Buddhist idealism, and counted only a few generations of students after Jōkei.

It is true that some of the Japanese scholars had tried to give an international and universal character to the study of logic. For example, Genshin sent his work, "Short Commentaries on the Four Contradictions in Logic" (*Immyō Ronsho Shisōi Ryakuchūshaku*) through Sung merchants to disciples of Master Hung-tao of the Tz'u-ên Temple in China, and wished "to distinguish, in detail, between right and wrong, and to enlighten them".[8] But this was an exceptional case. In Japan, logic was transmitted from a master to only one disciple, and it was prohibited to communicate it to others. For example, in the Kamakura period, when Jōkei (1155–1213) gave his work "Short Commentary on Logic" (*Myō hon-shō*) to his disciple, Ryō-san, he wrote: "I made only one copy. But, because I cannot disappoint those two people, I gave the first half (seven volumes) to the Vicar-General of the Tōhokuin, and the second half (six volumes) to the Preceptor of the Kōmyōin. By mutual agreement each can borrow the other half and make copy of it. While any of the two is living, *the number of copies should not be increased.* When you transmit it in future, you must choose a person who in religious caliber has the same disposition as you. In answer to these instructions, Ryō-san pledged: "So long as I live, even two copies, to say nothing of many, will not be permitted to be made of this book. Even if a noble lord orders it, or if an influential man of the world urges it, *there will never exist many copies.* In short, other men will not be allowed to copy it. And, after my death, it will be transmitted to a man of religious caliber among my disciples, and even to such a one I will not transmit it, if he is a worldly, unlawful, or unjust man". Moreover, if he breaks this pledge, "may all of the punishments of the God Kasuga afflict me in every pore of my body." Since then, this Commentary was kept in the *secret treasury-box* of the Kasuga Shrine in the Kōfukuji Temple and transmitted to chosen disciples only under very strict rules. A later document dealing with the transmission of this book (dated 25. 12. 1256) said that "This book should be the secret of the Temple, inaccessible to outsiders".

Also, Shinken closed the postscript of his "Short account of the Real Essence of the Predicate" (*Hōjisō-yōmonshō*) by the following words: "My disciples to whom this book will be transmitted should keep it in greatest secrecy".[9] And Ryōben has among his writings a book the title of which is "Of the Secret Account of the Transmission of Logic" (*Inmyo Sōjō Himitsushō*). We know therefore that the Buddhist logic was transmitted secretly. On the mark-papers inserted into copies of these books, we can sometimes see the names of the people to whom the book was transmitted, and we sometimes meet on these papers the warning "Absolute Secrecy". In Japan, therefore, logic was adopted as a secretly transmitted catechistic technique not to be generally disseminated. This prevented logic from becoming universal science.

We must pay particular attention also to the social fact that Indian logic, in Japan, had been studied only by learned Buddhist priests, not by the Japanese people generally. Even these learned priests applied logic only to the interpretation of Buddhist philosophical works. These learned priests did not use logic for other subjects. It goes without saying that the mass of the Japanese people and many Buddhist priests were unacquainted with the Buddhist logic. In short, the sacred writing of logic was reduced to an apparatus for interpretation of scriptures.

In the fourth place, because of the fact that the Japanese *inmyo* was a continuation of the Chinese version of logic, it has consequently exegetical character, and did not have the character of logical inquiry. Nineteen books were written, in Japan only, to comment on the Four Contradictions, working from just that part of Tz'u-ên's "Great Commentary on Logic" (*Inmyō Daisho*)[10] which had dealt with them. Non of these books, however, was a logical interpretation of this problem.[11] This was probably inevitable, because the commentary of Tz'u-ên itself did not offer a logical interpretation of the Contradiction, and it had been respected as the highest authority by Japanese students. These commentaries on logic had, in general, fallen to the level of exegetic commentaries on words, and hundreds of commentaries, produced during more than one thousand years, had almost nothing to contribute to the development of logic. None of them has made efforts to set forth a well-organized logical system based upon the author's own thinking.

In the fifth place, the study of logic in Japan, as in China, did not treat the problem of the critical study of knowledge. On this point, it was quite different from the logic of Dharmakīrti and others in India. Because the Japanese studied logic only through the Chinese translation, the Indian ideas that had not been introduced into China were inaccessible to the Japanese.

[The Japanese scholars, like their predecessors in China, scarcely studied logical works of Dignāga, founder of Buddhist logic in India. His principal work, the *Pramāṇasamuccaya,* once translated into Chinese, was lost very soon without ever being utilized. Hsüang-chuang translated a compendium by Dignāga, called the *Nyāyamukha,* into Chinese, but few Chinese and Japanese scholars seem to have ever studied this work. The *Nyāyapraveśaka,* which Japanese scholars looked upon as their exclusive authority, is only a poor synopsis of the *Nyāyamukha*. Tibetan Buddhists, on the other hand, have kept studying the more important and more voluminous works of Dharmakirti, the brilliant successor of Dignāga. more voluminous works of Dharmakirti, the brilliant successor to Dignāga. We owe to the Tibetans the important informations about Buddhist logic in

Thus in Japan, just as in China the logic of Indian Buddhism could not take root and develop. No book on logic has been written in the native Japanese language. Cursed by secret transmission also, a knowledge of logic could not have spread widely among the Japanese. Another point to be noted is that, in Japan, logic had nothing to do with mathematics and natural sciences. Even in native Japanese mathematics, we cannot find any trace of the influence of logic. It was not simply that logical thinking was not developed among the Japanese people, the significance of exact logic was not realized by them at all. And it was far more difficult for them to develop their own logic, independently from Indian logic. It is asserted frequently that, in the Tokugawa period, a logical thinking appeared in some Japanese scholars, for example, in Miura Baien (1723–89) but all that we can discern in him is a way of thinking similar to Hegelian dialectics.[12] Miura did not know formal logic. He had no connection with the tradition of the Indian logic.

It seems ordained by history, almost predestined, that logical thinking is beyond the power of the Japanese people. Since the Meiji era, Western formal logic has been introduced into Japan, and included in the curriculum of a junior college education. But, in Japan, the study of logic has made rather poor development, compared with development in other fields of culture. While an enormous number of philosophic works have been produced since the Restoration, they are mostly of the essay genre and consequently not always written with logical precision. Excellent works on logic written by Japanese are very few. And little philosophical thought has appeared which exhibits logical thinking in the sense of formal logical structure.

---

1) The first four volumes of Kakuken (覺憲)'s *Inmyō-shō* (因明抄) 5 vols. were made for preparation for the assertion at the Jion-meeting. Ennen (緣圓) wrote at the postscript of his work *Ichi-in-i-shi* (一因違四): "I have copied this work so that the Jion-meeting of this year will be finished without trouble by the merit of copying".

2) Jakuhyō Koya 姑射若氷: (歌合と因明 *Utaawase to Inmyō*) *Misshū Gakuhō* (密宗學報), June, 1920. No. 84

3) *Yat kṛtaṃ tad anityam dṛṣṭaṃ yathā ghaṭādir iti.*
Yan nityam tad akṛtakam dṛṣṭaṃ yathākaśādir iti. (Śaṇkarasvāmin's *Nyāyapraveśaka*)

4) K. Kishigami 岸上恢嶺: *Gōtō Inmyō Nisshōriron Kachuū* (鼇頭因明入正理論科註), 1888. K. Kira 雲英晃耀: *Kanchū Inmyō Nisshōriron-shō* (冠註因明入正理論疏), , vol. II, p. 9, vol. III, p. 4.

5) A Buddhist commented as follows:
「因明ニテハ、辭ヲ巧ミニ廻セハ理ハ非ニテモ勝ニナリ、辭ノ廻シ様ガ拙ケレバ理ハ是ニテモ負ニナルナリ。故ニ因明ニテハ利ロナ者ハ勝チ、鈍ナモノ負ケニナリテ、眞實ノ道理ハ顯シ難シ」(因明犬三支 三枚裏)
"As for Buddhist logic, one who is proficient in using ornate expressions skilfully can win in a debate even if his assertion is wrong. On the other hand, one who is awkward in expression is defeated even if his assertion is reasonable. So in Buddhist logic clever people win, whereas dull ones lose, and truths are difficult to manifest themselves". (*Inmyō Inu-sanshi*, p. 3 b.)

6) Daitō Shimaji 島地大等: *Nihon Bukkyō Kyōgaku-shi* (日本佛教教學史), pp. 231, 282.

7) Having pointed out the fact that in ancient Japan the scholarship of Buddhist logic highly flourished, Chikū (癡空) at the end of the Tokugawa period said: "Nowadays people who make it their own business to debate with others have come not to know even the names of the three members of syllogism (=the two propositions and conclusion). It argues the decline of Buddhist scholarship". (Inmyō Inu-sanshi) p. 4 b.

8) *Eshin Sōzu Zenshū* (慧心僧都全集), vol. V. p. 284.

9) These materials have been drawn from Tokujō Ōya (大屋德城)'s article: 鎌倉時代の因明研究 in *Mujintō* (無盡燈) vol. 21, 1916, Nos. 11, 12. p. 937.

10) This work is a commentary by Jion (Tz'u-ēn) on Śaṇkarasvāmin's *Introduction to Logic* (*Nyāyapraveśaka.*)

11) Hakuju Ui 宇井伯壽: *Indo Tetsugaku Kenkyū* (印度哲學研究), vol. I, pp. 255, 265.

12) H. Saegusa 三枝博音: *Miura Baien no Tetsugaku* (三浦梅園の哲學), pp. 204–209.

(4) Some hopes for development of logical thinking in Japan

We need not despair completely, however, of the capacity of the Japanese people for logical thinking, a way of thinking of a people is simply a tendency and is capable of being reformed. There is evidence for this in the fact that modes of expression in the Japanese language have gradually been growing more and more strict and precise in recent years. Although it is true that Japanese hithertofore has not been fit for philosophical thinking, it may improve in future in this respect. On the other hand it may also be remembered, that Leibniz himself was unable to compose his philosophical works in German, although he wrote in a wonderful style both in Latin and French; that is to say, the German language could become philosophically significant only after the efforts by a few later scholars, such as Wolff, Kant and their followers. We cannot also forget that the middle high German poets, e.g. Wolfram von Eschenbach, had to express their ideas far more concretely, and consequently less philosophically, than the modern German poets, such as Goethe, Schiller, Novalis and others did. In other words, the German language was not fit for philosophical thinking at the beginning, but it was elaborated by some eminent persons, including Meister Eckhart in the thirteenth century. Terms such as "Begriff" or "Vernunft" would never have gained their philosophical implication without the systems of German idealism. In the same way the Japanese may make progress in terms of logical expression. This hope finds support by the Japanese linguistic trend in recent years toward more and more precise expression. Japanese adaptation to Western ways of expressing thought is recently remarkable, although it is questionable whether it means always improvement.

The fact that Buddhist logic did not fully develop in the past can be ascribed to the illogical character of its immediate source, the Chinese *inmyō*. In spite of this there are the Japanese tried on several points indicating a development in Japan beyond the Chinese logic. We can mention an interesting, if rather trivial, example. In the Chinese logic, the word "*shūhō* (*tsung-la* 宗法 *pakṣadharma*) represents the predicate of an assertive proposition (*tong* 宗, major term, P., *sādhya*) as well as the predicate of a causal proposition (*yin* 因, middle term, M, *sādhana*). The Chinese technical terminology did not distinguish between the two. Even if there were at first a distinction made between the two uses through pronounciation, this distinction could not be preserved for a long time in a country using the Chinese language in which pronounciation rather frequently changed. The Japanese, distinguishing the two terms in pronounciation, read in voiceless sound *Shūhō* in one case where it means the predicate (P) of assertive proposition, and in voiced sound (*Shūbō*) in other case where it means the predicate (M) of causal proposition. Moreover, before the Meiji era, there were several scholars who had mastered[1] the Indian formal logic and had actually applied it to the study of Buddhist ideas. As an example we can mention the name of Rinjō (1751–1810) and Kaijō (–1805), of the Buzan school of the New Shingon sect. Surely logic can be disseminated and developed among the Japanese people, if we endevor seriously.

There are some cases of Japanese in the past who were willing to use terms of Buddhist logic, even if in changed meanings. For example, it has been asserted that the word "*rippa*" (立派 magnificent, splendid) is a phonetic equivalent to "*ryūha*" (立破 assertion and refutation in a debate) and that, "*mutai*" (無體) unreasonable also is due to Buddhist logic.[2] Although it is doubtful whether this assertion or conjecture is right or not, it is an established fact that there were some men of letters who explained it that way. It means that some ideas related to logic were not alien to common people although they were not fully aware of the exact meaning of them.

Taking these facts into consideration, we believe that logic can be disseminated and developed among the Japanese people, if we endeavor seriously in a right way. Logical improvement will not be impossible for us in future although it is fraught with many difficulties.

---

1) Hakuju Ui 宇井伯壽: *Bukkyō Ronrigaku* (佛教論理學), p. 168.

2) "今の世に物を飾る事をりっぱにすと云ふは立破の字音也。本は己を立て人を破る義なるが，一轉して今の如く用ゐるなるべし。" (俚言集覽 増補) "成佛遲速の立破には道雄道昌も口を閉じ………" *Heike Monogatari* (平家物語，宗論). In other MSS. or versions, the words 'りっぱ', '立波', '流派' are used instead of '立破'. Y. Yamada mentioned other materials copiously in addition. (*op. cit.* in *Geirin* '藝林'), vol. 3, Nos. 1, 2
As for 無體: 「立敵倶ニ有リト覓得ル名目ヲ因ニ用ルヲ體ト云フナリ。立敵倶ニ許サズ有リモセヌ名目ヲ因ニ用ルヲ無體ト云フナリ。」 *Inmyō Inu-sanshi* (因明犬三支) p. 19. But this term seems not to have been so important in original Indian Buddhist logic.

(5) Intuitive and emotional tendencies

Although the Japanese language, as already explained, is unsuitable for logically precise expression, it is well adapted to the expression of intuition and of individual emotion. On this point, Dr. Watsuji says: "In Japanese, the expression of feeling and will comes to the foreground. And, owing to this characteristic, what man understands in his direct and practical action is extremely well preserved [in language]. One of the modes of expression conspicuous in Japanese literature, surely owes its high degree of development to this characteristic of the Japanese language. This mode consists in connecting words and phrases together which exhibit no connection of cognitive meaning simply according to identity or similarity of pronunciation, and moreover through the connection of their emotive and affective content, achieving the expression of one complete concrete emotion. It seems to me that this characteristic is nothing more or less than a characteristic of the Japanese spirit".[1]

The Japanese themselves have been conscious of this characteristic for a long time. Yamanoue-no-Okura called Japan "the land where the spirit of language prospers". In Japan, almost everybody is a poet, and can compose and criticize *tanka* (the verse of thirty-one syllables) or *haiku* (the verse of seventeen syllables). But between the Japanese and other peoples there is a great difference in the significance of poetic expression.

The illogical character of the Japanese and their emphasis on the emotional mood are revealed in the form of their poetic expression. A conspicuous difference appears when Japanese poetry is compared with that of another Eastern people, the Indians, to say nothing of poetry in Western language. In Indian poetry, the subject and the predicate are distinguished, and also the relation between the principal and subordinate clauses is clearly recognized. And these characteristics are probably due to the special character of the Sanskrit language. Accordingly, so far as the linguistic materials used in it are concerned, it is almost not different from prose, except for a flavor of poetical emotion produced by rhyme. In the Japanese *tanka,* on the contrary, it is a common phenomenon that the subject and the predicate are hardly distinguished and that the relation between the principal and the subordinate clauses is not clear. Although some tankas are composed with logical precision,[2] they are, in the aesthetic opinion of the Japanese, rather poor in artistic value. And in *haiku,* where the abridgment of wording is carried to an extreme, words are cut down to a still shorter form, consquently the emotional mood which is conveyed by each single word has greater importance.

As pointed out already, in Japanese, the same judgment can have various expressions, and among these expressions exists a very delicate difference of emotional implication. And as has been pointed out, in Japanese the use of honorific expressions has become very complicated; it is an error, furthermore, to think that honorific language reflects only personal status in the feudal hierarchy. Rather it is often used in order to lend an air of grace and courtesy to the expression. For example, the miso soup is called '*o-mi-o-tsu-ke*', and the foot '*o-mi-ashi*', through the addition of two or three honorific particles. Furthermore, in some cases, for example, '*o-shiroi*' (face-powder), and '*o-mocha*' (toy), the honorific expression merges into the word and becomes an integral part of it. this point, Dr. Yaichi Haga gives the following explanation: "Essentially, honorific expression is not always used to show reverence. In some case, it is used to express affection, or to speak gracefully. Moreover, so long as honorific words exist, if we do not use them, we are regarded as vulgar. Consequently, men of upper classes and men of refined manners use polite words even toward their inferiors".[3]

Owing to this way of thinking, Japanese thought did not develop in the form of intellectual and systematic theories, rather it was apt to be expressed in the form of intuitive and emotional arts.

Ancient books of Japanese history written in the Japanese language, for example, *Ō-kagami, Mizu-kagami, Ima-kagami* and lastly *Masu-kagami,* are literary works rich in feeling. On this point, Japanese historiography is quite different from that of the Chinese. The Chinese people interpret and criticize historical facts from moral and political standpoints. The Japanese, however, describe the historical facts with artistic feeling. And, while the Chinese word '*Chien*' (mirror) 鑑, used frequently in the title of the books of Chinese history, for example, in *Tzu-chih-t'ung-chien,* means a reflection of moral and political principles, the Japanese word '*kagami*' (mirror), although it reflects the objects as they really are, has no moral implication.

This characteristic way of thinking was revealed also in the process of assimilation of Buddhism in Japan. When Buddhism came to Japan as a synthesis of religion, art, and philosophy, the Japanese people adopted a very peculiar emotional attitude toward it. The Japanese of those days took in only what were congenial to them. Particularly they were charmed by the aesthetic impressions of the statues of the Buddha, and, above all, they are struck by its solemn magnificence. Accordingly, they devoted themselves chiefly to plastic arts. Since then, in the Nara and the succeeding periods, the Japanese drew religious ecstasy chiefly from Buddhist arts. In Buddhist meetings, arts of all kinds, music, dancing, literature, etc., were used synthetically. Here, the Japanese were immersed in the ecstasy, as if they are in the Pure Land of Amitābha (*Gokuraku*) without taking leave of earthly existence.

St. Myōe used the word '*sukigokoro*' to express the ecstatic taste for the beautiful and the pure. This taste, coming in contact with the objects and driven by inspiration, expresses itself in poetry. Consequently, for him, poetry was almost Buddhism itself. "Considering the men of all ages", he said, "there exists not a single case that a tasteless and shameless double-dealer succeeded in becoming a Buddhist. This fact was stated clearly by the Buddha in sūtras, and further it was expounded in treatises. Therefore, there is no doubt about it. I have never seen the books of physiognomists, but, when I judge the character of other people by their faces, surmising it from the sayings of the Buddha, I was right eight or nine times out of ten. Through all ages the eminent Buddhists emerge out of men of taste. Although the poems both in Chinese and Jāpanese and the poetical dialogues in Japanese are not Buddhism as they are, those who have taste for these things are certain to extend their taste to Buddhism and become the wise and highly kind men. Even if the men of worldly mind succeed in having the appearance of virtuousness through their study, there remains some flavor of baseness, for they always look after their own interests and suffer from excessive attachment. Buddhism should be taught to those who, from childhood, has delicate taste and truthful heart".[4]

Of course, the unity of literature and religion was protested by many Buddhists. According to one of them, Dōgen, Buddhism should be practiced as Buddhism itself, and the literature has no use for genuine devotees of Buddhism. "The people who pursue the Way should not read the books of doctrinaire sects and other religions. If they should like to read something, they should read the collection of sayings (*Goroku*). The other books must be put aside for the time".[5] Accordingly he prohibited to keep other books than those relating to Buddhism in the dormitories of Buddhist temples. "In the dormitories, the books of mundane affairs, astronomy, geography, other religions, poems and verses, should not be kept".[6] Herein we can hear the voice of the traditional spirit transmitted from the day of early Buddhism in India. But, in spite of this declaration, Dōgen was a great poet. His Chinese poems are lofty and elegant, while his *tankas* are vibrating with warm sympathy with nature.

A monk of the Zen sect, Suzuki Shōsan, defended and admired his poetical greatness. "A man asks:—Dōgen wrote a *tanka* at Kitano at the night of August the fifteenth, 'Although I hope and expect to live and enjoy autumn again, I cannot sleep this night for the beauty of the moon'. Isn't this *tanka* unworthy of such an eminent devotee, for it expresses the attachment to the moon?

"Master (Suzuki) answers: —You are wrong. Dōgen diverted himself by writting *tankas*, for he was well versed in the Way of *tanka*. We should sing of the moon and flowers from the bottom of our heart. You seem to think it will do only if you say 'No delusion should be harbored; Everything should be relinquished' ".[7]

It may be unnecessary to enumerate the cases of other men. In Japan, the eminent religious men wrote Chinese poems and Japanese *tankas*. (This phenomenon stands out when compared with the case of Buddhist philosophers in India. For example, Nāgārjuna, Vasubandhu, and Dignāga did not leave any lyric or pastoral poem. They only amused themselves by expressing abstract theories of their philosophy in verse). Thus, the *tanka* is particularly important as the expression of Buddhist thought in the Japanese language, because it reveals clearly the characteristic way of thinking of the Japanese people. Among the Buddhist *tanka,* some are nothing but the expression in thirty-one syllables emotionally equivalent to some one sentence in sūtras.[8] But the majority of them use intuitive and concrete expression, that is, they use particular illustrations in order to express the universal, the abstract ideas and general propositions of Buddhism. This fact will be shown clearly by the following examples.

"The Three Worlds are but One Mind" is transfigured to 'The dews fall on thousands of grass-leaves of every field, but they are the same dew of the same autumn'.

"The Meditation on the Doctrine of the Middle Way" is transfigured to 'In contemplation, the clouds clear up from the sky of my mind, and there, in its void, remains only the moon'.

"Eternal time has passed since I really became the Buddha" is transposed to 'By the river flowing far and long, we may know of its inexhaustible source'.

"The Precept that Thou Shalt Not Steal" is transfigured to 'Along the witewave-swelling (*shiranaminotatsu*) stream of Mt. Tatsuta, you should not break even a twig of a maple-tree, if not permitted by its owner. Or else you shall have a bad name (*naga-tatsu*) of shameless robber (*shiranami*)'.

"The Precept that Thou Shalt Not Commit Adultery" is illustrated as 'You must content yourselves with enjoying the beautiful sight of a mountain spring. Do not go beyond that. Do not scoop and soil water, even if it is overflowing'.

"The Identity of Mind and the Buddha" is given its emotional equivalence in 'I am floating and sinking among the waves undistinguishable from the mandarine duck or the sea-gull'.

The "alphabet" verse (Iroha-uta), commonly ascribed to Kōbō, is one of the best examples.

Although fragrant in hue,
(blossoms) are scattered.
For everyone, life is impermanent.
This morning I crossed the uttermost limit,
and I am not intoxicated.

This is the Japanese translation in verse of a hymn which had been transmitted since the day of Early Buddhism in India. The original hymn means that 'Whatever is phenomenal is impermanent; Their essential quality is appearance and disappearance; When these appearance and disappearance repose, tranquility is comfort'. In the Japanese 'alphabet' verse, these abstract expressions were changed to emotional expressions, which use as materials the intuitive and concrete figures, such as 'gay', 'hue', 'crossing', 'uttermost limits', 'dreams', 'intoxicated', and conceal abstract theories behind them.

Thus, to interpret Buddhist ideas in poems, the Japanese people, using concrete materials, appealed to intuition and added to the ideas the flavour of emotional moods. In the Indian versification of Buddhist doctrines, on the contrary, contents are almost always abstract and general propositions, and the composition is systematic, with the subject and predicate. It is philosophy disguised in verse-form. For example, one of the philosophers of the Indian Buddhism, Nāgārjuna, in the above-mentioned hymn in verse, says: "We preach that the dependent origination is the voidness. It is temporary being dependent (upon something else). It is the Middle Way itself".[9] This poem has nothing that is poetic in essence.

It has been frequently suggested that the Japanese people love purity and undefiledness.[10] And, they are proud of this fact. In Shintō, "purity" is one of the most important virtues from the oldest times. Although almost all peoples love this virtue, too, what is meant by "purity" differs considerably between the Japanese and the other peoples. In the former, "purity" is expressed by phenomena such as frequent bathing, daily sweeping and dusting, purification ceremony (*misogi*), great exorcism (*ō-harai*), image for redemption (*katashiro*), dislike of defiledness, abstinence (*monoimi*), tidiness of the appearance. All of these are concrete acts known intuitionally, which appeal to senses and unsophisticated sentiment. Their aim is not purity in the metaphysical or religious sense, based on a poignant consciousness of sinfullness. In this sense, the Japanese people are essentially different from the Indians. The Indians value religious and metaphysical purity more than sensuous purity. It was one of the ideals of Early Buddhism that the monks who renounced the world should collect the thrown-away tatters and wear them. Though in ragged clothes, they believed that they could attain spiritual purity. The clothes were called "Funzōe" ("Lavatory-clothes"). It was said that "They are thrown away and not unlike lavatory clothes. And furthermore, they belong to no one. Therefore, they are called 'lavatory clothes'".[11] To the Japanese, however, it is unbearable to wear such clothes. The Japanese clergymen kept the name of "lavatory clothes", but its substance has been changed to neat and tidy clothes. Dōgen emphasized the duty to clean body.[12] And, although Buddhism has shaped one of the main currents of Japanese culture in the past, the common people are rather inclined to consider that the temples and clergymen are impure. This view is deep-rooted, perhaps owing to the fact that the Japanese people have never valued spiritual and religious purity and they loved sensuous purity. And this corresponds to one of the characteristics of Japanese ways of thinking, that is, lack of consciousness of the universal.

---

1) Tetsurō Watsuji 和辻哲郎: *Zoku Nihon Seishin-shi Kenkyū* (續日本精神史研究 Supplement to Research in Japanese Intellectual History) p. 393.
2) e.g. Shikishimano Yamatogokoroo Hitotowaba Asahini-niou Yamazakura-bana 敷島の大和心を人とはば朝日に匂ふ山櫻花.
3) Yaichi Haga 芳賀矢一: *op. cit. Kokuminsei Jūron* 國民性十論 p. 211.
4) *Toganoo Myōeshōnin Ikun* 栂尾明惠上人遺訓 (*Kokubun Tōhō Bukkyō Sōsho* 國文東方佛教叢書, *Hōgo-bu* 法語部, p. 57)
5) *Shōbōgenzō Zuimonki* 正法眼藏隨聞記 vol. II (Iwanami Bunko ed. pp. 37–38).
6) *Kichijyōzan Eiheiji Shuryō shingi* 吉祥山永平寺衆寮箴規.
7) *Ro-an-kyō* 驢鞍橋 pt. 2, no. 62.
8) e.g. Heijō-zedō 平常心是道 Makotoshiku Hotokeno Michio Tazunureba Tada Yonotsuneno Kokoro Narikeri まことしく佛の道を尋ぬればたゞ世のつねの心なりけり.
(*Zoku Kokinshū* 續古今集 ch. 8.)
9) *Chūron* 中論 (The *Madhyamaka-śāstra*) 24, 18.
10) Cf. Yaichi Haga: *op. cit. Kokuminsei Jūron* pp. 182–204. Ginō Tanaka 田中義能: *Shintō Gairon* 神道概倫 p. 80.
11) *Daihōshakukyō* 大寶積經 vol. CXIV. 糞掃衣比丘品 (*Taishō*. vol. 11, p. 646 c)
12) *Shōbōgenzō* 正法眼藏, Senmen 洗面.

(6) Lack of ability of forming complicated ideas

Among the Eastern peoples, while the Indians were rather inclined to attach importance to the universal, the Japanese emphasized the individual. This difference in the way of thinking is revealed in various fields of thinking of the two peoples.

The best illustration of this fact is supplied by the poetical expression of objects. In Sanskrit, the cloud (*megha*) is often called "*jalada*" or '*aṃbuda*" (water-giver), the bird "*vihaṃga*" (flyer in the air), the elephant "matamga" (meditative walker), the lotus "ambuja" (the flower which grows out of water). All of these are compound words, formed out of two words. And the fact that the last-added word is derived from the root of verb gives an abstract character to this compound word. The concrete and phenomenal meaning is brought about on the basis of this abstract meaning of the words of which a compound is made. As shown by these examples, the Indians loved abstract expression. But, in the Japanese language, the same things are expressed by words, whose origin is obscure, at least to the consciousness of their users, and consequently, whose abstract meanings have been lost, such as "kumo" (cloud), "tori" (bird), "zō" (elephant), "hasu" (lotus).

The Japanese language is, generally speaking, very poor in imaginative words based on abstract and universal ideas. By bringing concrete and particular objects in contact with abstract ideas, which are constituent elements of the ideas to be expressed ultimately, Japanese inspires particular and emotional moods. The use of "Makura-kotoba" (lit. pillow-words) in *tanka* and other literary works offers revealing examples.

> "By these *bows of catalpa,* we have made up our mind to *shoot* (*iru*) enemies and to expect not to return from this battle. So we write down the names of those who will certainly *join* (*iru*) the dead". Here the three words are chosen.
>
> "My mother very often smoothed down my *black-as-a-crow* hair (nubatama-no-kuro-kami), but certainly she never dreamt that the day would come when this hair would be cut down".

The "association-word", which is used quite often in literary works, is another example of this characteristic.

Consequently, the imaginative power of the Japanese people, from the oldest times, has been limited to, and has never stepped over, the concrete and intuitive world of nature. "The ancient Japanese", says Dr. Tsuda, "are generally poor in imaginative power, the power to shape concrete fantasy".[1] And this tendency, we may say, runs through the Japanese literature to the present day. Accordingly, the Japanese people have never developed titanic myths. In this, they are like the Chinese. "Among our people, who have not formed the idea of God with human personality, it was only natural that the deity saga (*Göttersage*) has not been developed".[2] In this respect, the Japanese literature, shallow and unimaginative in general, is diametrically opposed to the Indian literature, although both are products of the same East.

The characteristic way of thinking, which has been pointed out, determined the form of assimilation of Buddhism, too. The Buddhist sūtras have never been translated into Japanese before the Meiji Restoration. This means that Buddhist thought of the Indians has hardly penetrated as a whole into the life and thought of the Japanese people.

The lack of imagination was revealed in the process of transformation of the Jōdo religion (the sect of the Pure Land of *Amitābha*). The Nembutsu, "Keeping the Buddha in mind" practiced by the Japanese is different from the *nembutsu* preached in India. In the latter case, for example, in Early Buddhism, then, in the Great *Sukhāvatīvyūha-sūtra* and the *Amitāyurdhyāna-sūtra,* it chiefly consists in praying for the Buddha, recalling its sublime features. The Amitābha, created by imagination of the Indians, had extraordinarily gigantic features.[3]

"The body of Buddha Amitāyus is a hundred thousand million times as bright as the colour of the *Jambūnada* gold of the heavenly abode of Yama; the height of that Buddha is six hundred thousand *niyutas* of *koṭis* of *yojanas* innumerable as are the sands of the river Ganges.

The white twist of hair between the eyebrows all turning to the right, is just like the five Sumeru mountains. The eyes of Buddha are like the water of the four great oceans; the blue and the white are quite distinct. All the roots of hair of his body issue forth brilliant rays like the Sumeru mountains. The halo of that Buddha is like a hundred millions of the Great Chiliocosmus; in that halo there are Buddhas miracurously created, to the number of a million of *niyutas* of *koṭis* innumerable as the sands of the Ganges; each of these Buddha has for attendants a great assembly of numberless Bodhisattvas who are also miraculously created.

Buddha Amitāyus has eighty-four thousand signs of perfection, each sign is possessed of eighty-four minor marks of excellence, each mark has eighty-four thousand rays, each ray extends so far as to shine over the worlds of the ten quarters, whereby Buddha embraces and protects all the beings who think upon him and does not exclude (any one of them)".

Then, the *nembutsu* of the Indians was to contemplate this gigantic features of the Buddha by vivid imaginative power. The *nembutsu* preached by the Chinese, for example, by Ten-dai Daishi, Chih-i, had the same character. But, being transplanted into the Japanese soil, it was changed to the invocation of Amitābha following the teaching of Shan-tao of China.

Even in Japan, there was a clergyman who preached that the Nembutsu consists in contemplation of features of the Buddha. (Shikisōkan). It was Genshin. He said: "The novice cannot practise the discipline of contemplation of the profound (esoteric) .... The various sūtras preach the merit of (contemplation of) features of the Buddha. Therefore, now is the time to practice this discipline". His *nembutsu*, however, went a step further toward the *nembutsu* as invocation of Amitābha. He especially emphasized the importance of the *nembutsu* on the death-bed. "Even a man of lowest rank, if he practices "*Jū-nen*" which is the repetition of the name of Amitābha ten times, he can be re-born in the Pure Land of Amitābha". His interpretation og *Jū-nen* is altered from that of the Jōdo cult in China. According to Tao-ch'ue in China, "To recall the whole features or the partical features of Amitābha, to contemplate them in reference to objects at that occasion, during ten moments of thought with no intervention of other ideas—this I call Jū-nen". But, according to Genshin, "The so-called Jū-nen, although variously interpreted, is to repeat, with heart and soul, 'Oh! save me, thou Amitābha!' ten times".[4]

The *nembutsu* as invocation to the Amitābha by mouth acquired its absolute significance in Hōnen, the founder of the Jōdo sect. It was not easy for the unimaginative Japanese to contemplate, as preached by sūtras, the features of Amitābha, created by the imagination of the Indians. Hōnen perceived this difficulty. "Even if you try to contemplate the features of Amitābha, it will be difficult for you to visualize them as clearly as flowers and fruits of cherry, plum, peach, and damson".[5] Therefore, he prohibited the *nembutsu* as contemplation of the features of Amitābha. "Nowadays, the devotees should not practice contemplation. Even if you try to contemplate the features of Amitābha, it will be difficult to visualize its image as sculptured by Unkei or Kōkei". Therefore, according to Hōnen, "The Original Vow of Birth in the Pure Land of Amitābha cannot be accomplished by various disciplines, for example, image-making, tower erecting, etc., but by the sole discipline of the repetition of the name of Amitābha, because the Original Vow is pledged to receive far and wide the whole mass of people". It was for these reasons that he turned to and relied on the *nembutsu* of Shan-tao of China.

In "the Panegyric of the Birth in Pure Land" (*Ōjō-Raisange*) of Shan-tao, we can find the following dialogue. "Question: —You do not allow the contemplation, but exhort only the invocation. Why, and in what intention, do you rely on such a practice?

"Answer: —Now, all the people are obstructed by heavy burdens. Their mind is too rough-structured to contemplate a subtle object (that is, Amitābha). Furthermore, their spirit is always oscillating in mid-air. Consequently, compassionating that they can hardly accomplish their contemplation, the Great Sage (Buddha) exhorts the exclusive invocation to his name. It is owing to the easiness of invocation that the people can go to be born in the Pure Land of Amitābha only through the continuous practice of this discipline".[6]

Shinran followed this standpoint of Shan-tao and Hōnen. He thought it was inconceivable for us, ordinary men, to contemplate the features of Amitābha. "O deadly sinner! Invoke Amitābha alone! He is taking hold of us. Though our eyes of flesh cannot clearly see him owing to our sins, yet is his mercy constantly present to illuminate our minds".[7]

And Ippen said, "We should not try to see the Amitābha, except through invocation to him. Invocation is the true seeing Amitābha itself. The Amitābha seen by the eyes of flesh is not the true Amitābha".[8]

Why this difference appeared between the Indian and the Japanese Nembutsu? It is because that the spiritual aptitude of the former consists in overflowing imagination and the love of the subtle introspective analysis of psychology, while the latter, lacking this aptitude, are inclined to depend solely on concrete symbols.

In this, we can find the cause of the difference between the Japanese Pure Land cult and the Indian bhakti religion. The first, having never been given to wanton imagination, could not develop frantic or ecstatic rituals. (Although such a tendency was not absent, it was regarded as an exceptional phenomenon and rejected by the Pure Land cult in general.)

The characteristic way of thinking, which we pointed out in the process of transformation of the Pure Land cult, can be recognized in case of *zazen* (*dhyāna,* to sit in contemplation), too. The Indians, in *samādhi,* silent meditation and abstraction of thought, kept something in mind, for example, imagined that the universe is like space, or that it is larger than space, or that, on the contrary, it is smaller than a grain of rice, or that the soul is as large as a thumb. This type of discipline had been practised in Buddhism as well as in Brahminism, since the days of the philosophers of the Upanishads. It was to keep the Buddha or truth in mind or to recall the Past Life. It may be called *the Zazen as contemplation of features.*[9]

In the Japanese Zen sect, however, Zazen aims at detachment from discriminative knowledge, regardless of whether it is in the form of the deliberation of catechetic questions assigned by master, or in the form of endeavoring to do away with conceptualization. What Dōgen adopted as his motto was the precept: "Practice only sitting".

The Japanese people, as mentioned already, are inclined to loathe theoretical argument. This tendency has influenced the character of the Japanese philosophy in the past. The learning of exegesis and interpretation was enjoyed as ornamental literature in China, but the Japanese endeavoured to grasp their essentials to utilize them for practical understanding.

Examples of this characteristic can be found in the process of assimilation of Buddhism. The commentary on sūtras by Prince Shōtoku of Japan is not pedantic at all. It is brief and to the point. But, the Chinese reference book which Prince Shōtoku made use of, the commentary of Chia-hsiang Ta-shih Chi-tsang of China, mentions many meanings in the interpretation of just one word. We cannot recognize, and the author does not try even to demonstrate, which of these meanings is the correct one. Therefore, so far as the purpose of clear exposition is concerned, the Commentary of Prince Shōtoku is superior, as Fujaku had pointed out.[10] Of course, we cannot find this characteristic in all of commentaries written by Japanese Buddhists. But, compared with the general tendency of the Chinese commentaries, the majority of the Japanese commentaries are rather succinct summaries. Not only the Japanese studied the scholastic doctrines of the *Vijñaptimātratāsiddhi* or *Abhidharmakośa* in great detail, but also they wrote on them many commentaries which are brief and to the point.

It seems that the study of Confucianism in Japan showed the same tendency. The positivist scholars in the Ching period, who devoted their life to the exact philological study of Chinese classics, had never tried to summarize its results and to expose their essentials. But, the Japanese Confucians of the Archaist (Kogaku) school, inferior to the Chinese in the exactitude of their philological study, were very skilled in summarizing results of their study and leaving them to the posterity.[11]

Thus, Japanese scholars concentrated their energies to get promptly to a conclusion. Their attitude may be called practical. In the past, they were very weak in critical observation of nature and its logical reconstruction. The cause of this attitude can be found in the fact that the Japanese generally loathed complicated, structural thinking and estimated practical value above all things.

The tendency of aversion to complicated, structural thinking was revealed, also in the system of the Buddhist doctrines in Japan. In the critical classification of various sects according to their doctrines, the Chinese arranged them hierarchically, for example, by the fiive periods and the eight categories of Śākyamuni's teaching, or by the five and ten divisions of Buddhism of the Hua-yen school. The Japanese, on the contrary, simply distinguished doctrines of their own sect on the one hand, from those of other sects on the other. The Shingon sect calls itself "esoteric school" and all of other sects "exoteric schools". The Zen sect summarizes other sects under the name of "doctrinaire sects". The Pure Land sects contrast their own school of "the immediate salvation by faith in Amitābha" with the other ordinary schools of "the way of holiness by the process of practice". The complicated and hierarchical classification of the Chinese has never been adopted by the Japanese Buddhists. (Although this type of simple classification had already appeared in China, we must point out that the Japanese like especially to classify things by the simple types.)

It has been said that the Japanese people are adept in imitation and sterile in invention. They are apt not to try to understand foreign culture from its principle and structure. They import precipitately only those parts which can be put into practical use. How abundant, in fact, Japanese culture in the past was in such superficial imitations!

The originality of Japanese Buddhism has frequently been asserted by Japanese scholars. But it means chiefly that it simplified the Buddhism of the Continent and popularized it. It is rare that it criticized the Continental Buddhism from its principles and structure.

The practical character of Japanese Buddhism is also frequently emphasized. It is true that, owing to its simplification, its disciplines could be practised with ease by common people, and that it penetrated into their everyday life. But there was danger of sacrificing theory for practice. For example, Dōgen said, "Buddhists should not discuss the relative merits of various doctrines or the relative profundity of various tenets. It is sufficient for them to know the truthfulness of disciplines".[12]

The Japanese people, because of the lack of ability in forming complicated, structural thinking, are inclined to reject the "doctrine of expediency", one of the most characteristic doctrines of Buddhism. Buddhism's original standpoint of "Preach according to each man's nature" permits clergymen to preach different doctrines to different persons, that is, to preach a doctrine suitable to each person. Eminent Buddhists in

India were not worried about contradiction between these different doctrines adopted for "expediency". Chinese Buddhists conspicuously preserved this standpoint. But Japanese Buddhists who were of peculiarly Japanese character, for example, Hōnen, Shinran, and Nichiren, rejected this standpoint. They preached the same and consistent doctrine. Furthermore, Dōgen expressly opposed the doctrine of expediency. "If a man asks about the essence of the doctrine and disciplines, certainly monks should answer by truth. They should not answer by false expediency, considering that his caliber is not sufficient, or that the truth cannot be understood by this uninitiated and unlearned man. The true meaning of the precepts of Bodhisattva is that, if the man of calibre of "the Smaller Vehicle" asks about the Way of "the Smaller Vehicle", they should answer by the Way of "the Greater Vehicle". It is the same with the precepts for salvation, laid down by the Buddha during his life. The false doctrine of expediency is really not useful. The final (ultimate) true doctrine alone is useful. Accordingly, they should answer only by truth, without considering whether it will be understood by the questioner or not".[13]

The attitude of the rejection of expediency can be discerned plainly in Nichiren also. All sūtras, except the Hokke Sūtra, preach the doctrine of expediency, and, therefore, must be rejected, he asserted. "In the Hokke Sūtra, it is preached in the beginning that 'the Exalted One will certainly preach the truth, after he taught the various doctrines for a long time, and then, that 'There exist neither two doctrines nor three doctrines. The doctrine of expediency of the Buddha must be rejected'. And also that 'Rejecting expediency in earnest', or 'You shalt not believe in any of the hymns of other sūtras'. Therefore, since then, the Good Law that 'There exists only one vehicle of the Buddha' is the Great Law which can accomplish the salvation of the mass of the people, and the sutras other than the Hokke Sūtra have no use at all".[14]

Characteristically Japanese Buddhists were single-minded. This may have some relation to the fact that the Japanese, as mentioned already, valued the virtue of honesty. And the special emphasis put on this virtue by Buddhists and common people in Japan, is, for one thing, owing to their aversion to complicated thinking in human relations. Compared with other peoples, the Japanese are generally simple and faithful, and not adept in political and diplomatic bargaining. Probably, there may exist some relations between this characteristic and the above-mentioned way of thinking.

Already in the Tokugawa period, Tominaga Nakamoto, defining the spiritual characteristic of the Japanese, said, borrowing the word of the Analects of Confucius, that they were honest, did not stick to complicated etiquette, and value straightforwardness.[15] And Matsumiya Kanzan said, "In our country, the nature of the people is simple and honest", and "The teaching of gods" is "the doctrine of simplicity and honesty". These reflections seem to be quite correct.[16]

---

1) *Jindai shi no Kenkyū* (神代史の研究 Study on the History of Ancient Japan) p. 593.
2) *Ibid.*, p. 595.
3) *Kanmuryōju-kyō* 觀無量壽經.
4) Taijō Tamamuro 圭室諦成: *op cit. Nihon Bukkyō-shi Gaisetsu* p. 107.
5) Shinkō Mochizuki 望月信亨 (ed.): *Hōnen Shōnin Zenshū* 法然上人全集 p. 531.
6) *Taishō*. vol. 47. p. 439 a.
This is also quoted in the *Kyōgyōshinshō* pt. 2.
7) *Shōshinge* 正信偈
8) *Ippen Shōnin Goroku* 一遍上人語錄.
9) Cf. *Daimuryōju-kyō* 大無量壽經 pt. 1.
10) Tetsurō Watsuji 和辻哲郎: *op. cit. Zoku Nihon Seishin-shi Kenkyū* pp. 88–89; 103–104.
11) Kōjirō Yoshikawa 吉川幸次郎: Gakumon no Katachi 學問のかたち (*Sekai* 世界 May, 1946.)
12) *Shōbō Genzō* 正法眼藏 *Bendōwa* 辨道話.
13) *Shōbōgenzō Zuimonki* 正法眼藏隨聞記 vol. VI. (Iwanami Bunko ed. p. 108).
14) *Nyosetsu Shugyōshō* 如說修行鈔.
cf. *Myōichini Gozen Gohenji* 妙一尼御前御返事.
15) *Shutsujyōkōgo* 出定後語 ch. 8. *Jinzū* 神通.
16) *Sankyō Yōron* 三敎要論 p. 2.

(7) Fondness for simple symbolic expressions

Poor imagination corresponds to fondness for simple expression. From the oldest times, the Japanese are inclined to loathe complicated expressions and to love simple and naive expressions.

The Japanese language, as pointed out already, is very poor in words expressing complicated and abstract conceptions. Consequently, even to this day, they use the Chinese words, in most cases, to express abstract ideas.

In art, this tendency can be discerned obviously, too. The impromptu short verse, like *haiku* and *tanka,* is cherished by the Japanese. In the history of Japanese poetry, the long verse (chōka) is reduced to short one (tanka), and then to shorter one (haiku). The extremely short form of artistic expression is characteristically Japanese and the like of it cannot be found elsewhere. Moreover, long verse forms like epic poetry have never prospered in Japan. Not to mention the cases of Greek and Teutonic peoples, the Indians produced an epic of more than one hundred thousand verses, the *Mahābhārata*. Such an achievement was inconceivable in case of the Japanese. In the Japanese literature, lyric poems and scenery sketches have been highly developed, but poems of grand style, with dramatic plots full of turns and twists, have made only a poor development.

Not only in poetry but also in architecture, we can recognize the characteristic love of simplicity. The Japanese have imported various formative arts from Indian Buddhism, indirectly through the hands of Chinese and Koreans. As seen in the magnificient splendour of golden Buddhist altars and mural paintings of temples, the complicated sculptures of transoms, the fantastic statue of Goddess of Mercy (Avalokiteśvara) with a thousand arms, the square diagram of figures (Maṇḍala) with complicated and delicate structure—all of them had, in general, a very complicated structure. But, such an art could hardly penetrate into the life of the common people. The Japanese could not abandon the simple and unpainted wooden architecture of ancient style, in many shrines as well as in the Great Shrine of Ise. And, even in architecture of Buddhist temples, the various sects of the Kamakura period turned to rather simple style. Also, in the Zen-influenced taste of the tea-ceremony house, we can discern naive simplicity. The Japanese grave-marker (*sotoba*), which is a symbolic imitation of the gigantic cairn of the Indian people (stupa), is nothing but a very small wooden tablet.

This simplicity, however, does not always mean an obliteration of complexity. In some cases, especially under the influence of the Zen cult, the Japanese endeavored to infuse unlimited complexity into this simplicity. This tendency is conspicuous especially in art, such as architecture, drawing, and poetry. For example, the void, which gives no positive expression, in fact, has a very important meaning. Even in the etiquette and conversation of everyday life, it is really a very positive expression to utter nothing and to mention nothing. Of course, this tendency was an ideal. This ideal was realized by the Chinese people, who loved complicated thinking and whose spiritual life was greatly influenced by the Zen cult. When introduced into Japan, however, this, too, took the course of simplification.

Thus, the Japanese people, in general, loathe the expression of complicated thinking, have been unable to think or imagine the objects in relation to universal structure. For example, in India, as well as in China, the worship of stars prospered, and myths and legends concerning them were numerous. The Chinese worshipped the Stars of the Cowboy (Altair) and of the Weaver (Vega). But the primitive Shintō in Japan, although it contained many and various folk-religions as in the case of other peoples, did not worship stars.[1] When the Japanese imported the Chinese worship of stars, the star of the Weaver was identified with the Japanese Goddess of the Weaver (*Amenotanabatahimenokami*), and its worship was transformed to the Festival of the Weaver (*Tanabata-matsuri*). In short, stars were not holy and austere gods for the Japanese. They were lovely and intimate heroes and heroines of familiar legends. The Japanese could not produce the sublime metaphorical expression of Kant, who compared moral axioms to stars.

Thus, because complicated symbols were not used by the Japanese in their thinking, the philosophical theories of the Indian and Chinese Buddhism were too profound, abstruse and complicated to penetrate into the life of the common people in Japan. Consequently, they had to be simplified.

The Japanese, in assimilating Buddhism, did not depend upon its philosophical doctrines. Of course, the clergymen of large temples were engaged in philosophical debates and wrote a great number of books. The common people, however, demanded concrete and empirical clues rather than philosophical theories. Although they extolled the Hokke Sūtra and the *Suvarṇaprabhāsasūtra,* they could not understand their philosophical theories. They valued only the incidental contents of sūtras, that is, their magical elements. The same attitude persists up to this day.

In fact, the Japanese Buddhism simplified doctrines, separating them from the study of philosophical theories, and transcended scholastic systems of doctrines.

The Buddhist sects of the Nara period, which, as a whole, introduced and studied the Chinese doctrines, could not be propagated among common people. The Tendai and Shingon sects, introduced at the beginning of the Heian period, followed, in the main, the doctrines of Chinese sects of the same name. The Tendai sect, however, made an original development as time passed. This sect, developing the theory of the Truth of All The Beings: on the basis of the Hokke Sūtra., divided this sūtra into two parts, that is, the first fourteen chapters (*Shakumon*), relating to the purpose of the Buddha's earthly life and various teaching, and the following fourteen chapters (*Honmon*), relating to the final revelation of the Buddha as eternal one. And the discipline of the contemplation of truth through these two gates (*Mon*) was called *Shikan* (the tranquility and contemplation of mind). But the new Tendai school of the Kamakura period went a step further. In its critical classification of doctrines of various sects, it relied on the fourfold criteria. They asserted that the first three criteria—(1) the doctrines delivered before the Hokke Sūtra (*Nizen*), (2) the doctrines delivered in *Shakumon,* (3) the doctrines delivered in *Honmon*—should be "discarded". Then, and only then, the last and the true criterion—the contemplation of the absolute truth (Kan)—arises. This standpoint clearly values the practice based on the non-discriminative wisdom above complicated, theoretical wisdom.

In Japan, Pure Land Buddhism also developed in the sole direction of belief in, and reliance on Amitābha. The Pure Land Buddhism which has been prevalent in China up to this day is conflated with Zen Buddhism and other various forms of faith. In Japan, however, the faith in, and reliance on Amitābha has been preserved in a pure form.

The devotional faith in Pure Land became prevalent in the Kamakura period. But even before that, in fact, throughout the Heian period, the devotees of this cult were numerous.[2] But, it was Hōnen that advocated the doctrine of invocation to the Pure Land of Amitābha (*Jōdo-nembutsu*) on the theoretical ground, detaching it from other doctrines. Hōnen preached as follows: The period of degeneration and extinction of the Buddha-law (*Mappō*) has come. Men cannot attain higher perception (*Satori*) by various disciplines. They shall be given salvation only through faith in Amitābha. Renounce the spirit of self-relying disciplines; shut the gate of silent meditation and cultivation of virtues; ignore all of the devices; throw away the whole knowledge; and concentrate in the one discipline of invocation to the Buddha.[3] Thus, Hōnen advocated to "renounce, shut, ignore, and throw away", one of the most famous assertions in the history of the Japanese Buddhism. Rejecting all of the other doctrines, he chose the doctrine of *Jōdo-nembutsu* (The Choice of *Nembutsu* as the Original Vow of the Buddha).

The disciples of Hōnen went further in the direction of simplification of Pure Land cult. One of them advocated the following extreme doctrine: "Saint Hōnen repeated the *nembutsu* seventy thousand times a day. But it is only external expediency. In its interior, there exists a true meaning, unknown to ordinary men. What I call true is this: — If you penetrate into, and believe in, the Original Vow of Amitābha, and repeat his name only once, you can go, at once, to be born in the Pure Land of Amitābha. Thus, the practice of the Pure Land cult will be accomplished. You can go to the Pure Land, if you invoke only once. You need not invoke many times. And the ultimate meaning is to penetrate into, and believe in, the Original Vow".[4] There appeared some who went so far as to say: "Those who want to repeat invocation do not, in fact, believe in the Vow of the Buddha".[5]

In the direction of simplification, Shinran, too, went further than Hōnen. According to him, invocation to the name of Amitābha, that is, "Oh save me, thou Amitābha!" (*Namuamidabutsu*), is the essence and idol of the fundamental sūtra, *the Large Sukhāvatīvyūha-sūtra.* To understand words or sentences of this sūtra, is not so important. The consummation of faith consists in invocation to Amitābha. Hōnen advocated that the name of Amitābha should be repeated sixty thousand times a day, but Shinran rejected this doctrine as meaningless. Although he inherited the term of the pure and exclusive discipline, he changed its meaning completely. "You should believe, with exclusive and single heart, in the Original Vow that we can go to be born in the Pure Land of Amitābha if we say '*Namuamidabutsu*' only once. This discipline can be called the pure and exclusive discipline".[6] "The exclusive heart referred to in the Commentary (the *Sanzengi* of Zendō) is nothing but the single heart. It expresses that we should not have two hearts . The exclusive discipline referred to is nothing but a single discipline. It expresses that we should not have two disciplines".[7]

Thus, the doctrine of *one-time-nembutsu* reached its climax in Shinran. Although it had been embraced by many devotees of the Pure Land cult before him, it was Shinran that gave it a theoretical expression.[8]

Since then, Ippen, the founder of the Ji sect, advocated the *nembutsu,* too. According to a legend, he, on his death-bed, "burnt down, with his own hands, the books in his possession, and said that all of the holy doctrines of the whole life of the Buddha was reduced to *nembutsu*".[9] Rennyo, too, valued "the image of Amitābha than his statue, his name more than his image".[10]

Then, in the Japanese Pure Land cult, the invocation of "*Namuamidabutsu*" had the central significance. On this point, it was quite digerent from the *nembutsu* practiced by the Chinese. The Chinese clergymen greet each other, saying "Amitōfo" (Amitābha). But it has only accessory significance.[11]

As the Pure Land cult was simplified in the direction of *nembutsu,* the doctrine of the Tendai sect, which embraced the teaching of the Hokke Sūtra, was simplified in the direction of *"Daimoku"* (the heading of the sūtra).

In the Japanese Tendai sect, it was considered difficult for common people to understand the philosophical theories of the Hokke Sūtra. Dengyō is said to have preached: "For ordinary men, who are born among the extremely inferior men of the lowest status in the period of degeneration and extinction of the Buddha-law, it is vain to endeavor to pretend to be an ascetic figure that is fresh and unobscured by nature. The men of superior disposition and wisdom should practise disciplines and acquire merits. For those of inferior disposition and wisdom, the Buddha has bequeathed the panacea that summarizes his holy teaching of all his life—the five words of *Myō-hō-ren-ge-kyō* (the Sūtra of the Lotus of the Good Law). Therefore, this heading was preached to be propagated far and wide among the multitude of all spheres of existence during the last five hundred years of the period of degeneration and extinction of the Buddha-law". Thus, according to Dengyō, the panacea for salvation of the common people is not the philosophical theories of the Hokke Sūtra, but its heading of five words, *Myō-hō-ren-ge-kyō.* Then, before the appearance of Nichiren, in the new Tendai doctrine of the Kamakura period, it was preached that, to attain salvation, it was sufficient to practise only the invocation to the heading of the Hokke Sūtra, not the troublesome contemplation, for example, the simultaneous contemplation from the view points of 'void', 'fictions' and 'middle', or the contemplation of the three thousand spheres in one thought. "If you repeat *Namumyōhōrengekyō* on your death-bed, you can, by virtue of the Three Powers of the Good Law, attain the illuminated mind and deliver yourself from the burden of birth and death".[12] "The contemplation of the three thousand spheres in one thought, on your death-bed, is nothing but the invocation to the Hokke Sūtra of the Good Law. (*Myō-hō-ren-ge-kyō*). Myō corresponds with one thought, Hō with the three thousand spheres. Therefore, these two are synonymous with the three thousand spheres in one thought. On your death-bed, you should just repeat Myō-hō-ren-ge (-kyō) with your whole heart".[13] And, in fact, the devotees, who repeated only this heading, were already numerous in the Heian period.[14]

It was Nichiren, however, that pushed this doctrine unto its "logical" conclusion. "In the Hokke Sūtra", he said, "you should consider that the reading of the whole eight volumes, or one volume, or one chapter, or one hymn, or one sentence can have no more merits than the reading of one heading".[15] "This sūtra, I think, states that the assignment of one heading or one hymn is sufficient as duty of the devotee, and decides that the time of its practice must be the time when you rejoice whole-heartedly in the doctrine. Generally speaking, the gigantic treasury of Buddhist scriptures of eighty thousand volumes or the vast sūtra of eight volumes (Hokke Sūtra) exists only to preach these five words .... Only by the repetition of Namumyōhōrengekyō, you can atone all your sins and have all blessings".[16] Pushing the argument to the extreme regardless of historical connection of the various doctrines, we can say that the religion of Nichiren, so far as the love of simplicity is concerned, is nothing but the replacement of the name of Amitābha by the heading of the Hokke Sūtra. Nichiren said: "The saying of 'Embrace only this sūtra' (which is preached in the Hokke Sūtra), does not mean a study of the whole sūtra. It means only that we should embrace only the heading, with no intervention of other sentences".[17] Clearly this is not the original standing of the sūtra. The simplification that the invocation to the heading is sufficient for salvation, has been never seen in other countries. And, with this simplification, the sect of exclusive faith in the Hokke Sūtra was established, a phenomenon also unseen in other countries.

Thus, the devotees of Nembutsu as well as of the 'Heading' have relied on the simple symbol of faith. Then, we must consider the case of the Zen cult. Eisai, the introducer of the Zen of the Rinzai sect, brought the other various cults into his Zen cult. But Dōgen, who introduced the Zen of the Sōtō sect, taught repeatedly to "endeavor exclusively to sit in meditation (*dhyāna, zazen*)". He said "The study and practice of the doctrine of Zen cult is the Freedom from the burden of body and soul (*shin-jin-datsuraku*). Incense-burning, adoration, *nembutsu*, confession, sūtra-reading are unnecessary. It is necessary only to sit in meditation".[18] Once a man asked Dōgen if the devotees of Zazen might practise the disciplines of magical formulae of the Shingon sect or of tranquility and contemplation of mind of the Tendai sect as well. He answered: "When I asked my Master about the true secrets, while I was in China, he said he had never heard that the Great Masters of all ages and all countries, who had transmitted the Buddha-seal, had practised those disciplines. In fact, if you don't concentrate yourself in one discipline, you can never attain even one wisdom".[19]

Therefore, according to Dōgen, the idle study of the doctrines was meaningless. "It is the same in the case of sūtras. In spite of their immensity, we should believe in and devote ourselves to one hymn or one sentence. We cannot understand the eighty thousand (doctrines)".[20] "The erudition and extensive reading are unattainable for us. We must renounce this design resolutely. We should concentrate ourselves in one discipline only, learn the views and usages, and follow the practices of the predecessors, with no pretention of a teacher or a leader".[21]

Dōgen preached that the clergymen should concentrate themselves in only one discipline with their whole body and soul. "Even the men of world should not practice many disciplines simultaneously so as to be adept in any of them. Rather they should practice only one discipline so as to be more adept in it than other people .... If they want to practise the various disciplines of the vast Buddha-doctrine, they cannot accomplish any of them. Even when they concentrate themselves in one disciplinc, its accomplishment during their life is difficult for their miserable caliber by nature. Then, the devotees should endeavour to concentrate themselves in one discipline exclusively".[22] When, Ejō, one of his disciples, asked him what discipline, among the Buddha-law, he should practise whole-heartedly, Dōgen answered: "Although it must be decided according to man's nature and disposition, it is Contemplation that has been transmitted and practiced exclusively from ancient masters. This discipline can conform to all kinds of nature and be practiced by all sorts of dispositions". Thus, he was opposed to one of the traditional doctrines of Buddhism, the doctrine that preaching must conform to the nature of each digerent person (*Taiki-seppō*).

On this point the Zen cult advocated by Dōgen is diametrically opposite to that of the Chinese. In Chinese Buddhism almost only the Zen cult has become prevalent since the Sung period, but they practised various disciplines including the Pure Land cult and the esoteric cult of the Shingon sect, and occasionally the disciplines of Early Indian Buddhism (Vinaya-piṭaka) also. To Dōgen, however, this was unbearable psychologically. So he simplified Buddhism in the direction of only one discipline of Contemplation.

Although Dōgen objected to the loud repetition of Nembutsu by the multitude of the devotees of the Pure Land Buddhism, comparing it to the voice of frogs, he sympathized completely with the exclusiveness of their disciplines. Kūamidabutsu, who had been a famous scholar of the exoteric and esoteric teachings, retiring from the world and living in a hermitage of Mt. Kōya, devoted himself to Nembutsu. When, one day, a clergyman of the esoteric school visited him and asked him about the esoteric doctrines, he said: "I have forgotten everything. I do not remember any word".[23] Dōgen admired the thoroughness of this discipline. Therefore, he agreed with the devotees of the Japanese Pure Land Buddhism, so far as the reliance on simple symbolic expression is concerned.

It has been frequently pointed out that the Zen cult exerted an enormous influence on the culture of *samurais* (*Bushidō*). The extreme simplicity and frugality of life and deeds of Zen priests might have captivated *samurais*. *Samurais* risked their life on the battle-field, where scholastic doctrines of Buddhism were of no use. Therefore, the simple doctrines of "We do not value words" (Fu-ryū-mon-ji) or "We point to human mind directly" (Jiki-shi-nin-shin) appealed to them. The spiritual trainings of the Zen sect, which could control human mind completely for its simplicity, can be practiced by *samurais*.

In the Chinese Zen cult, no legend existed that Zen clergymen taught to warriors the readiness for death. In Japan, on the contrary, such legends are abundant. One of the reasons of this peculiar phenomenon may be the transformation of the Zen cult in Japan, that is, its simplification. Furthermore, the Zen cult exerted a great influence on the various fields of Japanese culture, for example, architecture, painting, seventeen syllable verse (Haiku), flower arrangement, tea ceremony, etc.. It was also owing to the fact that the Zen cult in Japan had wholly abandoned the complexity and prolixity and contained infinite significance in its negative silence.

The simplification of complicated doctrines can be recognized also in the various old sects of Buddhism, early introduced into Japan. The idealistic philosophy of the Hossō sect was too difficult and complicated to be understood by common people. Therefore, Jōkei (1155–1213) advocated that the ignorant people, who could not understand doctrines of idealism, should, at least, repeat always the Praise, transmitted and taught by the Three Great Sages: "The devotee of the Mahāyāna contemplates that the contents of all objects are nothing but the creation of mind, and then he effaces his own views as the external objects. That is to say, he contemplates fully that all are nothing but the content of ideas created by himself. Thus, remaining within himself, he knows that the objects are not existent, and furthermore, that the cognizing subject is not existent. Then he can attain, for the first time, the state of liberty, free from everything".[24] In the Kegon sect, too, Myōe taught that, in the case of common believers, it was not necessary to understand the doctrines, but to repeat "Homage to the Three Jewells and the Mind of Enlightenment; May my prayer come to be realized to perfection here as well as hereafter". or "Alas, the Three Jewells! Save me in my after-life".[25]

The cult of Maitreya, which prospered in the Kamakura period, taught the same doctrines as the Pure Land Buddhism under the influence of the faith in Amitābha. "If we practise the vow of abstention only for a moment, we can have superior happiness in our after-life, and if we invoke the name of Maitreya just once, we can go to be born in his Pure Land in some life or other. Its practice is very easy and its virtue is most great. Only by virtue of the Original Vow of the Benevolent Lord, we can share its merits. This pleases all the Great Sages and it is craved by all ordinary men".[26] "According to the teaching of the Ascent Sūtra, it is very easy to be born in the Paradise of Maitreya (Tuṣita). If we crave this ascent only for a moment, and if we practise invocation just once, we can attain our cherished desire".[27] And in the Heian period and thereafter, there had been many devotees who had faith in Kṣitigarbha-bodhisattva and repeated only his name.[28] The faith in the *dhāraṇī*, especially Kōmyō-shingon-dhāraṇī or Hōkyōin-dhāraṇī, was propagated among the common people. And, so far as the way of thinking is concerned, the creed of itinerant priests (Shugen-dō) was the development of this direction of simplification, too. "The itinerant priests, though they have En-no-Gyōja and Jōzō-kisho as their predecessors, are only the devotees of one *dhāraṇī*".[29] The understanding of the whole content of Shingon-dhāraṇī was not demanded. It was sufficient for them to repeat any of those *dhāraṇīs*.

The tendency of fondness for simple symbols appeared in the process of adoption of Buddhist ideas by Japanese Shintoists in the Ancient and Medieval times. It has been already mentioned that the moral ideas of Shintō was influenced by Buddhism. Shintō, in the process of its development as religion, advanced from the cleanness of the body to the idea of cleanness of spirit. This "internal cleanness" was expressed by moral virtues of "sincerity" and "honesty".[30] The virtues of gods of Shintō were admired through these virtues. But we can find these terms in the Buddhist sūtras. Besides, the benevolence and wisdom, admired as virtues of gods, are, of course, the Buddhist terms. Therefore, it is not too much to say that almost all of the terms of the central virtues of the Medieval Shintō were derived from Buddhist sūtras. It must be mentioned, however, that Shintoists never adopted the doctrines of Buddhism indiscriminately. Only the virtues, which had originally existed as germs in Shintō, were brought to the definite consciousness and expression by the help of Buddhist philosophy. The Shintoists did not take in the speculative, schematized and generalized classifications of virtues of the Indian Buddhism, such as the Four Noble Truths, the Eight Right Ways, the Twelve Nidānas, the Six Pāramitās. They took in the virtues straightforwardly, which were considered congenial to Shintō. Consequently, they hardly endeavored to interpret the relation between these virtues systematically and speculatively.

We have demonstrated through the process of assimilation of Buddhism that the Japanese people are inclined to give direction to their practice through very simple symbols. This tendency reappeared, it seems, in the introduction of Christianity from the period of the Civil Wars to the beginning of the Tokugawa period. The Japanese Christians devoted themselves to simple symbols of Christianity. The trampling of the holy image (*Fumi-e*) on this psychological ground served its purpose as a loyalty test at the time of the Christian Inquisition.

We may say that the religion is always simplified when it is popularized. In the West, Christianity was simplified, for example, to making the sign of cross, or to repetition of abreviated passages of Bible. Therefore, it may be said that the simplification is the phenomenon universal to popularization of all religions. The Japanese religions, however, preached that it is sufficient only to rely on simple symbolic expressions. This remarkable characteristic may correspond to the fact that Buddhism was more popularized in Japan than in other countries.

This tendency of thinking persists to this day. If we look back to the trend of Japanese thought in recent years, we can realize that the complete reliance upon simple symbols has been one of the most deep-rooted attitudes of the Japanese people.

---

1) cf. Yasusada Hiyane 比屋根安定: *Nihon Shūkyō Shi* (日本宗教史History of Japanese Religions) pp. 248 & 400.
2) Saburō Iyenaga 家永三郎: *Chūsei Bukkyō Shisō-shi Kenkyū* (中世佛教思想史研究 A Study on Buddhist Thoughts in Medieval Age) p. 42.
3) cf. *Risshō Ankokuron* 立正安國論.
4) *Kangotōroku* 漢語燈錄 vol. X. *Hokuetsu ni Ttsukawasu Sho* 遣二北越一書 (*Taishō*. vol. 83, p. 169 b).
5) Shōkaku 聖覺: *Yuishinshō* 唯信鈔 (*Taishō* vol. 83), p. 915 b.
6) *Mattōshō* 末燈鈔, last part.

7) *Kyōgyōshinshō* 教行信證 pt. 2.
8) Saburō Iyenaga: op. cit. p. 34.
9) *Ippen Shōnin Goroku* 一遍上人語錄.
10) *Rennyo Shōnin Goichidaiki Kikigaki* 蓮如上人御一代記聞書 no. 69.
11) Daijō Tokiwa 常盤大定: *Nihon no Bukkyō* (日本の佛教 Buddhism in Japan), p. 43.
12) *Shuzenji Sōden Kuketsu* 修禪寺相傳口決 vol. 1. (*Dengyō Daishi Zenshū* 傳教大師全集 vol. III, p. 666). But this book is actually not written by Saichō.
13) *Ibid.* vol. II, (*Dengyō Daishi Zenshū* vol. III p. 679)
14) Saburō Iyenaga: *op. cit.* p. 95.
15) *Gassui Gosho* 月水御書.
16) *Shōgu Mondō Shō* 聖愚問答鈔 pt. 2.
17) *Shishin Gohon Shō* 四信五品鈔.
18) cf. *Shōbōgenzō* 正法眼藏, Gyōji,b 行持下.
19) *Ibid. Bendōwa* 辦道話.
20) *Ibid.* Bukkyō 佛經.
21) *Shōbōgenzō Zuimonki* 正法眼藏隨聞記 vol. I. (p. 14).
22) *Ibid.* vol. I. (p. 20; 21).
23) *Ibid.* vol. II. (p. 41).
24) Daitō Shimaji 島地大等: *Nihonbukkyō Kyōgakushi* (日本佛教教學史 History of Buddhist Doctrine in Japan) p. 224.
25) *Ibid.* p. 366.
26) *Miroku Kōshiki* 彌勒講式 (*Taishō.* vol. 84. p. 889 a).
27) *Shaseki Shū* 沙石集 ch. 2. pt. 2.
28) Saburō Iyenaga: op. cit. p. 42.
29) *Shin Sarugaku-ki* 新猿樂記 (*Gunshoruijū* 群書類從 vol. IX. p. 348).
30) cf. supra. ch. 2, pt. 12.

(8) The lack of knowledge concerning the objective order

The Japanese people value human relations above all things and make little of objects unless they are related to the human relations. Owing to this attitude, they cannot study things enough as objectively existing things.

This tendency can be discerned in the linguistic expression of the Japanese. In the first place, the Japanese language, as already mentioned, is not adequate to exact objective statement. Of course, this does not mean that the foundation for the recognition of the objective order is totally lacking in their linguistic expression. As one of the foundations, which can be used as a basis for such cognition, we may mention the distinction between the noun and the adjective in Japanese. The ancient Indian and the Chinese language had none of such a strict distinction. Therefore, we must distinguish them through the meaning of words or through context. These languages, so far as linguistic expression is concerned, do not distinguish between the judgment of classification and judgment of attribution. In Japanese, however, the nouns which are indeclinable words, are distinguished from adjectives, which are declinable words. Therefore, we can recognize at once the distinction between the individual-substantive and the universal-attributive. On this point, it resembles the Western languages. And, like them, it attracts our attention to the order or law of the objective world of nature.

The Japanese people, however, owing to the above-mentioned characteristic way of thinking, are inclined to grasp this order or law in relation to human relations. They do not grasp it as law of objective things. This tendency has been strengthened especially through the illogical character of the Japanese language. Consequently, the thinking of the Japanese people has not been developed in objective and logical direction. Rather the direction of expression and description of individuality has been emphasized. From the oldest times, the spiritual life of the Japanese has been concentrated chiefly in moral and art, not in objective knowledge. While literature and history written in Japanese are many and excellent, the scientific books in Japanese are few. In the theoretical cognition, the Japanese people thought and wrote, mostly, in the Chinese language.

The indifference toward objective cognition is reflected in the usage of Japanese language. In the original Japanese language, there is no word that expresses the object as opposed to the subject. The word "*mono*" means the person as subject as well as the thing as object. In such a situation, it cannot be expected that the word "*shiru*" (to know) will be developed to denote the cognition of objects as existing apart from the knowing subjects. In other words, the emphasis is put rather on the understanding of inner experiences and on the mutual understanding among men, as shown by the usage of "*Nasake-o-shiru*" (to understand the feeling) and of "*Hito-to-shiri-au*" (to understand each other). It is chiefly directed toward the expression of human existence. The pure Japanese language has no word corresponding to "knowledge" or "cognition".[1] Therefore, it occurred hardly that the Japanese people attained scientific self-consciousness, that is, the perception of things as distinguished from perceiving subjects.

This characteristic appears also in the syntax. In the Indo-European languages, the subjective case of noun, in the neutral singular, takes the same form as its objective. This is explained as follows: originally, the neutral nouns were not used as subject and consequently did not have the subjective form. Then, when they came to be used as subject, the independent subjective form was not created, and the objective form was used as subject. Perhaps, in the ancient times, objective things might not be personified and consequently were not used as subject. And while the Indo-European languages passed this stage early, the Japanese language has not completely emerged from it yet. In the Japanese sentences, the subject is, in most cases, a human being or personified subject of action. And, in customary usage, the composition of the passive voice is rare, that is, the objective things or the object of action are rarely used as subject.

And the Japanese people, in general, did not give objective representation to the self as subject of action. In Japanese, "*mizukara*" (self) is not a noun, but an adverb, that is, it was not perceived as an abstract conception. The word "*onore*" (self) is often used as noun, but it is rare that it is used as subject. Therefore, the Japanese have never used words, which mean self, for example, "*ware*", "*onore*", "*mizukara*", as philosophical terms, as in the cases of the other civilized peoples. To express the self-examination common in Buddhist philosophy, they relied on the Chinese terms, such as "*ga*" or "*goga*" (吾我 self), used in the Chinese version of sūtras.

Thus, the Japanese people seldom looked squarely at the objective reality as sharply distinguished from knowing subjects. It may be called their common way of thinking. It is often said that they are practical and adept in techniques of action, but they are rather weak in the objective observation of the basis of their practical action, because they are too anxious to accomplish their action. It is partially owing to this characteristic that they have been inclined, from the oldest times, to follow foreign ideas with an uncritical mind.

Although mentioned already, it is worth while to repeat that the Japanese in general have never attained the full consciousness of the importance of reasoning. Owing to the poor development of reasoning power, they used to depend exclusively upon senses and to concern themselves only with what was passing under their eyes. Frois, who came to Japan as Christian missionary in the sixteenth century, said that the common people in Japan "will accept nothing but the concrete demonstration which can be seen by eyes and taken by hands".[2]

In the history of technology also the Japanese people have valued intuitive perception (*Kan*) more than scientific observation based on structural thinking. They were apt to rely on dexterity of artisans rather than on exact calculation by machines. For example, the proper temperature of hot water, in which a forged sword (*katana*) is immersed, is kept in absolute secrecy by swordsmiths, who cut down the arms of men who tried to steal this secret. Thus, the temperature has been transmitted from a master to a disciple, as a secret which must be understood only through intuition.

On account of these situations, the natural sciences have almost never been established on the foundation of the original Japanese thinking. Even in Japan, some pioneers were aware of this fact. For example, Shiba Kōkan said: "The people of this country don't like to investigate the laws of universe..... They are shallow-minded and short-sighted".

The natural sciences were begun in Japan only through the introduction of sciences of Holland (*Ran-gaku*). And it is said that they were not understood structurally from fundamental principles, but it was introduced rather from the standpoint of utility. Moreover, the importance of natural sciences was hardly recognized. Motoori Norinaga, admitting that "the learning of the country called Holland" was the universal science common to all countries, still asserted "the superiority of the Emperor's Land".

In Japan, the science of cognition of nature had no mathematical foundation. Fukuzawa Yukichi said, "Comparing Confucianism of the East with Civilization(ism) of the Occident, we find that two things are lacking in the East. The first is, among material things, mathematics. The second is, among immaterial things, the independent spirit". What he called "mathematics" seems to be the modern mathematical physics.[3] This characteristic, although not limited to Japan only, seems to have been rather conspicuous in the way of thinking of the Japanese people. In the Japanese of the past, they were inclined to neglect the rational perception of laws of the objective world of nature.

Generally speaking, the Japanese have never studied scientifically the language which they use everyday. Before the Restoration of Meiji, they had no system of model grammar. During the Tokugawa period, the Japanese language was not included in the curriculum. In India, the case is diametrically opposite, and the grammar was taught regularly. It seems that, in Greece and Rome, the people received the education of grammar of their own language, although in lesser degree when compared to India.

The way of thinking to acquire knowledge, not in objective order, but in human relationship can be seen in the process of introducing Indian logic. This has been discussed already. (What has been pointed out here cursorily has been admitted by many as one of the characteristics of the ways of thinking of the Japanese. However, in the process of introduction of Buddhist thought we cannot find out easily any fact which corresponds to this very feature. It seems to be due to the fact that, as Buddhist culture in China had little to do with sciences, there occurred no phenomenon of modification, when imported into Japan. The relationship between Indian Buddhism and science should be investigated independently.)

---

1) Tetsurō Watsuji 和辻哲郎: *op. cit. Zoku Nihon Seishinshi Kenkyū* pp. 411–412 & 405.

2) Frois: *Japanese History* p. 449, (Saburō Iyenaga 家永三郎: *op. cit. Chūsei Bukkyō Shisōshi Kenkyū*) p. 142.

3) Masao Maruyama 丸山眞男: *Fukuzawa ni okeru Jitsugaku no Tenkai* 福澤に於ける「實學」の轉回 (*Tōyō Bunka Kenkyū* 東洋文化研究 No. 3) p. 7.

Chapter 4. Problem of shamanism

The weakness of the critical spirit of the Japanese, as was already pointed out, allowed the continuance of old ideologies that should have been abolished or modified by radical social changes. Although we have seen many social changes in the course of history, these changes have not reached the remote villages. In out-of-the-way corners, therefore, there persist, or occasionally crop out anew the most primitive ways of living and thinking, of which Shamanism is one. As is widely recognized, in the Asiatic continent there was prevalent Shamanism. This was a religious form in which certain individuals had privileges of wielding spiritual power, and communicating with evil spirits. In terms of Shamanism, we can characterize the ancient Japanese religion also.

Before the introduction of cultures from the continent, mediums occupied the central position in the Japanese religious world. Since the mediums were always descendants of powerful gods, they could, as was generally believed, exercise evil spirits by themselves, because they had inherited divine powers. Hence these mediums, or those qualified families certain members of which could be mediums, were revered by the community. They belonged to a special, honorable class, and common people managed their affairs in accordance with oracles, or the advice of the mediums. In connection with this, we may suppose that charms and divinations, or something of the sort, were popular among the Japanese from time immemorial.

Now let us inquire into the problem what modification had Buddhism under the influence of such a peculiar religious form in the course of its introduction. Orthodox Buddhism repudiates all of these shamanistic tendencies. Early Buddhism denied the spiritual powers peculiar to the Brahmins who were in charge of exorcism and sacred rites. This ban was also placed on magic and like matters. It was, furthermore, said that one must not believe in dream-reading, palmistry, horoscopes, and divination from the cries of birds and beasts.[1] On the other hand, Buddhism could not be propagated among the lower classes of the Japanese people, which preserved, without radical changes, the old shamanistic tendency: yet, in the case of the propagation of Christianity in the Occident, the new religion brought about a great revolution in European society. In Japan, at every critical moment when the ruling classes had lost their control over the peasantry, there became influential the primitive or shamanistic trends which lay hidden from earliest times.

Let us, then, consider the problem historically. First, at the time when Buddhism was introduced into Japan, it had to have, so as to be diffused among the common people, a shamanistic character, since the shamanistic religious modes were then influential. The Ritsu sect, having preserved the manners of Conservative Buddhism, had little influence over the Japanese. The sect did not compromise met with great favor among the people, some other sects of Buddhism met with great favor among the people, because they made concessions to the shamanistic tendency to a considerable degree.

The most striking phenomenon in Buddhism as it was introduced into Japan was that there were relatively many nuns to the number of priests. This may have been due to the fact that great importance was attached to nuns, paralleling the importance of female mediums who had particular qualifications to serve the gods.[2]

As a new religion, Buddhism was compelled to meet the popular requirement that it should be effective in exorcism. The Japanese type of Buddhism was largely one of prayer and exorcism. It mainly aimed at praying for benefits and wealth in this world and the next, in the interest of the state as well as of individuals. Even the reading of sūtras was considered to have exorcistic significance. Even the most philosophic Buddhist schools could not be secure in their positions unless they compromised with this tendency. Although Ekan introduced the doctrine of the Sanron sect, members of which inferred always with extreme logical accuracy, it is said that he himself prayed for rain, on the occasion of a long drought, and when he obtained a heavy rain, Empress Suiko appreciated very much his service and appointed him a bishop. Nevertheless, the philosophic sects of Sanron and Hossō were ultimately not diffused among the Japanese. Sects which could spread all over the country had to adopt shamanistic or magical interpretations of Buddhism.

If we look at the course of the diffusion of Buddhism, we note that the new religion was, in the first place, accepted by the nobility to meet its requirements in the mid-sixth century. The nobility at that time constructed many temples for the purpose of praying for the prosperity and permanency of their aristocratic life. Prayers were addressed to Śākyamuni for recovery from sickness and long life, to Avalokiteśvara for protection from evil, and also to the other Bodhisattvas: Bhaiṣajya, Maitreya, The Four God-kings, etc. From the Suiko feriod on, there were erected many statues of Avalokiteśvara. As for sūtras, the *Suvarṇa-prabhāsa Sūtra*, the *Saddharmapundarika* or Hokke Sūtra (especially *"Avalokiteśvara Sūtra"*), *"Ninnā-prajñā-pāramitā Sūtra*, the *Bhaiṣajyaguru Sūtra*, and so on, were recited; but this was for the main purpose of supplication, for health, long life and recovery, for the sūtras were believed to be pregnant with magical power. After the centralization of political power in Japan, there was a vigorous advocacy of the principle that Buddhism should have as its object the protection of the state, the tranquility of the Imperial Court, and the wealth of the people. This was based upon the popular belief that the State should be guarded, that people's life should become easier by the miraculous virtue which might be given in reciting and copying sūtras and treating monks and nuns by dinner.

It was almost the same with the Heian period down, excepting that the esoteric school then was more popular than the earlier schools of Buddhism. About the 7th and the 8th centuries, as far as we know now, one hundred and thirty seven scriptures of esoteric teaching were imported, including such fundamental scriptures of that type as the *"Mahāvairocana-sūtra"*, the "Kongōchōkyō", the "Susiddhi-sūtra".

Apart from Buddhas, Bodhisattvas, gods and spirits mentioned in the above scriptures, there were, as objects of worship, the bodhisattvas of esoteric lineage: Kannon with Eleven Faces, Kannon with Nine Faces, Kannon with Thousand Hands, Amoghapāśa, Kannon with Horse-head.

Beautiful-sight Kannon, Vajragarbha (Bodhisattva), Peacock-King (*Mahāmāgūrī*), five powerful Bodhisattvas, and so forth. Buddhistic morality had sometimes its manifestations in the decree of liquor prohibition as well as of forbidding the taking of all animal life, but they were only under the particular circumstances of drought, deluge, indisposition of His Majesty and the other national calamities. This was, after all, *an application in the Buddhist Mould of the theocratic way of thinking* peculiar to the Japanese antiquities. Various Buddhistic services in the Court were of the same magical significance as Shintō rituals. They just bore the same meaning as the rituals of Shintō purification in their motives and purposes.

> It is noteworthy that, in Japan, the Imperial family and the nobility were in a close connection with esoteric schools. The instances that the members of the Imprial family and Court nobility became devout believers were too many to be enumerated one by one. These converts believed solely in the esoteric teaching, including not only the Shingon sect but also the Tendai sect. So many instances of the conversion of the governing class members to esoteric sects had been seen neither in India nor in China. This is a reason why we have given a guess that the shamanistic and theocratic tendencies were disguised in the Buddhistic forms of the time.

A characteristic of Japanese Buddhism, thereupon, was the overwhelming predominance of Shingon esoterics over the religious world, at least before the Restoration.[3] Unlike the other Buddhist schools, the esoteric schools are recognized as the one which deals with magic and divination forbidden by the orthodox Buddhism.[4] Although the Shingon esoterics originated in India and then was transmitted to China, there remains little trace of it in these countries, whereas in Japan remain the esoteric rituals and manners even now. The esoteric doctrine, had it taken its source in China, was so highly developed in Japan that it came to be almost a new and nearly original one as for its content. The Tendai sect, although it was in opposition to the Shingon sect, had, from the beginning, adopted the esoteric teaching,[5] whose color had grown rapidly upon the sect after Jikaku Daishi (Ennin) and Chishō Daishi (Enchin).[6] As for esoteric studies, two scholastic lineages were formed, namely— "The esoterics of the Tōji sect (*Tōmitsu*)" handed down in the Tōji Temple of the Shingon sect and "The esoterics of the Tendai sect (*Taimitsu*)" transmitted in the

Tendai sect. The former adopted the doctrine of the Kegon sect and the latter went by the doctrine of the Tendai sect.

These two lineages were divided into the legitimate line and collateral line, respectively; and furthermore, various interpretations of esoterics were given birth in each legitimate line. Shingō and Eison—these two scholars, though they had been reared in the "Tōmitsu" school, interpreted the esoterics by the idealism of the Hossō sect. Their interpretation has been called "Esoterics of the Hossō sect (*Sōmitsu*)". By the doctrine of the Kegon sect as well, Kōben (of the Kegon sect) gave a new interpretation of it, which is "the esoterics of the Kegon sect (*Gonmitsu*)". Moreover these esoteric schools exerted an influence upon the Zen sect. For example, Eisai founded "the esoterics of the Zen sect (*Zenmitsu*)" by adopting "*Taimitsu*". Benni introduced "*Tōmitsu*" into the doctrine of the Zen sect. The esoteric rituals has been held also in the Rinzai sect. Dōgen persistently repudiated all of these esoteric interpretations, but, after the time of Keizan Jōkin (the founder of Sōjiji Temple), the esoteric rituals were adopted by the Sōtō sect so that its order might be able to propagate the teaching all over the country. In general, the esoteric modifications of Zen by secret transmission became popular from the Muromachi period onwards.

At the mid-Tokugawa period, however, Hakuin inaugurated reforms in the Rinzai sect so as to eliminate the esoteric elements of the teaching. Moreover, since Menzan and Manzen of the Sōtō sect advocated returning to the spirit of Dōgen, the magical factors in the teaching have been growing weaker, yet never abolished. All things considered, the magical or esoteric factors that were in reality alien to the essence of Zen supported the Zen sect in Japan. As collateral lines of esoterics, there are two major ways of ascetic practice of "*Shugendō*", namely—Shingon Ascetic Practice on the part of "*Taimitsu*" and Tendai Ascetic Practice on the part of "*Tōmitsu*". Further, there exists in Mt. Hiei a discipline, as distinguished from the above mentioned, of pilgrimages to sacred peaks.

The Buddhism that was popular among common people took the same course of development. Everywhere various magical formulae were recited. In former days—during the reign of the Empress Kōken in the Nara period, there were constructed innumerable pagodas named as "Million Pagodas" to which printed Dhāraṇīs were consigned.[7] From the Kamakura period onwards, common people came to believe in magical formulae, to copy Dhāraṇīs and consign them to "Towers for sūtras" or "Towers for the repose of souls", which were erected on all sides at that time.[8] Especially at the very Kamakura period, *Benzaiten* (*Sarasvatī*) was evoked and deified as a god of wealth at Enoshima, Itsukushima, Chikubushima, Amakawa, Minomo, Seburiyama, and so on. "Step in once this sacred place", praised a "*Noh*" song, "and you will have inexhaustible wealth in this world, and then will you be rewarded with a secure position in the other world, from which you will never fall".[9] *Dakiniten* (*Ḍākinī*), *Daikokuten* (*Mahākāla*) and the like who are gods of wealth came to be believed in as well. And as it is well known, the phenomenon of worship for *Fudō* (*Acala*) and *Shōten* (*Gaṇeśa*) is universal even nowadays.

Thus the esoteric devotion got into the very daily life of the Japanese people. If you read some literary works before the Restoration, you will find there that the Buddhistic conceptions are mainly esoteric.

The esoteric schools had prime reference to prayers. So as to get superior effects of these prayers the ascetic disciplines in retirement in forests were required. Gyōson (1054–1135), an ascetic famous for prayer at the Heian period, "did not spend a night in his private room after he entered the priesthood, but was staying in the main building of the temple for several nights on end so as to pay homage to Maitreya.... In these days, he made his pilgrimages to all of the sacred places—the secluded places in Mt. Ōmine, Mt. Katsuragi and so forth which are famous for their esoteric effectiveness. Thus he devoted his life for more than fifty years".[10]

A striking feature of Japanese esoterics was their mystical view on the famous priest, Kūkai. Such a view had nothing with the earlier esoterics in the continent. Kūkai died at Kongō-buji Temple of Mt. Kōya in March 21st, 835 A.D. But the believers in the Shingon sect say: he just then *entered the meditation* (*samādhi*) looking for the time of the descent of Maitreya the Buddha. Kūkai did not die. He is as yet *alive*. So, at a fixed time, a properly qualified high priest comes and changes Kūkai's gown in the inner sanctuary, where Kūkai is supposed to be still staying in meditation. What is the condition of Kūkai the great teacher of Buddhism now? It is a great secret that laity should not talk about.

Since such a mystic view has not been maintained but in Japan, we cannot help thinking that it sprang solely from the way of thinking peculiar to the Japanese people that has made much of magical conceptions and the spiritual prestige of particular individuals, to which we will refer later on.

In looking over the "Kamakura Buddhism", we find in the first place that the doctrine of Nichiren preserved the most of former Buddhistic elements. Though he persistently denounced the Shingon esoterics, his teaching was much the same as it, as far as the aim of prayers was concerned. He placed great emphasis upon the superiority of prayers in terms of the Hokke sūtra over those in the other sects.[11] "If all the people only recite 'Homage to the Sūtra of the Lotus of the Good Law' in chorus", he said, "They will see that branches won't sway about to the wind and clouds won't fall to pieces in rain. Then it will be a return to the Golden Age. There will be revealed the Cause of immortality of man and thing. Moreover, thanks to a promise of 'peace and tranquility in this life', they will escape an accursed misfortune and get a means of longevity".[12]

Such a thought of his had something with the very Sūtra itself that promoted the esoterical ideas like this in its every page. This fact enabled the doctrine of Nichiren to be easily disseminated among the people having the shamanistic thinking habit. There are much controversies among Nichiren's followers on the significance of prayers in his doctrine, but, in reality, many of them prayed, being fascinated by the self-suggestive behavior in repetitive reciting of "Adoration to the Lotus Sūtra". Besides, Nichiren identified himself with Viśiṣṭa-cāritra Bodhisattva predicated in the Hokke Sūtra. This daring claim was likely to have been founded upon the Japanese way of thinking to recognize willingly spiritual prestige in particular individuals. Moreover, when we consider that there is any trace neither in Indian nor in Chinese Buddhism of such a religious custom as to recite in chorus or demonstrate beating fan-shaped drums, we are compelled to suppose some impact of Shamanism on the doctrine of Nichiren.

In the continent the Zen sect approved no prayer from the beginning. In Japan, either, for some time after its introduction there was no prayer, except particular cases. Rankei Dōryū, Gottan Funei, Daikyū Shōnen, and Shigen Sogen offered scarcely any prayers, to say nothing of Dōgen. Even their patrons never forced upon the Zen priests to pray for any benefit, before the reign of Hōjō Tokiyori and Tokimune. This tradition, however, was broken down by the Japanese thinking habit to seek help through prayers. In the meanwhile, the Zen sect of Eisai and his lineage came to have strong coloring of esoterics including prayer. From the time of Hōjō Tokimune onwards, the nobility, patrons of Zen sect, assailed priests with demands for prayers, whenever they worried themselves even over the trivialities. Thus the temples of Zen sect were going to be a sort of seminary of prayers.[13] Dōgen, the introducer of the Sōtō sect, having repudiated magic or exorcism, could hardly be supported by the generality; whereas, after his death, the order of the sect became influential all over the country. This sudden change can solely be explained from the fact that Keizan Jōkin, his spiritual descendent, adopted the esoteric ceremonies.

The Pure Land (Jōdo) teaching, as opposed to the other sects, denounced magic or exorcism originally, asserting that looking to such magical resources was against the original vow of Amitābha Buddha. There is nevertheless no denying that the Japanese teaching of Pure Land had some coloring of magical practice. We have already pointed out that the Chinese teaching itself was likely to be partly esoteric in later periods, because the calling of its principal idol was "Amida", which was an exotic and incomprehensive sound-copy of the original symbol "Amitābha", instead of the "Buddha of Eternal Life", a Chinese word, which would have been much easier to be comprehended by the Chinese.

This trend was carried over into the Japanese teaching of Buddhism. For example, the "*Nembutsu*" (to praise the Name of Amitābha), prevalent among the Japanese common people, was noticeably shamanistic. At the mid-Heian period, Saint Kūya initiated the '*Odori-Nembutsu*', that was dancing to the drum or gong on the street in reciting "*Nembutsu*" or hymns in Japanese. The practice enjoyed general popularity at that time. By the power of "*Nembutsu*", it is said, Kūya conquered venomous serpents and beasts and repulsed robbers. And this was widely applauded by the people at large.[14] As evidenced in the writings of Fujiwara Kanezane, it was also because of magical powers that Hōnen had Fujiwara Kanezane converted to his sect.[15]

Jōdo sect, founded by Hōnen, came of itself to have esoteric coloring afterwards. Shōgei, the real founder of Jōdo sect in Kantō Area, worked mysteries named "mysteries to be initiated through fivefold means". Even nowadays the priests of Jōdo sect recite their hymns in Sanskrit, saying "the principal magical prayer of Amitābha Tathāgāta". This is the same as that used in the Shingon sect. This enigmatic formula transmitted in unintelligible transcription alone runs as follows when translated into our language: I will devote my life to Buddha, Law, and Order. I will devote my life to the Holy Tathāgāta of Eternal Life, the honorable Enlightened One. Om, the Immortal, the Immortal Life, the Immortal

Appearance, the Immortal Mother's Womb, the Immortal Power' ". After this enumeration, it concludes with the prayer: "Perish all of Karmas one by one, *svāhā*". This certainly is a magical formula. Aside from the original vow of the teaching, the sect has been considerably esoteric as it has been practised.

At the Kamakura period there was another promote rof *'Odori-Nembutsu'* (Invocation to Amitābha in Dancing). It was Saint Ippen, the founder of Ji sect. *"The Mirror of Nomori"* referred to him as follows: A priest, named Ippen, misunderstood the doctrine of *Nembutsu*, taking "dancing-ecstasy" for the high command to dance. The orthodox performance of *Nembutsu* lay for him in dancing and keeping time with the hands and feet. Furthermore, inspired by the utterance to the effect that a simple mind will enter easily the Pure Land of Amitābha, he became naked and had not a stitch of clothing upon his body pretending that one should reject any artificiality. Just like a crazy one he condemned anyone he ever hated. And yet all people, high and low, strove to be the foremost of his audience and were loud in praise of his conduct like a prosperous market.

Although the episode remains to be confirmed, there may be no room for doubt that *'Odori-Nembutsu'* was popular with the contemporaries. Down at the Tokugawa Shogunate a religious custom of bowl-beating remained yet to be in practice. Now we have to remember that "Shaman" which the word 'Shamanism' derived from means a skipping man. We shall, then, be justified in saying that it was into such an *'Odori-Nembutsu'* that the teaching of Pure Land was modified in terms of Shamanism in Japan.

Against the shamanistic or magical tendencies a gallant resistance was put up by the Jōdo-shin sect. It stood by its view that no permission should be given to look to exorcism or prayers and to choose a lucky day or lucky star.[16)] Nevertheless, another form of Shamanism was sought for by its believers. (The most outstanding group of them was *Hijihōmon* especially *Okura-monto*, of Jōdo-shin sect.) *"Odori-Nembutsu"* was sometimes performed by a part of the believers, in spite of a strict decree against it. There appeared, at the Ashikaga period, such a heretic view as that praying to Amitābha would cure any disease. It was in the same line of mystical thinking as the custom of drinking water of the Pope's bath-tub.

To recognize magical power in human voice is common to primitive people. The Indian Buddhism, especially its esoterics of the seventh and eighth centuries onwards, developed a similar thinking. But, in Japan, all of religious sects have been unwittingly governed by this magical thinking.

The Japanese have been disposed to regard funeral services as of great importance from the oldest times, and nowadays a funeral is of important significance to Buddhism itself. The Japanese funeral was a surprise to the Europeans who came over at the beginning of Modern Ages. Yet, in the time of original Buddhism, monks were never in charge of any funeral for the secular devotees. Buddhists in India expected no salvation of the dead from funeral services, which were to be held by Brāhmins. It was a common attitude of the leaders of the original Buddhism to "jeer and scoff at the magical formulae recited by Brāhmins".[17] (The Scripture of original Buddhism tells us that the Buddha himself forbade monks to participate in a funeral. Another resource says that one would go to Heaven after his death, thanks, not to a funeral, but to his virtue. At any rate, monks did not want to bother about such secular ceremony as funeral services.

And yet, as times went on after the in of Buddhism into Japan, Buddhism was believed by the generality, on account of its metaphysical character, to have a bearing upon the phenomenon of death, and have some influence on the repose of souls. Then at some date after the Heian period appeared some clergymen who took charge of funeral services for secular persons, so as to ameliorate the financial conditions of temples. Finally, the Tokugawa Shogunate bound all the people to Buddhist temples so that people might keep strictly the decree of the Prohibition of Christianity. As a consequence, every person has had a connection with the Buddhist temple, and that connection has been chiefly through funeral services. Thus a funeral comes to be taken for one of the most important Buddhist ceremonies nowadays. (The great temples in Nara, however, stick to the old Buddhist tradition, and do not participate in funerals even at present. It is the same with great Chinese temples.) So it may be a bitter irony that the real Buddhist circles in Japan count as the most essential social function of themselves what the monks of original Buddhism jeered at as nonsense. [Such a change may have occurred to other world-religions also. It requires further comparative studies.]

But, in fact, it is meeting the requirements of the generality. The Japanese people herein enjoy magical effects of Buddhism as well. These effects are produced by reciting the sūtras in melodious classical Chinese, the meaning of which common people can not understang. Not only the Indians but also the Chinese were able to understand the import of sūtras in their mother tongue. In Japan, however, the classical Chinese foreign to the Japanese does not convey any meaning except to learned persons. Yet in actual Buddhist services the long words of classical Chinese fascinate all the attendants by sheer melodiousness without allowing them any understanding.

The last question to be asked is whether or not there is any relation between Shamanism and Confucianism in Japan. The Japanese did not always adopt Chinese thoughts as they were. The time-honored religious modes in Japan repudiated not only the idea to change dynasty, but also the Chinese manners of religious service and the ideas of gods, including the supreme Heaven. They, however, were noticed to have some affinities with the trichotomy of the divine (God of Heaven, gods of earth and ghosts of men) in the *Chou Li,* and with the differentiation between prayer and retribution in the *Li Chi* (the Book of Rituals). Especially the this-worldly character of Confucianism based upon the family system met with the favor of the Japanese people.[18)]

The greatest foe, however, of Confucianism was the shamanistic tendency in Japan. Confucianists, although they originally denounced magic or exorcism, could not reject wholly the Japanese thinking habit oriented towards Shamanism. Some of the Japanese Confucian scholars, for example Ogiu Sorai, modified considerably the fundamental attitude of Confucius to keep silent about supernatural gods, when Ogiu said, "There is evidence for that Confucius himself approved the existence of spiritual beings. So, whoever denies the spiritual beings does not believe in Confucius".[19)] We, however, find in *the Analects of Confucius* a sentence as follows: "the subjects on which the Master did not talk, were extraordinary things, feats of strength, disorder, and spiritual beings". According to the interpretation of the Chinese scholar, it means that Confucius did not talk on any phenomenon beyond our sensory perception. But Ogiu explained the same sentence as follows: "Confucius, though a saint, was a man as well. Presumably he could not help being interested in ghost-tales. Indeed, in every-day talks, he must have referred, from time to time, to the existence of ghosts. But, as a precept, he did not encourage such a reference".[20)]

As for studies of Chinese classics, more energy was devoted to the study of the Books of Changes than to the study of the Books of Rituals. This may have some connection with the above-mentioned tendency.

From the Heian period onwards, not only Buddhism but Shintō adopted the Chinese Dualism or the Principle of positive and negative. It was a magical teaching by which one could master the art of divination, hydromancy, anthroposcopy, astrology, etc. It had a doctrine of the positive and the negative, and also of the five elements. In China, the teaching, having deified "T'ien-i", "T'ai-po", "God of Mt. T'aishan" and so forth, held the fetes of "One's Star", "Fatal Destiny", "Three Cycles", and, at the same time, was in charge of magical practice. The Chinese Dualism, though a magical teaching, had a theoretical construction, nevertheless: Having been introduced into Japan, however, the teaching lost its coherent doctrine of the positive and the negative. With no reference to doctrinal consideration, many Japanese, high and low, monastic and secular, believed in the magical teaching.[21] The Chinese Dualism, then, was nothing but a superstition in Japan. And yet its influence upon Japanese customs can still be discerned in the popular belief in fatalism as well as in the habit of avoiding an ominous direction.

Hence, upon Chinese thoughts also, we recognize the impact of Shamanism, though not so strong as the one upon Buddhism which we have fully discussed already.

Such shamanistic or magical tendencies will, with the course of diffusion of scientific knowledge, disappear sooner or later. Full investigation, however, is required by the problematic situation of the post-war period in which heretic religions of this sort have been growing.

---

1) e.g. *Suttanipāta*, 927.
2) Ryōnin Sekiguchi 關口亮仁: *Waga Kuni ni Okeru Bukkyō-Juyō ni tsuiteno ichi Kōsatsu* (我國に於ける佛教受容についての一考察 "An Observation on the Introduction of Buddhism into Japan"), in the quarterly *Shūkyō Kenkyū* 宗教研究, vol. IV, No. 1, p. 210 ff.
3) "The practice of Shingon and Tendai are fittest for Japan". (*Keiranshūyōshū* 溪嵐拾葉集, vol. 9 (*Taishō*. vol. 76, p. 539)).
4) cf. *Shugenshiyōben* 修驗指要辯 (*Nihon Daizōkyō* 日本大藏經 *Shugendō Shōsho* 修驗道章疏 vol. III), p. 7.
5) Dengyō Daishi himself introduced Esoteric Buddhism. *Daitō Shimaji* 島地大等: *Tendai Kyōgakushi* (天台教學史 History of Tendai Doctrine) p. 260 f.
6) *Ibid.* p. 345.
7) Some of them have been preserved in the Hōryūji Temple.
8) Taijo Tamamuro 圭室諦成: *Nihon Bukkyōshi Gaisetsu* 日本佛教史概說, pp. 278, 279.
9) *Yōkyoku* 謠曲, Enoshima 江島.
10) *Kokonchomonshū* 古今著聞集.
11) cf. *Kitōshō* 祈禱鈔.

12) *Nyosetsu-shugyōshō* 如說修行鈔.
13) Taijō Tamamuro: op. cit. p. 192.
14) *Eulogy to Kūya*, in *Zoku Gunshoruijū* 續群書類從, vol. VIII.
15) Tokujō Ōya 大屋德城: Some doubts on Fujiwara Kanezane's Faith and *Jūnen-gokuraku-iōshū*, *Shirin* 史林, vol. IX, No. 1, p. 26.
16) This purport is expressed in the chapter Hōben-keshin-do of Shinran's *Kyōgyōshinshō*. Shundai Dazai said to the same effect. (*Seigaku Mondō* 聖學問答, in *Nihon Rinri Ihen* 日本倫理彙編 compiled by Tetsujirō Inouye 井上哲次郎 and Yoshimaru Kaniye 蟹江義丸 vol. VI, p. 292.)
17) *Saṃyutta-nikāya*, ed. by the Pali Text Society, London, vol. IV, p. 118.
18) Naoichi Miyaji 宮地直一: *Jingishi Taikei* 神祇史大系, p. 37.
19) *Benmei* 辨名 pt. 2., in *Nihon Rinri Ihen*, vol. VI, p. 84.
20) Kōjirō Yoshikawa 吉川幸次郎: *op. cit. Shinajin no Koten to sono Seikatsu* 支那人の古典とその生活 p. 156.
21) Rei Saitō 齊藤勵: *Ōchō-jidai no Onmyōdō* 王朝時代の陰陽道 p. 39.

Chapter 5. The acceptance of actuality

(1) Apprehension of the absolute in the phenomenal world

In the first place, we should notice that the Japanese reveal, just in the act of the grasp of the Absolute, the attitude to lay a greater emphasis upon the intuitive sensible concrete rather than universals and the attitude to lay an emphasis upon the fluid, incipient character of the events. This way of thinking may come to regard the phenomenal world itself as the Absolute and to reject the recognition of the Absolute existing over and above the phenomenal world. What is widely known among post-Meiji philosophers as the "theory that the phenomenal is actually the real" has a deep root in Japanese tradition.

It was characteristic of the religious views of the ancient Japanese that they believed spirits to reside in all kinds of things. They personified all kinds of spirits other than those of human beings, concerning them all as ancestral gods, tending to view every spirit as noumenon of gods. It is such a turn of thought that gave birth to the Shintō shrines, for in order to perform religious ceremonies the gods and spirits were fixed in certain specified places. The most primitive form of this practice consists in the invocation and worship of spirits in some specific natural object, e.g., mountain, river, forest, tree, or stone. Forms of worship of ancient times were generally of this character. Herein, also lies the original significance of the "divine hedge" and "rock boundary". Even to this day there remain shrines that are merely of this type.[1]

This way of thinking is what runs through the subsequent history of Shintoism down to this day. "Nowhere is a shadow in which a god does not reside. Peaks, ridges, pines, cryptomerias, mountains, rivers, seas, villages, plains, and fields, everywhere there is a god. We can receive the constant and intimate help of these spirits in our tasks, many courtiers are passing".[2] Senge Takasumi, the priest of the Shintoism of the great shrine of the Izumo with such a pantheistic point of view, praised as follows: "There is not a direction in which a god does not reside, even in the wild waves' eight hundred folds or in the wild mountain's bosom".[3]

Buddhist philosophy likewise was received and assimilated on the basis of this way of thinking. To begin with, the Tendai sect in Japan is not the same as in China. The Tendai scholars in medieval Japan, using the same nomenclature as that used in the continental Buddhism, arrived at a system of thought that is distinctly original. This is what is called *Honkaku Hōmon* which asserts that the aspects of the phenomenal world are the Buddha. The world *Honkaku* or Enlightenment appears in the Chinese translation of the *Mahāyāna-śraddhotpāda-śāstra* (*Daijyōkishin-ron*) which was originally composed in India. In the continent, this word meant the ultimate comprehension of what is beyond the phenomenal world, whereas in Japan the same word was brought down to refer to what is within the phenomenal world. In this way, the characteristic feature of the Tendai Buddhism in Japan consists in their laying an emphasis upon things rather than principles. The Japanese Tendai scholars were not very faithful to the original texts in the Chinese Tendai. They sometimes interpreted the original texts in rather unnatural way, their interpretation being based upon the standpoint of the Phenomenal Absolute.[4]

It is natural that the Nichiren sect, which is an outgrowth of the Japanese Tendai, also lays an emphasis upon such a turn of thought, Nichiren asserts that the crux of Buddha's thought is revealed in the *Jyuryōbon* chapter (Duration of Life of the Tathāgata) of the Hokke Sūtra, saying, "In the earlier half of the whole sūtra, the ten directions are called the pure land and this place the soiled land, while, (in this Jyuryōbon part), on the contrary, this place is called the main land and the pure land in the ten directions the soiled land where Buddha has made an incarnation".[5] The Nichiren sect states that, while the Tendai sect from China onward takes the standpoint of "Action according to principles", Nichiren emphasized "Action according to things".

The way of thinking that seeks for the Absolute in the Phenomenal World plays an effective role in the assimilation of Zen sect as well. The Zen Buddhism in Dōgen seems to have been influenced by the Japanese Tendai Buddhism. This fact has often been alluded to by the specialists but has not been fully explored. Here I shall point out a few examples which reveal the above-mentioned way of thinking. The Chinese translated "*dharmatā*"[6] in Sanskrit as "the real aspect of all things". This concept refers to the real aspect of all kinds of phenomena in our experience, and, therefore, is composed of two distinct, contradictory elements, "All things" and "the real aspect". But, the Tendai Buddhism, gave this phrase an interpretation of "All things are the real aspect" and took the view-point that the phenomena are the reality. Dōgen gave a different twist to this interpretation and emphasized that "the real aspect is all things". He means to say that the truth which people search for is, in reality, nothing but the real world of our daily experience. Thus he says, "The real aspect is all things. All things are this aspect, this character, this body, this mind, this world, this wind and this rain, this sequence of daily going, living, sitting, and lying down, this series of melancholy, joy, action, and inaction, this stick and wand, this Buddha's smile, this transmission and reception of the doctrine, this study and practice, this evergreen pine and ever unbreakable bamboo".[7]

When one asserts "all things are the real aspect", the predicate being of a larger denotation, the real aspect seems to contain something other than all things. But in the expression "the real aspect are all things", the meaning is that there is nothing that is not exposed to us.[8] For Dōgen, therefore, the fluid aspects of impermanence is in itself the absolute state. The changeable character of the phenomenal world is of absolute significance for Dōgen. "Impermanence is the Buddhahood....[9] The impermanence of grass, trees, and forests is verily the Buddhahood. The impermanence of the person's body and mind is verily the Buddhahood. The impermanence of the (land) country and scenery is verily the Buddhahood". (*Syōbōgenzō*)[10] In other places, Dōgen says, "Death and life are the very life of the Buddha", and "These mountains, rivers, and earth are all the sea of the Buddhahood". In the Hokke Sūtra also Dōgen finds the same vein of thought. "Of the Hokke Sūtra.—The cry of a monkey is drowned in the sound of the rapid river. These are preaching this sūtra, this above all. He who attains the purport of this sūtra will discern the preaching of the doctrine in the voices on the auction sale in the mundane world and to change the line our Buddha's voice and form in all the sounds of the rapid river and colors of the ridge". (*Sanshō-Dōei*)

The same vein of thought is found in the Chinese poet Ssu Tung-p'o's poem: "The voice of the rapid is verily the wide long tongue (of the Buddha). The color of the mountains is no other than the pure chaste body. At night we have perceived eighty four thousand verses (of the sermon in natural phenomena). How should they be later revealed to other people?" This way of thinking is generally found in the Japanese Zen Buddhism. In the words of Mujū, "Mountains, rivers, earth, there is not a thing that is not the reality".[11)]

Starting from such a view-point, Dōgen gives some phrases of the Buddhist scripture interpretations that are distinctly different from the original meaning. There is a phrase in the *Mahāparinirvāṇa sūtra*[12)] that should be interpreted as "He who desires to know the meaning of the Buddhahood should survey the opportunity and conditions and wait for the opportunity to come. If the opportunity comes, the Buddhahood will be revealed of itself". Thus Buddhahood is here regarded as something possible and potential. To this concept, Dōgen gives a twist, and reads the phrase "survey the opportunity and conditions" as "makes a survey in terms of opportunity and conditions" and the phrase "if the opportunity comes" as "the opportunity has already come". His interpretation of the original passage becomes, in this way, something like the following. "Buddhahood is time. He who wants to know Buddhahood may know it by knowing time as it is revealed to us. And as time is something that has already arrived to us, Buddhahood also is not something that is to be sought in the future but is something that is realized where we are".[13)]

In such a way, Dōgen makes an effort to free himself from the idealistic viewpoint held by some Mahāyāna Buddhists of India. In the Chinese *Avataṃsaka-sūtra,* there is a phrase, "In all the three Worlds there is only this one mind".[14)] The original Sanskrit text is as follows: "All that belongs to these, three worlds is only mind. What the Buddha discriminatingly talked of as the Twelve Existence-Relations depends, in reality, solely upon the mind".[15)] But Dōgen in Japan states that the meaning of a "in the three worlds only mind",[16)] should be interpreted as "these three worlds are as they are regarded". He explicitly rejects its idealistic interpretation and asserts that "it is not that the three worlds are verily the mind". In another place, he makes a comment that, the mind and its object, which stand in an inseparable relation, may not be conceived in hierarchical terms as one subordinating the other. "The mind rightly interpreted is the one mind which is all things and all things which are the one mind".[17] And in another place, Dōgen says, "There is not the one mind apart from all things, and there are not all things apart from the one mind".[18]

Dōgen is critical of the Zen Buddhism of China. He chooses from the Chinese Zen Buddhism only those elements which he thinks fit for his own standpoint.

In the words of a Chinese Zen Buddhist, Yao-shan (751–834) there appears the phrase "at a certain time". Dōgen interprets this phrase unjustifiably as "Being time" and comments as follows: "So-called 'Being Time' means that time already is being and all being is time".[19] Taking this opportunity, Dōgen goes on to his unique philosophy of time. According to his philosophy, the every changing, incessant, flow of time is the ultimate Being.

Again and again Dogen emphasizes that the true reality is not something static but something dynamic. "It is a heretical doctrine", Dogen says, "to think the mind mobile and the essence sedate. It is a heretical doctrine to think that the essence is crystal clear and the appearance changeable".[20] Or again "It is a heretical doctrine to think that in essence water does not run, and the tree does not pass through viscissitude. The Buddha's way consists in the form as it is and the state as it is. The bloom of flowers and the fall of leaves are the state as it is. And yet unwise people think that in the world of essence there should be no bloom of flowers and no fall of leaves".[21]

Dōgen criticizes the Chinese Zen Buddhist Ta-hui who taught that both the mind and essence are over and above birth. According to him, Ta-hui wrongly taught that "the mind is solely perception and conceptualization, and the essence is pure and tranquil".[22] Here is revealed contrast between the static way of thinking in the Chinese and the dynamic way of thinking in the Japanese. Dōgen rejects the viewpoint of the *Vimalakīrti-sūtra.*

The *Vimalakīrti-sūtra* is the scripture regarded as especially important in China and Japan, nevertheless Dōgen has quite a low opinion of the significance of the silence of Vimalakīrti, which generally is highly commended.

"The reason why in Vimalakīrti there have not yet been found the light and merit is because he has not entered priesthood. Should he enter priesthood, he would have the merit. The masters of Zen of the T'ang and Sung periods not having mastered the doctrine of their sect, indiscriminately recommended Vimalakīrti, whom they considered to be good in action and good in speech. They are a despicable lot, not knowing the spoken teachings of the Buddha and being ignorant of the discipline of the Buddha. Among them there are even many of those who misconceive that the ways of Vimalakīrti and the Buddha are identical. They know neither the doctrine of the Buddha, nor the way of the founder, nor do they even know or estimate Vimalakīrti. They say that Vimalakīrti's silent revelation to Bodhisattvas is identical with the silent dispositions of the Tathāgata. This proves that they do not at all know the doctrine of the Buddha and they are not competent in practice .... The silence of the Tathāgata and the silence of Vimalakīrti are beyond comparison". According to him mere silence or a mere expression of negation does not stand for any ultimate significance.

"Evil men mostly think that speech and action are temporary things which have been set up by illusions, while silence and non-action are the truth. That is not the doctrine of the Buddha. That is what is conceived by those who have heard by hearsay the teachings of the scriptures of Brahma-deva and Īśvara-deva".[23)]

The negative and static character of Indian philosophy in general is rejected here. Consequently, the Buddhism preached by Dōgen is rather somewhat different in its content from what was emphasized by the Indian Buddhists in general or by the Chinese Zen sects in general.

The inclination to live contentedly in this given phenomenal world appears also in the modern sectarian Shintoism. The founder of the Konkō sect, for instance, teaches, "whether alive or dead, you should regard the heaven and earth as your own habitation".[24)] Itō Jinsai criticizes and metamorphoses the Chinese Confucianism just in the same way as Dōgen criticizes the Chinese Zen sect and changes the form of (or emphasizes some particular ideas of) Zen thought. Jinsai regards the heaven and earth as the evolvement of a great activity, where nothing but development exists, *and completely denies what is called death.*

" '*The Book of Change*' says 'The great virtue of the heaven and earth is called life'. It means that living without ceasing is nothing but the way of the heaven and earth. And in the way of the heaven and earth there is no death but life, there is no divergence but convergence. Death is the end of life, and divergence is the termination of convergence. That is because the way of the heaven and earth is one with life. Though the bodies of ancestors may perish, their spirits are inherited by their posterity, whose spirits are again inherited by their own posterity. When life thus evolves, without ceasing, into eternity, it may rightly be said that no one dies".[25]

According to him the world of reality is nothing but action, and action is in itself good.

"Between the heaven and earth there is only one reason: motion without stillness, good without evil. Stillness is the end of motion, while evil is the change of good; and good is a kind of life, while evil is a kind of death. It is not that these two opposites are generated together, but they are all one with life".[26]

Ogiu Sorai, a worthy rival as he was to Itō Jinsai, admires Jinsai's activism as "the supreme knowledge of a thousand years". He also rejects and denounces the static character of the doctrine of Chu-tsu. Most of the Japanese Confucianist scholars, even when they follow the doctrines of Chu-tsu, never choose the dualism of reason and atmosphere. All of the characteristically Japanese scholars believe in the atmosphere as the fundamental mode of existence. They unanimously reject the quietism of the Confucianists of the Sung period.[27]

The way of thinking that recognizes the absolute significance in the phenomenal world seems to be historico-genetically oriented by the Japanese attitude of love of nature. The Japanese in general loved rivers, mountains, grass and trees, and longed for nature.[28] The Japanese adore flowers, birds, grass and trees for the patterns of their *kimono*, and they are fond of the delicacies of the season, keeping their natural forms as much as possible in cooking. Within the house, flowers arranged in a vase and dwarf trees are places on the alcove, flowers and birds are engraved in the transom, simple flowers and birds are also painted on the sliding screen, and in the garden they have miniature mountains built and water drawn. The literature is also closely tied up with the warm affection toward nature. "*Makura no Sōshi*" begins with the general remarks about the four seasons and then goes into the description of the scenic beauties of the seasons and human affairs.

Of essays of this kind there are many. If the poems on nature should be set aside from among the collections of Japanese poems, how many pieces would there be left? Seventeen-syllable-shorter-poems cannot even be thought of, should they be dissociated from objects of nature.

The love of nature, in the case of the Japanese, is tied up with the tendencies of the love of minute things and of the esteem for delicate things. Contrast the Japanese love of individual flowers, birds, grass and trees with the British enjoyment of the spacious view of the sea and the countryside and their preference of dogs and cats among domestic animals.[29] Such a contrast seems to be originated from their respective national traits.

The Japanese have been lovers of natural beauties since ancient days. Occasionally they sing songs in praise of grand scenic beauties. But even then the grandeur of the scenery is reduced to its miniature form. To illustrate:

"When going forth I look for from the Shore of Tago,
How white and glittering is
The lofty Peak of Fuji,
Crowned with snows!"[30]
"As the tide flows into Waka Bay,
The cranes, with the lagoons lost in flood,
Go crying towards the reedy shore".[31]

They enjoy nature as it is reflected in their narrow and compact confines of vision, which is particularly evident in the following poem.

"In my garden fall the plum-blossoms—
Are they indeed snow-flakes
Whirling from the sky,"[32]
"The nightingale sings
Playing at the lower branches
Of the plum-tree of my garden,
Lamenting the fall of the plum-blossoms".[33]

In this respect the Japanese love of nature somewhat differs from the Chinese attachment to the rivers and mountains. This point may be best illustrated by the comparison of the following two poems. Dōgen writes:

"Flowers are in Spring, Cuckoos in Summer,
In Autumn is the moon, and in Winter,
The pallid glimmer of snow".

The meaning of the above poem coincides with what is intended by the Chinese verse of "*Wu-men-kuan*" (by Wu-men Hui-k'ai).

"A hundred flowers are in Spring, in Autumn is the moon,
In Summer is the cool wind, the snow is in Winter;
If nothing is on mind to afflict a man,
The best season that is for the man".

In the latter the "cuckoos" in the former is replaced by the "cool wind", which gives an entirely different effect. The cool wind and cuckoos are both sensible objects, but while the former gives the sense of unlimitedness and boundlessness, the latter gives a limited and cosy impression.

Such a characteristically Japanese element is still better exemplified by Ryōkan, who composed the following poem on his death-bed.

"For a memento of my existence
What shall I leave, (I need not leave anything)
Flowers in the spring, cuckoos in the summer,
and maple-leaves
in the autumn"

"maple-leaves" are felt to be far closer to ourselves in distance than "the moon". Herein we recognize the difference, amidst the similarity of the love of nature, between the Chinese preference of the boundless and distant and the Japanese preference of the simple and compact.

The Japanese garden typically exemplifies the Japanese attitude of expressing the natural scenery in a miniature scale. In this respect, the Indians are quite different. They too love nature and construct gardens (udyāna, ārāma), where they plant grass and trees and lay out wells and springs, but they never try *to imitate natural rivers and mountains on the smaller scale.*

The tender love of animals traditionally runs in the vein of the Japanese, but that love is concentrated on minute lovable living things.

"A copper pheasant warbles out.
Listening to its voice I thought,
Could it be the father calling?
Could it be the mother calling?"

To bring up the "copper pheasant" is very Japanese. In contrast, the peoples of India and the South-Asiatic countries are fond of such a phantastic story as to abandon oneself to a hungry tiger who attacks one. But such a story, an expression of benevolence toward living things as it is, is not quite congenial to the poetic sentiments of the Japanese, although both peoples wanted to express the idea of benevolence towards living beings.

The Indian ascetics also composed poems in praise of nature. They enjoy and extol nature as the sanctury beyond human attachments, afflictions and bondages. In their case, nature is conceived to be something opposed and *negative* to human elements.

"Before and behind, if there be none but oneself,
That is a great tranquility for the lone dweller of the wood.

Let me now go to the forest commended by the Buddha,
Since such is the place where solitary single-minded
Ascetics take their delight.
Let me clean my arms and legs
And go alone and return alone to and from
The cool forest in full-bloom
And the chilly cavern of the mountain,
When the breeze is cool and fragrant,
Sitting on the top of the mount, ignorance I shall annihilate.
At the chilly mountain slope, within the blossom-covered forest,
Let me enjoy the tranquility of deliverance
And take delight in it".[34]

In the case of the Japanese, however, priests and laymen alike are attached to nature which is but one with human beings and enjoy that attachment to their hearts' content. Even when they sit on stones under trees for the purpose of getting away from the afflictions of the mind and body, once they find flowers they enjoy and take delight in the flowers.

"Making the shades of trees
My dwelling-place,
A flower-gazer
I naturally become".[35]

Even Dogen, who took a Spartan attitude toward human desires, had a tender heart for natural beauties.

"The peach blossoms begin
To bloom in the breeze of the Spring;
Not a shadow of doubt
On the branches and leaves is left".
"Though I know that I shall meet
The autumnal moon again,
How sleepless I remain,
On this moon-lit night".

The Japanese esteem the sensible beauties of nature, wherein they seek the revelations of the absolute world.

"Cherry-blossoms, falling in vain,
Remind me of the Treasure-plants,
That adorn the paradise".[36]

There is no inkling of a view that regards the natural world as cursed or gruesome. Dōgen says: "There are many thousands of worlds comparable to the sūtras within a single spade of dust. Within a single dust there are innumerable Buddhas. A single stalk of grass and a single tree are both the mind and body (of us and Buddhas)".[37]

Relevant to such an idea was the conception prevalent in the Medieval Japan that even the grass and the tree are spirited and consequently they are eligible for being saved. The idea that even the things of "no-heart" (the objects of nature that have no spirits) can become Buddhas, based upon the Tendai doctrines, was particularly emphasized in Japan. This constituted an important theme for study in the Japanese Tendai sect, and the idea was inherited also by the Nichiren sect.[38] Nichiren sought the superiority of the Hokke Sūtra in its recognition of the eligibility of the grass the the trees to become Buddhas. There appears time and again among the Japanese Buddhist writings the following stanza: "When a Buddha, who has attained enlightenment, looks around the universe, the grass, trees and lands, all become Buddhas".[39] In 'Noh" songs we often come across such an idea which was taken for granted socially and religiously in those days. "The voice of Buddhahood of such a holy priest makes even the grass and trees predestined to become Buddhas. .... Even the grass and trees have attained the effect of becoming Buddhas, being led by the power that mankind are bound to be reborn into the Pure Land only if they invoke the Buddha's name and practice *nembutsu* prayer. .... Had it not been for the teachings of Buddhahood, the spirit of the decayed willow-tree which is impermanent and soulless would not have attained the Buddhahood". ("*Yugyō Yanagi*") The "Noh" song, "*Kochō*" (Butterflies) relates the story of an insect becoming a Buddha owing to the power of the Hokke Sūtra; "*Kakitsubata*" (Iris), "*Yugyō Zakura*", (The Cherry-tree of the Itinerant) "*Fuji*" (The Wisterian), and "Bashō" (The Banana-tree) describe the grass and trees becoming Buddhas; and "*Sesshō Seki*" (The Stone Destroying Life) is about the stone becoming a Buddha by being given a holy robe and bowl. More recently, a *jōruri* (a balled-drama) called "*Sanjūsangendō Munagi no Yurai*" has for its main theme a story of a willow-tree becoming a Buddha, based upon the religious faith of the Jōdo-shin sect.

"The Honganji Temple flourishes in the age of corruption,
The Tradition of Amitābha allows no regression;
The last effect of Buddhism is bound to last
For the coming five hundred years,
The grass, trees and lands all become Buddhas".[40]

The oral tradition of the medieval Tendai sect of Japan pushed the idea of the grass and trees becoming Buddhas so far as to preach "the non-becoming Buddhas of the grass and trees". According to this theory, everything is by nature a Buddha, that is to say, to attain enlightenment through the ascetic practice is one and the same thing as being a Buddha without recourse to the ascetic practice. Not only the grass and trees but also rivers, mountains and the earth are themselves Buddhahood already possessed intact. There is no becoming a Buddha in the sense of coming to be something separate and different in nature. That is the reason why the non-becoming of Buddhahood was preached.[41] The logical conclusion of the idea of the acceptance of the given reality is herein crystalized.

Indian Buddhism also admits the spirituality of the grass and trees. Not only that, the various schools of Indian philosophy adopted such a view.[42] But most of the Indian philosophies maintain that all the living things attain the state of deliverance through enlightened intelligence (vidyā), and not that the grass and trees become Buddhas as they actually are.

Such a tendency of thinking as discussed above seems to be still effective among the Japanese even in these days when the knowledge of natural science prevails. For instance, the Japanese generally use the honorific expression "o" prefixed to the names of various objects, as in the cases of "o-cha" (the honorific wording of tea) and "o-mizu" (the honorific wording of water). Probably there is no other nation on earth who use such an honorfic expression prefixed to the names of everyday objects. It is not conceived to be anything extraordinary by the Japanese themselves. It should not be regarded merely as an honorific expression, but it should rather be considered to be a manifestation of the way of thinking that seeks the *raison d'etre* and sacredness in everything that exists. According to the comments made by Westerners, "everything is Buddha" to the minds of the Japanese.

Then where these characteristics of the Japanese to grasp the absolute in accordance with the given phenomenal world, or to love nature as it is, come from? In Japan, because the weather is mild, the landscape benign, and the nature appears to be relatively benevolent to men, men love nature, instead of abhorring it, and feel congenial to it, instead of having a grudge against it. Consequently nature is thought as what is one with men, rather than what is opposed to men. This seems to account for the prevalence of the afore-mentioned characteristics of the thought-tendency of the Japanese.

---

1) Naoichi Miyaji 宮地直一: *Jingi-shi Taikei* 神祇史大系pp. 6 & 9.
2) Yōkyoku 謠曲 *Taisha* 大社.
3) *Fūkyō Hyakushu Kōsetsu* 風教百首講說 (Genchi Katō 加藤玄智: *Shintō no Shūkyō Hattatsushiteki Kenkyū* 神道の宗教發達史的研究 p. 935).
4) cf. 摩訶止觀 vol. I, pt. 1. (*Taishō*. vol. 46. p. 1 c).
Eun Mayeda 前田慧雲: *Tetsugakukan Kōgiroku* 哲學館講義錄 (*Shigaku Zasshi* 史學雜誌, 1923, pp. 373–374).
5) *Kaimokushū* 開目鈔 pt. 2.
6) See 羅什譯「中論」ch. 18, 7th gāthā: Saddharma-puṇḍarīka-sūtra (ed. by Unrai Ogiwara) p. 251, *l.* 25.; Aṣṭasāharsikā (Comp. Unrai Ogiwara) p. 51, *l.* 15.; p. 572, *ll.* 2–3; p. 666, *l.* 7; etc.
7) *Shōbōgenzō* 正法眼藏 Shohō-jissō 諸法實相.
8) See 法華玄義 vol. VIII, pt. 2. (*Taishō* vol. 33, p. 783 b).
9) *Shōbōgenzō*, Shōji 生死.
10) *Ibid.* Busshō 佛性.
11) *Shasekishū* 沙石集 vol. 10. pt. 1.
12) This Sentence was conposed in China based upon such sentences as「乳中有酪 衆生佛性亦復如是, 欲見佛性, 應當觀察時節形色.」and「以諸功德因緣和合得見佛性, 然後得佛」in 大般涅槃經 vol. XXVIII. (*Taishō*. vol. 12, p. 532 a & p. 533b).
13) *Shōbōgenzō*, Busshō.
14) 八十華嚴 vol. XXXVIII, 十地品. (*Taishō*. vol. 10, p. 194 a).
十地經 vol. (*Taishō*. vol. 10. p. 553 a).
15) *Bonbun Daihōkōbutsu-kegonkyō Jūjibon* 梵文大方廣佛華嚴經十地品 (ed. by Ryūkō Kondō 近藤隆晃) p. 98.
16) *Shōbōgenzō*, Sangaiyuishin 三界唯心.
17) *Ibid.* Sokushin Zebutsu 卽心是佛.
18) *Shōbōgenzō*, Butsukōjōji 佛向上事.
19) *Shōbōgenzō*, Uji 有時.
20) *Ibid.* Setsushin Setsushō 說心說性.
21) *Ibid.* Hosshō 法性.
22) *Ibid.* Setsushin Setsushō.
23) *Ibid.* Sanjūshichihon Bodaibunpō 三十七品菩提分法.
24) Yasusada Hiyane 比屋根安定: *Nihon Shūkyōshi* 日本宗教史 pp. 828–829.
25) *Gomō Jigi* 語孟字義 vol. I, p. 3.
26) *Dōjimon* 童子問 vol. II, up. 39.
27) Junsei Iwahashi 岩崎遵成: *Sorai Kenkyū* 徂來研究 p. 449.
28) Cf. Yaichi Haga 芳賀矢一: *Kokuminsei Jūron* p. 91 ff.
29) R. H. Blyth (the "*Cultural East*" No. 1, 1947, p. 45).
30) *Mannyōshū* 萬葉集 vol. III (318).
31) *Ibid.* vol. VI, (919).
32) *Ibid.* vol. V, (822).
33) *Ibid.* vol. V, (824).
34) *Theragāthā* 537, 538, 540, 544, 545.
35) Emperor Kazan 花山天皇 (*Eiga Monogatari* 榮華物語 Mihatenu Yume みはてぬ夢)
36) Emperor Kazan (*Zoku Kokinshū* 續古今集, Shakukyōka 釋敎歌).
37) *Shōbōgenzō*, Hotsumujōshin 發無上心.

38) Nichiren also wrote a book named *Sōmoku Jōbutsu Kuketsu.* (草木成佛口決).
39) This *gāthā* is not found in 中陰經. Perhaps, some one composed this *gāthā* based upon this sūtra.
40) Daijō Tokiwa 常盤大定: *Nihon Bukkyō no Kenkyū* 日本佛教の研究 p. 107 ff.
41) H. Ui: *Bukkyō Hanron* (佛教汎論 An Outline of Buddhism) 2nd vol., p. 337.
42) See supra. pt. II, Section 2, ch. 9 g.

(2) This-worldliness

While religions of the world very often tend to regard this world, as the land of impurity and the other world, as the blessed land of purity where one seeks the Heaven of eternal happiness, primitive Shintoism recognizes the intrinsic value here in this world. Each one of the Japanese people is considered to be descendant of gods and goddesses. In primitive Shintoism, one can find no profound reflections either upon the soul or upon death.

The ancient Japanese called the soul '*tama*'. Man's *tama* can function independently from their bodies, and assist the achievement of their work. Various ideas about *tama* are nothing more than the expositions of its utilities in worldly enterprises. One's *tama* is supposed to remain in this world and to continue functioning after one's death, and essentially no distinction is drawn about one's *tama* before and after one's death.[1]

According to the Japanese mythology, nothing is said about the future world. Indeed, there was an idea expressed that after one's death, one goes to the land of the night. That is supposed to be a dark underground place. When one dies, one is naturally buried underground, so it is common to every country, that there exists the concept of Hades. And it is also natural that death is universally abhorred. But it appears that the ancient Japanese were not afraid of death. They never worried about life after death. The Japanese mythology as a whole is attached to this world and makes much of this life.[2] Consequently, such metaphysical concept as the law of cause and effect (i.e. merit and reward) is lacking. They regarded death as impurity, and enjoyed solely with the life of this world.

As far as this-worldliness itself is concerned, Chinese religions such as Confucianism and Taoism are also rightly called to be this-worldly. Even the Zen sect is touched with its influence. In the case of the Japanese primitive Shintoism alone, it was mingled with animism, Shamanism and the thought-tendency to attach great importance to social nexus, and thus it came to assume a number of deviations and variations.

Once men became conscious of philosophical or metaphysical doubts, however, they could no more rest assured with such easy-going religious faith. They felt an internal urge to search into some deeper truth about men. It was in an answer to such spiritual demand that Buddhism flowed into this country. They could not but turn to Buddhism for a guide in such reflection.

It was only natural, when Buddhism was introduced to Japan, that there were those who rejected it and those who supported it. In the first place, among those who rejected it, there was a marked tendency for the glorification of this world. Ōtomo Tabito sang as follows:

This life of ours, let me enjoy;
In the other life I do not care,
An insect or a bird,
Or whatever I shall become.

This is to make fun of the Buddhist theory of the transmigration of the fictitious soul. The following poem is an apparent resistance to the Buddhist theory of the mutability of phenomenal things:

Everything alive is said
To be death-bound;
If it be so, let me be happy,
So long as I am alive.

He admired and adored the life of a hedonist and despised the Spartan life of moral austerity.

It is better to drink
And to weep in drunkenness,
Than to talk like a sage;
Ugly is the man who never drinks,
But pretends to be wise;
Scrutinizing his face, I've found,
What a monkey-face he has!
It is worse to say nothing,
And to pretend to be wise,
Than to drink and weep in drunkenness.

In contrast to Buddhism as an imported system of culture, the traditional Japanese culture was too weak to resist it. Was it then probable, as Buddhism was transplanted into this country and spread among the people, that the traditional Japanese way of thinking tended toward this-worldliness should have completely given its way to Buddhism? Buddhism, like a flood of water rushed forth from a broken dam, spread all over Japan within a very short time. It, however, was impossible for Buddhism completely to change the inclination for this-worldliness of the Japanese general public. On the contrary, it was the Japanese themselves that transformed Buddhism which they accepted from the continent, into a religion centered upon this world.

With the advent and spread of Buddhism, the Japanese came to think of life after death. But even then Buddhism was accepted as something this-worldly. All through the Nara and Heian periods, almost all the sects of Buddhism aimed at tangible profits in this world and they mainly depended upon incantation and magic. (This point was already pointed out in the third section, "Problems of Shamanism".)

The stūpa in India and the great image of Buddha at Nara in Japan might be called representative edifices that symbolize the proserity of Buddhism supported by the state-power in the respective countries. The stūpa is a large mound where the ashes of great men or saints were buried. The formative arts in India are crystalized into the stūpa, a symbol of death, while those in Japan are concentrated into the image of Buddha, a vivid symbol of the *living* ideal man. While the Indians search for the truth of humanity through the channels of death, the Japanese try to express it intuitively through the channels of life and embody the truth of humanity therein.

The Japanese way of thinking centering upon this world transformed even the Buddhist doctrines. According to the views of Indian Buddhist believers, all the living things are repeating themselves in an infinite process of transmigration of the soul; and a life in this world is but an infinitesimal period within that eternally circulating process. Even Śākyamuni himself was able to practice religion in this world and to become a Buddha only as a retribution to the multitude of good deeds accumulated in his countless lives in the previous existence world. Such practice, as was accomplished by Śākyamuni, cannot be achieved by an ordinary man within one life-time, but he has to continue his practice through many life-times. It was not that all the Buddhist believers in India believed thus, but the common men in India were of such opinion. Buddhism, however, was at first transformed by the this-worldly Chinese, and then again it was steeped even more deeply by the Japanese in the color of this-worldliness. There are many sects of Japanese Buddhism which emphasize that even ordinary men would be able to become Buddhas, should they attain enlightenment in this world (*Sokushin Jōbutsu*).

According to Saichō (Dengyō-Daishi), in his classified comments on various doctrines of Buddhism, Hīnayāna Buddhism is a circuitous teaching, since it advocates practice of religion through countless lives in an immensely long span of time. Some sects of the Mahāyāna Buddhism also preach that one should practice religion through similarly long periods of life, so they are of no use to the Japanese people of his time. Mahāyāna Buddhism in general directs the way in which an ordinary man can become a Buddha straightforwardly (A Direct Way). And it is the doctrine of the Hokke Sūtra that gives the fullest expression to such an idea. (The Great Straight Way)[3] Saichō used the phrase, '*Sokushin Jōbutsu*' (to become a Buddha being alive in the human body).[4] Such an idea was as old as Buddhism itself, but the use of such a phrase seems to have been initiated by Saichō. But in the theory of '*Sokushin Jōbutsu*' preached by Saichō, the doctrine of this worldliness was not thoroughgoing enough. It was the Japanese scholars of the Tendai sect who later pushed it to its extreme. The Tendai doctrine in China did not allow a man to become a Buddha through this life alone. Even if such be recognized, it is generally supposed to be the consequence of the ascetic practice accumulated through many lives, and one can become a Buddha only at the rudimentary status of the perfect religion. Hardly a hundred years had elapsed after the introduction by Saichō of the Tendai sect into Japan, when a Tendai scholar, Annen, began to preach not only that one could become a Buddha in this world, but also that one could become a Buddha through one life's ascetic practice and would be permitted to be a Buddha being alive in the human body.

"At the beginning, according to a sacred priest, or according to the scriptures, learning that an affliction is nothing but an enlightenment, one achieves the Intelligence of a Buddha without overcoming one's afflictions. Learning that the mundane existence is nothing but Nirvāṇa, one becomes a Buddha in the form of 'name-identity', into which the effect of the mundane existence turns out to be. That is why it is called enlightenment and also becoming a Buddha. If one's body does not become a Buddha, neither does one's mind. If one's mind has already become a Buddha, so does one's body *en suite*".[5]

This-worldliness was plainly expressed by Kūkai, the founder of the Japanese Shingon sect. According to Kūkai, the world and humanity both consist of six constituent elements; earth, water, fire, wind, sky, and intelligence. Their essence is the absolute truth (the World of the Law) and they are in such relationship as never to obstruct (or oppose) one another. It follows that mankind and Buddhas are equal, and they are identical in their essence. It is preached that if one should follow such a reason, making figures with one's hands, reciting incantations, or concentrating one's mind, then the three deeds of man, body, mouth and mind, would be directly identified with those of a Buddha. He specifically wrote a book called the *"Commentaries on Becoming a Buddha being Alive in the Human Body"*. He supports the doctrine of esoteric Buddhism: "One could attain the status of great enlightenment with the body that was born by one's parents".[6]

It is needless to say that the doctrine of Nichiren, a development of the Japanese Tendai sect and influenced by esoteric Buddhism, stressed becoming a Buddha being alive in the human body. "The gate to the truth called 'Becoming a Buddha being alive in the human body' ought to be studied as a matter of great importance by the scholars of the world. My own disciples in particular should keep this matter in mind above anything else. During these twenty-seven years between the fifth year of Kenchō and the third year of Kōan, I have stated in various places a great many gates to enter the truth. But all the gates lead up just to this one".[7] "Should we recite, with the sincerity of our hearts, 'Nammyō-hōrenge-kyo', the Perfect One in the body of the Law, the eternal fundamental basis, viewed from which everything is not made etc.—all of them would come and gather upon ourselves. That is the reason why the most devoted of the devoted followers of the true practice could become a Buddha, whether or not they take leave of their bodies".[8]

Running as a parallel to such a view in ecclesiastical doctrines, popular religions are also based upon this-worldliness. As an illustration, the religious faith in Jizō, a guardian deity of children (Kṣitigarbha-bodhisattva) became popular after the Heian period, for the reason that the common men in Japan looked to great benevolence of the deity who would save ordinary men just as they were.

"Kṣitigarbha-bodhisattva, since he is unfathomably benevolent, does not live in the Pure Land. Since his connections with human beings are so deep that, he does not call for divine death. He only makes the place of the evil as his own habitat, and makes friends solely with sinners".[9]

A question may be raised here. One might argue that in Japan Pure Land Buddhism was very popular, and even the Nichiren sect, under its influence, used the phrase "The Sacred Mountain which is the Pure Land".[10]

The Pure Land Buddhism in Japan, however, was not always other-worldly. The Pure Land Buddhism of the Heian period, it cannot be denied, was inclined to regard practical life as worthless and to attach prime importance to a life of seclusion. But in the case of Hōnen, he is decidedly on the side of asserting this world. Once a warrior came to him and confided Hōnen with what troubled his mind: he could not reconcile his religious belief as a believer of the Jōdo sect with his duty as a *samurai* to fight on the battlefield. Hōnen answered him as follows: "The original vow of Amitābha is not concerned whether one's predisposition is good or evil, or whether the religious practice is more or less. Since it does not depend upon the purity or impurity of the body, or time, place or opportunities, the occasion of death is of no consequence. Even sinners, as sinners, are eligible for rebirth in the Pure Land, if they should invocate the name of Amitābha. This is the miracle of the original vow. As for those born into the families of warriors, who fight in war and lose their lives therein, only if they should invocate the name of Amitābha, they would be assisted by the original vow and would be welcomed by Amitābha into the Pure Land. This you should never doubt".[11]

Moreover, the Jōdo-shin sect, from the standpoint that assures anyone to be reborn into the Pure Land only if one has faith in Amitābha in daily life, strives to realize the absolute significance within the life of this world. It attaches great importance to the phase of coming back to this world as in contrast to the phase of going to the Pure Land. Such a standpoint gave rise to more or less distorted interpretations of the phrases in the scriptures.[12]

The point that the Jōdo sect is meant to attach great significance to and to give a theoretical basis to positive action in this world was already elaborated. But according to the Pure Land Buddhism in India, this world is supposed to be the impure land smeared with dirt, where no ordinary men could ever practice religion. In order for the ordinary men to attain Nirvāṇa, they ought to be born in the next life into the Pure Land, which is the better world, where they should, under the guidance of Amitābha, listen to the doctrine of the Buddha and practice asceticism. According to the Japanese Pure Land Buddhism, especially the Jōdo-shin sect, in contrast, to be born into the Pure Land is identical with attaining Nirvāṇa. (To be reborn into the Pure Land is nothing but Nirvāṇa.) So it might as well concluded that the Japanese Pure Land Buddhism enhanced the position of this world, which is the impure land, to the position tantamount to what was considered by the Indian followers of the Pure Land Buddhism to be the delightful Pure Land. This should also be attributed to the this-worldly inclination of the Japanese people.

It is too rash, however to conclude that the Pure Land Buddhism in Japan is competely this-worldly. An element of escapism cannot be denied of its existence. The attitudes of resignation and submission in every matter of life were imposed upon people under the feudal regime, since, it was told, everything was predetermined as the consequence to the causes in one's previous life. In comparison with the Pure Land Buddhism of India and of China, such element of escapism-from-this-world was relatively weak in that of Japan, and became even less influential toward the modern period.

The this-worldly idea of becoming a Buddha being alive in the human body is also conspicuous in the Japanese Zen sects. Dōgen straightforwardly asserts that to attain enlightenment is not the function of the mind but *that of the body.*

"Does one attain the enlightenment by means of the mind or by means of the body? The masters of dogmas say that mind and body are of one, so even if they assert that one attains the enlightenment through the body, it is because, it is implied, mind and body are of one and the same thing. It is not clear, therefore, that it is the body that does so. Now, from our own standpoint, we attain the enlightenment through the mind and body together. Even in that case, as long as we deliberate upon the doctrine of a Buddha with our minds, we shall not attain the enlightenment even for ten thousand aeons and a thousand lives. At the moment when we set our minds free and abandon our deliberation and understanding, then and there only do we attain it. It is told that by looking at things one enlightens one's mind and by hearing sounds one attains enlightenment. These are also achieved through the body. Should one sit in meditation intently enough, abandoning all the deliberations and intelligence of one's mind, one would be able to become intimate with the enlightenment. It follows then that *to attain the enlightenment is certainly to attain it with the body.* This is what I recommend, knowing that, it is according to this, that one should sit intently".[13]

Dōgen recognized the uniqueness of Zen, in contrast to other doctrines, exactly on this point: to attain enlightenment with the body.

In parallel with this, there is Nichiren's assertion to the effect that "The Hokke Sūtra should not only be read in the mind, but should be read in the body". The Japanese Buddhism is, as to have been dwelt, strongly imbued with an activistic and practical tendency, which is tied up with those points related above.

Toward the latest period of Mahāyāna Buddhism in India, it was maintained that predisposition for a Buddha (possibilities to become an enlightened person) is constant and is not subject to change (the constancy and the unchangeability of predisposition for a Buddha). Dōgen tying up his own as he is to that assertion, expresses his own view somewhat differently. The changing and fluctuating phases of the phenomenal world, he asserts, are themselves predispositions for a Buddha. "Grass, trees, bushes and woods are changeable, that is, they are predispositions for a Buddha. Men, things, body and mind are changeable, that is, they are predispositions for a Buddha. Countries, rivers and mountains are changeable, that is because they are predispositions for a Buddha. Anuttara-Samyaksaṃbodhi (the supreme enlightenment) is changeable since it is a predisposition for a Buddha. The great perfect Nirvāṇa is a predisposition for a Buddha since it is changeable".[14)]

The this-worldly character of the Zen sect is also embodied by the Japanese Zen priests in the later periods. Suzuki Shōsan, for instance, taught the general lay believers as follows: "To pray for a happy future does not mean to pray for a world after death. It means to be delivered from afflictions really and now and thus to attain a great comfort. Then, where do you think those afflictions come from? They are originated merely from the love of your own body. Had it not been for this body of yours, from what should you suffer? To be delivered, therefore, from this body of yours is to become a Buddha".[15)] His disciple, Echū, also states that Buddhism ought to be what is useful to this real world. "The law of the Buddha is supposed to serve only the future life and to be *of no use for today's affairs.* Followers, therefore, only think of their future happiness, and none of them knows how to control evils within those today's minds of their own and to eliminate afflictions. This is a great misconception".[16)]

The medieval Shintoist theories adopted their terminology mainly from Buddhist scriptures. But Shintoism, being essentially this-worldly, accepted only the *this-world-central* aspect which appears only in the incidental remarks at some peripheral parts of the scriptures, rejecting the *the-other-worldly* aspect of Buddhism. The "*Hōki-Hongi*",[17)] one of the five books of Shintoism that provided the foundation for the Shintoist theology of the Ise Shrine at the Medieval period, states that if men should accomplish the supreme virtues of absolute sincerity and integrity, such condition would be realized as "being in peaceful harmony, sun and moon being clear and bright, wind and rain coming in due time and the nation being enriched and the people given secure". Then, it goes on to say, the armed forces would be no more necessary. These sentences are based upon the following part in the *"Daimuryōju-kyō* (The Larger *Sūkhāvatī-sūtra*): "Wherever a Buddha goes there is no country, town, hill or village that is not enlightened by him. Sky and earth are in peaceful harmony, and sun and moon are clear and bright. Wind and rain come in due time and there is no calamity. The nation is enriched and people are secured and no armed forces are ever used. Virtues are respected, benevolence is promoted, and courtesy and humility are practiced in earnest". Originally, the "Daimuryōju sūtra" instructs the existence of the Pure Land and the vow of Amitābha Buddha, and the essence of its teachings is to give meanings to the activities of this world by transcending this world. The Japanese Buddhists, on the contrary, regarded the above-mentioned sentences as advocating 'national defense' and laid great importance to them, while *Shintoists selected only this-worldly teaching out of Pure Land scriptures.*

Consequently, the union was quite facile between Shintoism and the Buddhist idea of becoming a Buddha alive in the human body.

"The shrine of gods
Is the body of my own,
Inhaling breath being the Outer Shrine,
Exhaling breath being the Inner Shrine".[18)]

This-worldliness became even stronger as the time proceeded into the Tokugawa period. The this-worldly and anti-religious tendencies were already manifest among the merchants' thought at the early Tokugawa period. "It is unnecessary to pray for a happy future when one is already in one's fifties. ... It is even more unbecoming to spend days and nights, on the pretext of praying for a happy future, abandoning one's family and boasting to go worshipping at a temple. ... In this life one should use one's discretion above anything else not to lose one's reputation". (The Will of Shimai Sōzen, a merchant of Hakata)[19)] It needs no particular mentioning that the this-worldly tendency became especially preeminent during the Modern period in Japan and it even caused the emergence of materialism.

The Indian theory of the transmigration of the soul was also adopted, but even this theory sometimes underwent transformation into asserting this world. To illustrate this point, let me quote from the famous description of Kusunoki Masashige at the time of his death.

"Masashige, in his seat, asked his brother Masasue: 'It is told that the good or evil of one's future life depends upon what one desires at the time of one's death. What is your wish among the nine worlds?' Masasue, laughing heartily, answered: 'It is my wish to be born as the same human being seven times in order to annihilate the emperor's enemy'. Masashige, looking supremely delighted, said: 'A most sinful evil wish as it is, I myself also with the same. Let us then be reborn into men and accomplish this wish of ours'. Thus pledging each other, they stabbed each other and fell upon the same pillow".[20]

According to the general view of the Indians, it is desirable *to be delivered* from this world. But here in Japan, while accepting the theory of the transmigration of the soul on one hand, they wish, on the other hand, *to be reborn into this world.* The concept of loyalty in China was the loyalty of one's life-time, in accordance with the Confucian theory. Chu-ko-k'ung-ming declares, in his "*Go Suishi-no Hyō*" (the second letter to the emperor at the time of mobilizing the army): "I, Your Majesty's humble servant, bending myself most humbly like a ball, shall exert my best effort and shall cease only after I am dead". In contrast with this, Kusunoki Masashige states: "I wish to be reborn seven times in order to serve (the emperor) most loyally". The idea of "Serving one's country by getting born seven times" was herein established, and it was made most of by the latter-day nationalists.

Ryōkan (Ninshō Bodhisattva), famous as a reviver of the Ritsu sect during the Kamakura period, was a welfare worker who founded a charity hospital to take care of invalids. When he was at Saidaiji Temple, taking pity on a leper, he repeatedly carried him on his own back to the city and begged for him whatever he wanted. Being deeply gratified with his deeds of benevolence, the invalid said to him in his death-bed: "I shall certainly be reborn into this world and become my master's humble servant in order to reciprocate my master's virtuous deeds. (As a mark for my master to identify me,) I shall have a scar left on my face". Sure enough, in the later years of Ninshō's life, there appeared among his disciples a man with a scar on his face, who served him as an attendant. People said, it was told, that he was the leper regenerated.[21] Whereas the mankind are supposed to transmigrate through the six spheres of existence on account of their good and evil deeds, according to the Indian Buddhist view of life and death, here in Japan, ordinary men are acknowledged *to be reborn into this world,* should they make vows to be so.

The Japanese had been this-world-central and optimistic long before the advent of Buddhism. It was because of the fact that such a view of life remained long with them that the ideas to regard this world as the stained and impure land could never take root. The theory of impurity as preached by Buddhism, therefore, was never adopted by the Japanese in its original form.

It is the first lesson for the ascetics of Hīnayāna Buddhism to recognize one's body as impure. Here the body is regarded to be the source of all evils and hindrance to the practice of the Way. Dōgen, however, revised this interpretation. According to him, to contemplate is to be actualized in one's practice in everyday life. "So-called contemplation is everyday activities of sweeping the ground and the floor".[22] That should exactly be conceived as identical to 'recognizing one's body as impure'. Moreover, in that case one is expected to transcend the dichotomy of purity and impurity. "It is not a dichotomous argument of purity or impurity". Consequently, the theory of impurity emphasized by the Indian Buddhism was not welcomed by the Japanese in general. "An opinion like the theory of impurity", commented Tominaga Nakamoto, "is based upon the mores of the Indians. On this land such a view is not accepted by people".[23]

Pessimism was another world view which never took a precise form in Japan. After the implantation of Buddhism into Japan, there appeared in "the *Manyōshū*" some poems, under the influence of Buddhist thoughts. But even these are no more than the lamentations of the changeability and transiency of man and things. To illustrate:

> To what shall I liken this life?
> It is like a boat,
> Which, unmoored at morn,
> Drops out of sight
> And leaves nothing behind.

The fear of death, as shown in the early Buddhism and Jainism, is conspicuously absent here. Let us listen to the confession of a Jain pessimist.

> "Living things torture living things.
> Behold, great fears of the world!
> Living things abound with afflictions.
> Human beings cling to lust and passion.
> They go to self-destruction with their frail helpless bodies".[21]
> "It is a great fear, affliction, I say.

Living beings are trembling in all the directions".[25]

Such profound outcries were never heard from the Japanese. Dōgen argues even against pessimism itself.

"The mundane existence is nothing but the life of the Buddha himself. Should one loathe and try to abandon it, that is precisely to lose the life of the Buddha. Should one stay with it and cling to the mundane existence, that also would mean to lose the life of the Buddha".[26]

As far as the number is concerned, there are innumerable poems composed in Japan to express Buddhist thought. But as far as the profound sense of pessimism is concerned, there are quite few expressing such a view, except for a limited minority of the people. Also lacking are the philosophical poems, expressing straight-forwardly the rational laws such as suffering, non-ego, and emptiness.

Ours is different from the pessimism of the Occidental people. In the West pessimism means to become wearied of the existence in this world. In the case of the Japanese, in contrast, it means to be wearied only of complicated social fetters and restrictions from which they wish to be delivered. Consequently, the sense of pessimism is pacified as soon as one comes to live close to the beauties of nature, far apart from the human society. Saigyō, escaped as he had from the world, enjoyed flowers and the moon, spending the rest of his life in travelling around on foot. Kamo-no-Chōmei, wearied as he was of this world, enjoyed nature and was contented, living a life of seclusion in his hermitage. St. Gensei of Fukakusa, and more recently, Ōtagaki Rengetsu also enjoyed nature, despite the fact that they loathed to be mingled with wordly affairs. Pessimism, as shown in these cases, is given its vent in the form of attachment with nature.[27]

"Changeable is this world,
So may be the cherry blossoms,
Falling in my garden".[28]

"Brief is this mortal life ——
Let me go and seek the Way,
Contemplating the hills and streams undefiled!"[29]

Not only were they attached to nature, but they *kept warm spots in their hearts for companions* and never ceased to long for humanity, in the midst of their hermitage. Saigyō, in his life of a solitary traveller, enjoyed tranquility and yet in his heart he yearned for life, which he had abandoned on his own accord.

"Weary as I am
Of this world,
When autumn comes
And the moon shines serene,
I feel I should like to survive".
"Wearied of this world
Why should I be?
Those once I loathed
Today my delight turn out to be".

Even Bashō's life as a solitary wanderer was deeply imbued with longing for companions. "What a lazy old man I am! Usually, being annoyed by visitors, I have pledged my heart not to see or to invite others. Nevertheless, on a moonlit night or on a snowy morn, how unreasonable it is of me to long for a companion".[30] In Kenkō, the author of the "*Tsure-zure-gusa*", the attachment to the worldly affairs is especially deep-rooted. That such a sentiment was not limited solely to some men of letters in the past is clear enough, when we look into our own minds a little deeper.

---

1) Yaichi Haga 芳賀矢一: *Kokuminsei Jūron* p. 70.
2) *Ibid.* pp. 65–67.
3) Ryōchū Shioiri 鹽入亮忠: *Dengyō Daishi to Hokekyō* 傳教大師と法華經 (in *Nihon Bukkyō no Rekishi to Rinen* 日本佛教の歷史と理念 comp. by Seiichirō Ono & Shinshō Hanayama), p. 117 ff.
4) See Hokke Shūku (by Saichō) 法華秀句 vol. II (*Dengyō Daishi Zenshū* 傳教大師全集 vol. II. pp. 265–266 & p. 280.)
5) *Sokushin Jōbutsugi Shiki* 卽身成佛義私記 (*Tendaishū Sōsho* 天台宗叢書 *Annen Senshū* 安然撰集 vol. II, p. 210.)
6) This is the words in Bodai Shinron 菩提心論 which is said to have been written by Nāgārjuna.
7) *Myōichi-me Gohenji* 妙一女御返事.
8) *Jushiki Kanjō Kudenshō* 授職灌頂口傳鈔.
9) *Shasekishū* 沙石集 vol. II. pt. 1.
10) 'The Sacred Mountain' here is a Japanese equivalent for *Gṛdhrakūṭo*. See *Jimyō Hokke Mondōshō* 持妙法華問答鈔; *Toki dono Gohenji* 富木殿御返事 etc.
11) *Hōnen Shōnin Gyōjō Ezu* 法然上人行狀畫圖 26.
12) Cf. *Yuishinshō Mon-i* 唯心鈔文意.
13) *Shōbōgenzō Zuimonki* 正法眼藏隨聞記 vol. II.
14) *Shōbōgenzō*, Busshō 佛性.
15) *Roankyō* 驢鞍橋 last pt. p. 71.
16) *Sōan Zakki* 草庵雜記 pt. II. p. 26.
17) *Shintō Gobusho* 神道五部書 in *Kokushi Taikei* 國史大系 vol. VII. p. 31.
18) *Hikosan Shugen Saihi Injin Kuketsushū* 彥山修驗最祕印信口決集 pt. 1. (*Nihondaizōkyō* 日本大藏經, *Shugenshōshobu* 修驗章疏部 pt. 2. p. 533 & p. 549.)
19) Masatomo Manba 萬羽正朋: *Nihon Jukyōron* 日本儒教論 p. 89.

20) *Taiheiki* 大平記 vol. XVI.
21) *Genkōshakusho* 元亨釋書 vol. XIII.
22) *Shōbōgenzō*, Sanjūshichihon Bodaibumpō 三十七品菩提分法.
23) *Shutsujō Kōgo* 出定後語, vol. XXV. Zatsu 雜
24) *Āyāraṅga*, herausgegeben von W. Schubring, I, 27, 1, 28 f.
25) *Ibid.*, I, 1, 6, 2 (S. 5, l, 8.)
26) *Shōbōgenzō*, Shōji 生死.
27) In details See. Yaichi Haga: op. cit. pp. 91–116.
28) *Mannyōshū* 萬葉集 vol. VIII. (1459).
29) *Ibid.*, vol. XX. (4468).
30) Cf. Ichirō Hori 堀一郎: Inton Shisō ni okeru Ningensei eno Shibo 隱遁思想に於ける人間性への思慕 *Yearning for Humanity in Asceticism*) (*Teiyū Rinri* 丁酉倫理, nos. 7–8, 1947).

(3) The acceptance of man's natural dispositions

I have already pointed out that the Japanese in general are inclined to search for the absolute within the phenomenal world or in what is real. Among all the natures that are given and real, the most immediate to man is the nature of man. Hence they tend to esteem highly man's natural dispositions.

Just as the Japanese are apt to accept the external and objective nature as it is, so they are inclined to accept man's natural desires and sentiments as they are, and not to strive to repress or fight against them.

Love was the most favorite theme of the ancient poetry. The love of the ancient Japanese is sensual and extremely open. The true meaning of life existed for them in love. In general, the expression of their sentiments are direct and open, and there is no suppression perceivable from outside.

Such a tendency later went through some variations according to periods and classes, nevertheless, it remained as a relatively distinctive characteristic of the people. The collections of poems in Japan, for instance, are rich in love-poems. This seems to be vastly different from the cases of the Indian or the Chinese peoples.

Motoori Norinaga (1730–1801), the great scholar of Japanese classics, recognized the distinction of the Japanese from the Chinese in this respect:

"The fact that the *Book of Poetry* (*shih*-ching) lacks in love-poems manifests the customs of the people of that country [China]. They only make outward show and try to appear manly, concealing the womanishness of their real selves. In contrast, the abundance of love-poems in this empire reveals the way to express one's genuine dispositions".[1]

In India there is an abundance of love-poems. Nevertheless, the Indians in general sought the ultimate and absolute meaning beyond passions of love, which ought to be annihilated. So the acceptance of love as it is may be taken to be the unique characteristics of the Japanese, distinguished from other civilized peoples of Asia.

How does this tendency determine the way of adopting foreign cultures?

The ethical theories of Confucianism tended originally to asceticism, which was no doubt inherited by the Japanese Confucianists. Among them, however, there were those who tried to accept man's natural dispositions. *The Tale of Genji* and *The Tale of Ise* were the favorite books of such scholars as Ogiu Sorai (1666–1728) and Hori Keizan (1688–1757). Sorai recognized the intrinsic value of these literary works, whose value should not be obscured by the immoral themes of the content.[2] He also maintained that since poetry expressed natural feelings, its far-fetched moralization as done by the Chinese moralists was not permissible.[3] In this respect his attitude is in conformity with that of scholars of Japanese classics.[4]

Accepting as he is the view that the *Book of History* (Shu-ching), among the *Five Books,* relates the 'Great Teachings and Laws of Ancient Wise Kings', he comments upon the *Book of Poety* (*Shih-ching*) as follows:

The *Book of Poetry* is another matter. It is composed of the language of songs, just as the later day poetry is. Confucius edited it as for wording. And the scholars studied it as for wording. That is why Confucius says: If you do not study the *Book of Poetry,* you have nothing to say. In the later day periods, one has come to study the *Book of Poetry* in the same fashion as one reads the *Book of Writing,* and they regard the former as an exposition of the principle of punishing vice and rewarding virtue. That is why one is at one's wit's end when one comes to interpret the lascivious poem of Cheng-wei. The moral teachings of justice are so rare in this *Book of Poetry* that they are negligible. If the laterday Confucianists' opinion be granted true, then why should the sage have resorted to such a roundabout way (of presenting the principle of punishing vice and rewarding virtue), instead of writing directly a separate book of instruction? So the opinion of those Confucianists is that of those who are ignorant of the essence of poetry. The preface to the *Book of Poetry* was written in the spirit of comprehending the proper meanings of poetry. .... The laterday scholars, losing grip of the original spirit of Confucianism, wrote large and small prefaces. This is most despicable. The words of poetry touch upon the subject-matters from the government to the street and also to the countries of many a lord. Is there any place in the world where the difference does not exist between the noble and the low, man and woman, the wise and the foolish, and the beauty and the ugly? Through poetry, one can comprehend the changes of the world, the customs of people, human feelings and the phases of things. Its language is elegant and gentle, being akin to sentiments, its expression delicate. The matters of poetry are all trivial and trifling and there is nothing that inspires the spirit of pride. Herein lies, however, the key for the wise man to comprehend the fools, for the brave man to understand the woman, for the kings to know their people, and for the age of prosperity to perceive the age of devastation".[5]

Dazai Shundai (1680–1747) called man's natural feelings the real feelings, which he defined to be "likes and dislikes, suffering and rejoicing, anxiety and pleasure, etc." And he maintains: ". . . . There is not a single human being devoid of these feelings. Either for the great or the petty, the noble or the low, there is no difference in this respect. Love of one's parents, wives and children is also the same among the noble and the low. Since these feelings are originated from the innate truthfulness, never stained with falsity, they are called the real feelings. . . . ."[6] His standpoint is pure naturalism.

"There are no double-dealings in the deeds overflowed from the natural dispositions, wherein the inside and outside are so transparent that they are one and the same thing. The natural dispositions are the innate true nature of men. Those deeds done without being taught, without learning, without forcing but with freedom from all thoughts are the works of the natural dispositions. This is called truthfulness. And this is the meaning of the golden mean".[7]

In the realm of reality, however, there exists certain regulations of conduct, to which only one should conform. But within one's inner self one can think whatever one pleases.

"According to the way of saints, one is called to be a man of noble character, only if one does not act against propriety but observes decorum concerning the body, (regardless of) whether or not one sees a woman and fancies her in the mind as a good woman and takes a pleasure in her beauty. That is exactly what is to be called to discipline one's mind with proper decorum".[8]

Apparently this is a metamorphosis of Confusianism in Japan. Discarded herein was the traditional attitude of the ancient Chinese Confucianism which refused to interpret the love poems of the *Book of Poetry* as such, and tried, instead, to interpret them as the poems of political and moralistic lessons. He defiantly declared: "I would rather be a master of acrobatic feats, than to be a moralist".[9]

As to the proper behavior of a married couple, the Chinese Confucianism taught, 'there is a discrimination between man and wife', which stressed a distinction according to the hierarchical order of husband and wife. The Japanese Confucianists like Nakae Tōju (1608–1648), however, emphasized rather the harmony of husband and wife. "The husband should be righteous, while the wife should be obedient, and when both are in this manner in perfect harmony, that is the meaning of the way of discrimination".[10]

Hirata Atsutane (1760–1843) also rejected the Chinese thoughts in general, but he interpreted the 'Doctrine of the Mean' ('*Chung-yung*') as a doctrine of naturalism and as such he adopted it.

"Anyone knows perfectly well by nature, without borrowing others' teachings, that gods, the lords, and parents are respectable and the wife and children lovable. Teachings of the way of humanity, complex as they appear to be, are in fact originated from this simple fact. .... The '*Chung-yung*' says 'The destiny predetermined in the heaven is called natural dispositions. To comply with those natural dispositions is called the Way. And to practice the Way is called teachings'. Its meaning is that at the time of man's birth man is provided with the inborn true feelings of benevolence, justice, propriety and intelligence. .... These are called dispositions. .... Not to falsify or to distort them is the true way of humanity. One should train and regulate the one inborn way so that no evil heart should come out. To illustrate this with a near-by example, our countrymen are by nature brave, just and straight, and that is what we call *Yamato-gokoro* (the spirit of Japan) or *Mikuni-damashii* (the soul of this country) .... Since the True Way is as facile a matter as this, one should indeed stop acting like a sage and completely abandon the socalled mind or, the way of enlightenment, and all that are affected and Buddhaish. Let us, instead, not distort or forget this spirit of Japan, the soul of this country, but train and regulate it so that we may polish it up into a straight, just, pure and good spirit of Japan".[11]

The naturalistic tendency as mentioned above determines also the mode of acccpting Buddhism.

Onkō (Jiun-Sonja 1718–1804), a Buddhist of the modern period, to whom credit should be given for propagating Buddhism among the common people, preaches that morality means to follow man's natural dispositions.[12]

In the case of Onkō, he accepted man's natural dispositions emphasizing his ability to control his lower desires and sentiments. Naturalism in this sense, however, never became popular among the Japanese at large as an influential guiding principle in reality. Naturalism in the sense of satisfying man's desires and sentiments, instead, was a predominant trend in the Japanese Buddhism.

The Ritsu sect with its two hundred and fifty precepts was introduced also into Japan but it never became widespread as it was in India and China. Even the ascetic practices of the Ritsu sect (similar to those of the early Buddhist orders), which were far from being austere compared with those of the Indian ascetics, had too much of inhibitory elements to man's natural dispositions and instinct to be accepted by the majority of the Japanese. (These ascetic practices are still strictly observed today in Ceylon, Burma, Siam and Cambodia.) The Japanese Buddhism inclined to hedonism. The practice of the ceremony of prayer, for instance, was meant to the aristocrats of the Heian period for worldly pleasure. "In front of Prince Spring, the fragrance of the plum blossoms wafts faintly, mingled with the scent from inside the bamboo blind, and makes one feel as though one were in the land of a living Buddha".[13] For them, a Buddhist mass in this world was in itself the Pure Land, the Paradise. In fact, it meant merely *"to have a pleasant evening,* having the fine-voiced chant sūtras for them".[14]

Such a tendency finally led to the repudiation of disciplines.

"Ganjin (Chien-chen) of the Ryūkōji (Lung-hsing) Temple of T'ang propagated the Right Law of disciplines and initiated the Buddhist confirmation of that Law, which in the course of time came to be neglected. Since the Medieval period, the Buddhist confirmation has become only nominal, and people gather from various countries merely to run about the ordination platform of the temple. They know nothing of the large and small disciplines, nor do they try to learn anything of the regulations about the infringement of these disciplines. Instead, they merely count the years after taking orders, and let themselves degenerated into the priests who accept services for nothing. The observance of abstention and disciplines has thus come to its end".[15]

The repudiation of disciplines was especially popular among the followers of the Jōdo sect.

"Those who practice the invocation to Amitābha alone say playing the game of *go* (game) or that of *sugoroku* (a kind of backgammon) is no breach of their teachings. *A clandestine sexual intercourse* or the eating of meat and flesh is no hindrance to the rebirth into the Pure Land. The observance of disciplines in the age of degeneration is the tiger in the street. That ought to be dreaded; that ought to be detested. Should one be afraid of sins and shrink from evils, such a one would certainly be a man who never believes in the Buddha".[16] The Pure Realm teachings, preached by Hōnen (1133–1212), disregards the distinction between the observance of disciplines and the infringement of disciplines. It lays emphasis solely upon the practice of the invocation of Amitābha. "If one who eats fish should be reborn into the Pure Land, a cormorant would certainly be the one. If one who does not eat fish should be reborn into the Pure Land, a monkey would indeed be the one. Whether or not one eats fish does not count, but it is the one who invocates Amitābha that is bound to be reborn into the Pure Land".[17]

It was Nichiren (1222–1282) who was keen enough to point out that the Jōdo sect of Japan had turned into something entirely different in practice from that of China.

"According to Zendō (*Shan-tao*)'s *Gate to the Meditation,* it is said: 'Make a vow not to touch with your hand, not to put into your mouth wine, meat and five spices. Pray that your body and mouth be attached instantly by the venomous pox, should you breach these words'. These sentences mean that those men and women, nuns and monks who try to practice invocation of Amitābha should abstain from wine, from fish and flesh, and from five spices such as a leek, a scallion and others. Those invocators, who do not observe this, shall be attached by the venomous pox in this life and shall fall into the inferno. Disregarding this warning, the men and women, the nuns and monks who practice invocation of Amitābha, drink wine and eat fish and flesh to their hearts' content. Is it not like swallowing a sword?".[18]

The tendency to ignore disciplines seemed also to be evident among the Zen sect. The "*Nomori no Kagami*" (by Fujiwara no Arifusa, 1294) has the following passage rebuking the Zen sect: "By abusing the precedents of those who had attained enlightenment took some wine, meat, five spices, etc. for their own excuse, even those who have not yet attained that stage dare do the same shamelessly".[19]

It is a well-known fact that after the Meiji Restoration, practically all the sects of Buddhism broke off from the disciplines. So it amounted to this: for the followers of the Pure Land Buddhists, it is enough to invocate Amitābha; for the followers of the Nichiren sect, to chant the title of the Lotus Sūtra; for some of the others, to chant certain sūtras and to repeat *dhāraṇīs*.

The most outstanding sample of the repudiation of the disciplines is *drinking*. The Indian Buddhists considered drinking as a very serious religious sin. That was why 'no drinking' was counted among the five disciplines and was ordained to be strictly observed not only by priests and ascetics but also by the general lay believers. In India the discipline of no drinking was well observed from the time of the early Buddhism to that of the Mahāyāna Buddhism. (The late degenerated period of the esoteric Buddhism was an exception). In China also strictly observed was this discipline of no drinking. On its arrival to Japan, however, the discipline was forsaken.[20] Hōnen, in reply to the question: "Is it a sin to drink?", answered: "In truth you ought not to drink, but drinking is after all a custom of this world".[21] Either Shinran or Nichiren considered drinking not necessarily evil. Nichiren preached, "Drink only with your wife, and recite *Nam-myō-hō-renge-kyō* (Adoration to the Lotus Sūtra)!"[22] The Shugen sect maintained that if one puts a slip with the following magic formula, even the evil wine is transformed into the good wine.

"The gods know, and
Pray gods also drink
The Pure-water wine
Of the Mimosuso River".[23]

Together with drinking, the sexual intercourse between men and women also had its place in Buddhism in Japan. As has already being recognized in the Japanese literary works, a novel like *The Tale of Genji* describes lascivious scenes and immoral characters, which are considered to be not lacking in beauty. Herein lies one of the traditions of Japanese literature, which clearly distinguishes them from the ethical views of Confucianism. Buddhism also is tinged with the same tendency. Toward the period of the degeneration of Buddhism in India, certain immoral rituals were practiced by some Buddhists, but among the Buddhists in China such a thing almost never occurred. Even the esoteric Buddhism was transmitted into China in its purified form, which was then transplanted by Kōbō into Japan. The Japanese followers of the Shingon sect, which was founded by Kūkai (Kōbō Daishi 744–835), kept their purity in their daily practice of asceticism. Toward the end of the Heian period, however, there emerged such a heretical religion as the Tachikawa group. They identified the sexual intercourse with the secret meaning of becoming a Buddha being alive in the human body. Such immoral secret rituals appear to be prevalent in various districts from the beginning to the middle of the Kamakura period. The decadent elements of the Indian esoteric Buddhism at the age of degeneration, once almost perfectly purified in the Chinese esoteric Buddhism, was revived once again in Japan. However limited that influence might be, such a difference of the respective characteristics cannot be ignored.

The tendency similar to the Tachikawa sect also manifested itself in the Jōdo sect. An example of such is the so-called *Sōzoku-kaie no Ichinengi* (which assured salvation and expiation for those who observe the Doctrine of One Thought). It preaches as follows:

"What is called *ichinen* (one thought) reads that two persons become united in one thought. When man and woman are held together and both feel good, they cry out once in unison *Namu-ami-dabutsu,* that is exactly what the Doctrine of One Thought (*ichinengi*) means. So those who remained single, being afraid that they were unable to be born into the Pure Land, sought their mates".[24]

Even Nichiren, a priest of good conduct, says as follows: "It is the internal evidence that the object and knowledge are two different things and at the same time they are one and the same thing. These are extraordinarily important Gates to the Doctrine. There are the meanings of the phrases: the affliction is nothing but enlightenment; the mundane existence is nothing but Nirvāṇa. Man and woman, in copulation, chant *Nam-myō-hōrenge-kyō* (Adoration to the Lotus Sūtra)——that is exactly what we call the affliction is nothing but enlightenment, the mandane existence is nothing but Nirvāṇa".[25] This is not what Nichiren preached in one of his books of doctrines in his serious mood, but quoted from a passage in his letter to a certain warrior. This way of teaching, Nichiren seems to have thought, was congenial to the Japanese.

Up until now, Shōten (Gaṇeśa) and Aizen Myōō (God of Love) are widely worshipped as the objects of popular religion for the consummation of one's love. Shōten, or the God of Ecstacy was originally Gaṇeśa in India, adopted and metamorphosed by the esoteric Buddhism. The images of Gaṇeśa now existent in India are by no means obscene. Such a religious custom of worshipping the images of the elephant-faced god and goddess in an embrace is confined perhaps to Japan and Tibet only.

It was in the similar manner that the entirely different meanings were bestowed upon those phrases which originally signified the fundamental ideas of Buddhism. Chikamatsu Monzaemon, the famous playwright (1653–1724), in describing lovers on their way to committing suicide, celebrates the beauty of their last moments as follows: "Adieu to this world, adieu to the night. .... The remaining one toll is the last sound of the bell they hear on earth; 'tranquility is comfort' is its sound".[26] *'Shinjū'* is a phenomenon peculiar to Japan and it is impossible to convey its real sentiment with such Western expressions as a 'double suicide' or 'Selbstmord eines Liebespaares'. But in any case, whereas the phrase 'tranquility is comfort' (*vyupaśamah sukham*)[27] meant originally both in India and in China the denial of worldly afflictions, it is now used in Japan for expressing the ultimate state of the worldly consummation of the sexual love.

The various literary works of the Tokugawa period show that the words which originally stood for the sacred ideas of Buddhism came to be used as the cryptology to suggest the scenes of lust and dissipation. Such instances of sacrilege never occurred either in India or in China. They are the phenomena perhaps peculiar to Japan.

Whereas the majority of the Indians and the Chinese in general are trying to distinguish the world of religion from that of the lusts of the flesh, there is a latent tendency among the Japanese to identify the one with the other. In this way the *same characteristics as mentioned before in respect to the form of accepting Confucianism* are also said to be present in respect to that of accepting Buddhism.

Even the traditional and conservative Buddhists in India were aware of the fact that the disciplines are hard to be observed strictly in its original form but they undergo changes according to the difference of time and place. "The Buddha announced to various priests, 'Although these disciplines are constituted by me, it is not necessary that you should use them all, if you find them not pure in other districts. As to disciplines that are not established by me, you should not hesitate to practice them all, if it is necessary to do so in other districts' ".[28]

In spite of these concessions made by the Buddha, there is no other race in the Asiatic countries than the Japanese that have forsaken almost all of the Buddhist disciplines. How should we account for this fact?

We shall later dwell upon the tendency of the Japanese to hold fast to the specific and closed social nexus. The repudiation of disciplines may seem on the surface to be incompatible with such a tendency. But these two are not necessarily in conflict. The disciplines are not always in agreement with common-sense morals. The eating of meat and flesh was permitted under certain circumstances by the early Buddhism, whereas it was prohibited by most of Mahāyāna Buddhism. Drinking was prohibited both in Hīnayāna and Mahāyāna Buddhism. The marriage for the priest was not allowed except for the esoteric Buddhism in later periods. These are important problems from the standpoint of religion, but from the point of view of defending the interests of the closed social nexus, they do not count very much. Quite prevalent among the Japanese is the double-barreled attitudes of ignoring the disciplines on the one hand and of self-sacrificing devotion to the interests of the closed social nexus on the other. Such an attitude gave rise to their idea that the assertion of natural desires and the repudiation of the disciplines do not necessarily mean the throwing away of the moral order.

The lack of the guiding spirit is often talked about and people frequently allude to the corruption of religionists. But such a phenomenon is more deep rooted than the mere responsibilities of religionists. They are imbedded in the Japanese way of thinking from the past.

We have reflected mainly upon the domain of religion, but the similar ways of thinking seems to be prevalent in other domains also.

---

1) In *Tamakatsuma* 玉かつま vol. 10, *Motoori Norinaga Zenshū* 本居宣長全集 vol. 4, p. 236. See also Muraoka Tenshi 村岡典嗣: *Motoori Norinaga* 本居宣長 p. 430 ff.—Motoori's judgment on the *Shih-ching* is based, of course, on the moralizing interpretation of the songs in that book given by the Confucianists.

2) See Junsei Iwahashi 岩橋遵成: *Sorai Kenkyū* (徂徠研究 Study on Ogyū Sorai), p. 433.

3) *Ibid.*, p. 331 f.

4) See, e.g. Motoori Norinaga, *Genji Monogatari Tama-no-ogushi* 源氏物語玉のをぐし, *Motoori Norinaga Zenshū* vol. 5, p. 1135 ff.

5) In *Bendō* 辯道, *Nihon Jurin Sōsho, Ronben-bu* 日本儒林叢書論辯部 p. 14.

6) In Dazai's *Keizai-roku* 經濟錄 vol. I, fol. 10.

7) In *Seigaku Mondō* 聖學問答 3, quoted in Inoue Tetsujirō 井上哲次郎, *Nihon Kogakuha no Tetsugaku* (日本古學派の哲學 Philosophy in Japanese Classical Study Group), p. 693.

8) *Ibid.*, quoted in Inoue *op. cit.* p. 698.

9) In *Gakusoku* 學則 7, quoted in Iwahashi (op. cit. p. 231.)

10) In *Okina Mondō* 翁問答 1, a, *Tōju Sensei Zenshū* 藤樹先生全集 vol. III, p. 76.

11) In *Kodō-taii* 古道大意 3, *Hirata Atsutane Zenshū* 平田篤胤全集 vol. VIII. p. 69.

12) See his various versions of "The Words of the Teaching in Kana (the Japanese alphabet)". *Jiun-Sonja Zenshū* 慈雲尊者全集 vol. 3.

13) From the *Genji Monogatari* 源氏物語, quoted in Yasusada Hiyane 比屋根安定: *Nihon Shūkyō-shi* (日本宗教史 History of Japanese Religion), p. 410.

14) From the *Eiga Monogatari* 榮華物語, quoted in Y. Hiyane *op. cit.* p. 410.
15) *Shaseki-shū* 沙石集 vol. III b, ed. by Ebara Taizō 穎原退藏, p. 106.
16) *Kōfukuji-sōjō* 興福寺奏狀, in *Dai-Nippon Bukkyō Zensho* 大日本佛教全書 vol. CXXIV, p. 107.
17) *Hōnen Shōnin Gyōjō-ezu* 法然上人行狀畫圖 vol. XXI, in *Jōdo-shū Zensho* 浄土宗全書 vol. XVI, p. 240.
18) *Shōgu Mondō-shō* 聖愚問答鈔 in *Shōwa Shinshū Nichiren Shōnin Imon-zenshū* 昭和新修日蓮上人遺文全集 vol. I, p. 474.
19) Fujiwara Arifusa 藤原在房: *Nomori no Kagami* 野守鏡 vol II, in *Gunsho-ruijū* 群書類從 2nd ed., vol. XXI, p. 263.
20) See Butsujō Kokushi 佛頂國師: *Daibai-zan Yawa*: 大梅山夜話 in *Zenmon Hōgo-shū* 禪門法語集 vol. II, p. 603 f.
21) *Hōnen Shōnin Gyōjō-ezu* vol XXII, in *Jōdo-shū Zensho* vol XVI, p. 20.
22) In his letter to Shijō Kingo (四條金吾殿御返事), in *Shōwa Shinshū Nichiren Shōnin Imon-zenshū* vol. II, p. 1407.
23) In *Shugen Shimpi Gyōhō Fuju-shū* 修驗深祕行法符呪集 vol. VII, Nihon *Daizōkyō Shugen Shōso-bu* 日本大藏經修驗章疏部 vol. II, p. 101.
24) *Nembutsu Myōgi-shū* 念佛名義集 vol. II, in *Jōdo-shū Zensho* vol. X, p. 376.
25) In his letter to Shijō Kingo, in *Shōwa Shinshū Nichiren Shōnin Imon-zenshū* vol. I, p. 866.
26) At the end of his play *Sonezaki Shinjū* 曾根崎心中, in *Kindai Nihon Bungaku Taikei* 近代日本文學大系 vol. VI. p. 247 f.
27) Jakumetsu-iraku 寂滅爲樂.
28) In *Shibun-ritsu* 四分律 vol. XXIII, (*Taishō* vol. XXII, p. 153 a); see also *Shibunritsu Sampan Gyōji-shō Jo* 四分律删繁行事鈔序 (*ibid.* vol. XL, p. 2 a.)

(4) Emphasis on the love of human beings

The tendency of the Japanese to accept the given reality manifests itself especially in the form of the acceptance and high esteem for man's natural dispositions. As has been already mentioned, the Buddhist ideas were preached with a close reference to the matters of love and sexual love is considered not to be incompatible with religious matters.

The tendency to esteem man's nature gave rise to the love of human beings in reality. Not only the significance of the real body was recognized, but also the idea of taking good care of one's body became prominent in Japanese Buddhism.[1]

"Question: The sūtra says one could not be Bodhisattva[2] unless one serves Buddhas by burning one's own body, elbows and fingers. What is the meaning? Answer: The burning of one's body, elbows and fingers is metaphorically used to mean elimination of the three darknesses of the branch, the leaf and the root..... If one eliminates these three darknesses, one becomes a Bodhisattva (a future Buddha who wants to save all living beings)..... If one should try to serve the Buddhas by burning one's sensual body, would any Buddha receive it?"

Here practices actually followed among the Buddhists both in India and China were completely denied by the Japanese Buddhists.

The Japanese lay special emphasis upon the love of others. Kumazawa Banzan, a famous Confucianist of the Tokugawa period, calls Japan 'The land of benevolence'.[3]

The love of others in its purified form is named 'benevolence' (Skrt. maitrī, karuṇā). This idea was introduced into Japan with the advent of Buddhism, and special emphasis was laid upon it in Japanese Buddhism.

Among many sects of Japanese Buddhism, the Pure Land Buddhism (Jōdo sects), a religion which typically emphasizes benevolence, enjoys great popularity. The Pure Land Buddhism preaches the benevolence of Amitābha Buddha who saves even the bad man and the ordinary man. Most of the high priests of the sect have especially benign looks.

The emphasis upon the deeds of benevolence is recognizable also in other sects.

The Japanese accepted the practice of the strict disciplines handed down from early Buddhism in the form of the 'Ritsu sect'. This sect followed rather a seclusionist method of ascetic practice. Later, however, with its development into Shingon-ritsu sect, a priest like Ninshō (1217–1303) launched upon such social welfare works as to save the suffering and the sick. He dedicated his whole life to the service of others. For this he was even criticized by his master, 'he overdid benevolence'.[4]

It was a breach of the ancient disciplines to dig ponds or wells or to save medicine and clothing for the sick or to accumulate money for them, but he never let himself be influenced by this.[5]

Needless to say, the idea of benevolence had an important significance in Chinese Buddhism. The Zen Buddhism, however, that was developed as the Chinese people's Buddhism, did not seem to emphasize the idea of benevolence too much. To confirm this, there is not a single reference made to the word "benevolence" in such well-known scriptures as '*Shinjin-mei*' (The Epigram of Faith), '*Shōdōka*' (the Songs of Enlightenment), '*Sandō kai*' (The Compliance with the Truth), and the '*Hōkyō-zanmai*' (the Precious-Mirror Meditation),[6] To go back still further, nothing is said about it in what is supposed to be the teachings of Bodhidharma.[7]

It is probably that the Chinese Zen sect, under the influence of Taoism and other traditional ideologies of China, was inclined to seclusion and resignation and neglected the positive approach of practicing deeds of benevolence. Such is my general impression, though a final conclusion cannot be drawn until we have made a thorough study of the general history of the Chinese Zen sect.

At the time the Zen sect was brought into Japan, however, it came to emphasize the deeds of benevolence, just as the other sects in Japan did. Eisai, who introduced Rinzai-zen, put the idea of benevolence at the foremost. In a reply to the question whether the Zen sect was too much obsessed by the idea of the void, he says: "To prevent by means of self-discipline the evil from without and to profit others with benevolence within. This is what Zen is".[8] As for the rules for ascetics of the Zen sect, he teaches: "You should arouse the spirit of great benevolence...and save mankind widely with the pure and supreme disciplines of the Great Bodhisattva, but you ought not to seek deliverance for your own sake".[9] Soseki (Musō Kokushi), Suzuki Shōsan, Shidō Bunan, and other Zen priests represent a positive repulsion against the seclusionist and self-satisfied attitude of the traditional Zen sect. They stress, instead, the virtue of benevolence.

Dōgen, although he does not often use the word, 'benevolence' overtly, chooses for instruction the phrase, 'speak kindly to others', (the words of affection) from among the various Buddhist doctrines of the past. "Speaking words of affection means to generate the heart of benevolence and bestow upon others the language of affection, whenever one sees them. To speak with the heart, looking at mankind with benevolence as though they were your own children, is to utter words of affection. The virtuous should be praised, the virtueless pitied. To cause the enemy to surrender, or to make the wise yield, words of affection are most fundamental. To hear words of affection in one's presence brightens one's countenance and warms one's heart. To hear words of affection in one's presence pleases one's countenance and warms one's heart. To hear the words of affection said in one's absence goes home to one's heart and soul. You should learn to know that words of affection are as powerful as to set the river on fire".[10]

In addition, he puts emphasis upon the virtues of giving, altruism and collaboration, at the bottom of which flows the pure current of affection.

The spirit of benevolence was not only preached by the Buddhists, but it also made its way into Shintoism and was tied up with one of the three divine symbols of the Japanese imperial family. It was also popularized among the general public and came to be regarded as one of the principal virtues of the *samurai*.[11]

The love of others by no means comes out of self-complacency. On the contrary, it goes with a humble reflection that I, as well as others, am an ordinary man. This had already been stressed by Prince Shōtoku at the beginning of the introduction of Buddhism into Japan.

"Forget resentment, forsake anger, do not become angry just because some one opposes you. Every one has a mind, every mind comes to a decision, and decisions will not always be alike. If he is right, you are wrong; if you are not quite a saint, he is not quite an idiot. Both disputants are men of ordinary mind; who is decisively capable of judging an argument between them? If both are wise men or both foolish men their argument is probably a vicious circle. For this reason, if your opponent grows angry, you had better be all the more cautious lest you too should be in error. Although you might think you are quite right, it is wiser to comply with the other man".[12]

Out of this emerged the spirit of tolerance, which shall be discussed in the next section.

A problem remains whether or not this tendency to stress love is inherent to the Japanese people. That there is no god of love in Shintoism was once criticized by a famous Buddhist scholar, which caused a great sensation among the Shintoists. They presented some counter-evidence, which seemed far from convincing. This issue cannot be settled as yet, but requires further investigation. But a general impression is that the spirit of benevolence was introduced into Japan probably with the advent of Buddhism and exerted a renovating influence upon the mental attitude of the Japanese. And within this limit, it may be asserted that there exists a certain element of humanism in the thinking of common man in Japan.

The love of human beings seems to be closely tied up with the love of the beauties of nature, which is as old as the people themselves.

1) *Bassui Zenji Hōgo* 抜隊禪師法語 p. 51, ed. by D. T. Suzuki 鈴木大拙.
2) A bodhisattva is a future Buddha who wants to save all living beings.
3) *Shūgi-washo* 集義和書, vol. 10.
4) *Kōshō Bosatsu Kyōkun Chōmon-shū* 興正菩薩教訓聽聞集, in *Kokubun Tōhō Bukkyō Sōsho* 國文東方佛教叢書, Hōgo-bu, pp. 99–100.
5) Nissaggiya-pācittiya 18–20; 23; 28; Pācittiya 10–11. cf. H. Nakamura, in *Nihon Rekishi* (日本歴史 The Japanese History), 1949, Nov.–Dec.
6) H. Ui: *Zenshū-shi Kenkyū* (禪宗史研究 A Study on the History of Zen Sect), pp. 3 ff. Tokyo, Iwanami.
7) Founder of Chinese Zen Buddhism.

8) *Taisho*. vol. 80, p. 7 b.
9) *Ibid*. p. 12 a.
10) *Sōtō Kyōkai Shushōgi* 曹洞教會修證義.
11) H. Nakamura: *Jihi* (慈悲 Benevolence), Kyoto, the Heirakuji, 1956, passim.
12) The Seventeen Article, Constitution of Prince Shōtoku, X.

(5) The spirit of tolerance

The Japanese are said to be distinguished for her spirit of torelance from the ancient days. Although there must have been instances of inter-racial conflicts in the prehistoric Japan, there exists no archeological evidence, that their armed conflicts were very violent. According to the classical records also, the Japanese treated conquered peoples tolerantly. As for the tales of wars there are many, but there is no evidence that conquered peoples were made into slaves *in toto*. Even prisoners were not treated as slaves in the Western sense of the word. Although there remains some doubt as to whether or not there existed a slave-economy in ancient Japan, the percentage of the slave-servants was very small in the whole population. It may be safely concluded, therefore, that slave labor was never used on a large-scale basis.

Such a social condition gives rise to the tendency to stress the harmony between the members of a society rather than the dominance controlled by power relationship. This is not to deny entirely the presence of the latter relationship in Japanese society since the olden days. The social restrictions and pressures upon the individual might have been indeed stronger in Japan than in many other countries. Nevertheless in the consciousness of each individual Japanese, the spirit of conciliation and tolerance is preeminent.

Ancient Japanese society had a system of government by religious ritual. In contrast to Judea, which was also a system of government by religious ritual, in Japan the sense of harmony of the community pervaded the whole climate of social consciousness. Jehovah is the God of Jealousy, of Revenge, and of Justice, but not of Love. It was through the crucifixion of his only son that Jehovah turned himself into the God of Love. But among the gods and goddesses worshipped in the ancient Japanese festivities, harmony and love were the keynotes of the atmosphere. The gods and goddesses called one another their "loving" ones. They are said to have "got drunk with wine and fallen asleep", or "played together for eight days and for eight nights".

The spirit of tolerance of the Japanese made it impossible to cultivate deep hatred even toward sinners. In Japan there existed hardly any cruel punishments. Since crucifixion appeared for the first time in Japanese history during the Age of Civil Wars, it was presumably started after the advent of Christianity and suggested by it. Burning at the stake seems to have been practised during the reign of Emperor Yūryaku (457–479), but it went out of use afterwards to be revived occasionally during the modern period.[1] In the medieval West, the condemnation at the stake was officiated under religious authority, which never happened in Japan. During the Heian period, capital punishment was out of practice for more than three hundred years until the War of Hogen (1156) took place.[2] Although this may be attributed to the influence of Buddhism, there has hardly been any period in any other country marked with the absence of the death penalty.

For the Japanese, full of the spirit of tolerance, *eternal damnation* is absolutely inconceivable. A Catholic priest, who forsook Christianity under the persecution of the Tokugawa Government, condemned the idea of the eternal damnation preached in Christianity. He said that as to the reward and punishment in the other world, if God be the Lord of Benevolence, he ought to condemn Himself rather than condemning human beings and punishing them for their sins. From among the doctrines of Christianity the idea of the eternal damnation was especially hard for the Japanese to comprehend. M. Anezaki commenting on this point, says: 'This is the outstanding line of demarcation between Judaism and Buddhism'.[3] This also reveals one of the characteristic ideas long held by the Japanese.

The idea of "being beyond deliverance forever" was also hard for the Japanese to comprehend. The Hossō sect, a school of Buddhist Idealism, advocates "the difference of five predispositions". Among men there are five differences, one who is predisposed to become a Bodhisattva, one to become Enkaku (*pratyekabuddha,* one who attains self-complacent enlightenment), one to become *Shōmon* (śrāvaka, an ascetic of Hīnayāna Buddhism), one who is not predisposed, and one who is beyond deliverance. Such an idea of discrimination was not generally accepted by the Japanese Buddhists. Prevalently accepted, instead, was the view, "All men are predisposed to become Buddhas".

A question may be raised here as follows. Is not the spirit of tolerance prominent among the Japanese an influence of Buddhism rather than an intrinsic Japanese characteristic? Before the advent of Buddhism the

Japanese also resorted to atrocities. Are not Emperor Buretsu (499–506) and Yūryaku described as violent and ruthless? The reason why the death penalty was abandoned during the Heian period was that the ideal of Buddhism was realized in politics. Even in present-day Japan, statistics prove beyond question that in the districts where *Haibutsu Kishaku* (the abolition of Buddhism by violence immediately after the Meiji Restoration) was committed the cases of the murder of one's close relatives are high in number, whereas such cases are relatively few where Buddhism is vehemently supported. The conversely however, it may also be true that because the Japanese were inherently tolerant and conciliatory, the infiltration of Buddhism into the peoples' lives was rapid. It is often pointed out by cultural historians that the Chinese people as a whole are inclined to ruthlessness and cruelty, in spite of the fact that the Buddhist influence has a longer history in China than in Japan. In Tibet, despite its being the country of Lamaism flying the banner of Buddhism, the severest of punishments are still in use.[4] Thus it may be concluded that the Japanese had originally possessed the spirit of tolerance and forgiveness to some extent, which was extremely strengthened by the introduction of Buddhism, and was again weakened in recent years by the aggrandizement of the secular power on the one hand and by the decline of faith in Buddhism on the other.

The fact that the Japanese are richly endowed with the spirit of tolerance and conciliation while they lack in the tendency for the intense hatred of sins also transformed the Pure Land Buddhism. According to his eighteenth vow Amitābha Buddha will save the whole of mankind out of his great benevolence, excepting only "those who committed five great sins and those who condemned the Right Law (= Buddhism)". Zendō (*Shan-tao*) of China interpreted the sentence as meaning that even great sinners, under the condition that they be converted, could be reborn into the Pure Land. Introduced into Japan, these exceptions were later considered as problematic, and came to be completely ignored by Hōnen. "This (salvation) includes all that are embraced in the great benevolence and the real vow of Amitābha, *even the ten evils and five great sins not being excluded,* and those who excel in those practices other than that of invocation of Amitābha being also included. Its meaning is to believe in what are revealed in the invocation of Amitābha for once and also for ten times".[5] "You should believe that even those who have committed the ten evils and the five heinous sins are eligible for rebirth in the Pure

Land, and yet you should shrink from the slightest of all the sins".[6] As far as the surface meaning of the sentence is concerned, Hōnen is diametrically opposed to the Indian men of religion who compiled the Dai-mu-ryō-ju Sūtra (*Sukhāvatī-vyūha-sūtra*). Out of such an inclination of thinking was formulated the so-called "view of the eligibility of the evil ones for salvation" (the view that the evil are rightfully eligible for salvation by Amitābha Buddha). This view may not be what Shinran really meant. But the fact that such a view was generally considered to be the fundamental doctrine of the (Jōdo) Shin sect cannot be denied.

Such a way of thinking amounts to this: however evil one may be, one is always saved, provided that one is dead. The dead are called "Buddhas" by the Japanese. The dead, however heinous their earthly crimes, are completely free from all responsibility for them, and the most wicked are sometimes considered to be extraordinary spiritual entities. This give rise to the strange phenomenon that the spirits of murderers and burglars are enshrined, or their graveyards are crowded with worshippers.

What are the rational bases for such a spirit of tolerance and conciliation? The tendency to recognize the absolute significance in everything phenomenal leads up to the acceptance of the *raison d'être* of any view held in the mundane world, and ends up with the connivance of any view with the spirit of tolerance and conciliation.[7]

Such a way of thinking appeared from the earliest days of the introduction of Buddhism into this country. According to Prince Shōtoku, the Hokke Sūtra (*Saddharmapuṇḍarīka-sūtra*), supposed to contain the ultimate essence of Buddhism, preaches the doctrine of the One Great Vehicle and advocate the theory "that any one of a myriad of good acts leads to one thing, the attainment of Enlightenment".[8] According to the prince, there is no innate difference between the saint and the most stupid.[9] Every one of them is primarily and equally a child of the Buddha. Prince Shōtoku regarded secular moral teachings as the elementary gate to enter Buddhism. He uses the expressions 'heretical doctrine' and 'pagan religion', but those expressions are borrowed rather from the traditional Indian terminology. He does not mean by them the doctrines of Lao-tzu and Chuang-tzu or Confucianism.[10] His interpretation of Buddhism is characterized by its all-inclusive nature. Only through taking into consideration of such a philosophical background, one is able to understand the moral idea of the prince when he says, "Harmony is to be honoured".[11]

It was this spirit that made possible the emergence of Japan as an unified cultural state.

Prince Shōtoku's philosophical standpoint is represented by the expressions, 'The One Great Vehicle' and 'The Pure Great Vehicle', which are supposed to have originated in the Hokke Sūtra. Ever since Saichō (Dengyō Daishi) introduced the Tendai sect, based upon the Hokke Sūtra, the Hokke Sūtra has come to constitute the backbone of Japanese Buddhism. Nichiren said; "Japan is single-heartedly the country of the Hokke Sūtra", and "For more than four hundred years since Emperor Kanmu, all the people of Japan have been single-heartedly devoted to the Hokke Sūtra". These words of Nichiren are not necessarily to be regarded as a selfcentered interpretation. Considering that the Pure Land Buddhism (Jōdo sect) and the Zen sect even, not to mention the Nichiren sect, are evidently under the influence of the Tendai doctrine, there is much truth in these assertions of Nichiren. Among the poems composed by various emperors on Buddhism, the subject-matter is overwhelmingly concerned with the doctorines of the Hokke Sūtra. The thought-tendency characteristic to the Hokke Sūtra which tried to accept the *raison d'être* of all the practices of Buddhism led to the extremely tolerant and conciliatory attitudes to various ideas..

Toward the end of the Heian period, there were those among ordinary men who prayed for the rebirth into the Pure Land through the merit of their observance of the Hokke Sūtra.

"All those who act in accordance with the *Hokke,* covering themselves with the armour of forbearance and not clinging to the dew-like life of mundane existence, shall climb upon the lotus dais".[13]

The idea of climbing upon the lotus dais is not to be found in the Hokke Sūtra itself. It shows rather the fusionist characteristic of the religious faith of the period.

Kōben (1173–1232) of the Kegon sect put together various faiths of both exoteric and esoteric Buddhism. There is no unity, no central focus in his religion, whose content is most heterogenious. "This high priest never limited himself to the teaching of one saint, but practiced in turn the religions of one saint after another". What is the cause of this? According to his own interpretation. "Each attains well-rounded enlightenment according to his customary practice. Since there is not just one customary practice (but many), the well-rounded enlightenment also cannot be just one".[14] He recognized the *raison d'être* of multiple religious faiths.

Owing to such a spirit of tolerance and conciliation, the development on a single continuum of various sects was possible within Japanese Buddhism. In India today, there is no Buddhist tradition extant. In China uniformity was established in Buddhism, where the Zen sect fused with the Pure Land Buddhism was the only remaining religious sect, while the traditions of all the rest of the sects almost went out of existence. In Japan, by contrast, there still exist many traditional sects which can no longer be found in China or in India.

In spite of the highly sectarian and factional tendency of the various religious sects keeping their traditional differences intact, the contempt of other sects was mutually prohibited by Japanese Buddhists. Even Rennyo (1415–1499) of the Jōdo-shin sect, which is supposed to be inclined toward monotheism and exclusionism, warns: "You ought not make light of shrines", or "You ought not slander other sects and other teachings".[15] Suzuki Shōsan, a Zen priest, ordains: "In this monastery the right and wrong of the world or the relative merits of other sects ought not to be talked about".[16] Jiun admonishes his disciples: "The right and wrong or the high and low of the teachings of other sects should not be discussed".[17]

Such an attitude of tolerance might have been handed down from early Buddhism. It is noteworthy that, despite the sectarian and factional tendency of the Japanese, they did not want to dispute with their opponents. Realistically speaking, the accomodation of Shintoism and Buddhism might have very well been an expedient measure taken in order to avoid possible friction between the traditional religion and the in-coming Buddhism, which came to be accepted as a national religion. It may also be said that it was political considerations that made Hōnen and Rennyo warn against rejecting sects other than their own. As far as subjective consciousness of each man is concerned, however, it is right to assert that the spirit of tolerance was the most influential factor. The most easily thought of instance of intolerance in Japan in the past is the Nichiren sect. But even this sect embraces many non-Buddhistic gods of India and of Japan and has adopted some elements of Shintoism and of popular faiths. The Jōdo-Shin sect appears to concentrate on pure faith in Amitābha, prohibiting religious practices other than the invocation of Amitābha. Nevertheless, this sect commends the worship of such a human being as the chief abbot and other fetishistic practices related to it.

An attitude of tolerance determined the all-inclusive and conciliatory nature of Japanese Buddhism. The ascendency of Buddhism in Japan in the course of more than ten centuries was entirely different from that of Christianity in the West. Buddhism tolerated various primitive faiths native to Japan. The clear notion of paganism was absent in Japanese Buddhism. The gods in the native Japanese popular religion, who should have been considered as pagan gods from the standpoint of Buddhism, were reconciled with Buddhism as 'temporary manifestations' (incarnations) of the Buddha. Along this line of thought a theory, called *Honji-Suijaku-setsu* was advanced in which the Shintoist gods were maintained to be temporary incarnarnations of the Buddha. Emperor Yōmei is said "to have believed in Buddhism and at the same time worshipped gods of Shintoism".[18] Precisely what Shintoism means in the above quotation needs to be clarified, since in the Nara period the idea of the accomodation of Shintoism and Buddhism had already come to the fore. According to this school of thought, the god rejoices in the Law of the Buddha and defends Buddhism, but since the god is an entity in the mundane world just as other human beings are and is not free from affliction, he also seeks salvation. The Nara period saw many a shrine-temple built. The Imperial message of 767 A.D. stated that the auspicious signs appeared, thanks to the Buddha, the Japanese gods and goddesses of the heaven and earth, and the spirits of the various emperors.

Thereafter, during the Heian period, (794–1192 A.D.) there were few shrines that did not have shrine-temples built in their confines, where Buddhist priests performed the morning and evening practices of reciting sūtras, and served shrine gods and goddesses together with Shintoist priests. The structure of the shrines was taken after that of Buddhist temples. At the Iwashimizu-Hachiman Shrine, whose construction was promoted by the priest Gyōkyō, the religious service was performed after the fashion of the Buddhist mass, and almost all the officials there in service were Buddhist priests. Simple offerings being offered, surplices and Buddhist utensils being dedicated, the whole rituals of the shrine were very much akin to those of a temple. Later on the shrines of Gion, Kitano and Kumano followed suit. Therein established was the institution of the shrine-temple, whose gods were named the gods of abstinence.

Deep-rooted, however, was the belief among the common men in the native gods and goddesses, to which Buddhists had to reconcile. The status of gods and goddesses were then enhanced to such an extent that they were entitled Bodhisattvas, and the recitation of Buddhist sūtras was performed in front of their altars. The gods and goddesses were thus exalted from the status of strayed mankind to that of the persons who were on their way toward enlightenment, or to the status of those who save mankind. The priests like Saichō and Kūkai sought access to the shrines and respected them, and at the same time they tried to make their own sects prosperous by utilizing the influence of the shrine. When Saichō pioneered the divine mountain of Hiei in Ōmi, where the spirit of Ōyamagui-no-Mikoto had rested for ages, to construct the Enryakuji temple, he enshrined therein the god of Ōmiwa, whom he named the god of Ōhiei and entitled him Sannō (the Mountain-God). Jikaku (784–864) founded the Akayama-Myōjin Shrine. Kūkai, who constructed the Kongōbuji Temple at the divine place of the Nifutsuhime Shrine, according to an old folk tale, prayed for the assistance of Nifu-Myōjin while he tried to pioneer mountain Kōya.[19] He is also said to have made the Inari Shrine into the guardian god of the Tōji Temple. These stories relate the history of ancient divine areas being turned into the sacred regions of Buddhism and of the shrines therein being attached with some newly fabricated interpretations of their origins related to Buddhism. The motivation for these peculiar endeavors for reconciliation, as I take it, was the building-up of the security of the confines and estates of the Buddhist temple through the clever maneuvering of the popular faith in native gods and goddesses. During the years of Bunji (1185–1189), Chōgen (Shunjō-bō) thought it an effective gesture to confine himself in the Ise Shrine and thus to appeal to the people's religious sentiments, for the realization of his great vow to solicit contributions for the reconstruction of the Tōdaiji Temple.[20]

The idea that the Japanese native gods are the temporary manifestations of the Buddha first appeared in the classical writings of the years of Kankō (1004–1012 A.D.), in the middle of the Heian period. After the reign of Emperor Gosanjō, a question was raised as to what the fundamental basis was, whose manifestations were those native gods and goddesses. During the period of the Civil Wars between the Genji and Heike Clans, each god or goddess was gradually alotted to his or her own Buddha, whose incarnation he or she was supposed to be, until at last during the Shōkyū years (1219–1222), the idea was established that the god and the Buddha were identical in the body. "There is no difference between what is called a Buddha and what is called a god".[21] Shōgun Ashikaga Takauji (1305–1350), in his letter of a vow dedicated to the Shrine of Gion, says: "Although a Buddha and a god are said to be different in the body, they are the inside and outside of the self-same thing".[22] The doctrinal organization of the theory that gods and goddesses were the temporary manifestations of Buddhas or Bodhisattvas was completed during the Kamakura period and its ideological gist was kept intact up to the Meiji Restoration.

The Buddhists of the Medieval period genuinely respected Shintoist scriptures, which they studied with sincerity and piety. Almost all the representative Shintoist scriptures extant today, such as *Kojiki, Nihonshoki, Kogo Shūi,* and others were copied by medieval Buddhist priests and thus transmitted to the posterity.[23]

What is the way of thinking that made such an accomodation of Buddhism and Shintoism possible? The influence of the traditional character of Buddhism cannot be denied, and it is particularly important to point out the influence of the idea of the One Vehicle manifested in the Hokke Sūtra. The Imperial Rescript of November of the year 836 A.D. says: "There is nothing more superior than the One Vehicle to defend Shintoism".[24] It goes without saying that Nichiren, who expressed his absolute allegiance to the Hokke Sūtra, also showed his genuine loyalty to the Japanese gods and goddesses. Even the Jōdo-shin sect, which was originally opposed to the gods and goddesses of Shintoism, tempered their oppositions to a more conciliatory attitude after Zonkaku (1290–1373). The theoretical basis for such a rapprochement was provided not by the triple-sūtras of the Pure Land Buddhism but by the Tendai doctrine based upon the Hokke Sūtra.

The Japanese native gods, exalted as they are from natural religious deity, kept their own distinctive existence intact. In this respect they differ completely from the occidental counterpart such as the ancient German religion, a trace of which was slightly maintained in the form of Christmas festivity within Christianity. The Japanese never considered it necessary to repudiate their religious faith in the native gods in order to become devoted followers of Buddhism. In this manner they brought about the conception of 'God-Buddhas'. It is generally noticed even today that the ardent Buddhist is at the same time a pious worshipper of Shintoist gods. The majority of the Japanese pray before the shrine and at the same time pay homage to the temple, without being conscious of any contradiction.

The same relationship as exists in the mind of the Japanese between Shintoism and Buddhism also holds true in the relationship between Buddhism and Confucianism. When the continental civilization was transplanted into Japan, Buddhism and Confucianism were simultaneously introduced, but there seems to be no theoretical conflicts taking place in the minds of the Japanese or no ideological warfares occurring on Japanese soil. On the contrary, Yamanoue Okura (d. 733), a famous poet, took a conciliatory standpoint that despite the difference existing between Buddhism and Confucianism, they amount to the same thing: "Although their ways of guiding are two, both lead up to the one and only one attainment of enlightenment".[25]

After the dawn of the Modern era, Confucianism came to flourish with the political backing of the ruling class, and from then on a doctrine was widely advocated to assert the unity of the three religions, i.e., Shintoism, Confucianism and Buddhism.

During the Tokugawa period *Kanazōshi* (popular novels written in the Kana characters) and other similar writings were extremely popular among the common folk. Most of them were written from the Buddhist point of view, with some exceptions written from the Confucian standpoint. The most famous of those were *The Tale of Kiyomizu, The Tale of Kiyomizu Continued, The Tale of Gion, The Tale of Daibutsu,* and others, all of which were written mainly from the view-point of the unity of the three religions. This was in spite of the fact that the Shintoist and Buddhist priests were deeply involved in sectarian and factional conflicts. The common men reconciled and fused those religions on whose difference the priests insisted. Otoo Fujii comments as follows: "What a close contact Confucianism and Buddhism were made to have in the *Kanazōshi*? Among the scholars conflicts and controversies were many in advocating their respective doctrines, but among the common men they were made to fuse and compromise. The Japanese are by nature inclined to rapprochement without threshing out an issue. No one has as yet taken up a noteworthy controversy between Confucianism and Buddhism, but, instead, there are already many who advocate the unity of the three religions".[26] Such a theoretical standpoint was represented in its most consistent form *Sekimon Shingaku,* which exerted the greatest influence upon common men. Scholars like Tejima Toan, Ishida Baigan (1685–1744), Nakazawa Dōni (1735–1803), Shibata Kyūō (1783–1839) belonged to this school, from whose standpoint they were cynical about the conflicts of various sects.

Such a conciliatory attitude seems ultimately to originate in our national traits. When the Christian civilization penetrated into our society after the Meiji Restoration, those who welcomed it were not necessarily Christians. For common men in Japan there was nothing about Christianity that was incompatible with their traditional religion. That was the reason, it appears to be, why the Christian culture became considerably widespread despite the extremely small minority converted into the Christian religion.

Perhaps social scientists will in the end furnish us with statistical proof for my suggestion that the Japanese are a tolerant race. My own impression comes, as I have shown, from the study of documents and personal observation.

Thanks to the spirit of tolerance, a massacre of heathens never took place in Japan. In this respect, the situation differs vastly in Japan from that of the West. As far as religion is concerned, the idea of 'harmony' is a distinctive quality in this country. There were, indeed, some seemingly exceptional cases, the country-wide one being an overall and thoroughgoing persecution of Christians, the second being the persecution of local Jōdo-Shin believers, and the third being a severe suppression of Nichiren and the Non-Receiving-and-Non-Giving sect[27] (one of the Nichiren sects, which refuses to receive alms from and give alms to those other than the believers of the *Hokke Sūtra*). These, in fact, were far from being religious persecutions in the Western sense of the word. These sects were suppressed and persecuted simply because the ruling class feared the subversion that might be worked by these sects upon a certain human nexus, or the feudal social order ordained by the ruling class. A mere difference of religious faith was generally no matter of consequence for the Japanese unless it was considered to be of any damage to the established order of human nexus, whereas in the West a religious difference in itself could give rise to a conflict between opposing parties.

A new problem may be introduced here. If any of the different thoughts and religions can claim its own *raison d'être,* then how can one determine their relative value, and what is the criterion of evaluation?

As has already been pointed out, the inclination to regard as absolute a limited specific human nexus naturally brings about a tendency to disregard a universal law of humanity that every man ought to observe at any place at any time. Instead, the standard of the evaluation of good and evil is identified here with the consideration of appropriateness or inappropriateness of a conduct in reference to the present situation of the particular human nexus to which one happens to belong.

That Japan is the supreme country of all the countries of the world and that to defend such a country is of the absolute religious significance were maintained particularly by the Shintoist thinkers. "The Great Japan is the country of gods. Founded by the heavenly ancestor is this country; transmitted for long by the Sun Goddess is the reign of this country. Such things happened only to this country of ours. There is nothing comparable to them in other countries. That is why this country is called the country of gods".[28] These words were taken as a motto up to quite recently. According to Urabe Kanetomo, who advocated Shintoist Monism, it is said: "Shintoism is the root of all the teachings. Those two doctrines (Confucianism and Buddhism) are differentiations of Shintoism".[29] It goes without saying that the movements of the Shintoists and the scholars of the Japanese classical literature of the Motoori and Hirata schools had much to do with propagandizing and convincing people of such chauvinistic ideas as mentioned above. There were some, among the Shintoists and the scholars of the Japanese classical literature themselves, who expressed their opposing opinions, but such a tendency was too weak to combat the general trend of thought.

It was not that Shintoists were completely lacking in universalistic character. That Shintoism is not the way of Japan but that of all nations is maintained mainly by sectarian Shintoists. The Kurozumi sect and the Misogi sect emphasize that "the four seas are brothers"; the founder of the Misogi sect teaches, "You should regard people of the world as your own parents and children"; the founder of the Revisionist sect (Nitta Kunimitsu) advocates, "You should expand this sect to all nations", and "You should treat all nations as one family and one body". The Konkō sect, in particular, worships as its principal god "the Golden God of the Universe", which has never appeared in the classics of our country, and which leads us to think that the Konkō sect itself is a world religion. "Under heaven there are no outsiders" is advocated by the founder of the Konkō sect. The Shrine Shintoism in general, however, has never been inclined to universalism, except for those cases where the Buddhist idea of benevolence was adopted.[30]

What was then the attitude of the Japanese in accepting the universalistic doctrines of foreign countries? The attitude to accept a foreign religious thought as universal and international and the attitude to regard Japan as absolute are by no means compatible. When the former attitude was accepted, the latter would have to be rejected. But even then was influential the tendency to think in conformity with the limited human nexus of Japan.

Such an inclination of thinking determined also the pattern of the acceptance of Buddhism. At first Buddhism was accepted, by Prince Shōtoku and a group of bureaucrats under his control, as a universal teaching that everyone should follow. Buddhism was estimated thereby as 'the terminating end of four lives (four kinds of all the living creatures) and the ultimate religion of all nations', and among the three treasures of the Buddha, the Law, and the Brotherhood (saṅgha), the Law or the religious doctrine was especially esteemed. They preached, in consequence, "Why should any period or any man not reverence this law?"[31] According to Prince Shōtoku, 'The Law' is "the norm" of all the living creatures, 'the Buddha' is in fact 'the Law embodied', which 'being united with Reason' becomes *saṅgha*. So, according to this way of teaching, everything converges to the one fundamental principle called 'the Law'.[32]

Even among the various sects of Buddhism during that characteristically Japanese period of Kamakura, the sense of the universality of 'the Law', as preached in Buddhism, was not lost. Dōgen (1200–1253), the Zen master, says: "Because there is the Way, Buddhas and their forerunners are comprehended. Without the Way there is no comprehension. Because there is the Law, things are originated. Without the Law nothing is originated".[33] Here too the Law and the Way are used interchangeably. Shinran himself quotes a sentence by Ryūju (Nāgārjuna): "See, enter and acquire the Law, and live in the solid Law, and don't tilt or move".[34] Nichiren also esteems the Hokke Sūtra as the Truth more highly than he does the Buddha. "I am asked why I should make the prayer of the Hokke Sūtra, instead of the Buddha (Shākya Muni), the principal object of worship. I answered that....while the Buddha is the originated, the Hokke Sūtra is the originator. While the Buddha is the body, the Hokke Sūtra is the spirit".[35] "The Hokke Sūtra is just as superior to a Buddha as the moon to a star and as the sun to artificial light".[36]

Among the Japanese, however, there is a strong tendency to understand such a universal law only in reference to some particular or specific phase of things. Moreover, the Japanese sought a standard of the evaluation of different thoughts in the direction of laying emphasis upon the historical and topographical specificity or particularity.

In Japan, the Tendai doctrine, which laid foundation for the doctrines of other sects of Buddhism in Japan, puts emphasis upon 'Things', while in China the doctrine of the same sect regards 'Reason' as most important. By 'Things' are meant phenomenal *specificities or particularities* limited in time and space. Shimei (Ssu-ming), a Chinese Tendai scholar, preached that the first half (*Shakumon*) of the Hokke Sūtra explains the perfect Truth in conformity with the Law of Reason (the perfect Reason), while the second half (*Honmon*) of the Sūtra exposes 'the perfect Truth' in accordance with phenomena (the perfect Thing). Even this latter truth expresses for him the eternal Buddha. In contrast, Eshin, a Japanese Tendai scholar, while accepting this two-fold interpretation, interpreted 'the perfect Reason' as to mean the comprehension of the multiplicity of the phenomenal world through the indiscriminatory Truth (*Sessō Kishō*), and 'the perfect Thing' as to mean the revelation of the Truth through the multiplicity of phenomena.[37)]

The tendency to attach more importance to things rather than to reason is one of the characteristics of the Japanese Zen sect, contrasted to that of China, and the teachings of the Japanese priests like Dōgen and Hakuin (1685–1768) prove it.

Based upon such a way of thinking, most of the Buddhist sects in Japan teach that doctrines should always be made 'apropos of the time'. Especially the idea of the age of degeneration penetrated deep into the core of the doctrines of various sects, which admitted that they were in the age of degeneration and religious doctrines ought to be made suitable to it. Each of the sects ended up in claiming the superiority of their respective sūtras or doctrines, since they are most suited to the age of corruption. This fundamental tendency is most manifested in the teachings of Nichiren, based upon the Japanese Tendai doctrine. He lays special emphasis upon the particularity and specificity of the truth of humanity. "The learning of just one word or one phrase of the Right Law, only if it should accord with the time and the propensity of the learner, would lead him to the attainment of the Way. The mastery even of a thousand scriptures and ten thousand theories, if they should not accord with the time and the propensity of the one who masters them, would lead him nowhere".[38)] Nichiren's evaluation of sectarian doctrines is called 'The Five Standards of Religion'. It sets five standards from which to evaluate. The deepness or shallowness and the superiority or inferiority of all the Buddhist doctrines originated from the Buddha, these five standards being the teaching (of the sūtra), the propensity (the spiritual endowments of the learner), the time (the demand of the time), the country (where the doctrine is practiced), and the order (before and after the propagation of the doctrine, or the preceding circumstances under which the doctrines have been practiced). Nichiren concluded, judging from those five standards, that the Hokke Sūtra was the most superior.[39] Saichō regarded the time and the country as important factors, but he did not go so far as to establish them into basic principles. It was Nichiren who presented them in a clear and distinct form, and it was Nichiren who first put forth 'the circumstances' before and after the propagation of the doctrine. The tendency of the Japanese Tendai sect to lay emphasis upon the thing was brought to its extremity by Nichiren, and such a method of evaluation has hardly been found either in India or in China. Herein lies a reason why Nichirenism in the past was so easily tied up with nationalism.

Such a particularistic way of thinking as discussed above seems to be a general trend during the medieval period. The *Gukanshō*, for instance, often uses the word 'reason', which by no means signifies the universal reason that applies to any country of the world, but which means each of the historical manifestations of reason peculiar to Japan. The historical manifestation, where political and religious factors are closely entangled, are not analyzed from a universal standpoint, but are classified according to the particular periods of development.

The characteristic which can be found in the process of the introduction of Buddhism also applies to the case of Chinese thought.

The doctrine of Chu-hsi (1130–1200) was said to be established by Hayashi Razan (1583–1657) as an official doctrine in Japan, but it was by no means in its original form that he introduced it. According to Chu-hsi, 'the Atmosphere' (*ch'i*) is the material principle that originates all physical phenomena, while 'Reason' (*li*) is their metaphysical basis. According to Hayashi Razan, however, 'Reason' is nothing more than *Japanese Shintoism,* which is a characteristically Japanese interpretation of the original doctrine. "The Way of Gods is nothing but Reason (*li*). Nothing exists outside of Reason. Reason is the truth of nature". The Way of Gods meant by him is the *Way of Emperors* handed down from the Sun Goddess. "In our country since the Sun Goddess, the god has been succeeded by the another god, the emperor has been succeeded by the another emperor. Why should the Way and the Way of Gods be two different things? This is what is meant by that Reason is identical with the Spirit".[40] He shares with Shintoists the view that "this country is the Country of Gods".[41] He denies the universal law of man as man. Instead he maintains, "I have never heard that there is anything to be called a Way other than that of the lord and the father".[42]

Such a way of thinking was not confined to Hayashi Razan, an official spokesman backed up with governmental authority, but was also recognizable in Nakae Tōju, a grass-roots scholar. He stressed that Confucianism is the absolute 'Way' universally applicable to the whole world, but at the same time he considered that the manifestations of the "Way" are relative to time, space, and the hierarchal status to which each man belongs.

"Since Confucianism is originally the ancient way of gods, there is no place in the world where ships and cars can reach, where human power prevails, where the heaven overhangs, where the earth covers, where the sun and the moon shine, where the dew and the frost fall, and where the high-spirited dwell, that Confucianism is not practiced. The manners and etiquette as laid down in Confucian writings cannot be observed as they are, but it depends upon the time and the place...."[43]

He preaches that "the manners and etiquette to associate with others" should be practiced "according to the custom of the particular country and the particular place".[44] He conceived that for the Japanese to follow *Japanese Shintoism* means to observe the way of gods in accordance with the primordial principle.

Kumazawa Banzan (1619–1691), his disciple, believed the same way. For him there is only One Way, namely the way of gods of heaven and earth, the manifestations of which differ according to different countries. An unbroken line of Emperors in Japan and revolutionary changes of dynasties in China are not the reflections of the difference in the way but in the national character. "In Japan naturally there are excellences peculiar to Japan".[45]

A Confucian scholar as he was, he attached great importance to Shintoism as the Way of Japan. "The Way of Gods of the heaven and the earth is called the great way. In Japan there exists the way of gods in accordance with our climate". "The Japanese Way of Gods in accordance with our climate can be loaned to, nor borrowed from, China or barbarians".[46]

These ways of thinking by the Confucian scholars run parallel to Japanese Buddhists in their recognition of Japanese Shintoism. The only difference between them seems to lie in that the Confucian scholars are not so strongly conscious of the historical peculiarity of the doctrine (e.g., idea to regard the present period as the age of degeneration) as Buddhists are, although they make much of the topographical peculiarities of the doctrine. (This by no means applies to all the Confucianists. Dazai Shundai's attitude of contempt toward Shintoism as a paganism is similar to the attitudes of the people of other races when a universal religion is introduced. So Dazai's attitude cannot be called characteristically Japanese. But the ways of thinking of the other scholars mentioned above may be rightly said to be uniquely Japanese.) The tendency of Japanese Buddhism to put 'Things' before 'Reason', as already discussed, also appears in the formation of the Japanese Confucianism. Ogiu Sorai emphasized facts rather than theories, and stressed the superiority of the former to the latter.[47]

If both Buddhists and Confucianists emphasize that in Japan there ought to be the way appropriate to Japan, and if they push that theory to its logical conclusion, will it not become meaningless for them to remain to be Buddhists or Confucianists? It amounts to this that for the Japanese it is enough to observe the *Way of Japan,* even when the righteousness of both Confucianism and Buddhism for guiding man to the right conduct is to be taken for granted. Such a logic was presented by Imbe Seitsū, a Shintoist. He never rejects Buddhism or Confucianism as flatly as Motoori Norinaga or Hirata Atsutane does. On the contrary, he recognizes the raison d'être of Confucianism and Buddhism by saying that they are "both more or less different but good ways". As for Shintoism he maintains, "Shintoism is the Right Way of this country. It respects the great order and honors clear reason, and does not repudiate the beginning as the beginning and never ceases to move".[48] That is to say, Shintoism, since it is the *Way of Japan,* should be relied upon. The scholars of the Japanese classical literature in the Tokugawa period go so far as to reject entirely the raison d'être of Confucianism and Buddhism. Kamo Mabuchi (1697–1769) maintains that Confucianism is of no use *for Japan* by saying, "While the teachings of Confucius have never been put into practical use even in China, whose (Confucianism) foundation these teachings are, of what use could it be, should it be brought to Japan?"[49] Such a view was later pushed to its extreme by the scholars of Japanese classical literature.

Those scholars who claimed to be independent either from Buddhism, Confucianism or from Shintoism also followed suit. For instance, Tominaga Nakamoto (1715–1746), an Ōsaka merchant scholar and free thinker, advocated 'the true Way' or 'the Way of Way' which was defined to be "the Way that should be practiced in the present-day Japan".[50] In order for the "true Way" to be realized, it should be limited both in time, i.e., 'the present-day' and in space, i.e., 'Japan'. Thus his theory evidently claims that 'the Way' as the principle of human existence manifests itself in the form inevitably determined historically and topographically. He denounces as "the ways against the true Way"[51] the Shintoism advocated by his contemporary scholars of the Japanese classical literature, the Confucianism taught by the Confucianists, and the Buddhism preached by the Buddhists, because, he says, all of them took no notice of the historical and topographical peculiarities of human existence.

We are now led to conclude that it was a distinctive characteristic of the Japanese scholars to use the idea of 'the historically determined present-day Japan' as the measuring rod of evaluating all the systems of thought.[52] Such an attitude cannot be found either in India or in China.

When such a way of thinking is pushed to its extreme, it ends up, in its emphasis upon *special specificity,* with ethno-centricism or supernationalism, and in its emphasis upon the specificity of the time, with opportunism, which leads one to compromise with a given particular situation. It is easily turned into a tendency to neglect the universal law that ought to be observed by anyone at any place. Any system of thought inclined to disregard the universal cannot attain universality among the systems of thought of mankind. It cannot find a sympathizer among other nations. It is extremely difficult to assimilate other nations from the bottom of their hearts with the Japanese thought. For that reason in the field of thought, Japan has had very little to offer to the culture of the world. In the field of art, especially of fine arts, however, Japan has contributed a great deal to the world. Take, for instance, the influence that the Japanese fine arts have exerted upon those of the West. The influence in this direction remains unerasable. As far as the world of thinking is concerned, however, Japan's influence is completely negligible.

An objection may be raised as follows:
Since the works of art are appreciated through intuition, their merits can be easily recognized by other nations. Since here the language is the medium of communication, however, it is difficult for one nation to understand the thought of the other, such an objection does not hold. In spite of the fact that a considerable number of works of the Japanese thought have already been translated and the contemporary Japanese philosophy has partly been introduced to foreign countries, in some case by the Japanese government and in some case by the government- sponsored organizations, they have exerted very little influence upon the thought of

other countries. The imposing attitude on the part of Japan was repulsed by other nations. In the case of the Indian thought or of the Chinese thought, in contrast, no comparable efforts for introducing them abroad by the respective governments have been exerted. Nevertheless, their influence is preeminent upon the thoughts of other nations. The spread of Buddhism over the Eastern countrits was not endorsed by any political or military force. The same is true with the propagation of Indian religions in the South Sea countries. Confucianism was not imposed upon Japan by the Chinese government, but it was voluntarily accepted by the Japanese people. The influence of Chinese thought upon the Western trends of thought of the Modern Enlightenment and the contribution of the Indian thoughts to the Modern Romantic philosophy and literature have left traces too deep to be wiped out. But has Japan contributed anything to the world?

Japan failed, even before the Pacific War, in her effort to propagate Shintoism, Japan's own religion, among Asiatic countries. The cause of the failure is quite clear: since Shintoism is the tribal religion of the Japanese, it is an impossible enterprise from the very beginning to try to substitute it for the tribal religions of other peoples. The various sects of the Japanese Buddhism also sent their missionaries to other Asiatic countries, which are also bound to fail. Why was it? It was not Buddhism itself, which originally is a universal religion, but the "Japanized" Buddhism that was unanimously rejected by the people of the Asiatic countries.

The inclination of thinking to lay too much emphasis upon particular facts or specific phases amounts to the stand-point of no-theory or anti-theory. It ends up with the contempt of rational thinking and the worship of uncontrolled intuitionism and activism. Herein lies the cause of the failure of Japan in the past, and the danger still lies in these directions today. In order not to repeat the same failure, we ought from now on to learn to seek universal "reason" through specific "facts".

---

1) See Yaichi Haga 芳賀矢一: *Kokuminsei Jūron* 國民性十論 p. 257.

2) The only parallel to this may be found in some ancient Indian countries to the west of the Ganges, as we are told in Fa-hsien's 法顯 *Fa-kuo-chi* 佛國記 and Hsüan-chuang's 玄奘 *Hsi-yü-chi* 西遊記 vol. 2.

3) See Masaharu Anesaki 姉崎正治: *Kirishitan Hakugai-shi-chū no Jimbutsu-jiseki* 切支丹迫害史中の人物事蹟 p. 476 f.

4) See Tōkan Tada 多田等觀: *Chibetto* (チベット *Tibet*), p. 113 ff.: Bunkyō Aoki 青木文教: *Chibetto Yūki* (西藏遊記 Travel in Tibet), p. 165 ff.

5) In his *Ōjō-taiyō-shō* (往生大要抄 An Outline of How to be Reborn into the Pure Land), *Shōwa Shinshū Hōnen Shōnin Zenshū* 昭和新修法然上人全集 p. 61 f.

6) *Hōnen Shōnin Gyōjō Ezu* (法然上人行狀畫圖 Illustrations of the Doings of St. Hōnen), vol. 21, in *op. cit.* vol. 16, p. 241.
7) See Ichirō Hori 堀一郎: *Shinkō no Heizonsei ni tsuite* 信仰の並存性について in *Rinri* 倫理 No. 543, Oct. 1948.
8) See Shinshō Hanayama 花山信勝: *Hokke-gisho no Kenkyū* 法華義疏の研究 p. 664 ff. This doctine is called *the Teaching of Manzen Dōki.*
9) *Ibid.* p. 117 f.
10) *Ibid.* p. 460.
11) In his *Jūshichi-jō no Kempō* (十七條憲法 The Seventeen Article Constitution).
12) In the *Kyōkijikoku-shō* 教機時國鈔, *Shōwa Shinshū Nichiren Shōnin Imonzenshū* vol. 1, p. 450.
13) The *Ryōjin Hishō,* a diary ascribed to Emperor Go-Shirakawa (1127–1192). In *Nihon Koten-zensho* 日本古典全書 vol. 2, p. 71 f.
14) See his *Keiranshūyō-shū* 溪嵐拾葉集, quoted in Taijō Tamamuro 圭室諦成: *Nihon Bukkyō-shi Gaisetsu* 日本佛教史概說 p. 221.
15) In his *Go-bunshō* 御文章 3, 10; see also *ibid.* 2, 3; in *Kōchū Rennyo Shōnin O-fumi Zenshū* 校註蓮如上人御文全集, p. 56 ff., cf. p. 24 ff.
16) In the *Sekihei-kahō* (石平家法 Disciplines of the Monastery at the Sekihei Mountain) quited in Motosue Ishida 石田元季: *Edo-jidai Bungaku Kōsetsu* 江戸時代文學考說 p. 14.
17) In the *Kōkiji-kitei* (高貴寺規定 The Regulations of the Kōkiji Temple), Article no. 13, quoted in Daijō Tokiwa 常盤大定: *Nihon Bukkyō no Kenkyū* 日本佛教の研究 p. 526.
18) In the chapter on Emperor Yōmei in the *Nihonshoki.*
19) See Zennosuke Tsuji 辻善之助: *Nihon Bukkyō-shi no Kenkyū* 日本佛教史之研究 p. 96 ff.
20) *Ibid.* p. 56.
21) In the *Ōmi Daifukuji-monjo* 遠江大福寺文書, quoted in Tsuji *op. cit.* p. 175.
22) See Yasusada Hiyane: *op. cit.* p. 634.
23) See Kanshi Kagamishima 鏡島寛之: *Chūsei-bukkyōto no Jingikan to sono Bunka* 中世佛教徒の神祇觀とその文化" in *Shūkyō-kenkyū* 宗教研究 1940, p. 813.
24) *Shoku-nihonkōki* 續日本後紀 vol. 5, Asahi Shimbunsha 朝日新聞社 ed. p. 94.
25) In his preface to a poem in *Manyōshū* 萬葉集 vol. 5, in *Kokka Taikei* 國歌大系vol. 2, p. 156.
26) In *Edo-bungaku-kenkyū* 江戸文學研究 p. 14.
27) Fuju Fuse-ha 不受不施派. This branch of the Nichiren sect, founded in 1595 by the bonze Nichiō 日奥, was forbidden together with the Christian religion in 1614.
28) Kitabatake Chikafusa (1293–1354), in his *Jinnōshōtōki* (神皇正統記 *A* History of the Legitimate Line of the Divine Emperors), bk. 1, *Gunsho-ruijū* vol. 29, p. 1.
29) Quoted in Hiyane *op. cit.* p. 679 f.
30) This material has been quoted from Genchi Katō 加藤玄智, *Shintō no shūkyō-hattatsushi-teki Kenkyū* 神道の宗教發達史的研究 p. 950 f. and Hiyane *op. cit.* p. 816 ff.
31) From Prince Shōtoku's Seventeen-Article Injunction.
32) See his *Shōmangyō-gisho* 勝鬘經義疏, ch. *Ichijō* 一乘; cf. Shinshō Hanayama: *Nihon no Bukkyō* 日本の佛教 p. 202 ff.

33) In the *Eihei-shingi, Bendō-hō* 永平清規, 辦道法, *Dōgen Zenji Shingi* 道元禪師清規, ed. Dōshū Ōkubo 大久保道舟, p. 43.
34) In the *Kyōgyōshinshō* 教行信證 Ch. 2, *Taishō Shinshū Daizōkyō* vol. 83, p. 591 a.
35) In the *Honzon Mondō-shō* 本尊問答鈔, *Shōwa Shinshū Nichiren Shōnin Imonzenshū* vol. 2, p. 1721 f.
36) In his *Letter to the nun Kubo* 窪尼御前御返事, *ibid.* vol. 2, p. 1768.
37) Daitō Shimaji 島地大等: *Tendai Kyōgaku-shi* 天台教學史 p. 492.
38) In his *Sado-gosho* 佐渡御書, *Shōwa Shinshū Nichiren Shōnin Imon-zenshū* vol. 1, p. 842.
39) In the *Kyōkijikoku-shō* and the *Shōgu Mondō-shō, Shōwa Shinshū Nichiren Shōnin Imon-zenshū* vol. 1, p. 447 f. and p. 579 f. In his two-volume work, *Senji-shō* 撰時鈔, Nichiren elaborates on how other sects are not fit for his time, see *Shōwa Shinshū Nichhiren Shōnin Imon-zenshū* vol. 1, p. 1189–1241.
40) *Honchō-jinja-kō* 本朝神社考, quoted in Masatomo Bamba 萬羽正朋: *Nihon Jukyō-shi* 日本儒教史 p. 103 ff.
41) In the preface to the *Honchō-jinja-kō, Razan Sensei Bunshū* 羅山先生文集 vol. 2, p. 118.
42) *Razan Bunshū* 羅山文集 vol. 56.
43) *Okina Mondō* vol. 3, *Tōju Sensei Zenshū* vol. 3, p. 248.
44) *Ibid.* p. 251.
45) In his *Miwa Monogatari* 三輪物語 vol. 7, *Banzan Zenshū* 蕃山全集 vol. 5, p. 67. Elsewhere he says: "If Chinese Sages should come to Japan they would subscribe to Shintō which has been our traditional Way". (*Banzan Zenshū* vol. 1, p. 12).
46) Quoted in Hiyane, op. cit. p. 943.
47) See Saburō Ienaga 家永三郎: *Chūsei Bukkyōshisō-shi Kenkyū* 中世佛教思想史研究 p. 104, and Iwahashi, *op. cit.* p. 301.
48) *Jindai-Kuketsu* 神代口訣, quoted in Hiyane *op. cit.* p. 660.
49) *Kokuikō* 國意考, *Kamo Mabuchi Zenshū* 賀茂眞淵全集 vol. 10, p. 368.
50) *Okina no Fumi* 翁の文, ch. 6.
51) *Ibid.* Ch. 1.
52) We do not contend that the Japanese thinkers mentioned above did not admit the universality of the Way. Kumazawa Banzan, for instance, said: "The Way is the Way of all gods, heaven and earth. It is universally valid throughout the whole world, China and Japan" (*Shūgi-washo* 集義和書 Ch. 11, *Banzan Zenshū* vol. 1, p. 286).

(6) Cultural multiplicity (consisting of several strata still preserved) and weakness of the spirit of criticism

The Japanese, owing to their tolerant and all-embracing nature, absorbed the heterogeneous cultures of foreign countries without much repercussion. They try to recognize the raison d'être of each of these different cultural elements, and at the same time they endeavor to preserve what has been inherited from the past. They seek unity while permitting the co-existence of heterogeneous elements.

Such a tendency may be found in various fields of culture.

First, let us take up the language, which is a common denominator to any nationality group. There are in Japanese a great many words of foreign origin. All the important concepts are expressed in Chinese characters. A considerable number of Western words have recently been introduced. Even the numerals, which are not easily changed in other languages, were adopted from Chinese. Those words adopted from foreign languages are sometimes made to stand for different meanings, but on the whole the original meanings are retained. There are often those cases where the archaic Japanese words are preserved in speech but they are represented by Chinese characters in writing. The absorption of so many foreign words into the system of a native language as the Japanese have done is quite rare among the languages of civilized nations.

Those words adopted from Chinese or Western languages are on the whole nouns. By suffixing postpositions to these nouns, something similar to case-declension is effected, and also the nouns are turned into adverbs or adjectives. By adding a verb '*su*'[1] to nouns, they are turned into verbs. These operations prove that foreign words are adopted essentially as nouns and are used as the materials of language as such. The main features of the Japanese language have undergone no considerable change but the old form, in its syntax, has been faithfully preserved.

That is exactly the attitude of the Japanese in accepting foreign cultures. They are extremely sensitive in adopting and absorbing foreign cultures. But, in fact, a foreign culture is adopted as a constituent element of the Japanese culture. Whatever the intention and outcry of the men in charge of its adoption might be, in the reality of a social and cultural fact, it was accepted in so far as its value was recognized as a means and material. Such an attitude gave rise to the conception of "the Japanese spirit and the Chinese learning". Such a traditional standpoint of the Japanese is the key to understand their cultural multiplicity.

There are various aspects to cultural multiplicity. In the field of politics in Japan, no radical revolution has ever taken place since ancient times. The ruling class of one period does not end up with a complete decline. The ruling class of the past, whose political hegemony has already been lost, may still command respect of the people as the preserver of the ancient cultural tradition and of spiritual authority. Such a political phenomenon has never been found either in India, China or Tibet. Such a tendency appears to be found somewhat among the Ural-Altaic peoples, but Japan is the most outstanding of the cases.[2]

Multiplicity is also found in the mode of living of the Japanese, in their clothing, eating and dwellings. In the field of arts also, unity is somewhat maintained in the juxtaposition of conflicting elements old and new. In the field of religion, different modes of belief, conflicting with one another in their respective peculiarities, not only coexist in the community, but operate at the same time within the life of *the selfsame individual person.*

It must indeed be a practical merit of the Japanese to let live the individual differences and peculiarities of conflicting elements of culture and at the same time to bring forth a concrete unity among them. In many cases, however, such a unity is based upon rapproachement for convenience's sake and in the mood of opportunism. Hampered by their own inclination to accentuate the social nexus and their illogical mentality, the Japanese are often lacking in the radical spirit of confrontation and criticism.

Such a weakness shows itself in the practical social behavior as in politics and in other fields, but the weakness is most pronounced in the field of thought where logical confrontation is indespensable. As for Buddhism, the life of the present-day priests and believers is completely changed from what it was before the Meiji Restoration. Consequently, there exists an abysmal gap between the old doctrine and the reality of the present-day living, but few try to bridge that gap with reflective thinking. Ideological chaos is most revealing as to the issues about disciplines. For instance as long as one remains a Buddhist, drinking is absolutely prohibited, whether one is a priest or a believer. But the breach of that discipline is taken for granted in Japan.[3] Marriage would not be permitted to the priest, except for the priest of Jōdo-shin sect, should the teachings and conduct of the Japanese founders of the various sects be observed as the absolute authority. The alternatives are either to follow strictly the examples of the founders or *to repudiate their authority* by positively declaring their standpoint to become a priest under the lay condition just as done by a part of the priests of the Mahāyāna Buddhism, the priests of Nepal, Tibet, or those of the Jōdo-shin sect. Such a decision based upon thorough-going logical judgement is never thought of by the Japanese Buddhist. They *don't want to do any theoretical reflection* upon the discrepancy, of which they sometimes become aware, between the doctrine vocally upheld and the conduct actually undertaken. (Such a mental phenomenon runs parallel to the intellectual-historical fact of the lack of critical studies when the Western philosophical thoughts were introduced and rashly absorbed after the Meiji Restoration).

The lack of the spirit of criticism in the theoretical field corresponds to the lack in the field of literature, of the will-power to drive home to the reader's heart a concept or an idea, however abstract it may be. Yaichi Haga writes: "There is scarcely any inclination in the mind of the Japanese to go to extreme in getting angry with the world, in deploring, in being cynical, or in being snobbish. That is the reason why the literature of our country is simple".[4] Even the Buddhist works of literature, favored by the Japanese people, are mostly lacking in their thoroughgoingness.

Even the Medieval period, when Buddhist thought most deeply penetrated into the minds of the people, the Japanese were not serious in their religious consciousness. In the *Ryōjin Hishō*, a collection of Buddhist songs, the songs that express gnawing consciousness of sin are extremely rare. In stead, most of them represent the moods of humour and optimism.

"An insect, weaving at the Eastern Gate
 of the Pure Land,
Lives in the cross-beam of the Gate.
He hastily weaves a robe of prayers,
 In the burning light of the Pure Land."[5]

An essay of Kamo no Chōmei (12th–13th cent.), known to be a representative work of Buddhist literature, also shows the lack of thoroughgoingness.

"In the spring the fragrant wistaria waves its blossoms like the lavender clouds that lead to the Pure Land in the west. In the summer the cuckoo brings to my mind the journey of death to the other world. The autumnal cicadas sing a melancholy song as if they were lamenting their fleeting life. In the winter I gaze in meditation at the snow, as it falls and as it melts, which reminds me of sins committed and purged. I let myself rest and relax whenever I feel too lazy to practice nembutsu prayers or to recite sūtras".[6]

The writer simply enjoys himself here with the changes of nature from one season to another, and there is neither any serious sense of sin and confession of sin, nor absolute devotion to the Buddha. In order to concentrate themselves on ascetic practices the Indians made various devices to torment themselves with, such as the 'five heats' by making fire burning at four sides around themselves under the burning heat of the summer sun, or sitting on the floor where splinters are made to stand upside down. Such a single-mindedness in the pursuit of ascetic practice has scarcely been found among the Japanese. It is utterly inconceivable either for the Chinese or for the Indians to recommend, as the Japanese do, as a representative work of Buddhist literature a confession of an idle hermit who "feels too lazy to practice nembutsu prayers or to recite sūtras". Commenting on this essay, Yoshio Yamada (1873–1958) says: "Although the author, led by the Buddhist philosophy, realized the impermanence of the phenomenal world, and thereupon escaped from this world, he neither resented Heaven nor cursed the world, but he simply secluded himself in a hermitage and found a kind of passive comfort in that state of his own. Consequently, both of his view of the impermanence of the phenomenal world and his pessimism appear to be half-hearted. Is that because of the fact that the Japanese are by nature optimists?"[7]

Kenkō (1283–1350), an essayist, the author of the *Tsurezuregusa* admires the ascetic practices of Buddhism, but at the same time he frankly expresses his desire for wordly pleasures. "Though I know it to be a temporary abode, a congenial dwelling place pleases me. .... A man who does not cherish love's pleasures, however excellent he may be in thousands of other things, is extremely riotous. He is like a wine-cup which is made of precious stone but without the bottom".[8] Japanese literature seems to have a grudge against describing a hermit who repudiates the properties of his own through and through. In this respect they are vastly different from those of Indian Buddhism.

The lack of thorough-going theoretical reflection goes hand in hand with the humourous and comic attitude of the Japanese. We need not go into detailed discussions on this point here, since it has repeatedly been pointed out elsewhere.[9] Here it suffices to mention that even such a serious subject as Buddhism is turned into something to be laughed at.

The fact that a Buddhist priest was made into an object of a scornful mirth was as old as the "Ten Thousand Leaves Anthology (*Manyō-shu*)".

"Don't tether a horse
To a stubb of a whisker,
A little bit grown
On the shaven face of a monk,
Don't pull it hard,
Lest, 'ouch', the monk may cry".[10]

Such a tendency to treat the affairs of Buddhism as the object of derision became especially pronounced in the modern period. Zen priests were then described as the heroes of comic stories. And they were supposed to write back and forth witty poems. This may be taken as a metamorphosis of the Zen catechism, but it was welcomed by the Japanese who love to make poor puns. Ikkyū is the prototype of such a priest and he is described as the hero of a series of funny stories called "Ikkyū Pieces".[11] Musō was also made into a comic hero. It was not confined to the Zen priests, but even the austere and pious St. Gensei of the Nichiren sect was made up into the author of a facetious literature called the *Fresco of St. Gensei,* which is an utter disgrace to such a respected man of religion. It was neither from the respect for Gensei nor from the positive intention for defaming Gensei that the real author tied up his own ludicrous stories with the honourable name of Gensei. He wanted simply to make his witticism more effective.[12]

In the same fashion, even a serious discussion is related in a humourous frame of mind. Hakuin, who spread and gave local color to the Zen teachings, preached in a way quite vulgar, and full of wit and humor.

"My name is Odawara Yūsuke, and I was an apothecary before I was born, that is, since my parents' generation. To force a sale is under the ban, I know, but pray listen to my telling you the effect of my medicine. The medicine I advertise is called the pill-of-becoming-a-Buddha-by-comprehending-one's-own-true-nature, and contains the direct heart of man. Should you use this medicine, you would get rid of tormenting sickness, and the pains of the vicissitudes of the three worlds and the sorrows of the transmigration of the soul in the six spheres would be allayed .... To this country, the Master Senkō introduced it first, and later on twenty-four excellent apothecaries came out. Still later, Master Daitō at Murasakino was used by the Emperor. At that time there appeared an apothecary who made the medicine called the pill-of-revelation and the pill-of-secrecy, and who contested with the pill-of-becoming-a-Buddha for the supremacy of effectiveness. By the imperial ordinance, Daitō debated with the apothecaries of the Mii Temple, Nara, the Mt. Hiei and their vicinities to the victory of the former. Priest-Emperor Hanazono sent an imperial messenger to Ibuka of Mino to call for the Master Kanzan, and honourably taking this medicine, the Priest-Emperor bestowed upon him an imperial wine-cup as a prize. Hanazonoya Shop is indeed the name of my own head family. To tell you the recipe for this medicine, first we cut down with an axe the oak tree of Shao-chou, beat it in the mortar of the Sixth Patriarch, dip the Seiko water of Ma-tzu, knead it on the octagonal plate of Daitō, put on the one hand of Hakuin, make it round with the finger of Chü-ti, wrap it up with the white paper of Hsüan-sha, and on that paper we write the superscription of the pill-of-becoming-a-Buddha-by-comprehending-one's-own-true-nature, of Hanazonoya Shop, of the Rinzai district, of the Zen sect. Should you gulp this pill, you would vomit something called an empty intelligence and the poison remains in your body through your life-time. If you chew it well enough and then swallow it and keep it at the bottom of your navel, when you go out or come back, or when you stand up or sit down, then you will never feel happy even if you get reborn into the paradise or never feel pain even if you fall into the hell. I am not to talk ill of other medicines, but the pill-of-the-six-characters (*Namu-amida-butsu*), recently on sale, may be nourishing for the ordinary man, if you take it before breakfast and after supper, but it will never, I assure you, be effective to alleviate the agony of death. It is of this kind of pill that people call the pill of becoming a Buddha for the moment of death. This kind of pill costs you three cents apiece. But as for my own pill, it costs you not a cent. Let me cut the further story, but why not try it now?"[13]

The high priests of India or China never preached Buddhism in such a way as this.

As the earlier stage of the Edo period, a person called Nyoraishi wrote a book named *An Account of Hundred and Eight Chō.*[14] This book asserts that each one of the three doctrines, Confucianism, Taoism and Buddhism, which is the central doctrine of all, has one *ri* (*ri* in Japanese stands both for *reason* and *a measure of distance*). And if each one of the three doctrines has one *ri*, and one *ri* stands for thirty-six *chō*, then the three doctrines together make up one hundred and eighth *chō*. Thus the book was named after such a play on words.[15] In this ludicrous way the unity of the three doctrines was preached and accepted by the public. Such a thing does not seem likely to take place among other peoples, but it is quite deep-rooted among the Japanese.

It is noteworthy to point out that the Japanese turn into ridicule indiscriminately a Buddha, the Seven Deities of Good Luck or whatever else is transplanted from abroad. But they never deride their own ancestoral gods.[16] Such a double-barrelledness was originated, as was pointed out in the above, from the lack of religious-consciousness on the one hand, and the emphasis upon the social nexus and the lineage on the other.

The Japanese with the above mentioned characteristics give the impression of much less profundity than the Chinese to Western observers.[17] And while the Japanese themselves were boasting that they had successfully synthesized the cultures of the world, actually they have simply resorted to uncritical and opportunistic attitude of compromise, leaving borrowed cultures in irrelevant juxtaposition.

---

1) In colloquial Japanese, "*suru*" (to do).
2) See B. Spuler, *Die Goldene Horde*, and id., *Die Mongolen in Iran.*
3) At the rededication of a famous Buddhist temple in October, 1958, the numerous sake barrels piled up as offerings in front of the temple and the booths advertising various brands of whisky certainly were in contrast to the original teaching of the Buddha.
4) *Op. cit.* p. 121.
5) In the *Ryōjin Hishō* vol. II., l.c. p. 104.
6) *Hōjōki* (方丈記 The Private Papers of Kamo no Chōmei of the *Ten-Foot-Square-Hut*), Iwanami Bunko edition p. 61 f.
7) In the introduction to the Iwanami Bunko edition of the *Hōjōki*, p. 4.
8) *Tsurezuregusa* 徒然草 Ch. 10, (*Nihon Koten-bungaku Taikei* 日本古典文學大系 vol. 30, p. 97.)
9) See Yaichi Haga: *op. cit.* p. 126 ff.
10) *Manyō-shū* No. 3846.
11) See Otoo Fujii 藤井乙男: *Edo Bungaku Kenkyū* (江戸文學研究 A Study on Literatures in Edo Era) p. 70 ff.
12) *Ibid.* p. 108 ff.
13) *Kenshō-jōbutsu-gan-hōsho* 見性成佛丸方書, in *Zenmon-hōgo-shū* vol. 2, p. 239 ff.
14) *Hyakuhacchōki* 百八町記.
15) See Motosue Ishida 石田元季: *Edojidai Bungaku Kōsetsu* (江戸時代文學考說 A Sturvey on Literatures in Edo Era) p. 9.
16) See Yaichi Haga: *op. cit. Kokuminsei Jūron* p. 142 ff.
17) See, for instance, H. Keyserling, *Reisetagebuch eines Philosophen* p. 583.

PART V. THE WAYS OF THINKING OF THE TIBETAN PEOPLE

Characteristics of Tibetan Ways of Thinking as Revealed in Cultural Phenomena, Especially in the Process of Accepting Buddhism

In Tibet, a barren highland situated at 8,000 metre above sea-level, surrounded by lofty mountains in four directions, where heavy storm is blowing and ice and snow cover the land during two third of a year, mankind has established a unique culture. Lamaism, governing over the common people with its great religious power, has produced many religious texts and architectural structures. Referring to the characteristics of Tibetan culture, Max Weber said as follows:

> "Due to the existence of the military service system of the old Chinese style and of the monastic order of Lamaist priests who live side-by-side with the common men who are required to enter military services, pay taxes and offer donations, there has been produced a culture in this land where there is, from the standpoint of capitalistic rentability, no possibility of producing great architectures due to its basically unfavorable natural conditions. The dissolution of this system spells out an end to their destiny as they have traditionally believed".[1]

Indeed, in this vast highland of no value from the standpoint of a capitalistic economy, there has flourished a unique culture.

Furthermore this religious culture of Tibet contains an element of universality. Lamaism had influence more or less upon the vast inland area of Asia convering the interior of China proper, Mongolia, Manchuria and Central Asia.[2] This fact is quite remarkable in comparison with what little influence Japanese religion has had upon foreigners inspite of the fact that the Japanese are very proud of their religious heritage.

The kind of religious and economic phenomena that are presented in the Tibetan highlands are not easy for the Japanese to understand, a fact to which the Japanese need to pay more attention. (Surely the Tibetan race is of quite little value from political, military or economic viewpoint, but as far as the ways of thinking are concerned, it is of great value and worthy to be investigated).

---

1) Max Weber: *Aufsätze zur Religionssoziologie*, II, S. 316.

2) Lamaism has been introduced into Europe, too. On account of the conquest of the 'Golden Horde' i.e. the Russia proper, by the Buddhist kings of Tartary, Buddhism has been propagated there and is thus still living in European Russia. Among Kalmaks in the basin of the Volga River, there are some people who call themselves Buddhists. (L. A. Waddell: *The Buddhism of Tibet or Lamaism*, London, 1895, p. 9.)

Due to the lack of many oppotunities to see the original texts of Tibetan works, and to the fact that not many studies have been made along this line, it is rather difficult to carry on a serious study of the Tibetan ways of thinking. Tibetology in Japan has been making some progress during the last two decades. But most scholars consider it a subsidiary work to their main field of concern which is Indology or Buddhology. Such being the case, the following study consists of but a brief survey.

Chapter 1. Introduction

Peculiarity of the Tibetan culture is due not a little to the physical surroundings of the land. Isolation from the neighbouring countries by the walls of the world-famous high lands made Tibet a land of mysteries. Being a vast barren land of poor natural resources, of seriously cold climate which refuses to produce food stuff to any great quantity, she could but nourish only a limited amount of people. Such geographical climatical conditions have had their influence in establishing customs characteristically Tibetan, and also in conditioning the ways in which they have accepted Buddhism.

Chapter 2. Weakness of consciousness of association among individuals

With regards to the family system, one of the most secluded institutions devised by humanity, curious customs carried over since the pre-historic days can be still witnessed in Tibet.

First of all, the practice of polyandry must be mentioned.[1] If a bridegroom were to have brothers, his bride is automatically married with her brothers-in-law. She is the co-wife to all the brothers. The qualification to be possessed of the co-wife is limited only to those sons of the same mother. If a woman were to have a sexual contact beyond this limitation, she is regarded as adultress. When she bears a child, however, only the eldest husband is called his or her father, while the others are called uncles irrespective of who the actual father is. Such a custom seems to strike us against our normal sense of morality, but Tibetans think it as a rather ideal form of family.

Why was such a system adopted in Tibet? Rev. Aoki who had lived in Tibet for some years once said as follows:

(1) Being a barren land, Tibet cannot nourish so big a population. Polyandry is quite suitable to limit the increase of population.

(2) Officers and merchants are often obliged to go out of home for a long duration due to the difficulties ensuing from their journeys through the mountain wilderness. In such a case the wife stays home with the remaining brothers with whom she may be bedded.

Polygamy is also observed. For example the King Sroṅ-btsan-sgam-po is reported to have had five wives. Polygamy, however, was rather a common custom among the ruling classes in the world of pre-modern periods. The peculiarity of Tibetan polygamy today lies in its form, that is, one of the pre-requisites is that wives should be sisters born of the same mother. It is practical especially for noble families which have no son but daughters.

Actually, however, most Tibetans adhere to monogamy; polyandry or polygamy being rather an exceptional arrangement. However, the existence of such a system should not go unnoticed. The system seems to show the unique way of thinking of the Tibetans. That is to say, although the Tibetans do have a concrete idea of a family they are not sensitively consciousness of the personal bond between man and woman.

Another example can be cited. A Tibetan re-marries immediately after the death of his or her partner, and as a result there is said to be almost no widow nor widower in Tibet. In a land adhering to such a custom, marriage often means not more than sexual relation rather than a realization of a spiritual bond. Such Tibetan custom is quite the opposite to the 'suttee'-custom of the Indians.

These customs did not change even after the introduction of Buddhism. High priest lamas were obliged to admit so. And the Tibetans, in their turn, did not accept the Buddhism 'of rigorous moralism'. Chinese Buddhists once tried to propagate their own brand of Buddhism into Tibet, but were soon expelled by the natives.[2] The strict morality of Chinese Buddhism could not take root in Tibet. What was accepted by the Tibetans was the Buddhism of worldly enjoyment which sometimes leads people to engage in sexual enjoyment, i.e. the corrupted form of Indian Esoterism.

To attach importance to sexual enjoyment is one of the prominent characteristics of Tibetan Buddhism. For the Buddhist mendicants, their goal is to enter the absolute state through the practice of meditation, a state which is usually expressed in negativism. Lamaism, on the contrary, expresses its highest goal through the image of deities in sexual union as the symbol of the greatest pleasure (*mahā-sukha*). This image of coupled deities is referred to as the 'Excellent Pleasure (*bde-mchog*)'. This idea seems to have its origin in a Hindu image of Śiva and Kālī (=Durgā) in '*saṃyoga*' (union).[3] Also the *liṅga* is regarded as something sacred. Though there is no '*liṅga*'-worship in Tibet, we sometimes find there a scene of religious dancing with a *liṅga* in hands.

Even Tsoṅ-kha-pa, the reformer of Lamaism in the 14th century, could not stamp out the practices described above. Consequently, the Tibetan's concept of family lineage is not strongly imbedded in their mind. Ancestor-worship is hardly noticed in Tibet except in a form of a mass for the dead, similar to the Japanese *Segaki* ceremony. The term 'ancestor worship' has no equivalent in the Tibetan vocabulary. Each Tibetan home keeps the Buddha's image in a niche or an altar, but unlike the Japanese and the Chinese, the Tibetans never keep ancestral tablets (Jap. *ihai*) or portraits of their ancestors in it. (As for the lack of consciousness with respect to the inheritance of property, which is somehow relating to the present subject, the reference will be made afterwards).

Also Tibetans have no fixed mythology about the origin of their race. Some of them believe that they are the descendants of the King Pāṇḍu who is spoken of in the *Mahābhārata*, the great epic of India, while others say that they are the descendants of a Rākṣasī and a monkey who lived in the Himālaya who is believed to be the incarnation of the Bodhisattva Avalokiteśvara. These facts, i.e. the lack of a fixed mythology about the origin of the race and its connection to Indian mythology, seem to show that they are not quite conscious of the genealogy of their race.

The idea of the national ancestor such as Sun Goddess of Japanese is also lacking in the Tibetan consciousness. Surely they venerate the three kings, Sroṅ-btsan-sgam-po, Khri-sroṅ-lde-btsan and Dar-pa-chen, but merely as the three great ancestors who made Tibet prosperous. National consciousness, too, is lacking.

Consequently the Tibetans do not pride themselves as the chosen people or as those who live in the center of world civilization as the Chinese did. They rather respect India as the land of the sages, and regard their country as a remote region of the world.[4)]

What then is the basic idea of morality among the Tibetans whose consciousness of association among individuals, as well as the concept of a genealogical recording of their race or nation are not well developed? The answer lies in their unconditional submission to Lamaism.

Lamaism is the Tibetan form of Buddhism. Buddhism was officially introduced into Tibet during the rule of Sroṅ-btsan-sgam-po (in th early 7th cent. A.D.). The king became a devout Buddhism, welcomed Buddhist monks from India and China, and ordered them to translate the scriptures into the Tibetan language. At the same time he sent Thon-mi-saṃbhoṭa to India to study Sanskrit. On his return to Tibet, the king asked him to establish an official Tibetan script and to compose the Tibetan grammar. Then about a century later, Esoteric Buddhism entered Tibet during the rule of the King Khri-sroṅ-lde-btsan (755–781 A.D.), when two Indian pandits, Śāntirakṣita and Padmasaṃbhava were said to have come to Tibet and performed miracles, quelled the curse of demons, etc., by the power of '*mantra*'-practice. Since then Tibet welcomed great Indian monks, who came to Tibet successively, and thus Esoteric Buddhism florished in Tibet.

The uncontested predominancy of Esoteric Buddhism, however, resulted in the extreme degeneration of Buddhism in Tibet. It was Tsoṅ-kha-pa (1357–1419 A.D.) who reformed this degenerated form of Buddhism. He established a religious atmosphere based upon a code of Buddhist precepts. His reformed school was called the Yellow-Caps (*shwa-ser*) in contrast to the traditional school which was called the Red-Caps (*shwa-dmar*). His first disciple, Dge-ḥdun-grub, was renowned for his virtues and regarded by the Tibetans as the incarnation of Avalokiteśvara. As the chief abbot he was endowed by the official title of *Dalai-lama,* a title which has been handed down to the present 14th Dalai-lama. The Yellow-Caps are predominant in Tibet at present, and the Dalai Lama, residing at Mt. Potala in Lha-sa, the capital of Tibet, was the chief abbot of Lamaism and the King of Tibet as well, before his departure for India as a refugee.

Tibetans submit themselves in absolute obedience to Lamaism disregarding the essense of individual existence within the framework of social nexus. Such a pattern of behavior directs one, inwardly, to submit unconditionally to a particular personality believed to be endowed with religious charisma, and, outwardly, to adhere to the Lamaistic social order. These two aspects of behavior shall be examined below.

---

1) According to recent studies, details of the polyandry in Tibet is as follows: "Though large percentage of marriages belongs to monogamy, not so negligible percentage of polyandry is recognized among the *agricultural* Tibetans. Among the Tibetans the idea of *generation hierarchy* is feeble, but the idea of *gradation of natural age* is remarkable. A polyandrous wife comes from another clan, who has brothers as her plural husbands in many cases. But in fewer cases, a set of plural husbands is composed of uncle and nephew. And even paternal polyandry, in which a father and his real sons have a common wife, if she is not an actual mother of the sons, is reported by some travellers. These three kinds of polyandry have a common denominator. If they put importance on the difference in generation hierarchy as is the case of the Chinese culture, then the fraternal relationship will be quite different from the avuncular or paternal relationship in its meaning. However, if they endow more importance to the gradation of natural age, neglecting the general hierarchy, then the three kinds of relationship means only one kind of age gradation, irrespective of whether they are paternal, avuncular, or fraternal.

Among a set of plural husbands, only one is dealt with as the main husband, who can be called an *accentuated husband.* However, this status of accentuated husband is not always occupied fixedly by a certain brother or an uncle, but moves from an elder to a younger. And usually an accentuated husband coincides with a housemaster. It means that the status of a housemastership also slides from an elder to a younger. And the transmission of the status of housemaster usually takes place in the age of fourty years or so. Accordingly the system of polyandry is a device which is to charter a more able younger male kinsman as a leader in the household, avoiding the friction between wives. Usually the average age of the climax talent is so young that real sons of the previous housemaster are too young to take leadership in the family, when the ability of his father passed the stage of climax talent.

In conclusion, polyandry is an adaptative form to the principle of talent mobility on the one hand. It is also a trial to heighten the stability of a household on the other hand, through which they try to avoid some crisis of their life. Therefore usually polyandry is prevalent only among the agricultural Tibetans, not among the nomadic Tibetans. Because the needs of property accumulation and familial cooperation are stronger in the former than in the latter".

Jiro Kawakita, *The Japanese Journal of Ethnology,* vol. 19, No. 1 (1955) and Nos. 3–4 (1956).

2) Waddell: *op. cit.*, p. 31; C. Fr. Koeppen: *Die Religion des Buddha*, 1859, II, S. 71.
3) Jitsugyō Kai 甲斐實行: *Ramakyō to Mandara* (喇嘛教と曼荼羅 Lamaism and Maṇḍala), *Shūkyō Kenkyū* 宗教研究, New Series vol. IV, No. 6, pp. 141 ff.
4) Ekai Kawaguchi 河口慧海: *Chibetto Bukkyō no Tokuchō* (西藏佛教の特徵 The Characteristics of Tibetan Buddhism), in the *Chūō-shidan* 中央史壇, for the 12th year of Taisho era, (1923) p. 497.

Chapter 3. Absolute submission to a religiously charismatic individual

The Tibetan attitude of absolute submission to a religiously charismatic individual is directed toward the personality of the lamas (*bla-ma*).

The Tibetan term *'bla-ma'* literally means 'a high (*bla*) person (*ma*)', and is identical with the Japanese concept of *'shō-nin'* (上人) in its literal sense. Actually, however, it is the Tibetan counterpart for the Sanskrit word *'guru'* (teacher), or sometimes for *'kalyāṇa-mitra'* (a friend of virtue). *'Bla-ma'* was originally an appelation for high priests or president of a monastery, but now-a-days it is used by any disciple in calling his master. Thus, the term means 'a master' or 'a teacher'.

An unique and important characteristic of Lamaism, which distinguishes it from other schools of Buddhism, is that the living lama is more highly revered than the Buddha or the Dharma. On this point, Rev. Tada explains as follows: "There is a saying which is usually recited by Tibetan monks: 'Before Lama's origination, there was not even the name of the Buddha. All the Buddhas of thousand eons existed in dependance on the Lama'. It means that we can know about the existence of Buddha and his teaching only through the Lama's instruction, and only through that can we follow the Buddhist practices; therefore Lama is the real teacher who enables us to enter the right path and leads us to enlightenment; all the Buddhas in the past, too, having received Lama's instruction, believed in Buddhism, practised it, and attained enlightenment. In this case the term *'lama'* seems to have kept its original meaning, i.e. 'master'.

A more important concept is added to this term in the sense of 'one's own master who saves him'. Namely a master is regarded by his disciples as something more venerable than the Triple Jewel. Disciples are requested to pay homage first to Lama, then to Buddha, Dharma and Saṅgha, not only as a matter of concept, but also in actual practices. Therefore, for the Tibetan Buddhists, the objects of worship are the 'Four Jewels' instead of the usual 'Three Jewels'. This is the principal doctrine of Lamaism, and to take refuge in these Four Jewels is one of the characteristics which distinguish Lamaism from other schools of Buddhism. Lamaism was established and developed on the basis of such a faith.

In a further developed form of this concept, Lama is regarded as the synthesis of the Triple Jewel. That is to say, they believe that the Jewel of the Lama is not the same as the other three, but is the unity or the substratum of them all. Lama is the substratum of all the virtues, the basis of all the paths, and the root of merits. To serve a Lama is nothing but to pay homage to the Triple Jewel. This service is to be conducted in meditation and practice, since it is not only the best way to accumulate the root of virtues but also the shortest way to acquire enlightenment. Therefore the followers should try to satisfy their Lama materially and spiritually as well. For pursuing this duty, they are required to be prepared even to sacrifice their lives".[1]

Here the living Lama is regarded as the Absolute. Lama is said to be the personal manifestation of the three virtues, wisdom, compassion and power, each of which is usually held to be represented by the Bodhisattva Mañjuśrī, Avalokiteśvara and Guhyarāja, respectively. In a yoga practice called '*Bla-maḥi rnal-ḥbyor*', mendicants, sitting in front of an image of Lama, meditate upon the identity of Lama with Vajrasattva, and in accordance with this meditation, they are expected to receive a miracle by which they can get rid of all the miseries of this world.[2]

Lamaists never speak of their master's name in front of others. They refer to their master not by name, but abstractedly or with explanation of the meaning of his name so that hearers can judge who is the master. In case the sign of Lama's name is required for document, etc., they do it with a preface: though I feel it pain to scribe my master's name.[3] Thus they hesitate even to utter the Lama's name.

Before Tsoṅ-kha-pa's reformation, a kind of caste system was observed among the Lamaist priests who were actually married although it was not officially recognized, and the priesthood was maintained by hereditary rights. Priests of the Yellow-caps, the reformers, practised celibacy, and today, only the Red-caps still retain this custom. Even in this case, however, the qualification to be a successor is given only to the son who is at the same time a disciple of his father. Unless he has gained the described qualification by study and practice, he can not succeed the priesthood. Therefore the transmission of priesthood is not always by heredity. Here, too, we can observe the way of thinking that the religious charisma is more important than blood.

In a society where a charisma is regarded important, we can not expect educational training to permeate all strata of society. In Tibet, only special individuals are allowed to write books and articles.[4]

What then is the character of the lama hierarchy? It is divided into two classes: ordinary monks and noble monks. Of them 'the noble monks' means those who had entered the order through recognition as incarnated Lamas. Their number is about thirty in each monastery and they are treated respectfully because they are believed to be the incarnations of virtuous Lamas.[5] Thus the noble monk does not mean the monk born of the nobility, but one who is personally qualified to be treated as a noble. Contrary to the manner in which monks of noble families were accorded special treatment in Japan, the Tibetan lamas placed importance not to family origin but to individual charisma.

The highest sovereignty of Tibet is in the hand of the Dalai Lama, while the Bkra-śis Lama (=Paṇ-chen bla-ma) possesses merely a part of the territory. According to the religious idea commonly accepted by Tibetans, however, Dalai Lama is believed to be the incarnation of the Bodhisattva Avalokiteśvara, while the Bkra-śis Lama, that of the Buddha Amitābha. The Dalai Lama has therefore received an honorific title of 'the Holy Avalokiteśvara' (Ḥphags-pa Spyan-ras-gzigs). On the basis of a common belief in Indian Buddhism that Avalokiteśvara saves all the living beings by means of his incarnations in thirty-three forms, the Tibetans believe that each Dalai Lama is reincarnated in this world in the form of a baby forty-nine days after his death.[6]

For the first several generations, each Dalai Lama gave prophecy on the name of place where he is to be reincarnated after his death, and there was no difficulty to discover his successor. In later days, however, a Dalai Lama passed away without giving prophecy, and the subordinates were obliged to seek his successor by means of an oracle. Since then the oracle method has become customary. The most famous place for oracle today is Nechung (Gnas-chuṅ) near the Ḥbras-phuṅ monastery, followed by the three monasteries of Bsam-yas, Dgaḥ-ldan and Lha-mo. In each of these monasteries, there is enshrined the Protecting Deity to whom the priest asks for an oracle about the successor to the Dalai Lama. The decision is made after considering the contents of the messages received from these four monasteries. Sometimes each messenger announces different oracle. A unanimous choice among the four is hardly expected. Therefore, if there were more than two candidates selected by this method, the officers nourish them till the age of four or five. During this period, the candidates are examined of their faculty and behaviour, then the officers will render their final decision. If the final decision is still difficult to be reached, they are called to come to Lhasa where officers select one of them by lot. The lot-drawing is held in the public hall in the presence of high government officers, secular and ordained, and the Chinese ambassador to Tibet. In the process of lot-drawing, however, there are rooms for plot. Sometimes the oracle is misled by corruption, sometimes bribery to the high officials or to the Chinese ambassador causes trickery in the lot drawing. Amount of bribes often holds the key to the final decision. "There is no social disorder because, fortunately, neither the Dalai Lama himself nor the people know about the fact that such a plot ever existed".[7]

Thus the Dalai Lama, the highest sovereign in both religion and state, is determined not by hereditary rights but by the commonly held belief in rebirth.

The belief in rebirth also plays an important role in determining the religious charisma of common lamas. Virtuous lamas are believed to be the incarnations of such and such lamas of ancient days.

The belief in rebirth or incarnation is, needless to say, of Indian origin. It was prominent especially among Indian Mahayanists, who believed in the doctrine that Buddhas and Bodhisattvas manifested themselves in various forms in order to save all living beings. But they had no belief, as in Tibet, that an individual of certain qualification is the incarnation of a certain Buddha or Bodhisattva of the past. For Indians, the question was on the general possibility of incarnation. They therefore admitted the existence of numberless incarnations. For Tibetans, on the contrary, the problem was limited to particular personalities of certain qualification. Here is observed the transformation of a thought pattern of the Indians, who attached importance to universality of things, to the Tibetan way of thinking, which attached importance to individual differences. Moreover, this transformation is observed not in the form of attachment of importance to the worldly authority based upon blood or hierarchy as in China and Japan, but to the religious charisma of the individual, the selection of which is based upon the belief in rebirth.

The same way of thinking exerts a great influence on the daily custom of the Tibetans. They, who attach no great importance to blood lineage, are likely to mistreat the body of a deseased at times of the funeral. "The head is tilted down between the knees, and the knees are tied firmly to the breast, making the body nothing but a solid mass of matter which is wrapped up in a dirty blanket and is placed at a corner of the room. On a fixed day, they hand it over to a carrier at early dawn. Neither relative nor pupil accompanies it. It is quite different from the elaborate funeral ceremonies observed in Japan. The Tibetans regard a body without a spirit as something like a solid clay of no value. Thus the body is carried near a rocky cavern, where condors live, and the body is offered to them for consumption".[8)]

The Tibetans may not be able to imagine the Japanese custom of regarding the body as the Buddha's image and reciting scriptures in front of it.[9)] Here is a contrast of the way of thinking between two peoples who accepted the same Esoteric Buddhism: The Japanese attaches importance to blood lineage, while Tibetans completely ignore it.

What is important for the Tibetans is the soul, the substratum of transmigration. "Generally, at the death of a Lamaist, they never offers incent and flowers for the dead, but ask the fortune-teller about the situation of the dead in the other world. If he is announced to be with Avalokiteśvara, they make an image of the same Bodhisattva and offer incent and flowers in front of the image".[10)]

The ceremony of the returning of the departed soul to this world is observed in Lamaism. It consists of a kind of a mass for the dead similar to the Japanese *Segaki* ceremony.

According to the reports of Hedin and other travellers to Tibet, there is 'a sage of the cave'. He is reportedly said to enter a cave, enclosing himself inside it, leaving only an opening sufficient to receive food, and continues to live in solitude in the place of no light forever. When the supplied food is found untouched, people outside recognize his entrance into *Nirvāṇa,* and open the entrance and perform the funeral for the sage. Some sages are reported to have lived about five or six years under such condition, while another, more than twenty years. Many sages perform this asceticism and die in the conviction that it is one of the short ways to liberation.[11)]

Not even the Indians observed such a cruel form of ascetic practice, which is completely different from the Zen training of Japan. Such asceticism seems possible only in the belief that the soul must be revered even at the cost of the body.

This way of thinking, i.e. to attach importance to the soul as the substratum and to ignore the body, is also observed in the manner of keeping Buddhist discipline.

Buddhism, especially Mahayana Buddhism, prohibits eating meat because of its emphasis on the spirit of compassion. In Tibet, however, Buddhists could not help eating meat due to extreme climatic and other unfavorable natural condition. They eat boiled mutton or yak meat by cutting it into pieces with a knife. Sometimes they eat raw meat with blood dripping down. Dried meat freezed in winter is also supplied for the table. Thus Tibetan dishes are full of meat. Even today, it is reported, people often come across the sight of robed monks purchasing meat. Thus the precept which prohibited eating meat was not adhered to in Tibet.[12] The only exception is that they never eat fish because they 'don't like the idea of depriving the fish of their lives'. On the same token, they don't eat bird. They interpreted the precept as follows:— that to kill a big beast like a yak is not sinful because the meat of a yak can supply enough food for many, while to deprive small animals like birds or fish of their lives for the purpose of eating is quite sinful.

The economic life of the Tibetans is also influenced by the same way of thinking. They have little desire to transmit their personal property to their relatives after death. The legacy of an unmarried monk is offered as donation at his death. (In Japan such legacy will be handed over to his relatives or disciples.) In the case of a noble monk, the amount of donation at time of his death is quite big, since he was in a position to accummulate quite an amount of property. Following the monk's way, many laymen, too, donate one third or one fifth of their property after death. And such habit of donation is said to make the otherwise poverty-stricken Tibetan economy run smoothly.

The way of thinking characterizing the importance of religious charisma can be directed to one with worldly authority. For example, when the British and the Russian competed for the dominance of Tibet at the beginning of this century, a Mongolian lama called Dorjief, who studied in Russia, approached the Dalai Lama with special message of the Russian Emperor and was thereby able to sway the Lhasa Government favorably to the interest of Russia. In order to arouse a pro-Russian feeling among the Tibetans, he preached 'the Pure-Realm theory' and said that 'the Pure Realm' means Russia, which lies in the West, and that the Russian Emperor is actually the incarnation of the Lord Amitābha. He further interpreted that as Tibet is the land of Avalokiteśvara, who is partially of the body of the Lord Amitābha, Russia and Tibet are but one and inseparable, therefore, Tibet should ally herself with Russia.[13] The religious charisma ascribed to a particular personality is more effective to move the Tibetans than economic interests.

The same way of thinking, however, frequently contributes to the corruption of human morality. Because Esoteric Buddhism permits monks to approach women, high priests of the Red Caps are allowed to have contact with many women and those women, who bear a child of a lama, and their child as well, are believed to be sacred. Such belief and practice lead the monks to indulge in lewdness and create a vitiated atomosphere. This practice is still observed particularly in the Khams province and the provinces near Mongolia.

---

1) Tōkwan Tada 多田等觀: *Chibetto* (チベット *Tibet*), pp. 2–3.
2) *Ibid.*, pp. 3–4.
3) *Ibid.*, p. 5.
4) Hakuyū Hatano 羽田野伯猷: *Zōgai Chibetto Seiten Mokuroku Hensan ni Tsuite* (藏外チベット聖典目錄編纂について "On the Compilation of a Catalogue of Tibetan Works on Buddhism" in the *Bunka* 文化, July 1944, p. 465.)
5) Tōkwan Tada: *op. cit.*, pp. 27–29.
6) Bunkyō Aoki 青木文教: *Chibetto-yūki* (西藏遊記 A Record of Journey in Tibet), p. 105. He calls himself an *'avatāra'*. (Waddell: *op. cit.*, p. 242.)
7) Bunkyō Aoki: *op. cit.*, p. 247 ff.
8) Tōkwan Tada: *op. cit.*, p. 24. In case of the Dalai Lama, Tibetans treat his dead body exceptionally with great care. (Bunkyō Aoki: *op. cit.*, p. 343 ff.)
9) Rev. Chiken Sumita, a high priest of the Higashi-Honganji temple, Japan, said, as one of his dying wishes, that the recitation of scripture should be performed in front of the Buddha's image. It is an exceptional case in Japan.
10) Tōkwan Tada: *op. cit.*, p. 26.
11) Yōkichi Takayama 高山洋吉 (tr.): *Chibetto-Tanken-ki* (西藏探檢記 A Record of the Expedition to Tibet), pp. 73 ff.
12) Tōkwan Tada: *op. cit.*, p. 89; Bunkyō Aoki; *op. cit.*, pp. 192, 326.
13) Bunkyō Aoki: *op. cit.*, p. 169.

Chapter 4. Absolute adherence to the Lamaist social order

Tibet is at present within the dominion of the People's Republic of China. Actually, however, she was always an independent state of absolute monarchy under the rule of the Dalai Lama. The Dalai Lama was the head of Lamaism, but, at the same time, he maintained the political power of the land. Thus he was the ruler of both the religion and the state.

Being a nomadic people living in a desert highland, the Tibetans were originally divided and ruled by several tribal heads. In later days, kings had arisen among such tribal heads, but they maintained no systematic political organisation. It was Lamaism that organised Tibet for the first time into one political unit. The rôle of Lamaist monks was important in the making of Tibet and they are sometimes compared to that of the Catholic priests in the age of the Germanic migration in the Western history. Till the end of the 9th century A.D., the sovereignty of Tibet was in the hand of the king, who protected the monastic order of Lamaism. Later on, however, the sovereignty was gradually transmitted to the hand of the Lamaist high priests, among whom the Dalai Lama established his permanent sovereignty at about the 15th century A.D. and became the actual king of Tibet.

The idea of patriotism and loyalty do exist among the Tibetans but it is based upon religious faith. That is to say, Tibetan patriotism is based upon the faith that Tibet is a sacred religious country and that the Dalai Lama, the sovereign of Tibet, is an incarnation of the Bodhisattva Avalokiteśvara. Therefore neither patriotism nor loyality to the king can exist apart from Lamaism, and to do something for the sake of the country or king is synonymous for to do something for the sake of their religion.

As Tibet is the Lamaist kingdom, the priests play an important rôle both in religious and secular affairs. They are trained in the details of both affairs and actively participate in political matters. Tibet in the early 20th century was said to be governed by a Central Government, which consisted of three premiers and four ministers who controlled both civilian and military officials in the central and provincial governments. The government was responsible to the Dalai Lama and endeavored to carry out his will politically as well as religiously. It was ruled that one of the premiers and one of the ministers must always be a monk. Such rule was also observed among the posts occupied by sub-officials and local boards. Number of officials was such as totaled about 175, which consisted of both priests and laymen. Among the local boards, the lay-officials took charge of economic affairs, while the priest-officials took care of religious and educational affairs. Lay-officials were usually in charge of judicial affairs, but sometimes the priests helped them.[1)]

Buddhist priests in India and China had seldom taken share in political matters directly as government officials. Chinese priests were concerned only with the administration of religious affairs. In Japan, even the administration of religious affairs was in the hand of secular authorities. Therefore, in the history of Buddhism it can be said that it is rather an unusual phenomenon to observe Buddhist priests taking an active part in governmental administration in their official capacity. Also it is to be observed that in most Buddhist countries a strong political consciousness or a controlling force has never developed with the inevitable result that an organized hierarchy could not be established. Tibet was an exceptional case.

What then is the relation between the Lamaist rule and the social hierarchical order in Tibet?

The hierarchy in Tibet is roughly divided into the nobility and the commoners. The latter is again divided into three: high, middle and low, according to occupational differences. Among them the nomads constitute the largest group, followed by the peasants and merchants. The artisans are placed at the lowest level of the Tibetan hierarchy. The nobles, being descendants of feudal lords, are possessed of extensive lands, but are not possessed of the right to manage them. Their lands are governed by officials sent by the Central Government. During the reign of the fifth Dalai Lama, at which time the central government was established, feudal lords lost their lands but instead obtained the right to become government officials with the status of nobility. Thus they have occupied the positions of lay-officers in the government exclusively, until recently, when the posts of government official were open to the commoners as well. On the contrary, any priest could be a priest-officer, irrespective of his origin, nobility or commoner, but he was required to be a graduate of the school of priest-officers. This fact shows the existence of a confidential belief in the religious charisma besides the feudalistic way of thinking in Tibet.

Influenced probably by such thought of hierarchical order, the Tibetan language keeps honorific form to some extent. Personal pronoun differs according to the speaker's attitude towards the person spoken of. Some nouns and verbs have their honorific form besides the usual one. For example, *lus*, the Tibetan term for 'body', is replaced by *sku* when it denotes a body of a respected person. (e.g. *saṅs-rgyas-kyi sku*, Buddha's Body)[2]

Due to the absolute power of Lamaism, the Tibetans accept with ease what are quite irrational to the eyes of modern people. For example, all the priests and monks in Tibet, more than 40,000 in number, have no tax-duty. Lhasa is the taxless area because it is a holy place. "Such arrangement seems quite unfair in comparison to the people living outside Lhasa who are suffering from heavy taxes. But to suffer is, they believe, the result of *karma* in former births, and owing to the services to lamas in this life, they will be able to attain a happy life in the next birth in accordance with the disappearance of *karma*".[3]

Because of the unique culture of Lamaism, the Tibetans regard their country religiously and as something particular, and have therefore developed a consciousness of exclusion towards foreigners.

First of all, the Tibetans call their country 'the land of the lotus flower'. They compare the Chos-khaṅ Palace of Lhasa to the calyx of a lotus flower, and the mountains surrounding the lands as its petals. (the calyx of a lotus flower signifies the Buddha's seat or Paradise. This idea is akin to the fact that the Japanese followers of Esoteric Buddhism consider Mt. Koya the seat of the central monastery of Esoteric Buddhism in Japan, as the lotus flower with the eight petals.)

The Tibetans believe that Tibet is the Pure Land of Avalokiteśvara. They say, Buddha Śākyamuni once gave prophecy to Avalokiteśvara, saying: "Beyond the Himalaya there live the people to be saved. Go there instantly and save them". This prophecy is recorded in the *Mañjuśri-paramârtha-nāmasaṃgīti*.[4] Here, they think, what is meant by 'the land beyond the Himalaya' is Tibet, and hence Tibet is the world entrusted to Avalokiteśvara, and the Tibetans and Avalokiteśvara stand in the relation between the people to be saved and the saviour.

It was probably due to this conviction that the Tibetans have come to believe the successive Dalai Lamas, the sovereigns of Tibet, as the reincarnations of Avalokiteśvara, and called their palace in Lhasa, 'Potala', after the name of Avalokiteśvara's Pure Land. They are pleased to have been born in such a holy land of Avalokiteśvara and desire to be reborn in Tibet. We cannot overlook the existence of the wishes among common people for the rebirth in the Pure Land of Amitābha or in the Tuṣita

Heaven of Maitreya. Generally, however, they regard their country as the ideal world.

Tibetan exclusivism is the result of such an idealisation of their country. It is rather caused by a religious idea, but not by the thought of territorial possession as seen among other races. Although they have no idea of 'the centre of the world civilisation' as has been observed above, they believe that their country is the proper land for Buddhism. They further believe that due to Buddha's grace, this Buddhist land is secure, and even if a disaster were to occur,[1] it would easily be removed, and everyone would be able to enjoy equally the life of peace and quietness; therefore, if foreigners entered this land, the pure Buddhist land would be instantly spoiled, the people would lose their happiness, receive the Buddha's punishment, and would fall into misery forever. Such a strong belief is the basis of their exclusivism.[5]

Thus the Tibetans prohibit the entrance of foreigners into their country. When they find strange travellers, they will at once chase them out of Tibet. Some explorers were killed by them. Tibetans who try to invite foreigners are punished in a cruel manner.

---

1) Bunkyō Aoki: *op. cit.*, p. 253, and according to his personal instruction.
2) e.g. H. A. Jäschke: *Tibetan Grammer*, New York, 1954, pp. 35–36.
3) Tōkwan Tada: *op. cit.*, p. 118.
4) *Ibid.*, p. 80 (cf. Tōhoku Catalogue No. 360).
5) The above is according to the reports of Rev. Aoki and Tada. It seems quite opposite to the report of Ekai Kawaguchi referred to in the previous section. A common way of thinking in both reports, which superficially contradictory to each other, is the belief in religious charisma. Therefore it may be interpreted that there is a consistent way of thinking inspite of the different forms of each idea due to historical and geographical conditions.

Chapter 5. Shamanistic tendencies

The Bon Religion prevailed in Tibet prior to the introduction of Buddhism. This religion is a form of Shamanism having originated somewhere in Central Asia, and was probably conveyed to Tibet in the company of racial migration. It is animism in character. It teaches that there exist numberless free spirits in the universe, whose motion causes good or ill fortune. Through prayer, people ask these spirits to remove ill fortune and bring good fortune. These spirits reveal their will before the people through mediums. At first a medium performs ceremony in order to have the spirit within his body. When the spirit transmits itself into the body of the medium, the latter loses his personality and the spirit reveals itself and conveys a command or prophecy through the mouth of the medium. The spirit sometimes manifests various miracles beyond human imagination. Thus it recovers people from ill, and turns misfortune into a blessing. There was no organized doctrine in the Bon Religion.[1]

The introduction of Buddhism caused the Bon Religion to decline. But accepting Buddhist doctrines, it still lives side by side with Lamaism in the hearts of the Tibetans. The relation between the Bon Religion and Lamaism is quite similar to that between Shintoism and Buddhism in Japan. There are also similar characteristics between Shintō ceremonies and those of the Bon Religion. In the Bon Religion, there is no shrine as in Japan, but the place where gods are considered to live is regarded as holy, and a tower is built in such a sacred place, and the way to that place is adorned with sacred rope (*'shimenawa'* Jap.). (In Shintoism, shrine construction was an art that developed at a much later period.) Sacred dance and music of the Bon Religion is also very similar to that of Japan. A Lama priest who visited Japan some years back expressed his impression when he observed the *Kagura*-dance held at the Ise shrine, sayiny, "It is just like the sacred dance of the Bon Religion". Nowadays the Bon Religion has accepted Buddhist terminologies, compiled scriptures, and maintains temples.

What then is the difference of the ways of thinking between the Bon Religion and Shintoism both of which are of shamanistic origin?

It is really not so simple to answer this question. We shall compare some of characteristics of both religions, though it may be quite superficial. Respect to purity and emphasis on simplicity observed in Shintō is absolutely lacking in the Bon Religion. Not only the Bon Religion, but the Tibetans in general are much fond of complexities and colors in decorating things as are observed particularity in their paintings. As for the virtue of honesty, there seems to be no clear tendency in Tibet. Rev. Aoki who lived in Tibet a long time confessed that he could not understand the Tibetan characters. Virtue of love, though it is sometimes said to be lacking in Shintoism, is surely emphasised particularly in the medieval age under the name of 'compassion' (*karuṇā*) due to the influence of Buddhism. But in Tibet, inspite of their acceptance of Buddhism, people are by nature of violent character. The existence of cruel penalties justifies this statement. Of course the Tibetans, especially the educated ones, are said to be quite gentle except for the primitive mountain inhabitants. Although the cruel forms of penalties which existed in the past are said to be no more, after their prohibition by the 13th Dalai Lama, nevertheless, the long existence of cruel forms of punishment suffices to reveal to us an aspect of the Tibetan habitude. The seemingly cruel behavior of the Tibetans is probably due to their habit of hunting and the general nomadic life they lived.

Buddhism, which took the place of the Bon Religion, was not heterobeneous to the latter but quite homogeneous. Being of esoteric character, it was, in a sense, more shamanistic than the Bon Religion, and thus was able to replace the Bon Religion. Most scriptures translated into the Tibetan language are those concerning Esoteric Buddhism. This newly introduced Esoteric Buddhism was a developed form of Tantrism in India which attached importance to the practice of ceremonies associated with alcoholic drinking and magic and regarded sexual enjoyment as of the highest value. Tsoṅ-kha-pa, in his reform program, tried to remove these elements out of Lamaism, but he was not able to uproot them completely.

On the contrary, the traditional, conservative Buddhism which prohibited enchantment, ceremony, magic and divination did not find room in Tibet. In the Tibetan Tripiṭaka, there are included thirteen scriptures translated from the Pāli Canon. Out of these thirteen, nine scriptures belong to the *Parītta-saṃgaha,* i.e. the collection of scriptures and phrases which are believed, among Southern Buddhists, to be effective to drive out evils and invite good luck, and are equivalent to the *Mantra-piṭaka* of the Dharmâkara school.[3] It seems to denote the fact that the Tibetans selected only those of magical character out of the Pāli scriptures of early Buddhism.

The practice of *dhyāna*-meditation was also introduced into Tibet, but it was observed merely among the more sincere monks in monasteries, while the people in general relied upon esoteric ceremonies.[4]

Such circumstances still remain basically unchanged today. People believe the existence of the demon of ill-health which invades the human body. When they fall ill, they ask a priest for fortune-telling, and then worshipping gods and Buddhas, they offer a prayer to remove the illness. The objects of their worship are not limited to the Buddha Śākyamuni and Amitābha, but inclusive of Mahāvairocana, Mahābhaiṣajyaguru and all the other Buddhas and Bodhisattvas in various worlds of ten directions, as well as the gods in heaven and on earth, demons and serpants. In a Lamaist temple, these objects of worship are enshrined side by side without order. Among them, gods and demons are mostly of Bon origin. As the Tibetans absorbed Buddhism, they became to be regarded as the protectors of Buddhism.

These gods and demons are believed to take possession of selected persons, who thus become mediums or magicians. When a medium or magician is consulted on marriage, journey, or on the fortune of a new-born child, he, with bloodshot eyes, foaming mouth, utters words and sentences scarcely comprehensible, which are interpreted afterwards into a horoscope.

The belief in demons is still held side by side with the utilization of modern technology. In their belief, there is a demon of eclipse who deprives the sun or moon of light. In order to kill the demon, they perform a ceremony against the demon, recite charms and discharge a gun towards the eclipsed sun or moon. Unless this is done, they are convinced that the sun or the moon would lose its light and the world would become dark forever.[5)]

Buddhism was accepted by the Tibetans only to the degree that it adapts itself to the Tibetan ways of thinking. Consequently, Lamaist priests are almost indifferent to the propagation of the Buddhist doctrine. They scarcely engaged themselves to missionary work. Even in Lhasa, preaching is held only twice or thrice a year and the number of those who attend the sermon is not more than two or three hundred at each time. "The real experience in the truth is, in Lamaism, to be secret, and hence, to preach to the common people is considered rather a debasement of the truth".[6)]

Thus the common people[7)] are almost indifferent to sermons. There are exceptional cases, however. For example, families of high position may invite an intimate lama to their home on special occasions to hear him. In Tibet, preaching does not mean propagation, but is merely a part of a ceremony.

On the other hand the recitation of scriptures is very popular among the Tibetans. Every home invites lamas for this purpose.

The unique method for seeking a new Dalai Lama referred to previously seems to be somehow related to this ancient shamanistic way of thinking. According to the view-point of the Tibetans, Lamas must be possessed of a supernatural power resulting from their perfect practice on Esoteric Buddhism which makes them immortal. Therefore their death means merely the change of body or the shift of place for life from one body to another. Thus, the Tibetans seek for a new-born child at the death of a Lama, welcome him as the reincarnated Lama, and render service with pious attitude to him as if to the former Lama. Thus is established a religious custom unique to the Tibetans.

The same shamanistic method was used till recent days even at times which required an important decision conserning state affairs. The state magician of the Tibetan Government, who lived in the Nechung (Gnas-chuṅ) monastery, had much influenced the cource of Tibet's internal and external policy by his predictions. His greatest influence was seen when a search was conducted for a new Dalai Lama. His office was established during the reign of the fifth Dalai Lama. A very fateful part was played by one of the State Magicians in the political developments which led up to the British military expedition into Tibet in 1904. The State Oracle was consulted regarding the measures to be taken, and he suggested that a certain mountain, situated a short distance within the Sikkimese territory, should be occupied by the Tibetan troops, as this mountain, by its magical qualities, would stop further advances by the British. The move, however, did not meet with success as the Tibetan troops were easily defeated. He seems to have been still of the opinion that eventually the Tibetan army would be victorious. Therefore the Tibetan Government refused to negotiate with the advancing British forces for such a long time. This policy was reversed only after Lhasa had been captured. The Dalai Lama removed the State Magician from his office due to the false prophecies he had made previously.[8)]

Thus the destiny of Tibet was controlled by a supernatural power even in recent times.

---

1) Tōkwan Tada: *op. cit.*, p. 168 ff.
2) According to Bunkyō Aoki's information, who guided this lama.
3) Susumu Yamaguchi 山口益 Chibettogo no Keitō (西藏語の系統 Tibetan Language), pp. 33–35. (Contained in the Iwanami Kōza 岩波講座, *"Tōyō-shichō* 東洋思潮").
4) According to Rev. Tada's information, the *Bhadracaryā-praṇidhāna*, the *Manjuśri-paramārthanāmasaṃgīti*, the *Sitātapatrā-dhāraṇī** are most oftenly used for ceremony, but the *Saddharmapuṇḍarīkā* is scarcely recited.
* *in detail*
1. the *Bhadracaryāpraṇidhāna* (Tōhoku Nos. 1095, 4377)
2. the *Mañjuśrijñānasattvasya-paramârthanāmasaṃgiti* (Tōhoku No. 360)
3. the *Ārya Tathagatôṣṇīṣasitātapatrā nāma aparājitadhāraṇī* (Tōhoku No. 593)

5) Bunkyō Aoki: *op. cit.*, p. 334.
6) Tōkwan Tada: *op. cit.*, p. 39; cf. Bunkyō Aoki, *op. cit.*, p. 230.
7) The following is according to Rev. Aoki's instruction.
8) R. Nebesky de Wojkowitz: State Oracle of Tibet. *The Modern Review*, 1950, December, pp. 479–480.

Chapter 6. Logical tendencies

The Tibetan language belongs to the same family as the Chinese, and is by natural not of logical character, nor suitable for abstract expression. For example, it has no word for 'size', a concept which can only be expressed by 'big and small' (*che-chuṅ*). Under the influence of Sanskrit, however, Thon-mi-saṃbhoṭa systematised the Tibetan language and gave it a logical character to some extent. Tibetan logical character is prominently shown in the mode of acceptance of Buddhism.

Firstly, we shall examine the character as appeared in the method of translation of Sanskrit.

If a Sanskrit word contained two ideas, they are expressed in two words in the Tibetan language. For example, the Sanskrit word *pariṇāma*, which means the process of changing and its result as well, is translated into Tibetan as *yoṅs-su hgyur-ba* and *yoṅs-su gyur-pa*, respectively. Thus the Tibetans distinguish the result of an action from its process.

A long Sanskrit compound word difficult to be analyzed is often explained clearly in Tibetan. For example:

'Buddha-kṣetra-vyūha-ananta-praṇidhāna-prasthāna-parigṛhīta',[1] (buddha—land—adornment—unlimited—vow—entrance—being embraced), a Bahuvrīhi-compound showing a qualification of the Bodhisattva, is translated into Tibetan in the following way:

saṅs-rgyas-kyi shiṅ-gi bkod-pa mthaḥ-yas-par smon-pa-la ḥjugs-pas yoṅs-su gzuṅ-ba.

By this translation, we are able to understand the clear meaning of this compound-word that "(a Bodhisattva who is) embraced by (the mind) enters into the vow for unlimited adornment of the Buddha's land". Thus Tibetan is indispensable for understanding Buddhist Sanskrit texts. The Indians, using Sanskrit which is logical by nature, made obscure expressions by using too many compounds, while the Tibetans, using a primitive and illogical language, made it possible for us to understand such expressions through their language. We can not but acknowledge the efforts of the Tibetans who were fairly successful in expressing the logic and the exactness of the Sanskrit words through the medium of the Tibetan language which is generally far from clarity in logic.[2] (The efforts of the Tibetans in this respect may be suggestive for the Japanese to improve the illogical character of their language.)

The same logical tendency is observed also in the way of accepting Buddhist ideas. The Tibetans translated a good number of works on logic (Nyāya). The Sde-dge edition of the Tibetan Tripiṭaka contains 66 works on Nyāya, some of which are quite voluminous. It is in remarkable contrast to the fact that the Chinese Tripiṭaka retains only a few Nyāya texts, e.g. the *Yin-ming chêng-li-mên-lun* (因明正理門論) (*Nyāyamukha*), the *Yin-ming-ju-chêng-li-lun* (因明入正理論) (*Nyāyapraveśaka*), all of which are simple textbooks. These Tibetan translations are indispensable for the study of Buddhist logic in view of the fact that many Sanskrit originals are lost.[3]

The Nyāya doctrine introduced into Tibet is mainly that of Dharmakīrti, who dealt with epistemology. The Tibetans are said to have conducted a critical examination on the theory of direct perception (*pratyakṣa, mṅon-sum*) taught by him.

The Tibetans utilized the Nyāya doctrine for practical purposes. Discussions are held among student-monks in the monasteries by means of the Indian logic of dialogue in order to examine the Buddhist doctrine, a matter which was rather different in China and Japan where logic remained merely as a branch in which it helped one in the preparation of making a commentary on one of the Buddhist texts but was not actually put into full practice.

The course of logic in Lamaist monasteries continues for about four years,[4] during which time students are required to learn by heart all the two thousand verses of the *Pramāṇavārttika* (*Critique on knowledge*), the masterpiece of Dharmakīrti.[5] This text is regarded as the basic scripture (*mūla*) on logic, and is the only one text in Tibet concerning logic written by an Indian logician.[6] There are a lot of Tibetan commentaries on it, of which some present rather unique theories. The Tibetans study them by means of summaries composed by Tibetan logicians of the ten schools. Inspite of the existence of many commentaries by Indian writers, they study logic only through the commentaries and summaries made by their fellow countrymen and pay no attention to those of Indian origin.

Notable here is the fact that only the *Pramāṇavārttika* of Dharmakīrti is studied and all the other works of him and of Dharmottara, who developed the Buddhist logic established by Diṅnāga and Dharmakīrti, are almost forgotten by the Tibetan logicians. Why is this so? According to Vostrikov, it is said that the Tibetans attach special importance to Chapter II of the *Pramāṇavārttika,* which discusses validity of knowledge in general, although in actuality, it is a commentary on the verses concerning the prayer to the Buddha written by Diṅnāga, and is devoted to the discussion of Mahāyāna Buddhism designed to prove that the Buddha is the Absolute, the Omniscient (*sarvajña*) and the *Manifested Knowledge* (*pramāṇabhūta*). In other words, in this chapter Buddhism is defended and established as a religion. Therefore, the Tibetans' attitude toward logic was basically religious; logic was merely an *'ancilla religionis'*, the servant of religion, as far as they were concerned. Therefore, the most suitable and acceptable section of the book was this chapter which attempted to establish a pure faith in the Omniscient and Absolate through a critical examination of matters, while Dharmakīrti's other works and those of Vasubandhu, Diṅnāga and Dharmottara, were conceived to have stood in the standpoint of agnoticism as far as their analysis of the Buddha as the Omniscient was concerned.

Although this view expressed by Vostrikov, which has been accepted by Stcherbatsky, is still uncertain as to whether it reveals the true state of the minds of the Tibetans, two schools of thought existed in Tibet concerning the relation between logic and religion. Kun-dgaḥ-rgyal-mtshan (1182–1251, the fifth Great Lama of the Sa-skya monastery, alias Sa-skya Paṇḍita), the founder of one of the schools on logic in Tibet, was of opinion that logic is a secular science and contains, like medical science and mathematics, not a single element of Buddhism. The same was the opinion of the famous historian, Bu-ston Rin-po-che. On the contrary, the Dge-lugs-pa Sect (the Yellow Caps), which is the only powerful sect today, rejects this opinion and maintains that the logic of Dharmakīrti offers a firm foundation to Buddhism as a religion.[7]

Actually, however, logic did not develop so much in Tibet. Dharmakīrti's system is its final development. His situation in Tibetan logic can be compared to that of Aristotle in European logic; and Tibetan works on logic, to those of Scholaticism in medieval Europe. Their main interest was in the strict definition of technical terms, establishment of scholastically detailed rules of their use, and expression of all kinds of scientific thinking by means of syllogism.

Logic is regarded in Tibetan monasteries as the fundamental study. School course begins with logic. A textbook on logic used in a monastery starts with the following sentences:

"kha-dog yin-na dkar-po yin-pas khyab zer-na/
pad-ma-ra-ga kha-dog-chos-can dkar-po yin-par thal/
kha-dog yin-pas phyir/
rtags ma-grub/
ciḥi phyir/ ——— "

(If it is asked) "Must it be white if it were a color"
Proposition: (It follows:) 'A ruby possessed of colour is white'.
Reason: Because it is (possessed of) colour.
(To this argument, the answer:) The evidence is not established.
(Questioner:) Why?

As it can be observed from the above catechism, the textook is here going to teach an error contained in the argument with respect to general and special concepts. To our surprise, this textbook is used in Tibetan monasteries for *the exercise of children of about ten years of age.*

Tibetan lama-students often conduct a symposium in the same manner as in India according to the manner of the Nyāya-dialogue and the victors are awarded prizes. Thus logic is utilized in Tibet as the rule for expediting discussions.

The logical and systematical way of thinking is also evident in the way of accepting the *śūnyatā*-theory, the fundamental doctrine of Mahāyāna Buddhism. The *Prajñāpāramitā,* the principal scripture of this theory, is quite a long unsystematic one. Maitreyanātha (4th cent. A.D.) organized its contents and composed a commentary called the *Abhisamayālaṅkāra,* on which Haribhadra again wrote commentaries.[8] Depending solely on the commentaries of Haribhadra, the Tibetans attempt to understand the *Prajñāpāramitā.*

It was Nāgārjuna who gave philosophical basis to the theory of *śūnyatā.* However, his *Madhyamaka-kārikā* does not maintain a system in spite of the fact that it shows a sharp logical approach. Therefore, the Tibetans rather prefer the *Madhyamakāvatāra* of Condrakīrti of the Nāgārjuna school to Nāgārjuna's *Madhyamaka-kārikā* itself, because the former discusses the Mādhyamika theory in a more organized manner. Moreover, notable is that those texts liked by the Tibetans are written according to the rule of Nyāya logic. Even the texts on grammar are explained systematically by means of the Nyāyic argument.

According to Rev. Tada, the subjects mainly studied in the monasteries are the Mantras, Nyāya and Abhidharma philosophy. Works on history are not read so much, although a fairly good number of works on this subject are written by the Tibetans. Among the works concerning Hīnayāna Buddhism, the *Abhidharmakośa* is read and studied in particular. As for the Vijñāna theory, only the *Trisvabhāva-nirdeśa* is carefully studied as they believe it to be the best to lead one to emancipation, while almost no attention is paid to the *Triṃśikā* and the *Viṃśatikā* with the exception of the commentaries written on them by Tsoṅ-kha-pa. The Dalai Lama recites the *Abhisamayālaṅkāra*, the *Madhyamakāvatāra* and the *Pramāṇavārttika* every morning, whose contents he knows by heart perfectly, and reads the texts on Esoteric Buddhism in the evening.

The Tibetans show their logical character in their critical attitudes even towards the Esoteric Buddhism introduced from India. Mahāyāna Buddhism in general formulates the theory of the Triple Body of Buddha, i.e. (1) the Absolute Body (*dharmakāya*) being the universal truth itself, (2) the Body of Bliss (*saṃbhogakāya*) being the body endowed with the perfect virtues as the result of religious practice in the previous lives, and (3) the Apparitional Body (*nirmāṇakāya*), being the incarnation manifested to this world in order to preach the doctrine for the sake of living beings. Moreover it maintains that to preach the doctrine to the living beings is the work of the Body of Bliss or the Apparitional Body, but not of the Absolute Body. In Esoteric Buddhism, however, the doctrine is asserted to be preached by the Abosolute Body (*Dharmakāya*) as the ultimate truth, and this is regarded as showing the philosophical superiority of Esoteric Buddhism over other systems. The Tibetans at the beginning accepted this theory as it was taught. (The case is the same as the Shingon school in Japan.) But the Yellow Caps, the reformers of Tibetan Buddhism, refused to accept this traditional theory, saying:

"The *Vajrasūtra* of Kālacakra of the Anuttara-yogatantra school, to which we pay our highest respect, was taught by Buddha Śākyamuni at Dhānyakaṭaka on the request of King Candrabhadra of Saṃvara State in the north. (The theory that the Dharmakāya itself preaches the doctrine) is not based on historical facts. It is fantasic and quite contrary to the fact to maintain such a theory. It is merely a production of verbal expression. Therefore we can not accept that theory".[9]

Referring to this point, Rev. Kawaguchi makes a comment as follows:

"If this theory (of the Yellow Caps) is acknowledged, the doctrine of the Old sect of Shingon Esoterics of Japan will lose its ground. The preaching of the Dharmakāya is one of the important elements with which they maintain themselves to be superior to other sects. In reality, the preaching of the Dharmakāya is difficult to be maintained, unless it was preached by the Body of Bliss. As far as the Dharmakāya is regarded as the abstract truth pervading the universe, it is difficult to maintain, without encountering a contradiction, that it is endowed with the power to preach, because the all-pervading truth is the one and absolute, while the activity to preach requires such entities as the subject and object".

It was probably the spirit of pursuing logical thoroughness that caused the Tibetans to assume such a critical attitude as seen in the doctrine of the Yellow Caps.

Not all the Tibetans can be characterised as logical, but it is at least clear that the intellectual people were aiming at a logical exactness in thinking and writing.

Above is an outline or a brief observation concerning the characteristics of the Tibetan ways of thinking the information of which was extracted from a limited source of material. The author believes, however, that within these pages can be found some of the unique characteristics of the ways of thinking of the Tibetans in comparison to other Eastern peoples.

---

1) The *Mahāvyutpatti*, ed. by Ryōzaburō Sakaki 榊亮三郎, No. 859. (Chinese equivalent to this Sanskrit is 持入無量諸佛國土莊嚴願 (bringing about (?)—numberless—Buddhas'land—adornment—vow).)

2) e.g. A Tibetan sentence: "*ṇaḥi gcen-po thams-cad bod-kyis bsad*" can be translated in two ways.
   a) Tibetans killed all my brothers.
   b) All my brothers were killed by Tibetans.
The copula '*yin-pa*' is here to be supplied.

3) Cf. Tensen Yamagami 山上天川: *Bukkyō-ronri no Kenkyū to Chibetto-zokyō* (佛教論理の研究と西藏々經 Studies on Buddhist logic and the Tibetan Tripiṭaka), *the Wayūshi* 和融誌, 1908, vol. XII.

4) Tibetan lama-students are required to study the five courses in the monastery, which require twenty years. Of them, the first three years are devoted to the studies in logic. (Tōkwan Tada: *op. cit.*, pp. 31 ff.)

5) According to Rev. Tada's information, the studies in logic in Tibet are based upon the *Pramāṇavārttika* alone, while the *Nyāyabindu* and the *Pramāṇaviniścaya* are scarcely studied.

6) The following is according to Th. Stcherbatsky: *Buddhist Logic,* vol. I, 1932, pp. 38, 57, 58.

7) *Ibid.* p. 46. This is to be compared to the fact that Japanese and Chinese Buddhists had never maintained logic to be a secular science. In these countries, logic was studied entirely on the line of 'theology'.

8) According to Rev. Tada's instruction, students are required to learn by heart a short commentary of Haribhadra on the *Abhisamayālaṅkāra* (Tōhoku Catalogue No. 3793). It maintained an almost equivalent authority as the holy scriptures. Haribhadra belonged to the line of Bhavya (Bhāvaviveka), but his idea of *śūnyatā* is different from Bhavya's and rather near to that of Candrakīrti.

9) Ekai Kawaguchi 河口慧海. *Nihon-Bukkyō to Chibetto-Bukkyō tono Busshin-kwan no Sōi ni tsuite.* (日本佛教と西藏佛教との佛身觀の相違について On the difference of Buddhology between Japanese and Tibetan Buddhism), *the Gendai-Bukkyō* (現代佛教,) March, 1928, p. 31.

PART VI. CONCLUSIONS

Chapter 1. General consideration of the ways of thinking of East Asian peoples

(1) Various cultural phenomena and the ways of thinking of East Asian peoples

Regarding various cultural phenomena, is it possible for us to recognize the features of the ways of thinking common to the peoples of the East? In Japan as well as in the West we often hear people maintain that a certain trait is "Oriental". In connection with this, let us inquire into the meaning implied by this term.

First of all, it is generally said that in the East man's individual existence is not fully realized, but that the individual is subordinated to the universal. Hegel, for instance, asserted that God or the Absolute in the East has the feature of "das Allgemeine".

"The fundamental principles of the various religions of the East are that the single 'Substanz' per se is 'das Wahrhafte', and an individual has no value within itself, nor is it capable of attaining any value so long as an individual holds itself, while standing against 'das Anundfürsichseyende' which is absolute; that an individual is only capable of assuming true value by uniting itself with the 'Substanz' when this individual, however, is no more a 'Subjekt' but is dissolved into the unconscious".[1)]

And as to the difference between the Eastern and Western thoughts he says thus:

"On the contrary, with Greek religion or Christianity 'Subjekt' is aware of its freedom; and we ought to think in this manner".

In the philosophy of the East, however, "The negation of the finite is existent. But that negation is the one in the sense that an individual only attains its freedom in unity with what is substantial".

Hegel had only a limited knowledge of the classics of the East, acquired through his reading of translations; his views, however, are shared by most of the Western people even nowadays.

To what extent then are Hegel's statements to be considered true? Indeed, in the East a blind subordination to authority in some form or other was conspicuous. Is it possible for us to assert that in the West "the self was free" and devoid of such subordination? The complete, blind faith in authority during the Middle Ages in the West and the subsequent destruction of heterogeneous culture did not occur in the East. Was the phenomenon of 'being united with the Substanz', as Hegel called it, not conspicuous, in some cases, in the West rather than the East?

It is often said that the peoples of the East are *intuitive* and accordingly, not systematical nor orderly in grasping things; in contrast the Westerners are said to be *inferential* or *logical,* and that they try to grasp things systematically and orderly. Indeed, the ways of thinking of the Chinese or the Japanese may be characterized as 'intuitive'. But in the case of the Indians this label is hard to apply. For example, the intricate arguments of the Abhidharma literature is logical; and can never be called intuitive. There is no need to refer to the difficult literature of theology in order to point out how far removed from intuitive grasping is that complicated, fantastic and strange sentiment found in Indian paintings and sculptures. That sentiment urges us to form a complicated association of ideas, and leads the spectator into a strange, fantastic atmosphere.

Secondly, it is often asserted that the ways of thinking of the Eastern peoples are *synthetic,* while that of the Westerners *analytic.* The Chinese word, for instance, gives us the impression that it is synthetic, but it may well be placed on the stage prior to analysis. So long as it has yet to pass through the process of analysis, it would hardly be called synthetic. On the other hand, it is generally recognized by scholars that the Indians showed a great skill in the analysis of philological or psychological phenomena. We can not say that the Westerners have a tendency only to be analytical. For example, the Indian grammar was most advanced in the analysis of words and phrases, but very weak in its consideration of the synthetic construction of sentences. While, on the other hand, Greek grammar has left an excellent achievement concerning syntax dealing with the synthetic field of words and phrases. Therefore, it is unjustifiable to characterize the ways of thinking of the Eastern peoples simply as being synthetic.

Then, let us consider the problem of *knowledge.* Max Weber says, "The premise which is common in the last analysis to all philosophies and soteriologies in Asia is that knowledge—whether it be that of books or mystical gnosis—is the only absolute way leading to the supreme bliss of this world as well as of the next world. A careful examination would reveal the fact that "knowledge" does not mean to know the things of the world, nature, social life nor laws regulating both of them. Rather, it is the philosophical knowledge of the 'meaning' of life and of the world. It is naturally understood that such a knowledge can not be replaced by Western empirical learning, and that it should never be sought by means of empirical learning, if we are to do justice to the purpose proper to the learning".[2)]

Indeed, it is true that knowledge as conceived by the East Asian people had a strong inclination to bear out the definition given above. But in the history of Western thought, we are able to note the existence of a similar inclination. The word gnosis itself which is used here is Greek. And a gnostic inclination is also seen in various religions in the West part of Asia, and is not peculiar to India and China alone. In the West, too, it explicitly revealed itself in the Neo-Platonians such as Plotinos, and it is considered to be traced back to Platon. It is generally presumed that such philosophical schools might have been influenced by Indian or Persian philosophy or thought, but this relationship is yet to be clarified. Under the influence of Greek philosophy the Gnostics arose as a movement to elevate the Christian faith to the level of knowledge. Likewise in the Middle Ages, such an inclination is said to be noticeable in some of the Mystics who were regarded as heretics, such as Tauler or Eckhart.

Let us consider the next problem. There are some people who maintain that all the principal religions of the world came into existence in Asia; therefore, if we label the whole area including the West part of Asia "East", East might be said to be *religious*, whereas Europe (and America) or the West non-religions. Such a view was fairly dominant in Japan prior to the Pacific War, and it has never completely disappeared. However, as pointed out above, among the East Asian races, the Indians in particular are extremely religious, but the spiritual disposition of the Japanese or the Chinese could never be termed religious. On the contrary, there is some evidence that the Western people are far more religious than the Japanese or the Chinese.

In the same way, the contention that has repeatedly been made that the Western civilization is '*materialistic*', while the East Asian civilization is '*soulful*' or '*spiritual*', is erroneous. A non-religions race can never be '*soulful*' or '*spiritual*'. The ancient Western civilization and especially modern civilization, which restored the old, were highly superior in the research and application of material nature, and consequently, the West with all its power made an advancement toward the East. The East Asian peoples, menaced by this invader labeled the West 'materialistic'; on the other hand, it has characterized the less advanced East itself as 'soulful' or 'spiritual'. As far as the feeble capability of controlling material nature is concerned, a similar feature can be seen in the aborigines of Africa as well as of America. It is in no way peculiar to East Asia alone. Furthermore, the justification for defining the East as 'internal' or 'subjective', and the West as 'external' or 'objective is highly questionable.

Furthermore, it would be a very superficial observation to describe the East as 'being ethical', for ethics is a part of every and any society. Observing that some of the traditional ethics of the Japanese and Chinese are not practiced in the modern West, some conservative Japanese, trying to preserve the ethics of old, made this characterization. In connection with the above observation, it is often advocated that Eastern thought is to be regarded as metaphysical, and that the basis of the Eastern thought is 'nothingness'. This results in the frequent use of the phrase 'Nothingness peculiar to the East'.[3] It goes without saying that 'nothingness' was propounded in the philosophies of Lao-tzu and Chuang-tzu. On the contrary, Indian philosophy generally inquires into the 'existent'. (The meaning of 'existent', however, is different from that of Greek philosophy, as heretofore pointed out.) In Indian philosophy in general, there is a thought tendency that the 'existent' can only be substantiated on the basis of 'what is existent'. In the case of Śaṅkara, the ultimate being of the world is the 'existent', and it is rather the phenomenal world which is void, so that his thought is diametrically opposed to the thoughts of Lao-tzu and Chuang-tzu, as far as literal understanding is concerned. In Buddhism, especially in Mahāyāna Buddhism, 'voidness' is expounded but it is different from 'nothingness'; this fact is often emphasized by the Indian Buddhists.[4] These two ideas were either identified or confused when the method known as Ko-i 格義 (The evaluation and interpretation of Buddhism through the doctrines of Chinese thoughts, such as Confucianism, Tao-ism etc.) was practiced after the introduction of Buddhism into China. Chia-hsiang-tai-shih 嘉祥大師,[5] however, repeatedly affirmed that Buddhist 'voidness' and the 'nothingness' of Lao-tzu's or Chuang-tzu's were not to be equated. Therefore, it is very dangerous for us to qualify the whole of Eastern thought with the term 'nothingness peculiar to the East'. (However, if the term is used to refer to one part of the thought, there would be no objection. Or if a modern philosopher sets up such an idea as a result of his contemplation, then he is free to do so, but this has nothing to do with verified thought.) Moreover, it could not possibly be averred that the East is metaphysical and the West is not so. Among the East Asian peoples, most of the Chinese and the Japanese in particular have been much more non-metaphysical than the Westerners.

Returning to the fundamental problem of the ways of thinking, it is often said that the Westerners are *rationalistic,* while the East Asians are *irrationalistic.* Such characterizations seem to have acquired general acceptance and usage especially after World War II. It is particularly emphasized that the Japanese are irrationalistic. Indeed, the Japanese are ill-fitted for the systematical and logical way of thinking, and we have already pointed out their irrational character. But when we consider it more deeply, in practice the Japanese generally tend to follow certain laws. As it was pointed out, a devotion to a particular ethical system is a general tendency, upon which they laid a criterion of the evaluation of value. Accordingly, in this sense we can say that rationality did exist—if "rational" is the correct term.

At first sight the Chinese give us the impression of being irrational. The way of expression in the Chinese language is extremely ambiguous, and the historical fact that there has never been a development of logic among the Chinese seems to support this view. To be *illogical,* however, is not necessarily to be irrational. It is widely known that Chinese thought, due to its rationalistic character, exerted a great influence upon the philosophy of enlightenment of the modern West. Max Weber says, —"Confucianism is extremely rationalistic since it is bereft of any form of metaphysics and in the sense that it lacks trace of nearly all religious basis—to such a degree that it is questionable whether it is proper to use the term 'religious ethics'. At the same time, it is more realistic than any other systems outside of J. Bentham's ethical system in the sense that it lacks and excludes all measures which are not utilitarianistic".[6] Concerning this point clarified here, it is the Chinese rather than the Westerner who is far more rationalistic. And it is solely due to this rationalistic character that Chinese thought inspired the thinkers of the period of enlightenment such as Voltaire and Wolff and came to serve as their weapon against the shackles of the Middle Age traditions.

Although the Indians did not achieve any remarkable development in the field of natural science as in the West, they conducted far more elaborate speculations than the Westerners of the old and Middle Ages with respect to fields such as the analysis of psychological phenomena or that of linguistic structures. The Indians are highly rationalistic in so far as their ideal is to adhere to eternal laws concerning past, present and future. The thought represented by the aphorism, 'credo quia absurdum', or 'I believe because it is absurd' had no chance to appear in India. The Indians are, at the same time, logical since they generally have the tendency in their thinking to give import to the universal; they are at once logical and rationalistic. On the contrary, religions of the West are irrational and illogical. This is what is acknowledged by the Westerners themselves. For example, Schweitzer, a pious and most devoted Christian, says,

"Compared to the logical religions of the East Asia, the evangel of Jesus is illogical".[7)]

On this point, the East is more rational and conversely, the West is more illogical. A rationalistic attitude is seen consistent in Dharmakirti's logic or the natural philosophy of the Vaiśeṣika school of India. Consequently, we cannot imprudently adopt the classification that the East is irrationalistic and the West rationalistic.

It is to be noted here that there is an effort being made to make a distinction between the rationalism of East and West. For example, Max Weber says,

"The practical rationalism of the West is extremely different in nature from that of the East, notwithstanding the outward or actual similarity of the two. The post-renaissance rationalism was especially rationalistic in the sense that it abandoned the restrictions of tradition and believed in the power of reason existent in nature".

This statement appears to be well grounded. The thought tendency, however, which was bent on disregarding traditional authority or restriction appeared as early as the turbulent days of the so-called "Ch'un-ch'iu" 春秋 to the beginning of "Ch'in" 秦 in China, and in India it was conspicuous in urban society during the period of the advent of the Buddha, and even afterwards it was propagated by naturalistic philosophers and logicians. In modern Japan as well, the germination of free thought is faintly perceived. Accordingly indeed it is a fact beyond doubt that disregard for conventional authority and restriction was dominant in the modern West, and was weak in East Asia, but this is merely a difference of degree or quantitative distribution; it is not a difference in essence. And even if that thought tendency was influential in the modern West, it was not so in the Middle Ages; therefore, it would be improper to distinguish the East and West on this point.

In connection with this, a *nostalgic conservatism* is very conspicuous among the Chinese, and it can also be seen to a considerable degree among the Japanese, while in India it was once partly forsaken. In the case of the Moslems, who make up a fairly large part of the Indian race, on the surface have disengaged themselves from the religions peculiar to the Indian race; therefore nostalgic conservatism can not be called a general feature of the East Asia. Although this nostalgic conservative character is partly common to both the Indians and the Chinese, the former is prone to be united with the universal law underlying the past, present and future, while the latter is inclined to revere a particular example as a precedent. Thus, the basis of these two similar nostalgic character harbors difference in outlook or thought.

Again with relation to this, we might think that the character of the East Asians is to grasp things *passively*. That this is a conspicuous feature of the way of thinking of the Chinese and the Indians was pointed out in the above. Among the same East Asians, however, the Japanese in particular are highly sensitive to the transition of things. That Buddhist teachings and Confucian learnings alike have been transformed into something dynamic in character since their introduction to Japan was also pointed out. Therefore, it is impossible to sum up the ways of thinking of the East Asians in general as merely being 'passive'. And authough those of the Westerners might indeed be called 'dynamic', the idea of evolution or development in phenomenal existence or in history has manifested itself clearly only in modern times and could not possibly be said to have existed from the past age.

It is often pointed out that India, China, and Japan are climatically situated in the monsoon zone, so that the thought tendency of the three countries has some climatic trait common to them. People living in this zone are generally passive and submissive to objective nature and lacking in the will to conquer it by means of rational and measured thinking, and as they make a move en masse, they are easily subordinated by a specific authority and they dislike to assert themselves positively. Accordingly, when various thoughts are found opposed to one another, they are likely to recognize their raison d'être and to compromise and synthesize, rather than to adopt one of them alternatively to the exclusion of others.

Therefore, it is often contended that in contrast to the Western thought the spirit of tolerance and mutual concession is a salient feature of Eastern thought. The religion of the West emphasizes the struggle for the sake of religion.

"If any man come to me, and hate not his father, and mother, and wife, and children, and brethren, and sisters, yea, and his own life also, he cannot be my disciple". (Luke, 15–26)

"I am come to send fire on the earth; and what will I, if it be already kindled?—— Suppose ye that I am come to give peace on earth? I tell you, Nay; but rather division: For from henceforth there shall be five in one house divided, three against two, and two against three. The father shall be divided against the son, and the son against the father; the mother against the daughter, and the daughter against the mother; the mother in law against her daughter in law, and the daughter in law against her mother in law". (Luke, 12–49∼53)

Such aggresive thought as mentioned above did not appear at all in the religions of East Asia. Throughout the religious world of India a tranquil and peaceful atmosphere has prevailed from time immemorial. Gotama and Mahāvira ended their lives in peace. Perceiving the fact that in China a perfect freedom of faith has been preserved since ancient times, Voltaire, who was called the 'apostle of the freedom of faith', was utterly fascinated by Chinese law.[8] Although in Japan, the principle of the freedom of faith has not fully been realized where political influence was exerted, due to the interference of the state, the hatred against the heretic has been mild among the people in general. Even the Jōdo Shin sect, the most clear-cut sect in its uncompromising attitude toward the other faiths, advises that in order to spread the faith it is wiser to wait calmly for a suitable opportunity rather than to force the situation.[9]

With the Indian people, a self-conscious reflection as to the impact of one self against other selves was not clearly revealed. Underneath this fact lies the view that all men are one. And such a view as this seems to be perceived in the other races of the East Asia as well, though in different degrees.

The idea of tolerance and mutual concession is based on the standpoint which admits the compatibility of manifold different philosophical views of the world. According to our foregoing, the Indians are prone to tolerate the co-existence of philosophical thoughts of various types from the metaphysical viewpoint; the Chinese are inclined to try to reconcile and harmonize them from a political and practical viewpoint; and the Japanese tend to emphasize the historical and physiographical features of such diverse thoughts. The interference with religions on the part of the state was not very notable in India, but in China it was conducted to a considerable degree, and in Japan it was occasionally extreme. Consequently, we hesitate to sum up these stand-points with the adjective 'Asiatic'. While in the West in modern times, the spirit of tolerance and mutual concession was preached especially by the thinkers of the Enlightenment or Pietists, in Asia, especially Iran, heretical views on religion were relentlessly persecuted.

Particularly, it is often pointed out by Westerners that Eastern thought has a tendency foword *escapism* and that it is rather indifferent toward social and political action. They say that Christianity preaches the importance of practice within this world but religions of the East Asia teach man to shun this world.[10] Such criticism seems to have become common in the West. In relation to this, especially concerning the traits of the religions of Asia, Max Weber says,

"Indifference to the world was the attitude taught them,——be it in the form of external escapism, or be it expressed in actions indifferent to this world, although taking place in this world. Accordingly, it is resistance toward the world and the practices of oneself".[11] According to Max Weber,

"The fundamental creed of Protestant ethics in the modern West is 'inner-wordly' asceticism. It attempted to rationalize this world ethically by accepting the will of God positively, rather than to tend toward escapism as in the case of meditation.[12] Daily conduct is elevated, through rationalization, to the level of godsent vocation, and this is also man's assurance of happiness. In contrast with this, religions of the East are nothing but a herd of the meditative, fanatic or insensitive devotees and they regard any inner-worldly practice as nonsense and are anxious to leave this world. Not that Buddhist monks have no practice at all, but, since their ultimate objective was to escape the 'circle' of transmigration (saṁsāra), their conduct could never have undergone any thorough, inner-worldly rationalization".[13] Indeed, the ethics of Protestantism may have been as described by Max Weber. But Western thought in and prior to the Middle Ages has not always been characterized by an attitude of inner-worldly rationalization. 'A herd of the meditative, fanatic or insensitive devotees' did exist in the West in the past as well as in the East. And regarding the fact that the religious men of the East were conducting *inner-worldly activities,* this book only referred to in part although it is a fact beyond doubt. The religion that pervaded the various countries of East Asia was Mahāyāna Buddhism which stresses such *inner-worldly activities.* And we can see in the religion of Iran a tendency toward the worldly.

In relation to this, it is often asserted that the East Asian people follow nature and attempt to realize the identification of man and nature; whereas the Westerners attempt to conquer nature. The attempt on the part of man, however, to assert himself and to conquer nature was not uncommon in East Asia. In China and India as well, the construction of canals, banks, water tanks, and ramparts was undertaken. On the other hand yearning for nature appeared also in the West, in which people sought to return to the nature. Accordingly on this point also, it is very difficult for us to make a clear distinction between the two spheres. Concerning problems of philosophy, the opposition of subject and object, for instance, was already taken up in ancient Indian philosophy. The reason why natural science has made remarkable progress in the West, especially in modern times will be considered on another occasion. In any case, the attitudes toward nature as found in the West and the East are difficult to difine or distinguish.

Max Weber states that during or prior to the Middle Ages, the ascetic life in the Christianity of the West had been tinged with a *rational* character.

"Its object was to overcome the 'natural state' (status naturae), to rid man of his dependence upon the power of irrational impulse and upon nature and the world, to subordinate man to the rule of a deliberate scheme, and to place man's conducts under the incessant self-examination and the *evaluation* of ethical significance".

"Herein lies the world-historical significance of the monk's life of the West in contrast to that of the East Asia—viewed not from the whole of it, but from the general type thereof—".[14] From the view-point of the rationalization of life, however, the workaday practices at Zen monasteries in Japan are extremely rationalistic, and as was pointed out before, the social work of Japanese priests prior to the Middle Ages were very extensive. Therefore it is the author's opinion that it is difficult to make a clear distinction between the East and the West on this particular point.

After having examined what have heretofore been designated as features peculiar to Eastern thought, we find ourselves in reality incapable of recognizing a difinite trait which can be compared with that of the West. It appears possible for us to recognize a few similarities common to the nations in East Asia; however, it is impossible to regard them as general features, comparing them with those of Western thought as if they were non-existent in the West. These features were regarded as 'Eastern' because they were conspicuous in certain countries in a certain period or among certain peoples. Accordingly it is also certain that those features are not without some truth.

Thus we must acknowledge the fact that there exists no single "Eastern" feature but rather that there exist diverse ways of thinking in East Asia, characteristic of certain peoples but not of the whole of East Asia. This can be affirmed by way of comparison between the cultures of the East Asian nations, and by noting the fact that Buddhism was received by various nations of East Asia according to the character of the recipients; this clearly testifies to the reality of this view-point. In other words, Buddhism whose basic principle is universality and transcendency over the distinction of social classes and nations, has been taken in with certain modifications, modifications which were made according to the features of the ways of thinking of each recipient nation.

Of course, there can be similarities of the ways of thinking between the Buddhists of various nations, even if they may differ in nationality, since Buddhism is a world religion and it has especially exercised a profound influence over the spiritual and social life of the East Asian nations. Buddhism, in so far as it is Buddhism, must be basically consistent wherever it may be found. (The problem of general or common features of Buddhists is not treated within this book, for the problem is of a different nature.) It is only natural that a generality should be perceived so long as an overwhelming part of the nations of the East Asia are Buddhists. However, we can not make a generalization of this fact as to the East Asian nations as a whole.[15] Because the East Asian nations are not all necessarily Buddhists. To say that there are similarities and parallelisms among Buddhism of the East Asian nations is not tantamount to showing the parallelisms and similarities of the East Asian nations as a whole. Whether the conclusions regarding the Buddhists as a whole are applicable to, for instance, the Indians in general—they are non-Buddhists—must be considered separately.

According to the above considerations, the inevitable conclusion is that *there are no features of the ways of thinking exclusively shared by the East Asians as a whole.*

Furthermore, if the ways of thinking differ according to each nation, then the cultures formed by these nations would be heterogeneous to each other. Already a scholar has observed that the three nations; India, China, and Japan, have established respectively their own distinct culture.[16] As far as the ways of thinking or folk-traits of each nation are concerned, it seems proper for us to admit such a remark as this.

---

1) Hegel: *Vorlesungen über die Geschichte der Philosophie*, herausgegeben von Michelet, S. 135–136.

2) Max Weber: *Aufsätze zur Religionssoziologie* II, S. 364–365.

3) As to the positive inquiry into the idea of "nothingness" in the East Asia, confer Kumataro Kawada's 川田熊太郎 *Muno Shisōno Keitōronteki Kenkyū* (無の思想の系統論的研究 Systematic Study on the Thought of "Nothingness".) (Sanseidō 三省堂 *Bukkyō Shisō Ronshū* 『佛教思想論集』 pt. 1).

4) Already in India 'śūnyatā' was liable to be misunderstood as 'nothingness' or 'nihil'. Those who attacked the Mādhyamika school that advocated the doctrine of śūnyatā, identified śūnyatā with nothingness, and argued that the Mādhyamika school is nihilist (*nāstika*) since it advocates nihil, negating everything. (*Madhyamakavṛtti*, pp. 475, *l.* 8; 490, *ll.* 1–2). If we take the connotation of śūnyatā as nothingness, then the Mādhyamika school becomes an advocate of a doctrine that would destroy Buddhism; therefore, even within Buddhism there appeared antagonists of the doctrine of śūnyatā. (*Mādhyamika Śāstra*, 24. 1–6). According to Candrakīrti's commentary the Mādhyamika school was viewed as 'absolute nihilist' (*atyantanāstika*, *op. cit.* p. 159, *l.* 4) or 'one who views everything as nothing' (sarvanāstika, p. 159, *l.* 11) or 'basic nihilist' (*pradhānanāstika*, p. 329, *l.* 12). The Sarvāstivādins of Hīnayāna Buddhism viewed the Mādhyamika school as 'one who argues that everything is nothing' (阿毘達磨顯宗論 vol. XXVI, *Taishō.* vol. 29, p. 901 b). The Sautrāntika also denounced it saying that 'one who has a middle mind' (*Madhyamakacitta*) is 'one who denies the existence of the substance of all things' and since he is obsessed with 'a prejudice that everything is non-existent' (*sarvanāstigrāha*), the doctrine of this school is one of the two heretical views within Buddhism, side by side with the Vatsīputrīyas which admit pudgala. (俱舍論 vol. XXX. p. 6–b. *Abhidharmakośa*, trad. par Poussin, IX, 271, note). Furthermore the Mādhyamika school is viewed by the Vijñānavādins as an 'extreme view' (*ekāntavāda*) which holds that even the sense-consciousness (*vijñāna*) is non-existent. (*Triṃśikā*, p. 15, *ll.* 13–16. 成唯識論 vol. 1. p. 1–b, 同上 述記 vol. 1. *Taishō.* vol. 43. p. 236–b–c.) It is only natural that most of the Western scholars call the "*Prajñāpāramitā Sūtra*" or the doctrine of the Mādhyamika school nihilism since such criticisms were already expressed in India. Against such criticisms, however, Nāgārjuna, founder of the Mādhyamika school, says, "You are ignorant of the function in śūnyatā, the meaning of the śūnyatā and śūnyatā

itself". (*Mādhyamika Śāstra;* 24. 7) According to Candrakīrti's commentary, he says, "The meaning of the word 'nothing' (abhāva) is not that of the word 'śūnyatā', and yet, you denounce us assuming that the meaning of the word 'nothing' is equal to that of the word 'śūnyatā'. Therefore, you are equally ignorant of the meaning of the word 'śūnyatā'". (p. 491, *l.* 15 f. also cf. places before and after this passage). The object of the Mādhyamika Śāstra is not to elucidate the nothingness of all things but śūnyatā itself. (p. 239, *l.* 8). Nāgārjuna states that the philosophy which considers śūnyatā as nothingness is false, and argues that we should not identify the śūnyatā doctrine with the view of nothingness (*abhāvadarśana*). (p. 273, *l.* 12 f.; *Madhyamakāvatāra,* p. 77). He also says, "We are not nihilists. We clarify the unique way which leads to the castle of Nirvāṇa by rejecting the two extreme views of 'existence' and 'nothingness'. (p. 329, *l.* 13). Indeed śūnyatā and nothingness do appear to resemble each other as the other schools contend, but those who advocated the doctrine of śūnyatā make a clear distinction between the two ideas.

5) Being different from Lao-tzu's nihil, Śākyamuni's way is transcendent of the four heretical prejudices (『三論玄義』 p. 9–b), but since Lao-tzu 'advocated the way by expounding nothingness', Chia-hsiang-tai-shih says that we must distinguish Buddhist śūnyatā from Laotzu's nothingness. (*ibid.* p. 12–a).

6) Max Weber: *op. cit.* I. S. 266.

7) Albert Schweitzer: *Das Christentum und die Weltreligionen,* S. 52.

8) Sueo Gotō 後藤末雄: *Shina Bunka to Shinagaku no Kigen* (『支那文化と支那學の起源』 Chinese Culture and the Origin of the Chinese Study) p. 418.

9) What have we to do if in one family there are members whose faith differ from the others? According to "*Myōkōnin-den*", the analects and records of devout followers of Jōdo Shin Shū, we can see many of such cases. A woman who married a Nichiren believer became a devotee of Jōdo Shin Shū; however she continued to worship for two years the image of the Amida Buddha. One day she was discovered by her husband, who was impressed by her devotion and eventually became a devotee. (初篇下, 常州忠左衛門の條). A man by the name of Gozayemon who lived in the Ban-shū province was constantly persuading his wife to become a Buddhist, but he always met with indifference. However, by chance he succeeded in making his wife a Shinshū believer. (二篇上). Such ways of proselytism as mentioned above are in vivid contrast with those of the Western religions which I mentioned previously.

10) For example, Schweitzer: *op. cit.* S. 30 f.

11) Max Weber: *op. cit.* II, S. 367.

12) Concerning ethical rationalization of the present world, Max Weber asserts that the East Asians are lacking in the ethical character in respect to identifying profession with duty. Prof. Kwanji Naitō, however, positively proved by citing the Ohmi merchants that this view of Max Weber's was incorrect. (*Shūkyō to Keizairinri—Jōdo Shin Shū to Ōmishōnin* (「宗教と經濟倫理—淨土眞宗と近江商人」 Religion and Economical Ethics—Jōdo Shin sect and Merchants in Ōmi. *Nippon Shakaigakukai Nempō* 日本社會學會年報 Shakaigaku (社會學) vol. 8. 1941. pp. 243–286).

13) Max Weber: *op. cit.* I, S. 263–264.

14) Max Weber: *Die protestantische Ethick und der Geist des Kapitalismus*; Jap. Tr. by Tsutomu Kajiyama, p. 143.

15) Vivekānanda, the religious reformer of modern India, visited China and Japan in 1893, and is said to have been moved by the fact that in various temples the manuscripts and epitaphs written in ancient Indian letters had been preserved and to have strengthened his faith in the *spiritual unity of Asia*. (Romain Rolland: *La Vie de Vivekananda*, I, p. 42). However, this unity points to the universality of Buddhism. Therefore the unity of Asia is to be recognized within this context, i.e. the universality of Buddhism.

16) Sōkichi Tsuda 津田左右吉: *Shina Shisō to Nippon* (支那思想と日本 Chinese Thought and Japan).

Chapter 2. The universal character and the particular character of East Asian thought

(1) The concept of the "East" and previous comments on it

We have clarified in the previous chapter that there is no way of thinking generally applicable to the East Asians. Why then are such phrases as 'East Asian thought' or 'East Asian culture' used as if they were axiomatic concepts? The reason in my opinion is as follows: The Japanese people were thrown into spiritual confusion due to their abrupt acceptance of the Western culture after the Meiji Restoration. In Japan prior to this period Chinese and Indian thought intermingled with the traditional Japanese thought, and they existed in harmony, in oblivious of contradictions. As a result, this relationship was applied to both Chinese thought and Indian thought in general, and furthermore, in general Japanese thought was regarded as being not in conflict with Chinese and Indian thoughts. Thus, the phrase 'East Asian thought' came to be applied to these countries, as identical with them. The people advocating the necessity of preserving the old Japanese cultural tradition especially emphasized the importance of the East Asian thought; at the same time, almost invariably, such people have been 'Orientalists'. Admittedly, an exclusive minority with nationalistic tendencies did their utmost to rid Japanese culture of the remains of the influence coming from the Indian and the Chinese cultures. This faction maintained that they would pay their respect to things proper to Japan. But as the predominant part of old Japanese culture owed much of her substance to India and China, such a narrow-minded attitude was not shared by the intellectuals at large. They paid instead their attention to the similarity and affinity between the old Japanese culture and the culture of East Asia in general. Accordingly, despite the difference of geographical space between 'Japan' and 'the East

Asia', the conflict between them has been scarcely felt. Along with the attitude which maintained the superiority of Japanese culture, the following view was generally held: "The Japanese are the most ingenious race in regard to taking in foreign culture. They took in and assimilated the essence of the culture of the East Asia. Buddhism and Confucianism are examples. Hereafter Japan must take in Western civilization and thereby build a new culture". Such a view as this served to justify the identification of the cultures of East Asia and Japan.

However, as we have pointed above in this book, the way in which the Japanese received the cultures of India and China was led to serious distortions; they did not take in and assimilate them in their entirety. There is apparantly a fundamental discrepancy between the old Japanese culture and the cultures of other countries in East Asia. We must not overlook this fact.

Taking notice of this situation, it has already been observed even by the Japanese scholars on East Asia that the culture of East Asia is far from being a unified entity. "Whatever amount of space may be allotted to the area which should be called 'East Asia', as far as the cultural significance is concerned, it has never existed from old times as a unified world, there has existed no single history called the history of East Asia, and accordingly, it is fundamentally impossible for us to assume that there is a single culture to be called the culture of East Asia".[1] The scholars who advocate the view such as above negate the singularity of East Asia but admit that of the West: "On the whole, the West has evolved, moved by a single world and history, though the nations existing therein had their own singular racial traits and were not without their own national histories".[2] At the same time it is emphasized that the Western culture is at once world culture. "At present, modern culture, world culture, that is to say, Western culture is not standing in opposition to the culture of Japan, but rather it is immanent in her and can be considered as Japanese culture itself".[3] This view expressed by a respected scholar on East Asia is shared and supported by a good number of intellectuals at present. However, when such an observation is analysed, it is found that there are two premises presupposed: (1) the singularity of the Western culture, (2) the identity of the Western culture with the world culture. These two premises are formulated to destroy the idea of the singularity of the culture of East Asia. We must, however, examine and criticize these two premises.

First, concerning the singularity of Western culture, there is no doubt that European countries since the past ages developed a culture keeping a close connexion with one another spiritually and materially. However, can we rightfully claim that Western culture is a single, unified entity? Western culture may be traced back to two cultural currents: Greek and Hebrew, but it is a sheer historical fact that they conflicted with each other. These two currents were compromised and blended with each other in the Middle Ages somehow or other, but in modern times a minority of the Westerners or certain materialists or natural scientists came to part with the Hebraic religious thought. Furthermore, in Western culture, there are included a number of things heterogeneous to one another and we have already pointed out that the features of the ways of thinking which are generally called 'Oriental' are also found among the ways of thinking of the Westerners.[4] It is one think to admit that there was a close relationship among the Western nations and it is another to acknowledge *the singularity of the ways of thinking* of these nations. Therefore, as far as the ways of thinking are concerned, we must disavow the singularity of the West as we did in the case of the East. The singularity of the West is in the final analysis nothing but that of type or an approximation. In some cases it can never be established either.

Next, let us deal with the contention that Western culture can be equated with the world culture. It is generally acknowledged that the unification of the world was accomplished by the Western nations with their realization of dominance over the world in recent times. It goes without saying that no people or nation can exist isolated from the West politically or economically. In other fields as well such as learning, art, etc. the influence of Western culture is decisive. This is the reason it is generally thought that the world was unified and at the same time westernized. The unification of the world, however, is only conspicuous regarding man's efforts to control, and utilize material nature; while on the side of language, ethics, religion, art, customs, etc. the spiritual traditions of each nation can be altered only with much difficulty. For instance, the Westerners arrived in India for the first time towards the end of the fifteenth century and at last she came to be ruled by them. In spite of their skilfull ruling policy, the Christian population in India is about six million, which is only a little over one sixtieth of the whole population; the majority of Indians professing Christianity consists of either the outcast from the Hindu society or the lowly, while the majority of the whole populace embraces the popular faiths, derived from ancient times. In China the situation is somewhat similar. The fact that the nations of the East refuse to be altered easily in their ways of thinking or their mental tendency even in the face of the thought or cultural influence of the West should not be characterized merely as the backwardness or retardation of the East Asian people. Some scholars report that the characters of the ways of thinking which have been delineated above mainly in terms of how Buddhism was received presented themselves in the case of Christianity as well. If it were true, then it follows that the ways of thinking of various nations have been unexpectedly firm enough to retain their existence to this day.

The East Asian people or its culture is not in its entirety retarded or backward. In some cases it is as advanced as the West. For example, it is common to the West, India, China, or Tibet that culture has developed from the integral language form to the analytical one. We have referred to this fact above. In some phases, the principal nations of the world have gone through a common process of progress. Such a common process of progress is also seen in the fields of religion, ethics, social institutions, political organizations, etc. The problem of the spirit of the times shall be discussed upon in another thesis. Hereafter the research into various nations as seen from the view-point of their interrelationship is necessary. In different times, there are different social structure and different forms in the contrast of social classes. In spite of that, there is something unchangeable that has survived to this day, and here, I have attempted to define this. I never mean to say that something climatic or stationary is superior to the characteristics which are historical, time-honoured, or of social classes. Even while the world is making its progress in the same direction, the racial distinction will not be dissolved. And as long as the racial distinction keeps its existence, the Western nations or the Western culture should be considered as being one particular culture.

---

1) Sōkichi Tsuda 津田左右吉: *Shina Shisō to Nippon*, p. 178.
2) *Ibid.* p. 148.
3) *Ibid.* p. 179.
4) cf. the previous chapter.

(2) East Asian thought and its universality

It may be noted that those who contend that westernization is at once universalization have the following view in mind: "Cultures of East Asia are subordinate after all to the Western culture. The characteristics of various ways of thinking of the East Asian people are to be overcome some day by those of the Westerners. The Western culture is in possession of universality, while the Eastern culture is not". For example, Max Weber says, "The cultural phenomena which promoted the development of universal meaning and applicability happened to appear in the West, and that in the West alone". And he has conducted a sociological research into almost all the religious systems the world over in the light of the question 'Upon what kind of chain of conditions was the above fact dependent?'[1] In Japan on the other hand, Dr. Tsuda observed likewise that the Chinese thought, for example, is incapable of assuming universality.[2] However, what is meant at all by 'being incapable of assuming universality'? It is natural that the natural-scientific knowledge or techniques which arose in the modern West should be understood or assimilated with ease and without change. But with respect to other cultural fields, is it possible for us to say that anything born of the culture of the West is capable of assuming universality, whereas all the cultural products of other nations are not? When we look back over the history of mankind, we can see the traces of Eastern influence upon the West. It is often observed that in the Bible there are seen traces from the stories of the Buddhist scriptures or that a part of Greek philosophy was influenced by Indian philosophy; These assertions may be vague and have not been fully worked out. However, the fact that in the parables or stories current in the Middle Ages of the West the influence of the Indian civilization is seen was acknowledged by scholars.[3] Among others the fact that the concept of the Buddhist 'Bodhisattva' was transferred to the West and made canonized Catholic saint could not be overlooked in spite of its triviality.[4] There is also the fact that the life-story of the Indian Śākyamuni was brought over to the West, where it was transformed into that of one of the Catholic saints; subsequently, it was carried to Japan by 'Kirishitan' missionaries, but neither Buddhists nor Christians were aware of its background.[5] In modern times, however, by means of translations Eastern thought became increasingly familiar to the West. Since then the influence of Eastern thought over the thought-formation of France[6] and Germany was indeed remarkable. The Chinese thought especially served as an impetus to the Enlightenment thought-tendency and inspired such people as Voltaire and Wolff. Likewise, Indian thought contributed to the formation of Romanticism in Germany. The movement by the brothers Schlegel, the philosophy of Schopenhauer, the thought of Keyserling in modern times, etc. could not be imagined without the influence of Indian thought. W. von Humboldt spoke highly of the Indian *Bhagavadgītā* as the most beautiful and most profound philosophical work in the world; Schopenhauer called the *Upaniṣads* 'The consolation of my life and death' and found therein the fountainhead of his thought; Keyserling concluded his book '*Reisetagebuch eines Philosophen*' with the following lines. "The turmoil of the world after the great war could only be saved by the Bodhisattva Ideal".; Prof. Charles Morris, a philosopher in the present-day America, has given the name 'Maitreyan Way' to the path upon which the world should tread in the future. In the present-day America an interest in Eastern thought has increased from the view-point of pragmatism. Northrop's studies are said to have been done from such a view-point. In England, Germany or America, groups of people have appeared who call themselves 'Buddhists', though very small in number, and have formed small organizations.[7] Thus, if Eastern thought should come to be understood more deeply, we could not deny the possibility of its further influence being revealed.

Even within the confines of East Asia, a great cultural interchange was accomplished in the past. Buddhism spread over the almost whole of Asia. To what extent Confucianism regulated the actual life of Japan is yet to be studied; however, there is no doubt that it held a kind of regulating-power in the actual, social life of Japan. According to a Confucian, it was not until the beginning of introduction of Confucianism that the moral code prevailed in Japan.[8] Confucian scholars such as Ogiu Sorai, Dazai Shuntai, Yamagata Shūnan, etc. thought in this way: In ancient Japan there was no philosophy which can be regarded as ethics and it was not until the advent of Chinese Confucianism that morality came into being. Particularly, Dazai Shuntai believed that in Japan from the beginning moral or ethical awareness never existed, and it was not until the introduction from China of the 'Way of the Sage' or 'The teaching of Sage' that the Japanese became ethical: "In Japan from the beginning there has never been such a conception as 'the way'. In recent years, however, Shintoïsts are said to be solemnly preaching the 'way of our country' as if it be profound, yet whatever they are preaching are all fabrication and nonsense of later times. The fact that there are no Japanese equivalents to the letters, 仁, 義, 禮, 樂, 孝, 悌, is the proof that there was no such concept as 'the way' (道) in Japan, for whatever originally existed in Japan have their own Japanese equivalent and so the lack of Japanese equivalents reveals that their origin is not to be placed in Japan. From the times of the gods to somewhere around the fortieth Emperor, for want of decorum marriages were held among parents, children, brothers, uncles, and nieces. In the meantime a communication was started with foreign countries with the result that *the way of the Sage of China* came to be spread in this country, and on all matters people are now following the example of China. Since then the people of this country came to know decorum and to become aware of the way of human society and have ceased to do act like animals. The most lowly of society at present regard the people who have behaved against decorum as nothing better than beasts: this is because of *"the prevalence of the teaching of the Sage"*.[9]

While from the view-point of the Buddhists, prior to the introduction of Buddhism, Japan was utterly in the dark; it was not until that time that people were saved and Buddhism and its enlightening virtues were received with rejoicing. For instance, Rennyo expressed his feeling of joy in the following manner:

"The spread of Buddhist teachings in this country can be traced back to the time of the Emperor Kimmei when Buddhist teachings arrived in Japan. The Tathāgata's teaching was not wide-spread prior to that time; people did not hear at all the way to Enlightenment. Having been born in an age when the Buddhist teaching is wide-spread, we are now fortunate enough to have heard the way of deliverence from the world of birth and death, though we do not know what good causes brought this happiness about. Indeed we are able to meet that which is difficult to meet".[10]

Nichiren also says:

"In ancient days prior to the advent of Buddha-Dharma, people knew neither of the Buddha nor of the Dharma. Yet after the struggle between Moriya and Jōgū Taishi (Prince Shōtoku), some people came to believe it and others did not".[11]

How can we contend that there was no universality in the teaching which impressed the people as being the universal teaching? Those who deny the singularity of the East are prone to disavow the universality of the Eastern thought. But logically speaking, it apparently is inconsistent to deny the universality of the thought while disavowing the singularity of the East, dividing it into a number of units, and at the same time recognizing a mutual (or unilateral) influence among those units. We must avoid this logical conflict. We deny the singularity of the East but affirm the establishment of a number of units. And it is because of this that we should like to acknowledge a *universal significance* in various thought-systems established in East Asia. It is by no means that all these systems have universality, but that we should recognize it in some part of them. What part of them have universality would depend on the nature of the times.

If we take the stand-point of those who would favor an impartial examination of the thoughts which mankind has produced, it follows that we could not possibly say that the Western thought alone is universal and those of the other nations have no universal significance. The ancient Greeks or at least a part of them[12] had acknowledged that the philosophical thoughts of the other nations had likewise their individual significance. Also among the modern philosophies of the West there were a good number of people who held such a view.[13] Nevertheless, there are some who would attribute universal superiority especially to Western thought alone. It is because they wish to display the power of the modern West to control nature or they are fascinated by it alone.

Indeed it is a fact beyond doubt that the modern world is being unified as a perfect world by dint of the political and military pressure of the West, but this does not affirm the insignificance of the cultures of the non-Western nations. In the ancient West, for instance, Greek culture still held its position of leadership even under the political and military rule of Rome, while India was gorgeously adorned by the flowers of culture, in spite of the oft-repeated dominance by foreign races during her long history. We ought not to disregard the cold fact that culture is subject to the political, military pressure, but at the same time we must not forget the nobility of man which no power can subdue.

Customary and conventional as the phrase may be, if we remember this fact, it would not be meaningless for us to emphasize the significance of 'East Asia' of the present. There is a great significance in knowing East Asia and developing its culture. Originally such concepts as East Asia, the East, or the Orient were set in opposition to the Occident. In spite of their obscure connotation, these words became to be used of their own accord by the races that have long been subjected to the oppression by the military and political superiority of the Westerners; this was an attempt to preserve their respective cultural traditions. Indeed the famous slogan 'Asia is one' uttered by Okakura Tenshin is not free from inaccuracy and is not in accordance with the reality of the history of thought. But the nations of East Asia, which have long cherished the desire to preserve and develop the respective cultures of their own, have inadvertently connected themselves with this slogan, because of the common feeling that *they shared the same objective.* It was a sort of repulsion aiming at defending their respective cultures against the rule of the West.

The desire on the part of various nations to preserve and develop their respective cultural traditions is justifiable. We ought to respect this desire. In that case, however, it behooves each nation to see to it that while being critical against foreign cultures they remain critical of their own indigenous culture. That is, with modesty and self-awareness a new culture should be formed through enlightened criticism.

The neglect of criticism and the mere affirmation and preservation of the past would be tantamount to annihilating one's own culture. While, if it affirms foreign cultures uncritically, this would be merely blind acceptance, and consequently, no positive contribution toward forming a new culture for mankind will have been made.

Standing on such a position, studies in East Asia would make something more than the mere tastes by dilettanti and positively be able to contribute to forming a fresh culture, and it should do. There have by now been such people as would regard the learning and its method established in the modern West as the only and the absolute ones and such thought-tendency seems to be as yet fairly influential at present. This may be only natural but we ought to be critical as well of the learnings of Modern West. The learning in the future must be formed and developed with the results of studies in the Eastern culture being reinforced.

---

1) Max Weber: *Aufsätze zur Religionssoziologie*, Einleitung.

2) "The political and moral teachings formed in ancient times (of China) have long been traditional without losing their prestige as a thought of intellectual society; such a thought, however, should not merely be applied for the other nations, but it would be extremely difficult to be understood as a thought by them". (Sōkichi Tsuda: *Shina Shisō to Nippon*, p. 8).

3) M. Winternitz: Geschichte der indischen Litteratur, II. S. 226–267.

4) Bodhisattva is Budsaf in Persian, which came to be identified with Joasaf, one of the saints of the Catholic church.

5) The contents of "*Acta Sanctorum*" (published in Japanese translation in 1591), the story of St. Joasaf and one of the translations in Kirishitan literature, show a striking identity with the life-story of the Buddha. (cf. Noritsugu Muraoka 村岡典嗣: *Kirishitan Bungaku-shō* 吉利支丹文學抄 pp. 51–88; Masaharu Anesaki 姉崎正治: *Kirishitan Dendō no Kōhai* 切支丹傳道の興廢 pp. 390–391).

6) As for the influence of Chinese thought over France; cf. Sueo Gotō 後藤末雄: *Shinabunka to Shinagaku no Kigen* (1933).

7) As for the Buddhism in the West: cf. Kaigyoku Watanabe 渡邊海旭: *Ōbei no Bukkyō* (歐米の佛教 Buddhism in Western Countries). The titles of books published in Germany for the purpose of study and propagation of Buddhism are contained in Hans Ludwig Held's "*Deutsche Bibliographie des Buddhismus*" (München, 1916), according to which the number amounts to as many as 2544. Westerners have also appeared who renounced the world and conducted positive activities after being ordained bhikkhus. British bhikkhu, Ānanda Metteya and German bhikkhu, Nyānatiloka are the most well-known. In Germany, too, several organizations such as Gemeinde um Buddha were established, whose activities were withheld by the Nazis during the last war, but now they have reportedly started again their vigorous activities.

8) Hisashi Uda 宇田尚: *Nippon Bunka ni Oyoboseru Jukyō no Eikyō* (日本文化に及ぼせる儒教の影響 The Influence of Confucianism upon Japanese Culture) p. 340 ff.

9) *Bendōsho* 辨道書.

10) Rennyo 蓮如: Jōgai Ofumi 帖外御文 (Yūshō Tokushi 禿氏祐祥: *Rennyo Shōnin Ofumi Zenshū* 蓮如上人御文全集 p. 76).

11) Hokkeshō 法華鈔

12) "Megasthenes, Seleukos Nikator's contemporary, clearly writes in the third chapter of his book "India", as follows: Verily whatever were taught about nature by the ancient people (of Greece) were taught likewise by the philosophers of the other countries: among Indians by Brakhmana (Brahmans) and in Syria by Iudaios (Jews)". (Clemens of Alexandria, *Strom.* I. p. 305. D. (Ed. Colon. 1688); quoted from *Megasthenis Indica, Fragmenta collegit commen ta tionem et indices addidit,* ed. E.A. Schwanbeck, Fr. 42.

13) It is a well-known fact in the history of philosophy that Schopenhauer was absorbed in the Upanisad scriptures through their translations, under the influence of whom Deussen wrote a history of Philosophy of all the nations of the world, that is, *Allgemeine Geschichte der Philosophie.* Therein he falls short of describing in detail the philosophical views in China and Japan due to the linguistic difficulties, he shows due concerns about them. As far as the interest in various thoughts of the world is concerned, works such as G. Misch's "*Der Weg in die Philosophie*" or Keyserling's "*Reisetagebuch eines Philosophen*" would be in the same category. In Masson-Oursel's "*La philosophie comparée*" is contained a positive contention on this point. American philosophers, as in the case of Emerson or Royce ("*The world and the individual*"), have also deep interest in Indian philosophy.

(3) Comparative study of ways of thinking and philosophy

A comparative study of ways of thinking of the East Asians, at the same time, should be compared critically with that of Western philosophy. It goes without saying that we must compare above all the complete philosophical system of East Asia with that of the West. Deussen once stated thus: "Suppose that there exists a certain planet in the solar system, say, Mars or Venus, inhabited thereupon by human beings or other beings with their culture flourishing and with an established philosophy.

Suppose we come to know their philosophy through one of the beings living there, who had entered into the sphere of our terrestrial gravitation after being shot out in a bullet. In that case we might undoubtedly take an enormous interest in the results of their philosophy, and we might carefully compare and examine the philosophies of theirs and ours. If there should be some difference, we would determine which side is true, and if it should be found that there is no difference between the two, then this would imply that the truth of the outcome of the philosophical contemplation of both sides had been substantiated. Although in this case we would have to take into account the natural and inevitable sophistication of pure reason, as Kant put it. This may be a wishful thinking, but we have a similar situation in Indian philosophy, for Indian philosophy has taken a course of development independent of Western philosophy".[1]

He then proceeds to say, "Here, people may question as follows: We are living in an age which has attained such a remarkable stage of development, that would it not be a childish and inappropriate attempt for us to learn something from the ancient Indians? To know the view of the world of the Indians, however, is profitable. We are enabled thereby to realize that we have fallen into a great prejudice on account of the whole system we have established about religion and philosophy, and that besides the way of understanding things established by Hegel as the only possible and reasonable one, there exists as yet another one totally different from Hegel's".[2]

Deussen's allegation affords a number of problems over which we must ponder. As we are concerned in this book with *the ways of thinking of various nations,* we shall not treat here the significance of comparative philosophy.[3] Instead, we would here especially lay stress on the following point:

As is seen in the modern Western philosophy, the concept of philosophy, which is required for instance by Kant, is not the 'technical concept' (*Schulbegriff*) but the 'general human concept' (*Weltbegriff, conceptus cosmicus*). He was not merely looking for the 'epistemological system which was to be sought for only as a learning, and which regard as its object nothing more than the unity of knowledge, that is, the logical perfection of cognition'. With him, the ideal of philosophy was to be the 'learning of the relationship between all the cognitions and the essence of human reason'. A philosopher was not the technician of reason but the legislator of human reason (*Gesetzgeber der menschlichen Vernunft*).[4]

Therefore, for him the truth to be given by the supreme philosophy is *nothing but what is already known by common people.* It may perhaps be due to such a standpoint that in his metaphysics the commonsensical view about religio-ethics held by the Westerners in general is seen emerging.

In the 'a priori dialectics' in his work *Kritik der reinen Vernunft,* Kant made an inquiry into the nature of such ideas as mind, freedom, God, etc. and contended that it is not the concept of understanding but that of reason, therefore in regard to natural cognition it is not structural as in the case of category, but regulative, and that there is a danger of our bringing about an image in case we misuse the idea structurally, misunderstanding the meaning of it. According to his philosophy, however, an idea is in no way an image. It is the misuse of an idea that brings about an image. Therefore, he rejected the natural reality of an idea, but recognized the metaphysical reality thereof. And it is considered that therein is grounded his practical philosophy.

It is really due to the fact that he followed the 'general human concept' that he recognized the metaphysical reality of such an idea. It is not for certain whether he himself was aware or not but anyway that was a traditional religio-ethical concept among the Westerners which made him set up such an idea. Such an idea is not necessarily taken for granted among the East Asians in general. For example, the thought which recognizes the metaphysical reality of soul has been rejected by Buddhism. Buddhists are trying to ground the establishment of ethics without setting up the idea of immortality of soul as a condition. As for the idea of God, both Buddhists and Jains disapprove the creator God of the universe. In Eastern thought in general, especially in Indian thought, gods are possessed of no meaning of any importance. Indian people generally are inclined to base their ethics on *the domain free from God's authority.* Such a view as this did not enter into Kant's philosophical sight. As has been done from various view-points, the attempt to understand Kant's thought merely as an epoch at which starts a stage of development to be made by mankind's society and thought is onesided. As far as this point is concerned, Kant's philosophy is after all nothing but a philosophical and theoretical expression of the Westerner's commonsensical, ethico-religious idea.

What we have said in the above is only an example, but in any case if we introduce various ways of thinking of the East Asians into philosophical speculation, then it would afford a clue for the critical consideration of the philosophical thoughts of the West.

If, however, we should admit any of the philosophical thoughts of the West indiscriminately, then it would be nothing but *a blind adherence to authority* which is conspicuous among the Japanese intellectuals. What the German philosophers have taken out as the 'general human concept' (*Weltbegriff*) was after all restricted by the historical tradition of the German people's human life, spiritual and social, so that the attempt to enforce the concept in Eastern society, admitting an universal significance only in it and neglecting their circumstances, is a kind of non-critical attitude in the formation of culture. Among what the Western philosophers have taken up as the 'general human concept', there are not a few that seem to a majority of Japanese to have been transformed into the 'technical concept'.

By reflecting upon the seemingly irrelevant ways of thinking of the East Asians, we can be *critical* of the philosophical thoughts of the West.[5] And as a result of the criticism, we would be able to acquire an efficient basis for our march toward the establishment of a new and true philosophy.

---

1) P. Deussen: *Die Sûtras des Vedanta,* 1920, Vorrede S. 5–6.
2) P. Deussen: *Allgemeine Geschichte der Philosophie,* I, 1. S. 36.
3) As for the matter of comparison of Indian philosophy with Western philosophy alone, P. Deussen's *Allgemeine Geschichte der Philosophie* (2 Bände) treated it for the first time, and then S. Radhakrishnan's *Indian Philosophy* (2 vols. 1923, 1930) often took it into account. Rudolf Otto's *West-Östliche Mystik* (Gotha, 1929) clarifies the similarity and difference of the mysticisms of the East and West, comparing Śankara's metaphysics with those of Eckhart and Fichte. The comparison of Kant's categorical imperative with that of Prabhākara is discussed in detail by Th. Stcherbatsky in *Festgabe Hermann Jacobi* (Bonn 1926, S. 369 f.). These researches were introduced in Yenshō Kanakura's 金倉圓照 *Indo Tetsugaku to Seiyō Shisō* (印度哲學と西洋思想) (*Risō*「理想」No. 172, June 1947) and therein the significance of the comparative study of the thoughts of East and West is treated.
4) Kant: *Kritik der reinen Vernunft,* S. 866 f.
5) For instance, Rickert characterized Historical Science as 'idiographisch' and Natural Science, 'nomothetisch'. But as we have already considered in this book, the ways of thinking of the Chinese is 'idiographisch', while that of the Indians, 'nomothetisch'. As far as at least the etymology of these two terms derived from Greek is concerned, this judgment can safely be done. Therefore, if such characteristics of the ways of thinking of the East Asians are taken into account, there is a need for the discussion about learning made by Rickert and the Germans after him to be reflected upon once again.

Chapter 3. The cognitive basis and the existential basis for the difference of ways of thinking

In the above we have first of all taken out the traits of ways of thinking of various nations in respect to their forms of expression of judgment and deduction used by various nations in East Asia, and then considered how these traits are expressed in various cultural phenomena and how they have influenced Buddhism, as a universal religion, to assume different phases. In that case, we have adopted the method to draw out other traits deductively, if possible, from among some traits seen in expression-forms of judgment and deduction. The former method proved to be the means to know the latter. Therefore, the traits seen in expression-forms of judgment and deduction are the cognitive basis (ratio cognoscendi, jñāpaka hetu).

Here arise several questions: What is the existential basis (ratio essendi, kāraka hetu) which brings about the difference of ways of thinking among nations? By what cause was such a difference of expression-forms or ways of thinking brought about?

These questions could never easily be solved here, because they are difficult questions which concern the foundamentals of not only philosophy but of all the sciences of humanities. We shall just confine ourselves to trying to cover, in our consideration, the field over which we have already treated. Then the general glimpse which we had from a limited range of observation might help us in solving these questions.

We could think of various matters as what cause various nations to have differences of ways of thinking. First of all, the features of ways of thinking seem to have nothing to do with the blood or lineage of nations. That is to say, the features of ways of thinking and racial ones do not coincide. Being left to live among a greater and mightier race, a minority group naturally become assimilated in the people around it and finally come to show the same trait of ways of thinking as that of the former, as is seen, for instance, in the familiar case of the Japanese emigrants who went abroad to settle. The fact that even the self-same Aryan race which was divided into East and West, that is to say, the Europeans and the Indians have come to show different features of ways of thinking, was already pointed out. In a way it seems that the Indians are not the pure Aryans but a hybrid of the Aryans and the aborigines, hence such differences appear; however, there is also evidence to the contrary. Although the inhabitants of North-West India are keeping even at present the pure Aryan blood, they have already discarded the religion of their ancestors and embraced Mohammedanism. Accordingly, there is no intrinsic relationship between the physiological and racial lineage and the ways of thinking.

Here comes up in our consideration the difference of climatic environment.[1] It is believed that by such causes as climate, weather, geology, the nature of the soil, natural view, etc. of a certain locale, the difference of ways of thinking among races might have been brought about, and that the difference of ways of thinking between the Europeans and the Indians in the Aryan lineage might have been derived from or dependent upon such a climatic environment. Even climatic environment, however, does not possess a singular or decisive influence over the difference of man's ways of thinking. If so, then the theory of climatic determinism would be established. But the real facts testify to the opposite case. It sometimes happens that the self-same race living in one and the same climatic environment changes its ways of thinking under the influence of the thought of the other nations. Although the ways of thinking of one nation are durable and hardly changeable, they can yet be changed to a considerable degree under the influence of the other nations. This fact could easily be understood if we go through the history of each nation. If we stick to the climatic environment alone as its decisive cause, then we could never explain the change of ways of thinking or the thought-patterns of a nation.

Also in this connection, no geographical environment or position makes a decisive factor, either. As is often said, India and China belong to the Continent, so that the nature of cultures born there is continental, while that of the Japanese culture is insular. Truly they create such an impression. Among others Japan is an island nation out of the reach of any great foreign invasion, so that she has preserved the ancient culture and even keeps such cultural products intact as have already been lost in the mainland of Asia. In the Ceylon island, to cite another instance, the most primitive of all forms of Buddhist orders in other countries has been preserved. Therefore, it is true that an island nation is characterized by the conservatism which preserves the traditional ancient culture intact, but a nation in the continent is not without such a conservative character. The anti-progressive character of the Chinese nation is such as has often been pointed out. And it is a matter of wonderment that a part of the Indians still preserves the Vedic culture as it was established three thousand years ago. Anti-progressivism or conservatism is seen in any of the countries mentioned above. Accordingly it is impossible for us to draw a conclusion that the geographical environment or position, continental or insular, is the only factor which determines the difference of the ways of thinking of peoples.

Here the possibility to think in the following way might be justified: Ought we not recognize the existential basis of the difference of ways of thinking, not in the natural scientific conditions such as race, blood, climatic environment, but in the conditions which rather have something to do with man's actual conduct and yet are materialistic? What emerges here is a theory which attaches great importance to the economic conditions in social life of humanity. Historical materialism may be an example of such a theory. Since the criticism of materialism would constitute an independent theme of study, it is impossible for us to refer to it here. As a result of our study into the ways of thinking of the East Asian peoples, we shall not hesitate to conclude as follows: *The theory of materialistic view of history or economic view of history is incapable of explaining in its entirety the fact of the difference of ways of thinking varying according to the people.* Needless to say, the materialistic view of history emphasizes that the sum total of the productive relations in a certain period, or the economic structure of society makes the basis of reality upon which is established the juridical and political upper-structure and in accordance to which is also formed a certain social consciousness. Despite the fact that it affords a number of solutions to the problems about social organization or social thoughts, it does not always sufficiently explain the other problems. As a matter of fact, to what extent will, from the standpoint of the materialistic or economic view of history, be ejplained the difference of ways of thinking among peoples which was brought about in our studies? For example, it could never be explained in terms of the difference of productive types that there is such a totally opposed variance of ways of thinking as evidenced by the fact that the Chinese race which attaches importance to singularity, while the Indian race does so to universality, and in contrast to the Chinese race which is empirical, sensuous and realistic, the Indian race is imaginative, other-worldly and metaphysical. It is said that in the East Asian society people generally inherited the same type of agricultural production from ancient times and that there is little digerence in its types among nations. This is the very reason why the phrase 'Asiatic productive type' is used as if taken for granted by economists and sociologists, though, of course, it is true that on the other hand a question is raised thereto. In economics the 'Asiatic productive type' might well be admitted, but so far as the ways of thinking is concerned, we shall reject the use of the word 'Asiatic' as a clear and unquestionable concept. According to what we have examined before in this book, the ways of thinking are varied according to every nation. The concept of the 'Asiatic productive type' does not explain the ground upon which the difference of ways of thinking existing among Asian nations has been based. Consequently, as far as this point is concerned, the materialistic view of history or the general economic view of history has exposed its fatal weak point.

In this connection, it is often maintained by scholars that the underdevelopment of cities in East Asian society is the actual basis upon which was produced the characteristics of East Asian thought. '*Polis*' or '*civitas*' was never made in East Asia, and the 'bourgeois' in its true sense of the word has never existed in East Asia. '*Shimin*' (citizen) is nothing but a translated word. '*Chōnin*' is not identical with citizen.[2] But the underdevelopment of civic society might have been the actual basis for the appearance of the thought-characteristic *common to the general* East Asian nations, but it is impossible for us to explain thereby the *difference* of ways of thinking among nations.

After such considerations, the following thought emerges; namely, a religious ideology is the determining factor of the singularity of the social and economic life of each nation. Apparently this thought has an intention to correct other thoughts such as the materialistic view of history. Max Weber, a representative of such a progressive view, says: "The 'world-image' created by an 'idea', just like a switch man, used to determine the track on which the motive of interest moved man's conducts".[3] Attaching great importance[4] to the influence dealt by religious ideas on the social life or economical ethics, he examined the relationship between religion and social life with almost all the important nations of the world. The result of his study must be highly valued, but along with it, and apart from religion, we cannot neglect the characteristics of ways of thinking seen in every nation. As for the Indians, they have a general characteristic perceived commonly in Hindus, Jains, and Moslems, and as for the Chinese, they have a characteristic of ways of thinking perceived equally among the devotees of Confucianism, Taoists, and Buddhists, and it often happens that the same person proves to be the follower of many religions. The case is the same with Shintoism, Buddhism, and Christianity in Japan, in which there is a tendency characteristic of Japan transcending the distinction of all religions. As has often been pointed out in this book, it often happened in the past that a foreign religion has wholly transformed the ways of thinking of a nation, and at the same time the ways of thinking peculiar to a nation have on the contrary changed the foreign religion itself.

Therefore, besides that, we have to pay our attention to the fact that, in order to bring about a difference of thought type, the historical circumstances of a nation count to a great extent. We have already pointed out the fact that the view of the Indians about human relations favors the identity or fusion of one and others, in contrast to the ancient Westerners' view which is extremely hostile and antagonistic. The formation of such a difference of the thought-form is considered to be due to the difference of the historical formation-process of the society which the ruling race formed in India and in the West. In the case of the West, the Greeks, for instance, formed their '*polis*' after conquering the preceding race. They, as adventurers, had come to invade amidst a foreign race, and made first of all a safety-zone encircled by stone walls so as to keep the common enemy out of their own world. Thereby they thought that they would succeed to protect themselves against the power of the dead souls of the enemy, being at the same time protected against the assault from the living enemy around them, so long as they hid themselves therein.[5] Against their expectations, however, the Aryans who invaded India did not face any such violent resistance on the part of the aborigines, so that their society was least menaced by the aborigines. They constructed *puras* (fortresses) on hills, wherein they only confined themselves on emergencies, such as by the enemy invasion or flood, and at ordindary times living outside them. The difference of historical background in regard to social formation such as this seems to be regulating the ways of thinking of every nation long enough down to the latter days. The difference of historical background, however, could be effected or, on the contrary, deepened by the historical changes there-after. Consequently it is not possessed of any absolute significance either.

Such being the case, the question; —What is the existential basis which determines the characteristics of a people's ways of thinking?— yet remains unsolved. It is then questioned: Are not the expression-form of judgment and deduction we adopted as *the cognitive basis* to know the characteristics of ways of thinking, working at once as *the existential basis?* Generally speaking, since the grammar and its syntax which regulate the expression-form of judgment and deduction do not easily change,[6] they are not only expressive of the characteristic of ways of thinking of a nation but also they in return regulate them for all time. In other words, it is probable that the ways of working of a thought might in return be qualified by its language-form. Therefore, as far as this point goes, the expression-form by a language of thought also makes the existential basis with the characteristic of ways of thinking of a people. But this relationship is in no way of absolute nature. A grammar or a syntax might change on account of social unrest or of a contact with foreign languages. In such cases, the ways of thinking could have undergone a change. The change of ways of thinking of a nation depends upon the times.

According to the above considerations, we could say in the last analysis, as the conclusion as follows: There is no such thing as the fundamental principle which supports the characteristic of ways of thinking of a people. Various elements, as mentioned above, being related *in multi-fold ways* and exerting an influence, caused the ways of thinking of a people to be fixed. If we deal with the question of the existential basis which brings about the difference of ways of thinking, there would be no way left for us but to take the standpoint of pluralism. The attempt to find out an isolated cause looks alluring but it is destined to fail to grasp the reality of affairs. We are obliged to recognize in this case also the principle of "Things are born of various conditions" which Buddhism put forth against the monistic metaphysical theory. In what order, then, do these elements make themselves felt? This is a question to be contemplated upon once again in the future. Here we cannot dwell upon this question in detail, and even if we try to get a general perspective, it would perhaps be difficult for us to acquire an isolated response thereto. Since the thinking function is one of the mental phenomena within the reality of man's conduct and practice, it might have to be said that it is qualified by how man stands at a certain point of time. Man is a historical being and is all the time subject to the current of history from the past, so that he should heed to the necessity of history, and at the same time, it seems that therein are contained not a few moments of chance. For instance, such an accidental event in which a nation gets into contact with another, one could bring about an unexpected change of affairs of grave nature that the nation in question had never expected.

The ways of thinking of a people has the function to be qualified by what were created by man, and at the same time to qualify them in return. In some cases we can also see the phase on which each one of the above-mentioned sundry cultural factors is in return characterized and formed by the characteristic of ways of thinking of a people. It is an independent theme of study for us to clarify how the mutual qualifications from both sides are done. In this book, however, we shall have practically attained the objective of study, if we succeeded to clarity the following two points: In the first place, that *there are some characteristics different one from another* as to the ways of thinking of the East Asian nations. In the second place, that with regard to a people, there is a *certain logical connection* among these characteristics.

Attention should also be paid in this connection to the fact that in the history of every people there is a distinction of periods, such as the ancient, the middle, and the present, according to which the ways of thinking of peoples naturally differ. This fact we do not mean to deny. But at the same time we also ought to recognize the fact that in every nation there is an especial thought-tendency which has long been preserved throughout these historical stages. Hereafter the more communication progresses and the closer intercourse between nations become and the world becomes unified, the less would become the disparity of ways of thinking among nations. Notwithstanding this fact, however, it would never be easy for us totally to disjoin ourselves with the traditional characteristics of the past, or it might prove to be an impossibility. In order to balance variations in the ways of thinking of nations and to create a new-world culture, we need first of all to reflect upon and ascertain the characteristics of ways of thinking of peoples beforehand. Of course, it goes without saying that we should equally consider how they underwent changes in the course of history. The over-all renovation of ways of thinking of nations would never easily be accomplished by merely taking external or institutional measures such as renovations of land ownership, economic, and political systems. For the purpose of building a new culture aspiring for truth, a rigorous criticism of the ways of thinking of nations ought to be made.

---

1) The reason why I have brought out here the concept of "climatic environment" is to prevent misunderstanding by making a distinction, as a makeshift, between this and Dr. Watsuji's concept of 'climate'. According to his climatology, climate is in no way a mere natural phenomenon. He says:

"Furthermore we can find the climatic phenomena in all the expressions of man's life such as literary arts, fine arts, religions, customs, etc. All this would be but a natural state of affairs, so long as climate is the expression of man's own understanding of himself". (*Fūdo* 風土 p. 12) What I am analyzing here in connection with the problem of the existential basis of the difference of ways of thinking, however, is the climate as a *natural environment* to the last. Therefore, I used another word for it for the sake of distinction.

2) According to Max Weber, there is a reason significant in the spiritual history in that cities made a progress in their particular fashion in the West. First, the western cities are a cooperative society formed by the pact based on the voluntary will. A city in the West was at the beginning created as a defensive body, the principle of which is that it should be defended by self-fortification of the *body itself*. Everywhere except in the West, monarch's army preceded the coming into being of cities. In the West, however, the coming into existence of the army to be armed under the order of soldier-monarch or the separation of soldiers and the means of war, was only effected in the modern times, but in Asia it was started from the very beginning. They say that the reason is that in East Asia, Egypt, West Asia, India, or China, the river-improvement problem was of grave concern for the nation; therefore a powerful monarchism and bureaucracy were caused to appear. The second reason is said to be that in East Asian societies, ecclesiastical institutions were established which monopolized magical tricks and exercised a ruling power. (This statement is based on the explanation by Prof. Toratarō Shimomura 下村寅太郎).

3) Max Weber: *Aufsätze zur Religionssoziologie*. I, S. 252.

4) "Although the extent to which the social influence under some economical and political conditions wields upon religious ethics was, in some isolated cases, fairly grave, the characteristic of such ethics is basically given by the side of religion. Before anything else it primarily depends on the contents of religious message or god's testament.——In any religion the vicissitude of the class which instructs the society in its teaching counts greatly, and on the other hand, once the type of religion is fixed it would extensively exercise a great influence over various heterogeneous types of way of life". (Max Weber: Die Wirtschaftsethik der Weltreligion, *Aufsätze zur Religionssoziologie*. I, S. 240–241) As for the reason why the caste-system was established in India, he explains thus: "Originally the union of the creative caste-orthodoxy with the doctrine of karma or the theodicee peculiar to the Brahmins, was a direct product of the rational and ethical thinking, and it *is not that of economical 'condition' of any sort*. And it was not until this thought-product came to be unified with the traditional social order with the thought of transmigration (*saṃsāra*) as an intermediary that such an order came out to reign over the thinking and aspiration of the people in question and to produce a firm basic-form to dispose religiously and socially every low professional group and the mean classes. (*Hinduismus und Buddhismus*, S. 131.)

5) Tetsurō Watsuji 和辻哲郎: *Homērosu Hihan* (ホメーロス批判 Criticism on Homeros, p. 40.)

6) Even in a language, the vocabulary or words used in that language is most liable to change, whereas grammatical rules or ways of expressions are comparatively hard to change. Even when fairly a large number of foreign words are adopted, it is quite rare that the grammatical system should come to be affected by foreign countries. Accordingly, a grammar is preserved for all time and so the vitality of tradition in grammar is comparatively strong. (*Hashimoto Shinkichi Hakase Chosakushū* 橋本進吉博士著作集 vol. 1. p. 348 ff. Kokugo to Dentō (國語と傳統 National language and Tradition)).